ISBN 978-1-330-70613-8
PIBN 10094890

1 MONTH OF
FREE
READING

at

www.ForgottenBooks.com

By purchasing this book you are eligible for one month membership to ForgottenBooks.com, giving you unlimited access to our entire collection of over 1,000,000 titles via our web site and mobile apps.

To claim your free month visit:

www.forgottenbooks.com/free94890

English
Français
Deutsche
Italiano
Español
Português

www.forgottenbooks.com

Mythology Photography **Fiction**
Fishing Christianity **Art** Cooking
Essays Buddhism Freemasonry
Medicine **Biology** Music **Ancient
Egypt** Evolution Carpentry Physics
Dance Geology **Mathematics** Fitness
Shakespeare **Folklore** Yoga Marketing
Confidence Immortality Biographies
Poetry **Psychology** Witchcraft
Electronics Chemistry History **Law**
Accounting **Philosophy** Anthropology
Alchemy Drama Quantum Mechanics
Atheism Sexual Health **Ancient History**
Entrepreneurship Languages Sport
Paleontology Needlework Islam
Metaphysics Investment Archaeology
Parenting Statistics Criminology
Motivational

A TREATISE

ON THE

LAW OF CONTRACT

BY

C. G. ADDISON

AUTHOR OF "THE LAW OF TORTS"

THIRD AMERICAN, FROM THE SEVENTH LONDON EDITION
OF LEWIS W. CAVE, Esq.

BY

JAMES APPLETON MORGAN

OF THE NEW YORK BAR. AUTHOR OF "THE LAW OF LITERATURE;" AMERICAN EDITOR
OF "DECOLYAR ON GUARANTY," &C. &C.

VOL. II

NEW YORK

JAMES COCKCROFT & COMPANY

1876

TOBITT & BUNCE,
PRINTERS AND STEREOTYPERS,
131 WILLIAM STREET.

1264

CONTENTS OF VOLUME II.

BOOK II.

THE LAW OF PARTICULAR CONTRACTS.

CHAPTER I.

THE CONTRACT OF SALE.

CONTENTS.

SEC. 3.—*Of contracts for the sale of incorporeal property.*

CHAPTER II.

THE CONTRACT OF LETTING.

CHAPTER III.

CONTRACTS FOR SERVICES.

CONTENTS.

THE

LAW OF CONTRACT

BOOK II.

THE LAW OF PARTICULAR CONTRACTS.

CHAPTER I.

THE CONTRACT OF SALE.

SECTION I.

OF CONTRACTS FOR THE SALE OF LANDS.

507. *Contracts of sale.*—The contract of purchase and sale is founded upon a mutuality of engagement or upon mutual promises, the promise or undertaking of the one party to sell being the consideration for the promise of the other to buy. It is completed and rendered binding, consequently, if properly authenticated, by the bare consent of the parties, and ranks amongst that class of contracts called bilateral contracts. It is essential to the creation of a contract of sale that there be a price consisting of a sum of money to be paid by the buyer to the seller; for, if " there is an agreement that I shall sell you my horse for one of your books, this agreement does not constitute a sale, but a different kind of contract, viz., an exchange." (*a*) [1]

508. *Sale of lands and corporeal hereditaments.*—We have already seen that no action can be brought whereby to charge any person upon any contract for the sale of lands, tenements, or hereditaments, or any interest in or concerning them, unless the contract, or some memorandum or note thereof, is in writing, and signed by the party to be charged therewith, or by some other person by him lawfully authorized to sign it; but that it is not necessary to show that the memorandum of the agreement has been signed by both the parties to it, in order to render the one who has signed it liable upon the contract. The note or memorandum need not be drawn up in technical language, or in words of form; but both the subject-matter of the sale and the price to be paid for it must be specified; and it must also mention who is the purchaser. (*b*) If, therefore, upon a treaty for the

(*a*) Pothier, Obligations, No. 6.

(*b*) Bayley, J., Saunders v. Wake-field, 4 B. & Ald. 501. Blagden v. Bradbear, 12 Ves. 466. Seagood v.

[1] All that is essential to the sale of a chattel, at common law, is the agreement of the parties that the property in the subject-matter should pass from the vendor to the vendee, for a consideration given or promised to be given by the vendee. 2 Parsons on C., ch. iv. sec. 1. Taking of goods for a price promised to be paid on approval, without returning them, constitutes a sale. Spickler v. Marsh, 36 Md. 222. When, upon purchase of a chattel the purchaser gave his note, under a parol agreement that the chattel should belong to the sureties until the note was paid, the agreement effects to a change of title from the seller to the sureties direct, and not from the seller to the purchaser and then to the sureties. Worthy v. Cole, 69 N. C. 157. It is also essential to the contract of sale that the seller must have a vested interest or title in the thing sold. One may not sell " all the halibut that may be caught by the master and crew of the schooner R., on the voyage on which she is about to proceed." Low v. Pew, 108 Mass. 347.

purchase and sale of an estate, the owner writes a
letter which amounts to a distinct offer to sell the
property upon certain terms, and the party to whom
the letter is addressed answers it and accepts the offer
within a reasonable period, the contract is complete ;
and an action for damages may be maintained upon
it, or the owner may be compelled to perform it in
specie. (*c*) But, if there has not been a clear offer
and acceptance of one and the same set of terms,—if
the property has not been clearly described and defined, or any material particulars are left unsettled
between the parties,—there is not a concluded contract, capable of supporting an action for damages or
specific performance. (*d*) Where a draft agreement
had on the back of it, " We approve of this draft," and
this was signed by the intended parties to the agreement, it was held that it merely amounted to evidence
of something they intended to agree to, and not to
an actual agreement. " If the words," observes Lord
Tenderden, " imported an agreement, there would
never be any necessity for any other instrument." (*e*)
" Still," observes Lord St. Leonards, " where the
parties themselves, not being professional persons,
sign such a memorandum, it is a question to be decided in each case whether they signed in that form
as simply approving of the draft as such, or whether
they intended to give validity to it as an agreement."
(*f*) " It is not necessary that the note in writing, to
be binding under the statute, should be contemporary
with the agreement. It is sufficient, if it has been

Meale, Pre. Ch. 560. Ogilvie v. Fol-
jambe, 3 Mer. 53. Skelton v. Cole, 1
De G. & J. 596. Boyce v. Green,
Batt. 608.

    (*c*) Coleman v. Upcot, 5 Vin. Abr.

527, pl. 17. Dunlop v. Higgins, 1 H
L. C. 381 ; 12 Jur. 295.

    (*d*) Kennedy v. Lee, 3 Mer. 451
Thomas v. Blackman, 1 Coll. Ch. 312

    (*e*) Doe v. Pedgriph, 4 C. & P. 312.
    (*f*) Sugd. Vend. 14th ed. 144.

made at any time and adopted by the party afterwards; and anything under the hand of the party expressing that he has entered into the agreement will satisfy the statute, which was only intended to protect persons from having oral agreements imposed upon them." (*g*)

509. *Signature of the writing.*—The various modes of signing contracts by the party to be charged, so as to satisfy the requirements of the Statute of Frauds, have already been considered.

510. *Sales by auction.*—In the case of sales by auction, the assent of the parties to the contract of sale is manifested, as we have already seen, by the knocking down of the auctioneer's hammer. The bidding is a mere offer to buy at the price named by the bidder, which offer may be retracted at any time before the hammer is down and the offer has been accepted. (*h*) A stipulation in the conditions of sale, to the effect that no person shall retract their biddings, would not, at common law, prevent the bidder from retracting, if he thinks fit so to do, before his offer has been accepted and a contract has been actually made. The vendor may, if he thinks fit, be his own auctioneer; but he can not, unknown to the bidders, privately depute a third party to attend the sale and bid progressively for the property on his account, as a defensive precaution to prevent it from being sold at an undervalue. ' The employment of a single person to bid on behalf of the vendor will avoid the sale, unless the fact is notified to the assembled bid-

---

(*g*) Shippey v. Derrison, 5 Esp. 192.   Warlow v. Harrison, 28 L. J., Q. B.
(*h*) Payne v. Cave, 3 T. R. 148.   18 ; 29 Ib. 14.

' *Ante*, vol. i. p. 41, and cases cited in note 2.   Brent v. Green, 6 Leigh, 16.

ders. (*i*)[1] And, if the vendor publicly reserves to himself the right "to make one bidding and no more,"
through a person who is named, and then secretly
employs another person to make general and repeated
biddings, this is a fraud and imposition upon the
parties who attend the sale, and entitles the person
who is eventually declared the purchaser to abandon
the contract. (*k*) Formerly, there was a conflict between the courts of law and equity in respect of the
validity of sales by auction, where a puffer had bid,
although no right of bidding was reserved, the former
holding that all such sales were absolutely illegal, and the
latter giving effect to them under some circumstances,
although the rule was unsettled ; (*l*) but, by the 30 &
31 Vict. c. 48, s. 4, "whenever a sale by auction of
land would be invalid at law by reason of the employment of a puffer, the same shall be deemed invalid
in equity as well as at law." Sect. 5 of the same Act
requires that the particulars or conditions of sale shall
state whether the land is to be sold without reserve,
or subject to a reserve price, or whether a right to bid
is reserved. If it is stated that land will be sold without reserve, or to that effect, it is unlawful for the
seller to employ any person to bid at the sale, or
for the auctioneer knowingly to take any bidding

(*i*) Parke, B., Thornett v. Haines, 15 M. & W. 372. Green v. Baverstock, 32 L. J., C. P. 181.

(*k*) Rex v. Marsh, 3 You. & Jerv. 331.

(*l*) Mortimer v. Bell, L. R., 1 Ch. 10 ; 35 L. J., Ch. 25.

[1] Steele v. Ellmaker, 11 Serg. & R. 68; Towle v. Leavitt, 3 Fost. (N. H.) 360 ; Wolfe v. Luyster, 11 Hall 149; Latham v. Morrow, 6 B. Mon. 630. But see *contra*, Pennock's Appeal, 2 Harr. p. 446; Staines v. Shore, 4 Ib. 200; Nearie v. Williams, 8 How. 134; 3 Story, 611; Towle v. Leavitt, 3 Fost. (N. H.) 360; Moncrief v. Goldsborough, 4 Har. & McHen. 282.

from such person. If a right to bid is reserved, the
seller, or any person on his behalf, may bid as he may
think proper. (*m*)   But there is a distinction between
a reserved bidding and a reserved right to bid, and in
order to reserve to the vendor the right to bid up to
the reserve price, such right must be expressly stipulated for ; it is not sufficient to state in the conditions
that the sale is subject to reserved bidding. (*n*)   The
effect of employing anyone to bid when the sale is
" without reserve is, that the sale is void, and the purchaser is entitled to recover back his deposit from the
auctioneer." (*o*)   The term " without reserve " is understood " to exclude all interference by the vendor, or
those coming under him, with the right of the public
to have the property at the highest bidding." Any
arrangement, therefore, between the vendor and a
third party, the result of which is to prevent the
property from being sold under a fixed sum, will
render the sale null and void. (*p*)   When the vendor
inserts in the conditions of sale that the property is to
be sold " without reserve," he, by so doing, contracts
with the highest bona fide bidder that the sale shall
be without reserve.   If, therefore, a bid is made by
or on behalf of the vendor or the owner of the
property, the latter may render himself responsible in
damages to the highest bona fide bidder for a breach
of the conditions of sale. (*q*)   But the auctioneer is
not responsible for a breach of the condition, unless
he has himself made a representation false to his

(*m*) 30 & 31 Vict. c. 48, s. 6. These
sections are not to affect sales of land
under the order of the Court of Chancery.

(*n*) Gilliat v. Gilliat, L. R., 9 Eq.
60 ; 39 L. J., Ch. 142.

(*o*) Meadows v. Tanner, 5 Mad. 34.

Thornett v. Haines, 15 M. & W. 367.
Warlow v. Harrison, 1 El. & El. 295,
316 ; 29 L. J., Q. B. 14.

(*p*) Robinson v. Wall, 16 L. J., Ch
401.

(*q*) Warlow v. Harrison, *supra.*

knowledge, and has thereby induced the plaintiff to incur expense and loss, as there is no contract between the auctioneer and the highest bidder that the property offered for sale shall be knocked down to him. (*r*)

As, on the one hand, the seller can not employ secret bidders to run up the price, and delude the purchaser with a fictitious contest, so, on the other hand, if a purchaser by his conduct induces other persons not to bid, the sale will not be binding on the vendor. (*s*) [1] Where the known agent of the vendor was employed by the purchaser to attend a sale by auction and bid for him, and was thought by the assembled company to be a puffer, which deterred other persons from bidding, and the estate was knocked down to the agent, under the false impression that he was acting for the vendor, the Court of Chancery refused to assist the purchaser to enforce the contract, as the employment of the vendor's agent by the purchaser had hurt the sale, and had been detrimental to the vendor. (*t*) As soon as the hammer of the auctioneer is down, and the bidding has been accepted, an agreement for the sale and purchase should be signed by the parties themselves, or by the auctioneer as their agent, inasmuch as sales by auction are, as we have before seen, within the Statute of Frauds, and must, whenever the subject-matter of the sale consists of an estate or interest in land, be authenticated by a signed writing. [2] The printed conditions of sale, containing

---

(*r*) Mainprice v. Westley, 6 B. & S.   316 ; 3 B. & B. 116.
420 ; 34 L. J., Q. B. 229.   (*t*) Twining v. Morrice, 2 Bro. Ch.
    (*s*) Fuller v. Abrahams, 6 Moore,   C. 331.

[1] Martin v. Runlett, 5 Rich. 541 ; Haynes v. Crutchfield, 7 Ala. 189.

[2] *Ante*, vol. i. pp. 296, 297, 298.

the terms on which the purchaser bids and the vendor accepts his bidding for the estate, form, when signed, a written contract between the vendor and purchaser, sufficient to satisfy the requirements of the Statute of Frauds; and the auctioneer's receipt for the deposit, signed by him, will amount to an agreement binding upon the seller, if it contains the names of the seller and purchaser, a description of the estate sold, and the price to be paid; or if it refers to the conditions or particulars of sale, so as to enable the court to read them together as one contract.[1]

When an estate is sold by auction in separate lots, a separate contract is created as to each lot. (*u*) But it is otherwise, if a contract is made for the purchase of several lots at one aggregate price; or if the several lots are so connected together that the possession of all is essential to the use and enjoyment of any one or more of them, and they have consequently been purchased by the vendee as one property. (*x*) We have already seen that an auctioneer effecting a sale by auction, or an auctioneer's clerk taking down the bidding, is deemed to be the authorized agent both of the vendor and purchaser, so as to be enabled to bind both or either of the parties by signing their names to the printed conditions of sale; but, until the hammer goes down, the auctioneer is exclusively the agent of the vendor; (*y*) and, when the sale is over, the auctioneer is no longer the agent of either party. (*z*) But he is not necessarily the agent of both parties; for it may be shown that the purchaser bought

---

(*u*) Emmerson v. Heelis, 2 Taunt. 38. James v. Shore, 1 Stark. 426. Roots v. Lord Dormer, 4 B. & Ad. 77.

(*x*) Chambers v. Griffiths, 1 Esp. 150. Gibson v. Spurrier, 2 Peake, N.

P. C. 49. Boyer v. Blackwell, 3 Anstr. 657. Dykes v. Biake, 4 Bing. N. C. 463; Sc. 345.

(*y*) Warlow v. Harrison, *ante.*

(*z*) Mews v. Carr, *ante.*

[1] *Ante,* vol. i., p. 320, 321, 322.

under an express contract between him and the vendor, and not under the conditions of sale. (*a*) The auctioneer generally puts down the purchaser's name in his catalogue or in the conditions or particulars of sale, with the amount of the bidding opposite the lot purchased; or he makes an entry of the particulars in his books, inserting the name of the purchaser. In either case the latter will be bound. If the conditions of sale are pasted up in a conspicuous position in the auction-room, the purchaser will be bound by the terms and conditions, although it can not be proved that he read them. (*b*) These conditions can not be contradicted, added to, or altered by verbal declarations made by the auctioneer at the time of the sale. (*c*) The reading of a lease at an auction by an auctioneer is no excuse for a misdescription of the terms of the lease in the particulars or conditions of sale. (*d*) If the estate is sold by order of the Court of Chancery and a bidder who is declared the purchaser sells again in the auction-room at an additional price, the court will order a re-sale. (*e*) If the auctioneer at a sale does not disclose the name of the vendor, but makes the contract in his own name, he will himself be personally responsible for the fulfillment of the contract. (*f*) [1]

511. *Of the enforcement of oral contracts for the*

(*a*) Bartlett v. Purnell, 4 Ad. & E, 794.

(*b*) Mesnard v. Aldridge, 3 Esp. 271. Bywater v. Richardson, 1 Ad. & E. 508.

(*c*) Higginson v. Clowes, 15 Ves. 521.

(*d*) Jones v. Edney, 3 Campb. 286. Flight v. Boote, 1 Bing. N. C. 370.

(*e*) Holroyd v. Wyatt, 2 Col. C. C. 327.

(*f*) Franklyn v. Lamond, 16 L. J., C. P. 221; 4 C. B. 637.

[1] A sale at auction to an association, of which the auctioneer is himself a member, is void. Kearney v. Taylor, 15 How. 494.

sale and purchase of estates.—If livery of seisin is
made to a purchaser under an oral contract for the
sale of a freehold estate, or of a leasehold estate exceeding three years in duration, and he is actually put
into possession of the property agreed to be sold to
him, yet he will have only an estate or lease at will, by
reason of the fourth section of the Statute of Frauds,
which enacts, as previously mentioned, that all estates
of freehold, or terms of years, or any uncertain interest
in lands, tenements, or hereditaments, made or created
by livery and seisin only, or by parol, and not put into
writing and signed by the parties creating them or
their agents, shall have the force and effect of leases or
estates at will only, excepting leases not exceeding
the term of three years from the making thereof.
But the purchaser so let into possession will be entitled to a conveyance of the estate ; and the court
will compel the vendor to execute such a conveyance,
notwithstanding the provisions of the Statute of
Frauds, on the ground that there has been a part performance of the contract, and that, possession having
been given and accepted in the fulfillment of the bargain, it would be fraudulent in either party to withdraw
therefrom without the consent of the other. (g) The
equity arising from part performance operates against
a company in like manner as against an individual,
the enactments of the Companies Clauses Act, 1845,
as to the mode in which contracts may be entered
into on behalf of a company, not precluding the enforcement against a company of the ordinary equity
based on part performance. (*h*) The mere naked

(g) Butcher v. Stapely, 1 Vern. 364.
Pyke v. Williams, 2 Ib. 455. Fon-
blanque, 175, n. Reynolds v. Waring,
1 Younge, 352. Caton v. Caton, L.
R., 1 Ch. 137, 148 ; 35 L. J., Ch. 292,
295.

(*h*) Wilson v. West Hartlepool Railway Company, 2 De G., J. & S. 475 ;
34 L. J., Ch. 241.

transfer of the possession of land alone is not, it has been said, sufficient to justify the courts in enforcing the performance of an oral contract for the purchase of the freehold and inheritance of such land on the ground that the transfer of the possession is a part performance of such oral contract. Acts done in performance, it has been observed, must be such as could have been done with no other view or design than to fulfill the particular contract sought to be enforced. (*i*) If, indeed, the change of possession is accompanied by the payment of money on the part of the occupier to the owner, under circumstances giving rise to the presumption that it was an installment of purchase-money, and not a rent paid in advance, there would undoubtedly be a part performance of a contract, which could be no other than a contract of sale. (*k*) So, if the change of possession has been accompanied by the exercise of acts of ownership, such as the expenditure of money in building, repairs, drainage, and lasting improvements, quite inconsistent with the notion of a contract for a yearly tenancy, it is evident, from the acts done, that there has been a part performance, either of a contract for the purchase of the fee, (*l*) or for the grant of a lease for a long term of years. (*m*) Such acts as are ordinarily introductory or anciliary to contracts for the purchase and sale of an estate or interest in land, such as the giving of directions for a conveyance to be prepared, making valuations, or fixing upon parties to value fixtures or

(*i*) Gunter v. Halsey, Ambl. 586. Cole v. White, cited 1 Bro. Ch. C. 409. Frame v. Dawson, 14 Ves. 388. Reynolds v. Waring, 1 Younge, 350. O'Reilly v. Thompson, 2 Cox, 273. Clinan v. Cooke, 1 Scho. & Lef. 22. Watt v. Evans, 4 Y. & Coll. 579. But see Wilson v. West Hartlepool Railway Company, 2 De G., J. & S. 475.

(*k*) Main v. Melburne, 4 Ves. junr. 720. Coles v. Trecothick, 9 Ib. 234.

(*l*) Borrett v. Gomeserra, Bunb. 94.

(*m*) Sutherland v. Briggs, 1 Hare, 26. Thornton v. Ramsden, 4 Giff. 519. Nunn v. Fabian, L. R., 1 Ch. 35 ; 35 L. J., Ch. 140.

stock, or the making of admeasurements, or the preparing of maps or plans, are not acts of performance of an oral agreement for the purchase or sale of an estate or interest in land, sufficient to take the contract out of the statute. (*n*)   But if "the purchaser of lands under an oral contract files a bill against the vendor to carry such contract into execution, and the vendor puts in an answer admitting the contract as stated, it takes it entirely out of the mischief of the Statute of Frauds, and, there being then no danger of perjury, the court would decree it to be performed." (*o*)

512. *Of the transfer of the estate in equity by the bargain before the execution of a conveyance.*—The execution of a simple contract in writing for the sale and purchase of an estate in fee, atlhough accompanied by livery and seisin, or delivery of possession of the land to the purchaser, does not, since the passing of the Transfer of Property Act, transfer to the latter the legal estate or interest agreed to be sold.   The written contract, if it amounts to a grant of the fee, would be a feoffment, and would be avoided by the section of the Act which enacts that "a feoffment (other than a feoffment made under a custom by an infant) shall be void unless evidenced by deed."   A right to have a conveyance of the land passes by the contract to the purchaser, but not any legal estate or interest in the land itself beyond an estate at will.   It is not necessary, however, for the alienation of property that there should be a formal deed of conveyance ; a contract for a valuable consideration, by which it is

(*n*) Clerk v. Wright, 1 Atk. 13. Cooke v. Tombs, 2 Anstr. 420. Whitechurch v. Bevis, 2 Bro. Ch. C. 559. Redding v. Wilkes, 3 Bro. Ch.

C. 400.   Phillips v. Edwards, 33 Beav. 440.

(*o*) Att.-Gen. v. Day, 1 Ves. senr. 220.   Gunter v. Halsey, Ambl. 586. Rondeau v. Wyatt, 2 H. Bl. 68.

agreed to make a transfer of particular specified property, passes the beneficial interest, provided the contract is one which would be specifically enforced. (p)
" The estate, from the signing of the contract, becomes
the real property of the vendee.   It is vendible as his,
chargeable as his, capable of being incumbered as his,
devised as his ; it may be assets, and will descend to
his heir." (q)   The purchaser, therefore, in such a case,
is said to have the equitable interest in the land,
whilst the vendor has the legal estate, and is deemed
to be a trustee for the purchaser, holding the land
upon trust to convey it to the latter upon the terms
and conditions of the contract of sale, (r) whilst the
purchaser is a trustee of the purchase-money for the
vendor. (s)

This transfer of the equitable ownership is naturally
accompanied with a corresponding transfer of the risk
of loss, so that, if lands and houses are agreed to be
sold, and the houses are burned down by fire, or
destroyed by an earthquake, between the time of the
making of the contract of sale and the execution of a
conveyance of the legal estate, the loss will fall upon
the purchaser, who will be compelled to accept a conveyance of the land without the houses, and to pay
the full amount of the purchase-money to the vendor;
(t) nor will he be entitled to the benefit of any insurance effected by the vendor in the absence of an
express stipulation to that effect in the agreement for
the purchase. (u)   So, if a simple contract be entered

(q) Lord Eldon, Seton v. Slade, 7
(p) Holroyd v. Marshall, 10 H. L.
C. 191 ; 33 L. J., Ch. 193.
Ves. 274.
(r) Davie v. Beardsham, 1 Ch. C. 39.
(s) Green v. Smith, 1 Atk. 572. Pol-
llexfen v. Moore, 3 Atk. 273.

(t) Harford v. Purrier, 1 Mad. 538,
539. Rawlins v. Burgis, 2 Ves. & B.
387. Paine v. Meller, 6 Ves. 353. Cass
v. Rudele, 2 Vern. 280.   Poole v.
Adams, 33 L. J., Ch. 639.
(u) Poole v. Adams, 33 L. J., Ch.
639.

into for the sale of an estate holden for two lives, and
one of the lives drops before the conveyance is executed, the loss will be the loss of the purchaser. (x) And,
if a man signs an agreement for the purchase of an
annuity, payable during the life of a third party, and
the latter " happens to die before the annuity is legally
transferred to the purchaser, the death can form
no objection to the specific performance of the
contract," (y) and the purchaser must pay his money,
although he can never enjoy that for which it was
agreed to be paid. If, on the other hand, any profit
or gain accrues, it will belong to the purchaser.
Therefore, if a reversionary interest is agreed to be purchased, and lives drop between the time of the making
of the agreement and the execution of a conveyance,
the purchaser will have the benefit of it. (z) If an
estate is sold for an annuity to be paid by the purchaser
during the life of the vendor, and the vendor dies
after the signing of the agreement and before the
execution of the conveyance, the purchaser will nevertheless remain the equitable owner of the property,
and will be entitled to call upon the heir at law of the
vendor for a conveyance of the legal estate ; and he
may thus acquire the property without the payment
of a single shilling of money. (a) But he must not
sleep over his rights. (b) And it must be observed

(x) White v. Nutts, 1 P. Wms. 62.
So by the civil law, "cum autem emptio et venditio contracta sit, periculum
rei venditæ statim ad emptorem pertinet, tametsi adhuc ea res emptori tra-
dita non sit. Itaque, si aut ædes totæ
vel aliqua ex parte incendio consump-
tæ fuerint, emptoris damnum est, cui
necesse est, licet rem non fuerit nactus,
pretium solvere. Sed et si post emp-
tionem fundo aliquid ad emptoris com-

modum pertinet : nam et commodum
ejus essedebet cujus periculum est."
Instit. lib. 3, tit. 24, § 3.

(y) Kenney v. Wexham, 6 Mad.
357.

(z) Ex parte Manning, 2 P. Wms.
410.

(a) Mortimer v. Capper, 1 Bro. C.
C. 156. Jackson v. Lever, 3 Ib. 604.

(b) Wyvill v. Bishop of Exeter. 1
Pr. 292.

that if the annuity becomes due before the death of the vendor, and the purchaser has neglected to pay it or tender payment, the court will render him no assistance. (*c*) But the simple contract of purchase and sale must, of course, be a complete and concluded contract, in order to transfer the right of property and the risk of loss to the purchaser. In the case of judicial sales by the court in the master's office, the contract of sale is not considered to be concluded until the master's report is confirmed as to the party who is the best purchaser, and the title is accepted, and in some cases not until the purchase-money is brought into court, or paid into the bank. (*d*) In order to transfer the right of property and the risk of loss, it must also appear that the vendor has a good title at the time of the making of the contract, or before the disaster happened, and that he was clothed with the estate or interest he agreed to sell ; for, if he had not himself got the estate, it can not of course have passed to the purchaser.

513. *Of the production and proof of the vendor's title.*—It is the first duty of the vendor, when an executory contract of sale has been concluded, to prepare and show to the purchaser satisfactory evidence of title. "An agreement to make out a good title is implied from every contract for the sale of realty ;" (*e*) and a purchaser is not bound to accept a doubtful title.[1] If no precise time is fixed within which the title is to be deduced, the vendor will have a rea-

(*c*) Pope *v.* Roots, 1 Bro. P. C. 370.

(*d*) Twigg v. Fifield, 13 Ves. 518. Vincent v. Going. 3 Dru. & W. 75. Mackrett v. Hunt, 2 Mad. 34, n.

(*e*) Hall v. Betty, 4 M. & Gr. 410 ; 5 Sc. N. R. 508. Dick v. Donald, 1 Bligh, N. S. 655.

[1] See Dearth v. Williamson, 2 Serg. & R. 500; Sweitzer v. Hummell, 3 Id. 228.

sonable time for its establishment. (f)[1]   He may, if
he thinks fit, stipulate for the sale of an estate with
such a title only as he happens to have ; and in such

(f) Sansom v. Rhodes, 6 Bing. N. C. 261 ; 8 Sc. 544.

[1] A vendor of land who has covenanted to convey on a day
certain, will not be in default until the party entitled to the
conveyance has demanded it, and having waited a reasonable
time for the preparation and execution of the deed, has demanded it a second time.   But if the first demand was refused,
a second will not be necessary.   Connelly v. Pierce, 2 Wend.
129 ; Blood v. Goodrich, 9 Wend. 68.
As to the essentiality of delivery to a deed, see Hulick v.
Scovil, 4 Gilm. 175 ; Church v. Gilman, 12 Wend. 656 ; Fairbanks v. Metcalf, 8 Mass. 230 ; Stiles v. Brown, 16 Vt. 563 ;
Fletcher v. Mansur, 5 Ind. 267.   Once delivered, a deed can
not be defeated by subsequent acts not conditioned in the
deed itself. Washburn on Real Property, vol. ii. p. 577. There
can be but one delivery of the same deed.   (Id.)   The deed
takes effect from the time of its delivery, not from its date,
though *prima facie* they are supposed to be identical.   Id. ;
Jackson v. Bard, 4 Johns. 230 ; Harrison v. Phillips Academy,
12 Mass. 455 ; Geiss v. Odenheimer, 4 Yeates, 278 ; Cutts v.
York Co., 18 Me. 190 ; Colquhoun v. Alkinson, 6 Munf. 515.
The delivery must be intentional.   If a deed be laid upon a
table by the grantor in the presence of the grantee, with the
intention of the latter taking it, that is a good delivery ; but
if the grantor laid it down with no such intention, the
grantee's taking it up does not amount to a delivery.   Washburn, vol. ii., p. 604 ; Methodist Church v. Jaques, 1 Johns.
Ch. 456.   But see Fisher v. Beckwith, 30 Wis. 55, holding
that when a grantor has been guilty of negligence in having
made, signed, and acknowledged the deed, and keeping or
depositing it in a place where he knew the party named as
grantee might possess himself of it if so disposed, he is
estopped from setting up in title against an innocent purchaser for value.   And see as to what is not a delivery,
Deanesney v. Graveline, 56 Ill. 93 ; Duncan v. Pope, 47 Ga.
445 ; Stanton v. Miller, 65 Barb. 58 ; Ford v. James, 2 Abb.
(N. Y.) App. Dec. 159. Delivery by a corporation will
ordinarily consist in the attaching thereto of their common
seal by their consent.   Washburn, vol. ii. p. 578.   If they authorize their attorney to deliver it, it is not their deed until
formally delivered by him (Id.).   Delivery to the authorized

a case the purchaser will be bound to take whatever interest the vendor has in the premises, whether free-hold, leasehold, or copyhold. (*g*)   The vendor must

(*g*) Freme v. Wright, 4 Mad. 364. Duke v. Barnett, 2 Coll. C. C. 337.

agent of a corporation, is a delivery to that corporation. Western R. R. v. Babcock, 6 Met. (Mass.) 356.

A delivery of a deed to the agent of the grantee, to be held while he considers whether or not to accept, is no delivery. Ford v. James, 2 Abb. (N. Y.) App. Dec. 159. In Hatch v. Hatch, 9 Mass, 307; and Foster v. Mansfield, 3 Met. (Mass.) 412, a father made a deed to his son, and left it in the hands of a stranger, to be delivered to the son after his (the father's) death, and the delivery was held good, although it was not regarded as an escrow by the grantor; and see O'Kelly v. O'Kelly, 8 Met. (Mass.) 439. See as to what will be considered as an escrow, Marsh v. Austin, 1 Allen 238; Hulick v. Scoville, 4 Gilm. 176; Buffum v. Green, 5 N. H. 71; Belden v. Carter, 49 Day 66; Ruggles v. Lawson, 13 Johns. 285; Morrison v. Kelly, 22 Ill. 626; Wheelright v. Wheelright, 2 Mass. 447; Foster v. Mansfield, 3 Met. 412; Wisson v. Stevens, 4 Ired. Eq. 557; Oliver v. Stone, 24 Ga. 63; Cincinnati, &c., R. R. v. Iliff, 13 Ohio St. 249; Church v. Gilman, 15 Wend. 656; Mallett v. Page, 8 Ind. 364; Guard v. Bradley, 7 Id. 600; Stewart v. Weed, 11 Id. 92; Berkshire, &c., Ins. Co. v. Sturges, 13 Gray (Mass.) 177; Phillips v. Houston, 5 Jones (Id.) 302; Boody v. Davis, 20 N. H. 140; Cloud v. Calhoun, 10 Rich. (1 Eq.) 358; Mitchell v. Ryan, 3 Ohio St. 382; Bullit v. Taylor, Miss. 741; Boardman v. Dean, 34 Pa. St. 252.

But there can be no delivery without an acceptance on the part of the grantee, and an act of delivery and acceptance must be mutual and concurrent. Washburn, vol. ii. p. 581; Mitchell v. Ryan, 3 Ohio St. 386; Jackson v. Bodle, 20 Johns. 184; Dikes v. Miller, 24 Tex. 417.

Mere proof of acceptance at a time subsequent to the act of delivery will not give validity to a deed unless, the act of delivery were one in its nature continuing until acceptance, *e. g.*, such as leaving a deed on deposit, to be accepted by the grantee at his election. Maynard v. Maynard, 10 Mass. 456; Rennell v. Weyant, 2 Har. 501; Elsey v. Metcalf, 1 Den. 326; Jones v. Bush, 2 Harring. 1; Church v. Gilman, 15 Wend. 656; Jackson v. Dunlap, 1 John's. Cas. 114; Canning v. Pinkham, 1 N. H. 353; Buffum v. Green, 5 N. H. 71; Hulick

furnish, at his own expense, an abstract of his title,
consisting of a written statement containing with
sufficient fullness the effect of every instrument which

v. Scovil, 4 Gilm. 177 ; Lloyd v. Giddings, 7 Ohio, 2.   But see
Mitchel v. Ryan, 3 Ohio St. 377.

A deed handed to a party to see if it is satisfactory ; or to
an attorney, with the remark that it was not to be binding
until something else was done, is not a delivery of that deed.
Graves v. Dudley, 20 N. Y. 76 ; Black v. Shreve, 13 N. J. L.
457. And consult Parker v. Parker, 1 Gray 407 ; How v.
Dewing, 2 Id. 476 ; Philadelphia, &c., R. R. Co. v. Howard,
13 How. 334 ; Worrall v. Muva, 1 Seld. 229 ; and it may be
shown by parol evidence that a deed has not been delivered.
Black v. Lamb, 1 Beasl. (N. J.) 116 ; Black v. Shreve, 13 N.
J. L. 457 ; Roberts v. Jackson, 1 Wend. 478 ; though where a
deed is found in a grantee's hands, the presumption is that it
has been delivered ; Clarke v. Ray, 1 Harr. & J. 319 ; Ward v.
Lewis, 4 Pick. 518 ; Ward v. Ross, 1 Stew. (Ala.) 136 ; Canning v. Pinkham, 1 N. H. 353 ; Cutts v. York Co., 18 Me. 190 ;
Green v. Yarnall, 6 Mo. 326 ; Houston v. Stanton, 11 Ala.
412 ; Chandler v. Temple, 4 Cush. 285 ; Southern Life Ins. Co.
v. Cole, 4 Fla. 359 ; though it may be shown to have been
surreptitiously obtained.   Den v. Farlee, 1 N. J. 279 ; Morris
v. Henderson, 37 Miss. 501 ; Adams v. Frye, 3 Met. 109 ;
Williams v. Sullivan, 10 Rich. Eq. 217 ; Little v. Gibson, 39
N. H. 505 ; Black v. Shreve, 13 N. J. 459 ; but not if delivered
to a stranger ; Church v. Gilman, 6 Wend. 656. Depositing the
deed in the post office has been held to be a delivery ; Mc-
Kenney v. Rhodes, 5 Watts. 343 ; where the grantor has parted
with all control of the deed, and it is upon its face beneficial
to the grantee, its acceptance will be presumed, even if the
delivery was made to one without previous authority to receive it—that is, if the person claiming the deed show affirmatively that the grantee was *in esse* when the delivery was
made ; Hulick v. Scovil, 4 Gilm. 190 ; Beasley v. Atwill. 2
Cal. 231, 236 ; Wall v. Wall, 30 Miss. 91.   When a grantor,
after executing a deed ready for delivery, retains it, by agreement with the grantee, it is neither a delivery nor an acceptance ; Jackson v. Dunlop, 1 Johns. Cas. 114 ; but if, under
those circumstances, the grantor declared that he delivered it,
it has been held to be a delivery.   Stewart v. Weed, 11 Ind.
92 ; Souverbye v. Arden, 1 Johns. Cas. 253, 255 ; Scrugham
v. Wood, 15 Wend. 545.

constitutes part of his title. (*h*)   The abstract ought
to show the state of the title for at least sixty years
immediately preceding the contract of sale. (*i*)   And,

(*h*) Oakden v. Pike, 34 L. J., Ch.   Ex. 175; 42 L. J., Ex. 108.
620. Want v. Stallibrass, L. R., 8   (*i*) Cooper v. Emery, 1 Phill. 388.

No particular words are necessary to accompany a delivery.   Maynard v. Maynard, 10 Mass. 456.   See in this connection, Mitchell v. Ryan, 3 Ohio St. 377, where title was held
to have passed to an infant daughter from her father, who
died before she knew that the deed had been made to her.   As
to delivery by means of registration in the register's office, see
Parker v. Hill, 8 Met. 447; Jackson v. Leek, 12 Wend. 107;
Barns v. Hatch, 3 N. H. 304; Denton v. Perry, 5 Vt. 382;
Harrison v. Phillips Academy, 12 Mass. 455; Jackson v.
Phipps, 12 Johns. 418; Jackson v. Richards, 6 Cow. 617;
Elsey v. Metcalf, 1 Denio, 326; Hedge v. Drew, 12 Pick. 141;
Powers v. Russell, 13 Pick. 69, 77; Parker v. Hill, 8 Met.
447. A delivery after record is good; Porter v. Buckingham,
2 Harring. 197; Baldwin v. Maltsby, 5 Ired. 505; Stillwell v.
Hubbard, 20 Wend. 44; Rathbun v. Rathbun, 6 Barb. 98;
Oliver v. Stone, 24 Ga. 63; Berkshire M. F. Ins. Co. v.
Sturgis, 13 Gray, 177; Boardman v. Dean, 34 Penn. St. 252;
Boody v. Davis, 20 N. H. 140; Shaw v. Hayward, 7 Cush. 174;
Mills v. Gore, 20 Pick. 28.

In certain states a deed made to a married woman, without
her husband's consent, is void as to her; Foley v. Howard, 8
Clarke (Iowa) 36; Melvin v. Proprietors, 16 Pick. 167;
though a wife, after her husband's death, can not verbally
waive or disclaim a grant made to them both during his life-
time; Washburn on Real Property, vol. ii., p. 583.   The relationship of a party to whom the deed is delivered, may be such
that the law will presume an acceptance; as a delivery to a
father for his daughter; Bryan v. Wash, 2 Gilm. 557; or to a
cestui que trust, who was the beneficiary under the deed;
Souverbye v. Arden, 1 Johns. Ch. 240; Jaques v. Methodist
Church, 17 Johns. 577; S. C., 1 Johns. Ch. 456; Cloud v. Calhoun, 10 Rich. Eq. 362; Morrison v. Kelly, 22 Ill. 612.

Remaindermen can take under a deed poll delivered to a
tenant of the estate, though a stranger to the deed.   Phelps v.
Phelps, 17 Md. 134.   Where the deed conveys an estate to one
which is defeasible upon contingency, and the same is thereupon to go over to another, as a contingent limitation, or
there is a contingent remainder limited after the expiration of

upon a sale of leasehold property without any condition protecting the vendor against the production of
deeds, the vendor is bound to produce the lease which

a particular estate, a delivery of the deed to the first taker is a
delivery as to all who may be to take under it.   Folk v. Varn,
9 Rich. Eq. 303.   In the case of several grantees mentioned
in one deed, it may be delivered to one on one day, and to
another on another, and so take effect as to all.   Washburn on
Real Property, vol. ii. p. 583.   But, unless so expressed by
the grantor, a delivery as to one is not a delivery as to all.
Hannah v. Swarner, 8 Watts. 9.   A class of cases is treated
by Washburn (on Real Property, vol. ii. p. 583), where debtors and insolvents deliver deeds in assignment to third persons, for the benefit of creditors.   In one such case, Merrills v.
Swift, 18 Conn. 257, the deed took precedence of an attachment, though not actually received and accepted by the creditor until after the attachment was made; and see Wilt v.
Franklin, 1 Bin. 502.   A deed in a grantee's hands is never an
escrow, although the title may pass, unless, under peculiar
circumstances.   Fairbanks v. Metcalf, 8 Mass. 230, 238;
Brown v. Reynolds, 5 Sneed, 639; Cin. Wil. & Z. R. R. v.
Iliff, 13 Ohio St. 249–254.   And see, as to conditional delivery of bonds, Lawton v. Sager, 11 Barb. 349; Williams v.
Green, F. Moore   ; Foley v. Cowgill, 5 Blackf. 18; Gilbert
v. N. A. Ins. Co., 23 Wend. 43.   In the case of an escrow
some condition is essential, upon performance of which the title
vests.   Millett v. Parker, 2 Met. (Ky.) 608, 616; Worrall v.
Munn, 1 Seld. 229; Wight v. Shelby R. R., 16 B. Monr. 4.
And consult M. & I. Plank Road Co. v. Stevens, 10 Ind. 1.   A
delivery to a party vests the title as the deed of the grantor.
Herdman v. Bratten, 2 Harring. 396; State v. Chrisman, 2
Ind. 126; Plank Road Co. v. Stevens, 10 Id. 1; Black v.
Shreve, 13 N. J. 458; Cincinnati, &c. R. R. Co. v. Iliff, 13
Ohio St. 249; Wheelright v. Wheelright, 2 Mass. 447; State
Bank v. Evans, 3 Green, 155; Foster v. Mansfield, 3 Met. 412;
O'Kelly v. O'Kelly, 8 Id. 434; Shaw v. Hayward, 7 Cush. 175;
Jackson v. Catlin, 2 Johns. 248, 259; Jackson v. Sheldon, 22
Me. 569; White v. Bailey, 14 Conn. 271; Hinman v. Booth,
21 Wend. 267; Green v. Putnam, 1 Barb. 500, 504; Frost v.
Beekman, 1 Johns. Ch. 297; Evarts v. Anges, 4 Wis. 351;
Ruggles v. Lawson, 13 Johns. 285; Shirley v. Ayres, 14 Ohio,
307; Jackson v. Rowland, 6 Wend. 666.   A deed sent inclosed
in a letter to a third person, to be delivered to a grantee upon

is the root of his title, although the lease is more than sixty years old. (*k*) The vendor is not bound to abstract, at his own expense, deeds more than sixty years old, when a good title for sixty years is apparently deduced. But, when any circumstance transpires throwing a serious doubt upon the title as deduced, the vendor must then be at the expense of bringing forward further and earlier evidence to remove the doubt. A delivery of the vendor's title-deeds themselves is not equivalent to the delivery of an abstract of title. (*l*)[1] But the right of the purchaser to have

---

(*k*) Frend v. Buckley, L. R., 5 Q. B. 213; 39 L. J., Q. B. 90.

(*l*) Horne v. Wingfield, 3 Sc. N. R. 340.

---

his paying a certain sum, is an escrow; Clark v. Gifford, 10 Wend. 310; Gilbert v. N. A. Ins. Co., 23 Id. 43; State Bank v. Evans, 3 Green, 155; Millett v. Parker, 2 Met. (Ky.) 616. If an escrow be delivered before the condition is performed, no title will pass. Stiles v. Brown, 16 Vt. 563, 569; Jackson v. Sheldon, 22 Me. 569; State Bank v. Evans, 3 Green, 155; Rhodes v. Gardiner, 30 Me. 110; unless the grantee holding it convey the land to a bona fide purchaser, ignorant of the fact as to the delivery. Blight v. Schenck, 10 Penn. St. 285; Peter v. Wright, 6 Ind. 183; Souverbye v. Arden, 1 Johns. Ch. 240. Everts v. Agnes, 4 Wis. 343; Cincinnati, &c. R. R. v. Iliff, 13 Ohio St. 249; Southern, &c. Ins. Co. v. Cole, 2 Fla. 359. If a feme covert deliver a deed as an escrow, and become discovert before the second delivery, such second delivery will give no validity to the deed, the first being void. Washburn on Real Property, vol. ii. 587. And as to when the party who makes the deed dies before the event happens, which was to make it effectual, see Jackson v. Catlin, 2 Johns. 248, 259; Hatch v. Hatch, 9 Mass. 307, 310; Jackson v. Rowland, 6 Wend. 666; Shirley v. Ayres, 14 Ohio, 309; Ruggles v. Lawson, 13 Johns. 285; Carr v. Hoxie, 5 Mason, 60; Evans v. Gibbs, 6 Humph. 405; Frost v. Beekman, 1 Johns. Ch. 257.

[1] A question may arise in England, under certain circumstances, as to who has a right to the custody of title deeds. But probably under the American system of registration no such question would arise (Williams on Real Property, 375;

an abstract may, of course, be waived ; and, if the
agreement for the purchase provides for the delivery
of an abstract to the purchaser at the vendor's expense,
this stipulation may be waived by an acceptance on
the part of the purchaser of the title-deeds themselves,
and a perusal and consideration of them and approval
of the title on the part of the purchaser's attorney or
counsel ; but the fact of the approval and of the
waiver of the delivery of the abstract must be established through the medium of letters and written evidence of the same legal character and importance as
that by which the contract itself is authenticated, and
can not be established through the medium of oral
testimony.

A proviso that, in case the vendor can not deduce
a good title or the purchaser shall not pay the money
on the appointed day the agreement shall be void,
does not enable either party to vitiate the agreement
by refusing to perform his part of it. The meaning
is that, if the vendor can not make out a title, the
purchaser shall be at liberty to be off the bargain ; and
so e contra, if the purchaser is not ready with the
money, the vendor may refuse to carry out the contract ; but "the purchaser can not say, 'I am not
ready with my money ; therefore I will avoid the contract ;' nor can the vendor say, ' My title is not good ;
therefore I will be off.' " (*m*) Where there is a
proviso that, if the purchaser shall raise objections to
the title which the vendor shall not be able or willing

(*m*) Roberts v. Wyatt, 2 Taunt. 277.

Rawles' note ; Washburn on Real Property, vol. i. § 33). In
case of the granting of the fee the English deeds usually contain a clause in relation to the transfer of the title deeds, but
there is of course no necessity for such a clause with us. Id.
vol. ii. § 65.

to remove, the vendor shall be at liberty to rescind the contract, the vendor, when the objections are sent in, must determine which of the two courses he will adopt. If he expresses his willingness to remove the objections, he is forever thereafter precluded from exercising the option given him to rescind the contract. (*n*) If the time for making objections to the title is limited, the limitation is waived by the vendor's receiving and considering the objections after the time appointed, provided the fact can be established through the medium of letters or any evidence in writing. (*o*) Where, after notice of rescinding the contract, a correspondence on the title is continued under protest, this gives to the transaction the character of a treaty for the renewal of the rescinded contract. (*p*) If it is provided that no further evidence of the identity of the parcels shall be required beyond what is afforded by the title-deeds and documents abstracted, and the descriptions in the documents differ, the purchaser is entitled to further proof of identity. (*q*) If it is provided that no other title shall be required than that deduced by a particular abstract, the purchaser is not precluded from objecting to the title as it appears upon the face of the abstract. (*r*) If a party sells an estate without having a title, but before he is called upon to make a conveyance, gets such an estate as will enable him to make a title, that is sufficient. (*s*)[1]

(*n*) Tanner v. Smith, 10 Sim. 411.

(*o*) Cutts v. Thodey, 13 Sim. 206.

(*p*) Southcomb v. Bishop of Exeter, 16 L. J., Ch. 378 ; 11 Jur. 275.

(*q*) Flower v. Hartopp, 6 Beav. 476.

Nicholl v. Chambers, 21 L. J., C. P. 54.

(*r*) Sellick v. Trevor, 11 M. & W. 729.

(*s*) Thompson v. Miles, 1 Esp. 185.

[1] Tison v. Smith, 8 Tex. 147 ; Wilson's Estate, 2 Burr. 325

514. *Of the title to reality.*—An agreement to sell
a house or land generally, not specifying the estate or
interest of the vendor, is in contemplation of law an
agreement to sell an estate in fee : and the purchaser
may refuse to complete his contract, if the vendor is
unable to make out a title to, and convey, such an
estate. (*t*)   But, if the abstract of title, when delivered,
shows that the vendor is possessed only of a life estate
or a term of years, and the purchaser, after the delivery
of such abstract, proceeds with the purchase and accepts the title, the contract will be deemed to be a
contract for the sale and purchase of the estate and
interest disclosed upon the face of the abstract.   If the
agreement specifies the precise nature of the estate or
interest bargained for and agreed to be sold, and the
abstract discloses a title to a different estate in the
same land, and the purchaser accepts the title in writing, the contract for the sale and purchase of the first-
named estate will be deemed to be abandoned, and a
new contract set up for the purchase of the interest
disclosed upon the face of the abstract.   But an oral
acceptance of the title, and an oral agreement to accept such subsequently disclosed interest in lieu of the

---

(*t*) Hughes v. Parker, 8 M. & W. 244.

Whenever the grantor of a defective title afterwards acquires
a good title, it enures to the benefit of his grantee.   McCall v.
Coover, 4 Watts. & Serg. 151.   In Mays v. Swope (8 Gratt.
46), it was held that where a vendee of land discovered a technical defect in the title, and thereupon abandoned it, and
brought a bill to enjoin the collection of the purchase
money, he nevertheless could not refuse to accept the title
upon its being made perfect.   If a grantor convey the whole
of a tract of land of which he owns but a parcel—if he afterward come into possession of the rest, it enures to the
benefit of his grantee.   Tyson v. Passmore, 2 Burr. 122.

estate originally bargained for, can not be set up in opposition to the original contract. (*u*)   A contract to make a good title to an estate means, of course, a title both good at law and in equity. (*x*)   If, therefore, the vendor has only a naked legal title as a trustee, or a mere equitable interest without the legal estate, the contract as to title is not fulfilled. (*y*) '   A title may be good, and the purchaser be compelled to complete the purchase, although there may be no title-deeds to produce.   " There are good titles of which the origin can not be shown by deed or will ; but then you must show something that is satisfactory to the mind of the court, that there has been such a long, uninterrupted possession, enjoyment, and dealing with the property, as affords a reasonable presumption that there is an absolute title in fee-simple." (*z*)   If a conveyance to a purchaser has been accidentally burned, the vendor, if living, will be compelled to execute a fresh conveyance, and supply the defect in the title occasioned by the accident. (*a*)

515. *Of the period for which the title ought to be shown* —As an estate for life may last sixty years, and thirty years more may be required, in case of disabilities, to bar the claim of the remainderman, it is

---

(*u*) Deverell v. Lord Bolton, 18 Ves. 510.

(*x*) Maberly v. Robins, 1 Marsh. 258 ; 5 Taunt. 625. Jeakes v. White, 21 L. J., Ex. 265. Boyman v. Gutch, 7 Bing. 279.

(*y*) Elliott v. Edwards, 3 B. & P. 183. Cane v. Baldwin, 1 Stark. 65.

(*z*) Cottrell v. Watkins, 1 Beav. 365. Scott v. Nixon, 3 Dru. & W. 405.

(*a*) Bennett v. Ingoldsby, Finch, 262.

' A tender of title is not good from another than the vendor.   So, in a contract for sale, when part of the land belongs to a third person, the latter's tender to the purchaser of a deed of that part owned by him, with covenants of warranty from himself, is not a tender of the deed and covenants of the first vendor.   Cook v. Grant, 16 Sergt. & R. 198 ; and see as to delivery of a deed, *ante,* vol. i. p. 49 ; of an escrow, Id. p. 51.

obvious that the period of sixty years for which the title is, by the general practice of the profession, required to be carried back, is not too long, and that a purchaser would not be safe in limiting his researches to a shorter space of time. " By the Vendor and Purchaser Act, 1874 (37 & 38 Vict. c. 78), s. 1, in the completion of any contract of sale of land made after December 31, 1874, and subject to any stipulation to the contrary in the contract, forty years shall be substituted as the period of commencement of title which a purchaser may require in place of sixty years, the present period of such commencement ; nevertheless earlier title than forty years may be required in cases similar to those in which earlier title than sixty years may now be required." The Statute of Limitations (3 & 4 Wm. 4, c. 27), consequently, although it has made a sixty years' title, a better title than it was before, has in nowise abridged the time for which the title must be shown ; and every purchaser is still entitled, as we shall presently see, to the production of a sixty years' title on the part of the vendor. (*b*) An oral stipulation that the title is not to be made out, beyond a limited period can not, as previously mentioned, be engrafted upon a written contract which makes no mention of such a stipulation ; but, if a notice in writing to that effect can be proved to have been given to the purchaser prior to the making of the contract, the latter must accept the title as limited, unless he can show that he had refused to be bound by the notice, and had declined to treat on the terms sought to be imposed on him. (*c*)

516. *Title to leaseholds.*—If an agreement is made for the sale of leasehold property (not being a church lease), the vendor is bound to establish the

---

(*b*) Cooper v. Emery, 1 Phil. 383.   (*c*) Ogilvie v. Foljambe, 3 Mer. 65.

lessor's title to grant the lease, unless there is an express stipulation to the contrary in the contract ; and no agreement to dispense with the production of the lessor's title will be implied from the antiquity of the lease, (*d*) the shortness of the term for which the lease is granted, the small value of the property, or the absence of a premium. " By the Vendor and Purchaser Act, 1874 (37 & 38 Vict., c. 78), s. 2, it is enacted in the completion of any contract made after the 31st of December, 1874, and subject to any stipulation to the contrary in the contract, under a contract to grant or assign a term of years, whether derived or to be derived out of a freehold or leasehold estate the intended lessee or assign shall not be entitled to call for the title to the freehold." (*e*) But there is no such implied engagement in the case of a bargain for the purchase of an agreement for a lease. (*f*) If the vendor stipulates that he shall not be obliged to produce the lessor's title, this stipulation does not, of course, preclude the purchaser from taking any objection derived from another source to the validity of that title. (*g*) But, if the purchaser agrees to take the title that the vendor has, and to purchase the lease as holden by him, he will be precluded from objecting to the title. (*h*) The obligation to produce the lessor's title does not, it seems, extend to church leases and bishops' leases. (*i*) Upon the sale of a leasehold for lives, expressed to have been granted by a corporation in consideration of the surrender of a

(*d*) Frend v. Buckley, L. R., 5 Q. B. 213 ; 39 L. J., Q. B. 90.

(*e*) Souter v. Drake, 5 B. & Ad. 992; 3 N. M. 40. Hall v. Betty, 5 Sc. N. R. 508 ; 4 M. & Gr. 410. Purvis v. Rayer, 9 Pr. 488. Deverell v. Lord Bolton, 18 Ves. 505.

(*f*) Kintrea v. Preston, 1 H. & N. 357 ; 25 L. J., Ex. 287.

(*g*) Shepherd v. Keatly, 1 C. M. & R. 117.

(*h*) Spratt v. Jeffery, 10 B. & C. 249.

(*i*) Fane v. Spencer, 2 Mad. 438.

prior lease, the title to the surrendered lease must be shown. (*k*)   When a man professes to grant or sell a lease, it is, of course, understood to be a lease which the lessee or purchaser may insist upon as good against all the world.   If, therefore, a covenant or condition has been broken, and a right to re-enter has accrued to the superior landlord, and the vendor is unable to put the purchaser into possession of a good lease, he is responsible in damages for a breach of contract. (*l*)   If the consent of the original lessor is essential to the validity of the transfer or assignment of the lease to the purchaser, it is, of course, the duty of the vendor to procure that consent. (*m*)   When leaseholds, consisting of several houses held under the same lease, are sold in several lots to distinct purchasers, and the lease contains covenants affecting the whole, with a proviso enabling the landlord to re-enter in the case of the breach of any one covenant, the purchaser of one lot may be evicted without any default on his own part, but solely through the default of another purchaser. (*n*)   Very great inconveniences may arise and great risk be run of the loss of the entire purchase from such a state of circumstances: the covenants of the original lease, therefore, should be strictly examined.   When such covenants exist, the purchaser is not bound to accept the title with an indemnity. (*o*)

517. *Waiver of proof of title and of objections to title.*—Where a person contracted for the purchase of a lease of a public-house, and of the stock and goodwill, and entered into possession, paid part of the

(*k*) Hodgkinson v. Cooper, 9 Beav. 304; 15 L. J., Ch. 160.

(*l*) Penniall v. Harborne, 11 Q. B. 368; 17 L. J., Q. B. 94.   Nouaille v. Flight, 7 Beav. 521.

(*m*) Lloyd v. Crispe, 5 Taunt 249. Mason v. Corder, 7 Id. 9; 2 Marsh. 332.

(*n*) Patterson v. Long, 6 Beav. 597.

(*o*) Blake v. Phinn, 3 C. B. 976.

purchase-money, and mortgaged his interest, it was
held that he had waived his right to call for the production of the lessor's title. (*p*)[1] The mere taking
possession of lands and tenements under an agreement
for the purchase of them, before any abstract has been
delivered, or proof of title produced, does not, of
course, amount to a waiver of the purchaser's right to
have an abstract delivered and title proved in the
usual and ordinary course ; (*q*) nor does the taking
possession by the purchaser, after the delivery of an
abstract, amount to an acceptance of the title, where
the vendor has no title at all to the estate and interest bargained for and agreed to be conveyed. But,
if possession is given under the contract, and the
abstract of title is delivered, and the purchaser continues in possession for a lengthened period, making
no objections at all to the title, or only frivolous
objections, with a view of delaying payment of the
purchase money, the court will decree payment without going into any investigation of title, unless the
title is clearly shown to be bad. (*r*) Proof of title to
transfer the estate agreed to be sold is a condition
precedent to the vendor's right to the purchase
money ; and the court can not, of course, make a
purchaser accept a title which does not exist, and will
not compel him to pay the purchase money, when it
can not give him the estate for which he agreed to
pay it. (*s*) A purchaser can not be held to have

(*p*) Haydon v. Bell, 1 Beav. 337.   1 Mad. 310. Hall v. Laver, 3 You. &
(*q*) Burroughs v. Oakley, 3 Swanst.   C. 196.
171.   (*s*) Blachford v. Kirkpatrick, 6 Beav.
(*r*) Margravine of Anspach v. Noel,   236.

[1] One entering upon land, under a contract to purchase, or
those claiming under him, is estopped from denying his vendor's title. See Pyles v. Reeve, 4 Rich. 555.

waived objections to title because his counsel has approved of the title. (*t*)　And, even if he expressly accepts the title as satisfactory, such acceptance does not preclude him from subsequently showing that the vendor has no title at all, and that the acceptance had been made under a misapprehension and mistake. (*u*) If it is stipulated by the contract that objections to title are to be considered as waived unless made within a certain time, the time is made of the essence of the contract; so that, if the objection is not sent in within the time, the vendor has a right to take the benefit of the condition, and say that the title has been accepted, unless the abstract is so defective that no title is shown upon the face of it. (*v*)　If the purchaser takes possession under the contract, and afterwards rejects the title, he may be turned out of possession by the vendor, and can not, in general, claim compensation for improvements. (*y*)　Lastly, it may be observed that, whenever a third person, having any right or title to lands or tenements about to be sold, knows of the sale and of his own title, and neglects to give the purchaser notice thereof, " he shall never afterwards be admitted to set up such right to avoid the purchase ; for it was an apparent fraud in him not to give notice of his title to the intended purchaser ; and, in such case, infancy and coverture shall be no excuse." (*z*)　A purchaser may, by taking possession of the estate agreed to be sold to him after the delivery of an abstract apprising him of the existence of certain incumbrances, waive his right of objecting to

(*t*) Deverell v. Lord Bolton, 18 Ves. 505.

(*u*) Warren v. Richardson, 1 You. 1. Ward v. Trathen, 14 Sim. 82. Bousfield v. Hodges, 33 Beav. 90.

(*v*) Blacklow v. Laws, 2 Hare, 40.

Oakden v. Pike, 34 L. J., Ch. 620.

(*y*) Nicloson v. Wordsworth, 2 Swanst. 365.

(*z*) Savage v. Foster, 9 Mod. 38. Sharpe v. Foy, L. R., 4 Ch. 35.

the title, on the ground of the existence of such incumbrances. Where, for example, a purchaser took
possession of an estate after the delivery of an abstract of title, on the face of which it appeared that
part of the estate was subject to a right of sporting, it
was held that he had waived his right to object to
the title on the ground of the existence of such a
right. (*a*)

518. *Of the production of the title-deeds.*—After
the title, as disclosed upon the abstact, has been approved of and accepted by the purchaser or his legal
advisers, the title-deeds themselves must be produced
for inspection and examination and verification with
the abstract. If they are not produced, the purchaser
will not be bound to complete his purchase. In the
case of a sale of a copyhold estate, the copies of court-
roll are the documents of title, and must be furnished
to the purchaser for comparison with the abstract. (*b*)
The vendor is in all cases bound to produce and show
to the purchaser all deeds and writings in his possession or under his control that in anywise relate to or
concern the property agreed to be sold, whatever be
their date or age ; but he is not in general bound, as
we shall presently see, to furnish an abstract of any
deed of an earlier date than sixty years. If the deeds
abstracted refer to prior deeds, settlements, or wills
not in the possession or under the control of the vendor, and the absence of the deed so referred to throws
a serious doubt upon the title, the purchaser will
not be bound to complete his purchase. "When
the title under the conveyance which contains the re-
cital is fortified by sixty years' undisputed possession,
the loss of the deed recited throws no reasonable doubt

(*a*) Burnell v. Browne, 1 Jac. &   (*b*) Whitbread v. Jordan, 1 You. &
Walk. 168.   C. 318.

upon the title." (c)   If a deed or will in the abstract
professes to have been made in execution of a power
of appointment contained in a previous deed or will
more than sixty years old, and not abstracted, the purchaser will be entitled to call for the production of the
deed, if it is in the possession of the vendor, to see that
the power has been properly executed.   But, if there
has been sixty years' undisputed possession by the
parties entitled under the appointment, and the deed
creating the power is not in the possession or under
the control of the vendor, the presumption is in favor
of a valid execution of the power, and the purchaser
will be compelled to complete his contract, unless he
can bring forward evidence impeaching the validity of
the appointment, and throwing a reasonable doubt
upon the title.

519. *Loss of title-deeds after delivery of the abstract.*—If the title-deeds are destroyed by accident
after approval of the title, the vendor must furnish the
purchaser with the means of proving the actual existence of the deeds, their contents, and that they were
duly delivered and executed by all necessary parties. [1]

(c) Prosser v. Watts, Mad. & Geld. 60.   Moulton v. Edmonds, 29 L. J.,Ch. 131.

[1] The system of registering deeds prevalent in the United
States, and which in spite of efforts in Parliament and of able
publicists, has been steadily resisted in England (with the
exception, it seems, only of the West Riding of Yorkshire)
differs from the old enrollment of deeds of bargain and sale
required by the statute 27 Hen. viii. ch. 16, in that, with few
exceptions, the registration has nothing to do with the validity of the deed; and in Indiana (Gwair v. Doe, 7 Blackf. 210)
and in New York (Jackson v. Wood, 12 Johns. 74), this enrollment itself has been held to be unnecessary to the validity of
this description of deed.   Each state with us, however, has
provided for the appointment of public officers who shall
register the deeds of the jurisdiction, and preserve and per-
petuate such records for public reference, which thereafter are

If the abstract of title has been delivered and compared with the deeds themselves prior to their destruction, this may afford the means of proving the contents of the deeds; but it must then be shown who the at-

a public and constructive notice to all persons interested, of any prior conveyance, lien, or incumbrance, as effectual in law as if given personally to a party. Hill v. Epley, 31 Pa. St. 335; and see Morrison v. Kelly, 22 Ill. 610; Belk v. Massey, 11 Rich. (Law) 614; Godbold v. Lambert, 8 Rich. (Eq.) 155; Moore v. Jourdan, 14 La. An. 414; Nutting v. Herbert, 37 N. H. 346; Pomroy v. Stevens, 11 Met. 244; Mara v. Pierce, 9 Gray, 306; Dooley v. Wolcott, 4 Allen, 406; Billington v. Welsh, 5 Binn. 129; 4 Dane, Ab. 85; Watkins v. Edwards, 23 Texas, 443; Partridge v. McKinney, 10 Cal. 181; Stafford v. Lick, 7 Cal. 479; Hunter v. Watson, 12 Cal. 363; Helms v. May, 29 Ga. 121; Wyatt v. Elam, 23 Ga. 201; Berg v. Shipley, 1 Grant Cas. 429; Coleman v. Barklew, 3 Dutch. 357; Lea v. Polk Co. Copper Co., 21 How. 493.

The duty of registering the deeds is a ministerial one simply, and not a judicial one; and any instrument properly acknowledged by a magistrate (who must certify in effect that the maker who is personally known to him has appeared before him and acknowledged the same to be his voluntary act) is entitled to be copied upon the books of the registrar's office. This provision, although framed to prevent a fraudulent use of the record books, has not always proved effectual for that purpose; and it has been suggested, that, as in France and other countries, the magistrate who takes the acknowledgment be authorized to keep the original instruments, giving duplicates to the parties, which, in addition to our present system of registry, would, it is thought, make the forgery of instruments of title practically impossible. At present, a registration not in the proper district, or by an officer beyond the limits of his appointment, is void. Harper v. Tapley, 35 Miss. 510; Lynch v. Livingston, 8 Barb. 463; Harris v. Burton, 4 Harring. 66; Jackson v. Humphrey, 1 Johns. 498; Jackson v. Colden, 4 Cow. 287; Howard, &c. Association v. McIntyre, 3 Allen, 572; Thurman v. Cameron, 24 Wend. 91; contra, Ordiorne v. Mason, 9 N. H., 30.

The certificate, to entitle to registry, must show affirmatively that all acts required by the statute have been substantially complied with. Jackoway v. Gault, 20 Ark. 190; Bryan v. Reming, 8 Cal. 461. The certificate is, however, not so

testing witnesses were, and that the deeds were duly executed and delivered, and the purchaser must be furnished with the means of proof thereof, for the purpose of asserting his title and defending his possession.

conclusive that it can not be impeached. Jackson v. Schoonmaker, 4 Johns. 161; Dodge v. Hollinshead, 6 Minn. 46.

The certificate is received as evidence of its own genuineness, without its first being shown affirmatively by whom the certificate is made, if it be in proper form. Thurman v. Cameron, 24 Wend. 87; Thompson v. Morgan, 6 Minn. 295; Tracy v. Jenks, 15 Pick. 465. But it is competent for a party con testing the deed to show with what intent the grantor acknowledged it, in order to establish that the deed was only inchoate, and never fully executed and delivered. Hutchinson v. Rust, 2 Gratt. 394. In Minnesota the certificate of acknowledgment of a married woman, made by a magistrate upon a deed, may be controlled or contradicted by evidence. Dodge v. Hollinshead, 6 Minn. 25; Annan v. Folsom, Id. 300. But in Indiana such certificate is conclusive evidence. M'Neely v. Rucker, 6 Blackf. 397.

In certain states, viz. : Alabama, Iowa, Kentucky, Massachusetts, Mississippi, Missouri, New Jersey, Ohio, Rhode Island, South Carolina, and Virginia, it appears to have been held that the date of a deed is constructively the date of its registration. Mallory v. Stodeter, 6 Ala. 801; Dubois v. Young, 10 Id. 365; Warnock v. Wightman, 1 Green, 52; Hopping v. Burnam, 2 Id. 39; Gill v. Fannelleroy, 8 B. Mon. 177; Mass. Gen. Stat. ch. 17, § 93; McRaven v. McGuire, 9 S. & M. 34; Harold v. Simond, 9 Mo. 326; Davis v. Ownsby, 14 Mo. 175; Nichols v. Reynolds, 1 R. I. 30; Horsley v. Garth, 2 Gratt. 471; and see Quirk v. Thomas, 6 Mich. 76; McCabe v. Gray, 20 Cal. 509. A deed duly recorded is constructive notice of its existence, and its contents to all persons claiming what is thereby conveyed under the same grantor by subsequent purchase or mortgage, but not to other persons. Bates v. Norcross, 14 Pick. 224, 231; Tilton v. Hunter, 24 Me. 35; Little v. Megquier, 2 Id. 176; Crockett v. Maguire, 10 Mo. 34. See Flynt v. Arnold, 2 Met. 619; Whittington v. Wright, 9 Ga. 23; Shults v. Moore, 1 McLean, 520; Doe v. Beardsley. 2 Id. 412; Shaw v. Poor, 6 Pick. 85, 88. But the record is not constructive notice of its existence or contents, unless all the prerequisites prescribed by law in respect to its registration be observed, such as its acknowledgment or witnessing :

If no such proof is afforded, the purchaser is dis.
charged. (*d*)   If, after the making of the contract, the
purchaser is let into possession, and the contract is

(*d*) Bryant v. Busk, 4 Russ. 4.

Meighen v. Strong, 6 Miss. 177 ; have been complied with. Nor
would it be constructive notice, if the deed were on record in
any way not authorized by law, or if the instrument were not
required by law to be recorded.   Shults v. Moore, 1 McLean,
520; Isham v. Bennington Co., 19 Vt. 230; Choteau v. Jones,
11 Ill. 300; Herndon v. Kimball, 7 Ga. 432 ; Tillman v. Cow-
and, 12 S. & M. 262; Blood v. Blood, 23 Pick. 80; De Witt
v. Moulton, 17 Me. 418; Carter v. Champion, 8 Conn. 549;
Heister v. Fortner, 2 Binn. 40; Shaw v. Poor, 6 Pick. 88;
Cheney v. Watkins, 1 Harr. & J. 527 ; Doe v. Smith, 3 McLean,
362; Lewis v. Baird, Id. 56; Kerns v. Swope, 2 Watts, 75 ;
Graves v. Graves, 6 Gray, 391 ; Burnham v. Chandler, 15
Texas, 441; Bossard v. White, 9 Rich. Eq. 483; Galpin v. Abbott, 6 Mich. 17; McKean v. Mitchell, 36 Penn. St. 269; Dus-
saume v. Burnett, 5 Clark, Iowa, 95 ; Peck v. Mallams, 10 N.
Y. 518; Harper v. Barsh, 10 Rich. Eq. 149.   The registry of
a defective deed is no notice of title to any one.   Isham v.
Bennington Iron Co., 19 Vt. 245; Harper v. Barsh, 10 Rich.
Eq. 149.   So a record of a deed in a wrong county has no
effect as a notice.

The record limits by its terms the extent to which it will
be constructive notice to strangers where the condition of a
mortgage as written was for three thousand dollars, but as
recorded, it showed the condition to be three hundred dollars,
it was held to be a constructive notice as to three hundred
dollars only.   Beekman v. Frost, 18 Johns. 544; Frost v.
Beekman, Johns. Ch. 299 ; and see Chamberlin v. Bell, 7 Cal.
292 ; Baltimore, &c. v. White, 2 Gill. 444; Jackson v. Livingston, 10 Johns. 374; Brush v. Ware, 15 Pet. 93; Daughaday
v. Paine, 6 Minn. 452.   If an ordinary diligent search will inform the stranger of incumbrances, he is presumed to know
them; Flynt v. Arnold, 2 Met. (Mass.) 619 ; Gilbert v. Peleler,
38 Barb. 488; one purchasing of another who holds a recorded
deed, will acquire precedence over one holding a prior unrecorded deed, of which he was ignorant, although the holder
of such recorded deed knew of the existence of such prior
deed when he took his own, and could not himself have
claimed any precedence.   " But if the holder of the earlier
deed, have it recorded before the holder of a deed of a later

abandoned or rescinded and comes to nothing, the
purchaser can not be treated as a lessee, and can not
be compelled to pay rent, or to pay for the use, occu-

date but an earlier record, shall have actually conveyed the
estate to another, though he is ignorant of such earlier deed,
the record would be constructive notice to such purchaser from
the holder of the later deed, and defeat his precedency of
title." Washburn on Real Property, vol. ii. p. 595; and see
in the various states, Boynton v. Rees, 8 Pick. 329; Hagthor
v. Hook, 1 Gil. & J. 270; Adams v. Cuddy, 13 Pick. 460; Coffin v. Ray, 1 Met. (Mass.) 212; Trull v. Bigelow, 16 Mass.
406; Flynt v. Arnold, 2 Met. (Mass.) 619; Den v. Richman, 1
Green, 43; Schutt v. Large, 6 Barb. 373; Jackson v. Leek, 19
Wend. 339; Irvin v. Smith, 17 Ohio, 226; Martin v. Quattle-
bam, 3 McCord, 205; Lillard v. Rucker, 9 Yerg. 64, 73; Corliss v. Corliss, 8 Vt. 373; Turner v. Stip, 1 Wash. 319; Sicard
v. Davis, 6 Pet. 124; Van Rensselaer v. Clark, 17 Wend. 25;
Swan v. Moore, 14 La. Ann. 833; Morrison v. Kelly, 22 Ill.
610; Burkhalter v. Ector, 25 Ga. 55; Miller v. Chittenden, 2
Clarke (Iowa), 315; Blain v. Stewart, Id. 378; Ricks v. Reed,
19 Cal. 571; Ohio Life Insurance Co. v. Ledyard, 8 Ala. 866;
Doe v. Reed, 4 Scamm. 117; Givan v. Doe, 7 Blackf. 210;
Doe v. Beardsley, 2 McLean, 421; Hopping v. Burnam, 2
Greene, 39, 48; Applegate v. Gracy, 9 Dana, 224; Boling v.
Ewing, Id. 76; Nason v. Grant, 21 Me. 160; Dixon v. Doe, 1
S. & M. 70; Rogers v. Jones, 8 N. H. 264; Wark v. Willard,
13 Id. 389. Where there are several grantees, notice to the
one who takes the deed is notice to all. Stanley v. Green, 12
Cal. 148.

In Kentucky (Edwards v. Brinker, 9 Dana, 69; Ring v.
Gray, 6 B. Mon. 368), Tennessee (Washington v. Trousdall,
M. & Y. 385; Lillard v. Rucker, 9 Yerg. 64), and Virginia
(Guerrant v. Anderson, 4 Rand. 208), an unrecorded deed, if
known to a subsequent purchaser, is good notice to him, but
not against creditors, although known to him. It seems that
in Alabama, Georgia, Illinois, Kentucky, Mississippi, Missouri,
New Jersey, New York, Pennsylvania, and Virginia, a deed
duly recorded is prima facia evidence; and courts will presume
that all requirements necessary to give the record validity
have been complied with. But in the others it seems that the
deed must be proved as at common law, in order to be used in
evidence in matters involving its own validity.

In the following states: Alabama, Georgia, Illinois, Mis-

pation, and enjoyment of the property. (Post, ch. 2, s. 1.)

520. *Effect of misdescriptions.*—The vendor must

sissippi, Missouri, New Jersey, New York, North Carolina, Pennsylvania, and Virginia, a deed duly acknowledged seems admissible without further proof. Note to § 299, vol. ii. Greenleaf on Evidence. In Massachusetts, the registry copy of a deed of land is not admissible in evidence against the grantee therein, without notice to him to produce the original. Commonwealth v. Emery, 2 Gray, 80; Brown v. Boston, Id. 94. In Warren v. Wade, 7 Jones (L.) 494, it is said that an office copy of a deed inter partes executed in pais, and acknowledged and recorded in the courts of another state, is not such a record or judicial proceeding as can be authenticated under the act of Congress of 1794; though it might perhaps be included under the supplemental act of 1804. Greenleaf on Evidence, vol. ii. § 299, note. See Young v. Ringo, 1 Mon. 30; Toulmin v. Austin, 5 Stew & P. 410.

In Maryland the enrollment of a deed of bargain and sale is evidence of a title in an action of ejectment, without production of the original (Hunn v. Soper, 6 Harr. & J. 276); and in Indiana, Massachusetts, Mississippi, and New Hampshire, and other states, the registry or certified copies of deeds, without the authentication of witnesses, are evidence. Dickson v. Doe, 5 Blackf. 106; Cogan v. Frisby, 36 Miss. 178; Eaton v. Campbell, 7 Pick 10; Scanlan v. Wright, 13 Id. 523; Ward v. Fuller, 15 Id. 185; Farrarr v. Fessenden, 39 N. H. 268; Harvey v. Mitchell, 11 Fost. (N. H.) 582. A deed, even though not so acknowledged as to be entitled to record, may convey a title as against a grantor and his heirs. Blain v. Stewart, 2 Iowa, 383; Doe v. Naylor, 2 Blackf. 32; Gibbs v. Swift, 12 Cush. 393; Ricks v. Reed, 19 Cal. 571; but see in Ohio, Smith v. Hunt, 13 Ohio, 260.

A question of great importance to the American practicing lawyer, was discussed in Doe d. Beanland v. Hurst (11 Price, 475, 489–492), as to whether a deed respecting real estate will be presumed in a county where deeds were registered. The English Act (see Id. p. 492) for registering deeds and conveyances, in the West Riding of Yorkshire, provides that they be so registered to protect the grantee against subsequent bona fide conveyances or mortgages, and in effect is the same as the Registry acts in the United States. In that case a presumption of a grant of care in the West Riding was

be prepared and able to convey and transfer to
the purchaser an estate or interest substantially corresponding with that bargained for and agreed to be

urged as arising from certain circumstances, which was resisted
on the ground that the registry should determine the matter,
and that there was no registry of any such grant.   The omission was relied upon as effectually rebutting the presumption
The point does not appear to have been expressly decided, but to
have been left to the jury by Bailey, J.   On the argument at
bar, Rex v. Long Buckby (7 East, 45) was cited, and appears
to be conclusive that such a case presents as fair a subject of
presumption as any other.   In Rex v. Long Buckby, an indenture of apprenticeship had been lost, and was sought to be
proved by parol.   There was no evidence that it had ever been
stamped, and no registry of such stamping existed at the
stamp office where it would have naturally existed, had there
been no irregularity.   But the court held that after a lapse of
nearly twenty years, during which the indenture of apprenticeship had been acted upon as valid, the evidence of non-
registry was not *per se* sufficient to repel the presumption that
it had been properly stamped, but that it would rather presume that the stamping had been performed, and the registry
in the proper office omitted by mistake.   In Cowen and Hill's
notes to Phillips on Evidence, it is pointed out, as throwing
light upon the question as to the presuming of a deed of conveyance, where no registration of such deed exists, that the
case of the stamp is much stronger as to the presumption of
irregularity, than the case of the registry of a deed could be.
For " this was a case where without a stamp, the indentures
would have been a nullity to all intents, and where in the
regular course of things there must have been a registry.   It
was surely much stronger against the presumption that the
omission to register a deed of conveyance.   The latter are
valid as against the party without registry, and the grantee
being in possession, they would be valid against all the world,
purchasers and mortgagees included.   Governeur v. Lynch, 2
Paige, 300, 301, and cases cited.   Neither are registering acts
imperative, nor is there, in case of a deed, any great danger in
omitting to register.   It is entirely optional with the party,
and if purchasers or mortgagees are uninjured by lack of constructive notice, none others can complain.   Where notice
alone is the object, it is given by a change of possession to
the practice ; and an absolute deed may ordinarily be held

sold, both as regards the tenure and the situation and condition and natural advantages of the property. Any misdescription of the estate or interest, or of the

from the record without any danger. Indeed, this is often so' in practice. And it follows that there is nothing in the omission to register necessarily inconsistent with the common presumption, which involves the previous existence and loss [of the deed] and may equally well include the non-registry." Adverse possession, it seems, must be shown, before any presumption will be made in favor of a claimant. Wadsworthville School v. Meelze, 4 Rich. 347. Permissive possession will raise no such presumption. Roxbury v. Huston, 37 Maine, 42 ; and see Morgan's Best on Evidence, vol. ii., note 1, p. 48. In some of the states a time is prescribed within which a deed when recorded takes effect by relation back from its delivery, and gives it precedence over intermediate conveyances, even as to persons ignorant of such unrecorded deed. Washburn on Real Property, vol. ii. p. 593.

In Ohio such a time is six months for deeds, but mortgages must be recorded forthwith. The record of a deed recorded after the six months is constructive notice only after the actual time when it is made (Id.). In Kentucky, this time is eight months (Applegate v. Grace, 9 Dana, 217); and mortgages must be recorded in sixty days (Id. Dale v. Arnold, 2 Bibb. 605). In Mississippi the time is three months, but, if recorded after that, it is notice from the date of the registry (Id. McRaven v. McGuire, 9 S. & M. 34). In Georgia the time is twelve months, but if after the expiration thereof, the registry is notice from the time of the record, but does not date back to any prior time (Id. Helms v. O'Bannon, 26 Ga. 132 ; Anderson v. Dugar, 29 Id. 440). If two successive deeds are made of the land within the twelve months, but neither is recorded, the recording of the second deed after that time does not give it precedence over the first (Id. Doe v. Reddin, Dudl. (Ga.) 177; Martin v. Williams, 27 Ga. 406). The same rule, says Washburn, applies to the effect of a record in South Carolina (Id. Ledger v. Doyle, 11 Rich. (Law) 109). In Pennsylvania, where the time is six months, in the above case, if the second deed were taken without actual notice of the first, and were recorded first, it would have precedence over the one first executed (Id. Lightner v. Worney, 10 Watts. 407). Mortgages are to be recorded in sixty days (Poth v. Anstall, 4 Watts. & S. 307; Berg v. Shipley, 1 Grant Cas. 429; Souder v.

nature, or situation, or extent, or value of the property
in a material and substantial point, so far affecting the
subject-matter of the contract that it may reasonably
be supposed that, but for such misdescription, the contract would never have been made, at once releases the
purchaser from the bargain. (*e*) If the conditions
and particulars of sale provide that errors and misstatements shall not vitiate the sale, but that an abatement
shall be made in the purchase-money by way of compensation, the provision will extend only to unintentional errors and misstatements in matters of detail,
not amounting to fraud, (*f*) and not materially altering the nature of the subject-matter of the contract
itself; for no man is bound to take an estate or interest
essentially different from that which he agreed to purchase. (*g*) A general agreement to sell a house or

(*e*) Dimmock v. Hallett, L. R., 2
Ch. 21 ; 36 L. J., Ch. 146.

(*f*) Dimmock v. Hallett, L. R., 2
Ch. 21 ; 36 L. J., Ch.; 146. Whitte-

more v. Whittemore, L. R., 8 Eq.
603 ; 38 L. J., Ch. 17.

(*g*) Flight v. Booth, 1 Bing. N. C.
377 ; 1 Sc. 190.

Morrow, 33 Pa. St. 83). So in Ohio (Id. Northrup v.
Brehmer, 8 Ohio, 392). In New Jersey, in the case above
given, the time cited is six months, though the deed may
be recorded after, but not so as to affect a subsequent
bona fida deed, lodged for record before the first. If
the prior deed is lodged for record before the second, after
the expiration of the six months, it will take precedence of the
second (Id. Den v. Richmond, 1 Green, 43). The time is said
to be reduced to fifteen days by statute of 1820. 4 Kent Com.
457, note. In Alabama, the time is six months, but if the deed
is recorded afterwards, it is notice from the time of the record.
Mallory v. Stodder, 6 Ala. 801. If to secure the debt, the time
is three months. Washburn, note, p. 593, vol. ii. The times
allowed for recording deeds in Delaware, Tennessee, and
Indiana, are twelve; in Virginia, eight; and in Maryland,
North and South Carolina, six months. 4 Kent Com. 457.
In Massachusetts, in determining the question of precedence
between a purchaser or mortgagee and a creditor, no time is
allowed for the former, in which to record his deed. Cushing
v. Hurd, 4 Pick. 252.

land means, as we have already seen, that the owner of
the property will sell an estate in fee. The purchaser,
therefore, may refuse to complete the purchase, if the
vendor is unable to transfer a freehold property; but,
if he chooses to take such an estate as the vendor has
in the land, the latter will be bound to transfer his
whole interest to the purchaser. (*h*) And, if an abstract of title has been delivered to the purchaser, showing that the vendor has a different estate and interest
from that bargained for and agreed to be sold, and the
purchaser returns the abstract and accepts the title in
writing, the purchaser will be deemed, as we have already seen, to have assented to take the estate and interest disclosed upon the face of the abstract.

If an estate is subject to a right of sporting, or a
right of common, or a right to dig for mines, or a right
on the part of third persons to have extensive under-
ground watercourses, and to enter upon the land to
open, cleanse, and repair such watercourses, and the
purchaser contracts for the estate in ignorance of these
rights he may refuse to complete his purchase as soon
as he is aware of their existence ; and he can not be
compelled to take the estate with an abatement on
the amount of the purchase money. (*i*)[1] If a man
contracts for the purchase of a house and wharf, or a
wharf and jetty, he may refuse to take the house without the wharf, or the wharf without the house, or
without the jetty, if they are contiguous to each

(*h*) Bower v. Cooper, 2 Hare, 408.   (*i*) Shackleton v. Sutcliffe, 12 Jur.
199.

[1] But a covenant to a vendor to execute a deed in fee of
land, "free of all incumbrances," will not be held unperformed if there be a public road upon the land in question, at
least in absence of evidence to rebut presumption of knowledge in the purchaser.   Patterson v. Arthurs, 9 Watts, 152.

other, and were clearly intended to go together. (*k*) And, whenever mansion-houses, farms, woods, or meadows are sold together as one estate, and the hope of possessing the one was the inducement to the purchaser to buy the others, he may insist upon having the whole or none. (*l*) " The court wil determine as a jury would the question, ' Did or did not the party purchase the one with reference to the other? Would he or would he not have taken the one, had he not reckoned also upon having the other?'" (*m*) If a purchaser, has contracted for the purchase of a freehold interest, he is not bound to accept a copyhold estate, (*n*) nor a leasehold interest, however long the duration of the term. (*o*) If he has bargained for a fee-simple in possession, he is not bound to take a remainder in fee expectant upon the determination of a life estate, however advanced in life the tenant for life may be, or however liberal may be the compensation offered in the shape of an abatement of the purchase money. (*p*) If he has bargained for the purchase of a lease having eight years to run, he can not be compelled to take a lease of only six, although the vendor may offer him a proportionate reduction in the amount of the purchase money. (*q*) But, if there is only a slight difference in the duration of the term, as between the lease offered to be assigned and that bargained for —if it substantially corresponds with the description

(*k*) Peers v. Lambert, 7 Beav. 546.

(*l*) Poole v. Shergold, 2 Bro. C. C. 118. Gibson v. Spurrier. 2 Peake, 49. Dykes v. Blake, 4 Bing. N. C. 477 ; 6 Sc. 320. Chambers v. Griffiths, 1 Esp. 151.

(*m*) Casamajor v. Strode, 2 Myl. & Kee. 730. Lewin v. Guest, 1 Russ. 330.

(*n*) Hick v. Phillips, Pr. Ch. 575.

(*o*) Drewe v. Corp, 9 Ves. 368. Wright v. Howard, 1 Sim. & Stu. 190. Price v. Ley, 4 Giff. 235.

(*p*) Collier v. Jenkins, 1 You. 295.

(*q*) Farrer v. Nightingal, 2 Esp. 639. Long v. Fletcher, 2 Eq. Ca. Abr. 5, pl. 4.

given of it in the contract for the sale—the purchaser will be bound to take it, and the deficiency must be compensated for in an abatement of the price. (*r*) [1] If, therefore, the purchaser bargains for a term of ninety-nine years in land, and the vendor has only ninety-eight or ninety-seven years, the purchaser will be bound to take the smaller term, receiving a proportionate abatement in the amount of the purchase money. (*s*)

If a man has not the entirety of the estate he professes to sell, the purchaser is not bound to accept at a proportionate price the share which he actually has in the estate. And, if tenants in common of an estate contract for the sale of it, and one of them dies, the purchaser can not be compelled to take the share of the survivors without the share of the deceased. (*t*) If the purchaser elects to take such an interest as the vendor has in the land agreed to be sold, subject to a fair and proportionate abatement in the amount of the purchase-money, the vendor is not entitled to object to his so doing. The purchaser is entitled to take what he can get with compensation for what he ought to have had, but can not obtain, (*u*) provided the contract is capable of being carried out by a decree for specific performance. (*v*) Where, however, the purchaser knows that the land is in the occupation of a tenant he is affected with notice of the tenant's interest, and is not entitled to specific performance with

(*r*) Belworth v. Hassell, 4 Campb. 140.

(*s*) Halsey v. Grant, 13 Ves. 77. Mortlock v. Butler, 10 Ves. 305.

(*t* Att.-Gen. v. Day, 1 Ves. senr. 218.

(*u*) Wood v. Griffith, 1 Wils. Ch. C.

45. Thomas v. Dering, 1 Kee. 744, Graham v. Oliver, 3 Beav. 124. Barnes v. Wood, L. R., 8 Eq. 424; 38 L. J., Ch. 683.

(*v*) Price v. Griffith, 1 De G. Mac. & G. 80; 21 L. J., Ch. 78.

[1] King v. Bardeau, 6 Johns. Ch. 38.

compensation if the tenant has a lease. (*y*)   Quit
rents, being incidents of tenure, are proper subjects of
compensation by abatement of the purchase-money.
An omission, therefore, of the fact of an estate being
charged with a quit-rent will not invalidate the contract for the sale of it ; but it is otherwise if the charge
is a rent-charge. (*z*)

The following misstatements and misdescriptions
have been held so far material and important as to entitle the purchaser to refuse to complete his contract,
and to enable him to recover back his deposit, on the
ground that the vendor had not tendered him that
which he bargained for and intended to buy, although
the contract contained the usual provision that errors
and misstatements should not vitiate the sale,—*i. e.*, a
public-house described in the printed conditions as a
"free public-house," whereas it was held upon the
terms that all the beer should be taken from a particular brewer (*a*)—a lease described as containing a restriction against offensive trades, whereas it contained
a restriction, not only against offensive trades, but also
against some trades that were perfectly inoffensive (*b*)
—houses described as Nos. 3 and 4, whereas they were
Nos. 2 and 3 (*c*)—a reversionary estate described as
"absolute on the death of a person aged sixty-six,"
whereas the party was only sixty-four, and the reversion was not absolute (*d*)—a public-house and yard
described as being holden for a term, of which twenty-
three years were unexpired, at a rent of £55 per annum,
whereas the yard was held distinct from the public-
house, under a demise from year to year only, at an

(*y*) James v. Lichfield, L. R., 9 Eq.
51 ; 39 L. J., Ch. 248.

(*z*) Esdaile v. Stephenson, 1 S. & S.
22.   Bowles v. Waller, 1 Hayes, 441.

(*a*) Jones v. E iney, 3 Campb. 235 ;
339 ; Mood.

(*b*) Flight v. Booth, 1 Sc. 203 ; 1
Bing. N. C. 377.

(*c*) Leach v. Mullett, 3 C. & P. 115.

(*d*) Sherwood v. Robins, 3 C. & P.
& M. 194.

additional rent of £8 per annum (*e*)—a redeemable
estate, or a redeemable annuity issuing out of land,
described generally as "an estate," or "an annuity," no
notice being taken of its being subject to redemption
(*f*)—a plot of ground described generally on a plan,
without notice of any right of way over it, or right of
sporting, whereas it was held subject to a right of sporting, (*g*) or to a right of way on the part of the occupiers
of an adjoining house, their servants and families (*h*)—
leases described as containing particular covenants on
the part of the lessees, whereas no such covenants existed (*i*)—or described as leaseholds renewable by custom, when no custom to renew existed (*k*)—dwelling-
houses described as being holden on a ground-rent lease
at a net annual ground-rent of £42, whereas the rent
was a rack-rent (*l*)—a dwelling-house described as a
brickbuilt dwelling-house, whereas parts of the external
walls were composed of only lath and plaster (*m*)—a
steam factory described as being well supplied with
"water," whereas there was no natural supply, but all
the water was furnished at very great cost by a water
company (*n*)—a house described as being held at a
low ground-rent of £15 per annum, whereas the ground-
rent was £35 per annum (*o*)—a lease described as an
original lease, whereas it was an under-lease (*p*)—and
described as in the occupation of a tenant, whereas the
occupier was a hostile claimant (*q*)—meadows de-

(*e*) Dobell v. Hutchinson, 3 Ad. &
E. 356.

(*f*) Coverley v. Burrell, 5 B. & Ald.
357. Ballard v. Way, 1 M. & W. 520.

(*g*) Burnell v. Brown, 1 Jac. & W.
168.

(*h*) Dykes v. Blake, 4 Bing. N. C.
463; 6 Sc. 320. If the right of way is
patent and obvious, the principle of
caveat emptor applies. Bowles v.
Round, 5 Ves. 509.

(*i*) Waring v. Hogart, R. & M. 39.

(*k*) Newby v. Pinter, 17 Jur. 483.

(*l*) Stewart v. Alliston, 1 Mer. 26.

(*m*) Robinson v. Musgrove, 2 Mood.
& R. 92.

(*n*) Leyland v. Illingworth, 3 De G.
F. & J. 248; 29 L. J., Ch. 611.

(*o*) Mills v. Oddy, 6 C. & P. 728.

(*p*) Mason v. Corder, 2 Marsh. 336.

(*q*) Lachlan v. Reynolds, 23 L. J.,
Ch. 8.

scribed generally, without notice of any right of common over them, whereas one of the meadows was held subject to the exercise of such a right every third year (*r*)—a timber estate described as comprising a wood of sixty-five acres of fine oak timber-trees of the average size of fifty feet, whereas the average size of the trees appeared to be only twenty-two feet (*s*)—a sum in gross payable under a covenant described as a freehold ground-rent. (*t*) Where a purchaser surveyed the property with a plan in his hand which had been furnished to him by the vendors, and was naturally misled into thinking that the boundary included certain trees which it did not include, the court held that he had been misled by the fault of the vendors, and refused to decree specific performance against him. (*u*)

But, if the thing tendered to the purchaser substantially corresponds with the description given in the contract of sale, and there only exists some trifling defect, easily measurable by a pecuniary standard, the purchaser will be bound to complete his contract, on receiving a proportionate abatement of the purchase money. Thus, where a piece of meadow-land, imperfectly watered, was described by a vendor as " uncommonly rich water-meadow," and where a leasehold estate was represented to be nearly equal to freehold, being renewable upon a small fine, whereas the fine was a large one, it was held that the misrepresentation did not avoid the contract, but afforded ground for compensation to the purchaser. (*x*) And, if the purchaser must have known the true state and con-

(*r*) Gibson v. Spurrier, Peake's Ad. Cas. 49.

(*s*) Lord Brooke v. Rounthwaite, 5 Hare, 298 ; 15 L. J., Ch. 332.

(*t*) Robins v. Evans, 2 H. & C. 410 ; 33 L. J, Ex. 68.

(*u*) Denny v. Hancock, L. R., 6 Ch. 1; 40 L. J., Ch. 193.

(*x*) Scott v. Hanson, 1 Sim. 13. Fenton v. Browne, 14 Ves. 144. Trower v. Newcome, 3 Mer. 704.

dition of the property, and could not have been misled
or deceived by the misdescription, he will not be permitted to avail himself of it for the purpose of defeating the contract. So, too, if he proceeds with the
treaty after he is aware of the misstatement or misdescription, and makes no objection, he will be deemed
to have waived his right to object, and to have assented
to take the estate as it is, and not as it was described
to be, subject in certain cases to an abatement in the
amount of the purchase money. If the misrepresentation, moreover, does not in anywise affect the value
or enjoyment of the property, it will not invalidate
the contract. Thus, where fines payable to the lord
of a manor were described as arbitrary, whereas they
were both arbitrary and certain, but the annual
value of the property was correctly stated, it was held
that the purchaser had no ground for refusing to complete the purchase. (*y*) If the price of an estate is
not regulated by the acreage of the property, but by
its peculiar situation or advantitious value, and the
quantity is stated as mere matter of description or
opinion, and not as the result of actual admeasurement, the purchaser may be compelled to take the
estate, and will not be entitled to any abatement of
his purchase money, if the actual quantity falls short
of the estimated quantity. If the price has been
regulated by the acreage, and the quantity has been
innocently misrepresented by the vendor, "the purchaser has a right to have what the vendor can give,
with an abatement out of the purchase money for so
much as the quantity falls short of the representation.
This is the rule, though the land is neither bought nor
sold professedly by the acre, the presumption being
that, in fixing the price, regard was had on both sides

(*y*) White v. Cuddon, 8 Cl. & Fin. 785.

to the quantity which both supposed the estate to
consist of." (*z*)   But, where a mistake of quantity is
of such a nature that it can not fairly and equitably
be made the subject of compensation, it is not a case
for compensation, but a ground for avoiding the contract. (*a*)   If the purchaser has never seen the estate,
but relies solely on the representations made to him
by the vendor, and there is any great or material difference between the actual and represented quantity,
the purchaser will not be bound to complete his purchase.   The words, "more or less," or "thereabouts,"
will only cover a moderate excess or deficiency, and
will never be suffered to be the instrument of fraud.
(*b*)   If the vendor makes a mistake against his own
interest, as if he sells an estate with the timber, and
the timber is by mistake sold at too low a price, he
can not have the sale re-opened, and the purchaser is
entitled to his bargain. (*c*)

521. *Alterations in the condition of property.*—
The vendor must be prepared also to transfer the
estate in the same state and condition that it was in
at the time of the making of the agreement for the
sale; otherwise the purchaser may repudiate the contract and recover his deposit.   Thus, where the vendor
pulled down and removed a summer-house, it was
held that the purchaser might refuse to complete the
purchase and recover back the deposit. (*d*)   So, where,
after an agreement had been entered into for the
purchase and sale of an estate, and before the completion of the contract by the execution of the deed

(*z*) Hill v. Buckley, 17 Ves. 401.
King v. Wilson, 6 Beav. 129.

(*a*) Durham (Earl of) v. Legard, 34
L. J., Ch. 589.

(*b*) Day v. Fynn, Owen, 133. Winch.

v. Winchester, 1 Ves. & B. 377. Port-
man v. Mill, 2 Russ. 570.

(*c*) Griffiths v. Jones, L. R., 15 Eq.
279; 42 L. J., Ch. 468.

(*d*) Granger v. Worms, 4 Campb.
83.

of conveyance, the vendor cut down some ornamental timber, it was held that the purchaser might refuse to complete his contract. (*e*)   If a man contracts for the sale of the land and trees, the purchaser is not bound to take the estate without the timber. (*f*)   If it is stipulated that the purchaser shall pay for timber growing on the land, he must pay for all trees which are considered to be timber by the custom of the country. (*g*)

522. *Time and mode of performance.*—The time appointed for the conveyance of the legal estate, or the delivery of the abstract of title, or the performance of the other preliminaries, is not of the essence of the contract; and the parties, although precise days are fixed, will be allowed a reasonable time for performance, regard being had to all the circumstances of the case, and the nature of the title to be made. (*h*) If the vendor will not complete his part of the contract within a reasonable time, the purchaser may withdraw from the contract, and decline to have anything further to do with it. (*i*)

Time may, however, be made of the essence of the contract, before the sale, by a proper condition, (*k*) and after the sale, by giving a proper notice of completion or rescission by a limited time; (*l*) and, if it plainly appears to have been the intention of the parties that time should be of the essence of the contract, (*m*) or that the sale should be conditional, and

(*e*) Magennis v. Fallon, 2 Moll. 588.

(*f*) Duke of St. Albans v. Shore, 1 H. Bl. 280.

(*g*) Duke of Chandos v. Talbot, 2 P. Wms. 601. Aubrey v. Fisher, 10 East, 446.

(*h*) Hipwell v. Knight, 1 You. & Col. 416. Hearne v. Tenant, 13 Ves. 287.

(*i*) Macbryde v. Weeks, 22 Beav.

539.   Nott v. Riccard, Id 307.

(*k*) Hudson v. Temple, 29 Beav. 536; 30 L. J., Ch. 251.

(*l*) Taylor v. Brown, 2 Beav. 180. Wells v. Maxwell, 32 Beav. 408; 33 L. J., Ch. 45.

(*m*) Darnley (Earl of) v. London and Chatham, &c., Ry. Co. 33 L. J., Ch. 9.

be made to depend on the performance of the contract by an appointed period, the court will not decree
performance after the time has elapsed. (*n*)   Thus, in
a condition that objections to the vendor's title are to
be sent in within a given period, time is of the essence
of the contract. (*o*)   But, if a vendor does not deliver
the abstract of title within the time specified, the
purchaser is not bound to send in his objections within the specified time. (*p*)   Time is considered to be
material, and to a very considerable extent, to be of
the essence of the contract, from the nature of the
property or the surrounding circumstances, (*q*) as
where the subject-matter of the sale is exposed to
daily variations in value, such as stock, shares, scrip,
(*r*) reversionary estate, (*s*) mines, factories, and
buildings used for trading purposes, (*t*) and public
houses, (*u*) and in the case of contracts made with
ecclesiastical corporations, where the value of the subject-matter of the contract, and the persons who are
to participate in the benefit of it, are liable to con-
stant change. (*x*)   If a person, seeking to enforce a
contract for the sale of land, has himself been guilty
of delay—if he has slept over his rights, and allowed
an unreasonable time to elapse before seeking for
performance—the court will not assist him. (*y*)

(*n*) Reynolds v. Nelson, Mad. & Geld. 26. Hudson v. Bartram, 3 Mad. 440. Hipwell v. Knight, 1 Y. & C. 401. Ranelagh (Lord) v. Melton, 34 L. J., Ch. 227 ; 2 Dru. & Sm. 278.

(*o*) Oakden v. Pike, 34 L. J., Ch. 620.

(*p*) Upperton v. Nicholson, L. R., 6 Ch. 436 ; 40 L. J., Ch. 401.

(*q*) Roberts v. Berry, 3 De G. M. & G. 284. Tilley v. Thomas, L. R., 3 Ch. 61.

(*r*) Doleret v. Rothschild, 1 Sim. & Stu. 590.

(*s*) Newman v. Rodgers, 4 Bro. C. C. 391.

(*t*) Coslake v. Till, 1 Russ. 376. Walker v. Jeffreys, 1 Hare, 348.

(*u*) Cowles v. Gale, L. R., 7 Ch. 12 ; 41 L. J., Ch. 14.

(*x*) Carter v. Dean, &c., of Ely, 7 Sim. 211.

(*y*) Lloyd v. Collett, cited 4 Ves. 690. Guest v. Homfray, 5 Ves. 818. Watson v. Reid, 1 Russ. & Myl. 236. Colby v. Gadsden, 34 Beav. 416.

Where a purchaser agrees that if, " from any cause whatever," the purchase shall not be completed on the day fixed, he will pay interest, he must pay such interest, unless the delay has been occasioned by misconduct on the part of the vendor. (z)

Where time is of the essence of the contract, mutual promises or covenants between a vendor and purchaser, for the conveyance of an estate on the one hand, and the payment of the purchase-money on the other, at an appointed period, constitute mutual conditions to be performed at the same time ; so that, " one party was ready and willing, and offered to perform his part of the contract, and the other neglected or refused to perform his, he who was ready and willing has fulfilled his engagement, and may maintain an action for the default of the other, though it is not certain that either is obliged to do the first act." (a) It is a sufficient performance, however, of the vendor's part of the contract, if he is " ready and willing " to execute a conveyance, inasmuch as it is the duty of the purchaser to prepare the conveyance, and tender it to the vendor for execution, (b) unless the latter has previously declared that he will never execute it, or has refused to deliver the abstract, and intimated his intention not to complete the purchase, or has sold the estate to another person, or done any other act incapacitating himself from fulfilling his engagement. (c) The conveyance, when tendered, must be a conveyance of the estate and interest bargained for

(z) Williams v. Glenton, 34 Beav. 528 : 35 L. J., Ch. 284. Palmerston (Lord) v. Turner, 33 Beav. 524; 33 L. J., Ch. 457.

(a) Jones v. Barklay, Doug. 684.

Kingston v. Preston, cited Id. 691.

(b) Poole v. Hill. 6 M. & W. 835.

(c) Franklyn v. Lamond, 4 C. B. 637 ; 16 L. J., C. P. 221.

and agreed to be sold, or the vendor will not be bound to execute it. (*d*)

If one time has been appointed for the execution of the conveyance and another for the payment of the purchase-money, the mutual promises do not constitute mutual conditions, but the several acts must be strictly performed in the order of time agreed upon.   And, if a time is appointed for the payment of the purchase money, but no time has been specified for the execution of the conveyance, the purchaser is bound to pay the money at the time appointed, whether he has or has not obtained a conveyance of the property.   In such a case the execution of the conveyance is not a condition precedent to, or concurrent with, the payment of the purchase money ; and the vendor may consequently sue for the money, if it is not paid at the time appointed, without offering or expressing his readiness to execute a conveyance. (*e*)

523. *Enlargement of the time of performance.*— The time limited for the performance of a contract required to be in writing by the Statute of Frauds can not be extended by a mere oral agreement ; " for, to allow the substitution of a new stipulation as to the time of completing the contract, by reason of a subsequent oral agreement of the parties to that effect, in lieu of a stipulation as to time contained in the written agreement signed by the parties, is virtually and substantially to allow an action to be brought on an agreement relating to the sale of land, partly in writing, signed by the parties, and partly not in writing but by parol only, and amounts to a contraven-

---

(*d*) Vonhollen v. Knowles, 12 M. & W. 602.

(*e*) Mattock v. Kinglake, 10 Ad. & E. 50.

tion of the Staute of Frauds." (*f*)   Where a contract
for the sale and purchase of land provided that a good
title to the land should be produced, and a defect was
discovered in the title which could not be cured, and
the purchaser then agreed, by word of mouth, to
waive the defect, and take the land with such a title
as the vendor himself possessed, but afterwards, re-
penting his subsequent promise, he refused to complete the purchase, it was held that the oral waiver
could not be given in evidence ; that it had the effect
of creating a new contract, altogether different from
the original contract, and ought to have been authenticated by writing. (*g*)   But, even where time is of
the essence of the contract, it may be waived by the
conduct and actions of the parties, and by the contract being treated and acted upon as a continuing
contract after the appointed period. (*h*)

524. *Non-performance by the vendor.*—Where the
vendor has reserved to himself a right to rescind the
contract if the purchaser raises objections to the title,
which the vendor is unable or unwilling to remove,
the vendor can not refuse to complete the contract, if
the purchaser is willing to waive the objections he
has made. (*i*)   If the purchaser intends to sue for the
recovery of a deposit paid by him under the contract,
and for general damages, by reason of the non-performance of the contract by the vendor at the time agreed
upon, the purchaser should give the vendor notice of
his intention, and allow the latter a reasonable time,
from the date of the notice, to complete the contract.

(*f*) Stowell *v*. Robinson, 3 Bing.
N. C. 937 ; 5 Sc. 212.

(*g*) Goss v. Lord Nugent, 2 N. &
M. 35. Harvey v. Grabham, 5 Ad. &
E. 74.

(*h*) Webb v. Hughes, L. R., 10 Eq.
281 ; 39 L. J., Ch. 606.

(*i*) Turpin v. Chambers, 30 L. J.,
Ch. 470.

(*k*)   If there has been a general breach of contract
by the vendor, independently of the question as to the
time of performance, or the title to relief has been
barred by notice, an action is maintainable for the
recovery of the deposit, with interest, when the deposit
has been paid into the hands of the vendor himself.
If the vendor has no title to the property agreed to
be sold, or if he has a naked legal title, or an equitable
interest only, the deposit is recoverable, (*l*) unless
there is an express agreement to the contrary ; (*m*)
and so it is, if the estate is shown to be subject to an
equitable incumbrance. (*n*)   The purchaser, in these
cases, is entitled, as we shall presently see, to recover
the costs and expenses incurred by him in investigating the title ; (*o*) also the costs of preparing and tendering a conveyance where that has been done, and,
where the vendor has acted with bad faith, and willfully refused to fulfill his contract, damages for the
loss of his bargain.   It will be no defense to the action
that the vendor has a title at the time of the trial, or
after the commencement of the action. (*p*)   Where a
purchaser paid a deposit on a contract for the purchase of a lease of a house, and afterwards discovered
that the house was comprised with another in an
original lease, under which the lessor had a right to
re-enter for breach of covenant in respect of either
house, it was held that the purchaser might rescind
the contract and sue for his deposit and expenses. (*q*)
In order to entitle himself to maintain an action

(*k*) Parkin v. Thorold, 22 L. J., Ch.
175.   King v. Wilson, 6 Beav. 126.

(*l*) Maberly v. Robins, 5 Taunt.
625 ; 1 Marsh. 258.   Cane v. Baldwin,
1 Stark. 65.   Roper v. Coombes, 6 B.
& C. 534.

(*m*) Ashworth v. Mounsey, 23 L. J.,

Ex. 73.

(*n*) Elliot v. Edwards, 3 B. & P. 181.

(*o*) Richardson v. Chasen, 16 L. J.,
Q. B. 341.

(*p*) Cornish v. Rowley, 1 Selw. N.
P. 12th ed., 203.

(*q*) Blake v. Phinn, 3 C. B. 976.

against the vendor for the damages resulting from the non-execution of the conveyance, the purchaser must prove a tender of a conveyance to the vendor for execution, and his own readiness and willingness to pay the purchase-money, unless the vendor has incapacitated himself from executing a conveyance by selling the estate to another, and has thus discharged the purchaser from his obligation. (*r*) But it is not necessary for the purchaser to prepare and tender a conveyance, in order to entitle himself to maintain an action for the recovery of his deposit, and the expenses of investigating the title. (*s*) If the vendor's failure to make out a good title arises from circumstances over which he has no control, and is not the result of fraud or mala fides on his part, the purchaser will not be entitled to recover damages in respect of the presumed or fancied value of his bargain ; but if the vendor's conduct has been fraudulent, the case is otherwise. If the title has been made out and accepted by the purchaser, and the latter has then resold to a second purchaser, and the original vendor refuses to execute a conveyance on being tendered the purchase-money, the purchaser will be entitled, on tendering a conveyance, to recover the profit realized on the re-sale, and all the costs and expenses attending it, in addition to his costs of investigating the title. If the purchaser sues the vendor upon the contract, for the recovery of his deposit as part of the damages resulting from the vendor's neglect to complete the sale, he will be entitled to recover interest upon his deposit ; and he may also, in certain cases, recover interest upon the purchase-money, if it has been lying

---

(*r*) Knight v. Cockford, 1 Esp. 193.   (*s*) Lowndes v. Bray, Sugd. Vend. 14th ed., 364.

idle, awaiting the vendor's acceptance. (*t*)   But, if it should turn out that the contract was not binding upon the vendor, by reason of its not being properly authenticated by writing, or if the contract has been abandoned or rescinded by mutual consent, interest on the deposit can not be recovered, nor any of the costs and expenses incurred in the investigation of the title. (*u*)   It is frequently stipulated in contracts of the sale and purchase of estates that if either party shall neglect to fulfill his part of the contract, he shall pay to the other a fixed, ascertained sum of money, as the liquidated and agreed damages.   The amount so agreed to be paid may, as we have already seen, under certain circumstances and with certain qualifications, be recovered by action. (*v*)   And where the vendor is in default, the purchaser will generally be held to be entitled to a lien on the estate for his deposit and interest. (*y*)

525. *Non-performance by the purchaser—Forfeiture of deposit.*—In case of the non-performance of the contract by the purchaser, the deposit is generally forfeited, (*z*) but, to entitle the vendor to retain the deposit, he must show that he has faithfully fulfilled his own part of the contract, and has not done anything amounting to a waiver of his right to take advantage of the forfeiture.   If he has himself prevent-

---

(*t*) Farquhar v. Farley, 7 Taunt. 592 ; 1 Moore, 322.   Hodges v. Earl of Litchfield, 1 Sc. 443 ; 1 Bing. N. C. 492.   Gardom v. Lee, 34 L. J., Ex. 113.

(*u*) Walker v. Constable, 1 B. & P. 306.   Gosbell v. Archer, 2 Ad. & E. 500 ; 4 N. & M. 485.   Casson v. Roberts, 32 L. J., Ch. 105.

(*v*) *Ante.*

(*y*) Rose v. Watson, 33 L. J., Ch. 385.

(*z*) Palmer v. Temple, 1 P. & D. 387 ; 9 Ad. & E. 521.   Whether it would be held to be forfeited where no stipulation to that effect is expressed or can be inferred, would seem to admit of doubt, see Palmer v. Roberts, 9 Ad. & E. 508.   Casson v. Roberts, 32 L. J., Ch. 105.   Depree v. Bedborough, 4 Giff. 479 ; 33 L. J., Ch. 134.   Hinton v. Sparkes, L. R., 3 C. P. 161 ; 37 L. J., C. P. 81.

ed the purchaser from fulfilling the contract at the time appointed, or has himself asked for delay, or has induced the purchaser to incur the forfeiture by fraudulent statements and deceitful promises, he will not be permitted to take advantage of such forfeiture. (a) Where it was stipulated by the contract that objections to the title not made within twenty-one days should be considered as waived, and the deposit forfeited, and the vendor at liberty to re-sell in case of the non-completion of the purchase by the purchaser, and the vendor's solicitor received the objections long after the twenty-one days, and entered into a written correspondence respecting them, it was held that the vendor had waived his right to insist on the forfeiture of the deposit and to re-sell the estate. (b)   The personal representative of the purchaser, and not his heir, is the proper party to be made plaintiff in an action brought for the recovery of the deposit. (c)   A purchaser who is entitled to a return of his deposit can not be compelled to take the stock in which it may have been invested, unless the investment was made with his assent and direction, or under the authority of the Court.   His assent to the investment can not be inferred from the fact of notice having been given him thereof, and no reply having been made to such notice. (d)   A stipulation for the forfeiture of the deposit, in case of the non-completion of the contract by the purchaser, does not, as we have already seen, preclude the vendor from suing the purchaser for the recovery of the general damages resulting from the breach of contract ; but, if the deposit has been paid to the vendor and forfeited, it must be treated as so

(a) Carpenter v. Blandford, 8 B. & C. 575 ; 3 M. & R. 95.

(b) Cutts v. Thodcy, 13 Sim. 206.

(c) Orme v. Brougton, 4 Moo. & Sc. 417 ; 10 Bing. 533.

(d) Roberts v. Massey, 13 Ves. 561.

much money paid to the vendor on account of such
damages. (*e*)

526. *Deposits in the hands of auctioneers and
third parties.*—When a deposit has been paid into the
hands of an auctioneer, solicitor, or any third party,
the latter stands in the position of a stakeholder, and
is responsible for the payment of the amount to the
vendor in case of the completion of the contract, and
also for the return of it to the purchaser in case of the
abandonment of the contract, or the neglect of the
vendor to complete his part of it. The depositary,
therefore, should not part with the deposit until the
sale has either been abandoned, or has come to nothing, or until it has been duly completed and carried
into effect, and it appears by the result to whom the
deposit properly belongs. (*f*)   If he pays it over to
the vendor, and the title turns out to be defective, he
will be bound to make good the amount to the purchaser, (*g*) unless it appears to have been the intention of the parties that the amount should be paid
over to the vendor, and it has accordingly been done ;
(*h*) as, for instance, where the deposit is to be paid to
the vendor's solicitor "as agent for the vendor," in
which case the solicitor is not a stakeholder, but must
pay the deposit to the vendor on demand. (*i*)   If the
auctioneer makes away with the deposit, and becomes
bankrupt, the loss will in general fall upon the vendor,
who selects and appoints him, and constitutes him his
agent for the receipt and keeping of the money. (*k*)

(*e*) Ockenden v. Henly, El. Bl. &
El. 485.   As to when the forfeit of the
deposit can be treated as liquidated
damages, see Lea v. Whitaker, L. R.,
8 C. P. 70.

(*f*) *Post,* ch. 3. s. 1, STAKEHOLD-
ERS.

(*g*) Gray v. Gutteridge, 1 M. & R.
614.

(*h*) Hurley v. Baker, 16 M. & W.
26.

(*i*) Edgell v. Day, 35 L. J., C. P. 7.

(*k*) Annesley v. Muggridge, 1 Mad.
593.   Smith v. Jackson, 1 Mad. 618.

No notice need be given to the auctioneer of the
abandonment of the contract, or of the default made
by the vendor prior to the commencement of the
action against him for the recovery of the deposit. (*l*)
When the action for the return of the deposit is
brought against the auctioneer, interest thereon is not
recoverable by the purchaser, although the money has
been placed in the funds, and interest has been
made. (*m*) But it is otherwise, as we have already
seen, when the deposit has been paid to the vendor,
and the action for its recovery is brought   against
him.

527. *Rights of the vendor.*— Before the vendor
can maintain an action for the recovery of damages
by reason of the neglect of the purchaser to tender
and accept a conveyance of the estate and pay the
purchase money, he must produce and establish a
good title to the estate agreed to be sold, and
it must appear that he was ready and willing
to execute a conveyance thereof to the purchaser, on receiving payment of the purchase money.
(*n*) But, if he can prove this, he is entitled, as we
shall presently see, to recover all the damages he has
sustained by the breach of contract, and all the costs,
charges, and expenses he has incurred. Before he
brings an action to recover such damages by reason of
the non-payment of the purchase money at the time
appointed, he should give notice to the purchaser, and
require the latter to pay the money within a reasonable time. If the purchaser takes possession of the
estate, and receives the rents and profits, he will, in

(*l*) Duncan v. Cafe, 2 M. & W. 244.

(*m*) Harington v. Hoggart, 1 B. & Ad. 577. Curling v. Shuttleworth, 6 Bing. 121 ; 3 Moo. & P. 368. Gaber v. Driver, 2 Y. & J. 549.

(*n*) Martin v. Smith, 6 East, 555. Hallewell v. Morrell, 1 M. & Gr. 367. Poole v. Hill, 6 M. & W. 835. Phillips v. Fielding, 2 H. Bl. 132.

general, be compelled to pay interest on the purchase
money from the time that he became possessed of the
property.   If he neglects to fulfill his part of the contract at the time appointed, or within a reasonable
period after request, if no time was appointed, the vendor will be entitled, after a reasonable notice, to re-sell
the estate and sue for damages.   If a second purchaser
has taken a conveyance and paid his purchase money
without notice of a prior sale, he has equal equity with
the first purchaser; and, having clothed himself with
the legal estate, he comes within the rule that, where
parties have equal equity, he who has the legal title
shall prevail.   But, if such second purchaser had notice
of the first contract, the court will, if the first purchaser's right to a specific performance has not been
barred, compel such second purchaser to convey the
estate to the first purchaser.   To obviate difficulties
and objections to a re-sale, it has been usual to insert
in agreements for the sale of realty a stipulation to
the effect that, if the purchaser shall fail to complete
the purchase and pay the price at the time appointed,
the agreement shall be utterly void, and the vendor be
at liberty to re-sell the estate, and that the deficiency,
if any, by such re-sale, together with the costs and
charges attending the same, shall be made good by
the defaulter. (*o*)   This stipulation, and also a vendor's
notice of re-sale, may be waived, and the right to take
advantage of it lost, if objections to title made by the
purchaser have been considered by the vendor or his
attorney subsequently to the time fixed for the re-sale,
and if it can be shown, through the medium of written
evidence, that the vendor, after such time of re-sale
had elapsed, still continued to deal with the purchaser
as a purchaser, and still continued to treat the con-

(*o*) Ex parte Hunter, 6 Ves. 94.

tract as a subsisting contract. (*p*)   When the vendor
has re-sold and conveyed the property under these
circumstances, he will be considered as selling it for
the benefit of the original purchaser, for whom, by
the first agreement, he became trustee, and he will be
compelled to account to him for the purchase
money. (*q*)

528. *Damages from breach of contract for the
sale of realty—Non-performance by the purchaser.—*
If an estate agreed to be sold has been actually conveyed by the vendor to the purchaser, and has become
the property of the latter, and the vendor sues for
the non-payment of the purchase money, the measure
of damages is the price agreed to be paid, with interest; but, if no conveyance has been executed, and the
estate still remains the property of the vendor, the
measure of damages is the difference between the price
agreed to be paid and the marketable value of the
property; for the vendor can not have both the estate
and the purchase money. (*r*)   So long as the right of
property in the thing agreed to be sold has not passed
to the purchaser, the vendor is entitled, in case of the
non-completion of the contract by the purchaser, to
re-sell it;   and, if the re-sale has taken place within a
reasonable period from the breach of contract, the
difference between the price realized on the re-sale
and that agreed to be paid by the purchaser will be
the measure of damages which the vendor will be entitled to recover, in addition to the costs, charges, and
expenses of the re-sale.   If the vendor does not re-sell
the estate, but elects to keep it in his own hands, he
will then be entitled to recover the difference between
the agreed price and the presumed marketable value

(*p*) Cutts v. Thodey, 13 Sim. 206 ;   (*q*) Daniels v. Davison, 16 Ves. 255
1 Col. 223.   (*r*) Laird v. Pim, 7 M. & W. 478.

of the property, together with his costs, charges, and
expenses. Amongst these costs and charges may be
included the expense of making out the title ; for,
although the expense is, by custom and usage, de-
frayed by the vendor, yet that is done upon the understanding that the contract will be duly fulfilled by the
purchaser. In many cases of sales of realty there will
be no difference between the contract price and the
marketable value of the property agreed to be purchased ; and in such cases, if the vendor elects to keep
the property in his own hands, and not to re-sell it, he
will be entitled to recover nominal damages only in
respect of the loss of the purchase, in addition to the
costs and expenses he has incurred in carrying out
and completing his part of the contract. If the conditions of sale provide for the payment of a deposit by
the purchaser, and for the forfeiture of such deposit in
case of the failure of the purchaser to comply with the
conditions, the deposit must, nevertheless, be brought
into account by the vendor, if he seeks to recover the
deficiency on a re-sale of the property. (*s*)

529. *Damages from non-performance by the Vendor.*—If the action is brought by the purchaser in
respect of a breach of the contract by the vendor, the
nature and amount of the damages recoverable will
depend, to a certain extent, upon the existence or
non-existence or bad faith on the part of the vendor.
If the sale goes off because the vendor refuses to fulfill
his contract, the purchaser will be entitled to full
compensation for the loss of his bargain. (*t*) If the
vendor had reasonable ground for believing that he
was the owner of the property and had a right to sell

(*s*) Ockenden v. Henly, El. Bl. & El. (*t*) Ld. Campbell, C. J., Simons v.
485. But see Hinton v. Sparkes, L. Patchett, 26 L. J., Q. B. 199.
R., 3 C. P. 161 ; 37 L. J., C. P 81.

at the time he agreed to sell, but is prevented by an unexpected defect of title from completing his engagements, and is ready to do all that he possibly can to fulfill the contract, the purchaser will only be entitled to recover nominal damages, together with his deposit (if a deposit was paid), with interest, and the expenses he has in incurred investigating the title and searching for judgments. He can not recover damages in respect of the presumed or fancied value of his bargain over and above the price agreed to be paid, (*u*) nor the costs of any proceedings taken to enforce performance. (*v*) If he re-sells before he has investigated the title of his vendor, and the sub-contract fails by reason of a defect in that title, and not from any mala fides on the part of the original vendor, he will not be entitled to recover damages in respect of any profit that he would have realized on such re-sale ; for, " if premises for which a party has contracted are by him offered for re-sale too soon, that is at his own peril ; and the damage (if any) resulting from that offer arises from his own premature act, and not from the fault of his vendor." (*y*) If, however, the breach of contract arises, not from the inability of the vendor to make a good title, but from his refusal to take the necessary steps to give the purchaser possession pursuant to his contract, the purchaser may recover, not only the deposit and the expenses of investigating the title, but also damages for the loss of his bargain, which will be measured by the differ-

---

(*u*) Flureau v. Thornhill, 2 W. Bl. 1078. Sugd. Vend. 1077, 1078. Robinson v. Harman, 1 Exch. 855. Pounsett v. Fuller, 17 C. B. 676 ; 25 L. J., C. P. 145. Sykes v. Wilde, 1 B. & S. 587 ; 4 Id. 421 ; 30 L. J., Q. B. 325 ; 32 Id. 375. Bain v. Fothergill, L. R., 6 Ex. 59 ; 40 L. J., Ex. 34 Gray v. Fowler, L. R., 8 Ex. 249 ; 42. L, J., Ex. 61.

(*v*) Malden v. Fyson, 11 Q. B. 292.

(*y*) Bayley, J., Walker v. Moore, 10 B. & C. 421. Poth. OBLIGATIONS, No. 168.

ence between the contract price and the value at the time of the breach of contract ; and the profit which the purchaser could have made on a re-sale, will be evidence of this enhanced value ; (z) for if the vendor acts with bad faith, and fails to do all that it is in his power to do to perform and fulfill the contract, he will be bound to compensate the purchaser for all the loss he has sustained. If the title shown on the abstract has been examined with the deeds, and found correct, and the purchaser, acting upon the title so shown, enters into a sub-contract for the re-sale of the estate, and the original vendor then refuses to complete the first purchase, in consequence whereof the contract for the re-sale fails, the purchaser will be entitled to recover the profit that he would have realized on the re-sale, and all the costs and expenses attending it. And if the vendor has nothing at all in the shape of title, but has taken upon himself to offer an estate for sale, without having a shadow of interest in the land, holding himself out as the legal owner, when in point of fact he never was the legal owner, and could have had no reasonable ground for thinking so, if he had examined into his own rights, he must pay such damages as the purchaser has really sustained by not having that which the vendor contracted that he should have. (a)

Expenses incurred in getting a survey made of the estate, or plans prepared preparatory to the making of the contract, but before the contract was actually entered into, can not be recovered by the purchaser, nor can the expense of a conveyance prepared before

(z) Engel v. Fitch. L. R., 3 Q. B. 314 ; 37 L. J., Q. B. 145. Godwin v. Francis, L. R., 5 C. P. 295 ; 39 L. J., C. P. 121.

(a) Hopkins v. Grazebrooke, 6 B. & C. 31; 9 D. & R. 26. Sykes v. Wilde, ante.

the title has been approved of, and before it is known whether objections raised to the title can be answered by the vendor. (*b*)   And, if there has been no written contract of sale binding on the vendor, but the matter rests merely upon an oral agreement rendered invalid by the Statute of Frauds, the purchaser has no means of recovering the expenses incurred by him in investigating the title.   He may, however, recover the deposit and auction duty, as money paid upon a consideration that has failed. (*c*)

In the case of the non-performance of an agreement for the sale of an estate, damages for non-performance are not given in addition to specific performance, except where special damage has occurred from the delay. (*d*)

530. *Specific performance.*—As the estate agreed to be sold vests in equity in the purchaser from the time of the signing of the agreement, the court will in all ordinary cases, decree a specific performance by the vendor of all such acts as are necessary to be done by him to transfer the legal estate to the purchaser, and clothe the latter with the legal as well as the equitable ownership of the property, and thus carry the contract into complete effect.   If the vendor has no title, a specific performance can not be decreed, as he can not be compelled to convey an estate which he has not got. (*e*)   If, therefore, he has signed an agreement for the sale of property under the impression that he was seized in fee and it subsequently appears that he has only a life estate, a specific performance of the contract can not be decreed ; but the

(*b*) Hodges v. Earl Litchfield, 1 Sc. 443.

(*c*) Gosbell v. Archer, 2 Ad. & E. 500.

(*d*) Chinnock v. Ely, 34 L. J., Ch, 399 ; 2 H. & M. 221.

(*e*) Nicolson   v.   Wadsworth,   2 Swanst. 369.

purchaser may, if he pleases, have a decree for a conveyance of the life estate, with compensation by way
of reduction of the amount of the purchase-money. (*f*)
If the remainder, after the determination of the vendor's life interest, is vested in his wife for life, with
remainder to his son in fee, the court will not compel him to use his marital and parental authority to
to induce the wife and son to part with their interests
in the property. (*g*) Where a husband and wife
agreed to sell the wife's estate, the purchaser being
aware that the estate belonged to the wife, and the
wife afterwards refused to convey it, it was held that
the purchaser could not compel the husband to convey
his interest and accept an abated price. (*h*)   The
court will not compel a purchaser to take a doubtful
title ; and a title is regarded as doubtful where there
has been a decision adverse to it or the principle upon
which it depends, or a decision in favor of it which
the court is of opinion is wrong, or where there is a
known difficulty in the title, or when the validity of
the title depends upon a fact or facts of the exact accuracy of which the court has no means of judging. (*i*)

A contract established through the medium of
letters may be enforced in specie ; but it must appear
to be a complete and concluded contract ; (*k*) and it
must be sufficiently certain. (*l*)[1]   The courts grant
the decree only in those cases where there is a mutuality of obligation, and where the remedy is mutual.

(*f*) Barnes v. Wood, L. R., 8 Eq.
424 ; 38 L. J., Ch. 683.

(*g*) Howel v. George, 1 Mad. 6.

(*h*) Castle v. Wilkinson, L. R., 5 Ch.
634 ; 39 L. J., Ch. 843.

(*i*) Mullings v. Trinder, L. R., 10
Eq. 449 ; 39 L. J., Ch. 833.

(*k*) Huddleston v. Briscoe, 11 Ves.
591.   Stratford v. Bosworth, 2 Ves. &
B. 341. Cowley v. Watts, 17 Jur. 172.

(*l*) Rummens v. Robins, 3 De G. J.
& S. 88. Dear v. Verity, 38 L. J., Ch.
297.

[1] *Ante*, vol. i. p. 43, note 1.

If, therefore, an infant signs a contract for the purchase of an estate, the court will not decree specific perfor_ mance in his favor, because he is not himself bound by the contract, by reason of his infancy. (*m*) ' Specific

(*m*) Flight v. Bolland, 4 Russ. 301.   Hills v. Croll, 2 Phill. 62, n. (*b*).

[1] " If an infant has made a deed of a conveyance of land, inasmuch as he has parted with his seizin thereby, it has been held, and, it is believed, is the better doctrine, that he can only avoid it by re-entry, unless he has retained possession, or unless it was wild and vacant land, in which case a deed of it to a stranger would be a disaffirmance of his first conveyance." Washburn on Real Property, vol. i. p. 301 ; and see Worces_ ter v. Eaton, 13 Mass. 371; Whitney v. Dutch, 14 Id. 463; Roberts v. Wiggin, 1 N. H. 75 ; Murray v. Shankin, 4 Dev. & Bat. 289; Bool v. Mix, 17 Wend. 133; Jackson v. Burchin, 14 Johns. 124 ; Tucker v. Moreland, 10 Pet. 65.

It has been held that a deed, without a formal prior entry to regain seizin, would be sufficient. Cresinger v. Welch, 15 Ohio, 192 ; Scott v. Buchanan, 11 Humph. 468; Drake v. Ramsay, 5 Ohio, 251; Jackson v. Carpenter, 11 Johns. 539 ; Jackson v. Burchin, 14 Johns. 124, where the land was vacant; where the minor was all the time in occupation of the prem- ises. See Tucker v. Moreland, 10 Pet. 65. One who executes an agreement while too intoxicated to understand its meaning and effect, may avoid it. Washburn, vol. i., p. 304. Leases by married women are void, unless relating to their own sole property, over which, by chancery or the statute of the state where they live, they are authorized to act as femes sole. Smith, Land & Ten. 48; 1 Platt, Leases, 48; Murray v. Em- mons, 19 N. H. 483. So leases obtained by duress are voidable, but not void. Worcester v. Eaton, 13 Mass. 371. So, also, leases made by infants. Worcester v. Eaton, 13 Mass. 375 ; Scott v. Bu- chanan, 11 Humph. 468; Kendall v. Lawrence, 22 Pick. 540; Roof v. Stafford, 7 Cow. 179; Stafford v. Roof, 9 Id. 626; Rob- erts v. Wiggin, 1 N. H. 73; Tucker v. Moreland, 10 Pet. 71; Jackson v. Carpenter, 11 Johns. 539; Drake v. Ramsay, 5 Ohio, 251; Bool v. Mix, 17 Wend. 131. So a lease may be avoided for fraud. But if the lessee be the party defrauded, he must rescind the contract promptly, and so long as he retains pos- session of the premises, he is liable for the rent. McCarty v. Ely, 4 E. D. Smith, 375.

Infants' leases may be affirmed and made effectual by ratifi-

performance will not be decreed in favor of a person who has been guilty of an unreasonable delay in fulfilling his part of the engagement, or who has slept

tion, or disaffirmed and avoided, by the acts and declarations of the lessor, done or madé at the proper time. Right to disaffirm a lease is a personal privilege, and must be exercised by the lessor himself or his heirs, and not by a stranger. Worcester v. Eaton, 13 Mass. 371; Wheaton v. East, 5 Yerg. 61. The law permits an infant to disaffirm the sale of a chattel where it would not allow the disaffirmance of a conveyance of land, since he may do the one before arriving at age, but he can not disaffirm his deed of conveyance while an infant. " It would seem by the analogy there is between the chattel interest in a term for years, in which no seisin passes, and the property in personal chattels, that a lease may be disaffirmed by an infant before arriving at age, and from the well-settled principle that, though an infant can not defeat his deed until he is of age, he may enter and take the profits of the land while an infant. An infant lessor may enter and avoid his lease during his infancy. However this may be held by the courts, the following authorities are clear, that while an infant may not avoid his deed until after arriving at age, he may disaffirm and avoid a sale of a chattel, but he may enter and take the profits." Washburn on Real Property, vol. ii. pp. 305–306, citing Zouch v. Parsons, 3 Burr. 1808; Bool v. Mix, 17 Wend. 132; Scott v. Buchanan, 11 Humph. 473. Roof v. Stafford, 7 Cow. 179, to the effect that an infant can avoid neither as to personalty nor lands until of age, was overruled as to personalty, and affirmed as to lands, in Stafford v. Roof, 9 Cow. 628; Shipman v. Horton, 17 Conn. 481; Matthewson v. Johnson, 1 Hoff. Ch. 560. Though an infant may not avoid his deed till of age, he may enter and take the profits of the land. An infant must avoid his deed of lands after arriving at age, within the period of limitation for making an entry. Drake v. Ramsey, 5 Ohio, 251; Cresinger v. Welsh, 15 Ohio, 193; but see Richardson v. Boright, 9 Vt. 368; Holmes v. Blogg, 8 Taunt. 35; Kline v. Beebe, 6 Conn. 494; Scott v. Buchanan, 11 Humph. 468; 2 Kent Com. 238; Hoyt v. Underhill, 9 N. H. 436; which hold that he must do it, if at all, within a reasonable time after arriving at age. Still other cases hold that in order to make

for a lengthened period over his rights, and comes forward at last, when circumstances have changed in his favor, to enforce a stale demand. (*n*)　If the contract of sale provides that immediate possession shall be given to the purchaser, and possession is accordingly taken by him, and the vendor afterwards evicts him, the latter forfeits his right to a specific performance. (*o*)　If there is a mistake between the parties as to what was sold, or as to the quantity sold, or the price, the court will not interfere in favor of either of them. (*p*)　If there has been surprise on third parties at a sale by auction, and they have been deterred from bidding, or if the purchaser has made false statements which have kept persons away from the sale, the decree will not be granted in his favor ; (*q*) nor will it

(*n*) Lloyd v. Collett, 4 Bro. C. C. 469. Alley v. Deschamps, 13 Ves. 225. Southcomb v. Bishop of Exeter, 16 L. J., Ch. 378. Colby v. Gadsen, 34 Beav. 416. Moore v. Marrable, L, R., 1 Ch. 217.

(*o*) Knatchbull v. Grueber, 3 Mer. 124.

(*p*) Clowes v. Higginson, 1 Ves. & B. 524. Neap v. Abbott, Coop. Ch. Pr. 333. Malins v. Freeman, 2 Kee. 25. Durham (Earl of) v. Legard, 34 L. J., Ch. 589. Swaisland v. Dearsley, 29 Beav. 430. Day v. Wells, 30 Beav. 220.

(*q*) Twining v. Morice, 2 Bro. C. C. 330. Mortlock v. Buller, 10 Ves. 305.

his contracts binding as such, the minor must affirm them after coming of age, by some distinct act, with full knowledge that it would not be binding without such confirmation. Curtin v. Patton, 11 S. & R. 305 ; Thompson v. Lay, 4 Pick. 48 ; 2 Kent Com. 8th ed. 239, n. ; Hoyle v. Stowe, 2 Dev. & Bat. 320. So of a deed. Tucker v. Moreland, 10 Pet. 76.

See Houser v. Reynolds, 1 Hayw. 143, where an infant told the grantee to keep the deed, and that he would not take advantage of his infancy, upon coming of age. If an infant receive rent after coming of age for land leased by him in his minority, it is an affirmation of the lease. Cheshire v. Barrett, 4 McCord, 241 ; Smith v. Low, 1 Atk. 489. Where an infant vendor saw his vendee making extensive improvements upon the land, and said that he had been paid and satisfied, it was held a ratification. Wheaton v. East, 5 Yerg. 62.

be granted in any case where there has been a misrepresentation, fraud or deceit, or the plaintiff does not appear before the court with " clean hands ; " (*r*) nor where there has been a misapprehension by the defendant to which the plaintiff has by his acts, even unintentionally, contributed ; (*s*) nor where a person has been induced to sign an agreement whilst he was in a state of complete intoxication; (*t*) but, if the defendant was only a little drunk, and knew what he was about, and there was no fraud, the decree will be made. (*u*)   Where owners of a colliery contracted to purchase an estate without disclosing the fact that they themselves had got coal from under it and were liable for damages, the court declined to enforce the contract in their favor, although they had agreed to give the full value of the property. (*v*)   If a person knowingly contracts for the sale of an estate without a title, and the owner offers to make the seller a title, yet the court will not force the buyer to take it ; for every seller ought to be a bona fide contractor ; (*y*) but, if the vendor has contracted bona fide in ignorance of the defect of title, and procures a good title within a reasonable time, and then calls upon the purchaser to complete his contract, and the latter refuses, a decree for specific performance will be granted against the purchaser. (*z*)   Extravagance, unreasonableness, or inadequacy òf price, form no ground in general, for refusing the specific performance of a contract, unless

(*r*) Cadman v. Horner, 18 Ves. 10. Clermont v. Tasburgh, 1 Jac. & Walk. 120. Phillips v. Duke of Bucks. 1 Vern. 227.

(*s*) Baskomb v. Beckwith, L. R., 8 Eq. 100 ; 38 L. J., Ch. 586.

(*t*) Cooke v. Clayworth, 18 Ves. 12. Say v. Barwick, 1 Ves. & B. 195.

(*u*) Lightfoot v. Heron, 3 You. & C.

590.

(*v*) Philips v. Homphray, L. R. 6 Ch. 770.

(*y*) Tendring v. Loudon, 2 Eq. Cas. Abr. 680.

(*z*) Boehm v. Wood, 1 Jac. & Walk. 421. Chamberlain v. Lee, 10 Sim. 444. Eyston v. Simonds, 1 You. & C. C. C. 608.

" it is such as shocks the conscience and amounts in
itself to conclusive evidence of fraud in the transaction." (*a*)   But an exception is made in favor of heirs
dealing with their expectancies, and in the case of sales
of reversions by them, which are closely scrutinized and
generally discountenanced. (*b*)

Specific performance will also be decreed in favor
of a principal who purchased through the medium of
an agent, although the agency was not known or disclosed until after the contract had been signed, unless
there was some fraud or misrepresentation in the
matter. (*c*)

If the price to be paid for an estate is to be fixed
by a third party, there can, of course, be no action for
damages, or decree for specific performance, until the
price is fixed. (*d*)   Neither party can be compelled
to appoint an arbitrator to name the price; (*e*) and, if
an arbitrator is actually appointed, the death of either
party before award made will revoke the submission,
(*f*) unless there be mutual covenants between the
parties for themselves and their heirs, executors, and
administrators, for the conveyance of the estate and
payment of the money to be awarded to the vendor.
(*g*)   When the person who is to make the valuation
is named in the agreement for the sale, the court will
compel the vendor to permit the valuation to be made

(*a*) Coles v. Trecothick, 9 Ves. 246.
But see Baker v. Monk, 33 Beav. 419.

(*b*) Sugd. Vend. 14th ed. 276-287.
See, however, the 31 Vict. c. 4, s. 2, by
which no purchase, &c., made bona
fide, without fraud or unfair dealing,
of any reversionary interest in real or
personal estate, is to be opened or set
aside merely on the ground of undervalue.

(*c*) Hall v. Warren, 9 Ves. 605.

(*d*) Wilks v. Davis, 3 Mer. 507.
Vickers v. Vickers, L. R., 4 Eq. 529 ;
36 L. J., Ch. 946.

(*e*) Agar v. Macklew, 2 Sim. & Stu.
418.

(*f*) Blundell v. Brettargh, 17 Ves.
232.

(*g*) Belchier v. Reynolds, 2 Ken.
Ch. C. part 2, 87.

according to the contract. (*h*) If a party, having power to revoke the authority given to the arbitrator to name a price, exercises his power contrary to good faith, the court will not give him any aid or assistance in furtherance of his misconduct. (*i*) A revocation of the submission after it has been made a rule of court is a contempt. (*k*) If an action is brought for specific performance, and a valid contract of sale is clearly established, the court will grant an injunction to prevent either of the parties from doing any act which may be injurious to the estate, such as cutting down timber, removing boundaries, pulling down buildings and walls, presenting to a living, &c.; (*l*) and the vendor will, in general, be restrained from re-selling the estate and executing a conveyance of the legal estate in the property to a third person. (*m*) But, if the validity of the contract is brought into doubt, or there is good reason for thinking that a final and concluded agreement had not been entered into, the court will decline to interfere by way of injunction.

Sales by trustees will not be enforced by the court, if they are improvident sales. " If the trustee has been negligent, not taking that care to preserve the interest of his cestui que trust which he ought to have done, it will not permit the party dealing with him to take advantage of that negligence ; " for the court will not enforce any contract involving a breach of trust. (*n*) If trustees are authorized and empowered to sell

(*h*) Morse v. Merest, Mad. & Geld. 138.   Nicholson v. Knapp, 9 Sim. 26.   326.

(*i*) Pope v. Lord Duncannon, 9 Sim. 179.   (*m*) Echliff v. Baldwin, 16 Ves. 267.

(*k*) Harcourt v. Ramsbottom, 1 J. & W. 511.   (*n*) Ord v. Noel, 5 Mad. 440. Thompson v. Blackstone, 6 Beav.

(*l*) Crockford v. Alexander, 15 Ves.   472.

at the request of a tenant for life, the trustees have a
discretion which the court has no power or jurisdiction to control; and they can not, consequently, be
compelled to give effect to a contract entered into by
the tenant for life, without their concurrence, for the
sale of the estate. (*o*)   If trustees, acting in the exercise of a power of sale, make an agreement for the
sale of an estate, the contract binds the estate; and,
though by subsequent events it can not be executed
under the power, yet it will be decreed to be specifically performed by those who have acquired the interest in the estate bound by the contract. (*p*)   If an
agent, authorized to sell by public auction, sells by
private contract, a specific performance will not be
decreed against the principal, although the estate was
sold for a greater price than he required for it. (*q*)
An agreement by one of two joint tenants to sell his
share of the joint estate, amounts to a severance of
the joint tenancy; and a specific performance of the
contract will be decreed as against the survivor. (*r*)
A married woman can not bind herself by a contract
to sell her property; and, if a husband agrees to sell
his wife's lands, a specific performance can not be decreed against him. (*s*)

　　If, after making a contract of sale, the vendor has re-
sold the estate and executed a conveyance to the second
purchaser, and the latter has bought and accepted the
conveyance, and paid the purchase-money, in ignorance
of the first contract of sale, a specific performance of
such first contract will not be decreed.   But, if the
second purchaser has bought with notice of the first

(*o*) Thomas v. Dering, 1 Keen, 729.　　(*s*) Emery v. Wase, 8 Ves. 515.
(*p*) Mortlock v. Buller, 10 Ves. 315.　　Martin v. Mitchell, 2 Jac. & Walk.
(*q*) Daniel v. Adams, Ambl. 495.　　425.
(*r*) Brown v. Raindle, 3 Ves. 257.

sale, the first purchaser is entitled to a decree for a specific performance against the vendor and the second purchaser, the latter being considered to take subject to the equity of the first purchaser to have the premises conveyed to him at the price originally agreed upon. $(t)^1$ If the vendor re-sells, without having any right in equity so to do, he will be considered as a trustee for the purchaser, re-selling the estate for the benefit of the latter, and will be compelled to account to him for the purchase money. (u) If the vendor is seized in fee or pur autre vie, and dies before a conveyance is executed, his heir-at-law will be decreed to perform the agreement in specie, and will be compelled to execute a conveyance of the estate, (x) although the purchase money is not payable to him, but to the personal representatives of the vendor. If the latter is only tenant in tail, his agreement to sell can not be enforced in equity against the issue in tail, although he may have entered into the strongest covenants to that effect, and although a decree for specific performance may have been obtained against him in his life-time, and he may have died in contempt and in prison for not obeying the decree, and although he may have received part or even the whole of the purchase money; (y) for the issue in tail claim per formam doni from the creator of the estate tail, and not from the tenant in tail himself; and the court can not take away their rights by title paramount. But, if the entail is barred by the vendor in his life-time, and his estate is thus converted into a fee, then, as there are no issue in tail, a

---

(t) Daniels v. Davison, 17 Ves. 433. 199.

(u) Daniels v. Davison, 16 Ves. 255.

(x) Gell v. Vermedun, 2 Freem.

(y) Fox v. Crane, 2 Vern. 306. Frank v. Mainwaring, 6 Beav. 126. 3 & 4 Wm. 3, c. 74, s. 47.

^{1} Glover v. Fisher, 11 Ill. 666.

specific performance will be decreed as against his heir-at-law. By the 3 & 4 Wm. 4, c. 74, it is provided (S. 47) that, in cases of dispositions of lands by tenants in tail under that Act, the jurisdiction of courts of equity shall be altogether excluded in regard to specific performance and the supplying of defects in the execution of the powers of disposition given to tenants in tail by the Act, and that no disposition thereof by a tenant in tail in equity shall be of any force, unless such disposition would at law be an effectual disposition under the Act. This provision, therefore, prevents the court from treating a contract or covenant to bar an estate tail as an actual bar of the estate, and prohibits a decree for the specific performance of any such contract as against the issue in tail; yet it does not prohibit the exercise of the old power of enforcing a specific performance of a contract against the tenant in tail himself. By the 11 Geo. 4 & 1 Wm. 4, c. 36, s. 15, the court itself may execute the decree against a tenant in tail in custody for a contempt, (*z*)

531. *Payment of purchase money into court.*—In certain cases, where an action has been brought for a specific performance, and the purchaser has been let into possession of the property, the purchase money will be ordered to be paid into court. This has been done where an unexpected delay occurred in making out the title, and the purchaser insisted on his right to retain possession and receive the profits of the land during the delay (*a*)—where the purchaser became insolvent, and attempted to re-sell the estate (*b*)— where the purchaser, after being let into possession

(*z*) Sugd. Vend., 14th ed., 205.   (*b*) Hall v. Jenkinson, 2 Ves. & B.
(*a*) Gibson v. Clarke, 1 Ves. & B.   125.
500.

dealt improperly with the land, cut down timber and
underwood, and opened and worked mines (c)—where
the title was accepted, and the purchaser made frivolous objections, still keeping possession of the property.
In some cases where a purchaser retains possession,
and unexpected delay has occurred in the completion
of the title, an occupation rent has been fixed and decreed by the court, after deducting interest on the
deposit, (d) in others a receiver has been appointed,
(e) and in others the purchaser has been ordered to
give up possession or pay the purchase money into
court. (f)

532. *Assignment of contract to purchase land.*—
A vendor of land may receive the balance of the purchase money, and convey the estate to the purchaser
without regard to the receipt of a notice that the purchaser has agreed to assign the contract; for the
vendor is not bound to see that the purchaser carries
out his agreement with the sub-vendee; but it would
be otherwise if the vendor had notice that the contract
had been actually assigned, and that the sub-vendee
insisted on its being completed with him instead of
with the purchaser. (g)

533. *Invalid sales—Want of title in the vendor—
Eviction of the purchaser.*—We have already seen
that, whilst a contract of sale remains executory, and
before a transfer or conveyance under seal has been
executed, a purchaser is entitled to recover any deposit he may have paid, if it turns out that the vendor
is unable from want of title to transfer the estate or

(c) Cutler v. Simons, 2 Mer. 103.
Buck v. Lodge, 18 Ves. 450. Pope v.
Great Eastern Railway Company, 36
L. J. Ch. 60. But see Robertshaw v.
Bray, 35 L. J., Ch. 844.

(d) Smith v. Jackson, 1 Mad. 618.

(e) Hall v. Jenkinson, 2 Ves. & B.
125.

(f) Curling v. Austin, 2 Drew &
Sm. 129.

(g) Shaw v. Foster, L. R., 5 H. L.
321 ; 42 L., Ch. 49.

interest he has agreed to sell; and, if the whole purchase money has been paid in advance, the whole is recoverable. Thus, where a contract for the sale and purchase of the residue of a term of one thousand nine hundred years was entered into, and a deed of assignment of the lease prepared and executed by some of the vendors, and the purchase money paid and possession given, but, before the deed had been completely executed, it was discovered that the vendors had no title to the lease, and the purchaser was evicted, it was held that he was entitled to recover the purchase money, as the vendors had never transferred to him that which they had agreed to sell, and he to buy. (*h*)   But if, after a deed of conveyance has been executed, and the purchase money paid, it appears that the vendor had no title and the purchaser is evicted, the latter can not recover back the purchase money, or obtain compensation for the damages he has sustained, if the ordinary covenants for title are not inserted in the deed, and it does not appear upon the face of the conveyance that any particular estate or interest in the land was bargained for, and covenanted or agreed to be sold. For the purchaser might have protected himself by proper covenants for title; and if he has neglected to do so, he will be deemed to have been content to take such estate or interest in the land as the vendor actually possessed; and, having got that, he has got all he bargained for. (*i*)   If he might, by a careful investigation of the

(*h*) Johnson v. Johnson, 3 B. & P. 126. Farrer v. Nightingall, 2 Esp. 639. Cripps v. Reade, 6 T. R. 666. Cod. lib. 8, tit. 45, lex. 5.

(*i*) Bree v. Holbech, 2 Doug. 655. Johnson v. Johnson, 3 B. & P. 170. Duke v. Barnett, 2 Coll. C. C. 337. Wakeman v. Duchess of Rutland, 3 Ves. 235. Browning v. Wright, 2 B. & P. 23. Thackeray v. Wood, 34 L. J., Q. B. 226. Goodtitle v. Morgan, 1 T. R. 762. Roswell v. Vaughan, Cro. Jac. 197. Chapman v. Speller. 14 Q. B. 624 ; 19 L. J,. Q. B. 239. Delmer

title have discovered that he was buying another man's property and not the estate of the vendor, he is concluded by his own laches, unless there has been actual fraud on the part of the vendor. (*k*)

534. *Qualified covenants for title.*—If the vendor by the conveyance transfers the premises so far as he himself possesses them or can grant them, and covenants that, notwithstanding any act done by him, he hath in himself good right to grant and assure, &c., he limits his covenants for title to that which he actually has, or but for his own act would have had to convey, and does give a general and absolute warranty of title. (*l*)   So by the Scotch law, "When one sells with warrandice from fact and deed, the intention is not to sell the subject absolutely, which would be the same as selling it with absolute warrandice, but only to sell it so as the seller himself has it—that is, to sell what title and interest he has in the subject. The purchaser takes upon himself all other hazards ; and, therefore, if eviction happen otherwise than through the fact and deed of the disponer, he bears the loss." (*m*)

In the Roman law, if the vendor was not in the actual possession of the subject-matter of the sale, and was not clothed with the visible and apparent ownership of it, but sold only a naked title or right to a thing which was in the possession of a third party, it was considered to be the duty of the purchaser to inquire into the title of the vendor before he entered into the contract of sale. (*n*)   But, whenever a person

v. McCabe, 14 Ir. C. L. R. 377. Anon. 2 Ch. C. 19.   Maynard v. Moseley, 3 Swanst. 655.

(*k*) Anon., 2 Ch. C. 19.   Maynard v. Moseley, 3 Swanst. 655.

(*l*) Thackeray v. Wood, 33 L. J., Q.

B. 275 ; 34 L. J,. Q. B. 226.

(*m*) Craig v. Hopkins, 2 Collect. Decisions, 517, 518.   Brown's Law of Sale, 279.

(*n*) The maxim, "Caveat emptor, qui ignorari non dubuit quod jus

sold property of which he had the actual possession
and the visible and apparent ownership at the time of
sale, there was an implied warranty of title on the
part of the vendor; and, if the purchaser was evicted,
he had a claim to restitution of the price and to compensation for all the loss and damage he had sustained by the eviction ; (*o*) and, in the case of sales
of hereditary estates, the heir was bound by the warranty of his ancestor. (*p*)   By the Code Napoleon,
"although at the time of the sale no stipulation was
made respecting warranty, the seller is obliged by law
to warrant the purchaser against eviction and against
incumbrances not declared at the time of the sale."
(*q*)   "In the Scotch law," observes Mr. Bell,
"although there be no express stipulation of warrandice, there is an implied convention, where a full,
onerous consideration is given for the conveyance,
that the transference shall be effectual; and this not
merely to the effect of restoring the consideration
given, but of indemnifying the grantee in all respects
for the loss, &c., in case of eviction." (*r*)   In the
Roman law a formal stipulation was frequently superadded to the contract of sale by the parties, binding
the vendor to defend the possession of the purchaser,
and in case of eviction to pay him double the amount
of the price. (*s*)

By the common law the words "give" or "grant"

---

alienum emit " (Hobart, 99, Broom's
Maxims, 2nd edition), applies to the
question of title as between the purchaser of property sold by a person
who had no right to sell it and the
true owner who claims it, rather than
to the question of compensation as
between the vendor and his immediate
purchaser.

(*o*) Cod. lib. 8, tit. 45 (De Evictioni-
bus), lex 6.   Dig. lib. 21, tit. 2, lex. 1,
60, 70.

(*p*) Cod. lib. 8, tit. 45, lex. 20.
Domat, liv. 1, tit. 2, s. 10, 6.

(*q*) Code Napoleon, liv. 3, s. 3.
Pothier, Contract de Vent, No. 83 to
No. 233.

(*r*) 1 Bell's Com. p. 644.

(*s*) Dig. lib. 21, tit. 2, lex. 6.

in a deed of feoffment, or any equivalent words passing the estate, raised an implied covenant on the part
of the grantor to warrant, and defend, and secure to
the grantee the estate or interest granted, which implied covenant was annexed to the estate and ran
with the land, so that the right to take advantage of
it passed to the heirs and assigns of the grantee, who
might in case of eviction by title paramount, sue the
grantor upon the covenant.   Now, however, by the
8 & 9 Vict. c. 106, s. 4, it is enacted, "that the word
'give' or the word 'grant' in a deed shall not imply
any covenant in law respect of any tenements or
hereditaments, except so far as the word 'give' or the
word 'grant' may, by force of any Act of Parliament,
imply a covenant."   Consequently, if the purchaser of
an estate be evicted, he has no longer any remedy
against the grantor upon any implied covenant for
title or quiet enjoyment.   But, if the deed of conveyance recites that the vendor is seized of an estate in
fee, and that he has agreed to sell such an estate, this
amounts to an express covenant that he is so seized,
and has a right to convey such an estate to the purchaser; (*t*) and, if he was not seized in fee, and no fee
in the lands passed by the conveyance, he would be
responsible in damages for a breach of covenant.
Where a man had bought his own estate in ignorance
of his title, and accepted a conveyance thereof, and
paid the purchase money, the vendor was compelled
to repay the amount; "for, there being a plain mistake, the court can not suffer the vendor to run away
with the money in consideration of the sale of an
estate to which he had no right." (*u*)   If a man, having nothing at all to sell, bargains as if he had, and

(*t*) Severn *v.* Clerk, 1 Leon 122.   (*u*) Bingham *v.* Bingham, 1 Ves.
Bar oot v. Freswell, 3 Ke). 4f 5.   sen. 126.

thereby prevails on another party to become a purchaser and pay him money or give him a bond, that
is what is called a fraud in equity, although the vendor
might have thought at the time that he had something
to sell. (*v*)   Therefore, "if I sell you a thing which,
without the knowledge of either of us, has ceased to
exist, there will be no contract." (*y*)

If a vendor affirms that he is the owner of certain
property, believing what he says to be true, and so induces another party to buy, an action for deceit will
not lie against him, if the purchaser was furnished with
the means of ascertaining for himself the truth or falseness of the representation. (*z*)   The mere assertion by
a vendor that he has a good title, on the faith of which
the purchaser relies without investigation, is not necessarily such a misrepresentation as will preclude the
vendor from enforcing the contract, where at the time
of making the representation, he was ignorant of the
defect in his title. (*a*)   But, if the vendor knew at
the time that his title was defective, and kept back the
fact from the purchaser, this is a fraudulent concealment which avoids the contract ab initio, and entitles
the purchaser to recover back his purchase money ; (*b*)
and in such a case the court will not allow him to
force the title upon the purchaser, although in the
conditions of sale he has employed general words large
enough to include the defect. (*c*)   In every contract
of sale there is an implied undertaking or covenant,
according as the contract may or may not be under

(*v*) Hitchcock v. Giddings, 4 Pr.
141.

(*y*) Cod. lib. 4, tit. 38. Domat. liv.
1, tit. 2, s. 10, 24. Pothier, OBLIGA-
TIONS, No. 6. Tayler v. Caldwell, 3
B. & S. 837 ; 33 L. J., Q. B. 164.

z) Roswel v. Vaughan, 2 Cro. 196.

(*a*) Hume v. Pocock, L. ;R., 1 Ch.
379 ; 35 L. J., Ch. 731.

(*b*) Edwards v. M'Leay, Coop. Ch.
313 ; 2 Swanst. 287. Early v. Garrett,
9 B. & C. 932.

(*c*) Edwards v. Wickwar, *In re*
Brayne, 35 L. J. Ch. 48.

seal, that the vendor does not, at the time he assumes to be the owner of the property and to have a right to sell it, know that he is not the owner and has no right to sell ; and if the knowledge of his want of title can be brought home to him, there is a direct breach of this implied undertaking or covenant, which will enable the purchaser to recover all the damages he has sustained. (*d*) If an action is brought by a vendor to compel a specific performance by a purchaser of a contract of sale, and the purchaser pays the purchase money without putting in an answer, and afterwards discovers that he was deceived and defrauded by the vendor, he is not precluded from bringing an action against the latter and recovering damages, if he comes speedily after discovering the fraud. (*e*)

535. *Breach of covenants for title.*—If, after the purchase has been completed by the execution of the conveyance and payment of the purchase money, it is discovered that the vendor had no title to the estate he professed to sell, and the purchaser is evicted, and brings his action for a breach of the ordinary covenants for title and quiet enjoyment, the measure of damages will be the amount of purchase money paid for the estate, and all incidental damages flowing from the breach of contract, such as the costs and expenses of preparing the conveyance and investigating the title. If the breach has not been followed by any eviction of the purchaser, the latter should wait until the ultimate damage has been sustained by eviction; and he may then recover the whole amount of purchase money paid, with interest, and his costs and expenses; but he can not do this so long as he has not

(*d*) Peto v. Blades, 5 Taunt. 457. Furnis v. Leicester, Cro. Jac. 474. Crosse v. Gardner, Carth. 90. Harding v. Freeman, Styles 310. Warner v. Tallerd, 1 Rol. Abr. 91.

(*e*) Jendwine v. Slade, 2 Esp. 572.

been disturbed in his possession and enjoyment of the property. (*f*) " If," observes Domat, "the thing sold is diminished in value by the effect of time, or from other causes, so that it is worth less at the time of the eviction than the price paid by the purchaser, the latter is entitled to recover from the vendor only the diminished value as it existed at the time of the eviction ; for it is only in that value that the purchaser's loss doth consist. The diminution in value which preceded the eviction regarded only the purchaser, who ought not to be made a gainer by the eviction." (*g*)

If, between the time of the execution of the conveyance and the period of eviction, the purchaser has expended money upon the land in drainage, buildings, and improvements, he will not be allowed to recover from the vendor the amount of capital so expended, unless the latter has been guilty of a downright fraud in the sale of the estate; (*h*) neither could he by the common law recover the money so expended from the party who evicted him ; he sustained, therefore, in general, a dead loss of the amount. But, in equity, if the land was known to have been purchased for the erection of buildings, and the purchaser was evicted after having expended money in building, the purchaser had, in certain cases, a claim upon the land for the amount of his expenditure. (*i*) In the civil law, the purchaser was entitled to be reimbursed the money he had expended in improvements, and had a lien upon the estate for the amount. If the vendor had been guilty of a fraud

---

(*f*) 2 Saund. 181, b. Shep. Touch. 170. King v. Jones, 5 Taunt. 428.

(*g*) Domat. liv. 1, tit. 2, s. 10.

(*h*) Dallas. C. J., and Robertson, J., Lewis v. Campbell, 8 Taunt. 715 ; 3 B. & Ald. 392. Worthingion v. Warrington, 8 C. B. 134.

(*i*) Bunny v. Hopkinson, 29 L. J., Ch. 93 ; 27 Beav. 565.

in making the sale, and had knowingly sold the property of another man, he was bound to make good to the purchaser the capital expended by the latter ; but, if there was no fraud in the case, and the vendor sold under a mistake, it was considered that the expense of the improvements ought to fall upon the person who evicted, rather than upon the vendor ; (*k*) and the former consequently could not obtain possession of the estate without paying the value of the improvements. The vendor in this case had to idemnify the purchaser according to what the estate would have been worth at the time of the eviction, if it had not been improved ; and the evicting party had to make good the improvements, and was never allowed to reap the profit of them. " In making an estimate of these improvements," observes Domat, " we must set the expense of making them against the profits the purchaser has received from them, so that, if the profits he has received equal the expenditure of the principal and interest he laid out, there will be no reimbursement due, it being enough for the purchaser that he loses nothing. If the profits come short of the expenditure, the purchaser will be entitled to the difference." (*l*)   If the purchaser has not been evicted, but has entered into a fair compromise with the real owner or party having title paramount, he will be entitled to recover the whole amount paid by way of compromise, together with his costs and expenses. (*m*) If an estate has been sold as freehold, with a general

---

(*k*) Si mihi allenam aream vendideris, et in ea ego ædificavero, atque ita eam domisnus evincit ; nam quia po sum petentem dominum, nisi imp msam œdificiorum solvat, doli mali ιxceptione summovere, magis est, ut .a res ad periculum venditoris non pertineat.   Dig. ljb. 19, tit. 1, lex. 45, § 1.   Cod. lib. 8, tit. 45, lex. 16.

(*l*) Domat. liv. 1, tit.12, s. 10. Poth. Vent. No. 133–135. Cod. lib. 8, tit. 45. 1 Bell's Comm. 645.

(*m*) Smith v. Compton, 3 B. & Ad. 407.

covenant that the vendor is seized in fee, and the estate proves to be a copyhold estate, the measure of damages will be the difference between the value of a freehold and copyhold estate. (*n*)

536. *Non-payment of purchase money after the execution of a conveyance.*—If the conveyance expresses, contrary to the fact, that the purchase money is paid, though the legal estate passes, yet the purchaser will not be permitted to possess and enjoy the estate for his own use, benefit, and advantage, unless he pays down the purchase money. (*o*)

537. *Sale of pretenced titles.*—By the 32 Hen. 8, c. 9, s. 2, it is enacted that no person shall bargain for, buy, or sell, or obtain, or grant, or covenant to have any " pretenced rights or titles" of any person to any manors, lands, tenements, &c„ unless the person bargaining, selling or granting the same, or his ancestors, or the parties through whom he claims, have been in possession of the same, or the reversion or remainder thereof, or taken the rents or profits thereof, for one year next before the said bargain, sale, or grant. But persons in possession of manors, lands, &c., and in receipt of the rents and profits thereof, may buy (s. 4) or acquire the pretenced title of other persons afterwards to be made. " A pretenced right or title is where one is in possession or receipt of the rents and profits of lands, &c., as owner, and another that is out of possession claims them." (*p*) A person, therefore, who has been turned out of possession and deprived of the rents and profits of land to which he is entitled, has no saleable interest. He may enforce his right through the medium of an action ; and, when he has

(*n*) Gray v. Briscoe, Noy's R. 142.
(*o*) Winter v. Lord Anson, 1 Sim. & Stu. 444.

(*p*) Partridge v. Strange, Plowd. 88.

got possession of the land, he may then sell it ; but he can not sell or transfer his right of action. (*q*)

538. *Fraudulent concealment.—Avoiding sales of realty.*—Where a vendor, knowing that he has no right or title to property, or being cognizant of the existence of incumbrances or outgoings upon it, or of latent defects materially lowering its value in the market, sells it, and neglects to disclose such defects to the purchaser, (*r*) there is a fraudulent concealment vitiating the contract; and conditions of sale, not drawn bona fide, but intended to cover difficulties arising from such uncommunicated defects, will not preclude the purchaser from objecting to them. (*s*) So it is, where the vendor of a lease which becomes forfeited if the premises are not put into repair after notice, receives such notice, and then sells the premises in a dilapidated state without informing the purchaser of the notice. (*t*)   There may also be a fraudulent concealment by a purchaser which will vitiate a sale, as where a person having secret information of the death of one of two tenants for life, went and purchased the reversion without disclosing the fact to the reversioners of whom he bought. (*u*)   But in a general sale of an estate, if the vendor has said or done nothing to throw the purchaser off his guard or to conceal a patent defect, there is no fraudulent concealment on the part of the vendor. (*v*)   The purchaser has an op-

---

(*q*) Doe v. Evans, 1 C. B. 717 The 32 Hen. 8, c. 9, contains prohibitions against maintenance, champerty, and embracery.

(*r*) Edwards v. M'Leay, 2 Swanst. 287 ; Coop. Ch. G. 308   Peto v. Blades, 5 Taunt. 657. Wilson v. Fuller, and Fuller v. Wilson, 3 C. B. 58, 68. Shirley v. Stratton, 1 Br. C. C. 440.

(*s*) Jackson v. Whitehead, 28 Beav. 154. Hume v. Pocock, L. R., 1 Ch. 379 ; 35 L. J., Ch. 731.

(*t*) Stevens v. Adamson, 2 Stark. 422.

(*u*) Turner v. Harvey, 1 Jac. R. 169.

(*v*) Jones v. Bright, 3 Moo. & P. 175.   F. N. B. 94 C.

portunity of inspecting and judging for himself; and the principle of caveat emptor applies. (y) Where a meadow is sold without any notice being given to the purchaser of a public footway around the meadow and another across it, there is no fraudulent concealment on the part of the vendor. "Certainly," observes the Lord Chancellor, "the meadow is very much the worse for a road going through it; but I can not help the carelessness of a purchaser who does not choose to inquire. It is not a latent defect." (z) So, where property was sold which was represented as standing on a fine vein of anthracite coal, it was held that it was the business of the purchaser to inquire as to the extent to which the coal had already been worked. (a) On the other hand, the purchaser may use his own knowledge, and is not bound to give the vendor information of the value of the property; as, if an estate is offered for sale, and I treat for it, knowing that there is a mine under it, and the vendor makes no inquiry, I am not bound to give him any information of it. (b)

539. *Sale with all faults, or without allowance for any defect or error.*—If it be made a term of the contract that the subject-matter of the sale is to be taken with all faults, the term or stipulation will release the vendor from the obligation of disclosing all such defects as are susceptible of discovery by a rigid examination of the subject-matter of sale. (c) Where the vendor of a house, being conscious of a defect in the main wall, plastered it up and papered it over for the purpose of concealing it from the purchaser, it was

---

(y) Turner v. Harvey, 1 Jac. 178.   (b) Turner v. Harvey, 1 Jac. 178.
(z) Bowles v. Round, 5 Ves. 509.   (c) Pickering v. Dowson, 4 Taunt.
(a) Colby v. Gadsden, 34 Beav. 416.   779.

held that this was a direct fraud, which avoided the
contract of sale and enabled the purchaser to recover
back the purchase money. (*d*)

540. *Voluntary conveyances, gifts, and transfers
defrauding subsequent purchasers* are made void by
the 27 Eliz., c. 4, s. 2, and penalties are imposed (s. 3)
upon all persons who are parties or privies to such conveyances, &c.; but any conveyance, lease, &c., made
bona fide upon good consideration, is not invalidated.
This statute is to a great extent declaratory only of
the common law, which invalidates every voluntary
conveyance or gift and voluntary settlement of property
made without valuable consideration as against a subsequent purchaser for value of the same property, even
though he had notice of the prior voluntary conveyance or settlement; for, whenever the question is
between one who has paid a valuable consideration for
an estate and another who has given nothing for it, it
is a just presumption of law that such voluntary conveyance founded only on considerations of affection
and regard, if coupled with a subsequent sale, was
made to defraud those who should afterwards become
purchasers for a valuable consideration; and it is more
fit that a voluntary grantee should be disappointed
than that a fair purchaser should be defrauded. (*e*)
If, therefore, after marriage, either the husband or wife,
or both of them, make a conveyance of lands to the
use of themselves or their children, such conveyance
is absolutely null and void against a subsequent purchaser for value. (*f*)   But a deed can not be set aside
merely because it is a voluntary conveyance; and one

(*d*) Anon. cited by Gibbs, J., Pickering v. Dowson, 4 Taunt. 785.

(*e*) Doe v. Manning, 9 East, 59.
Clarke v. Wright, 6 H. & N. 849; 30

L. J., Exch. 113.

(*f*) Goodright v. Moses, 2 W. Bl.
1019. Butterfield v. Heath, 22 L. J.,
Ch. 270.

voluntary conveyance can not defeat another ; and it has been held that, if there be two voluntary conveyances or gifts of land by deed, the first voluntary conveyance is not annulled by the second, and that a purchaser from the second voluntary grantee or donee can not avoid the estate created by the first gift ; so that, if a man makes a voluntary conveyance or gift of land to A, and then devises the same land to B, and B sells to C for value, C has no title to such land, aad can not defeat the gift to A. (*g*)   A husband acquiring an estate by marriage, or under a post-nuptial settlement not made in pursuance of articles entered into before marriage, is not a purchaser within the meaning of the statute, and is not entitled to avoid a previous voluntary conveyance. (*h*)   In considering the operation of the statute, the court only considers whether the transaction is one purely voluntary, or whether it is one of bargain, and the mere quantum of consideration is not material. (*i*)   Evidence is admissible to show valuable consideration beyond what appears on the face of the deed. (*k*)   A conveyance, though voluntary upon the face of it, and at first void against a purchaser for value, may yet become valid by force of subsequent events ; (*l*) and consequently a purchaser is not bound to take a title with a voluntary settlement as a part of it, but may decline to complete, and may recover his deposit. (*m*)

541. *Fraudulent conveyances—Fictitious qualifications—Fictitious votes.*—By the 7 & 8 Wm. 3, c. 25, s. 7, it is enacted, that all conveyances of any messuages,

(*g*) Doe v. Rusham, 21 L. J., Q. B. 139 , 16 Jur. 359.

(*h*) Douglas v. Ward, 1 Ch. C. 99. Doe v. Lewis, 20 L. J., C. P. 180.

(*i*) Townend v. Toker, L, R., 1 Ch. 446 ; 35 L. J., Ch. 608.

(*k*) Townend v. Toker, *supra.*

(*l*) Prodgers v. Langham, 1 Sid. 133.

(*m*) Clarke v. Willott, L. R., 7 Ex. 313 ; 41 L. J., Ex. 107.

lands, tenements, &c., in order to multiply voices or
to split and divide the interest in any houses and lands
among several persons to enable them to vote at elections, shall be "void and of none effect;" and the 10
Anne, c. 23, s. 1, enacts that all estates and conveyances made to any person in any fraudulent or collusive manner on purpose to qualify him to give his
vote at elections (subject to conditions or agreements
to defeat or determine such estate, or to re-convey the
same), shall be deemed and taken, against those
persons who executed the same, as free and absolute,
and be holden and enjoyed by such persons, discharged from all manner of trusts, conditions, clauses
of re-entry, powers of revocation, provisoes of redemption, or other defeasances whatsoever for defeating
such estates or for the re-conveying thereof. A deed
may be void by statute, and yet it may not be competent to the parties thereto to set up its invalidity;
and it has been held that the true construction of
these two statutes is that, dealing only with the subject of parliamentary law, they prevent a man from
acquiring a right to vote which it was contrary to the
policy of the law he should acquire, but that they
leave the conveyance to operate upon the land freely
and absolutely in all other respects. (*n*) [1]

(*n*) Philpotts v. Philpotts, 10 C. B. 85.   Doe v. Roberts, 2 B. & Ald. 367.

[1] Says Dr. Washburn : "There is a class of conveyances
of lands which, though formal in all respects, and effectual
between the parties, are, by the policy of the law or by statute,
held to be void to a certain extent.   This embraces what are
known as fraudulent conveyances, where the intent of the parties to the same is to defraud the creditors or the subsequent
purchasers of the grantor, by means of such conveyance.   The
questions arising under this are usually referred to the statutes of
13 Eliz. ch. 5, and 27 Eliz. ch. 4, though these are said to be in affir-
mance of the common law, and, in one form or the other, prevail

542. *Conveyances and transfers constituting an act of bankruptcy.*—By the 32 & 33 Vict. c. 71, s. 6, a fraudulent conveyance, gift, delivery, or transfer of his

all over the United States. The first of these statutes relates to creditors, and provides, in general terms, that all conveyances of lands intended to defraud or delay creditors, shall, as to such creditors, be void. Story Eq. § 353–356; Sands v. Cadwise, 4 Johns. 536; Penneman v. Cole, 8 Met. 499. As to the question in these cases depends upon the bona fides with which the transaction takes place. A few general principles may be stated. In the first place, such conveyance, though fraudulent, is, if otherwise sufficient, and for a valuable consideration, valid as to all innocent purchasers not privy to the fraudulent intent. Thus, if a fraudulent grantee conveys the estate to a bona fide purchaser, for a valuable consideration, the conveyance is good, and the first grant may be purged of the fraud. Oriental Bank v. Haskins, 3 Met. 340; Jackson v. Henry, 10 Johns. 185; Somer v. Brewer, 2 Pick. 180; Clapp v. Torrell, 20 Pick, 247. So, though the grantor makes the conveyance with a fraudulent intent, it will not affect the validity of the transaction unless the grantee was cognizant of his intent, or participated in it. Bridge v. Eggleston, 14 Mass. 250; Harrison v. Trustees, &c., 12 Mass 462. And though the design be originally fraudulent, as to creditors, and known to the grantee, so as to be void as to creditors so long as the transactions had that character, yet it may become valid by being purged of the fraud by matter ex post facto, if the fraudulent intent is abandoned. Oriental Bank v. Haskins, 3 Met. 340; Verplank v. Sterry, 12 Johns. 552; Sterry v. Arden, 1 Johns. Ch. 261. But if vendor and vendee participate in the purpose of the vendor, to defraud or delay creditors, by conveying his land, it will be void as to such creditors, though a full and valuable consideration may have been paid for the same. Story Eq. § 369; Wright v. Brandis, 1 Ind. 336; Ruffing v. Tilton, 12 Ind. 260. In respect to conveyances that are voluntary, that is, made without a valuable consideration, the cases are not uniform. Such conveyances are not void as against subsequent creditors, where no intent exists to defraud such creditors, seems to be admitted. And while, as to previous creditors, different courts have applied different degrees of stringency in the rule, it may be laid down as a general proposition that if such conveyance be made to any person other than a child, it will be void as to

property or any part thereof made by a debtor, is an
act of bankruptcy. It is not necessary that the assignment should be fraudulent, in the strict sense of

existing creditors, and when made to a child, or as a settlement
upon a wife, whether it shall be void or not depends upon the
condition of the grantor as to his ability to pay his debts out
of his remaining property at the time of its being made. And
it may be added that such voluntary conveyances are uniformly
recognized as valid between the parties and their representatives. Sexton v. Wheaton, 8 Wheat. 229; Salmon v. Bennett,
1 Conn. 525; 1 Am. Lead. Cases, 49–85; Doe v. Hurd, 7
Blackf. 510; Bullitt v. Taylor, 34 Miss. 708, 737, and cases
cited in the argument; Story Eq. §§ 362, 364, 371; Reade v.
Livingston, 3 Johns. Ch. 500, 501; Hinde's Lessee v. Long-
worth, 11 Wheat. 199. See Washband v. Washband, 27 Conn.
424, for the distinction between an inadequate and no consideration, in its effect where grantor owes existing debts; in the
former the deed will be good, unless made with a fraudulent
intent. Where the conveyance is made with an actual fraudulent intent, it may be avoided by subsequent as well as previous
creditors. Parkman v. Welch, 19 Pick. 231. But see Bullitt
v. Taylor, 34 Miss. 740, 741. But that a voluntary conveyance,
made in good faith, will be good against a subsequent purchaser with notice, seems to be the better rule of law, as now
prevailing in the United States, though held otherwise in England. And it would not be good against a subsequent purchaser without notice, if for a valuable consideration. Story
Eq. § 427; Cathcart v. Robinson, 5 Peters, 264, 280; Beal v.
Warren, 2 Gray, 447; Doe v. Rushan, 17 A. & E. N. S. 724;
Jackson v. Town, 4 Cow. 603; Sterry v. Arden, 1 Johns.
Ch. 261. Another class of conveyances which were good
at common law, have been declared fraudulent, by statute,
under the doctrine of modern bankrupt and insolvent laws,
and that is, conveyances intended to give undue preferences
to creditors, and to prevent an equal distribution of a bankrupt's assets among his creditors. Penniman v. Cole, 8 Met.
500. And it may be added that, though the deed be
voluntary, and fraudulent in its intent, it is, nevertheless,
valid and effectual against the grantor and his heirs. Jackson v. Garnsey, 16 Johns. 189. In Bunn v. Winthrop a
voluntary deed settling lands, in which the grantor had a
chattel interest, upon a natural daughter, was sustained in a
court of equity, although, after executing it, but without deliv-

the term, in order to make it an act of bankruptcy. It is sufficient if the necessary effect of it is so to cripple the resources of the trader as to produce insolvency, and deprive him of the present power of satisfying his creditors. (*o*) [1]

SECTION II.

OF ORDINARY CONTRACTS FOR THE BUYING AND SELLING OF GOODS AND CHATTELS.

543. *Of the title to goods and chattels.*—The title to goods and chattels does not rest upon title-deeds, nor, in general, upon documentary evidence, but is founded, prima facie, upon visible possession and apparent ownership. (*p*) The mere possessor of goods by finding is entitled to hold them as against every person but the true owner,[2] and can convey an indefeasible title by sale in market overt, and a good title,

---

(*o*) *Ante.*

(*p*) Hiern *v.* Mill, 13 Ves. 122 ; T. R. 589, 750.

---

ery, the grantor sealed it up with his will, and retained the custody of it till his death. Bunn v. Winthrop, 1 Johns. Ch. 329; Souverbye v. Arden, 1 Johns. Ch. 255. And in respect to deeds obtained by duress or fraud at common law, if the party so obtaining a deed, which is duly executed in matter of form, convey the estate to a bona fide purchaser, ignorant of the duress or fraud, for a valuable consideration, the latter will hold the estate purged of such fraud or duress. Somes v. Brewer, 2 Pick. 184, 203 ; Worcester v. Eaton, 11 Mass. 379; Deputy v. Stapleford, 19 Cal. 302." Real Property, vol. ii., p. 59₂.

[1] See United States Bankruptcy Act, *ante*, vol. i., p. 660, note 1.

[2] 2 Parsons on Contracts, 97.

against everybody but the true owner, by sale not in market overt. (*q*) [1]

But possession is only prima facie evidence of title; and no purchaser can be secure of a safe title to the goods and chattels he buys, unless the purchase has been effected in market overt, nor even then, if the property he buys should happen to be stolen property. He may purchase a horse, or he may buy merchandise or furniture in the ordinary way of trade from a party in possession thereof; but, if the vendor was not the owner, and had no authority from the owner to sell, the purchaser will have no title whatever to the property he has bought as against the true owner, (*r*) unless the vendor was a

---

(*q*) Bridges v. Hawkesworth, 21 L. J., Q. B. 75. 311. Cooper v. Willomat, 1 C. B. 672, Dyer v. Pearson, 3 B. & C. 38; 4 D. & R. 648.

(*r*) Loeschman v. Machin, 2 Stark.

[1] We have no market overt in the United States (1 Parsons on Contracts, p. 520; Wheelwright v. Depeyster, 1 Johns. 479; Hosack v. Weaver, 1 Yeates, 478; Easton v. Worthington, 5 S. & R. 130; Lance v. Cowan, 1 Dana, 195; Ventress v. Smith, 10 Pet. 161; McGrew v. Browder, 14 Mart. (La.) 17; Roland v. Gundy, 5 Ohio. 202; Browning v. Magill, 2 Har. & J. 308; Dame v. Baldwin, 8 Mass. 518), but the original owner may claim his property wherever he finds it, and take it without any payment to the holder, any more than if the holder were the thief himself (Id.). Even an auctioneer selling stolen goods, and paying over the money to the thief in good faith, is liable in trover to the true owner of the goods. Hoffman v. Carrow, 22 Wend. 285). But if an owner is deceived into parting with his property, he might claim it from the taker, but if he voluntarily parts with it, he can not reclaim it from one who in good faith buys it of the fraudulent party; even if the fraud amounted to felony. Caldwell v. Bartlett, 3 Duer, 341; Jennings v. Gage, 13 Ill. 610; Malcom v. Loveridge, 13 Barb. 372; Keyser v. Harbeck, 3 Duer. 373. Williams v. Given, 6 Gratt. 268; Titcomb v. Wood. 38 Me. 561; Smith v. Lynes, 1 Seld. 41; Sawyer v. Fisher, 32 Me. 28.

factor or agent for the sale of goods as presently mentioned. By the French Code (art. 2279) the mere possession of movables is equivalent to title in all cases excepting where property has been lost or stolen ; and, as regards lost or stolen property, it is provided (art. 2280) that the party who has lost anything, or from whom it has been stolen, may reclaim it within three years from the party in whose hands he finds it, saving to the latter his remedy over against the person from whom he obtained it; but, if the actual possessor of the thing stolen or lost has purchased it in a fair or market, or at a public sale, or from a merchant who sells similar articles, the original proprietor can only procure it to be restored to him on repaying to the possessor the price which it cost him.

By the common law the right of property in, and the title to, goods and chattels may be transferred to a purchaser, as we shall presently see, by a contract of sale, without any delivery of the goods or payment of the price, so that, after the bargain has been concluded, the goods may become the property of the buyer, although they still continue in the possession of the vendor ; and, if the vendor sells them again by sale not in market overt, and actually delivers them to a second bona fide purchaser who pays him the price, yet the latter will have no title to the goods as against the first purchaser, although the first purchaser by leaving the goods in the hands of the vendor enabled him to commit the fraud. (*s*)   By the civil law actual tradition or delivery was essential to the transference of the ownership of moveables ; and no right of property passed to the purchaser until possession was given.

(*s*) Cooper v. Willomat, 1 C. B. 672.

As between the vendor and purchaser, the contract of sale so far altered the situation of the parties that, from the time of the making of it, the price became a debt due to the vendor, and the thing sold (when the sale was of an ascertained subject at an ascertained price) remained at the risk of the purchaser ; but the contract conveyed to the latter a mere JUS AD REM, or chose in action, and not the JUS IN RE or right of property. (*t*)   The vendor, so long as delivery had not been made, preserved as between himself and third parties the full dominion and ownership over the thing sold.[1]

543. "*Qui nondum rem emptor itradidit, adhuc ipse dominus est.*" (*u*) —Consequently, whenever the

---

(*t*) Troplong (De la Vente), vol. 1, p.   (*u*) Instit. lib. 3, tit. xxiv. § 3.
50, 4th ed.

[1] When the sale has been made but the goods have not passed, the vendor has no special remedy growing out of the relations of vendor and vendee : his remedies rather are the ordinary ones for breach of contract, and the measure of his damage the difference between the value of the goods at the time when the contract is broken and the contract price. Dana v. Fielden, 12 N. Y. 40; Gordon v. Norris, 49 N. H. 376 ; Deming v. Grand Trunk Railway, 48 N. Y. 455 ; Clement & Hawke M'f'g. Co. v. Meserole, 107 Mass. 362 ; Smith v. Berry, 18 Maine, 122 ; Donald v. Hodge, 5 Hayw. 85 ; Bailey v. Clay, 4 Rand. 346 ; Wells v. Abernethy, 5 Conn. 222 ; West v. Pritchard, 19 Id. 212 ; Connell v. M'Clean, 6 Harr. & J. 297 ; Gilpins v. Consequa, Peters C. C. 85, 94 ; Willings v. Consequa, Id. 172, 176 ; Shaw v. Nudd, 8 Pick. 9 ; Thompson v. Alger, 12 Met. 428, 443 ; Quarles v. George, 23 Pick. 400 ; Worthen v. Wilmot, 30 Vt. 555 ; Shepherd v. Hampton, 3 Wheat. 200, 204 ; Orr v. Bigelow, 14 N. Y. 556 ; Dey v. Dox, 9 Wend. 129 ; Davis v. Shields, 24 Id. 322 ; Stanton v. Small, 3 Sandf. 230 ; Mallory v. Lord, 29 Barb. 454, 465 ; Pitcher v. Livingston, 4 John. 15 ; Clark v. Pinney, 7 Cowen, 687 ; Gordon v. Norris, 49 N. H. 376 ; McHose v. Fulmer, 73 Pa. St. 365.   And the question as to the market value is for the jury. Smith v. Griffith, 3 Hill, 333 ; Blydenburg v. Welsh, 1 Bald-

same thing was sold by the same owner to two different individuals successively, he who was first put
into actual possession became the true owner.

545. *Sale in market overt.*—Our Saxon ancestors,
were greatly opposed to all private and secret transfers of property. By the laws of Athelstan all persons were absolutely prohibited from buying and
selling goods out of the open public market ; and by
the ordinances of other Saxon kings, no bargain and
sale, or exchange of goods and chattels, was allowed
to be valid, unless it was made publicly at a fair or
market, or in the presence of two or more credible
witnesses. (*x*)   Things purchased at shops in the city
of London in the ordinary way of trade have always
been considered to have been bought in market overt,
so as to exempt the purchaser from the obligation of
inquiring into the title of the shopkeeper to the goods
he sold. (*y*)   But shops in country towns, although
openly and notoriously used as public places of purchase and sale accessible to all comers, are not markets

---

(*x*) Ancient Laws and Institutes of
England, 14, 15, 87, 90, 116, 117, 120,
ed. 1840.   The Mirror, c. 1, s. 3.   2
Instit. 220.   Mosley v. Walker, 9 D.
& R. 863 ; 7 B. & C. 54.   Mayor, &c.,
of Macclesfield v. Chapman, 12 M. &
W. 18.

(*y*) Godb. 131, pl. 148. 5 Co. 83, b.
Lyons v. De Pass, 11 Ad. & E. 326.

---

win, 331, 340 ; Joy v. Hopkins, 5 Denio, 84 ; Furlong v. Polleys 30 Maine, 493 ; Hanna v. Harter, 2 Pike, 397.   In Furlong v. Polleys, 30 Me. 493, Shepley, C. J., held that "if it
appears that as goods of a kind like those sold could not be obtained at the time and place of delivery, and that no market
price there existed, the party entitled to damages must, upon
principle, be allowed to ascertain the market price at the near-
est and most suitable place where the goods could have been
purchased, and the difference between the market value there
at the time, and the price paid, adding the necessary cost of
their transportation to the place of delivery, would be the
measure of damages."

overt for the sale of the goods and commodities ordinarily sold or exposed for sale therein. (*z*)

A wharf in the city of London is not a market overt like a shop; (*a*) and a shop in London is not a market overt for the sale of any other commodities than those which are customarily bought and sold therein. (*b*) And the distinction must be observed between a sale over the counter to a customer of things exposed in a shop for sale, and a sale to the shopkeeper himself of things bought by him to be added to his stock-in-trade. The one may be a sale in market overt, but not so the other. If a servant, for example, steals his master's books, and goes and sells them to a bookseller in the city of London, the sale to the bookseller is not a sale in market overt, and the bookseller would acquire no right to the books as against the true owner from whom they had been stolen; (*c*) but, if after the books have been added to the bookseller's stock-in-trade, and exposed for sale in his shop in the city, they are purchased bona fide by a customer in the ordinary way of trade, the purchase would be a purchase in market overt, which would change the ownership and give the purchaser a title to the books, defeasible only on the conviction of the thief. So, if the hirer of household furniture takes it to a furniture-broker, and sells it, and receives the money, the sale does not alter the ownership, or give the broker any right to detain the

---

(*z*) Prior of Dunstable's case, 11 Hen. 6, 19, pl. 13; 25 pl. 2; 2 Brownl. 288. Harris v. Shaw, Cas. temp. Hardw. 349. Anon., 112 Mod. 521. Lee v. Bayes, 18 C. B. 601.

(*a*) Wilkinson v. King, 2 Campb. 335.

(*b*) Taylor v. Chambers Cro. Jac.

68. The Bishop of Worcester's case, F. Moore, 360. Clifton v. Chancellor, ib. 624; 5 Co. 83 b.

(*c*) White v. Spettigue, 13 M. & W. 603. Crane v. London Dock Company, 5 B. & S. 313; 33 L. J., Q. B. 224.

furniture from the owner who has let it out on hire ;
(*d*) but, if the furniture is brought into a furniture-
broker's shop in the city, and exposed for sale, and is
then bought by a customer in the ordinary way of
trade, the right of property is altered, and the owner
can not follow the subject-matter of the sale into the
hands of such second purchaser.   His remedy is either
against the party to whom he let out the goods, and
who is responsible for the breach of trust, (*e*) or
against the furniture-broker who bought from him.
(*f*)   The goods, moreover, must be corporeally present in the shop of the vendor at the time of the sale,
so that a sale by sample or a sale of goods to be
afterwards manufactured and sent from the manufac-
tory to the residence of the purchaser without ever
having been in the shop, is not a sale in market
overt. (*g*)

546. *Sale of stolen horses, goods, etc., in market
overt—Right of restitution.*—At common law the
ownership or right of property in goods sold in market overt was changed permanently by the sale ; and
the purchaser acquired an indefeasible title against all
the world : but, formerly by the 21 Hen. 8, c. 11, and
the 7 & 8 Geo. 4, c. 29, and now by the 24 & 25 Vict.
c. 96, s. 100, the property in all chattels which have
been stolen reverts, on conviction of the thief, to the
original owner from whom they were stolen, so as to
entitle him to maintain an action against the purchaser
for the goods, or the value of them, without obtaining
an order of restitution. (*h*)   The statutes 2 & 3 Ph

(*d*) Cooper v. Willomat, 1 C. B. 672.
Loeschman v. Machin, 2 Stark. 311.

(*e*) 18 Ed. 4, 23, pl. 5.   5 Hen. 7,
15, pl. 5.

(*f*) Peer v. Humphrey, 2 Ad. & E.
495.

(*g*) Crane v. London Dock Com.
pany, 5 B. & S. 313 ; 33 L. J., Q. B.
224.   Hill v. Smith, 4 Taunt. 520.

(*h*) Scattergood v. Sylvester, 15 Q.
B. 510; 19 L. J., Q. B., 447. And see
the 30 & 31 Vict. c. 35, s. 9.

& M. c. 7, and 31 Eliz. c. 12, provide for the sale of
horses in markets and fairs, and impose " sundry good
ordinances touching the manner of selling and tolling
horses for the purpose of repressing or avoiding horse-
stealing." They prevent the property in any stolen
horse from being altered by sale in market overt until
six months have elapsed from the time of the sale,
and enable the owner at any time afterwards to recover the horse on payment of the price to the purchaser. The names and addresses of all the parties to
contracts for the sale of horses are to be entered in
the toll-gatherer's book, together with the price of the
horse, its color, marks, etc.; and, if the requisites of
the Acts, as regards these and other particulars, are not
complied with, the sale is void. (*i*)

547. *Sale out of market overt.*—The rule of law,
that a person from whom goods have been stolen can
not bring an action against the thief for damages until
after he has prosecuted him for felony, does not prevent him from recovering from a third innocent person
property which has been stolen from him and sold to
the latter out of market overt. (*k*) It is said to be a
general rule of the common law, that a vendee out of
market overt can not acquire a better title than his
vendor. There are, however, some important exceptions to this rule. Where, for example, a man obtains
possession of goods through the medium of a pretended contract of sale, buying the goods and paying for
them by a cheque on a bank where he has no funds,
or by a fictitious bill of exchange, he himself has no
title to the goods after they have been demanded back
by the vendor; but, if he re-sells them and delivers

(*i*) Gibb's case, Owen, 27.   P. 249. White v. Spettigue, 13 M. &
(*k*) Lee v. Bayes, 18 C. B. 602 ; S.   W. 605. Stone v. Marsh, 6 B. & C.
C. nom. Lee v. Robinson, 25 L. J., C.   551.

them into the hands of a bona fide purchaser, before the vendor interferes to recover posession of them, the title of such bona fide purchaser can not be defeated. (*l*)   If, however, the party selling the goods obtained possession of them through the medium of false pretenses, and not by virtue of a contract of sale, the purchaser will have no title to the goods as against the true owner. (*m*)

If several joint owners of goods and chattels permit one of them alone to have the possession of the joint property, and the one so trusted with the possession sells to a bona fide purchaser, the latter will acquire a good title as against them all. (*n*)   If, too, the owner of goods has intrusted another with the possession of them, or with documentary evidence of title to them, for purposes of sale, and the party so intrusted has sold contrary to the express directions of the owner, the purchaser will nevertheless acquire a complete and perfect title by the sale.   If the owner of goods stands by and voluntarily allows another to deal with the goods as if he were the owner, and thereby induces some third party to purchase them, he can not afterwards, though he acted under a mistake, claim them from such third party. (*o*)[1]   But he may, in general, claim the price of them, if such price has not previously been paid over to the immediate ven-

---

(*l*) White v. Garden, 10 C. B. 919; 20 L. J., C. P. 167. Pease v. Gloahec, L. R., 1 P. C. 219.

(*m*) Kingsford v. Merry, 1 H. & N. 515; 26 L. J., Ex. 83.

(*n*) Morgan v. Marquis, 23 L. J. Ex. 21.

(*o*) Pickering v. Busk, 15 East, 43. Gregg v. Wells, 10 Ad. & E. 90. Waller v. Drakeford, 22 L. J., Q. B. 275.

[1] See Western Transportation Co. v. Marshall, 37 Barb. 509; Saltus v. Everett, 20 Wend. 267; Crocker v. Crocker, 31 N. Y. 507; Labdell v. Baker, 1 Met. 202; Wooster v. Sherwood, 25 N. Y. 278.

dor and apparent owner. (*p*) [1]   If goods are deposited in the hands of a warehouseman or wharfinger, and the owner sells them, and hands to the purchaser a delivery order or dock-warrant for their delivery, which is accepted by such warehouseman or wharfinger, and the purchaser then re-sells the goods, the original vendor can not prevent the delivery of the goods to the sub-purchaser, although the first purchaser has become bankrupt without paying the price. (*q*)   Having been a party to the creation of the title of the sub-vendor, he is bound by the re-sale.

548. *Sales by factors and agents.*—By the 6 Geo. 4, c. 94, s. 4, it is enacted, that it shall be lawful for any person to contract with an agent intrusted with goods, or to whom the same may be consigned for sale, for the purchase of such goods, and to receive the same of, and pay for the same to, such agent ; and such contract or payment shall be binding upon and good against the owner, notwithstanding the person dealing with the agent knew at the time that he was only an agent.   But the contract and payment must be made in the usual course of business ; and the party must not be aware of any want of authority on the part of the agent to sell or to receive the purchase-money.

549. *Legal authentication of executory contracts for the sale of goods and chattels.*—We have already seen that, by the seventeenth section of the Statute

---

(*p*) Dickenson v. Naul, 4 B. & Ad. 638.   Allen v. Hopkins, 13 M. & W. 94.   As to intrusting documents of title to factors and agents, see *post*, ch. 5, s. 3, FACTORS ACTS.

(*q*) Hawes v. Watson, 4 D. & R. 22.   Woodley v. Coventry, 2 H. & C. 164 ; 32 L. J., Ex. 185.   Knights v. Wiffen, L. R., 5 Q. B. 660 ; 40 L. J., Q. B. 51.

[1] See remarks as to this rule in Benjamin on Sales, 1st American Edition, § 64c.

of Frauds, it is enacted that no contract for the sale
of any goods, wares, and merchandise, for the price
of ten pounds sterling or upwards, shall be allowed
to be good, except the buyer shall accept part of the
goods so sold, and actually receive the same, or give
something in earnest to bind the bargain or in part
payment, or unless some note or memorandum in
writing of the bargain be made and signed by the
parties to be charged by such contract or their agents
thereunto lawfully authorized.[1]

[1] *Ante*, vol. 1, § 207.   References to the Statutes of Frauds
as re-enacted in the states, will be found in a note to page 332,
of vol. 1. " Earnest " is now generally understood as meaning
a part payment of the purchase money, under and to satisfy
the statute.   Howe v. Hayward, 108 Mass. 54.   Earnest must
be either money or money's worth.   Brown, Statute of Frauds,
§ 341 ; Artcher v. Zeh, 5 Hill, N. Y. 200.   The earnest must
not only be given, but accepted by the vendor.   Edgerton v.
Hodge, 41 Vt. 676, Hicks v. Cleveland, 48 N. Y. 84; Hawley
v. Keeler, 53 Id. 115; or his agent, Id.   The part payment
must be actual and not merely an agreement or condition to
pay.   Brabin v. Hyde, 32 N. Y. 519; Mattice v. Allen, 3 Keyes,
492 ; Teed v. Teed, 44 Barb. 96.   The part payment need not
be made at the time of the sale.   Sprague v. Blake, 20 Wend.
61 ; Thompson v. Alger, 12 Met. 435; Davis v. Moore, 13
Maine, 424; Gault v. Brown, 48 N. H. 183, 189. But see
Hawley v. Keeler, 53 N. Y. 114 ; Bissell v. Balcom, 39 Id. 275.
Nor can the part payment be made by merely crediting the
amount against another indebtedness of the vendor to the
purchaser.   Such a transaction is merely a contract, if anything, to pursue that mode of payment, and will have no
effect under the statute.   Clark v. Tucker, 2 Sandf. 157; Gilman v. Hill, 36 N. H. 319; Brabin v. Hyde, 32 N. Y. 519;
Mattice v. Allen, 3 Keyes, 492.   But it may be different in
case of a promise by the purchaser to pay the price to a creditor of the vendor, which promise, if accepted by the creditor,
who thereupon discharges the vendor, may be such a part payment as will satisfy the statute.   Cotterill v. Stevens, 10 Wis.
422.   Or the part payment may consist of a settlement for,
and an actual transfer of the title to, property previously delivered by the purchaser to the vendor.   Dow v. Worthen, 37
Vt. 108.

550. *Requisites of the memorandum of the contract.*—We have already seen that the note or memorandum of the bargain should disclose the names of the vendor and purchaser, or their agents (*r*)¹ the thing sold, and the price to be paid, if the price was fixed and agreed upon at the time of the making of the contract; (*s*)² but, if no price was

---

(*r*) *Ante.*

(*s*) Elmore v. Kingscote, 5 B. & C.

583; 8 D. & R. 343. Goodman v. Griffiths, *ante.*

¹ See note * to page 187 of Morgan's De Colyar on Guaranty, as to this rule in the case of the 4th section of the statute.

² That is to say, apparently, that a distinction is to be made between the contract itself and a memorandum of the contract; the contract may be made at one time, and the memorandum at a subsequent time. Indeed, the statute presupposes a parol contract which may be proved by parol, while the memorandum may be supplied by letters or other documents, written at certain times after the contract, and referring to it. Marsh v. Hyde, 3 Gray, 333; Gale v. Nixon, 6 Cow. 445; Williams v. Bacon, 2 Gray, 387; Lerned v. Wannemacher, 9 Allen, 412; Davis v. Shield, 26 Wend. 341; Coddington v. Goddard, 16 Gray, 436; Ide v. Staunton, 15 Vt. 690; Webster v. Lielly, 52 Barb. 482; Davis v. Moore, 13 Me. 424; Hunter v. Giddings, 97 Mass. 41; Jonness v. Mount Hope Iron Co., 53 Me. 20; Dana v. Hancock, 30 Vt. 66. But the writings must be attached or connected by their internal evidence; parol evidence can not be admitted for the purpose. Kurtz v. Cummings, 24 Penn. St. 25; Adams v. McMillan, 7 Porter, 73; Moale v. Buchanan, 11 Gill & J. 314; Williams v. Bacon, 2 Gray, 391; Johnson v. Buck, 6 Vroom (N. J.) 344; Knox v. King, 36 Ala. 367; Freeport v. Bartol, 3 Greenl. 340; Morton v. Dean, 13 Met. 385; Lerned v. Wannemacher, 9 Allen, 417; Smith v. Arnold, 5 Mason, 416; O'Donnell v. Leeman, 43 Me. 158; Fowler v. Rendican, 52 Ill. 405. Nor to vary the terms expressed in the writing. Reed v. Jones, 8 Wis. 392; Peers v. Davis, 8 Jones (29 Mo.) 184. But parol evidence is admissible to identify the subject-matter. Miller v. Stevens, 105 Mass. 518; Pike v. Fay, 101 Id. 134; Stoops v. Smith, 100 Id. 63; Swett v. Shumway, 102 Id. 367; Hart v. Hammett, 18 Vt. 127; George v. Joy, 19 N. H. 544; Gray v. Harper, 1

positively and definitely fixed and agreed upon, the
note or memorandum will be sufficient without any
statement of price, and the law will infer that a reasonable price was to be paid. (*t*) Any note or entry in
a book or ledger, or any letter, (*u*) acknowledging the
fact of the sale, mentioning the name of the vendor
and the thing sold, and signed by the purchaser or his
agent, will take the case out of the statute, although
it subsequently contains a repudiation of the bargain
on bad and insufficient grounds. (*x*) The contract
may also be authenticated and established through the
medium of bills of parcels, entries in books, letters, and
separate writings, provided they refer to each other
and to the same persons and things, and manifestly
relate to the same contract and transaction. (*y*) Where
divers articles ordered by the defendant were entered
in the plaintiff's order-book, and the defendant wrote
his name at the foot of the entry, it was held that the
entry and signature of the defendant might be taken
in connection with an entry of the plaintiff's name in

(*t*) Hoadley v. Maclaine, 4 M. &
Sc. 340; 10 Bing. 482.   Joyce v.
Swann, 17 C. B. N. S. 103.   Acebal
v. Levy, 4 M. & Sc. 217, 227, 229.
Valoy v. Gibson, 4 C. B. 864; 16 L.
J., C. P. 248.

(*u*) Buxton v. Rust, L. R., 7 Ex.
279; 41 L. J., Ex. 173.

(*x*) Bailey v. Sweeting, 9 C. B. N.
S. 843 ; 30 L. J., C. P. 150. McClean
v. Nicolle, 9 W. R. 811.   Newell v.
Radford, L. R., 3 C. P. 52 ; 37 L. J.,
C. P. 1.

(*y*) Saunderson v. Jackson, 2 B. &
P. 238.   Allen v. Bennett, 3 Taunt.
169.

Story, 574; Hill v. Rewee, 11 Met. 268; Foley v. Mason, 6
Md. 37; Swett v. Shumway, 102 Mass. 365; Noyes v. Canfield, 27 Vt. 29; Rhoades v. Castner, 12 Allen, 130; Dana v.
Fielder, 2 Kernan, 40.   See Morgan's De Colyar on Guaranty,
ch. 3, " What is a sufficient Memorandum in writing to Satisfy
the Requirements of the Statute."   And see a note to p. 179
of that chapter, as to the rules in the different States, as to
the expression of the consideration in the memorandum, as
required or dispensed with under the fourth section of the
statute.

the book showing the book to be his book, so as to establish the requisite written memorandum of the contract. (*z*)¹ Where goods were sold by auction to

(*z*) Sarl v. Bourdillon, 1 C. B. N. S. 195 ; 26 L. J., C. P. 78.

¹ The signature is to be by the party to be charged, and may be in pencil ; Clason v. Bailey, 14 Johns. 484; Draper v. Pattina, 2 Speare, 292; McDowell v. Chambers, 1 Strobh. (Eq.) 347 ; Merritt v. Classon, 12 Johns. 102 ; or stamped upon the paper, or by mark, see Meehan v. Rowke, 2 Bradf. 385 ; Campbell v. Logan, Id. 90 ; Morris v. Kniffin, 37 Barb. 336 ; Barnard v. Heydrick, 49 Id. 62 ; or by initials ; Sanborn v. Flager, 9 Allen, 574; Palmer v. Stephens, 1 Den. 471. The Christian name may be set out at length, expressed by initials, or left out altogether. Morgan's De Colyar on Guaranty, p. 205 ; Boardman v. Spooner, 13 Allen, 353 ; and see *ante*, vol. 1, § 215 ; or printed, Salmon Falls M'f'g. Co. v. Goddard, 14 How. 456 ; Merritt v. Classon, 12 Johns. 102 ; 14 Id. 484, per *contra*, Zacrisson v. Poppe, 3 Bosw, 171 ; and may be in an unusual place, as at the beginning, or in the body of the paper; Coddington v. Goddard, 16 Gray, 444 ; Battens v. Sellers, 5 Har. & J. 117 ; Fessenden v. Mussey, 11 Cush. 127 ; Penniman v. Hartshorn, 13 Mass. 87 ; M'Comb v. Wright, 4 Johns. Ch. 663 ; Anderson v. Harold, 10 Ohio, 339 ; Argenbright v. Campbell, 3 H. & Munf. 144, 198 ; Higdon v. Thomas, 1 H. & Gill, 139 ; Hawkins v. Chace, 19 Pick. 502. Though in some of the states the statute used the words " subscribed," and in these, it is said, the signature must appear at the end. See Davis v. Shields, 23 Wend. 322 ; 26 Id. 341 ; Vielie v. Osgood, 8 Barb. 130. The statute may be satisfied by an indorsement of the defendant's name on a mere draft of the agreement. Morgan's De Colyar on Guaranty, p. 205. And the contract made by the signature is good or not, at the election of the party who has not signed. M'Farson's Appeal, 11 Penn. St. 503 ; De Cordova v. Smith, 9 Texas, 129 ; Lansing v. Cole, 3 Green Ch. 229 ; Young v. Paul, 2 Stockt. Ch. 402 ; Ide v. Stanton, 15 Vt. 687 ; Shirley v. Shirley, 7 Blackf. 452 ; Barstow v. Gray, 3 Greenl. 509 ; Old Colony R. R. Co. v. Evans, 6 Gray, 25 ; Hawkins v. Chace, 19 Pick. 502 ; Penniman v. Hartshorn, 13 Mass. 87 ; Getchell v. Jewett, 4 Greenl. 350 ; Douglass v. Spears, 1 Nott & McC. 207 ; Adams v. McMillan, 7 Port. 73 ; Ballard v. Walker, 3 Johns. Cas. 60 ; Justice v. Lang, 52 N. Y. 323; The Same, 42 Id 494; Higdon v. Thomas, 1 Harr. & G, 139 ; Clason v. Bailey, 14 Johns.

an agent acting on behalf of an undisclosed principal, and the auctioneer wrote the initials of the agent's name, together with the prices, opposite the lots purchased by him, in the printed catalogue, it was held that the entry in the catalogue and a letter afterwards written by the principal to the agent, recognizing the purchase, might be coupled together to constitute and establish the requisite written memorandum of the contract. (*a*) ¹

(*a*) Phillimore v. Barry, 1 Campb. 513. Gibson v. Holland, L. R., 1 C. P. 1; 35 L. J., C. P. 5.

387 ; Dresel v. Jordan, 104 Mass. 412 ; Hunter v. Giddings, 97 Mass. 41 ; Newby v. Rogers, 40 Ind. 9 ; Smith v. Smith, 8 Blackf. 208 ; Cook v. Anderson, 20 Ind. 15 ; Davis v. Shields, 26 Wend. 340 ; Lent v. Padelford, 10 Mass. 236.

¹ Signature by an agent has been elsewhere treated (*Ante*, vol. i. §§ 57, 215). The American decisions holding that an auctioneer at a public sale, is the agent of both parties, to sign memoranda, are numerous. Harvey v. Stevens, 43 Vt. 655, 656 ; Brent v. Green, 6 Leigh, 16 ; White v. Crew, 16 Geo. 416 ; Anderson v. Chick, 1 Bailey Eq. 118 ; Adams v. M'Millan, 7 Porter, 72 ; Smith v. Arnold, 5 Mason, 414 ; Hart v. Woods, 7 Blackf. 568 ; Jenkins v. Hogg, 2 Const. Ct. Rep. 820 ; Bent v. Cobb, 9 Gray, 397 ; Gordon v. Sims, 2 McCord Ch. 164 ; Pugh v. Chesseldine, 11 Ohio, 109 ; Burke v. Haley, 2 Gilm. 614 ; M'Comb v. Wright, 4 Johns. Ch. 659 ; Johnson v. Buck, 6 Vroom (N. J.) 338, 342 ; Hathaway, J., in Pike v. Balch, 38 Maine, 302, 311 ; Morton v. Dean, 13 Met. 388 ; Cleaves v. Foss, 4 Greenl. 1. But the memorandum must be made and completed at the time of the sale. Horton v. McCarty, 53 Maine, 394 ; Gill v. Bicknell, 2 Cush. 355 ; Alna v. Plummer, 4 Greenl. 258 ; O'Donnell v. Leeman, 43 Maine, 158, 160 ; Smith v. Arnold, 5 Mason, 414 ; Horton v. McCarty, 53 Maine, 394. The auctioneer is the agent for the purchaser from the moment the hammer falls ; up to that time he is only the seller's agent, and may retract the bargain, as may the purchaser. Benjamin on Sales, 1st Am. Ed. § 270. After the sale is over, he is agent for the seller only, as before, Horton v. McCarty, 53 Me. 394. Or the auctioneer's clerk may sign these memoranda with the above effect. Smith v. Jones, 7 Leigh, 165. See Smith v. McGregory, 34 N. H. 414, 418, 419 ; Alna v. Plummer, 4 Greenl. 458 ; Meadows v. Meadows, 3

And, where a buyer wrote to the seller, " I give you notice that the corn you delivered to me, in part performance of my contract with you for one hundred sacks of good English seconds flour, at 45s. per sack, is so bad that I can not make it into saleable bread," and the seller replied, " I have your letter or notice of the 24th September, in reply to which I have to state that I consider I have performed my contract as far as it has gone," it was held that the first letter and the answer might be coupled together and incorporated, and were sufficient evidence in writing to satisfy the terms of the Statute of Frauds, and enable the buyer to sue the seller for the non-delivery of an article corresponding with that mentioned in the buyer's letter. (*b*)

But, if there is any material discrepancy between the letters and entries—if they describe the quality and quantity of the thing sold differently, or vary in the statement of the terms of the contract, and do not recognize the same contract and refer to the same transaction—they will fail in establishing the bargain. (*c*) Where the entry and the letter referred to different contracts, the one being evidence of an absolute

(*b*) Jackson v. Lowe, 7 Moore, 219, 228 ; 1 Bing. 9.

(*c*) Smith v. Surman, 9 B, & C. 561, 569.

McCord, 457 ; Gill v. Bicknell, 2 Cush. 558 ; Cathcart v. Keirnaghan, 5 Strobh. 129; Johnson v. Buck, 6 Vroom, 338, 342, 343. There is another party who may sometimes affix the signature and thereby make a valid contract, viz., a telegraph operator. See *ante*, vol. 1, note 1, § 22 ; Taylor v. Steamboat Robert Campbell, 20 Mo. 254 ; Durkee v. Vermont Central R. R., 29 Vt. 127; Henkel v. Pape, L. R. 6 Exch. 7; Leonard v. N. Y. &c. Tel. Co., 41 N. Y. 544 ; Beach v. Raritan &c. R. R. Co., 37 Id. 457 ; Rommel v. Wingate, 103 Mass. 327. Similar rules determine whether a contract has been made by letter. *Ante*, vol. 1, § 22, note 1, and Trevor v. Wood, 36 N. Y. 307; Story on Contracts, § 498.

and unconditional contract of sale, and the other of a qualified and conditional bargain, it was held that the plaintiff could not avail himself of the letter for one purpose—to bind the defendant within the statute— and renounce it for another purpose, but that he must take it altogether; and then it was no recognition, but a repudiation, of the contract sought to be established by the entry. (*d*) But, if the letter acknowledges the essential particulars of the contract, and then repudiates it on bad or insufficient grounds, there will, as we have seen, be a good memorandum of the bargain. (*e*)

551. *Brokers' bought and sold notes.*—When sales are effected through the medium of brokers acting between the parties buying and selling, the broker is the agent of both parties, and as such may bind them by signing the same contract on behalf of buyer and seller.[1] But, where the broker delivers notes of the contract materially differing in their terms, and there is no signed entry in the broker's books to cure the discrepancy, there is no proof of the assent of the parties to the same terms, and no valid bargain between them. (*f*) It is the duty, but not always the practice, of brokers to make a memorandum of the contract in their books,[2] to sign such memorandum, and to transcribe therefrom the bought and sold notes. If these notes

---

(*d*) Cooper v. Smith, 15 East, 103, 108. Richards v. Porter, 6 B. & C. 437. Archer v. Baynes, 5 Exch. 625; 20 L. J., Ex. 55.

(*e*) *Ante.*

(*f*) Grant v. Fletcher, 5 B. & C. 437. Heyman v. Neale, 2 Campb. 337. Gregson v. Ruck, 4 Q. B. 747. Thornton v. Kempster, 5 Taunt. 786, 788. But an unimportant or immaterial variation will not avoid the bargain. Maclean v. Dunn, 1 Moo. & P. 778, 779.

[1] See Shaw v. Finney, 13 Met. 453; Coddington v. Goddard, 16 Gray, 442; Henckley v. Arey, 27 Me. 362; Merritt v. Clason, 12 Johns. 102; Davis v. Shields, 26 Wend. 341; Suydam v. Clark, 2 Sandf. 133; Toomer v. Dawson, 1 Cheves, 68.

[2] Coddington v. Goddard, 16 Gray, 442.

are signed by the broker and agree, but differ from an
unsigned entry in the book, the notes constitute the
contract. If they agree, but differ from a signed entry,
and the signed notes so agreeing have been received
and adopted by the vendor and purchaser, they will,
it seems, constitute a new contract in substitution and
extinguishment of the contract evidenced by the signed
entry. (*g*) If they differ from each other, and one of
them agrees with the signed entry, the entry and note
agreeing with it may, it seems, be taken together as constituting the contract, to the exclusion of the other
note. [1] "A broker has only a special authority, not a

(*g*) Thornton v. Charles, 9 M. & & K. 22. Goom v. Aflalo, 9 D. & R.
W. 807, 808. Sievewright v. Archi- 148; 6 B. & C. 117. Thornton v.
bald, 17 Q. B. 103; 20 L. J., Q. B. Meux, 1 Mood. & Malk. 43.
535. Townend v. Drakeford, 1 Car.

[1] The broker is the agent of both parties. M'Comb v.
Wright, 4 Johns. Ch. 659; Morton v. Dean, 13 Met. 385;
Adams v. McMillan, 7 Port. 73; Meadows v. Meadows, 3
M'Cord, 458; Doty v. Wilder, 15 Ill. 407; Cleaves v. Foss, 4
Greenl. 1; Alna v. Plummer, Id. 248; Anderson v. Chick,
Bailey Eq. 118. But if the bought and sold notes vary, and
there is no signed entry in the broker's book, nor other writing, showing the terms of the bargain, there is no valid contract between the parties. Benjamin on Sales, 1st Am. Ed.
§ 301, and see Suydam v. Clark, 2 Sandf. 133; Parsons on
Contracts, vol. 1, p. 543. The bought note is addressed to the
purchaser, notifying him that the broker has this day bought
for him, &c.; the sold note is a similar statement addressed to
the vendor; each describes the goods, terms, &c.; and the signed
entry in the broker's own books must be simultaneously made
by him to satisfy the statute of frauds. Cabot v. Winsor, 1
Allen, 546. Parsons on Contracts, vol. 1, p. 543, says that the
bought and sold notes are the best evidence of the bargain.
"Where the contract is made through the agency of two
brokers, one acting for the vendor and the other for the purchaser, and the sold note given by the purchaser's to the
vendor's broker, states that the sale is made on account of the
latter, instead of his principal, the vendor may nevertheless
treat the contract as his own, and enforce it upon the terms of
the sold note."

general one ; and, if you employ a broker to buy one kind of goods, and he buys another, you are not bound by his act." (*h*)   In an action by the purchaser against the vendor on a contract made through a broker, it is sufficient for the purchaser to produce the bought note handed to him by the broker, and to show the employ- ment of the latter by the vendor. If the sold note varies from the bought note, it lies on the vendor to prove that variance by producing the sold note. (*i*) So, if the action be brought against the purchaser for not accepting goods sold, the sold note bearing the signa- ture of the broker acting for both buyer and seller is a sufficient memorandum of the bargain. (*k*)   An ap- parent variance between bought and sold notes may be explained by mercantile usage. (*l*)   Letters consti- tuting a sufficient contract to satisfy the Statute of Frauds are not abrogated and annulled by bought and sold notes differing from them, unless it plainly appears that the notes were to constitute the contract to the exclusion of the letters. (*m*)

552. *When the broker is himself liable upon the contract.*—A usage of trade to the effect that, when- ever a broker purchases or sells for his principal with- out disclosing the name of such principal, the broker himself is liable to be looked to as purchaser or seller, may be given in evidence to fix the broker on the contract. (*n*)

(*h*) Pitts v. Beckett, 13 M. & W. 743, 747.   Bostock v. Jardine, 34 L. J., Ex. 142.

(*i*) Hawes v. Forster, 1 Mood. & Rob. 368.

(*k*) Parton v. Crofts, 16 C. B., N. S. 11 ; 33 L. J., C. P. 189.

(*l*) Bold v. Rayner, 1 M. & W. 343.

Kempson v. Boyle, 3 H. & C. 763 ; 34 L. J., Ex. 191.

(*m*) Heyworth v. Knight, 17 C. B., N. S. 298 ; 33 L. J., C. P. 298.

(*n*) Humfrey v. Dale, 27 L. J., Q. B. 390.   Fleet v. Murton. L. R., 7 Q. B. 126 ; 41 L. J., Q. B. 49.

ᶦ See Raymond v. Proprietors, &c., 2 Met. 319 ; Winsor v. Griggs, 2 Cush. 210 ; Taintor v. Prendergast, 3 Hill, 72.

553. *Of the signature to the memorandum.*—The question as to what is and what is not a signing of a contract so as to meet the requirements of the Statute of Frauds has already been considered.[1]

554. *Acceptance and actual receipt of goods within the Statute of Frauds.*—We have already seen that " no contract for the sale of goods for the price of £10 or upwards is good, unless the buyer has accepted part of the goods sold and actually received the same, or given something in earnest," &c.[2] The acceptance of the goods may be either before or at the time of the receipt of them. Thus, if the purchaser selects the goods himself, and orders them to be sent to his residence or place of business, and the selected goods are sent and delivered to him or his servant, at the place indicated by him, there is evidence of an acceptance and an actual receipt of the goods within the meaning of the statute. (*o*)   If there has been an acceptance and an actual receipt of the thing only for an instant, the purchaser is bound by the bargain, and can not afterwards withdraw his acceptance and reject the article, except on the ground of fraud. Thus, where the purchaser selected some sheep from the plaintiff's flock, and had them sent down to his own residence, and there counted them over, and said, "It is all right," and then sent them into his field, and the day after refused to keep them saying they were not the sheep he bought, it was held that there was evidence for the jury of an acceptance of the sheep, and that, if the defendant had

(*o*) Cusack v. Robinson, 1 B. & S.   v. Ogden, 3 H. & C. 717 ; 34 L. J.,
299 ; 30 L. J., Q. B., 261.   Hodgson   Ex. 159.
v. Le Bret, 1 Campb. 233.   Kershaw

[1] *Ante*, vol. 1, § 214, and note 1.
[2] *Ante*, vol. 1, § 207.

once really accepted them, his rejection of them afterwards would be of no avail. (*p*) [1]   The acceptance
must be made with the consent of the vendor; and
if, after goods are delivered to a carrier consigned to
the vendee, and before any order has been given, or
act done constituting an acceptance of the goods, the
contract is rescinded, no subsequent act by the vendee or by his assignees in the event of his bankruptcy
will amount to an acceptance, so as to change the
property in the goods, without the consent of the
vendor. (*q*) [2]

To constitute an actual receipt as well as an acceptance of the goods, it must appear that the vendor
has parted with the possession of the goods, and
placed them under the control of the purchaser, so as
to put a complete end to all the rights of the unpaid
vendor as such. (*r*) [3]   Although, therefore, goods are

(*p*) Saunders v. Topp, 4 Exch.
390; 18 L. J., Ex. 374.
(*q*) Smith v. Hudson, 34 L. J., Q.
B. 145; 6 B. & S. 431. And see Bolton v. Lancashire Railway Company,
L. R., 1 C. P. 431; 35 L. J., C. P.
137.
(*r*) Cusack v. Robinson, *supra*.

[1] Gibbs v. Benjamin, 45 Vt. 124.   The question is not
whether he ought to have accepted them, or whether his reasons are frivolous, but whether he actually has accepted them.
There may be an acceptance without a receipt.   Prescott v.
Lockee, 51 N. H. 94.

[2] A carrier is an agent to receive, not an agent to accept.
Maxwell v. Brown, 39 Me, 98; Frostburg Mining Co. v.
New England Glass Co., 9 Cush. 115; Rodgers v. Phillips, 40
N. Y. 519.

[3] These acts need not be simultaneous; Bush v. Holmes, 53
Me. 417; Sprague v. Blake, 20 Wend. 61; McCarty v. Nash, 14
Minn. 127; Marsh v. Hyde, 3 Gray, 331; Damon v. Osborn, 1
Pick. 480; Davis v. Moore, 13 Me. 437; McKnight v. Dunlop, 1
Seld. 537; Richardson v. Squires, 37 Vt. 640; Danforth v.
Walker, Id. 239; Vincent v. Germond, 11 Johns. 283;
Sale v. Darragh, 2 Hilt. 184; Thompson v. Alger, 12 Met.
435; Chapin v. Potter, 1 Hilt. 360; but the intention to do
this must be clear; Brand v. Fockt, 3 Keyes, 409; Marsh v.

selected by a purchaser, and ordered to be sent to the
residence of the latter, yet, if the purchaser refuses to
take them in when they arrive, or the vendor gives the

Rouse, 44 N. Y. 643; Dole v. Stimpson, 21 Pick. 384; Shepherd v. Pressey, 32 N. H. 49; Shindler v. Houston, 1 Comst.
261; Young v. Blaisdell, 60 Me. 272; Gray v. Davis, 10 N.
Y. 285; Messer v. Woodman, 22 N. H. 172, 182; something
more than mere words is necessary; Shindler v. Houston, 1
Comst. 261; Dole v. Stimpson, 21 Pick. 384; Artcher v. Zeh,
5 Hill, 205; Denny v. Williams, 5 Allen, 3; Howard v. Borden, 13 Id. 299; Edwards v. Grand Trunk Railway Co., 54
Me. 111; Brabin v. Hyde, 32 N. Y. 519; mere words
which are part of the original contract, or employed as to its
carrying out, and not intended as an acceptance, are not sufficient; Shepherd v. Pressey, 32 N. H. 49. In Maxwell v. Brown,
39 Me. 101, Appleton, Ch. J., holds that there must further be
an acceptance and receipt by the purchaser, else he will not
be bound; and to that effect, see Boardman v. Spooner, 13
Allen, 357; Prescott v. Locke, 51 N. H. 94; Denny v. Williams, 5 Allen, 3; Shindler v. Houston, 1 Comst. 261; Gibbs
v. Benjamin, 45 Vt. 124, 130, 131; Johnson v. Cuttle, 105
Mass. 449. The question as to whether the facts of the case
amount to a constructive, acceptance is for the jury; Frostburg Mining Co. v. New England Glass Co., 9 Cush. 118;
Borrowscale v. Bosworth, 99 Mass. 381; Rappleye v. Adee, 65
Barb. 589; Sawyer v. Nichols, 40 Me. 212; Kirby v. Johnson, 22 Miss. 465; Bailey v. Ogden, 3 Johns. 399, 420; Parker
v. Wallis, 5 E. & B. 21; but if the facts are not in dispute, it
has been held that the court may instruct the jury as to
whether or not they constitute an acceptance; Shepherd v.
Pressey, 32 N. H. 56, 57. "It is for the court to withhold
the facts from the jury when they are not such as can afford
any ground for finding an acceptance; and this includes cases
where, though the court might admit that there was a scintilla
of evidence tending to show an acceptance, they would still
feel bound to set aside a verdict finding an acceptance on
that evidence." Browne, St. Frauds, § 321; Denny v.
Williams, 5 Allen, 5; Howard v. Borden, 13 Id. 299; and
see Prescott v. Locke, 51 N. H. 94; Snow v. Warner, 10 Met.
136; Chapman, J., in Denny v. Williams, 5 Allen, 3; Dole v.
Stimpson, 21 Pick. 384; Boynton v. Veazie, 24 Me. 286;
Gibson v. Stevens, 8 How. (U. S.) 384; Carver v. Lane, 4 E.
D. Smith (N. Y.) 168; Snow v. Warner, 10 Met. 132.

person carrying the goods directions not to leave them without receiving the money, and no money is forthcoming, and the goods are not left, there is no actual receipt of them by the purchaser. (s)

555. *Receipt for inspection and approval.*—When the specific articles have not been selected by the purchaser, there is no acceptance until he has had an opportunity of exercising his judgment with respect to the things sent ; for he can not be made the acceptor of whatever the vendor chooses to send him. (t) If, therefore, an intended purchaser merely receives the article on examination or trial, and returns it within ·a reasonable period, there is no acceptance.[1] And, if a small quantity, but no more of it than was absolutely necessary, has been experimented upon for the purpose of testing its quality, such user does not constitute an acceptance and receipt of the entire commodity. (u)[2] If a purchaser sends his servant for

---

(s) Baldey v. Parker, 2 B. & C. 37 ; 3 D. & R. 220.

(t) Hunt v. Hecht, 8 Exch. 817.

(u) Heilbut v. Hickson, L. R., 7 C. P. 438 ; 41 L. J., C. P. 228.

[1] In sales on trial, a failure to return the goods within the time specified, makes the sale absolute ; Johnson v. McLane, 7 Blackf. 501; Aiken v. Hyde, 99 Mass. 183; Hartford v. Sorghum Mfg. Co., 43 Vt. 528; or within a reasonable time; Moore v. Piercey, 1 Jones (L.) 131 ; Hunt v. Wyman, 100 Mass. 198; Buffum v. Merry, 3 Mason, 478; Ray v. Thompson, 12 Cush. 281 ; Jameson v. Gregory, 4 Met. (Ky.) 363; Chamberlain v. Smith, 44 Penn. St. 431; Witherby v. Sleeper, 101 Mass. 138; Sargent v. Gile, 8 N. H. 325; Porter v. Pettengill, 12 N. H. 300; Hurd v. West, 7 Cow. 752; Washington v. Jones, 7 Humph. 468; Johnson v. McLane, 7 Blackf. 501; Buswell v. Bicknell, 7 Me. 344; Perkins v. Douglass, 20 Me. 317; Holbrook v. Armstrong, 1 Fairf. 31; Walker v. Blake, 37 Me. 373; Crocker v. Gullifer, 44 Me. 491 ; Schlesinger v. Stratton, 9 R. J. 478.

[2] But see the ruling in Smith v. Love, 64 N. C. 439. If in the trial a portion of the goods are consumed, or used so

goods, and, after they have been brought to him, sends them back, there is no acceptance and receipt. And the delivery of the goods into the hands of the intended purchaser, and the unpacking of them by the latter, are not sufficient, if it appears that he has taken them and had them in his possession for no greater time than would reasonably suffice for him to examine the quantity and quality of the goods, and declare his approval or disapproval thereof. (*x*) Where the defendant gave an oral order for a bale of sponge, which was sent to him in the country by carrier, and the sponge was returned, accompanied by a letter from the defendant saying he had sent it back as he did not think it worth the price charged, it was held that there had been no acceptance and receipt of the sponge. (*y*) Where a pair of ear-rings at a sale by auction were knocked down to the defendant, and delivered into his hands, but in a few minutes he handed them back and declined the purchase, on the ground that he had been mistaken in the value of the stones with which they were set, it was held that, as by the conditions of sale the defendant had no right to remove the ear-rings until the deposit was paid, the mere delivery of them into his hands the moment he was declared the purchaser, was not of itself evidence of an intention to part entirely with the possession of them, and that consequently there was not a complete delivery nor an acceptance and actual receipt. (*z*) And, where the purchaser,

(*x*) Curtis v. Pugh, 10 Q. B. 111; 16 L. J. (N. S.), Q. B. 199. Jordan v. Norton, 4 M. & W. 155. Lucy v. Mouflet, 5 H. & N. 233; 29 L. J., Ex. 110.

(*y*) Kent v. Huskisson, 3 B. & P. 233, 235.

(*z*) Phillips v. Bistolli, 3 D. &. R. 822; 2 B. & C. 511.

as to make them second-hand, the question as to a fair trial is one for the jury. Benjamin on Sales, Am. Ed. § 596.

having inspected a heap of mixed bones, orally agreed to purchase a quantity of ox-bones and cow-bones, to be separated from the heap and sent to a place of deposit indicated by him, and the bones were forwarded there, and the purchaser went and inspected them, and then gave the vendor notice that he did not intend to take them, it was held that there was no acceptance and actual receipt of the bones by the purchaser. (*a*) But acceptance may be inferred from the goods having been kept an unreasonable time. (*b*)

556. *Acceptance and receipt where goods have been purchased by a bailee.*—Whenever goods are in the hands of a hirer or bailee of them, and an oral bargain is made by him for the purchase of the goods, and the purchaser then takes to the goods as such and changes the character in which he holds them, it is an acceptance as against him, and there will be a binding contract for the purchase of the goods; but, if the parol authority to take to the goods as owner, resulting from the oral bargain with the vendor, has been revoked, and the vendor has withdrawn from the bargain, a subsequent taking to the goods by the buyer is unauthorized and tortious, and can not be an acceptance, which to bind the bargain must be with the assent of the vendor. (*c*)

557. *Delivery at a named wharf* or at a railway-station pursuant to the verbal order of the purchaser, is no evidence of an acceptance and actual receipt within the statute. (*d*)

(*a*) Hunt *v.* Hecht, 8 Exch. 814. Coombs v. Bristol and Exeter Railway Company, 27 L. J., Ex. 402. Smith v. Hudson, 6 B. & S. 431 ; 34 L. J., Q. B. 145.

(*b*) Coleman v. Gibson. 1 Mood. & Rob. 168.

(*c*) Taylor v. Wakefield, 6 Ell. & Bl. 769.

(*d*) Hart v. Bush, 27 L. J., Q. B. 271. Smith v. Hudson, 34 L. J., Q. B. 145.

558. *Constructive acceptance.*—There may be a constructive acceptance, within the meaning of the statute, manifested by the exercise of acts of domination and ownership over things incapable of manual occupation and transfer from hand to hand. (*e*) If the purchaser sells, or offers to sell, the chattel, or deals with it in a manner which is inconsistent with the right of property and possession being in any one else but himself, his conduct affords evidence of an acceptance and actual receipt of the thing. (*f*) But it has been held that, so long as the vendor retains his right of lien for the price over the whole commodity sold, there can be no such acceptance and receipt as the statute requires. Thus, where the defendant, being on a visit at the plaintiff's house, orally agreed to purchase a horse of him for forty-five guineas, and the horse was taken out of the stable by his orders, and was mounted, galloped, and leaped both by himself and servant, and was afterwards cleaned by the latter, and various things were done to the animal by the defendant's directions, and the defendant then asked the plaintiff to keep the horse for him until he could send for it, and the horse died before it was fetched away, whereupon the defendant refused to pay the price, it was held that there had been no acceptance and receipt of the horse within the meaning of the statute, the plaintiff never having parted with the possession or control of the horse, or lost his lien for the price. (*g*) So where the defend-

(*e*) Williams, J., Bushel v. Wheeler, 15 Q. B. 445. Beaumont v. Brengeri, 5 C. B. 301. Parker v. Wallis, 5 Ell. & Bl. 28. Currie v. Anderson, 2 Ell. & Ell. 592 ; 29 L. J., Q. B. 87.

(*f*) Morton v. Tibbett, 15 Q. B. 428 ; 19 L. J., Q. B., 382. Edan v. Dudfield, 1 Q. B. 302. But see Castle v. Sworder, 6 H. & N. 832 ; 30 L. J., Ex. 310.

(*g*) Tempest v. Fitzgerald, 3 B. & Ald. 684. Carter v. Toussaint, 5 B. & Ald. 855. As to feeding of cattle by the purchaser's servant, see Holmes v. Hoskins, 23 Law T. R., Ex. 70.

ant ordered the plaintiff to make him a wagon, and, whilst it was in progress of construction, the defendant employed and paid a smith to furnish and affix certain ironwork thereon, and also a tiltmaker to put on a tilt, but the wagon still remained on the premises of the plaintiff, it was held that, as the acts relied on as acts of ownership were performed before the wagon was finished and capable of delivery, and the wagon afterwards remained on the plaintiff's premises to be finished by him, and the latter retained his lien upon it for the price, there had been no acceptance and receipt within the, meaning of the statute. (*h*) [1] Where the defendant came to a coppice where some ash trees were being cut down, and agreed to purchase the timber at so much a foot, and the trees were marked and numbered, and the defendant gave some directions to the workmen as to the mode in which they were to be cut, and the timber was measured, and the measurement communicated to the defendant, who then offered to sell the butts of the trees, declaring it to be his intention to convert the tops into building stuff, it was held that this was no acceptance and receipt of the timber by the defendant within the meaning of the statute, as the vendor had not lost his right of lien over it for the price. (*i*) [2]

(*h*) Maberley v. Sheppard, 3 M. & Sc. 436 ; 10 Bing. 99.

577 ; 4 M. & R. 455, 470. Acraman v. Morrice, 8 C. B. 449. Bill v. Bament, 9 M. & W. 40, 41.

(*i*) Smith v. Surman, 9 B. & C. 561,

[1] See Arnold v. Delano, 4 Cush. 38 ; South-western Freight Co. v. Stanard, 44 Mo. 71 ; South-western, &c. Co. v. Plant, 45 Id. 517.

[2] And so where the goods at the time of the sale are in the possession of a third person, such a delivery as will extinguish a vendor's lien would ensue upon the vendor, the purchaser, and the third person, agreeing that the third person shall cease to hold the goods for the vendor, and retain custody of them as the agent of the buyer. See Weld v. Came,

559. *Constructive possession by the purchaser and extinction of the right of lien.*—Possession of goods and chattels may be given up, and the right of lien extinguished, although the goods are never actually removed from the premises of the vendor ; (*k*) and it has been held that, if an oral bargain is made for the purchase of goods, and the purchaser desires the vendor to keep them in his possession for an especial purpose, and the vendor assents thereto, there may be

(*k*) Jacobs v. Latour, 2 Moo. & P. 205.   Martin v. Reid, 11 C. B., N. S. 730 ; 31 L. J., C. P. 126.

98 Mass. 152 ; Plymouth Bank v. Bank of Norfolk, 10 Pick. 459 ; Tuxworth v. Moore, 9 Pick. 349 ; Bullard v. Wait, 16 Grav, 55 ; Linton v. Butts, 7 Barr. 89 ; Parks v. Hall, 2 Pick. 212 ; Hall v. Jackson, 20 Id. 198.   The following cases as to constructive delivery are presented, as covering a variety of circumstances, and illustrating the rule in the different states on the subject : Terry v. Wheeler, 25 N. Y. 520 ; Bethel Steam Mill Co. v. Brown, 57 Me. 9 ; Webber v. Davis, 44 Me. 147 ; Morse v. Sherman, 106 Mass. 430, 432, 433 ; Barrett v. Goddard, 3 Mason, 107, 110 ; Hotchkiss v. Hunt, 49 Me. 213 ; Arnold v. Delano, 4 Cush. 33 ; Willis v. Willis, 6 Dana, 48 ; Hall v. Richardson, 16 Md. 396 ; Currie v. White, 1 Sweeny (S. C.), 166 ; Hooban v. Bidwell, 16 Ohio, 509 ; Frazer v. Hilliard, 2 Strobh. 309 ; Willis v. Willis, 6 Dana, 48 ; Crawford v. Smith, 7 Dana, 59, 60 ; Martin v. Adams, 104 Mass. 262 ; Merchants' National Bank v. Bangs, 102 Id. 295 ; Thayer v. Lapham, 13 Allen, 28, Foster, J. ; Page v. Carpenter, 10 N. H. 77 ; Buffington v. Ulen, 7 Bush. (Ky.) 231 ; Means v. Williamson, 37 Me. 556 ; Waldron v. Chase, 37 Id. 414 ; Merrill v. Parker, 24 Id. 89 ; Wing v. Clark, Id. 366 ; Bailey v. Smith, 43 N. H. 143 ; Felton v. Fuller, 29 N. H. 121 ; Rice v. Codman, 1 Allen, 377 ; Hurlburt v. Simpson, 3 Ired. (Law) 233 ; Olyphant v. Baker, 5 Denio, 379 ; Sweeney v. Ousley, 14 B. Mon. (Ky.) 413 ; Terry v. Wheeler, 25 N. Y. 520 ; Warden v. Marshall, 99 Mass. 305 ; Bigelow, C. J., in Gardner v. Lane, 9 Allen, 498 ; Marble v. Moore, 102 Mass. 443 ; Chase v. Willard, 57 Me. 157.

a constructive acceptance and constructive actual receipt, so as to satisfy the words of the statute. In cases of this sort, the question will be whether the vendor had the subject-matter of the sale in his own possession, retaining his right of lien for the price, or whether he had the bare custody of the chattel as the servant of the purchaser, having no possession and no right of lien. (*l*) Where a couple of horses had been sold by a livery-stable keeper at a fixed price, and the purchaser told the vendor that, as he had neither servant nor stable, the vendor must keep the horses at livery for him, whereupon the latter removed them from his sale-stable to his livery-stable, and there kept them at livery, it was held that this amounted to an actual delivery of the horses, that the vendor had parted with the possession of them, lost his lien for the price, and held the horses only as any other livery-stable keeper might have held them, having the bare custody of the horses, and not the right of possession. (*m*) And, where there was an oral bargain for the sale of a horse, and the vendor asked the purchaser to lend him the horse for a few days till he got another, and the purchaser agreed to this, and the vendor kept the horse for a week, and then sent it to the purchaser, who refused to receive it or pay for it, it was held that the purchaser by lending the horse to the seller had taken to it as owner, and that the possession of the vendor under the loan was the possession of the purchaser. (*n*)

560. *Acceptance of bills of lading, delivery orders, and dock-warrants.*—The acceptance of a bill of

---

(*l*) Castle v. Sworder, 6 H. & N. 828 ; 30 L. J., Ex. 310 ; overruling Castle v. Sworder, 5 H. & N. 285. Cusack v. Robinson, 1 B. & S. 299 ; 30 L. J., Q. B. 261.

(*m*) Elmore v. Stone, 2 Taunt. 458.

(*n*) Marvin v. Wallis, 6 Ell. & Bl. 735 ; 25 L. J., Q. B. 369.

lading of goods on board ship in transitu to the purchaser is not an acceptance and receipt of the goods,
unless the purchaser exercises dominion and ownership over the bill of lading, and deals with it so as to
transfer the right of property in the goods to some
third party. (*o*)   The acceptance and receipt also by
a purchaser of a delivery order or dock-warrant is not
an acceptance and actual receipt of the goods mentioned or comprised in such order or warrant, until it
has been presented to and accepted by the warehouse-
keeper or dock-keeper, and the latter has attorned to
the purchaser, and consented to hold the goods on his
account. (*p*)   Before the order or warrant has been
presented to, and accepted by, the warehouse-keeper,
it may be countermanded ; (*q*) but, as soon as it has
been presented to and accepted by him, the acceptance, whether made orally or by writing, and whether
it is or is not filed in the warehouse, constitutes the
warehouse-keeper the agent or trustee of the purchaser, and binds him to hold the goods at the disposal of the latter, and there is then an executed
delivery as much as if the goods had been delivered
into the purchaser's own hands, or had been removed
to his warehouse and there put under lock and key.
(*r*)   And, although the goods are not, at the time of
the acceptance of the order, in the actual possession
of the warehouseman, yet, if they afterwards come
to hand, he is bound to hold them at the disposal of
the party in whose favor the order has been made. (*s*)

(*o*) Meredith v. Meigh, 2 Ell. & Bl.
368 ; 22 L. J,. Q. B. 4Q3.   Currie v.
Anderson, 2 El. & El. 592 ; 29 L. J.,
Q. B. 87.

(*p*) Bendall v. Burn, 5 D. & R. 284 ;
3 B. & C. 423.   Farina v. Home, 16
M. & W. 119 ; 16 L. J., Ex. 75.

(*q*) Lockington v. Atherton, 7 M.
& G. 360 ; 8 Sc. N. R. 42.

(*r*) Pearson v. Dawson, Ell. Bl. &
Ell. 456.   Harman v. Anderson, 2
Campb. 242.   Dickenson v. Marrow,
14 M. & W. 713.

(*s*) Holl v. Griffin, 3 M. & Sc. 732 ;
10 Bing. 246.

The bailee of the goods can not, as between himself and the purchaser, after he has once accepted the order, deny the rights of the purchaser, unless the latter has become bankrupt or insolvent before the thing to be delivered has been identified and put into a deliverable state, and the unpaid vendor has interfered to prevent the delivery in the manner presently mentioned. (*t*) [1]

561. *Acceptance and receipt of goods by carriers, forwarding agents, and agents for custody.*—The acceptance and receipt of a carrier or wharfinger, or mere forwarding agent, appointed by the purchaser to be the vehicle of transmission to him, are not the acceptance and receipt of the purchaser, (*u*) unless the latter so deals with the carrier or forwarding agent as to convert him into an agent for custody holding the goods as the purchaser's servant or agent. [2]   When the pur-

---

(*t*) Gillett v. Hill. 2 Cr. & M. 536 ; 4 Tyr. 290. Gosling v. Birnie, 5 Moo. & P. 168.   Stonard v. Dunkin, 2 Campb. 344.

(*u*) Smith v. Hudson, *ante,*

---

[1] A bill of lading is in general a receipt or representation of the goods for which it is given, and its indorsement and delivery is such a constructive delivery of the goods as will divest a vendor's lien, though, in so far as it is a receipt, it might be competent to show under it that the goods were not of the same quality or number stated in the bill; Bissel v. Price, 16 Ill. 408; Wolfe v. Myers, 3 Sandf. 7; Sutton v. Kettell, 1 Sprague, 309; Shepherd v. Naylor, 5 Gray, 591; O'Brien v. Gilchrist, 34 Me. 554; Dickinson v. Ledge, 12 Barb. 102; Grimes v. Harwood, 9 Barb. 447; Wayland v. Mosely, 5 Ala. 430; McTyer v. Steele, 26 Ala. 487; or it might be shown by parol that the goods were not in the quality or good order mentioned in the bill when received; Ellis v. Willard, 5 Selden, 529; Barrett v. Rogers, 7 Mass. 297; Clark v. Barnwell, 12 How. 272. And see the rule as to bills of lading treated under the subject of stoppage in transitu, and will be found referred to *post*, this section, paragraph 597.

[2] See *post*, this section, paragraph 592; Shepherd v. Pressey

chaser refuses to receive the goods from the carrier, the latter holds them as the agent of the consignor from whom he received them, and there is no acceptance and actual receipt by the purchaser within the meaning of the statute, although the latter has directed the mode of conveyance, and pointed out the particular carrier to be employed. (*x*)   Where, therefore, an oral order had been given by the defendant to the plaintiff for two chests of tea to be sent by the usual conveyance, and the tea was shipped on board a vessel which was lost at sea, and the defendant refused to pay the price, it was held that the shipmaster was not the defendant's agent for the acceptance and receipt of the tea, and that, as the defendant had not himself accepted and received it, there was nothing to bind the bargain within the statute. (*y*)   And, where the defendant

---

(*x*) Astey v. Emery, 4 M. & S. 262.   v. Meigh, 22 L. J., Q. B. 401 ; 2 Ell. Norman v. Phillips, 14 M. & W. 277.   & Bl. 364.   Hart v. Bush, Ell. Bl. & (*y*) Hanson v. Armitage, 5 B. & Ell. 498. Ald. 557 ; 1 D. & R. 128.   Meredith

32 N. H 49 ; Maxwell v. Brown, 39 Me. 98 ; Frostburg Mining Co. v. New England Glass Co., 9 Cush. 115 ; Spencer v. Hale, 30 Vt. 315 ; Cross v. O'Donnell, 44 N. Y. 661 ; Quintard v. Bacon, 99 Mass. 185 ; Magruder v. Gage, 33 Md. 344 ; Foster v. Rockwell, 104 Mass. 167 ; Cobb v. Arundell, 26 Wis. 553 ; Everett v. Parks, 62 Barb. 9 ; Putnam v. Tillotson, 13 Met. 517 ; Orcutt v. Nelson, 1 Gray, 536 ; Janvrin v. Maxwell, 23 Wis. 51 ; Barrett v. Goddard, 3 Mason, 107 ; Weld v. Carne, 98 Mass. 152 ; Kirby v. Johnson, 22 Mo. 354 ; Johnson v. Cuttle, 105 Mass. 447 ; Boardman v. Spooner, 13 Allen, 353 ; Grimes v. Van Vechten, 20 Mich. 410 ; Rodgers v. Phillips, 40 N. Y. 519 ; Denmead v. Glass, 30 Geo. 637 ; Jones v. Mechanics' Bank, 29 Md. 287.   But a delivery to his carrier is delivery to the vendor, after acceptance by him ; Cross v. O'Donnell, 44 N. Y. 661 ; and there appears to be no reason why delivery to a warehouseman might not have the same effect ; per curiam, Hunter v. Wright, 12 Allen, 548.

gave an oral order for cider to be forwarded to his residence, and it was sent there by the wagon, but the defendant refused to take it in, and caused it to be lodged
in an adjoining warehouse not belonging to him, where
it remained, and no notice was given by the defendant
to the vendor of the defendant's intention not to take
the cider, it was held that there had been no acceptance
and actual receipt of the cider by the defendant. (*z*)
But, if a purchaser directs goods to be taken to a place
of deposit indicated by him, and they are accordingly
sent there, it is the same as if they are sent to his own
house. (*a*)¹ And a purchaser may, by his conduct and
course of dealing with the carrier, convert the latter
into an agent for custody holding the goods on his,
the purchaser's, behalf. (*b*)

562. *Part acceptance and actual receipt binding
the contract.*—If the defendant receives a portion of
the bulk, and keeps it, he is responsible in damages for
the non-acceptance of the whole of the commodity he
agreed to buy. (*c*) But, where the acceptance of a
part of goods sold is relied upon to take the case out of
the statute of frauds, it must be an acceptance of a
part of goods bought under one entire contract.
Where, therefore, the traveler of a mercantile house,

(*z*) Nicholle v. Plume, 1 C. & P.   (*b*) *Post.* Bushel v. Wheeler, 15 Q.
272.   B. 442.
  (*a*) Dodsley v. Varley, 12 Ad. & E.   (*c*) Gilliat v. Roberts, 19 L. J., Ex.
632.   410.

  ¹ Hunter v. Wright, 12 Allen, 548 ; or delivering the key
of a warehouse, may be a delivery of the goods ; Wilkes v.
Ferris, 5 Johns. 335 ; Chappel v. Marvin, 2 Aikens, 79 ; or "less
than this, where the goods are bulky, as for instance, a quantity of timber floating in a boom, or a large stack of hay."
3 Parsons on Contracts, 43 ; Jewett v. Warren, 12 Mass. 300 ;
Boynton v. Veazie, 24 Me. 286 ; Gibson v. Stevens, 8 How.
384 ; Calkins v. Lockwood, 17 Conn. 154. But see Shindler
v. Houston, 1 Denio, 48 ; 1 Comst. 261.

received an order in the country from a carpet-manu-
facturer for a cask of cream of tartar at a fixed price,
and also an order for two chests of lac dye, provided
they could be furnished at a given price, and reserved
to his employers a right to decline to fulfill the contract for the lac dye at the price named, if they
should think fit, and, the cream of tartar and the chest
of lac dye being forwarded, the manufacturer accepted
the cream of tartar, but refused to take the lac dye, it
was held that there were two distinct and independent
contracts of sale, and that the acceptance of the cream
of tartar could not take the contract as to the lac dye
out of the operation of the statute. (*d*)   Where a purchaser had ordered two dozen of port wine, and the
same quantity of sherry, to be returned if not approved,
and the vendor sent four dozen of each, and the purchaser kept thirteen bottles and returned the rest, it
was held there was no part acceptance of the whole
quantity, so as to take the wine returned out of the
operation of the statute. (*e*)   Generally speaking, however, when a person goes into a shop and buys various
different articles at the same time, he does not make
as many different contracts as there are articles purchased; (*f*) but there is one contract for the whole,
and the acceptance and receipt of any one of the articles so purchased will take the contract as to all of
them out of the operation of the statute.[1]   Where the

(*d*) Price v. Lea, 2 D. & R. 295; 1
B. & C. 158.

(*e*) Hart v. Mills, 15 M. & W. 85;
15 L. J, Ex. 200.

(*f*) Alderson, B., 12 M. & W. 38;
3 M. & W. 178.   Baldey v. Parker, 3
D. & N. 220; 2 B. & C. 37.

[1] 3 Parsons on Contracts, 44; in general, a delivery of a
part is a delivery of the whole, " if it be an integral part of one
whole, but not if many things are bought and sold as distinct articles, and some of them are delivered, and some of them are
not." Id. ; Seymour v. Davis, 2 Sandf. 239; Davis v. Moore,

traveler of a steel manufacturer, at Sheffield, took an oral order from an edge-tool maker, at Birmingham, for thirty-five bundles of common steel, at 34*s.*, and five bundles of cast steel, at 48*s.*, it was held that this was one entire contract, and that the acceptance of the common steel took the cast steel out of the operation of the statute. (*g*)   But, where growing crops were put up to auction in several lots, and separately knocked down to a bidder at separate prices, it was held that there was a distinct contract of sale as to each lot. (*h*)

Where a party under one contract purchases goods ready made, and orders others to be made, an acceptance of the former goods is a sufficient compliance with the Statute of Frauds and the 9 Geo. 4, c. 14, s. 7. (*i*)   If after a purchase, the purchaser draws samples from the bulk of the commodity, this amounts to an acceptance of it. (*k*)   Certain sugars in a warehouse were advertised for sale by auction, and samples of half a pound weight from each hogshead, drawn after the sugars had been weighed, were produced to the assembled bidders, and after the biddings were closed, the samples were delivered to and accepted by each purchaser, as part of his purchase, to make up the quan-

---

(*g*) Elliott v. Thomas, 3 M. & W. 176. Rohde v. Thwaites, 9 D. & R. 293 ; 6 B. & C. 388. Bigg v. Whisking, 14 C. B. 198.

(*h*) Roots v. Lord Dormer, 4 B & Ad. 77 ; 1 N. & M. 667.

(*i*) *Ante.* Lord Abinger, C. B., Scott v. Eastern Counties Railway Company, 12 M. & W. 38.

(*k*) Gardner v. Grout, 2 C. B., N. S. 340.

13 Me. 424 ; Mills v. Hunt, 20 Wend. 431. ' Where several owners make a joint sale, and one of them sells a part of his portion, the delivery of this is said to satisfy the statute as to all.'' 3 Parsons on Contracts, 44 ; Field v. Runk, 2 N. J. 523 ; and as to whether the delivery of the part is intended to be a delivery of the whole, is a question for the jury ; Pratt v. Chase, 40 Me. 269.

tity and weight of each lot, as specified in the catalogue, and it was held that the delivery and acceptance of the sample were an acceptance and receipt of
part of the things sold, so as to remove the contract
from the operation of the statute. (*l*)

563. *The acceptance takes the whole contract
out of the statute, leaving it open to the parties to
supply the terms of the bargain by oral evidence.*—
If, therefore, the contract is made defeasible on certain
conditions, the conditions will stand good as part of
the contract. Where a mare was sold on the terms
that, in case she should prove in foal, she should be
returned together with part of the price ; and the
mare was delivered and accepted, and afterwards
proved to be in foal, but the purchaser refused to
return her, it was held that the acceptance took the
whole agreement out of the statute of frauds, and that
the plaintiff might sue the defendant for the refusal to
return the mare. (*m*)

564. *What is earnest and part payment within
the second exception of the statute.*—The giving of
any quantity of money, however small, by way of
earnest or part payment, has the effect of taking the
whole contract out of the operation of the statute.
It binds the bargain as between the parties, provided
the other requisites necessary to the completion of a
contract of sale have been duly complied with, and
operates as a transfer of the right of property to the
purchaser. (*n*) The vendor can not sell to another,
until he has requested the vendee to remove the
goods and pay the price, and the latter has neglected

(*l*) Hinde v. Whitehouse, 7 East, B. 707 ; 25 L. J., C. P. 85. Collis v.
570. Talver v. West, Holt, 178. Botthamley, 7 W. R. 87.
(*m*) Williams v. Burgess, 10 Ad. & (*n*) Bach v. Owen, 3 T. R. 409.
E. 499. Tomkinson v. Staight, 17 C. Blakey v. Dinsdale, 2 Cowp. 664.

to comply with the requisition within a reasonable period. (*o*)   If there is a bargain for the sale of goods at a certain price, and subsequently an agreement that a debt due from the purchaser shall be wiped off from the amount of the price, and the debt is accordingly released and discharged, this may be equivalent to earnest and part payment. (*p*) The civil law respecting earnest provides that, " if earnest has once been given, the sale is perfected, whether the contract be in writing or be made merely by word of mouth."   " If the buyer neglects to perform the contract, he loses what he has paid as earnest ; and, if the seller makes default, he is bound to render to the buyer double the value of what he has received. But the price of the thing sold must always be fixed ; for without a price there can be no sale." (*q*)

565. *Transfer of the right of property in the thing sold.*—A contract for the sale of goods, wares, and merchandise, of the value of less than £10, and so not requiring authentication by a signed writing, or duly authenticated in the mode previously pointed out, may operate as a direct transfer of the ownership and right of property in the thing sold to the purchaser, or may amount only to an agreement for a future transfer, giving the purchaser a right of action against the vendor for a breach of contract, but not effecting any alteration of ownership.   When the bargain operates as a transfer of ownership, the sale is perfect and complete ; when it amounts only to an agreement to procure or manufacture an article of a given character and description, and then transfer it to the purchaser, and does not effect any immediate

---

(*o*) Langford v. Administratrix of Tyler, 6 Mod. 162.

(*p*) Walker v. Nussey, 16 M. & W.

306, 505 ; 16 L. J., Ex. 120.

(*q*) Instit. lib. 3 tit. 24. Cod. iv., tit. 38, 40.

alteration of ownership, the sale is imperfect and incomplete. A transfer to the purchaser of the right of property in the thing sold, is naturally accompanied by a transfer of the risk of loss, so that, if, between the time of the making of the bargain and the delivery, the thing sold is consumed or destroyed, without any neglect or want of care for its preservation on the part of the vendor, the loss is the loss of the purchaser, and he may be compelled, as we shall presently see, to pay the price, although he can never have the thing for which he agreed to pay it. (*r*) To constitute a perfect and complete sale, the precise thing sold must be ascertained and identified, except where the sale is of shares and undivided quantities expressly sold as such, and the price must be ascertained and fixed. Personal engagements may subsist between the parties; but there can be no transfer of ownership and risk, until such ascertainment and identification have been accomplished.[1]

566. *Imperfect sales of unascertained chattels.*— Until the parties are agreed on the specific individual goods, the contract can be no more than a contract to supply goods answering a particular description; and, since the vendor would fulfill his part of the contract by furnishing any parcel of goods answering that description, and the purchaser could not object to them if they did answer the description, it is clear there can be no intention to transfer the property in

(*r*) *Post.* As to loss of goods by   see Greaves v. Hepke, 2 B. & Ald. distress for rent after sale of them,   133.

[1] The risk of loss is in the purchaser, in an actual sale, while in an agreement to sell, the risk remains in the vendor; Benjamin on Sales, 1st Am. Ed. §§ 78, 314, 315; the risk of property follows the title; Taylor v. Lapham, 13 Allen, 26; Willis v. Willis, 6 Dana, 49; Joyce v. Adams, 4 Selden, 296; Terry v. Wheeler, 25 N. Y. 324.

any particular lot of goods more than another, until it is ascertained which are the very goods sold. (*s*) " Thus," observes Pothier, ' in the sale of things which consist in quantity and which are sold by weight, number, or measure, as if one should sell fifty quarters of corn out of a larger bulk in a granary, ten thousand weight of sugar, a hundred carp, &c., the sale is not perfect (so as to vest any right of property in the purchaser) so long as the wheat has not been measured, the sugar weighed, and the fish counted; for up to that time nondum apparet quid venierit. It does not sufficiently appear which is the wheat, which the sugar, and which the fish that constitute the object of the sale. . . . The sale is of an unascertained subject, and one which can not be ascertained but by the measuring, the weighing, or the counting. It is not, therefore, until these have been accomplished, that the thing sold remains at the risk of the buyer; for risk can only attach on an ascertained subject." (*t*) [1]

Although the vendor has given a delivery order, or a dock-warrant, to a warehouse-keeper, wharfinger, or bailee, having the custody of the goods, commanding him to deliver them to the purchaser, yet, so long as the precise quantity of goods to be delivered under the order has not been identified and ascertained, and separated from the mass of the commodity in bulk, the sale is not perfect and complete, and the right of property is not altered. Thus, where a vendor, hav-

---

(*s*) Blackburn on the Contracts of Sale, 122.   White v. Wilks, 5 Taunt. 178.   Logan v. Le Mesurier, 6 Moo. P. C. 116; 11 Jur. 1091. Heseltine v. Siggers, 1 Exch. 861.   Hale v. Rawson, 27 L. J., C. P. 191; 4 C. B., N. S. 85.

(*t*) Pothier, Contrat de Vente, No. 179.

[1] See *ante,* note 2, paragraph 564.

ing eighteen tons of Riga flax in mats lying at a wharf, sold ten tons thereof to a purchaser, and gave him a delivery order on the wharfinger for ten tons, which order was accepted by the latter, and entered in his books, it was held that the ownership was not altered, nor the right of property transferred from the vendor to the purchaser, until the flax had been weighed, and the precise quantity to be delivered under the order had been separated from the bulk and put into a deliverable state, and placed at the disposal of the purchaser. (*u*) [1] If, however, the bulk of the commodity has been identified, and the sale is a sale of an undivided quantity thereof, expressly sold as such at an ascertained price, the ownership of the share and the risk of the loss of the subject-matter thereof will pass to the purchaser, although the shares have not been separated and divided. (*x*) [2]

(*u*) Busk v. Davis, 2 M. & S. 403.   Moakes v. Nicholson, 34 L. J., C. P.,
Shepley v. Davis, 5 Taunt. 617.   273.
(*x*) *Post.*

[1] Until identification or "appropriation," the contract is merely executory, and the property does not pass ; Browning v. Hamilton, 42 Ala. 484 ; so the sale of a certain number out of a large lot of barrels of pork, stored in a cellar ; Scudder v. Worster, 11 Cush. 593 ; Warren v. Buckminster, 24 N. H. 336 ; but to the contrary, see Chapman v. Shepard, 39 Conn. 413 ; Pleasants v. Pendleton, 6 Rand. (Va.) 473 ; Waldron v. Chase, 37 Me. 414 ; Cushing v. Breed, 4 Allen, 380 ; Warren v. Millikin, 57 Me. 97 ; Hall v. Boston, &c. R. R. Co., 14 Allen, 439.   The decisions in the various states are far from uniform on this subject.   See Wood v. McGee, 7 Ohio, 466 ; Foot v. Marsh, 51 N. Y. 288 ; Redee v. Wade, 47 Barb. 63 ; Field v. Moore, Hill & D. 418 ; Ropes v. Lane, 9 Allen, 502 ; Golder v. Ogden, 15 Penn. St. 528 ; Waldo v. Belcher, 11 Ired. 609 ; Merrill v. Hunnewell, 13 Pick. 215 ; Gardner v. Dutch, 9 Mass. 427 ; Messer v. Woodman, 22 N. H. 172 ; Bailey v. Smith, 43 Id. 141 ; Hutchinson v. Hunter, 7 Barr, 140 ; Bell v. Farrar, 41 Ill. 400.
[2] *Post*, chapter 3.

567. *Contracts for the sale and manufacture of goods.*—Where any specific chattel is ordered to be made, the right of property is not vested in the party who gives the order, nor the right to the price in the vendor, until the thing ordered is completed and made ready for delivery, and has been approved of by the purchaser, or some person appointed on his behalf to inspect the materials and workmanship. The builder or maker is not bound to deliver to the purchaser the identical chattel which is in progress, although the purchase money may have been paid in advance, but may, if he pleases, dispose of it to some other person, and deliver to the purchaser another chattel, provided it answers to the specification or description contained in the contract. (*y*)   But, where the contract provides that the article shall be manufactured under the superintendence of a person appointed by the purchaser, and also fixes the payment by instalments regulated by particular stages in the progress of the work, the general property in the materials used, vests in the purchaser at the time when they are put together under the approval of the superintendent, or, at all events, when the first instalment is paid, subject to the right of the builder to retain the fabric, in order to complete it and earn the rest of the price ; and the rights of the parties are then in the same state as if so much of the article as is then constructed had originally belonged to the purchaser, and had been delivered by him to the builder to be added to and finished. (*z*)   And, when

(*y*) Atkinson v. Bell, 8 B. & C. 282; 2 M. & R. 301. Mucklow v. Mangles, 1 Taunt. 318. Laidler v. Burlinson, 2 M. & W. 615. Elliott v. Pybus, 4 M. & Sc. 389 ; 10 Bing. 512.

(*z*) Clarke *v.* Spence, 4 Ad. & E.

470. Woods v. Russell, 5 B. & Ald. 942. Bead v. Fairbanks, 22 L. J., C. P. 206 ; 13 C. B. 692. Wood v. Bell, 6 Ell. & Bl. 361 ; 5 ib. 772 ; 25 L. J., Q. B. 148, 321.

the article is completed and made ready for delivery, and has been approved of by the purchaser, the general property therein is transferred to the latter, although the chattel may remain in the hands of the builder for the purpose of receiving some subsequent additions and improvements. (*a*)

There is a great analogy, it has been observed by the civilians, between this description of contract of sale, and the contract of letting and hiring of work and labor; and we are told in the Digest, and in the Institutes, how to discriminate between the one and the other. If, it is said, the materials for the work, as well as the work itself, have been furnished by the workman, then the contract is a contract of sale. If, on the other hand, the employer has furnished the materials, and the undertaker of the work contributes his labor merely, the contract is a contract of the letting and hiring of labor. Thus, to quote an example from the Roman law, " If Titius should agree with a goldsmith for the making of a certain number of golden rings, of a specified size and weight, for ten aurei, the goldsmith to furnish both the gold and workmanship, the contract would be a contract of buying and selling. But if Titius should give his own gold, and agree to pay only for the workmanship, then the contract would be a contract of letting and hiring simply." (*b*) [1]

(*a*) Carruthers v. Payne, 2 Moo. & P. 441. Wilkins v. Bromhead, 7 Sc. N. R. 921.

(*b*) Dig. lib. 19, tit. 2, lex. 2. Instit. lib. 3, tit. 25, § 4, § 1. God. lib, 4,

tit. 65. Lee v. Griffin, 1 B. & S. 272 ; 30 L. J., Q. B. 252. Atkinson v. Bell, 8 B. & C. 277. Grafton v. Armitage, 2 C. B. 341 ; 15 L. J., C. P. 20.

[1] Considerable apparent diversity exists in the rule as to articles to be manufactured, where work and labor is to be done as to materials to be found in the United States; Erchelberger v. McCauley, 5 Harr. & J. 213 ; but it is believed

568. *Imperfect   sales—Unascertained   price.—* Moreover, although the subject-matter of the sale may be ascertained, and identified, and selected, and

that a reconciliation of them is not impossible ; see Gilman v. Hill, 36 N. H. 317 ; Abbott v. Gilchrist, 38 Me. 260 ; Cason v. Cheely, 6 Ga. 554 ; Gorham v. Fisher, 30 Vt. 428 ; Sewall v. Fitch, 8 Cow. 215 ; Cummings v. Dennett, 26 Me. 397 ; Dows v. Ross, 23 Wend. 270 ; Jackson v. Covert, 5 Wend. 139 ; Courtwright v. Stewart, 19 Barb. 455. In Story on Sales (p. 274, § 260 c.), it is said " that where the labor and service were the essential considerations, as in the case of the manufacture of a thing not *in esse*, the contract would not be within the statute ; where the labor and service were only in-cidental to a subject matter *in esse*, the statute would apply." Said Shaw, C. J., in Lamb v. Crafts, 12 Met. 356 ; " The dis-tinction, we believe, is now well understood.   When a person stipulates for the future sale of articles which he is habitually making, and which at the time are not made or finished, it is essentially a contract of sale and not a contract for labor ; otherwise when the article is made pursuant to the agree-ment ;" and see Smith v. New York Central R. R. Co., 4 Keyes, 180 ; Mixer v. Holworth, 21 Pick. 205 ; held that in case of an agreement with a workman to put materials together and construct an article for the employer, whether at an agreed price or not, though, in common parlance, it may be called a purchase and sale of the article, to be completed in future, it is not a sale until an actual or constructive delivery and accept-ance, and the remedy for not accepting, is on the agreement." See Clark v. Nichols, 107 Mass. 47, where an oral agreement to deliver certain timber sawed into a certain shape, was a sale of the timber, and not a contract to manufacture ; and see Hight v. Ripley, 19 Me. 137 ; Fickett v. Swift, 41 Me. 68 ; Crookshank v. Burrell, 18 Johns. 58 ; Cummings v. Dennett, 26 Me. 397 ; Abbott v. Gilchrist. 38 Id. 260 ; Edwards v. Grand Trunk Railway Co., 48 Id. 379 ; Pitkin v. Noyes, 48 N. H. 294 ; Prescott v. Lock, 51 N. H. 98.   So a contract to sell all the sheep pelts taken off by the seller, a butcher, be-tween certain months, was held to be a contract for the sale of goods, and not for work and labor.   Gilman v. Hill, 36 N. H. 313.   In Crookshank v. Burrell, 18 Johns. 58, a contract to make the woodwork of a wagon, was held to be a contract for labor and services, and not a sale.   In Sewall v. Fitch, 8 Cow. 215, a contract for nails of a certain pattern, not then

approved by the purchaser, yet, so long as anything
remains to be done, as between the purchaser and
vendor, for the purpose of ascertaining the price of
the article, the right of property and the risk of loss
are not altered. (*c*) ' Thus it has been said, " If I
sell you all my corn for 12*d.* a bushel, you may not

(*c*) 2 Wms. Saund. 122, note (*m*), ed 1871.

made, was held to be a contract for labor, and not within the
statute ; and see Robertson v. Vaughan, 5 Sandf. 1.   So a
contract for flour to be manufactured from wheat ; Bronson v.
W,iman, 10 Barb. 406 ; but in Downs v. Ross, a contract for
the sale of wheat, then in existence, to be delivered in six
days, notwithstanding portions of the same were to be cleaned
and threshed, was held to be a contract of sale (Cowen, J.,
dissenting) ; 23 Wend. 270.   It is believed that the above are
sufficient to guide the student to the distinction attempted in
these cases ; but see also Passaic Mfg. Co. v. Hoffman, 3 Daly,
495 ; O'Niel v. New York Mining Co., 3 Nev. 141 ; Gorham
v. Fisher, 30 Vt. 428 ; Mead v. Case, 33 Barb. 202 ; Gardner v.
Joy, 9 Met. 178 ; Parker v. Schenck, 28 Barb. 38 ; Cook v.
Millard, 5 Lans. 243.   Under a contract for supplying labor
and materials, no property passes while any thing remains to
be done, and while the thing to be manufactured is unfinished
or incomplete, unless the contrary be clearly expressed in,
or implied by, the terms of the contract ; Williams v. Jackman, 16 Gray, 517 ; Elliot v. Edwards, 6 Vroom, 265 ; and this
rule applies to property already *in esse*, as well as to property
to be manufactured ; Halterline v. Rice, 62 Barb. 593.   And
after the manufacture, the chattel must be accepted by the
purchaser before the title will pass ; Sandford v. Wiggins
Ferry Co., 27 Ind. 522 ; Merritt v. Johnson, 7 Johns. 473 ;
Gregory v. Stryker, 2 Den. 628 ; West Jersey R. R. Co.
v. Trenton Car Works, 3 Vroom, 517 ; Middlesex Co. v.
Osgood, 4 Gray, 447 ; Rider v. Kelley, 32 Vt. 268 ; McIntyre
v. Kline, 30 Miss. 361 ; Andrews v. Durant, 1 Kern. (N. Y.)
35 ; Blasdell v. Souther, 6 Gray 149, 152 ; Mixer v. Howarth,
21 Pick. 205 ; Gamage v. Alexander, 14 Tex. 414 ; Johnson
v. Hunt, 11 Wend. 139 ; Bennett v. Platt. 9 Pick. 558 ; Veazie
v. Holmes, 40 Me. 69 ; nor does tender thereof on the part of
the manufacturer, pass the title ; Moody v. Brown, 34 Me.
107.

' *Post*, note 1, at the end of this section.

take it before it is measured, whereby the number of
the bushels may be known, and also the certainty of
the sum which is to be paid for it, so that before the
certainty is known, it can not be adjudged any good
contract or agreement." Where a vendor sold the
bark stacked at Redbrook at £9 5s. per ton of 21
cwt., to be weighed before delivery, and 8 tons, 14
cwt. of the bark were weighed and delivered ; but, before the residue was weighed and the quantity thereof ascertained, a high flood arose and destroyed it, it
was held that the right of property in the unweighed
residue had not been altered, neither, consequently,
had the risk of loss. (*d*)   And, where several hundred bales of skins, containing five dozen in each
bale, were sold at 57s. 6d. per dozen ; and by the
usage of trade it was the duty of the seller to count
the bales before delivery, to see that each bale contained the number specified, and before any enumera-
tion the skins were destroyed by fire, it was held that
the seller must bear the loss. (*e*)   So, where 1,391
pieces of red pine timber measuring 50,000 feet, more
or less, were sold at the rate of 9½d. per foot to be
measured off before delivery, it was held that, until
a measurement had been effected, the sale was not
perfect and complete, so as to transfer the ownership
and risk. (*f*) [1]

So, observes Pothier, " if the sale is of all the
merchandise or corn stored in a particular granary at
so much per thousand weight, or so much a quarter,

(*d*) Simmons v. Swift, 8 D. & R.   (*e*) Zagury v. Furnell, 2 Campb.
703 ; 5 B. & C. 862. Martineau v.   239.
Kitchen L. R., 7 Q. B., 436, 454 ; 41   (*f*) Logan v. Le Mesurier, 11 Jur.
L. J., Q. B. 227.   Hanson v. Meyer,   1091.
6 East, 627.

[1] *Post*, note 1, at the end of this section.

the sale is not considered to be perfect, and the things
sold are not at the risk of the buyer, so long as they
have not been weighed or measured; for up to that
time the quantity has not been ascertained, and, the
price being determined only by each thousand weight
that shall be weighed, or each quarter that shall be
measured, there is no ascertained price until the
weighing or measuring shall have been accomplished;
and the sale, consequently, before that time, is not
sufficiently perfected for the risk of the things sold
to belong to the buyer; and he ought not to be
charged with it until the weighing and measuring
have been accomplished." (*g*) [1]

But the distinction must be observed between a
sale by measure or weight requiring the measuring or
weighing to be accomplished for the purpose of determining and fixing the price, and a sale of specific
goods in the lump at an ascertained price, accompanied with a representation or warranty of the weight
or quantity, where the weighing or measuring is necessary only for the purpose of satisfying the purchaser
that he has got the quantity bargained for. (*h*) The
mention of the quantity has no further effect in this
case than to oblige the vendor to make good to the purchaser any deficiency that may be found to exist. (*i*)
Moreover, if it appears by the terms of the contract
that it was the intention of the parties that the property should pass to the buyer, it will pass, although
the goods have still to be weighed, measured, or

(*g*) Pothier, Contr. de Vente, No.
309.   Dig. lib. 18, tit. 1, lex. 35.
(*h*) Swanwick v. Sothern, 9 Ad. &
E. 900. Gilmour v. Supple, 11 Moore,
P. C. 571.   Furley v. Bates, 33 L. J,   .

Ex. 43 ; S. C. nom. Turley v. Bates,
2 H. & C. 200.   Kershaw v. Ogden,
3 H. & C. 717 ; 34 L. J., Ex. 159.
   (*i*) Pothier, Vente, No. 310.

[1] *Ante*, note 2, §§ 565, 566.

tested, provided the subject-matter of the sale is ascertained and identified; (*k*) and there may be a
complete contract so as to pass the property in the
goods, although the price has not been definitely
agreed on, (*l*) or although the goods are still unfinished, (*m*) or unweighed. (*n*)

When the quantity is ascertained, the mere omission to add up the total contents according to weight
or measure, will not prevent the right of property
and the risk from passing to the purchaser. (*o*)   If
certain specific cases, bales, or packages of goods are
sold in the lump, at the customary and reasonable
price paid for such articles, the price is sufficiently
ascertained, and the right of property will pass,
although no definite sum has been agreed upon, and
the time or mode of payment has not been specified. (*p*) [1]

(*k*) Turley v. Bates, 2 H. & C. 200 ;
S. C. nom. Furley v. Bates, 33 L. J.,
Ex. 43. Martineau v. Kitchen, *ante.*

(*l*) Joyce v. Swann, 17 C. B., N. S.
84.

(*m*) Young v. Mathews, L. R., 2 C.
P. 127 ; 36 L. J., C. P. 61.

(*n*) Martineau v. Kitching, *ante.*

(*o*) Tansley v. Turner, 2 Sc. 241 ; 5 ·
Bing. N. C. 151.

(*p*) Valpy v. Gibson, 4 C. B. 837 ;
16 L. J., C. P. 248.   Joyce v. Swann,
17 C. B., N. S. 102. Hoadley v. Maclaine, 10 Bing. 482 ; 4 M. & Sc. 340.

---

[1] A price must be money paid or promised; Benjamin on
Sales, Am. Ed. §§ 2, 85.   The law will imply a reasonable
price when none is mentioned, but parol evidence is admissible to show that a price was actually agreed upon, in order to
establish the insufficiency of a memorandum which is silent
as to the price; Id. § 249 ; until the price is fixed there is no
contract; Id. § 87 ; even if it be the fault of one of the parties that no valuation was fixed, in which case, however, it is
for the jury to fix the value; Id. § 87; if the price can be
made certain, it will be sufficient; Fuller v. Bean, 34 N. H.
304.   In the civil law it was a settled rule that there could be
no sale without a price certain.   "Pretium autem constitui
oportet, nam nulla emptio sine pretio esse protest consed et
certum esse debet," was the language of the Institutes.   Lib.
3, tit. 23–1.   And it was a subject of long contest among the

569. *Perfect sales operating as transfers of the
ownership and risk.*—When the subject-matter of the
sale is ascertained and identified at the time the bar-

earlier jurisconsults whether the necessity for a certain price
did not render invalid an agreement that the price should be
fixed by a third person ; but Justinian put an end to the question by positive legislation : "Alioquin si inter aliquos ita
convenerit, ut quanti Titius rem æstimaverit tanti sit empta,
inter veteres satis abundeque hoc dubitabatur sive constat
venditio, sive non. Sed nostra decisio ita hoc constituit, ut
quotiens sic composita sit venditio, quanti ille æstimaverit,
sub hac conditione staret contractus; ut si quidem ipse qui
nominatus est pretium definierit, omnimodo secundum ejus
æstimationem et pretium presolvatur et res tradatur, et venditio ad effectum perducatur, emptore quidem ex empto actione,
venditore ex vendito agente. Sin autem ille qui nominatus
est, vel noluerit vel non potuerit pretium definire, tunc pro
nihilo esse venditionem quasi nullo pretio statuto. Quod jus,
cum in venditionibus nobis placuit, non est absurdum et in
locationibus et conductionibus trahere." These rules have
been adopted into the Code Napoleon. Art. 1591: "Le prix de la
vente doit être déterminé et désigné par les parties." 1592 :
"Il peut cependant être laissé à l'arbitrage d'un tiers; si le
tiers ne veut ou ne peut faire l'estimation, il n'y a point de
vente." Benjamin on Sales, § 89. "The language of the
civil law upon this subject is the language of common sense."
Story, J., in Flagg v. Mann, 2 Sumn. 538.

Differing rules have been adopted in the various states as
to whether this consideration must be expressed in the memorandum required by the statute. By the 19 and 20 Vict. ch. 97,
§ 3, in England its expression is no longer necessary. In
Alabama, ch. 1852, § 1551 ; California, L. April 19, 1850, ch.
4, § 8 ; Minnesota, R. S. 1866, ch. 41, tit. 2, § 6 ; Nevada, L.
1861, ch. 9, § 57 ; Oregon, C. C. tit. 8, ch. 8, § 775 ; and Wisconsin, R. S. 1849, tit. 20, ch. 76, § 2 ; it is expressly enacted
by statute that the consideration shall appear. In Indiana,
R. S. 1852, ch. 42, § 2 ; Kentucky, R. S. 1852, ch. 22, §§ 1, 2 ;
Massachusetts, G. S. 1860, part 2, tit. 6, ch. 105, §§ 1 and 2 ; but
this is not made expressly applicable to the 5th section of the
statute ; Packard v. Richardson, 17 Mass. 122 ; New York, L.
1863, ch. 464, p. 802, amending 3 R. S. p. 221, 5th Ed. ; and
Virginia, C. 1849, ch. 143, § 1 (8) ; the consideration may
appear, or may be proved by any other legal evidence. In

gain is struck, and the price is likewise agreed upon
and reduced to a certainty, the sale is a perfect and
complete sale from the time of the making of the bar-

Louisana the civil law prevails, and no consideration is necessary to be stated or proved. Ringgold v. Newkirk, 3 Ark. 96.
In those states whose statute couples the word "promise"
with the word "agreement," the courts, it will be observed,
have generally dispensed with the statement of the consideration. Browne on Statute of Frauds, 409, § 391; see also
Morgan's De Colyar on Guaranty, notes *, page 50, and *
page 24. In Georgia (Browne on Statute of Frauds, App. p.
514; T. R. Cobb, N. D. App. III.) and Maryland (Browne on
Statute of Frauds, App. p. 520 (Kelty's Report of English
Statutes, p. 242) the English statute, as unamended, is
still in force; and the rule in Wain v. Warlters, 5 East, 10,
that the consideration moving to the agreement must appear
in the writing (see Morgan's De Colyar on Guaranty, p. 176)
has received the sanction of the courts. Henderson v. Johnson, 6 Ga. 390; Hargroves v. Cooke, 15 Id. 321. In Maryland,
Sloan v. Wilson, 4 Harr. & J. 322; Elliot v. Giese, Id. 457;
Wyman v. Gray, Id. 409; Edelen v. Gough, 5 Gill. 103; Hutton v. Padgett, 26 Md. 228; but see Brooks v. Dent, 1 Md.
Ch. Dec. 530. In the states whose statutes are silent on the
subject, the point has been decided as seemed to its courts
"wisest in point of policy or most commended by authority."
Browne on Statute of Frauds, p. 408. Of the states not above
mentioned (all of which retain the word "agreement" in their
particular statute of frauds), the ruling in Wain v. Warlters
has been rejected in Maine, Levy v. Merrill, 4 Greenl. 189;
Gilligham v. Boardman, 29 Me. (16 Shep.) 81; Vermont,
Smith v. Ide, 3 Verm. 299; Patchin v. Swift, 21 Id. 297; Connecticut, Sage v. Wilcox, 6 Conn. 81; North Carolina, Miller
v. Irvine, 1 Dev. & Bat. 103; Ashford v. Robinson, 8 Ired. 114;
Ohio, Reed v. Evans, 17 Ohio, 128; and Missouri, Bean v.
Valle, 2 Mo. 103; but it has received the sanction of the courts
in New Hampshire, Neelson v. Sanborn, 2 N. H. 414; Underwood v. Campbell, 14 Id. 393; New Jersey, Buckley v. Beardsley, 2 South. 572; Laing v. Lee, Spencer, 337; South Carolina, Stephens v. Winn, 2 Nott & McC. 372, note *a*; per *contra*,
however, see Lecat v. Tavel, 3 McCord, 158; Michigan, Jones
v. Palmer, 1 Doug. 379; Wisconsin, Reynolds v. Carpenter, 3
Chand. 31; Taylor v. Pratt, 3 Wis. 674; Mississippi, Wren v.
Pierce, 4 Sm. & M. 91; Tennessee, Taylor v. Ross, 3 Yerg,

gain, and the right of property in the thing sold and
the risk of loss are transferred to the purchaser,
although the right of possession may continue in the
vendor until the purchase money has been paid or tendered. (*q*)   Where the vendor agreed to sell, and the
purchaser to buy, " a stack of hay standing in Canon-
bury Field, Islington, at the sum of £145, the hay to be
allowed to stand on the premises until the first of May
next, and not to be cut till paid for," it was held that
there was an immediate transfer of the right of property to the purchaser, and the hay having been accidentally destroyed by fire whilst it remained in the
possession of the vendor, that the purchaser must bear
the loss.   " If," observes Pothier, " things have been
sold per aversionem, that is to say, in the mass for a
fixed price, the sale is complete from the time of the
making of the contract, and the thing sold remains at
the risk of the purchaser, although it has not yet been
delivered to him, so that, if between the bargain and
delivery it should happen to perish without the fault
of the seller, the latter becomes released from his obligation to deliver, but the buyer is not, on account
thereof, released from his obligation to pay the contract price. (*r*)

570. *Selection and appropriation of goods to the
use of the purchaser.*—If the commodity was selected
in the bulk by the purchaser, the ownership and risk

(*q*) Bloxam v. Saunders, 4 B. & C.
948 ; 7 D. & R. 405.   Knight v. Hop-
per, Skin. 647.   Sweeting v. Turner,
L. R., 7 Q. B. 310 ; 41 L. J., Q. B. 58.
Si id quod venierit appareat, quid,
quale, quantum, sit et pretium, et pure
venit, perfecta est emptio.   Dig. lib.

8, tit. 6, lex. 8.   Noy's Maxims, ch. 42,
p. 88.   Bro. Abr. Contr. pl. 26.
   (*r*) Pothier, Contrat de Vente, Nos.
307, 308.   Tarling v. Baxter, 9 D. &
R. 272 ; 6 B. & C. 360.   Taylor v
Caldwell, 3 B. & S. 837 ; 32 L. J., Q
B. 164.

330 ; Kentucky, Ratcliff v. Trout, 6 J. J. Marsh. 606 ; Florida,
Doorman v. Bigelow, 1 Fla. 281.

pass as soon as the quantity sold has been separated from the mass and tendered to the purchaser, or placed at his disposal. Thus, where a quantity of turpentine was sold by auction at a fixed price per hundred-weight, to be delivered in casks, and taken at the net weight printed in the catalogue, the casks to be filled up by the vendor and removed by the purchaser, and all the casks were filled up except ten, and were placed in the vendor's warehouse at the disposal of the purchaser, and before they were removed, the whole quantity was consumed by fire, it was held that the right of property in the casks that had been filled up and placed at the disposal of the purchaser, had passed to the latter, and that he must stand to the loss; but as to the remaining quantity, which had not been selected and weighed and made ready for delivery, that it continued in the vendor and at his risk. (*s*)   And the right of property and the attendant risk may be transferred by the buyer to a third party by another contract of sale, although the price may not have been paid and the right of possession divested out of the original vendor. (*t*)   If the bulk of the commodity or the specific article bought and sold has not been selected by the purchaser and identified in the first instance, the sale may be rendered perfect and complete, so as to operate as a transfer of the property and risk, by a subsequent selection by the vendor and approval thereof by the purchaser, such subsequent selection and approval being the same as if the article had been fixed upon in the first instance; (*u*) but a selection by the vendor only,

---

(*s*) Rugg v. Minett, 11 East, 210. Aldridge v. Johnson, 7 Ell. & Bl. 899. Langton v. Higgins, 4 H. & N. 402. Langton v. Waring, 18 C. B. N. S. 315. Blackburn on the Contract of Sale, p. 128.

(*t*) Scott v. England, 14 L. J., Q. B. 43.

(*u*) Rhodes v. Thwaites, 6 B. & C. 388. Sparkes v. Marshall, 3 Sc. 185; 2 Bing. N. C. 775. Campbell v. Mersey Docks, 14 C. B. N. S. 412.

without the approval of the purchaser, will not transfer the property in the goods so selected. (*x*) [1]

571. *Delivery to carriers.*—If the vendor is authorized and empowered to select the goods and forward them to the purchaser, the selection by the vendor, and the delivery of the goods to a carrier to be conveyed to the purchaser, will have the effect of transferring the ownership and risk to such purchaser, provided there is a binding contract by note in writing, by part payment, or by part acceptance, and the selection is made according to the orders or authority given. (*y*) As soon as the goods are delivered into the hands of the carrier, in execution and fulfilment of a properly authenticated contract of sale,[2] the carrier becomes responsible to the purchaser to whom they are consigned, and there is an executed delivery, as we shall presently see, as well as a transfer of the ownership and risk ; (*z*) but if by the terms of the contract the delivery of the goods at their place of destination is made a condition precedent to the payment of the price, and the goods perish in the hands of the carrier, the vendor is not entitled to the price. (*a*) And if the purchaser's right to possession of the goods is made conditional on the prior performance of some act on his part, such as an acceptance of a bill of exchange, or the giving of a promissory note for the price, the

---

(*x*) Jenner v. Smith, L. R., 4 C. P. 270.

(*y*) Fragano v. Long, 4 B. & C. 221. Alexander v. Gardner, 1 Sc. 641 ; 1 Bing. N. C. 671. Browne v. Hare, 4 H. & N. 830 ; 29 L. J., Ex. 6.

(*z*) Anderson v. Clark, 2 Bing. 20. Bryans v. Nix, 4 M. & W. 791, 793.

Swain v. Shepherd, 1 Mood. & Rob. 223. Wiltshire Iron Company, In re, L. R., 3 Ch. 443 ; 37 L. J., Ch. 554.

(*a*) Ld. Cottenham, Dunlop v. Lambert, 6 Cl. & Fin. 621. Calcutta, &c., Steam Navigation Company v. De Mattos, 32 L. J., Q. B. 322 ; 33 L. J., Q. B. 214.

[1] *Ante*, note 2, § 564.
[2] *Ante*, note 2, § 559.

vendor may stop the goods in transitu, and resume the possession of them, if the purchaser neglects to fulfill the condition at the time appointed. (*b*) [1]

572. *Delivery under a bill of lading.*—Where goods are consigned to a merchant abroad under a bill of lading expressing that the goods are shipped by order and on account of the consignee, the property vests in the consignee from the time they are put on board. (*c*)   But if goods are delivered to a ship-master, to be carried under a bill of lading, whereby the latter undertakes to carry them for and on account of the vendor, and deliver them to the vendor at the port of destination, or to the assignee of the bill of lading, there is no transfer of the property until the bill of lading has been indorsed to the purchaser, (*d*) unless from all the facts it may fairly be inferred that it was the intention of the seller that the property in the goods should pass. (*e*)   Where goods destined for a foreign port are put on board ship, and the bill of lading and policy of insurance are handed over in exchange for a part payment, the property and risk in the goods forthwith vest in the purchaser. (*f*)

573. *Undivided shares.*—If things of quantity, such as corn, coals, &c., are laden on board a vessel, and the ship-master is directed to deliver certain ascertained but undivided quantities to different consignees, the

---

(*b*) Com. Dig. CONDITION (B. 13). Brandt v. Bowlby, 2 B. & Ad. 932. Moakes v. Nicholson, 19 C. B. N. S. 270, 34 L. J., C. P. 273.

(*c*) Brown v. Hodgson, 2 Campb. 35. Coxe v. Harden, 4 East, 211.

(*d*) Wait v. Baker, 2 Exch, 1 ; 17 L. J., Ex. 307. Jenkyns v. Brown, 14 Q. B. 503.

(*e*) Joyce v. Swann, 17 C. B. N. S. 84.

(*f*) Tregelles v. Sewell, 7 H. & N. 574.

---

[1] *Ante*, note 2, § 559.

latter have a right, as against the carrier, to the due
conveyance and delivery of their several undivided
shares of the cargo, although no right of property in
any specific measures of corn or coal can pass to
them until the cargo has been divided, and their several shares set apart for them and identified.   In cases
of this kind the goods are at the risk of the purchaser ; and, if the vessel is lost by perils of the sea, and
the whole cargo is destroyed, they must bear their
several proportions of the loss according to their several shares in the cargo, although those shares were
undivided.   In these cases they have a right of property in an undivided share, but not in any specific
ascertained portion of the cargo. (*g*) [1]

When everything that the seller is to do to complete the sale has been performed, the property and the
attendant risk pass to the purchaser, although the latter may not have got the right of possession of the
subject-matter of the sale, or perfect control over it,
by reason of the non-performance of some act to be
done exclusively by him, such as procuring wines and
spirits to be gauged by a custom-house officer, in
order to ascertain their strength preparatory to the
calculation of the duty, payment of the duty when
calculated and ascertained, or the non-performance of
any other act which it is incumbent on the buyer
alone to perform. (*h*)   But it is not competent to the
buyer to perfect the contract, and vest the property
in himself by the performance of acts which it is the

(*g*) Jenkyns v. Usborne, 7 M. &   Hinde v. Whitehouse, 7 East. 558.
Gr. 698.   Furley v. Bates, *ante*.   Sweeting v.
(*h*) Rugg v. Minett, 11 East, 210.   Turner, L. R., 7 Q. B. 310.
Studdy v. Saunders, 8 D. & R. 403.

[1] *Ante*, note 2, § 564.

duty of the vendor to perform, unless the acts are done with the sanction and by the authority of the vendor. (*i*)

574. *Conditional sale.*—If the article is to be selected by the vendor, or to be made or manufactured by him, and the purchaser makes its acceptance dependent upon his approval of it as regards workmanship, convenience, and taste, the latter will be entitled to reject it, if it does not meet his approval upon some one or more of the grounds stated. (*k*)[1] A contract for the sale of goods " on arrival," (*l*) or that may arrive, or be shipped, or loaded, (*m*) or expected to arrive, (*n*) is conditional on the arrival or shipping of the goods, so that, if no goods arrive or are shipped, there is no sale and no liability to deliver on the part of the vendor;[2] but if a man takes upon himself to sell goods expected to arrive by a certain ship, and the goods afterwards arrive consigned to some third party, so that the intended vendor has no power of disposing of them, he is precluded from setting up that, in addition to the contingency of their arrival, there was implied the further contingency of their coming consigned to him. Having dealt with them as his own, he can not be allowed to import into the contract a new condition, viz., that the goods on their arrival shall prove to be his; (*o*) for

---

(*i*) Acraman v. Morrice, 8 C. B. 459; 19 L. J., C. P. 57.

(*k*) Andrews v. Belfield, 2 C. B. N. S. 789. Lucy v. Mouflet, 5 H. & N. 229; 29 L. J., Ex. 110.

(*l*) Boyd v. Siffkin, 2 Campb. 325.

(*m*) Hayward v. Scougall, ib. 56.

Lovatt v. Hamilton, 5 M. & W. 639.

(*n*) Smith v. Myers, L. R., 5 Q. B. 429; ib., 7 Q B. 139; 39 L. J., Q. B. 210; 41 ib. 91.

(*o*) Fischel v. Scott, 15 C. B. 69. Gorrissen v. Perrin, 2 C. B. N. S. 701; 27 L. J., C. P. 29.

[1] Benjamin on Sales, Am. Ed. § 595.

[2] Nelcon v. Smith, 7 Vr. 148; Bendict v. Field, 16 N. Y. 597; Rerniers v. Redner, 2 Rob. (N. Y.) 11.

whenever the agreement is conditioned upon an event which happens, the vendor will be liable for non-performance, although he is prevented from fulfilling his contract by reason of some mistake or accident over which he had no control; for he ought to have provided against the possible contingency by his contract. If, therefore, he agrees to sell certain cases of East Indian tallow to be delivered to the purchaser on the safe arrival of a certain ship, and the ship arrives, but without the tallow, the vendor is responsible for the non-performance of his contract. (*p*) Where the plaintiff sold to the defendant a certain unascertained quantity of oil, part of a large quantity lying at the plaintiff's wharfinger's, and sent an order to the wharfinger to transfer the oil to the defendant, and the wharfinger made the transfer in his books to the defendant, and gave the plaintiff's clerk a paper acknowledging the transfer, and the clerk went with this paper to the defendant's counting-house, and demanded a cheque in payment, and was refused, but the defendant took and retained the paper, and sent to the wharfinger and obtained possession of the oil, it was held that, as there was no intention to part with the paper or the property in the goods without payment, there was no change of property in the goods in the hands of the wharfinger, and that the plaintiff was entitled to recover the oil or the value of it from the defendant. (*q*)

575. *Implied promises and undertakings resulting from executory contracts of sale.*—Although a bargain and sale may be so far incomplete and imperfect as not to operate as an immediate transfer of property, yet the engagements which naturally result

(*p*) Hale v. Rawson, 4 C. B. N. S. 85; 27 L. J., C. P. 189.

(*q*) Godts v. Rose, 17 C. B. 229; 25 L. J., C. P. 64.

from the contract are in existence as soon as it has been entered into. There is an implied promise or undertaking on the part of the vendor to put the vendee into possession of the thing sold without delay, if the contract makes no mention of the time of delivery, and a promise or undertaking by the vendee to accept the goods and pay the price on the delivery of the subject-matter of the sale by the vendor. There is also an implied undertaking, on the part of the vendor, of a specific chattel to be delivered at a future day, to take the same care of it as of a thing borrowed for his own use (*post*, ch. 2); and, if he wastes or re-sells the property, he is responsible in damages to the purchaser. (*r*)

576. *When the sale is a sale of particular classes and descriptions of goods* to be selected by the vendor, such as a sale of so many measures of corn, wine, oil, or fruit, and not of any specific ascertained parcel of goods, the vendor will fulfill his contract by furnishing any goods fairly answering the description given by him. When, on the other hand, the precise article intended to be bought and sold was ascertained and identified at the time of the making of the bargain, the vendor must deliver the identical thing so fixed upon and ascertained, and can not fulfill his contract by tendering or delivering anything else of a corresponding nature. If the purchaser, instead of going in person to a shop, and selecting the goods himself, sends an order describing what he wants, the vendor, if he accepts the order, must select and send an article which fairly corresponds with the description. Thus, where a purchaser forwarded a written order to the vendor for "scarlet cuttings," to be shipped on his account for the Chinese market, and

(*r*) Chinery v. Viall, 5 H. & N. 293; 29 L. J., Ex. 180.

the vendor sent on board a different article, it was held that the plaintiff was entitled to recover from the vendor all the loss he had sustained in consequence of his not having had in China the goods which he had ordered. (*s*)   So, where the purchaser sent an order in writing for "seventy-five barrels of best pork, branded Scott and Co.," a description of pork well-known in the market as cured by Scott and Co., and paid the ordinary price for the article, and the vendor sent an inferior commodity, cured by another person, it was held that the vendor was responsible in damages for having sent a different article. (*t*)   And, where one vendor had contracted to sell Skirving's Swede turnip seed, and another foreign refined rape-oil, it was held that they were responsible in damages for sending seed and oil which did not answer the description given. (*u*)   If, therefore, a ship owner supplies a ship ordered to be copper-fastened which is not copper-fastened, or if a diamond-merchant sells a piece of cut glass or crystal for a diamond, or a silversmith sells plated goods for silver, or if a merchant sells wine or beer described as " fit," or ordered by the purchaser to be " fit, for the Mediterranean," or " India market," and sends out a liquid which turns sour on the voyage, and is not saleable on its arrival as wine or beer, he is liable to an action for the breach of an implied undertaking to furnish the article described and ordered. (*v*)

577. *Mercantile usage.*—Where a contract was

(*s*) Bridge v. Wain, 1 Stark. 504. Gardiner v. Gray, 4 Campb. 144.

(*t*) Powell v. Horton, 3 Sc. 110 ; 2 Bing. N. C. 668.

(*u*) Allan v. Lake, 18 Q. B. 567. Nichol v. Godts, 10 Exch. 191. Simond v. Braddon, 2 C. B. N. S. 336 ; 26

L. J., C. P. 198.   Wieler v. Schilizzi, 17 C. B. 619.

(*v*) Fisher v. Samuda, 1 Camp. 189. Shepherd v. Kain, 5 B. & Ald. 240. Tye v. Finmore, 3 Campb. 461. As to implied warranties, see *post.*

entered into for the supply of a certain quantity of " best palm oil, usual tare and draft, wet, dirty, and inferior, if any, at a fair allowance," it was held that evidence was admissible to show that there was an established usage in the trade regulating the proportions of good and bad oil, and that the vendor under such a contract was bound to supply a certain proportion of the best oil. (*y*)

578. *Time of performance.*—If the sale is a sale of things of quantity generally, and no right of property in the things agreed to be sold passes by the bargain from the vendor to the purchaser, time will, in general, be of the essence of the contract, so long as the contract remains executory, and the purchaser will not be bound to accept and pay for the goods, if they are not tendered on the day specified; (*z*) [1] but if the sale is a perfect and complete sale of specific, ascertained chattels, and the ownership and right of property in the thing sold have been transferred by the bargain to the purchaser, time is not of the essence of the contract, and the vendor can not repudiate the sale, and re-vest the right of property in himself, and refuse to deliver the goods at a subsequent period on tender of the price, on the ground of the non-payment thereof at the time appointed, (*a*) unless the sale has been made conditional on payment at the time named. When different times are not expressly appointed for payment and delivery, the

(*y*) Lucas v. Bristow, 27 L. J., Q. B. 364.

(*z*) Gath v. Lees, 3 H. & C. 558. Coddington v. Paleologo, L. R., 2 Ex. 193 ; 36 L. J., Ex. 73.

(*a*) Martindale v. Smith, 1 Q. B 395. Wilmshurst v. Bowker, 8 Sc. N. R. 571 ; 7 M. & Gr. 882. Chinery v. Viall, 5 H. & N. 293 ; 29 L. J., Ex. 180.

[1] Sumner v. Parker, 36 N. H. 449; Haines v. Tucker, 50 Id. 307 ; Dwinel v. Howard, 30 Me. 258.

acts of payment and delivery are, as we have seen, concurrent, and constitute mutual conditions to be performed at the same time; (*b*) but if a precise time has been appointed for the payment of the price, and another and different time is fixed for the delivery, the acts are not concurrent, and do not constitute mutual conditions, (*c*) unless they are made so by custom and usage of trade. (*d*) If it appears to have been the intention of the parties that the sale should be void, and the right of property in the thing sold re-vested in the vendor, in case of the non-payment of the purchase money, or the non-delivery of the goods, on an appointed day, this does not enable the purchaser to say, " I am not ready with my money, therefore I will avoid the contract," nor the vendor to say, " I am not ready to deliver, therefore I will be off the bargain."

If the time appointed for delivery or payment is not of the essence of the contract, the delivery and payment must be made within a reasonable time after notice and request of performance; and if no time at all has been appointed for the performance of these acts, the vendor is bound to deliver within a reasonable period after request and tender of the price, and the purchaser must in like manner accept the goods and pay for them on delivery, or offer of delivery, being made by the vendor; and if the contract is not sought to be carried into effect within a reasonable period, either on the part of the vendor or the pur-

---

(*b*) Callonel v, Briggs, 1 Salk. 113. Lock v. Wright, 1 Str. 571; 8 Mod. 41. Withers v. Reynolds, 2 B. & Ad. 882. Atkinson v. Smith, 14 M. & W. 695.

(*c*) *Ante.* Thorpe v. Thorpe, 1 Salk. 171; 1 Raym. 665.

(*d*) Field v. Lelean, 30 L. J., Ex. 168.

chaser, it is deemed to be dissolved and abandoned by mutual consent. (*e*) '

When a particular day is appointed for the delivery of the goods, or the payment of the price, the party has the whole of the day, and if one of several days, the whole of those days, for the performance on his part of the contract; but he must do all he can to make the payment or perform the act at a convenient hour before midnight. Therefore, if he is to pay a sum of money, he must tender it a sufficient time before midnight for the party to receive it. If he is to deliver goods, he must deliver them in sufficient time for examination and receipt. If the payment or delivery is to be performed at a certain place on a specific day,

(*e*) Ellis v. Thompson, 3 M. & W. 457. Langfort v. Tyler, 1 Salk. 113. Domat (Sale), L. 1.   Lanyon v. Toogood, 13 M. & W. 27.

' And what is a reasonable time, is to be determined by all the circumstances of each case, and is a question of law. 2 Parsons on C., pp. 535, 661. Adams v. Adams, 26 Ala. 272; Crocker v. Franklin, &c., Mfg. Co., 3 Sumn. 530; Attwood v. Cobb, 16 Pick. 227; 5 Md. 121; Sawyer v. Hammott, 15 Me. 40; Howe v. Huntington, Id. 350; Atkinson v. Brown, 20 Id. 67; all other questions of reasonableness are questions of fact; but in the case of time, where a time is not mentioned, it is a presumption of law that a reasonable time is meant, and courts will treat such an agreement as if it had expressly stated that the thing contracted to be done should be done in a reasonable time; Crocker v. Franklin Mfg. Co., 3 Sumn. 530. But this statement of Judge Parsons (2 Contracts, pp. 535, 661), that the reasonableness of the time is a question of law, does not seem to be universally acquiesced in; it has been held that it may be a question for either or both according to circumstances; Attwood v. Clark, 2 Greenl. 249; Howe v. Huntington, 15 Me. 350; Kingsley v. Wallis, 14 Id. 57; Hill v. Hobart, 16 Id. 164; Murray v. Smith, 1 Hawks, 41; Greene v. Dingley, 24 Me. 131; Cameron v. Wells, 30 Vt. 633. Benjamin, in his work on sales (§ 700), says distinctly that such question is one of fact for the jury.

the tender must be to the other party at that place; and, as the attendance of the other is necessary at that place to complete the act, the law, though it requires the other to be present, does not require him to be present through the whole day; and therefore it fixes a particular part of the day; and it is enough if he is at the place a convenient time before sunset, so that the act may be completed; and if the party who is to perform tenders to the party present, or, if absent, if the tender is made, before sunset, that is sufficient. (*f*) Orders for goods to be delivered as soon as possible do not oblige the vendor who accepts the order to put everything else aside and execute it without any delay at all. He is only bound to execute the order within a reasonable time. (*g*)

579. *Enlargement of the time of performance.*— The time appointed for the performance of a contract of sale required by the Statute of Frauds to be in writing, can not be extended by an oral agreement, so as to enable a party to sue partly upon the written contract and partly upon the subsequent oral agreement. (*h*)

580. *Non-delivery of goods sold.*—If the contract is entire for the purchase of a certain quantity of goods, the vendor can not be compelled to deliver a part only of the goods; and if the purchaser declines to take the whole quantity he has ordered, the vendor may at once abandon the contract or sue for damages. (*i*) If the ownership and right of property in the thing sold, pass by the bargain to the purchaser, the vendor is not, as we have already seen, released from his obligation to

(*f*) Startup v. Macdonald, 7 Sc. N. R. 297; 12 L. J., Ex. 483; *ante.*

(*g*) Attwood v. Emery, 1 C. B. N. S. 114; 26 L. J., C. P. 73.

(*h*) Marshall v. Lynn, 6 M. & W.

109. Stead v. Dawber, 10 Ad. & E. 57; overruling Cuff v. Penn, 1 M. & S. 27.

(*i*) Kingdom v. Cox, 5 C. B. 522.

deliver the goods by reason of the non-payment of the price at the time appointed, unless the acts of payment and delivery have been made concurrent acts, and the sale is made conditional on the payment of the pur-chase money by an appointed period. If goods which have become the property of the purchaser by bargain are to be delivered at a future day, and before the day the vendor sells and delivers them to another, he is immediately liable to an action for damages at the suit of the first purchaser. (*k*)   If the goods are to be de-livered " forthwith," and the price is to be paid in a "fortnight" or "month," the delivery must be made without delay. (*l*)[1]   If a bought note specifies that certain goods have been "bought to be paid for by

---

(*k*) Bowdell v. Parsons, 10 East, 359. Hochester v. De la Tour, 2 Ell. & Bl. 688 ; *ante.*

(*l*) Staunton v. Wood, 16 Q. B. 638.

[1] The construction of words is of course for the court ; so the word "month" will be construed to mean a "calendar," and not a "lunar" or other month. Churchill v. Merchants' Bank, 19 Pick. 532 ; Thomas v. Shoemaker, 6 Watts. &,S. 179. Where a certain number of days is mentioned, they must be counted exclusively of the day of the contract. Weeks v. Hull, 19 Conn. 376 ; Bigelow v. Wilson, 1 Pick. 485 ; Wiggin v. Peters, 1 Met. 127, 129 ; Henry v. Jones, 8 Mass. 453 ; Blake v. Crowninshield, 9 N. H. 304 ; Avery v. Stewart, 2 Conn. 69 ; Aiken v. Appleby, 1 Morris, 8 ; Cornell v. Moulton, 3 Denio, 12 ; Farwell v. Rogers, 4 Cush. 460 ; Buttrick v. Holden, 8 Cush. 233 ; Oatman v. Walker, 33 Me. 71 ; Winslow v. China, 4 Greenl. 298 ; Howes v. Smith, 16 Me. 181 ; Ewing v. Bailey, 4 Scam. 420 ; Woodbridge v. Brigham, 12 Mass. 403. And it seems the act to be done must be done before midnight on the last day ; see McClartey v. Gokey, 31 Iowa, 505. Where two days are mentioned as "between the 15th and 28th," or "from the 15th to the 28th," both days are to be excluded from the running time ; Atkins v. Boylston, &c. Ins. Co., 5 Met. 440 ; Richardson v. Ford. 14 Ill. 332 ; Cook v. Gray, 6 Ind. 335 ; Newby v. Rogers, 40 Ind. 9 ; and the word "until" is ex-clusive ; People v. Walker, 17 N. Y. 502.

cash in one month," the buyer is entitled to call for delivery at any reasonable time from the making of the contract; but the vendor has no right to the money until the month has expired, unless a usage of trade, authorizing the vendor to keep possession of the goods until the day of payment arrives, can be established. (*m*)

If the goods are in the hands of a warehouse-keeper, wharfinger, or other agent, for safe custody, and are to be fetched away by the purchaser, and the goods are weighed and set apart for the purchaser, and the agent consents to hold them at the disposal of the latter, there is, as we have seen, a sufficient delivery on the part of the vendor; and, if the goods are improperly taken away by a third party, the vendor cannot then be sued for the non-delivery of them. (*n*) Where, by the terms of the contract, the goods were to be taken away at the purchaser's expense in fourteen days from the day of the sale, and the purchase-money was to be paid on or before the delivery of the goods, it was held that the seller was bound to deliver when called upon, at any time during the fourteen days, and had not fourteen days to deliver the goods, although the purchaser had fourteen days to take them away. (*o*) If goods are sold upon credit, upon the terms of immediate delivery and payment at a future day, and the purchaser suffers the vendor to retain possession until the period of credit has expired, and the money is not then paid, it has been said that the vendor's lien for the price revives, and that he will not then be bound to deliver the goods until he has received payment of the price. (*p*) If the purchaser has the option

(*m*) Field v. Lelean, *ante.*

(*n*) Wood v. Tassell, 6 Q. B. 234.

(*o*) Hagedorn v. Laing, 6 Taunt.

166.

(*p*) New v. Swain, 1 Dans. & Ll.

193. But see Parsons on Contracts,

of paying either by bill or cash, and he fails to give or tender a bill, he will be deemed to have made his election to pay cash. (*q*)

Some auctioneers sold two ricks of hay which had been distrained by a landlord for rent. By the conditions of sale, the hay was to be removed by the purchaser, and, the time specified for its removal being considered too short, the tenant gave a written permission for the hay to remain on the land for a longer period. The price of the hay was paid at the time of the sale, and a few days afterwards, the purchaser received from the auctioneers a written order, addressed to the tenant, requiring him to permit the purchaser to remove the hay; but the tenant then refused, and would not suffer him to come upon the land to take it. The purchaser then brought an action against the defendants for the non-delivery ; and the defendants pleaded that they did deliver possession to the plaintiff ; and it was held that this plea was supported by the facts; that the permission given by the tenant for the hay to remain on the land for the convenience of the purchaser amounted to an attornment from the tenant to the purchaser, and was equivalent to an express undertaking on the part of the tenant to hold the hay for the purchaser's use and at his disposal. (*r*)

581. *Rejection and non-acceptance of goods sold.*— If more goods are sent than the purchaser agreed to buy, under circumstances which seem to render it incumbent upon him to take the whole or none, he may refuse to receive any portion of the goods so sent,

p. 441. Blackburn on the Contract of Sale, p. 324, and Castle v. Sworder, 6 H. & N. 834 ; 30 L. J., Ex. 310.
(*q*) Schneider v. Foster, 2 H. & N. 4.

(*r*) Salter v. Woollams, Sc. N. R. 65, 67. Noy, 55. Wood v. Manley, 11 Ad. & E. 34. And see *post*, Constructive Delivery.

and is not bound to incur risk or trouble in selecting some of the things and sending back others. (*s*) So, also, a contract for the sale of cotton of a given quality, is not performed by a tender of a larger quantity, out of which the buyer is required to select those bales which answer the description of the cotton contracted for. (*t*) But, if the right of property in the subject-matter of the sale has passed by the bargain from the vendor to the purchaser, the latter is not justified in refusing to accept it and pay the price, by reason of its turning out on examination to be different from what it was supposed and intended to be, or by reason of some unintentional misrepresentation of the quantity or quality by the vendor, or some deterioration in the article between the time of the bargain and delivery. (*u*) Where the vendor agreed to sell, and the purchaser to buy, " the cargo prima donna as it stands, consisting of about 1,300 quarters Ibraila corn, at 30*s.* per quarter, the quantity to be taken from the bill of lading," and the bill of lading described the cargo as being 1,667 quarters ; and afterwards, when the corn came to be measured, it was found to consist of only 1,614 quarters, it was held that the purchaser must put up with the loss, as there had been no intentional misrepresentation, and no fraud on the part of the vendor. (*v*) If the right of property has not passed by the bargain, the purchaser can not be made responsible for the non-acceptance of the subject matter of the sale and non-payment of the price, unless the vendor can show that the article or chattel tendered for acceptance

(*s*) Levy v. Green, 1 El. & El. 969 ; 28 L. J., Q. B. 319. Cunliffe v. Harrison, 6 Exch. 903.

(*t*) Rylands v. Kreitman, 19 C. B. N. S. 351. Boswell v. Kilborn, 15 Moo. P. C. 309.

(*u*) Street v. Blay, 2 B. & Ad. 462. Dawson v. Collis, 10 C. B. 531. Parsons v. Sexton, 16 L. J., C. P. 184 ; 4 C. B. 907.

(*v*) Covas v. Bingham, 2 Ell. & Bl. 836 ; 23 L. J., Q. B. 27.

fairly corresponded in quantity and quality with the thing bargained for and agreed to be bought; for no man can be compelled to take more than he agreed to buy, or a commodity different from that which he purchased. (*y*)

If a purchaser has agreed to buy "about 300 quarters (more or less) of foreign rye, &c.," he is not bound to accept 350 quarters. (*z*)   If the vendor has agreed to sell, and the purchaser to buy, a certain quantity, "say not less than 100, &c.," the words amount to a contract to deliver at least the quantity specified. (*a*) If the quantity is to be between 1,800 and 2,200 quarters, the purchaser is not bound to accept more than 2,200 quarters, nor to accept less than 1,800. (*b*) If a man agrees to sell wool or sugar generally according to sample, and the sample exhibited is a sample of wool in good, dry condition, or a sample of fine white sugar, the purchaser will not be bound to accept damp and mouldy wool or moist brown sugar, unless it be proved that the sample was fairly taken from the bulk, and that the property passed by the bargain. (*c*) Nor is the purchaser bound to accept goods partly of the quality bargained for and partly of an inferior quality, if they are mixed together so that the whole bulk becomes of an inferior quality to that bargained for. (*d*)   If a vendor agrees to manufacture and deliver a specific chattel to a purchaser at a distant place, the vendee is not justified in refusing to accept

(*y*) Hart v. Mills 15 M. & W. 85 ; 15 L. J., Ex. 200.

(*z*) Cross v. Eglin, 2 B. & Ad. 106.

(*a*) Leeming v. Snaith, 16 Q. B. 275 ; 20 L. J., Q. B. 165.

(*b*) Tamvaco v. Lucas, 1 El. & El. 581 ; 28 L. J., Q. B. 153. Hoare v. Rennie, 5 H. & N. 27 ; 29 L. J., Ex. 73. Hibbert v. Shee, 1 Campb. 114.

Johnasson v. Young, 32 L. J., Q. B. 385.

(*c*) Sieveking v. Dutton, 3 C. B. 331 ; 15 L. J., C. P. 276.   Josling v. Kingsford, 13 C. B. N. S. 447 ; 32 L. J., C. P. 94.

(*d*) Nicholson v. Bradfield Union, L. R., 1 Q. B. 620 ; 7 B. & S. 747 ; 35 L. J., Q. B. 176.

it by reason of deterioration necessarily incident to the transit. (*e*) If the article was not inspected by the purchaser at the time of the sale, but was selected by the vendor, the purchaser has a right to inspect and examine it before acceptance; and if, on inspection, it turns out to be a different article from that which was bargained for and agreed to be sold, he may reject it. (*f*) But, if the article has been inspected and selected by the purchaser prior to the sale, or has been purchased with all faults, the purchaser has no right of inspection before payment. (*g*)

If a time for delivery is appointed, and the purchaser, before the time arrives, gives notice to the vendor that he will not accept the goods if delivered, such notice is not an immediate breach of contract, and does not enable the vendor immediately to bring action to recover damages. The vendor is " bound to wait until the time for delivery arrives, to see whether the purchaser will retract his refusal and receive the goods and pay for them." (*h*) But, when a bargain has been made for the manufacture of a certain specified quantity of goods to be supplied from time to time, and paid for after delivery, if the purchaser, having accepted and paid for a portion of the goods contracted for, gives notice to the vendor not to manufacture any more, as he has no occasion for them, and will not accept or pay for them, the vendor may without manufacturing and tendering the rest of the goods, maintain an action against the purchaser for

(*e*) Bull v. Robison, 10 Exch. 346 24 L. J., Ex. 165.

(*f*) Tye v. Finmore, 3 Campb. 461. Toulmin v. Hedley, 2 Car. & K. 157. Curtis v. Pugh, 10 Q. B. 111 ; 16 L. J., Q. B. 199. Lorymer v. Smith, 1

;B. & C. 1. Isherwood v. Whitmore, 11 M. & W. 347.

(*g*) Pettitt v. Mitchell, 4 M. & Gr. 836.

(*h*) Phillpotts v. Evans, 5 M. & W. 477. Ripley v. M'Clure, 4 Exch. 359.

damages. (*i*)   In an action on a contract of sale for
the non-acceptance of goods sold, the vendor must
show that he was ready and willing to deliver the
goods to the purchaser according to the terms of the
contract. (*k*)[1]

582. *Non-payment of the price—Goods bargained
and sold.*—A contract of barter can not be changed
into a contract to pay in money, unless the parties
come to a fresh agreement to that effect. (*l*)   If goods
are sold subject to a condition that, if the purchase
money be not paid by a particular day, they may
be re-sold by the vendor, and the loss on the re-
sale recovered from the purchaser making default, and
the right of re-sale is exercised, or if the purchaser has
refused to take and pay for the goods, and the goods
have been re-sold by the vendor, the vendor can not,
after such re-sale, recover the price of the goods, but
only the damage he has sustained by reason of the

(*i*) Cort v. Amberg., &c., 17 Q. B.
148 ; 20 L. J,. Q. B. 466.

(*k*) Boyd v. Lett, 1 C. B. 222.
Granger v. Dacre, 12 M. & W. 434.

Hannuic v. Goldner, 11 Ib. 856.

(*l*) Harrison v. Luke, 14 M. & W.
141. Atkinson v. Smith, Ib. 695.

[1] " Where a contract to deliver goods at a certain price is
broken, the proper measure of damages in general is the difference between the contract price and the market price of
such goods at the time when the contract is broken, because
the purchaser, having the money in his hands, may go into the
market and buy.   So if a contract to accept and pay for goods
is broken, the same rule may be properly applied, for the seller may take his goods into the market and obtain the current
price for them."   Benjamin on Sales, Am. Ed. § 758, and see
Ballantine v. Robinson, 46 Penn. 177 ; Ganson v. Madigan,
13 Wis. 67 ; Davis v. Shields, 24 Wend. 322 ; Whittemore v.
Coates, 14 Mo. 9 ; Northup v. Cook, 39 Id. 208 ; Haines v.
Tucker, 50 N. H. 307 ; Griswold v. Sabin, 51 Id. 167 ; Whelan
v. Lynch, 65 Barb. 329 ; Hewitt v. Miller, 61 Id. 571 ; Gordon
v. Norris, 49 N. H. 376 ; Haskell v. Hunter, 23 Mich. 305.

non-acceptance of the goods and non-payment of the price. (*m*)　If the price to be paid for the goods is to be fixed by the valuation or award of a third party, to be named by the purchaser, and the latter refuses to name or appoint such valuer, the vendor can not sue for the price, but must bring an action against the purchaser for refusing to make the nomination or appointment. (*n*)　Everything that is to be done on the part of the vendor to complete the sale, and transfer the ownership of the thing sold to the purchaser, and place it at his disposal, so far at least as to enable the latter to obtain possession of it, and deal with it as he may think fit, on payment or tender of the price, must be performed before an action for the price can be maintained. (*o*)

When the right of property in the subject-matter of the sale has passed by the bargain to the purchaser, the latter is not released, as we have already seen, from his obligation to pay the price, by reason of the vendor's neglect to deliver the goods at the time appointed for delivery, unless the time for delivery is of the essence of the contract, and it appears to have been the intention of the parties that the sale should be at an end in case of non-delivery on the day appointed. If the sale is a sale of an ascertained share of a particular chattel, such as a share of a coach or a horse, or a share of a butt of wine, or a cistern of oil, or a cargo of corn, sold as an undivided quantity at an ascertained price, the sale is complete, and the vendor is entitled to the price as soon as he has transferred his share and interest by a properly

(*m*) Lamond v. Davall, 9 Q. B. 1030; 16 L. J., Q. B. 136. Hore v. Milner, 1 Peake, 58.

(*n*) Thurnell v. Balbirnie, 2 M. & W. 786.

(*o*) Smith v. Chance, 2 B. & Ald. 753. Boswell v. Kilborn, 15 Moo P., C. 309.

authenticated contract. In sales of this kind, the ven dor only undertakes to sell and transfer the share, and to convey to the purchaser the same right to the undivided quantity that he himself possessed. He does not engage to put the purchaser into possession of the coach, or the horse, or to divide the wine, or measure off the oil or the corn, and put the purchaser into separate possession of the share.

583. *Goods sold and delivered.*—When goods and chattels have been actually delivered to, and received by, a third party, under circumstances fairly giving rise to a presumption that they were bought and sold, a jury may infer, as we have already seen, the existence of a contract of sale between the parties, although not one word was said about buying and selling, and no price was mentioned or fixed. (*p*) When an Act of Parliament, for the purpose of protecting buyers, prescribes regulations to be followed in the sale and delivery, the vendor can not, if he neglects to observe such regulations, recover the price. (*q*)

584. *Sale of goods on credit.*—If goods are sold on credit, the vendor can not sue for the price until the period of credit has expired, (*r*) unless the giving of credit has been made conditional on the perform- ance of some precedent act by the purchaser. If the goods are sold upon the terms that the purchaser is to give his acceptance at two or more months for the price, and are then delivered to the purchaser, and the latter refuses to give his acceptance according to the contract, the vendor can not forthwith bring an action for goods sold and delivered, but must either sue on the promise to give the acceptance, or wait

---

(*p*) *Ante.* Bennett v. Henderson, 2 Stark. 550   Coles v. Bulman, 6 C. B, 184.

(*q*) Cundell v. Dawson, 4 C. B. 378. (*r*) Paul v. Dod, 2 C. B. 800.   Price v. Nixon, 5 Taunt. 338.

the termination of the period during which the bill had to run. (*s*) If however, the goods are sold on the terms that the vendor is to have a bill at three months or cash, and the purchaser fails to give the bill, the vendor may at once sue for a fair and reasonable price in cash. (*t*) Where, by the terms of a contract of sale, the purchaser was to pay down £30 and £214 by bills of £30 each, payable in succession every three months, and the purchaser omitted to pay the £30 and to give the bills, it was held that the vendor could not maintain an action for the price of the goods until the expiration of the period at which the last bill would become due, but must sue on the special contract for the non-payment of the money and the non-delivery of the bills. (*u*) But where the defendant, when a portion of the goods has been delivered under the contract, repudiates the transaction and refuses to receive any more, the plaintiff has a right to treat the contract as rescinded, and to sue for the value of the goods which have been delivered. (*v*) If the contract is entire for the delivery of an undivided quantity of goods at a certain price by a certain time, the vendor can not, after delivering part of the goods, sue for the price of that part until the whole has been delivered ; but, if he delivers part, and such part is retained and used by the purchaser after the time for the delivery of the whole has expired, the purchaser is bound, notwithstanding the non-performance of the contract by the

---

(*s*) Mussen v. Price, 4 East, 147. Dutton v. Solomonson, 3 B. & P. 582.

(*t*) Rugg v. Weir, 16 C. B., N. S. 477. Nickson v. Jepson, 2 Stark. 227. And see *post*, Conditional Sales.

(*u*) Paul v. Dod, 2 C. B. 800 ; 15 L, J., C. P. 177.

(*v*) Bartholomew v. Markwick, 15 C. B., N. S. 711 ; 33 L. J., C. P. 145. Lee v. Risdon, 7 Taunt. 189.

vendor, to pay what the part retained and used by him may be reasonably worth. (*y*)

585. *Actual and constructive delivery of goods.*— The delivery of goods may be either real or symbolical, actual or constructive.[1] When the subject-matter of the sale is capable of manual delivery and occupation, such as a watch, a book, or a gun, and is actually transferred from the hand of the vendor to that of the purchaser or his agent, there is a real or actual delivery. So, if, being a bulky commodity, it is removed from the warehouse of the vendor to that of the purchaser, and placed under the power and control of the latter, there is an actual delivery. But, although there has been no manual transfer from hand to hand, and the goods have not been removed from the place where they were deposited at the time of the sale, if the vendor has handed the key of a box or warehouse where they were deposited, to the purchaser, in order that he may remove them, or has given to the purchaser a delivery order or warrant for their removal, and placed them at the disposal of the latter, there is a symbolical or constructive delivery, provided, at the time of the delivery of the key or warrant, the particular goods to be removed had been weighed out or measured, or separated from the bulk and identified, and nothing but delivery remained to be performed by the vendor in order to complete his part of the contract of sale. (*z*)[2]

(*y*) Oxendale v. Wetherell, 4 M. & R. 431.

(*z*) Chaplin v. Rogers, 1 East. 194. Greaves v. Hepke, 2 B. & Ald. 133.

[1] Sumner v. Hamlet, 12 Pick. 82.

[2] 2 Kent Com. 496; Crofoot v. Bennett, 2 Comst. 260. But a flock of sheep sold at so much a head, they to be counted after the sale, is a valid sale; Groat v. Gile, 51 N. Y. 431; and see Arnold v. Delano, 4 Cush. 33; Hyde v. Lathrop, 2 Abb.

When goods and chattels are incapable of manual
occupation and delivery, such as a haystack standing
in a meadow, the same strict evidence of transfer can

App. Dec. (N. Y.) 436; Kimberly v. Patchin, 16 N. Y. 330;
Foot v. Marsh, 51 Id. 288. But a contract to sell a "fare of
fish " does not change the property in the fish; Shaw v. Nudd,
8 Pick. 9; the general principle being that as long as any
operation of weighing, measuring, counting, or the like,
remains to be done, in order to ascertain the quantity, price, or
quality, to be delivered, there is no sale; Macomber v. Parker,
13 Pick. 175; Gibbs v. Benjamin, 45 Vt. 124; Hale v. Hunt-
ley, 21 Id. 147; Fuller v. Benn, 34 N. H. 290; Hutchings v.
Gilchrist, 23 Vt. 88; Prescott v. Locke, 51 N. H. 94; Messer
v. Woodman, 22 Id. 172; Gilman v. Hill, 36 Id. 311, 320;
Jones v. Pearce, 25 Ark. 545; Abat v. Atkinson, 21 La. Ann.
414; Bailey v. Smith, 43 N. H. 141; Kaufman v. Stone, 25
Ark. 336; Strauss v. Ross, 25 Ind. 300; McClung v. Kelley,
21 Iowa, 508; Mason v Thompson, 18 Pick. 305. But where it
appears from the circumstances that it was the intention of the
parties to make a sale without a measurement being ascertained, the rule may be different. So, in a case where a question arose as to whether certain timber lying in a mill-pond
at the end of a water-course had been delivered, where the
purchaser had signed a memorandum, as follows: "Received
of the vendor four shots of white oak plank, ... for
which I promise to pay him twenty-six dollars per thousand,
board measure. The above timber delivered in the mill-pond,"
&c., the seller signing, at the same time a writing acknowledging "that he had received of the purchaser two hundred dollars in part pay for 'the timber in question,' remainder to
be paid in ninety days from surveying. The canalage to be
paid by the purchaser, when he takes the plank and timber
from the pond;" and providing that the purchaser might procure a measurement of the timber by the superintendent of the
canal, and that he would abide by that measurement; it was
held that a jury would be warranted in finding such intention;
Reddle v. Varnum, 20 Pick. 175; and see Marble v. Moore, 102
Mass. 443; Stone v. Peacock, 35 Me. 385; where the ascertainment of the price is a mere mathematical computation, which
can have no further effect in bringing the minds of the contracting parties together, the sale may be considered as complete without it; see Adams Mining Co. v. Senter, 26 Mich. 73;
Tyler v Strong, 21 Barb. 198; Sewell v. Eaton, 6 Wis. 490.

not ordinarily be given, and it is enough for the vendor to show that the purchaser was himself to have fetched away the article, and that the vendor has given him the power and opportunity of removing it. (*a*)[1] But if the thing sold remains in the vendor's dwelling-house or warehouse, the mere circumstance that the vendor has placed the article at the disposal of the purchaser, and given him an opportunity of removing it, if he had thought fit, would not, it is apprehended, afford even primâ facie evidence of delivery. (*b*)   And it must be observed that the mere placing of goods at the disposal of the purchaser, or putting it in his power to remove them, will not in any case constitute a delivery, if the vendor retains his lien for the price, or possesses any dominion or control over them. (*c*)   Thus, if a contract

---

(*a*) Smith v. Chance, 2 B. & Ald. 755. Wood v. Manley, 11 Ad. & E. 35. Tansley v. Turner, 2 Sc. 238 ; 2 Bing. N. C. 151.

(*b*) Thompson v. Maceroni, 3 B. & C. 2.

(*c*) Goodall v. Skelton, 2 H. Bl. 316.

[1] This was the case in Dyer v. Libby, 61 Me. 45, the court saying, " The fact that it was one of the conditions of the sale that the plaintiff should haul the hay to the depot, is not inconsistent with the proposition that it might have been delivered so as to become the property of the defendant at the barn."   And see Comfort v. Kiersted, 26 Barb. 472 ; Southwestern Freight, &c. Co. v. Stanard, 44 Mo. 71 ; Dexter v. Norton, 55 Barb. 272 ; Bradley v. Wheeler, 44 N. Y.   ; McCrae v. Young, 43 Ala. 622 ; Kaufman v. Stone, 25 Ark. 336 ; Abat v. Atkinson, 21 La. Ann. 414 ; Browning v. Hamilton, 42 Ala. 484 ; Chase v. Willard, 57 Me. 157 ; Frost v. Woodruff, 54 Ill. 155 ; McDonald v. Hewett, 15 Johns. 349 ; Rapelye v. Mackie, 6 Cowen, 250 ; Russell v. Nicholl, 3 Wend. 112 ; Outwater v. Dodge, 7 Cowen, 85 ; Downes v. Thompson, 2 Hill, 137 ; Damon v. Osborn, 1 Pick. 476 ; Sewell v. Eaton, 6 Wis. 490 ; Watts v. Hendry, 13 Fla. 523 ; Houdlette v. Tallman, 14 Me. 400 ; Craig v. Smith, Sup. Ct. of Pa. 5 Law R. 112 ; Davis v. Hill, 3 N. H. 382 ; Woods v. McGee, 7 Ohio, 128 ; Jewett v. Warren, 12 Mass. 300 ; Decker v. Furniss, Hill & D. 611 ; Kein v. Tupper, 52 N. Y. 550 ; Ford v. Chambers, 28 Cal. 13.

has been entered into for the sale of oil, wine, or
brandy, and the portion to be delivered is separated
from a mass of the commodity in bulk, and put into
casks marked with the name of the purchaser, and
placed at his disposal, there is no delivery, if the article
remains at the time, and notwithstanding such trans-
position and appropriation, in the warehouse of the
vendor, and under his dominion and control. And if
a portion of the quantity so separated is actually delivered into the hands of the purchaser, this will not
vary the condition of the vendor, if the contract is
entire and indivisible, as he has a lien upon the residue,
and has not done that which is tantamount to a delivery of the whole.[1] But if the contract of sale is
divisible, and the portion removed can be referred to
a separate and distinct contract of sale, then the vendor
will be entitled to sue for the price of the portion so
handed over to the purchaser. (*d*)[2] If the goods,
however, are put into the possession of a third party,
on the understanding that they are not to be removed
by the purchaser until the price is paid, an action may,
it seems, be maintained by the vendor for the price of
them as goods sold and delivered. (*e*) A contract for
the sale of cotton of a given quality is not performed
by a tender of a larger quantity, out of which the buyer
is required to select those bales which answer the description of the cotton contracted for. (*f*)

(*d*) Holderness v. Shackels, 8 B. &
C. 621 ; 3 M. & R. 33.
(*e*) Dodsley v. Varley, 12 Ad. & E.
634.

(*f*) Rylands v. Kreitman, 19 C. B.
N. S. 351. Boswell v. Kilborn, 15 Moo.
P. C. 309.

[1] Russell v. Minor, 22 Wend. 259; Whipple v. Gilpatrick,
19 Me. 427; Hussey v. Thornton, 4 Mass. 405; Riley v.
Wheeler, 42 Vt. 528 ; Buckmaster v. Smith, 22 Id. 203; Allen
v. Delano, 55 Me. 113.
[2] See cases cited in last note.

586. *Proof of delivery*—The question of delivery, is a question of fact, and is to be determined by reference to all the surrounding circumstances, which must be looked at in order to see if there has been a virtual change of possession as well as a change of ownership. (*g*) The taking of samples, coopering casks, and the general exercise of acts of ownership by the purchaser over the subject-matter of the sale, in those cases where nothing but delivery remains to be performed to execute the contract, are circumstances from which an actual transfer of the possession of the article to the purchaser may be fairly presumed ; (*h*) but they are equivocal acts, open to explanation, and afford no sufficient or satisfactory proof of delivery, if they have been done without the knowledge or sanction of the vendor. (*i*) The marking of goods, and packing them up in boxes. or cloths, belonging to the purchaser does not constitute a delivery so long as the goods remain in the possession of the vendor, in as much as the latter has not, until he has actually parted with the possession of them, lost his lien for the price ; (*k*) and the delivery of part of the goods does not as before mentioned, operate as a constructive delivery of the whole, so as to deprive the vendor of his right to the possession of the residue until payment of the price. (*l*) The unpacking or unloading of goods for the purpose of inspection and examination by a purchaser who has not previously selected or examined them, is not necessarily an acceptance and taking pos-

---

(*g*) Blenkinsop v. Clayton, 1 Moore, 331.

(*h*) Wood v. Tassell, 6 Q. B 236.

(*i*) Dixon v. Yates, 5 B. & Ad. 313 ; 2 N. & M. 177. Craven v. Ryder, 6

Taunt. 433. See *post ;* Delivery Orders. Dock Warrants.

(*k*) Boulter v. Arnott, 1 C. & M 333.

(*l*) Bunney v. Poyntz, 4 B. & Ad. 568.

session of the goods by the purchaser so as to render him liable to an action for the price. (*m*) But if he lands and stores the goods, and keeps them an unreasonable time, or does more than is necessary to be done for inspection and examination, he makes the goods his own. (*n*)[1]

587. *Delivery to carriers.*—Although the acceptance and receipt of a carrier to whom goods are delivered to be conveyed to a purchaser, are not the acceptance and receipt of the purchaser within the meaning of the Statute of Frauds,[2] yet a delivery, by a vendor to a carrier, of goods sold, is a sufficient delivery to the purchaser to enable the vendor (if the contract of sale is properly authenticated by a memorandum in writing signed by the purchaser or by earnest or part payment), to maintain an action for the price. The delivery of the goods to the carrier operates as a delivery to the purchaser; the whole property immediately vests in him; he alone can bring an action for any injury done to the goods; and, if any accident happens to the goods, it is at his risk, (*o*) unless by the terms of the contract the transfer of the right of property and risk are made dependent on the arrival of the goods at their place of destination. (*p*) The only exception to the purchaser's rights over the goods is that the vendor, in case of the insolvency of the purchaser, may stop them *in transitu.* The placing

(*m*) Curtis v. Pugh, 10 Q. B. 111 ; 16 L. J., Q. B. 199. Toulmin v. Hedley, 2 Car. & K. 157.

(*n*) Chapman v. Morton, 11 M. & W. 540.

(*o*) Dutton v. Solomonson, 3 B. & P.

584. Gronin v. Mendham, 5 M. & S. 191. Lord Cottenham, Dunlop v. Lambert, 6 Cl. & Fin. 621. Tregelles v. Sewell, 7 H. & N. 574.

(*p*) Calcutta, &c., Steam Navigation Company v. De Mattos, *ante.*

[1] And see *ante*, § 576.
[2] *Ante*, § 561, and note.

of goods ordered on board ship is good evidence
of delivery, but not of acceptance and receipt within
the Statute of Frauds. The vendor, after he has once
parted with the goods in fulfillment of an absolute and
unconditional contract of sale, and placed them in a
course of transmission to the purchaser, can not, as
we have already seen, lawfully re-take them from the
carrier, unless the purchaser becomes bankrupt or insolvent whilst they are in the hands of the carrier, or
unless the goods have been sent merely on approval,
or under some special contract or conditional sale,
reserving to the vendor certain rights over the
goods. (*q*) [1]

588. *Damages for non-performance of a contract
for the sale of goods and chattels—Non-performance
by the purchaser.*—If a vendor brings his action
against a purchaser for the non-payment of the price
of goods sold and delivered at a fixed price, and the
delivery is proved, the measure of damages is obviously
the price agreed to be paid.[2] If no price was fixed
and determined upon, the measure of damages will be

(*q*) *Ante.* Wilmshurst v. Bowker,   8 Sc. N. R. 571; 7 M. & Gr. 882.
Key v. Cotesworth, 22 L. J., Ex. 4.

[1] And see *post*, section 597.
[2] The ordinary action of the vender against the purchaser,
where the default of payment does not rescind the contract,
is for goods sold and delivered. Messer v. Woodman, 22 N.
H. 172; Gordon v. Norris, 49 N. H. 382; Thompson v. Alger,
12 Met. 428; Gauson v. Madigan, 13 Wis. 67; Bement v.
Smith, 15 Wend. 493; Ockington v. Richey, 41 N. H. 279;
Sands v. Taylor, 5 Johns. 395. Payment by a check is a payment in cash, and if the check be dishonored, it seems this is
a breach of the condition of the sale. See Smith v. Miller,
43 N. Y. 171. As to payments by promissory notes, see
Clark v. Draper, 19 N. H. 419; Milliken v. Warren, 57 Me.
46; Arnold v. Delano, 4 Cush. 41; Thurston v. Blanchard, 22
Pick. 18.

the usual and customary price for goods of a similar character quality, and description. If the goods have not been delivered to the purchaser, but the ownership and right of property therein have been transferred by the bargain to the latter, and the vendor sues for the price of them as "goods bargained and sold," the measure of damages is, in like manner, the price agreed upon, which must be paid in full, without any deduction in respect of losses by fire, or tempest, or accident. But, if the right of property has not been divested out of the vendor, and transferred to the purchaser, the vendor can not bring an action for the price of the goods ; for he can not have both the goods and the price ; but he may sue the purchaser for his breach of contract in not accepting them, in which case the measure of damages will be the difference between the agreed price and the marketable value of the goods at the time they were tendered to, and refused acceptance by, the purchaser, in addition to the costs, charges, and expenses necessarily incurred by the vendor in fulfilling his part of the contract. If the market price of the article has declined after the making of the contract, and the purchaser gives notice to the vendor that he will not accept, the proper measure of damages is not the difference between the contract price and the market price on the day the notice was given, but at the time when the contract ought to have been fulfilled by the acceptance of the goods, if it had been carried into effect as originally intended. (*r*) If the goods have been resold by the vendor within a reasonable time after the breach of contract by the purchaser, the measure of damages will be the difference between the price agreed to be given and the price realized on

(*r*) Philpotts v. Evans, 5 M. & W.   145.   Startup v. Cortazzi, 2 C. M. & 475.   Boorman v. Nash, 9 B. & C.   R. 165.

the re-sale, with the costs and expenses of the re-sale ; but, if the re-sale has been unreasonably delayed until the market has fallen, the price realized on such re-sale will not afford a true criterion of the damage. (*s*)[1]

589. *Damages for non-performance by the vendor.*[2] —If a purchaser brings his action against the vendor for a breach of contract in not delivering goods sold, or not tendering them for acceptance, or for re-selling and converting them to his own use, the measure of damages will be the difference between the price agreed to be paid and the marketable value of the goods at the time and place when and where they ought to have been delivered to the purchaser. (*t*)

(*s*) Stewart v. Cauty, 8 M. & W. 162. Pott v. Flather, 16 L. J., Q. B. 366.   29 L. J., Ex. 180. Dingle v. Hare, 7 C. B., N. S. 145. Peterson v. Ayre, 13 C. B. 353.

(*t*) Chinery v. Viall, 5 H. & N. 288 ;

[1] And in Chicago v. Green, 9 Wall. 726, evidence that the plaintiff was left, by the breach of the contract, with a large amount of raw material on his hands, was also admitted as to the measure of damages.

[2] In the case of a steam-engine which was not delivered upon a certain day named in the contract, the rent of the factory, which would have been obtained had the engine been in its place, was recoverable as damages. Griffin v. Colver, 16 N. Y. 489 ; and see, Blanchard v. Ely, 21 Wend. 342; Freeman v. Clute, 3 Barb. 424. In McHose v. Fulmer, 73 Pa. St. 365 (said Sharswood, J.), "When a vendor fails to comply with his contract, the general rule for the measure of damages undoubtedly is the difference between the contract and the market price of the article at the time of the breach. This is for the evident reason that the vendee can go into the market and obtain the article contracted for at that price. But when the circumstances of the case are such that the vendee can not thus supply himself, the rule does not apply, for the reason of it ceases. The ordinary measure would not remunerate him when the article could not be obtained elsewhere. If an article of the same quality can not be procured in the market, its market price can not be ascertained, and we are without the necessary *data* for the application of the general rule. This is a contingency which must be considered

Where the defendant did not deliver a quantity of
iron in three equal proportions as agreed, it was held
that the true measure of damages in the absence of
proof by the defendant that the plaintiff might have
mitigated the loss, was the sum of the differences between the contract and market prices of each third of
the quantity on the respective dates at which they
ought to have been delivered. (*u*) If the contract is
for the sale and delivery of articles which can be

(*u*) Brown v. Muller, L. R., 7 Ex.   Johnson, L. R., 8 C. P. 167 ; 42 L. J.,
319 ; 41 L. J., Ex. 214.   Roper v.   C. P. 165.

to have been within the contemplation of the parties, for they
must be presumed to know whether such articles are of
limited production or not.   In such a case the true measure is
the actual loss which the vendee sustains in his own manufacture, by having to use an inferior article or not receiving
the advance on his contract price upon any contracts which
he had himself made in reliance upon the fulfillment of the
contract by the vendor.   We do not mean to say, that if he
undertakes to fill his own contracts with an inferior article,
and in consequence such article is returned on his hands, he
can recover of his vendor, besides the loss sustained on his
contracts, all the extraordinary loss incurred by his attempting
what was clearly an unwarrantable experiment.   His legiti-
mate loss is the difference between the contract price he was
to pay to his vendor and the price he was to receive.   This is
a loss which springs directly from the non-fulfillment of the
contract."   If the vendor knows that the purchase is made in
order to enable the buyer to fulfill an existing contract for re-
sale at a profit, the vendor is liable, if the non-delivery be his
fault, for the amount of such prospective profits ; Mossmere
v. New York Shot, &c., Co., 40 N. Y. 422 ; but the plaintiff
can not recover damages for his trouble and expense in procuring the contract ; Stevens v. Lyford, 7 N. H. 360 ; and see
Merrimack Mfg. Co. v. Quintard, 107 Mass. 127 ; Western
Gravel Road Co. v. Cox, 39 Ind. 260 ; 2 Chitty Contr. (11 Am.
ed.) 1325, note (*h*) ; Wolcott v. Mount, 7 Vroom, 262 ; Bridges
v. Stickney, 38 e. 361 ; Fox v. Harding, 7 Cush. 516 ; Masterton v. Mayor of Brooklyn, 7 Hill, 61 ; Philadelphia &c. R.
R. Co. v. Howard, 13 How. (U. S.) 307.

readily bought in the public market, the measure of damages is the difference between the agreed price and what it would have cost the buyer if he had gone into the market and purchased similar goods at the time the contract was broken. (*v*) But where, after breach of a written agreement to deliver goods, the buyer, at the seller's request, waited several months before buying goods in the place of those contracted for, it was held that the true measure of damages was the difference between the contract price and the price of the substituted goods, though this price was greater than that of such goods when the contract was first broken. (*y*) But if the goods are ordered in England by a merchant abroad, for the purpose of being exported and re-sold in a foreign market, and the order is accepted, and the vendor, knowing that the goods are required for a foreign market, undertakes to forward the goods, but neglects so to do, the measure of damages is not the difference between the agreed price and the marketable value of the goods in England, but between the price and the marketable value of the goods at the place where they would have been re-sold by the purchaser. (*z*) The purchaser can not recover as special damage the loss of anticipated profits in the home market ; nor, if he has contracted to re-sell the goods at a profit, can he recover such profit. (*a*)

If the vendor has a month, or any specific period

(*v*) Josling v. Irvine, *ante.* Jones v. Just, L. R., 3 Q. B. 197 ; 37 L. J., Q. B. 89.

(*y*) Ogle v. Vane (Earl), L. R., 2 Q. B. 275 ; L. R., 3 Q. B. 272 ; 36 L. J., Q. B. 77 ; 37 L. J., Q. B. 77.

(*z*) Bridge v. Wain, 1 Stark. 504. Borries v. Hutchinson, 18 C. B., N. S.

445 ; 34 L. J., C. P. 169. O'Hanlan v. Gt. West. Rail. Co., 6 B. & S. 484 ; 34 L. J., Q. B. 154.

(*a*) Williams v. Reynolds, 34 L. J., Q. B. 221, qualifying and restricting Dunlop v. Higgins, 1 H. L. C. 403, and overruling Waters v. Towers, 8 Exch. 401.

of time, allowed to him for making the delivery, and finds, before the time has elapsed, that he will be unable to complete the delivery, and gives notice to the purchaser that he refuses to proceed therewith, and the price rises, the measure of damages is the difference between the contract price and the higher price of the subject-matter on the last day of the period within which the delivery ought to have been made. (*b*) [1]　If the vendor of shares neglects to deliver the shares, or complete the transfer, the measure of damages is the difference between the price agreed to be paid and the market price on the day on which the sale should have been perfected ; and the purchaser is not entitled to damages in respect of a further advance of price taking place afterwards. (*c*)　In a case where the purchase-money had been paid in advance, the true measure of damages was held to be, not the amount of the purchase money, but the marketable value of the property at the time it ought to have been delivered to the purchaser ; for to that extent only was the purchaser damnified, unless he had sustained some special damage by reason of the non-delivery at the time appointed. (*d*)　But in the case of a contract for the sale and purchase of shares, when the vendor holds in his hands the money of the purchaser, and thereby prevents him from using it, and from buying other shares therewith, the proper measure of damages would seem to be the highest price for which the same number of shares might be purchased in the market, either on the day the contract was broken, or at any time between that

---

(*b*) Leigh v. Paterson, 8 Taunt, 540. Loder v. Kekule, 3 C. B., N. S. 140

(*c*) Tempest v. Kilner, 3 C. B. 253. Gainsford v. Carroll, 2 B. & C. 624.

Shaw v. Holland, 15 M. & W. 145.

(*d*) Dutch v. Warren, cited 2 Burr. 1011, 1012.　Valpy v. Oakeley, 16 Q. B. 941.

[1] See Merrimack M'f'g. Co. v. Quintard, 107 Mass. 127.

day and the day of trial, if the action has been brought without any unreasonable or improper delay. (*e*) When the action is not brought upon the special contract, but for the recovery of the purchase money, as money had and received, on the ground of a total failure of the consideration for the payment, the whole purchase money is recoverable. If special damage has been sustained by reason of the non-delivery, such special damage may, under certain circumstances, be recovered. (*f*)

If a bill has been given for the price of the goods, and the bill has been dishonored before delivery, nominal damages only are recoverable from the vendor in an action for not delivering the goods according to his contract. (*g*)

590. *Specific performance of contracts for the sale of goods and chattels.*—Performance of a contract for the sale of goods and chattels will not generally be decreed, not because of their personal nature, but because damages at law, calculated on the market price of the goods, are in general as complete a remedy for the purchaser as the delivery of the goods contracted for, inasmuch as with the damages, he may ordinarily purchase the same quantity of the like goods. (*h*) But a contract for the sale of a specific chattel, such as a barge or a vessel, (*i*) or a chattel having a "pretium affectionis" or a peculiar value resting on its individuality, such as "the Pusey Horn;" (*k*) St. Margaret's silver tobacco-box; (*l*) the silver altar-piece of the

(*e*) Owen v. Routh, 14 C. B. 337; 23 L. J., C. P. 105. Shaw v. Holland, *ante.* Sedgwick on Damages, 265.

(*f*) Black v. Baxendale, 1 Exch. 410.

(*g*) Griffiths v. Perry, 1 Ell. & Ell. 680; 28 L. J., Q. B. 204.

(*h*) Story's Eq. Jur. § 717. Buxton v. Lister, 3 Atk. 383. Pooley v. Budd, 14 Beav. 43.

(*i*) Claringbould v. Curtis, 21 L. J., Ch., 541.

(*k*) Pusey v. Pusey, 1 Vern. 272.

(*l*) Fells v. Read, 3 Ves. 70.

Duke of Somerset ; (*m*) the insignia and decorations of a lodge of freemasons ; (*n*) and old family pictures, (*o*) and heirlooms, (*p*) will be enforced in specie. A contract for the sale of 500 chests of tea is not a contract which can be specifically performed, because it does not relate to any chests of tea in particular ; but a contract to sell certain chests of a particular kind of tea deposited in a particular locality may be enforced in specie ; and the purchaser may obtain an injunction to prevent the seller from delivering it to any other person. (*q*) Wherever the object of sale is such that there is an uncertainty whether the purchaser can procure another chattel of the same kind and value, or the possession of it is desirable for certain purposes which no other chattel of the same kind will answer, a specific performance will be decreed. (*r*) [1]

(*m*) Duke of Somerset v. Cookson, 3 P. Wms. 389.

(*n*) Lloyd v. Loaring, 6 Ves. 773.

(*o*) Lady Arundell v. Phipps, 10 Ves. 139. Lowther v. Lowther, 13 Ves. 95.

(*p*) Earl Macclesfield v. Davis, 3. Ves. & B. 16.

(*q*) Lord Westbury, Holroyd v. Marshall, 33 L. J., Ch. 196 ; 10 H. L. C. 209.

(*r*) Falcke v. Gray, 29 L. J., Ch. 28.

[1] A court will decree specific performance wherever the article is of such a nature as that it can not be readily purchased, as in the English case of Thorn v. Commissioners of Public Works, 32 Beav. 490 ; where the articles were the arch stone, span-drill stone, and the " Bramley Fall " stone, of the old Westminster bridge ; Sarter v. Gordon, 2 Hill Ch. 126 ; Young v. Burton, 1 McMullan, 255 ; so contracts to deliver a certain sort of clay ; Forman v. Clark, 3 Stoct. (N. J.) 306 ; Clark v. Flint, 22 Pick. 231 ; or bank shares, Cowles v. Whitman, 10 Conn. 121 ; but where a quantity of articles are contracted to be delivered, some of which can be readily procured, and some of which can not, specific performance will be decreed as to them all ; McGowin v. Remington, 12 Pa. St. 56 ; but not of a contract to deliver stock, because stock ordinarily can be obtained in the market. Leach v. Forbes, 11 Gray, 506 ; Todd v. Tufft, 7 Allen, 371 ; Treasurer, &c. v. Commercial, &c. Co., 23 Cal.

591. *Abatement of the contract price.*—In contracts for the sale of goods and chattels, the agreed price may be reduced by evidence showing that the goods were not of the proper quality or description ; (*s*) and the purchaser is not, by reason of his having given such evidence, and obtained a reduction in the amount of the contract price in an action brought against him by the vendor, precluded from bringing his cross action to recover compensation for any special damage that he may subsequently sustain by reason of the breach of the contract. (*t*) Care, however, must be taken to mark the distinction between an action on the contract itself for the agreed price, and an action upon a bill of exchange or promissory note given by way of payment for the amount. In the former, the value only can be recovered ; in the latter, the party holding bills given for the price of the goods supplied can recover on them, unless there has been a total failure of the consideration. If the consideration fails partially, as by the inferiority of the

(*s*) Cutler v. Close, 5 C. & P. 337.　　(*t*) Mondel v. Steel, 8 M. & W. 858.
Allen v. Cameron, 1 Cr. .& M. 832.　　Rigge v. Burbridge, 15 M. & W. 598.
Turner v. Diaper, 2 M. & Gr. 241.

390 ; Ross v. Union Pacific R. R. Co., Wooler v. C. C. R. 26. But equity will not decree specific performance of a·contract of an actor to act ; Ford v. Jermon, 6 Phila. 6. " The reason," as was said by the court, Hare, J., in that case, "why the courts will not attempt to force an unwilling performer before the public, is the harshness of compelling obedience by imprisonment, and the difficulty, or rather impossibility, of knowing whether his obedience is real or illusory, when he finally consents to appear. In order to render such a decree effectual, it would be necessary to appoint a master whose duty it should be to frequent the theatre and decide whether the mistakes and incongruities by which the part might be disfigured, were in contempt of the order of the court or unintentional ; and see the question considered and cases cited in Morgan's Law of Literature, vol. 2, § 325.

article furnished, the buyer must seek his remedy by a cross action. (*u*) Thus, where a contract was entered into for the purchase of goods of "good quality and moderate price," and the price was estimated at £1,000, and bills were given for that amount, it was held to be no defense to an action on the bills that the goods turned out to be worth much less than the estimated price, and that the acceptor had paid on the bills more than the real value of the goods. (*v*) The contract also may be divisible ; but the security is entire.

592. *Of the vendor's lien for the price of goods sold.*—When different times are not expressly appointed for payment and delivery, the acts of payment and delivery are, as we have seen, concurrent, and constitute mutual conditions to be performed at the same time, so that the purchaser can not demand the thing sold without paying or offering to pay the price, nor the vendor the price without delivering or offering to deliver the subject-matter of the sale. " If I sell you my horse for £10, if you will have the horse, I must have the money ; or, if I will have the money, you must have the horse." (*y*) [1]

(*u*) Tye v. Gwynne, 2 Camp. 346. Moggridge v. Jones. 3 Camp. 38 ; 14 East, 486. Camac v. Warriner, 1 C. B. 357.

(*v*) Obbard v. Betham, M. & M. 483.

(*y*) Callonel v. Briggs, 1 Salk. 113. Lock v. Wright, 1 Str. 571 ; 8 Mod. 41. Withers v. Reynolds, 2 B. & Ad. 882. Atkinson v. Smith, 14 M. & W. 695.

[1] See Meany v. Head, 1 Mason, 319 ; Cornwall v. Haight, 8 Barb. 328 ; Bowen v. Burk, 13 Penn. St. 146 ; Milliken v. Warren, 57 Me. 46 ; Arnold v. Delano, 4 Cush. 38 ; Clark v. Draper, 19 N. H. 419, 421 ; Wilde, J. in Parks v. Hall, 2 Pick. 212 ; Barrett v. Pritchard, 2 Pick. 515 ; Burr v. Logan, 5 Harring, 52. But a lien may be waived by an agreement, express or implied ; Pickett v. Bullock, 52 N. H. 354. General delivery of a part of the goods is a sufficient delivery to destroy

593. *When the vendor may re-sell.*—If ascertained chattels have been bargained and sold by a properly authenticated contract, and the right of property has passed to the purchaser, the vendor can not, as we have already seen, rescind the contract and re-vest the right of property in himself, and re-sell the goods, by reason of the neglect of the vendee to take and pay for the goods at the time appointed; (*z*) but if the purchaser continues in default, and will not perform his part of the contract, the vendor may re-sell them within a reasonable period after he has given the purchaser express notice of his intention so to do.[1] A mere notice to remove the goods and pay the price will not justify the vendor in re-selling; (*a*) but if the latter gives to the purchaser a distinct intimation of his intention to re-sell in case of the non-removal and non-payment of the goods within a reasonable period from the receipt of the notice,[2] and the purchaser then

---

(*z*) Martindale v. Smith, 1 Q. B. 395. Milgate v. Kebble, 3 Sc. N. R. 358; 3 M. & Gr. 100. Wilmshurst v. Bowker, 8 Sc. N. R. 571; 7 M. & Gr. 882. Key v. Cotesworth, 7 Exch. 607; 22 L. J., Ex. 4. Page v. Cowasjee, L. R., 1 P. C. 127.

(*a*) Greaves v. Ashlin, 3 Campb. 426.

the vendor's lien; Buckley v. Furniss, 17 Wend. 507; Parks v. Hall, 2 Pick. 206; French v. Freeman, 43 Vt. 93; Haskell v. Rice, 11 Gray, 240; the giving of a promissory note is not such a payment as will divert a lien; Clark v. Draper, 19 N. H. 419; Thurston v. Blanchard, 22 Pick. 18; Arnold v. Delano, 4 Cush. 41; as to whether the indorsement of a bill of lading, dock warrant, or warehouse certificate will destroy a vendor's lien, see Arnold v. Delano, 4 Cush. 39.

[1] Haines v. Tucker, 50 N. H. 313; Redmon v. Smock, 28 Ind. 365; Saladin v. Mitchell, 45 Ill. 80; Rosenbaums v. Weeden, 18 Gratt. 785.

[2] Id. Girard v. Taggart, 5 Serg. & R. 19; Debble v. Corbett, 5 Bosw. 202; Newhall v. Vargus, 15 Me. 314; Neil v. Cheves, 1 Bailey (S. C.), 537; Warren v. Buckminster, 24 N. H. 336, 344; Pollen v. Le Roy, 30 N. Y. 558; Sands v. Taylor,

refuses to take and pay for the goods, he may fairly
be deemed either to have himself repudiated or abandoned the contract, or to be an assenting party to the
sale, or to have given the vendor an implied authority
to re-sell. (*b*)　If the goods are of a perishable nature,
and the purchaser refuses to receive them, the vendor
is entitled to re-sell them, to prevent their deterioration or destruction, after giving the purchaser due
notice of his intention.[1]

594. *Insolvency of the purchaser.*—When the purchaser becomes insolvent before the contract for sale
has been completely performed, the seller, notwithstanding he may have agreed to allow credit for the
goods, is not bound to deliver any more goods under
the contract until the price of the goods not yet delivered is tendered to him ; and if a debt is due to him
for goods already delivered, he is entitled to refuse to
deliver any more till he is paid the debt due for those
already delivered, as well as the price of those still to

(*b*) Maclean v. Dunn, 1 Moo. & P.   780, 781 ; 4 Bing. 722. Langfort v.
Tyler, 1 Salk. 113.

5 Johns. 395; Adams v. Mirick, cited in 5 Serg. & R. 32;
Girard v. Taggart, 5 Serg. & R. 19; M'Combs v. M'Kennan,
2 Watts & S. 216.

  [1] And this re-sale rescinds the original sale; see Warden
v. Marshall, 99 Mass. 305 ; Priest v. Wheeler, 101 Id. 479 ; and
the vendor sell them as the agent of the original purchaser,
and may recover of him the difference between the contract
and the re-selling price; Gordon v. Norris, 49 N. H. 383;
Haines v. Tucker, 50 Id. 313.　But the sale must be in good
faith, for the best procurable price, and in the most reasonable method that can be adopted to procure the best price,
whether it be private or public sale.　Crooks v. More, 1 Sandf.
297 ; Conway v. Bush, 4 Barb, 564; Pollen v. Le Roy, 31 N.
Y. 558; Appleton v. Hogan, 9 B. Mon. 69; Haines v. Tucker,
50 N. H. 307, 313.

be delivered. (*c*)[1] And it makes no difference in this respect whether the contract is for the sale of specific goods or for the sale of goods to be delivered by instalments. (*d*)[2]

595. *Countermand of delivery orders.*—Similarly, if possession has not been given, and the delivery completed, under a delivery order or dock-warrant, the vendor may, if the purchaser becomes insolvent before payment, countermand the order or warrant, although it has been accepted by the person to whom it is addressed, and require the latter to hold the goods on his, the vendor's, account, as before the order was made, provided the goods have not been re-sold, and the warehouse-keeper or bailee has not attorned, to the sub-purchaser in the manner presently mentioned. It has been holden that possession had not been given, and that delivery was not complete, so as to prevent the vendor from countermanding his delivery order by reason of the insolvency of the purchaser, in the following cases :—where ten tons of Riga flax were sold at £118 per ton, to be paid for by the purchaser's acceptance at three months, and the ten tons were to be separated from a larger quantity lying in bulk upon a wharf, and the vendor gave to the purchaser a delivery order on the wharfinger for the ten tons, which

(*c*) *Ex parte* Chalmers, *in re* Edwards, L. R., 8 Ch. 289.

(*d*) *Ex parte*, Chalmers, *in re* Edwards, *supra.*

[1] Or if he has agreed to receive the note of a third party in payment for the goods, and that party becomes insolvent; Roget v. Merritt, 2 Carnes, 117 ; Benedict v. Field, 16 N. Y. 595.

[2] See as to vendors' rights on bankruptcy or insolvency of the purchaser, Frazer v. Hilliard, 2 Strobh. 309; Jewett v. Warren, 12 Mass. 300 ; Rice v. Austin, 17 Mass. 204.

order was accepted by him and entered in his books, but, before the weighing and separation of the ten tons from the bulk, the purchaser became insolvent. (*e*)—where fifty tons of oil were sold at a fixed price ; and an order for the delivery thereof was given to the purchaser, and forwarded to the wharfinger who had the custody of the oil, but it was the custom of the trade for the casks to be searched by the cooper of the vendor, and for the broker of both parties to examine them to ascertain the foot, dirt, and water in each, with a view to certain allowances in respect thereof, and then the casks were to be filled up by the cooper at the expense of the vendor, and the purchaser became insolvent before these preliminary acts had been performed ; (*f*)—where a purchaser agreed to purchase the " small parcel of starch " belonging to the vendor, which he had seen lying at ʻthe warehouse of a third party, at £6, per cwt., to be paid for by bill at two months, fourteen days to be allowed for delivery, and the vendor gave a note to the purchaser addressed to the warehouse-keeper, directing him to " weigh and deliver " to the purchaser " all his starch," which order was forthwith lodged at the warehouse, and a large portion of the starch, on that and two subsequent days, was weighed and delivered to the purchaser, and removed pursuant to the order, but the purchaser became bankrupt whilst the residue remained unweighed in the warehouse, and the vendor countermanded the delivery of the unweighed residue. (*g*)

Where, on the other hand, 130 bales of bacon, lying at a wharf, were sold and weighed by the vendor, and set apart for the purchaser ; and the price

(*e*) Busk v. Davis, 2 M. & S. 402. (*f*) Wallace v. Breeds, 13 East.
Shepley v. Davis, 5 Taunt. 617.   522.
                                    (*g*) Hanson v. Meyer, 6 East, 625.

was ascertained, and was to be paid by bill at two months; and an order was given to the wharfinger to deliver the goods to the purchaser, who went to the wharf and presented the order, and with the assent of the wharfinger took possession of them and weighed the whole, and took away part, but became bankrupt before he had removed the residue, whereupon the vendor countermanded the delivery order, it was held that, the order having been executed, and the goods actually delivered under it to the purchaser, they had irrecoverably become the property of the latter. (*h*) And where a specified quantity of oats in a particular bin in a warehouse was sold at an ascertained price, and a delivery order was entered by the warehouse-keeper in his books, and the oats were transferred into the names of the purchasers, and there were no oats in the bin besides the oats in question, it was held that the delivery was complete by the transfer in the books of the warehouse-keeper. (*i*) Whenever the vendor has given the purchaser actual possession of the goods sold, all the vendor's rights over them are completely gone, although the things have not been removed from the vendor's premises. (*k*)

596. *Shares and undivided quantities sold as such.*—If the vendor himself is possessed only of an undivided share of a commodity, such as a quarter of a particular pipe of wine, or cistern of oil, or the half of a specific cargo of sugar in the hands of other part owners, or of a common bailee, and he sells his share and interest as an undivided quantity, just as he possesses it, and gives the purchaser credit for the payment of the price, and hands him a delivery

(*h*) Hammond v. Anderson, 1 B. & E. 895.
P. N. R. 69.
(*i*) Swanwick v. Sothern, 9 Ad. &

(*k*) Tansley v. Turner, *ante.* Cooper v. Bill, 34 L. J., Ex. 161.

order, which is accepted by the party having the custody of the property, the vendor can not, if the purchaser becomes bankrupt before payment, annul the sale and prevent his assignees from obtaining separate possession of his share. (*l*)

597. *Intervention of the rights of sub-pur-chasers.*—The indorsement and transfer of a delivery order from one purchaser to another will effect no change of possession of the goods, so long as the delivery order has not been presented to, and accepted by, the warehouse-keeper, or party holding the goods, as the agent of the vendor, and will not deprive the unpaid vendor of his right of countermand in case of the insolvency of the first purchaser. (*m*) If the vendor is his own warehouseman, and gives to the purchaser a delivery order, or an acknowledgment that he holds the goods on account of, or to the order of, the latter, he has a right to revoke the order and retain possession of the goods in case of the insolvency of the purchaser before actual payment, so long as the delivery order remains in the hands of the latter, and the goods have not been re-sold, and the rights of third parties do not intervene. (*n*) But if the goods have been re-sold, and the second purchaser has received from his immediate vendor, the first purchaser, a delivery order addressed to the original vendor, which has been accepted by him, the original vendor can not, after he has thus attorned to such second purchaser, refuse to deliver the goods to such second purchaser, pursuant to his acceptance, although the first purchaser to whom he sold, becomes bankrupt before delivery and before payment of the price, and

(*l*) Whitehouse v. Frost, 12 East, 614.

(*m*) M'Ewan v. Smith, 2 H. L. C.

(*n*) Townley v. Crump, 4 Ad. & E. 58 ; 5 N. & M. 606.

the goods were not weighed or measured over prior to the bankruptcy of the first purchaser. (*o*)   But it is otherwise if the original vendor has given his immediate purchaser, the sub-vendor, no delivery order or dock-warrant, and has not furnished him with any evidence of title, or in any way been a party to the sub-sale. (*p*)

598. *Of the vendor's right of stoppage* in transitu. —*Goods in the hands of carriers and forwarding agents.*—If the purchaser becomes bankrupt or insolvent before payment of the price, the vendor is entitled, so long as the goods are *in transitu*, and have not reached their final destination or come into the manual possession of the purchaser, or that of any other party whom he may have appointed his agent finally to take possession of and keep the goods for him, to re-take them and put himself into the same situation as if he had never parted with the actual possession of them. (*q*) [1]   And this right of the vendor

---

(*o*) Hawes v. Watson, 2 B. & C. 542. Green v. Haythorne, 1 Stark. 447. Stoveld v. Hughes, 14 East, 316. Pearson v. Dawson, 27 L. J., Q. B. 248.   Woodley v. Coventry, *ante.* Cooper v. Bill, 3 H. & C. 722 ; 34 L. J., Ex. 161. Knights v. Wiffen, L.

R., 5 Q. B. 660 ; 40 L. J., Q. B. 15.

(*p*) Craven v. Ryder, 6 Taunt. 433. Griffiths v. Perry, 28 L. J., Q. B. 204. Moakes v. Nicholson, 19 C. B., N. S, 290 ; 34 L. J., C. P. 273.

(*q*) Gibson v. Carruthers, 8 M. & W. 338–341.

---

[1] It was held in Rogers v. Thomas, 20 Conn. 54, that the insolvency or bankruptcy must occur between the dates of the sale and the stoppage ; but it has been said in Ohio, that the vendor may stop the goods upon discovering that the purchaser was insolvent at the date of the sale ; Benedict v. Schaettle, 12 Ohio St. 515 ; and see Naylor v. Dennie, 8 Pick. 198 ; Reynolds v. Boston & Maine R. R., 43 N. H. 589 ; Conyers v. Ennis, 2 Mason, 236 ; Buckley v. Furniss, 15 Wend. 137 ; S. C. 17 Id. 504 ; Biggs v. Barry, 2 Curtis, 259 ; Stevens v. Wheeler, 27 Barb. 663 ; Thompson v. Thompson, 4 Cush. 127, 134 ; Lee v. Kilburn, 3 Gray, 594, 600 ; Herrick v. Borst, 4 Hill, 650 ; Chandler v. Fulton, 10 Texas, 2 ; Benedict v.

is not defeated or destroyed by part payment of the
purchase money, or by the acceptance of a bill of
exchange or promissory note for part of the price. (*r*)
But it is strictly confined to the unpaid vendor of
goods sold, (*s*)[1] or to persons who stand in the position of an unpaid vendor, as, for instance, a merchant
who purchases goods on his own credit for another, (*t*)
and does not extend to persons who have forwarded
goods to a creditor by way of payment, or in satisfaction and discharge of a debt due to the consignee.
(*u*) The stoppage may be effected either by the
vendor himself or his authorized agent, but not by a
person who has no authority from the vendor to stop
the goods; and a subsequent ratification by the vendor
of an unauthorized stoppage is not equivalent to a
precedent authority, and will not cure the defect of
want of authority. (*x*)

Goods delivered to a carrier to be conveyed from
a vendor to a purchaser, are held to be *in transitu*;
although they may have been consigned to a carrier

(*r*) Hodgson v. Loy, 7 T. R. 440.
Feise v. Wray, 3 East, 93. New v.
Swain, 1 Dans. & Lld. Merc. C. 193.
Edwards v. Brewer, 2 M. & W. 375.

(*s*) Sweet v. Pym, 1 East, 4. Jenkyns
v. Usborne, 7 M. & Gr. 678.

(*t*) The Tigress, 1 B. & L. 38; 32
L. J., Adm. 97.

(*u*) Vertue v. Jewell, 4 Camph. 31.

(*x*) Bird v. Brown, 4 Exch. 796.
Hutchings v. Nunes, 1 Moo. P. C. N.
S. 243.

Schaettle, 12 Ohio St. 515; Blum v. Marks, 21 La. Ann. 268.
Or if the purchaser had died and his administrator received
the goods, the transit is ended and the goods can not be
stopped; Conyers v. Ennis, 2 Mason, 236.

[1] The right of stoppage *in transitu* is nothing more than
an extension of the vendors' common-law lien upon goods
for his price, and has no effect of itself upon the contract.
Rowley v. Biglow, 12 Pick. 313; Rogers v. Thomas, 20 Conn.
53; Atkins v. Colby, 20 N. H. 153; Grout v. Hill, 4 Gray,
361, 366; Jordan v. James, 5 Ham. 98; 2 Kent, 541; Chandler
v. Fulton, 10 Texas, 2; Newhall v. Vargas, 13 Me. 93, 104; S.
C. 15 Id. 315; Hunn v. Bowne, 2 Caines, 38, 42.

specially appointed by the purchaser to receive them, or may be under the charge of a general forwarding agent (y) of the purchaser, or in the hands of a packer, or wharfinger, or innkeeper, or any other middleman forming a mere link in the chain of communication or transmission from the buyer to the seller; and the *transitus* continues, into whatever hands they may happen to fall, until they have reached their destination, (z) or have been actually delivered to the consignee or his agent for custody, although the goods may have been shipped, and the prior carriage and wharfage dues paid, by the general shipping agent of the purchaser.[1] But goods are not *in transitu*, when they are journeying in the purchaser's own cart or carriage, under the custody or care of his own servant or agent. If the purchaser charters and despatches a vessel to a distant port to receive the goods, and they are put on board, the fact of their being *in transitu* will depend upon the character in which the master or commander receives them. If the charter-party amounts, as it generally does, merely to a contract for the carriage of merchandise, the cap-

---

(y) Slater v. Le Feuvre, 2 Sc. 146; 2 Bing. N. C. 81. Coates v. Railton, 9 D. & R. 593; 6 B. & C. 422.

(z) Bolton v. The Lancashire and Yorkshire Railway Company, L. R., 1 C. P. 431; 35 L. J., C. P. 137.

[1] The transfer of a bill of lading by the vendor to his agent, vests a sufficient property in the latter to entitle him to stop *in transitu* the goods in his own name. Seymour v. Newton, 105 Mass. 272; Newhall v. Vargas, 13 Me. 93; nor does it seem that he need any express authority to do so; Ib.; Bell v. Moss, 5 Whart. 189. The vendor's right is not impaired by his having negotiated bills given in payment for the goods; Donath v. Broomhead, 7 Penn. St. 301; Hays v. Mouille, 14 Id. 48; Stubbs v. Lund, 7 Mass. 453; Bell v. Moss, 5 Wheat. 189; Arnold v. Delano, 4 Cush. 33; and see Clark v. Mauran, 3 Paige. 373; Wood v. Roach, 1 Yeates, 177.

tain having the general control and management of the vessel, and continuing the servant of the ship-owners, the goods will be received by him in the character of a carrier, and will be in transitu. (*a*) But if the charter-party amounts to a demise or bailment of the ship, the charterer becoming the temporary owner, and the master or commander his servant or agent, the delivery of the goods on board will be a delivery to the charterer or purchaser, and the possession of the master his possession, and the vendor will have no right to re-take them, (*b*) unless the goods are shipped under a bill of lading reserving to the vendor the dominion and control over them.[1] If the vendee takes the goods out of the possession of the carrier into his own before their arrival at their destination, with or without the consent of the carrier, there seems no doubt that the transit will be at an end, although in the absence of the carrier's consent, there may be a wrong to him for which he would have a right of action. (*c*)

A delivery on board the purchaser's own ship and to his own master is not inconsistent with the vendor's annexing terms to the delivery by bill of lading, which may enable him to retain a right to claim the goods, and prevent delivery if the terms are not complied with. (*d*) Where goods shipped on board a vessel

(*a*) Rodger v. Comptoir d'Escompte de Paris, L. R., 2 P. C. 393 ; 40 L. J., P. C. 1.

(*b*) Bothlingk v. Inglis, 3 East, 397. Schotsmans v. Lancashire and Yorkshire Railway Company, L. R., 2 Ch. 332 ; 35 L. J., Ch. 100.

(*c*) Whitehead v. Anderson, 9 M. & W. 518.

(*d*) Ogle v. Atkinson, 5 Taunt. 750. Turner v. Trustees, &c., Liverpool Dock, 6 Exch. 543. Moakes v. Nicholson, 19 C. B., N. S. 290 ; 34 L. J., C. P. 273.

[1] Where the goods are carried by a ship chartered by the buyer, see Newhall v. Vargas, 13 Me. 93; Stubbs v. Lund, 7 Mass. 453; Rowley v. Bigelow, 12 Pick. 307.

were to be delivered to the purchaser " in the port of London," and the vessel arrived at her moorings in the river Thames, and the goods were put into the lighters of a wharfinger employed and paid by the purchaser, it was held that the *transitus* was not determined. (*e*) Neither is the *transitus* determined by the actual arrival of the goods in boats or lighters alongside the purchaser's wharf, if the boats and lighters are used merely as the vehicle of conveyance, and not as places of deposit and ultimate reception. (*f*) The *transitus* is not determined merely by the arrival of the goods at the place of destination, but is deemed to continue until they have come into the actual possession of the purchaser. If, therefore, they are in the hands of custom-house officers at the port of destination, or are placed in quarantine, the *transitus* is not determined, and the right of stoppage is not taken away. (*g*) If the goods are not addressed directly to the consignee, but to the vendor's own agent at the place of destination, accompanied by an order directing him to deliver them to the purchaser, the goods continue in the constructive possession of the vendor until they have been actually handed over to the purchaser, or until the vendor's agent has attorned to the latter and agreed to hold the goods on his account, and subject to his orders as previously mentioned.[1]

(*e*) Jackson v. Nichol, 7 Sc. 577 ; 5 Bing. N. C. 508.

(*f*) Tucker v. Humphery, 1 Moo & P. 378 ; 4 Bing. 516.

(*g*) Northey v. Field, 2 Esp. 614. Holst v. Pownall, 1 Esp. 240.

[1] The entry of goods in a custom-house, without payment of duties, is not a termination of the transit; Motram v. Heyer, 5 Den. 629; unless entered in the purchaser's name; Parker v. Byrne, 1 Lowell, 539 ; if deposited, but not entered, the transit is not ended ; Donuth v. Broomhead, 7 Pa. St. 301.

599. *Goods in the hands of the purchaser's agents for custody,* on the other hand, are not *in transitu,* but are in the actual possession of the purchaser, and can not be re-taken by the unpaid vendor. An agent for custody, as distinguished from a forwarding agent, is a person who has received goods by the direction and authority of the purchaser as a depositary or bailee invested with authority to receive goods and sell them for the purchaser, or to hold them generally on account of the latter, at his disposal, and not for the purpose of helping the goods on a stage further in a direct course of transmission to him. The delivery to such agent is a delivery to the principal, and the *transitus,* consequently, is determined as soon as the goods reach his hands; and, if the transit be once at an end, it can not commence *de novo,* merely because the goods are again sent up_n their travels towards a new and ulterior destination. (*h*) Where goods ordered by a purchaser for the Valparaiso market, were forwarded by railway to the shipping agents of the purchaser at Liverpool, and were put on board a vessel bound for Valparaiso, but were afterwards re-landed by order of an agent of the purchaser, to be re-packed, it was held that the *transitus* was determined, and that the goods had come into the actual possession of the purchaser. (*i*)[1]

(*h*) Dixon v. Baldwen, 5 East, 184.   (*i*) Valpy v. Gibson, 4 C. B. 837;
Ellis v. Hunt, 3 T. R. 464.   Leeds v.   16 L. J., C. P. 241.
Wright, 3 B. & P. 320.

[1] And see peculiar circumstances in Grout v. Hill, 4 Gray, 361; Stubbs v. Lund, 7 Mass. 453; Naylor v. Dennie, 8 Pick. 198. Calahan v. Babcock, 21 Ohio St. 281; Guilford v. Smith, 30 Vt. 49, 71, 72; Sawyer v. Joslin, 20 Vt. 192; Buckley v. Furniss, 15 Wend. 137. A vendee has, it seems, a right to intercept the goods and take them before they have arrived at their destination. See Jordan v. James, 5 (Ham.) Ohio, 88; Biggs v. Barry, 2 Curtis, 259; Atkins v. Colby, 20 N. H. 154;

600. *Conversion of a carrier, wharfinger, or packer, into the purchaser's agent for custody.*—So long as the carrier holds the goods as a mere instrument of conveyance, or in the character of a forwarding agent, the *transitus* continues, and the unpaid vendor has a right to stop them; but if the carrier enters expressly, or by implication, into a new agreement with the purchaser, distinct from the original contract for carriage, to hold the goods for the purchaser as his agent, not for the purpose of expediting them to the place of original destination pursuant to that contract, but in a new character for the purpose of custody on his account, and subject to some new or further order to be given by him, the *transitus* is at an end, and the goods are constructively in the possession of the purchaser, and can not be re-taken by the vendor. (*k*) ' But the assent of the carrier to hold the goods

(*k*) Whitehead v. Anderson, 9 M. & W. 518.

Wood v. Yeatman, 15 B. Mon. 270; Seccomb v. Nutt, 14 Id. 324, 327; Mohr v. Boston & Albany R. R. Co., 106 Mass. 67; Cabeen v. Campbell, 30 Penn. St. 254; Covell v. Hitchcock, 23 Wend. 611; Aguirre v. Parmelee, 22 Conn. 473. And a portion of the goods may be stopped even though the remainder have been delivered. Buckley v. Furniss, 17 Wend. 504.

' Whatever amounts to a delivery of the goods to the purchaser, puts an end to the transitus and defeats the right of stoppage; Guilford v. Smith, 30 Vt. 49; Cabeen v. Campbell, 30 Pa. St. 254; Mohr v. Boston & Albany R. R. Co., 106 Mass. 67; Sawyer v. Joslin, 20 Vt. 172; Hays v. Mouille, 14 Penn. St. 48; Biggs v. Barry, 2 Curtis, 259; Harris v. Pratt, 17 N. Y. 249; Pottinger v. Hecksher, 2 Grant, 109; Rowley v. Bigelow, 12 Pick. 307; if the carrier become the purchaser's bailee, of course the right is lost; Reynolds v. Boston & Maine Ry. Co., 43 N. H. 591; Atkins v. Colby, 20 Id. 154; the right can not probably be exercised; goods landed upon a wharf subject to the purchaser's disposition are delivered to the purchaser; Sawyer v. Joslin, 20 Vt. 172; and see a construction of a variety of circumstances, in Harris v. Pratt, 17 N. Y. 249; Covell v. Hitchcock, 23 Wend. 613; Mattram v.

II.—13

as an agent for custody on behalf of the purchaser
must be clearly established in order to put an end to
the *transitus* and deprive the vendor of his right to
stop the goods. A mere promise by the carrier to
deliver the goods to the purchaser as soon as they can
be got at is not enough to bring them into the possession, actual or constructive, of the purchaser. (*l*) If
the purchaser, having no warehouse of his own, is in
the habit of using the warehouse of his wharfinger, or
carrier, or packer, as his own, and making it the re-
pository of his goods until he has sold them or shipped
them for exportation, the *transitus* is at an end, and
the delivery is complete, when the goods arrive at that
warehouse and customary place of deposit ; although
they may immediately afterwards have received a fresh
destination by command of the purchaser. (*m*) Where
twenty mats of flax were sold by a merchant of Hull
to a manufacturer near Leeds, and were forwarded by
railway to Leeds, and arrived at the carriers' shed at
the railway terminus at Leeds, and it was the custom
of the carriers to give notice to the manufacturer of
the arrival of goods consigned to him, and for the
latter to send wagons to convey them to his mills to
be manufactured ; and, on the arrival of the flax,
notice was given to the manufacturer by letter that,

(*l*) Coventry v. Gladstone, L. R. 6
Eq. 44 ; 37 L. J., Ch. 492.

(*m*) Scott v. Pettit, 3 B. & P. 469.
Allan v. Gripper, 2 Cr. & J. 218.
Foster v. Frampton, 9 D. & R. 108 ; 6
B. & C. 107. Dodson v. Wentworth,
5 Sc. N. R. 832 ; 1 Smith's L. C. 5th
ed., 729–747. Cooper v. Bill, 3 H. &
C. 722 ; 34 L. J., Ex. 161. Rowe v.
Pickford, 8 Taunt. 83 ; 1 Moore, 526.

Heyer, 1 Denio, 487 ; Hays v. Mouille, 14 Penn. St. 48 ; Guil-
ford v. Smith, 30 Vt. 49 ; Buckley v. Furniss, 15 Wend. 137 ;
S. C., 17 Wend. 504 ; Hoover v. Tibbetts, 13 Wis. 79 ; Aguirre
v. Parmelee, 22 Conn. 473 : Sturtevant v. Orser, 24 N. Y. 538 ;
Markland v. Creditors, 7 Cal. 213 ; Pottinger v. Hecksher, 2
Grant, 309 ; Harris v. Hart, 6 Duer, 606.

unless the goods were sent for, they would remain at warehouse rent; and the manufacturer sent his cart, and took away ten of the mats, but before the others were removed, he became bankrupt; it was held that the goods had arrived at the place of destination, and had come into the constructive possession of the vendee, and that the *transitus* consequently was at an end. (*n*) But although the goods may have been landed and warehoused at a place commonly used by the purchaser as a place of deposit, yet, if the latter, finding himself to be in failing circumstances, has previously declared it to be his intention not to accept the goods, and not to take possession of them as owner, there has been no actual delivery, and the unpaid vendor's right of recovering possession has not been destroyed. (*o*) The vendor's right to stop *in transitu* can not be defeated by any claim of lien on the part of a carrier, wharfinger, or any other middleman, nor by a foreign attachment laid upon the goods by a creditor. (*p*)

601. *Stoppage of part of goods sold* under one entire contract of sale does not have the effect of revesting in the vendor that portion of them which has been actually delivered to the bankrupt purchaser; and a delivery of part will not have the effect of destroying the vendor's right of stoppage of the portion remaining undelivered. " What the effect of stoppage *in transitu* is," observes the Court of Exchequer, " whether entirely to rescind the contract, or only to replace the vendor in the same position as if he had not parted with the possession, and entitle him to hold

(*n*) Wentworth v. Outhwaite, 10 M. & W. 450, 451.

(*o*) James v. Griffin, 2 M. & W. 623. Nicholson v. Bower, 1 Ell. & Ell. 173; 28 L. J., Q. B. 97. Heinekey v. Earle,

8 Ell. & Bl. 428 ; 28 L. J., Q. B. 79.

(*p*) Crawshay v. Eades, 2 D. & R. 288. Oppenheim v. Russell, 2 B. & P. 42. Richardson v. Goss, Ib. 119.

the goods until the price be paid down, is a point not yet finally decided, and there are difficulties attending each construction. If the latter supposition be adopted (as most of us are strongly inclined to think it ought to be on the weight of authority), the vendor is entitled to retain the part actually stopped *in transitu*, until he is paid the price of the whole, but has no right to re-take that which has arrived at its journey's end. His right of lien on the part stopped is re-vested, but no more." (*q*)

602. *Notice of stoppage* in transitu.—The old rule of law, that a stoppage *in transitu* could be effected only by the corporeal touch of the goods, no longer prevails. (*r*) A notice to a carrier having charge of the goods is sufficient ; but, if given to an employer whose servant has the custody, it must be given at such a time and under such circumstances, that the employer may be able to communicate it to his servant in time to prevent a delivery to the consignee. (*s*) [1]

603. *Intervention of the rights of sub-purchasers.* —If the purchaser re-sells the goods whilst they are *in transitu*, and receives the price, and then becomes insolvent, the first vendor may stop the goods at any time before they have come into the possession of

(*q*) Wentworth v. Outhwaite, 10 M. & W. 452. Tanner v. Scovell, 14 M. & W. 35. Valpy v. Oakeley, 16 Q. B. 941. Ex parte Chalmers, in re Edwards, L. R,. 8 Ch. 289.

(*r*) Mills v. Ball, 2 B. & P. 457.

Litt v. Cowley, 7 Taunt. 169 ; 2 Marsh, 457. Hutchings v. Nunes, 1 Moo. P. C. N. S. 243.

(*s*) Whitehead v. Anderson, 9 M. & W. 518.

[1] The notice must require that the carrier hold the goods subject to the vendor's orders. Reynolds v. Boston & Maine Railroad, 43 N. H. 591 ; Bell v. Moss, 5 Whart. 189 ; Newhall v. Vargas, 13 Me. 93, 109 ; Mottram v. Heyer, 5 Denio, 629 ; Seymour v. Newton, 105 Mass. 272.

such second purchaser, and hold them as a security for the due payment of the original purchase-money, unless the second purchaser claims as the *bona fide* indorsee and holder of a bill of lading. As between a vendor and his immediate vendee, a bill of lading may be countermanded, in case of the insolvency of the latter, at any time before it has been actually executed, like any other order or direction to a common carrier. But as between a first vendor and *bona fide* sub-purchasers, the case is different. The first vendor, by indorsing and delivering a bill of lading to his immediate purchaser, accredits the title of the latter to the goods, and holds him out to the mercantile world as the owner of them; and the *bona fide* indorsement and delivery by such purchaser of such bill of lading to a second purchaser deprives the first vendor of all power and control over the goods, and destroy his right to stop *in transitu* as against the latter. (*t*)   If the assignee of the bill of lading, however, has given no value or consideration for the indorsement of such bill of lading, or if he knew of the insolvency of his vendor at the time he took the bill, he will be in no better situation than the latter. (*u*) and a pre-existing debt is not such a consideration for the indorsement of a bill of lading as to defeat the right of the unpaid vendor to stop *in transitu.* (*v*)

604. *Transfer by bill of lading,*—Goods will not pass to third parties by the mere delivery of a bill of

(*t*) Lickbarrow v. Mason, 6 East, 20 (*a*); 1 H. Bl. 357. Gurney v. Behrend, 23 L. J., Q. B. 265 ; 3 Ell. & Bl. 622 ; 1 Smith's Leading Cases, 459, 739. Slubey v. Heyward, 2 H. Bl. 504. Caldwell v. Ball, 1 T. R. 205. Hibbert v. Carter, Ib. 745. In re Westzinthus, 5 B. & Ad. 817. Jones v. Jones, 8 M. & W. 431. The Argentina, L. R., 1 'Ad. & Ec. 370. Pease v. Gloahec, L. R., 1 P. C. 219. The Marie Louise, L. R., 1 P. C. 219.

(*u*) Waring v. Cox, 1 Campb. 370. Cuming v. Brown, 9 East, 514.

(*v*) Rodger v. Comptoir d'Escompte de Paris, L. R., 2 P. C. 393 ; 38 L. J., P. C. 30.

lading without indorsement ; and the operation of the bill may be qualified and restricted by a conditional indorsement. (*y*) [1] The vendor may annex terms to the bill of lading preserving his control over the cargo and the jus disponendi of the goods on their arrival at their destination, although they may be shipped on board the purchaser's ship, and may be in the hands of the purchaser's shipmaster. (*z*)   Every consignee of goods named in a bill of lading, and every indorsee of a bill of lading to whom the property in the goods mentioned therein passes, has transferred to him all such rights of action and suit, and is subject to the same liabilities in respect of such goods, as if the con-

(*y*) Akerman v. Humphery, 1 C. & P. 57.   Mitchell v. Ede, 11 Ad. & E, 903.   Barrow v. Coles, 3 Campb. 92.
(*z*) Turner v. Trustees, Liverpool Dock, 6 Exch. 569.   Van Casteel v. Booker, 2 Exch. 708.   Jenkyns v. Brown, 14 Q. B. 503.   Berndtson v. Strang, L. R., 4 Eq. 486 ; Ib. 3 Ch. 588 ; 36 L. J., Ch. 879.   Fraser v. Witt, L. R., 7 Eq. 64 ; 37 L. J., Ch. 665.

[1] Otherwise than by a bona fide transfer of the bill of lading, a sale of the goods by the purchaser will not defeat the right of stoppage ; Kitchen v. Spear, 30 Vt. 545 ; O'Brien v. Norris, 16 Md. 122 ; Hays v. Mouille, 14 Penn. St. 48 ; Ilsley v. Stubbs, 9 Mass. 65 ; Stanton v. Eager, 16 Pick. 473 ; Gardner v. Howland, 2 Pick. 399.   And as to when the delivery may be without indorsement, see Walter v. Ross, 2 Wash. C. C. 283 ; Seymour v. Newton, 105 Mass. 275 ; Seccomb v. Nutt, 14 B. Mon. 324 ; Atkins v. Colby, 20 N. H. 154 ; Sawyer v. Joslin, 20 Vt. 172 ; Covell v. Hitchcock, 23 Wend. 611 ; Harris v. Hart, 6 Duer, 606 ; neither will an attachment of the goods for a debt of the consignee ; Seymour v. Newton, 105 Mass. 272 ; Hays v. Mouille, 14 Penn. St. 48 ; O'Brien v. Norris, 16 Md. 122 ; Calahan v. Babcock, 21 Ohio St. 281 ; Naylor v. Dennie, 8 Pick. 197 ; Buckley v. Furniss, 15 Wend. 137 ; Hause v. Judson, 4 Dana, 13 ; Wood v. Yeatman, 15 B. Mon. 270 ; Newhall v. Vargas, 13 Me. 514 ; Pratt v. Parkman, 24 Pick. 42 ; Winslow v. Norton, 29 Me. 414 ; Rowley v. Bigelow. 12 Pick. 307, 314 ; Stanton v. Eager, 16 Pick. 467, 474 ; Saltus v. Everett, 20 Wend. 268.

tract contained in the bill of lading had been made with himself; (*a*) and every bill of lading representing goods to have been shipped on board is conclusive against the master or person signing the same in the absence of fraud on the part of the shipper or holder. (*b*)

605. *Of the vendor's power of re-sale after stoppage* in transitu.—If a specific, ascertained chattel has been sold by a properly authenticated contract, so that the right of property has passed to the purchaser, the exercise of the right of stoppage *in transitu* will not at once have the effect of re-vesting the right of property in the vendor. (*c*) The assignees of the bankrupt purchaser are entitled to call upon the vendor to deliver the goods on being paid or tendered the price; but, if they refuse to take and pay for the goods, the vendor will be entitled to re-sell them in the same way that he is entitled to re-sell in ordinary cases after the refusal of a purchaser to take and pay for the things he has ordered and bought. If the sale is a sale of things of quantity generally, and the vendor will fulfill his contract by delivering any articles of the character and description mentioned in the contract, the vendor may, after he has recovered possession of the goods by the exercise of the right of stoppage, re-sell them; (*d*)' but he may be obliged to furnish other goods of a similar character and

---

(*a*) 18 & 19 Vict. c. 111, ss. 1, 3. The Figlia Maggiore, L. R., 2 Ad. & E. 106 ; 37 L. J., Adm. 52.

(*b*) Meyer v. Dresser, 33 L. J., C. P. 289.

(*c*) Martindale v. Smith, 1 Q. B. 395.

(*d*) Clay v. Harrison, 10 B. & C. 106.

' And should a balance of the original purchase money remain due him on his contract, after such sale he may recover it of the purchaser. Newhall v. Vargas, 13 Me. 514.

description to those originally bargained for, on tender of the price by the assignees.

606. *Sale of goods to one of several partners in trade—Dealings by one partner in fraud of the firm.*—A sale of goods of the same description as those ordinarily dealt in by the firm in the exercise of its trade to one of the partners who is known by the vendor, at the time of the sale, to be a member of the co-partnership, and is presumed by him to be dealing on account of the firm, is a sale to the firm at large, with whatever view the goods may have been bought by such single partner, and to whatever purposes they may subsequently be applied by him; and all the members of the firm, consequently, are liable for the payment of the price of them. (*e*) But, if the goods are not of the same character and description as those dealt in by the partnership in the way of its trade, and are not forwarded by the vendor to the place of business of the partnership, but to the private dwelling of the partner giving the order, and the goods have not reached the hands of the partnership, but have been appropriated to the private use of the partner ordering them, the vendor can not then look to the firm for payment. (*f*)   If an acceptance of a bill of exchange is given by one partner in his own name for goods supplied to the firm, and the partner giving the acceptance becomes bankrupt, and a portion of the amount of the bill is realized from his estate, the drawer may proceed against the other members of the firm, or against the partnership estate, for the balance due to him. (*g*) [1]

(*e*) Bond v. Gibson, 1 Campb. 185.   (*g*) Bottomley v. Nuttall, 5 C. B.,
(*f*) Story on Partnership, § 112.   N. S. 141 ; 28 L. J., C. P. 110.

[1] See *ante*, vol. 1, § 93, *et seq.*, as to Partners.

607. *Parties secretly interested in the subsequent disposition of goods purchased by one of them* on his own individual credit, are not necessarily liable for the payment of the price of them. Thus, where three parties agreed to bring out and publish a periodical called the Sporting Review, on their joint account, upon the terms that one of them, who was an author, was to write the book, and furnish manuscript and drawings, and another, who was a printer, was to furnish the paper for the work, and to charge it to the account at cost price, and was also to charge the printing at " master's prices," and the third, who was a publisher, was to publish the work, make and receive general payments, keep the accounts, and divide the profits between the three, and the printer ordered paper for the work, but became bankrupt before he had paid for it, whereupon the stationer sought to recover the price from the other two, it was held that they were not liable, as it was bought upon the individual credit of the printer. (*h*) Generally speaking, however, where goods are obtained for the joint use and benefit of several persons with their authority, they are all responsible as the real principals in the transaction, so that the full value of the goods may be recovered from any one of them, although they were purchased on the credit of the ostensible buyer alone. Where a publisher gave an order to a stationer to deliver to the defendant, who was a printer, " two hundred reams of super-royal paper for Jeremy Taylor's works, and seventy-two reams for Doddridge's Expositor," and the paper was delivered at the printer's office, and it was afterwards discovered that the printer was at the time of the giving of the order a partner with the publisher in

(*h*) Wilson v. Whitehead, 10 M. & W. 503.

both the works mentioned in the order, it was held that he was liable, together with the publisher, for the price of the paper. (*i*)

608. *Sub-purchasers of separate shares of goods sold.*—Where parties are not jointly interested in the disposal of goods when purchased, they can not be sued jointly, and one can not be made to pay the price of the whole, but each is separately responsible for his own separate share only of the things so bought. (*k*) Where three persons agreed amongst themselves to purchase jointly a quantity of oil on speculation, and Eyre, one of their number, was to go into the market and be the ostensible buyer, and the others were to share in the purchase at the same price which he might give, and Eyre accordingly bought the oil, but never paid for it, it was held that the other two persons could not be sued jointly with him as his secret partners in the transaction, that the agreement was a sub-contract to share severally in certain proportions in the purchase to be made by the ostensible buyer on his own credit, and that the failure of such buyer to pay the price did not render the two other sub-contractors responsible for the price of the whole bargain. (*l*)

609. *Sale of goods to registered joint-stock companies.*—A vendor who seeks to make a registered joint-stock company responsible for the payment of the price of goods delivered at the offices or ordinary place of business of the company, pursuant to the orders of officers of the company apparently intrusted with the management of the business of the company, is not confined to proving his case by the articles of association or the authorized regulations of the company; he may show that the whole of the shareholders

(*i*) Gardiner v. Childs, 8 C. & P. 345.   (*l*) Coope v. Eyre, 1 H. Bl. 37.
(*k*) Hoare v. Dawes, 1 Doug. 372.

have by usage or otherwise sanctioned contracts not sanctioned thereby. If the company has been in the habit of intrusting one director, or any public officer, or any shareholder, or other party with the duty of ordering goods required by the company in the exercise of its trade, or for carrying out the purposes for which it was registered, and has been in the habit of paying for goods supplied pursuant to the orders of such director, officer, or other party, the company will be responsible for the payment of the goods so ordered, whether that particular course of dealing is or is not sanctioned or authorized by the articles of association ; for, although they point out the mode in which the directors are to exercise their functions, and by which the company may be bound, yet the articles do not prevent them from binding themselves in some other way, and from appointing an agent and recognizing his contracts, and rendering themselves responsible as principals under the ordinary law of principal and agent.

610. *Avoidance of sales.*—It has been held that a sale by a debtor of the whole of his stock-in-trade to a bona fide purchaser for a fair price, does not neccessarily constitute an act of bankruptcy, though his creditors may be ultimately delayed or defeated, and the misapplication of the proceeds was contemplated by the trader at the time of the sale, because the trader gets a present equivalent for his goods. (*m*) It would be otherwise, however, if the assignee has express or implied notice that the bankrupt is selling with a fraudulent intention. (*n*)

611. *Of the promise or warranty implied from*

(*m*) Baxter v. Pritchard, 1 Ad. & E. 456. Graham v. Chapman, 21 L. J., C. P. 176. Bell v. Simpson, 2 H. & N. 410. Whitmore v. Claridge, 2 B. & S. 213 ; 33 L. J., Q. B. 87.

(*n*) Fraser v. Levy, 6 H. & N. 16.

a vendor that he does not at the time he sells know that he has no title of right to sell.—In Noy's Maxims it seems to be affirmed to be a principle of law that, if a man steals a horse and sells it on credit, and the owner takes it away from the purchaser before the price is paid, the thief may, nevertheless, sue the purchaser for the price. " If I take," it is said, " the horse of another man and sell him, and the owner take him again, I may have an action of debt for the money ; for the bagain was perfect by the delivery of the horse, et caveat emptor." (*o*) Such a proposition never could have been the settled law of this country. There are several ancient authorities opposed to it ; and all the modern decisions in our courts of justice are quite at variance with such a doctrine. It has always been held that, if a man sells a chattel, knowing it to be the property of another, and the purchaser is evicted, the vendor can not maintain an action for the price ; and, if the price has been paid over to him, the purchaser is entitled to maintain an action to recover it back. (*p*) If goods are sold by a person who is not the owner, and the owner is found out and paid for the goods, the vendor who sold them can not then call upon the purchaser for payment. (*q*) " If a man takes the goods of S tortiously and sells them to me for money as his own goods, and afterwards S takes them away from me, I may have an action on the case against my vendor." " If the vendor affirm that the goods are the goods of a stranger, his friend, and that, he had authority from him to sell them, and upon that B buy them, when in truth they are the goods of an-other, yet, if he sell them fraudulently and falsely on

---

(*o*) Noy's Maxims, 209, p. 89.

(*p*) Furnis v. Leicester, Cro. Jac. 474. Peto v. Blades, 5 Taunt. 657.

(*q*) Dickenson v. Naul, 4 B. & Ad. 638. Allen v. Hopkins, 13 M. & W. 102.

this pretense of authority, though he do not warrant them, and though it be not averred that he sold them knowing them to be the goods of the stranger, B shall have an action for this deceit." (*r*)   By the civil law, if the vendor knowingly sold a thing belonging to another person, the purchaser might sue for the recovery of damages without waiting for an eviction. (*s*)

612. *Warranty of title.*—" Where one having the possession of any personal chattel, sells it, the bare affirming it to be his amounts to a warranty of the fact: and an action lies on the affirmation; for his having possession is a color of title, and perhaps no other title can be made out. *Aliter*, where the seller is out of possession; for then there may be room to question the seller's title; and *caveat emptor* in such a case to have either an express warranty or a good title. (*t*)   " This distinction by Holt," observes BULLER, J., " is not mentioned by Lord Raymond, who reports the same case; and if an affirmation at the time of sale be a warranty, I cannot perceive a distinction between the vendor's being in or out of possession.   The thing is bought of him in consequence of his assertion; and, if there be any difference, it seems to me that the case is strongest against the vendor when he is out of possession, because then the vendee has nothing but the warranty to rely on. (*u*)

613. *Implied warranties of title on the part of*

(*r*) 1 Rolle Abr. 90 pl. 5 ; 91 pl. 7. See Pasley v. Freeman, 3 T. R. 59.

(*s*) Si sciens alienam vem ignoranti mihi vendideris, etiam priusquam evincatur, utiliter me ex empto acturum putavit in id, quanti mea interest meam esse factam. Dig. lib. 19, tit.

i, lex. 30, § 1.

(*t*) Medina v. Stoughton, 1 Salk. 210. Crosse v. Gardner, Carth. 90. Adamson v. Jarvis, 4 Bing. 73. Harding v. Freeman, Sty. 310. Rosewell v. Vaughan, Cro. Jac. 197.

(*u*) Pasley v. Freeman, 3 T. R. 58.

persons who sell as owners.—Wherever a man sells goods *as owner*, he impliedly undertakes and promises that the goods are his own goods, and that he has a right to make the sale and transfer he professes to make ; and if he was not the owner at the time of the sale, and was not selling his own goods but the goods of a third party, who subsequently claims them and deprives the purchaser of them, he is responsible in damages for the breach of such implied undertaking. (*x*) " By the civil law," observes BLACKSTONE, " an implied warranty was annexed to every sale in respect of the title of the vendor; and so, too, in our law, a purchaser of goods and chattels may have a satisfaction from the seller, if he sells them as his own and the title proves deficient, without any express warranty for that purpose." (*y*)   Such is the case in the Roman law, (*z*) the French law, (*a*) the Scotch law, and all the various systems of jurisprudence founded on the Roman code : and this, too, is the case in the American law, founded on the principles of our own common law. (*b*)   It has been decided by the Court of Exchequer that the law does not imply from the mere fact of the sale of a specific chattel any undertaking or warranty from the vendor that he is the owner of, or has a good title to, the thing he sells. (*c*)   But the Court of Queen's Bench has held that, whenever a man sells goods generally, and not in any particular character or capacity, such as auctioneer, agent, sheriff, pawn-

(*x*) Eichholz v. Bannister, 17 C. B. N. S. 708 ; 34 L. J., C. P. 105.   And see the French Cod. Civ. Art. 1599. Troplong, ch. 3.

(*y*) 2 Bl. Com. 451. 2 Kent's Com. 478. 2 Stephen's Com. 126.

(*z*) Cod. lib. 8, tit. 45. Dig. lib. 21, tit. 2.

(*a*) Cod. Civ. Art. 1626, Troplong, ch. 4, DE LA VENTE.

(*b*) Armstrong v. Percy, 5 Wend. 535. Blasdale v. Babcock, 1 J. R. 517. Sedgwick on Damages, 2d ed., 293. 2 Kent's Com. 478.

(*c*) Morley v. Attenborough, 3 Exch. 500 ; 18 L. J., Ex. 151.

broker, pledgee, &c., he must be taken to sell as
owner. (*d*) '

614. *Sales by sheriffs, agents, trustees, or persons*

(*d*) Lee, C. J., commenting on the   senr. 351). Simms v. Marryat, 20 L.
case of L'Apostre v. Le Plastrier   J., Q. B. 458.
(cited in Ryall v. Rowles, 1 Ves.

' The rule is unquestioned with us, and such title is taken
to be implied if the vendor have possession. Whitney v.
Heywood, 6 Cush. 82 ; Sargent v. Currier, 49 N. H. 310;
Storm v. Smith, 43 Miss. 497; Butler v. Tufts, 13 Me. 302;
Huntington v. Hall, 36 Id. 501 ; McCabe v. Morehead, 1
Watts & S. 513; Chism v. Wood, Hardin, 531 ; Bennett v.
Bartlett, 6 Cush. 225 ; Vibbard v. Johnson, 19 Johns. 78 ; Case
v. Hall, 24 Wend. 102 ; Dorr v. Fisher, 1 Cush. 273; Burt v.
Dewey, 40 N. Y. 483 ; Hoe v. Sanborn, 21 Id. 552 ; Thurs-
ton v. Spratt, 52 Me. 202 ; Hale v. Smith, 6 Greenl. 420;
Eldridge v. Wadleigh, 3 Fairf. 372 ; Payne v. Rodden, 4 Bibb.
304; Cozzins v. Whittaker, 3 Stew. & Port. 322 ; Inge v. Bond,
3 Hawks, 101 ; Mockbee v. Gardner, 2 H. & Gill, 176 ; Cool-
idge v. Brigham, 1 Met. 551 ; Sweet v. Colgate, 20 Johns. 196 ;
Reid v. Barber, 3 Cowen, 272 ; Vibbard v. Johnson, 19 Johns.
77 ; McKnight v. Devlin, 52 N. Y. 399, 401 ; Darst v. Brock-
way, 11 Ohio, 462 ; Lines v. Smith, 4 Fla. 47 ; Chancellor v.
Wiggins, 4 B. Mon. 201 ; Colcock v. Goode, 3 McCord, 513 ;
Ricks v. Dillahunty, 8 Porter, 134 ; Williamson v. Sammons,
34 Ala. 691 ; Gookin v. Graham, 5 Humph. 484; Scott v.
Scott, 2 A. K. Marsh, 215 ; McCoy v. Artcher, 3 Barb. 323 ;
Heermance v. Vernoy, 6 Johns. 5 ; per Shaw, Ch. J., in Dorr
v. Fisher, 1 Cush. 273 ; Emerson v. Brigham, 10 Mass. 202 ;
Bucknam v. Goddard, 21 Me. 71 ; Shattuck v. Green, 104
Mass. 42, 45 ; McCoy v. Artcher, 3 Barb. 233. The exception
is when the seller has no actual or constructive possession,
but a mere naked interest; Whitney v. Heywood, 6 Cush. 82 ;
and where the goods are in possession of a third party the
vendor buys at his own peril; Andres v. Lee, 1 Dev. & Bat.
Eq. 318; Emerson v. Brigham, 10 Mass. 202 ; Pratt v. Phil-
brook, 32 Me. 23 ; Scranton v. Clark, 39 N. Y. 220 ; Hunting-
don v. Hall, 36 Me. 501 ; McCoy v. Artcher, 3 Barb. 323 ;
Dresser v. Ainsworth, 9 Id. 619 ; Edick v. Crim, 10 Id.
445 ; Long v. Hickingbottom, 28 Miss. 772. If one knows he
has no title to what he is selling, he can not recover it from
the purchaser, but the purchaser himself is liable to the real

*assuming to sell in some special character or capacity,
and not as owners—*Caveat emptor.—Whenever a man
does not sell goods as owner, but in some special
character or capacity, and the purchaser has notice
thereof, he is bound to look into the title of his
vendor ; for there is not, under such circumstances,
any implied warranty of title on the part of the
vendor. (*e*) The latter merely undertakes and promises that he does not, at the time he sells, know of
any defect in his authority or title to sell; and he can
not be made responsible for the re-payment of the
purchase-money, unless it can be proved that he knew
he had no right or title to sell, and that consequently
his conduct was fraudulent. Thus, in the case of sales
by sheriffs of goods and chattels taken in execution,
the sheriff does not impliedly warrant his title to sell,
or warrant the purchaser against eviction; he merely
promises that he does not, at the time he sells, know
of any defect in his authority, or that he has no right
or title to sell. (*f*)[1]   So in the case of sales by pawn-

---

(*e*) Bagueley v. Hawley, L. R., 2 C.   (*f*) Chapman v. Spiller, 14 Q. B.
P. 625 ; 36 L. J,. C. P. 328.   621.

owner for detention and use of the property; Sweetman v.
Prince, 62 Barb. 256.   The implied warranty of title has been
held to extend to a prior lien or incumbrance; Sargent v.
Currier, 49 N. H. 310; Dresser v. Ainsworth, 9 Barb. 619;
there is no such implied warranty of title in a sale by executors or administrators, or trustees; Prescott v. Holmes, 7
Rich. Eq. 9 ; Blood v. French, 9 Gray, 197; Mockbee v. Gardner, 2 H. & Gill, 176 ; Ricks v. Dillahunty, 8 Porter, 133;
Forsythe v. Ellis, 4 J. J. Marsh. 298; Brigham v. Maxey, 15 Ill.
295 ; as to title implied, but not in the vendor at the time of
the sale, and whether it inures to the purchaser, consult Sherman v. Champlain Transportation Co., 31 Vt. 161.

[1] Davis v. Hunt, 2 Bailey, 412; Yates v. Bond, 2 McCord,
382 ; Puckett v. U. S., 19 L. Rep. 18; Rodgers v. Smith, 2
Cart. (Ind.) 526; Bashore v. Whisler, 3 Watts, 490 ; Stone v.

brokers of unredeemed pledges, the pawnbroker only warrants the subject-matter of the sale to be a pledge, the time for the redemption of which has expired. He does not warrant or promise that the pledgor had a title to pledge the article; nor does he impliedly warrant the purchaser against eviction. As he has sold in a special character or capacity, he impliedly sells and agrees to transfer his own title and interest in the subject-matter of the sale, and no more; and that being so, it is the duty of the purchaser to inquire into the title; and if he neglects so to do, and it subsequently appears that the pledgor had no title to pledge, nor the pawnbroker to sell, and the purchaser is evicted, he can not recover compensation for his loss, unless he can establish a case of fraud. (*g*)

615. *Sale by a vendor of such a title and interest as he actually possesses.*—A distinction has been made in some cases between a sale by a person who is in possession of the goods he sells and by a person who is out of possession, and sells merely his right or title to goods which are in the possession of a third party. Thus it is said that, if a man sells a horse, whereof another is possessed, without any covenant or warranty for the enjoyment, it is at the peril of him who buys; and the latter shall have no action at law for the recovery of his money, because he might have protected himself by the contract. (*h*) This is undoubtedly the case, if the possession of the third party is an adverse possession, and the title is disputed, and the vendor

(*g*) Morley v. Attenborough, 3   (*h*) *Ante.*
Exch. 500; 18 L. J., Ex. 151.

Pointer, 5 Munf. 287; The Monte Allegre, 9 Wheat. 694; Worthy v. Johnson, 8 Geo. 236; Hensley v. Baker, 10 Mo. 157; Bostick v. Winton, 1 Sneed. 525; Morgan v. Tencher, 1 Blackf. 10; 1 Parsons on Contracts, 594.

merely sells all the title and interest he possesses
submitting that title to the scrutiny or investigation
of the purchaser. But, if a man sells a thing in the
hands of a third party, absolutely as owner, and
receives the full value for it, he impliedly undertakes
to put the purchaser into possession of the subject-
matter of the sale. (*i*) By the civil law, the vendor
of rights to movables in the possession of third
parties, and of rights of action, impliedly warranted
that he had the right or title which he pretended to
sell or transfer; and, if he had no such right, the
sale was void, and he might be compelled to refund
the money he had received and make good the
damages sustained by the purchaser. (*k*) The vendor
of a debt impliedly warranted that the debt was due
to him, but not the solvency of the debtor. (*l*) If
the purchaser of a chattel, who had been sued and
evicted for want of title, neglected to give notice to
the vendor of the action brought against him, or if
he allowed judgment to go against him by default, or
defended himself negligently, or consented to a
reference without the knowledge of the vendor, he
was not permitted to proceed against the latter upon
the warranty, as the eviction might have resulted from
his own negligence. (*m*) But, where the purchaser,
at the time of the making of the contract, is afforded
the means of inspection and examination, there is no
implied warranty on the part of the vendor of the
peculiar character, quality, or condition of the thing
sold. The purchaser must judge for himself; and the
maxim of *caveat emptor* applies. (*n*) Where, how-

(*i*) Coe v. Clay, 5 Bing. 440; 3
Moo. & P. 59.

(*k*) Dig. lib. 18, tit. 4. Cod. lib. 4,
tit. 3.

(*l*) Dig. lib. 18, tit. 4, lex. 4.

(*m*) Dig. 21, tit. 2, l. 51, 53, 56. Cod.
lib. 8, tit. 45. Domat, liv. 1, tit. 2, s.
11, 21.

(*n*) Hall v. Conder, 2 C. B., N. S.
41.

ever, goods are sold under a certain denomination, the buyer is entitled to have such goods delivered to him as are commercially known under this denomination, though he may have bought after inspection of the bulk and without warranty. (*o*)

616. *Implied warranty where nothing is said respecting quantity or quality.*—Caveat emptor.—The law does not imply from the mere seller of an article in its natural state, who has no better means of information than the purchaser, as, for instance, where the goods are in existence and can be inspected by the buyer, (*p*)[1] and who does not affirm that the article is fit for any particular purpose, any warranty or undertaking beyond the ordinary promise, that he makes no false representation calculated to deceive the purchaser, and practices no deceit or fraudulent concealment, and that he is not cognizant of any latent defect materially affecting the marketable value of the goods. (*q*) "In the general sale of a horse, the seller only warrants it to be an animal of the description it appears to be, and nothing more; and, if the purchaser makes no inquiries as to its soundness or qualities, and it turns out to be unsound and restive, or unfit for use, he can not recover as against the seller, as it must be assumed that he purchased the animal at a cheaper rate." So, on the sale and transfer of wares and merchandise, if nothing is said

(*o*) Josling v. Kingsford, 13 C. B., N. S. 447; 32 L. J., C. P. 94.

(*p*) Jones v. Just, L. R., 3 Q. B. 197; 37 L. J., Q. B. 89.

(*q*) Bluett v. Osborn, 1 Stark. 384.

[1] So in the case of a sample, if the sample and the goods both have the same defect, there is no implied warranty that the goods have not the defect, even though, in both the sample and in the goods delivered, the defect was latent. Dickinson v. Gay, 7 Allen, 29.

as to the character or quality of the thing sold, the buyer takes the risk of all latent defects unknown to the seller at the time of the execution of the contract of sale, all that the seller answers for being that the article is, as far as he knows, what it appears to be. Where the plaintiff bought a quantity of hops of the defendant, who was not the grower, by sample taken from the pockets, and at the time of the sale the bulk fairly answered to the sample, and no inherent defect was perceptible or known to the defendant, the vendor, but the grower, in order to increase the weight of tbe hops, had fraudulently watered them after they were dried, and the effect of a proceeding of this kind did not usually become perceptible for several months, and was not known to the defendant at the time he sold the hops, but became manifest in a few months after the sale, whilst the hops remained in the plaintiff's possession, and rendered them un-saleable, it was held that there was no implied warranty on the part of the defendant that the hops were good, sound, and merchantable, at the time he sold them, and that, as the defendant had acted bona fide, he was not answerable for the loss. (*r*)

617. *Warranty of merchantable quality.*—Under a contract to supply goods of a specified description, which the buyer has no opportunity of inspecting, the

(*r*) Parkinson v. Lee, 2 East. 314. Emmerton v. Matthew, *post*. The sale of hops is regulated by the 48 Geo. 3. c. 134. the 54 Geo. 3, c. 123, and the 29 Vict. c. 37. By sect. 18 of the last-named Act every person who shall sell any hops in any bag or pocket having marked thereon any name. description, date, trade-mark, or symbol intended to indicate the name of the person by whom or the parish. county, or place where, or the year when, the said hops were grown, shall be deemed to contract that the said description, date, trade-mark, and symbol were genuine and true, and that such description, date, trade-mark, and symbol were in accordance with that and the therein recited Acts (the 48 Geo. 3, c. 134, and the 54 Geo. 3, c. 123).

goods must not only in fact answer the specific description, but must be saleable or merchantable under that description.[1] The maxim caveat emptor does not apply to a sale of goods when the buyer has no opportunity of inspection. (*s*)[2]

(*s*) Jones v. Just, *ante*.

[1] See Gallagher v. Waring, 9 Wend. 10; Gaylord M'f'g. Co. v. Allen, 53 N. Y. 518; Merriam v. Field, 24 Wis. 508; Hamilton v. Ganyard, 3 Keyes (N. Y.) 45; McClung v. Kelley, 21 Iowa, 508; Hyatt v. Boyle, 5 Gill & J. 110; Hanks v. McKee, 2 Litt. 227; Walton v. Cody, 1 Wis. 420; Lespard v. Vankirk, 27 Id. 152; Brenton v. Davis, 8 Blackf. 317; Chambers v. Crawford, Addison, 150; Howard ,v. Hoey, 23 Wend. 350; Moses v. Mead, 1 Denio, 378; 1 Parsons on Contracts, 578; Misner v. Granger, 4 Gilman, 69; Whitmore v. South Boston Iron Co., 2 Allen, 58; Leflore v. Justice, 1 Sm. & Mar. 381; Rogers v. Niles, 11 Ohio St. 48; Bird v. Mayer, 8 Wis. 362.

[2] See Gaylord M'f'g. Co. v. Allen, 53 N. Y. 515; where the purchaser is told by the seller to examine for himself, and does examine the merchandise, by cutting open as many bales as he chooses; it is not a sale by sample, and implies no warranty that the interior of the bales shall correspond to their exterior; Salisbury v. Stainer, 19 Wend. 159; and see Williams v. Spofford, 8 Pick. 219; Dickinson v. Gay, 7 Allen, 29. In Barnard v. Kellogg, 10 Wall. 383, the U. S. Supreme Court held that where a merchant in Boston placed certain wool which he had received from Buenos Ayres, on which he had made advances, in the hands of brokers for sale, with instructions not to sell unless the purchaser came to Boston and examined the wool for himself; and the brokers sent to the respnodents, who resided in Hartford, in the state of Connecticut, at their request, samples of the wool, and the latter offered to purchase it at fifty cents a pound, all round, if equal to the samples furnished, and this offer was accepted, provided that the respondents examined the wool on the succeeding Monday, and reported on that day whether or not they would take it, and the respondents agreed to this, and went to Boston and examined four bales in the broker's office, as fully as they desired, and were offered an opportunity to examine all the bales and to have them opened for inspection, but declined to do this, and concluded the purchase, and afterwards found some of the bales deceitfully packed, by placing in

When goods are sold by sample under circumstances in which, in the absence of a sample, there would have been an implied warranty that they were merchantable, such warranty is excluded only with respect to such matters as can be judged of by the sample. Where manufacturers contracted to supply to the plaintiffs a quantity of grey shirtings according to sample, each piece to weigh seven pounds, and goods according to sample and of the agreed weight were delivered and accepted, but it was afterwards discovered that the weight was made up by introducing into the fabric 15 per cent. of china clay, which made the goods unmerchantable, but which could not have been discovered by an ordinary examination of the sample, it was held that the implied warranty of merchantable quality was not excluded. (*t*) [1]

(*t*) Nusserwanjee Bomanjee Mody v. Gregson, L. R., 4 Ex. 49. Heilbutt v. Hickson, L. R., 7 C. P. 438 ; 41 L. J., C. P. 228.

the interior rotten and damaged wool and tags, concealed by an outer covering of fleeces in good condition, and demanded indemnity for the loss (it being conceded that the vendor had acted in good faith and knew nothing of the false packing of the bales): 1st. That the sale was not by sample ; 2d. that by the rule of the common law, where a person inspects for himself the specific goods sold, and there is no express warranty, and the seller is guilty of no fraud, and is neither the manufacturer nor grower of the goods sold, the maxim of *caveat emptor* applies ; and 3d. that since the law in such a case implies no warranty of quality—evidence of custom that such warranty is implied is inadmissible, and the custom or usage is invalid and void, especially so in the case before the court, as the parties were shown to have had no knowledge of the custom, and could not have dealt with reference to it.

[1] See *ante*, note 1, § 615 ; the sale must be made specifically and expressly with reference to the sample, or it will not be held to be a sale by sample ; Bierne v. Dord, 1 Seld. 95 ; the question as to whether a sale was by sample, was left to the jury in Atwater v. Clancy, 107 Mass. 369 ; and upon evidence

618. *Implied warranty where the vendor is told that the thing ordered is required for a specific purpose.*—If the vendor is informed that an article of a certain quality, character, or description, suited for some specified purpose, is required, the law implies a promise from him that he will supply to the purchaser an article of the quality, character, or description ordered, and reasonably fit for the purpose for which it is required. Where the plaintiff sent to the shop of the defendant, who was a rope dealer, for a crane rope, and the defendant's foreman went to the plaintiff's premises and took the necessary admeasurement, saw the crane, and was told that the rope was wanted for the purpose of raising pipes of wine, and the rope was brought and fixed, but it broke, and a cask of wine was precipitated into the street and wholly lost, it was held that the defendant, by accepting the retainer and employment under the circumstances, had impliedly undertaken to furnish a rope reasonably fit for the purpose for which it was ordered, and was liable for the damage occasioned by its breaking, although

---

that the seller, in the presence of the purchaser, put his hand into a package of tobacco and exhibited him some bunches, saying that he would warrant it to be all of the same quality as that exhibited, a jury may find the sale to have been one by sample, Id. See Gallagher v. Waring, 9 Wend. 20; Beebe v. Robert, 12 Id. 412; Boorman v. Jenkins, Id. 566; Sands v. Taylor, 5 Johns. 359; Williams v. Spofford, 8 Pick. 219; Hastings v. Lovering, 2 Id. 219; Borrekins v. Bevan, 3 Rawle, 37; Rose v. Beatie, 2 Nott & McC. 538; Moses v. Mead, 1 Denio, 386; Brower v. Lewis, 19 Barb. 574; Beirne v. Dord, 1 Seld. 95; 2 Sandf. 89; Hargous v. Stone, 1 Seld. 73; Bradford v. Manly, 13 Mass. 139; Henshaw v. Robins, 9 Met. 86; Oneida Manuf. Co. v. Lawrence, 4 Cow. 440; Andrews v. Kneeland, 6 Id. 354; Lathrop v. Otis, 7 Allen, 435; Messenger v. Pratt, 3 Lans. 234, Leonard v. Fowler, 44 N. Y. 289.

he was not in fact the maker or manufacturer of it, he having employed a ropemaker to execute the order, and the latter having, in his turn, employed a third manufacturer of ropes for the purpose. (*u*)

619. *Warranties by vendors who manufacture and sell an article to be used for a specified purpose.*—The law implies a promise or undertaking from a manufacturer that all goods manufactured and sold by him for a specific purpose, and to be used in a particular way, are reasonably fit and proper for the purpose for which he professes to make them, and for which they are known to be required. Thus, where a tradesman manufactured and sold copper sheathing for vessels, it was held that he impliedly warranted and undertook that the copper he manufactured was reasonably fit for the purpose of sheathing vessels; (*v*) and it would seem, indeed, that the mere seller of copper described as fit for sheathing vessels would be presumed to have a reasonable knowledge of the article so described and sold, and that the law would imply a warranty that the article was reasonably fit for the purpose specified. (*y*) Where a manufacturer invented and sold a " smoke-consuming furnace," and the defendant ordered it for his brewery, it was held that the law would imply no warranty that the machine was fit for the defendant's brewing-copper, and that the utmost that the vendor could be considered to undertake under such circumstances was that the machine would consume smoke, which it appeared to have done in other instances when applied to a different purpose.

620. " But," observes Lord Abinger, " if the

(*u*) Brown v. Edgington, ⌐ Sc. N. R. 496, And see Bigge v. Parkinson, 7 H. & N. 955; 31 L. J., Ex. 301.

(*v*) Jones v. Bright, 3 Moo. & P. 155; 5 Bing. 533.

(*y*) Gray v. Cox, 6 D. & R. 208; 4 B. & C. 108.

vendor had said, 'I will send you one of my smoke-consuming furnaces which will suit your brewery,' in such a case that would be a warranty that it should suit the brewery." (*z*) In an action for the price of a printing-machine, it appeared that the plaintiff had obtained a patent for a machine of which he was the inventor, which he called "Oliphant's patent two-colored printing machine," the object of which was to print calico of two colors ; that the defendant, hearing of the invention, wrote to the plaintiff to know the price, when the latter in reply said, "I undertake to make you a two-color printing machine on my patent principle ;" whereupon the defendant ordered the machine but could not make it print two colors, and therefore refused to pay the price ; but it was held that, as the defendant had got a machine made on the plaintiff's "patent principle," he had got all he had bargained for, and that there was no implied undertaking that it would, in the defendant's hands and under his management, answer the purpose for which he wanted it. (*a*) Where the defendant undertook to supply the plaintiff, who had entered into an agreement with the East India Company for the conveyance of troops to Bombay, with troop stores guaranteed to pass survey of the East India Company's officers, it was held that this express warranty did not exclude the warranty implied by law that the stores should be reasonably fit for the purpose for which they were intended. (*b*)

(*z*) Chanter v. Hopkins, 4 M. & W. 399. Camac v. Warriner, 1 C. B. 367. Prideaux v. Bunnett, 1 C. B., N. S. 616. Shepherd v. Pybus, 4 Sc. N. R. 444.

(*a*) Oliphant v. Bailey, 5 Q. B. 288 ; 13 L. J., Q. B. 34.

(*b*) Bigge v. Parkinson, 7 H. & N. 955 ; 31 L. J., Ex. 301.

[1] See Swett v. Shumway, 102 Mass. 365 ; Hogins v. Plympton, 11 Pick. 97.

621. *Implied warranties on sales of provisions.*—
Every victualler and dealer in provisions who sells
provisions impliedly warrants them to be wholesome
and fit for food. "If I come to a tavern to eat, and
the taverner gives and sells me meat and drink
corrupted, whereby I am made sick, an action lies
against him without any express warranty, because it
is a warranty in law." (*c*) If a man contracts to
supply victuals to a ship's crew, he impliedly warrants
them to be good and wholesome, and fit for the susten-
ance of man. But, where the purchaser examines
and selects the article himself, the vendor is not responsible for its being unwholesome, if he sold it
without fraud and in ignorance of its being unfit to
eat. (*d*) [1]

(*c*) Year Book, 9 Hen. 653. 1 Rolle
Abr. 90, P. pl. 2.

(*d*) Burnby v. Bollet, 16 M. & W.
644; 17 L. J., Ex. 190. Emmerton

v. Matthews, 31 L. J,. Ex. 139; 7 H.
& N. 586. But see Bigge v. Parkinson, 7 H. & N. 955; 31 L. J., Ex.
301.

[1] " In case of provisions it will be presumed that the vendor intended to represent them as sound and wholesome, because the very offer of articles for food for sale implies this,
and it may readily be presumed that a common vendor of articles of food, from the nature of his calling, knows whether
they are unwholesome and unsound or not. From the fact of
their being bad, therefore, a false and fraudulent representation may readily be presumed. But these reasons do not
apply to the case of provisions packed, inspected, and prepared for exportation in large quantities as merchandise;"
per Shaw, Ch. J., in Winsor v. Lombard, 18 Pick. 57; and
see French v. Vining, 102 Mass. 132, 136; Van Bracklin v.
Fonda, 12 Johns. 468; Marshall v. Peck, 1 Dana, 612; Humphreys v. Comline, 8 Blatchf. 508; Moses v. Mead, 1 Denio,
378; Hoover v. Peters, 18 Mich. 51; Divine v. McCormick,
50 Barb. 116; Davis v. Murphy, 14 Ind. 158; Osgood v. Lewis,
3 H. & Gill, 495; Emerson v. Brigham, 10 Mass. 197. It has
been held that there is no implied warranty in selling provisions as articles of merchandise, to one to sell again; Winsor v. Lombard, 18 Pick. 57; Mose v. Mead, 5 Denio, 678; Hart
v. Wright, 17 Wend. 267; Emerson v. Brigham, 10 Mass. 197.

622. *Sale by sample—Implied warranty.*—In all cases of sale by sample, there is an implied undertaking or promise on the part of the vendor that the sample is fairly taken from the bulk of the commodity ; but there is no warranty that the bulk is, at the time the sample is exhibited, of the same quality and description as the sample. (*e*) When there is a written contract of sale, or any note or memorandum of the bargain in writing, the circumstance of the sale being by sample, and of a representation having been made that the bulk corresponded with the sample, can not be imported into the contract and made use of by the purchaser, if the note or memorandum is silent as to the sample, unless the vendor knew of the defect, and there was consequently a deceitful and fraudulent representation ; for, wherever the contract is reduced into writing, the false affirmation or statement must be incorporated into the written contract to enable any of the contracting parties to avail themselves of it, unless it can be shown to have been false to the knowledge of the party making it, and therefore fraudulent. (*f*) If goods are sold by a written contract, which contains a description of their quality without referring to any sample, and the goods do not correspond with that description, the vendor can not exonerate himself from the consequences of the misdescription by showing that they corresponded with a sample exhibited at the time of the sale. (*g*)

(*e*) Ormrod v. Huth, 14 M. & W. 651. Sayers v. London and Birmingham Flint-Glass and Alkali Company, 27 L. J., Ex. 294.

(*f*) Meyer v. Everth, 4 Campb. 23.

Freeman v. Baker, 5 B. & Ad. 804. Moens v. Heyworth, 10 M. & W. 147.

(*g*) Tye v. Fynmore, 3 Campb. 461.

Hyland v. Sherman, 2 E. D. Smith, 234; Goldrich v. Ryan, 3 Id. 324.

But, where both parties intended the written contract to contain a stipulation that the article purchased was to be according to sample, and that stipulation is omitted by mistake, the purchaser may decline to accept the article if it does not agree with the sample. (*h*) Where goods have been sold by sample, evidence of a custom of trade, as to returning or making an allowance for such of the goods as do not answer the sample, is receivable. (*i*) [1]

623. *Warranty as to genuineness of articles with trade-marks.*—By the 25 & 26 Vict. c. 88, s. 19, in every case in which any person shall sell or contract to sell (whether by writing or not) to any other person any chattel or article with any trade-mark thereon or upon any cask, bottle, stopper, vessel, case, cover, wrapper, band, reel, ticket, label, or other thing, together with which such chattel or article shall be sold or contracted to be sold, the sale or contract to sell shall in every such case be deemed to have been made with a warranty or contract by the vendor to or with the vendee that every trade-mark upon such chattel or article, or upon any such cask, bottle, stopper, vessel, case, cover, wrapper, band, reel, ticket, label, or other thing as aforesaid, was genuine and true, and not forged or counterfeit, and not wrongfully used, unless the contrary shall be expressed in some writing signed by or on behalf of the vendor, and delivered to and accepted by the vendee.

(*h*) Borrowman v. Rossell, 16 C. B., N. S, 68 ; 33 L. J., C. P. 111.

(*i*) Cooke v. Riddelien, 1 Car. & Kirw. 561.

[1] But a custom of trade will not be allowed to reverse a rule of law ; Boardman v. Spooner, 13 Allen, 353 ; *e. q.*, a usage that a manufacturer is held not to warrant against latent defects ; Whitmore v. South Boston Iron Co., 2 Allen, 52 ; and see Dickinson v. Gray, 7 Id. 34 ; Dodd v. Farlow, 11 Id. 426.

624. *Warranty of description as to quantity or of the place or country of its manufacture.*—By the 25 & 26 Vict. c. 88, s. 20, in every case in which any person shall sell or contract to sell (whether by writing or not) to any other person any chattel or article upon which, or upon any cask, bottle, stopper, vessel, case, cover, wrapper, band, reel, ticket, label, or other thing together with which such chattel or article shall be sold or contracted to be sold, any description, statement, or other indication of or respecting the number, quantity, measure, or weight of such chattel or article, or of the place or country in which such chattel or article shall have been made, manufactured, or produced, the sale or contract to sell shall in every such case be deemed to have been made with a warranty or contract by the vendor to or with the vendee that no such description, statement, or other indication was in any material respect false or untrue, unless the contrary shall be expressed in some writing signed by or on behalf of the vendor, and delivered to and accepted by the vendee.

625. *Representations amounting to a warranty.* —Many representations and descriptions of the subject-matter of a contract are of such a nature and have been made under such circumstances, that the party making them may fairly be considered to warrant or vouch his knowledge of their truth and accuracy, so as to be estopped from afterwards setting up his want of knowledge. This is the case when the means of information are peculiarly within his reach, or he pretends to have informed himself upon the subject, and to know all about it, when in truth he knows nothing at all about it. (*k*)　　Where the

(*k*) Haycraft v. Creasy, 2 East, 103,　W. 155.　Fitzherbert v. Mather, 1 104. Moens v. Heyworth, 10 M. &　T. R. 15.

vendor of a ship published a written description of
the vessel, which represented the hull to be nearly as
good as when launched, whereas it was worm-eaten
and unseaworthy and the keel was broken, and it
appeared that the vendor had caused the description
to be written and circulated without having examined
the bottom of the vessel, and without knowing
whether the description was true or false, and the
vessel was afloat and the hull covered with water, so
that the purchaser had no means of examining the
hull himself, it was held that the vendor must be
considered to have warranted the fact to be as he asserted. (*l*)[1] If a jeweller represents a piece of crystal
to be a diamond, or a common stone to be a bezoar
stone, this would now be considered to amount to a
warranty of the fact to a purchaser, and the jeweller
would be responsible accordingly, whether he knew
the representation to be true cr false; (*m*) for,

(*l*) Schneider v. Heath, 3 Campb. 508. Pawson v. Watson, 2 Cowp. 788. Adamson v. Jarvis, 4 Bing. 73.

(*m*) Chandelor v. Lopus, Cro. Jac. 4, and the note, 1 Smith's Leading Cases 5th ed. 161.

[1] But it has been held with us that a description of
articles sold, contained in the bill of sale or elsewhere, is not
a warranty. See Carley v. Wilkins, 8 Barb. 557; Sweet v.
Colgate, 20 Johns. 196; Hotchkiss v. Gage, 26 Barb. 141; Barrett v. Hall, 1 Aiken, 269; Hastings v. Lovering, 2 Pick.
220; Seixas v. Wood, 2 Caines, 48; Whitman v. Treese, 23
Me. 213; Gosser v. Eagle, &c. Refinery, 103 Mass. 331; Daily
v. Green, 15 Pa. St. 118; Jennings v. Gratz, 3 Rawle, 168;
Carson v. Baillie, 19 Pa. St. 375; Wetherill v. Neilson, Id.
448; Borrekins v. Bevan, 3 Rawle, 23; Ender v. Scott, 11 Ill.
35; Hyatt v. Boyle, 5 Gill & J. 110; Hawkins v. Pemberton,
6 Rob. 42. But see the rule stated in the text asserted in
Winsor v. Lombard, 18 Pick. 60; Lamb v. Crafts, 12 Met.
355; Bradford v. Manly, 13 Mass. 139; Hastings v. Lovering,
2 Pick. 214; Morrill v. Wallace, 9 N. H. 11.; Wolcott v.
Mount, 7 Vroom, 262.

wherever the means of obtaining correct information lie peculiarly with the party making the assertion, and he asserts a falsehood to be the truth, not knowing whether it is or is not, he is as much responsible as if he had known the falsehood of what he asserted. (*n*) '

(*n*) Rawlins v. Wickham, 28 L. J., Ch. 192.

' An affirmation, at the time of a sale by the vendor, if it be not a mere expression of judgment or opinion, upon which he intends the purchaser shall rely, is a warranty; Rogers v. Akerman, 22 Barb. 134; Beeman v. Buck, 3 Vt. 53; Hawkins v. Berry, 5 Gilm. 36; McGregor v. Penn, 9 Yerg. 74; Ricks v. Dillahunty, 8 Port. 133; Towell v. Gatewood, 2 Scam. 24; Blythe v. Speake, 22 Texas, 430; Weimer v. Clement, 37 Penn. St. 147; House v. Fort, 4 Blackf. 296; Carter v. Black, 46 Mo. 384; Lawton v. Keil, 61 Barb. 588; Wolcott v. Mount, 7 Vroom, 262; Otts v. Alderson, 10 Sm. & M. 476; Kinley v. Fitzpatrick, 4 How. (Miss.) 59; Anderson v. Burnett, 5 Id. 165; Hanson v. King, 3 Jones (N. C.) Law, 419; McFarland v. Newman, 9 Watts, 56; Morrill v. Wallace, 9 N. H. 111; Henshaw v. Robbins, 9 Met. 83, 87, 88; Hillman v. Wilcox, 30 Me. 170; Bryant v. Crosby, 40 Id. 18; Ender v. Scott, 11 Ill. 35; Humphreys v. Comline, 8 Blackf. 508; Murphy v. Gay, 37 Mo. 535; Wilbur v. Cartwright, 44 Barb. 536; Bond v. Clark, 35 Vt. 577; Swin v. Denny, 4 Met. 151; Osgood v. Lewis, 2 H. & Gill, 495; Chapman v. Murch, 19 Johns. 290; Roberts v. Morgan, 2 Cow. 438; Whitney v. Sutton, 11 Wend. 441; Cook v. Moseley, 13 Id. 277; O'Neil v. Bacon, 1 Houst. 215; Beals v. Olmstead, 24 Vt. 114; Randall v. Thornton, 43 Me. 226; Hahn v. Doolittle, 18 Wis. 197; and this is generally a question of fact for the jury; see Tuttle v. Brown, 4 Gray, 457; Morrill v. Wallace, 9 N. H. 111; Stroud v. Pierce, 6 Allen, 413; Whitney v. Sutton, 10 Wend. 411; Foster v. Caldwell, 18 Vt. 176; Baum v. Stevens, 2 Ired. (N. C.) Law, 411; House v. Fort, 4 Blackf. 293; Duffee v. Mason, 8 Cow. 25; Whitney v. Sutton, 10 Wend. 411; Chapman v. Murch, 19 Johns. 290; Starnes v. Erwin, 10 Ired. 226; Fogart v. Blackweller, 4 Id. 238; McFarland v. Newman, 9 Watts, 56; Wolcott v. Mount, 7 Vroom, 262; Foster v. Caldwell, 18 Vt. 176; Bradford v. Bush, 10 Ala. 386; Humphreys v. Comline, 8 Blackf. 508; House v. Fort, 4 Blackf. 296; but the construction of a written contract is, of course, for the court; Brown v. Bige-

If the vendor of a house and the goodwill of a business represents the business done on the premises to
be greater than it really is, and so induces the purchaser to give more than the house or the goodwill is
worth, this amounts to a warranty of the fact stated,
although the statement may have been the result of
mistake, because the annual profit of the trade lies
peculiarly within the private knowledge of the vendor. (*o*)   It must be imputed to him that he knew
the fact ; and whether he did or did not is of no matter ; " he undertook to know, by undertaking to give
the description." (*p*)   A purchaser of a house gave
£7,350 for the house upon the faith of letters from the
vendor stating that, " the house was in so good a state
as not to require any repairs whatever," whereas the
house was, at the time the letters were written, affected
with the dry rot, and the floors gave way shortly after
the purchaser took possession of it ; and it was held
that the vendor was responsible to the purchaser for
such a sum as would put the house into the state he
had represented it to be in. (*q*)

626. *Representations not amounting to a warranty.*—But there is no warranty of the party's knowledge, or of the fact being as it is stated to be, if the
representation is made concerning some matter, the
knowledge of which lies as much within the power of
the one party as the other, and the correctness or incorrectness of which may be ascertained by the party
interested in knowing the truth by the exercise of or-

(*o*) Risney v. Selby, 1 Salk. 211.   (*p*) Calverly v. Williams, 1 Ves.
Mummery v. Paul, 1 C. B. 316. Tay-   junr. 212.
lor v. Green, 8 C. & P. 319.   (*q*) Grant v. Munt, Coop. Ch. C.
                                        173.

low, 10 Allen, 242 ; Watson v. Rowe, 16 Vt. 525 ; Stroud v.
Pierce, 1 Allen, 413 ; Smith v. Justice, 13 Wis. 600.

dinary inquiry and diligence, provided the representation is not made for the purpose of throwing the latter off his guard and preventing him from making those inquiries and examinations which every prudent person ought to make. (*r*) Thus, where a house was represented as a residence fit for a respectable family, the court said the purchaser might have seen the house and judged for himself, and he could not complain that the house did not answer the description, when ordinary diligence would have enabled him to make sure ; it was merely a puff. (*s*) So, where an estate was described as being within a ring-fence, but did not answer the description, and it appeared that the purchaser had gone over the estate before he entered into the contract, that he had lived in the neighborhood all his life, and must have known, at the time he made the bargain, whether the property did or did not lie within a ring-fence, it was held that there was no warranty and no deceit. (*t*) When a general warranty is given on a sale, defects which were apparent at the time of the making of the bargain, and were known to the purchaser, can not be relied on as a ground of action. (*u*) " If one sells purple to another, and saith to him, ' This is scarlet,' the warranty is to no purpose ; for that the other may perceive this ; and this gives no cause of action to him. To warrant a thing that may be perceived at sight is not good." (*v*)

627. *Representations of matters of opinion and belief.*—A representation, morever, frequently amounts

---

(*r*) Attwood v. Small, 6 Cl. & Fin. 338.   Clapham v. Shillito, 7 Beav, 146.

(*s*) Magennis v. Fallon, 2 Moll. 561.

(*t*) Dyer v. Hargrave, 10 Ves. 505. Cowen v. Simpson, 1 Esp. 290.

(*u*) Margetson v. Wright, 5 Moo. & P. 610 ; 7 Bing. 603 ; 1 M. & Sc. 622 ; 8 Bing. 454. Ekins v. Tresham, 1 Lev. 102.

(*v*) Baily v. Merrell, 3 Bulstr. 95.

to a mere statement of the party's own opinion and belief upon a matter concerning which the other contracting party is to exercise his own judgment, and does not amount to a positive affirmation or statement of a fact. Thus, if the vendor of a picture, submitted to the inspection and examination of the purchaser, states it to be the work of a particular artist, it is always a question for the jury to determine whether the statement amounted to a mere expression of the vendor's own opinion and belief upon a matter concerning which the buyer was to exercise his own judgment, or whether it was understood to be a positive affirmation or warranty of the fact. (*y*) Where a purchaser inquires for himself, and acts upon his own opinion, he can not say that he has been misled by the false statement of another; (*z*) and, if he inspects and examines the article for himself, and selects it after exercising his own judgment upon its character and quality, the vendor only warrants that the article is, so far as he knows, what it appeared to be, and what he believed it to be, at the time he sold it. (*a*) Thus, where the plaintiff, having heard that the defendant had some barley to sell, went to the defendant's counting-house, where a person who managed the defendant's business produced a sample of barley which he said was seed barley, and the plaintiff then looked at the barley, and said it was a good sample of seed barley, and bought it and it turned out that both parties were mistaken, and that the barley was not what was ordinarily known in the market as "seed barley," but

(*y*) Jendwine v. Slade, 2 Esp. 572. Lomi v. Tucker, 4 C. & P. 15. De Sewhanberg v. Buchanan, 5 C. & P. 343. Power v. Barham, 4 Ad. & E. 473 ; 6 N. & M. 62 ; 7 C. & P. 356.

Dunlop v. Waugh, Peake, 167.
(*z*) Jennings v. Broughton, 17 Jur, 905.
(*a*) Ormrod v. Huth, 14 M. & W. 664.

what was called " barley bigg," and it appeared that both parties had equal means of knowledge of the true character of the article, that both had believed it to be seed barley, and that it was bought and sold as such, it was held that what the defendant's servant said about the article amounted, under the circumstances, merely to an expression of his own opinion and belief about it, and did not amount to a warranty. (*b*)   But where the purchaser has not examined for himself, and has not relied upon his own judgment in the matter, but has acted upon the faith of the representation made to him, then the representation amounts, as we have seen, to a warranty of the fact. [1]

628. *Warranty on sales of horses.*—The owner of a horse who has used and driven it, or has had the means of doing so, has greater means of knowledge than a stranger who knows nothing about the animal. If, therefore, the owner offers the horse for sale, every representation that he makes to the buyer respecting the qualities and capabilities of the animal amounts to a warranty, although the word warrant is never used by him.   " If parties are dealing for a horse, and the seller says, ' You may depend upon it that the horse is perfectly free from vice,' that is a very sufficient warranty, though the word warrant was not used." (*c*)   If the purchaser of a horse tells the vendor in a letter, " You represented the horse to me as a five-year-old," and the defendant answers, " The horse is as I represented," this is evidence from which a warranty may be inferred. (*d*)   If a horse offered for

---

(*b*) Carter v. Crick, 4 H. & N. 416 ;   b.   Cave v. Coleman, 3 M. & R. 4.
28 L. J., Ex. 238.   (*d*) Salmon v. Ward, 2 C. & P.
(*c*) Thorogood's case, 2 Co. Rep. 9a,   211.

[1] See *ante.* note 1, § 624.

sale has a cough and running at the nose, and the vendor says that it is a mere cold, and that he will deliver the horse sound and free from blemish in a week, that amounts to a warranty to a purchaser that the horse has nothing more than a cold upon him. (*e*) " If a purchaser," observes BEST, C. J., "asks for a carriage-horse, or a horse fit to carry a lady, or a timid or infirm person, the seller who knows the qualities of the horse he supplies in answer to the demand, undertakes, on every principle of honesty, that it is fit for the purpose specified." (*f*) We have already seen that a warranty will not bind a man in a thing that is apparent, as to warrant that a horse has both his eyes, when he has manifestly lost one of them. (*g*) If, therefore, at the time of the sale of a horse, the animal is warranted sound in wind and limb, that is understood to mean saving those manifest and visible defects which were obvious to all observers; and, if the horse was manifestly blind or obviously lame, and the purchaser examined the animal before he bought it, and must have been aware of these patent defects, the vendor's representation will give no cause of action. But a purchaser who relies upon a warranty is not bound to make any particular examination of a horse before he buys, to ascertain whether a defect exists. If, relying upon a warranty, he omits to make any particular examination of the animal, and consequently fails to discover a defect which might have been ascertained by examination, he is, nevertheless, entitled to maintain an action; (*h*) and if a manifest defect is not necessarily of a permanent nature—if a horse has a cough and running at

(*e*) Liddard v. Kain, 9 Moore, 356.

(*f*) Jones v. Bright, 3 Moo. & P. 175.

(*g*) Ekins v. Tresham, 1 Lev. 102.

(*h*) Holyday v. Morgan, 28 L. J. Q. B. 9.

the nose, and the vendor says that it is merely a cold, and that the horse will be sound and well in a given time, and the purchaser buys in reliance upon the truth of the representation—the vendor, as we have seen, will be responsible in damages if the horse continues unsound and permanently diseased. (*i*) [1]

629. *Proof of warranties.*—It has been held that a warranty made orally, on the completion of a written contract of sale, can not be introduced as part of the contract, if the contract itself is silent as to the fact of the warranty, as it is a rule of law that oral evidence shall not be given " to superadd any term to a written agreement, for it would be setting aside all written contracts, and rendering them of no effect." But although a warranty can not be superadded to a written contract by oral testimony, yet, if it can be shown that the contract was induced by an oral warranty made by one of two contracting parties, which was false to the knowledge of the party making it, and was made for the purpose of throwing the other contracting party off his guard, and fraudulently obtaining his consent to the bargain, this is a circumstance altogether collateral to the contract, and the proof of it by oral testimony does not in anywise infringe upon the preceding rule of law. The oral evidence can not be received to show that the contract itself was different from that authenticated by the written instrument ; but it is admissible to show that

(*i*) Liddard v. Kain, *supra.*

[1] Roberts v. Jenkins, 21 N. H. 116; Burlon v. Young, 5 Harr. 233 ; and see Whitney v. Taylor, 54 Barb. 536 ; Foudren v. Durfee, 39 Miss. 324 ; Kornegay v. White, 10 Ala. 255 ; Brown v. Bigelow, 10 Allen, 244 ; Hook v. Stovall, 21 Geo. 69 ; Crouch v. Culbreath, 11 Rich. 9 ; Woodbury v. Robbins, 10 Cush. 520.

the assent of the party to the contract was obtained under false pretenses, and that the contract is bottomed in fraud, and has therefore no legal existence. Ex dolo non oritur contractus. The oral evidence of the false and fraudulent representation in such a case has not the effect of altering, varying, or adding to the written contract ; but admitting the contract in all its terms, it seeks to show that the party guilty of the fraud ought not to have the assistance of a court of justice for the enforcement of it. " If duress be pleaded, or a false reading of the deed, you avoid the deed at law by parol evidence : but then these facts are collateral to the import of the instrument ; they do not vary or alter it." The oral evidence is offered, not to affect the terms of the contract itself, but to destroy the remedy by way of action upon it. (*k*) An unstamped written agreement may be given in evidence to prove fraud, if it is used merely for the purpose of showing that a person paying money has been imposed upon. (*l*) Where representations which may amount to a warranty are contained in letters which constitute a contract of sale, evidence is admissible of the surrounding circumstances for the purpose of showing that no warranty was contemplated by the parties. (*m*)

630. *Construction of expess warranties.*—Where there was an agreement for the sale and purchase of all the naphtha the defendant might make during two years, " say from 1,000 to 1,200 gallons a month," it was held that these words did not amount to an undertaking or warranty that that quantity of naphtha

---

(*k*) Collins v. Blantern, 2 Wils. 347. Davis v. Symonds, 1 Cox. 405. Wright v. Crookes, 1 Sc. N. R. 698. Hutchinson v. Morley, 7 Sc. 341.

(*l*) Holmes v. Sixsmith, 7 Exch. 807 ; 21 L. J., Ex. 312.

(*m*) Stucley v. Bailey, 1 H. & C. 405 ; 31 L. J., Ex. 483.

should be manufactured and sold per month. (*n*)
But, where the agreement was to prepare and sell
"say not less than 100," &c., it was held that the
words did amount to a warranty or undertaking that
at least the quantity specified should be prepared and
sold. (*o*) Warranties of quantity and quality made on
sales of goods and chattels will be regulated by the
apparent intention of the parties at the time the contract was entered into.   There is no necessity that the
word "warrant" or "promise" should occur in the
bargain; but the promise or representation must form
part of the contract of sale. (*p*) Where a sale note
made on the purchase of a horse described the animal
as "a black gelding, about five years old, constantly
driven in the plough—warranted," it was held that, if
the word "warranted" had been placed at the commencement of the sentence, it would have extended
to the sex and age of the horse, and his fitness for the
plough; but as it concluded the sentence, it extended
only to the soundness of the animal, the preceding
sentences being merely descriptive of the horse, and
of the work to which it had been accustomed. (*q*)
And where the seller gave the purchaser a written
receipt for the purchase-money, describing the horse
as a bay gelding, got by Cheshire Cheese, warranted
sound, it was held that the warranty was confined to
the soundness of the animal, and did not extend to
the description of his parentage.   So, where a written
receipt described the horse sold as "a gray four years'
old colt, warranted sound in every respect," it was

(*n*) Gwillim v. Daniell, 2 C. M. & R.
61.

(*o*) Leeming v. Snaith, 16 Q. B. 275.
As to the effect of the words "about"
or ".more or less," see *ante.* Bourne
v. Seymour, 25 L. T. R. 162, " net

proceeds." Caine v. Horsfall, 1 Exch.
523.

(*p*) Hopkins v. Tangueray, 15 C. B.
138.

(*q*) Richardson v. Brown, 8 Moore,
338.

held that the warranty did not extend to the description of the age of the animal, and that if the parties
had meant to warrant the age as well as the soundness of the colt, the words should have been "warranted a four years' old colt, and sound in every
respect." (*r*)   Where, on the sale of a horse, the seller
signed the following warranty,—" Mr. C. bought of
Mr. G. G. a bay horse for ninety pounds, warranted
sound. £90. Warranted sound for one month,"—it
was held that the latter words limited the duration of
the warranty, and meant that it was to continue in
force for one month only, and that complaint of unsoundness must, therefore, be made by the purchaser
within one month of the sale. (*s*)   But the construction to be put upon contracts and representations of
· this description will be regulated by the surrounding
circumstances of each particular case, which must be
regarded in order that the true meaning and intention
of the parties may be discovered.[1]

631. *Warranties by agents.*—The general presumption is that, where a principal intrusts property
to an agent to sell, he authorizes him to make all
such warranties as are usual in the ordinary course of
that particular business of selling, and that, if it is

(*r*) Budd v. Fairmaner, 1 M. & Sc.   (*s*) Chapman v. Gwyther, L. R., 1
78. As to unsoundness, see Kiddell   Q. B. 643 ; 35 L. J., Q. B. 142.
v. Burnard, 9 M. & W. 670.

[1] Parol evidence is admissible to explain a warranty;
Bradford v. Manly, 13 Mass. 139; Atwater v. Clancy, 107 Id.
369; Hazard v. Loring, 10 Cush. 267; Frost v. Blanchard, 97
Mass. 155; not if the warranty be in a receipt, which is a complete contract. But see Niles v. Culver, 8 Barb. 205 ; Good-
year v. Ogden, 4 Hill, 104; Batturs v. Sellers, 5 Har. & J. 117 ;
Chapman v. Searle, 3 Pick. 38 ; or bills of parcels; Boardman
v. Spooner, 13 Allen, 353 ; Harris v. Johnston, 3 Cranch, 311 ;
Foot v. Bentley, 44 N. Y. 166; Sutton v. Crosby, 54 Barb. 80.

usual to sell with a warranty, he has an implied authority to warrant. (*t*)[1] The agent or servant of a horse-dealer has an implied authority to bind his principal or master by a warranty, even although (unknown to the buyer) he has express orders not to warrant; and evidence of an alleged custom among horse-dealers not to give a warranty where the purchaser obtained a veterinary-surgeon's certificate of soundness, is not admissible to contradict such implied authority. (*u*) But a servant intrusted on one particular occasion to sell has no implied authority to warrant so as to bind the owner. (*v*)

632. *Effect of a breach of warranty by the vendor.*—If it appears to have been the intention of the parties that a sale of chattels should be an absolute sale with a warranty, superadded, the purchaser can not an-

(*t*) Dingle v. Hare, 7 C. B., N. S. 145 ; 29 L. J., C. P. 148.
(*u*) Howard v. Sheward, 36 L. J., C. P. 42.

(*v*) Brady v. Tod, 9 C. B., N. S. 592 ; 30 L. J., C. P. 223. But as to this, see *ante.*

[1] Woodford v. McClenahan, 4 Gilman, 85 ; Bradford v. Bush, 10 Ala. 386 ; Peters v. Farnsworth, 15 Vt. 155 ; Boothby v. Scales, 27 Wis. 626 ; Skinner v. Gunn, 9 Porter, 305 ; Gaines v. McKinley, 1 Ala. (N. S.) 446 ; Bryant v. Moore, 26 Me. 84 ; Sandford v. Handy, 23 Wend. 260 ; Nelson v. Cowing, 6 Hill, 337 ; Hunter v. Jameson, 6 Ired. 252 ; Williamson v. Connaday, 3 Id. 349 ; Taggart v. Stanberry, 2 McLean, 543 ; Upton v. Suffolk, &c. Mills, 11 Cush. 416 ; Lane v. Dudley, 2 Murph. 119 ; Ezell v. Franklin, 2 Sneed (Tenn.) 236 ; Croom v. Shaw, 1 Fla. 211 ; Morris v. Bowen, 52 N. H. 416 ; Palmer v. Hatch, 46 Mo. 585 ; Randall v. Kehlor, 60 Me. 37 ; Fay v. Richmond, 43 Vt. 25 ; the agent may sell by sample and warrant ; Andrews v. Kneeland, 6 Cow. 353 ; but it is said, he may not warrant for the future, as, *e. g.*, that flour should keep sweet on a voyage to California ; Upton v. Suffolk &c. Mills, 11 Cush. 586 ; and see Randall v. Kehlor, 60 Me. 37 ; a broker may not, it seems, bind his principal by warranty ; Dodd v. Farlow, 11 Allen, 426 ; neither can an auctioneer ; Blood v. French, 9 Gray, 197.

nul the sale and return the thing sold, unless there has
been actual fraud, and the vendor knew, at the time of
the sale, that the thing sold did not answer the warranty ;
but, if the sale is conditional on the thing sold being
in accordance with the warranty, the purchaser will
be entitled to annul the sale, and return the article
and recover the price, if the condition is not fulfilled.
Where the plaintiff exchanged a watch with the
defendant for a pair of candlesticks, warranted to be
silver, which turned out to be base metal, it was held
that the defendant could not rescind the contract and
return the candlesticks and claim back his watch
without proving that the plaintiff knew that the
candlesticks were not silver at the time he gave the
warranty. (*y*)   Lord ELDON is reported to have said
that, if a person purchases a horse which is warranted
sound, and it afterwards turns out that the horse was
unsound at the time of the warranty, the buyer might
return the horse and bring an action to recover the
full money paid, but that the seller had a right to expect that the horse should be returned in the same
state he was in when sold, and not by any means
diminished in value. (*z*)   " It is, however, impossible,"
justly observes Lord TENTERDEN, " to reconcile this
doctrine with those cases in which it has been held
that where the property in the specific chattel has
passed to the vendee, and the price has been paid, he
has no right, upon the breach of the warranty, to
return the article and re-vest the property in the
vendor, and recover the price as on a consideration
which has failed, but must sue upon the warranty,
unless there has been a condition in the contract
authorizing the return, or the vendor has received

(*y*) Emanuel v. Dane, 3 Camp.   (*z*) Curtis v. Hannay, 3 Esp. 83.
300.

back the chattel, and has thereby consented to rescind the contract, or has been guilty of a fraud,
which destroys the contract altogether." " If these
cases," observes his lordship, " are rightly decided,—
and we think they are; and they certainly have
always been acted upon,—it is clear that the purchaser
can not by his own act alone, unless in the excepted
cases above mentioned, re-vest the property in the
seller and recover the price, when paid, on the ground
of the total failure of consideration." (*a*)   Where
goods are sold "guaranteed equal to sample," if the
sale is not of specific goods, such a clause is a condition going to the essence of the contract, and the
buyer may reject them if they are not equal to
sample ; but, where the sale is of specific goods, such
a clause is collateral to the covenant, and, if the goods
are not equal to sample, only entitles the buyer to a
reduction of the price, or to an action for damages.
(*b*)   If, however, the thing delivered does not answer
the description of that which was sold, if, that is, it
differs in kind and not in quality only, the buyer is
not bound to take it; and, if he has paid for it, he
may recover back the money as upon a failure of
consideration. (*c*)[1]

(*a*) Street v. Blay, 2 B. & Ad. 462.
Dawson v. Collis, 10 C. B. 153. Parsons v. Sexton, 4 C. B. 907 ; 16 L. J.,
C. P. 184. Toulmin v. Hadley. 2 C.
& K. 157. Foster v. Smith, 18 C. B.
160. Heyworth v. Hutchinson, L. R.,
2 Q. B. 447; 36 L. J., Q. B. 720.

Gottorno v. Adams, 12 C. B., N. S
566.

(*b*) Heyworth v. Hutchinson, L. R.,
2 Q. B. 451 ; 36 L. J., Q. B. 270.

(*c*) Azemar v. Casella, L. R., 2 C.
P. 431 ; Ib., 677 ; 36 L. J., C. P. 124.
263.

[1] The buyer may bring his action for breach of warranty at
once, without returning the goods ; but his continued possession of them, and their actual value would be considered in
estimating the damages ; 1 Parsons on Contracts, 591, citing
Cary v. Gruman, 4 Hill (N. Y.) 625 ; Voorhees v. Earl, 2 Id.
288; Comstock v. Hutchinson, 10 Barb. 211 ; Hitchcock v.

633. *Conditional and defeasible sales.*—If on the
sale of a horse it is part of the bargain that the
animal shall be taken back if it is unsound, or does
not answer the warranty, the purchaser will be
entitled to return the animal, and recover back the
purchase money, on proof of the unsoundness of the
horse. Where an agent intrusted to sell a mare, but
not being authorized to warrant her, refused to do so,
but at the time of the sale told the purchaser that, if
the mare was not all right, she was not his, and the
purchaser then paid the price and took away the mare,

Hunt, 28 Conn. 343 ; Krabton v. Kile, 21 Ill. 180. If he has
sold a part before the discovery of the breach, and therefore
can not return them, he may still rescind the sale, and will be
liable for the market value of what he does not return.
Shields v. Pettee, 4 Comst. 122. If the vendor refuses to receive them again, the purchaser may sell them, and recover
from the vendor the loss, if any, upon the resale, with the expense of keeping the goods and of the resale ; Buffington v.
Quantain, 17 Pa. St. 310 ; Woodward v. Thatcher, 21 Vt. 580.
" We should say, on the reason of the thing, that if the buyer
sells the goods with all proper precautions as to time, place,
and manner, to insure a fair sale, the vendor will be bound by
the price the goods bring, whether that be in fact equal to
their value or not; but this may not yet be established by
adjudication." 1 Parsons on Contracts, 593. " If he has a
right to return the goods, his tender of them completes his
right to sue for the price, whether the vendor receives them
or not." Id. Thornton v. Wynn, 12 Wheat. 193. But this right
to return for breach of warranty has been limited to cases of
fraud, or where the parties had so expressly agreed. Thornton v. Wynn, 12 Wheat. 183. In Pennsylvania, Kase v. John,
10 Watts, 107. In Tennessee, Allen v. Anderson, 3 Humph.
581 ; Carter v. Walker, 2 Rich. L. 40; Cary v. Gruman, 4
Hill (N. Y.) 625 ; Voorhees v. Earl, 2 Id. 288 ; Lightburn v.
Cooper, 1 Dana, 273. Breach of warranty has been held not
to be a bar to an action by the vendor for the price ; West v.
Cutting, 19 Vt. 536 ; Freeman v. Clute, 3 Barb. 424 ; delay in
returning may be construed as an acceptance by the purchaser
if occurring after the discovery of the deficiency in the goods.
Clements v. Smith's Administrators, 9 Gill, 156.

and, the animal proving to be unsound, he returned
her and sued for the price, it was held that there was
evidence for a jury of the sale being accompanied
with a condition authorizing a return of the mare and
enabling the purchaser to recover the price on proof
of her unsoundness; (*d*) so, where, pending a negotiation for a sale of hops, the growth of 300 acres,
the purchaser declared that he would not have the
hops if the bine had been sulphured, and required and
received a written undertaking from the vendor that
no sulphur had been used, and the hops were then
delivered to and received by the purchaser, and it was
then ascertained that sulphur had been used on five
acres by way of experiment without the knowledge
of the vendor, and that these sulphured hops were so
mixed with the unsulphured as to be undistinguish-
able, it was held that the purchaser had a right to
avail himself of the breach of the condition and
annul the bargain. (*e*) If a horse is sold on the
terms that the buyer is to have the horse a certain
time on trial, the sale is conditional on the purchaser's
approval of the horse after trial, so that, if he tries
the horse and then returns it, there is no sale. In
these cases the right of property in the specific thing
sold passes subject to a condition. If the condition
is fulfilled or waived, the sale becomes an absolute
sale; if it is not fulfilled or waived, the party in
whose favor and for whose protection the condition
was imposed is entitled to repudiate the contract and
return the subject-matter of the sale and recover the
price. (*f*) Where a mare was sold on the terms that,
if she proved in foal, she was to be returned, and the

(*d*) Foster v. Smith, 18 C. B. 156.   (*f*) Behn v. Burness, 32 L. J., Q.
(*e*) Bannerman v. White, 10 C. B.,   B. 204.
N. S. 844; 31 L. J., C. P. 28.

mare proved in foal, it was held that the vendor had
a right to have the animal returned to him. (*g*)
Where the sale is defeasible within a certain time, the
fact that the thing sold has within that time, and
without any negligence on the part of the purchaser,
ceased to exist, does not disable the purchaser from
avoiding the contract. Where a horse was sold with
a condition that he might be returned within a
specified time if he did not answer the description
given of him, and within the time the horse died,
without any negligence on the part of the purchaser,
it was held that the latter was ent'tled to rescind the
contract and recover the price of the horse which did
not answer the description. (*h*)

634. *Sale or return.*—When goods are sold under
a contract of " sale or return," the sale is a conditional
or defeasible sale. The right of property in the goods
passes to the purchaser subject to be divested out of
him and re-vested in the vendor by a return of the goods
to the latter, in accordance with the terms of the contract. If the goods are returned or tendered back to the
vendor within a reasonable time, the sale is annulled,
and the latter can not recover the price of them ; but
if the purchaser, having got possession of the goods,
fails to exercise his option of returning them within a
reasonable time, the contract is discharged of the condition, the sale stands as an absolute sale, and the
price of the goods may be recovered in an action for
goods sold and delivered. (*i*) So, if goods are
sold and delivered on the terms that the purchaser
is to have three or six months' credit, provided

(*g*) Williams v. Burgess, 10 Ad. &
E. 502.

(*h*) Head v. Tattersall, L. R , 7 Ex.
7 ; 41 L. J., Ex. 4.

(*i*) Moss v. Sweet, 16 Q. B. 493 ; 20
L. J., Q. B. 167, overruling Iley v.
Frankenstein, as reported, 8 Sc. N. R.
841.

he gives the vendor the security of a bill or note at
three or six months, and the purchaser refuses to give
the bill or note, the sale stands as an absolute sale, and
the price is immediately recoverable. (*k*)

635. *Redhibitory defects enabling a purchaser to
annul a contract of sale and recovered the price.*—It is a
maxim of the civil law, that " he who has sold one thing
for another, an old thing for a new, or a less quantity
than what he undertook to sell, is bound to take back
the thing or abate the price, and make good the damages sustained by the purchaser." (*l*) All defects which
deprived the purchaser of the use and enjoyment of
the subject-matter of the sale altogether, or which rendered it unfit for the purpose for which it was known to
be required, were, by the Roman lawyers, called red-
bibitory defects, because they gave rise to the redhibitory action, which was brought to compel the vendor
to take back the thing sold and refund the price. (*m*)
When the defects in the thing sold gave rise to a red-
hibition and dissolution of the sale, the vendor and purchaser were restored to the condition they were in
before the sale. The vendor was bound to restore the
price paid, with interest, and the purchaser was bound
to restore to the vendor the subject-matter of the sale
with all the profits and advantages he had reaped from
it whilst it was in his possession. (*n*) '

636. *Sales rendered avoidable on the ground of*

(*k*) Rugg v. Weir, *ante.*

(*l*) Domat. liv. I, tit. 2, s. 11, 15
Dig. lib. 18, tit. 1, lex. 45 ; lib. 19, tit.
1, lex 21, § 2.

(*m*) Dig. lib. 21, tit. 1, 21, 27. As
to redhibitory defects in the French
law, see Troplong, ch. 4, DE LA
VENTE.

(*n*) Factâ redhibitione, omnia in
integrum restituuntur, perinde ac si
neque emptio neque venditio inter-
cessit. Dig. lib. 21, tit. 1, lex. 60, l.
23, § 7.

' See *ante*, § 632, and note 1.

fraudulent misrepresentation.—It is not every willful false statement, made with full knowledge of its false-hood, that will amount in judgment of law to a fraud, so as to enable a purchaser to avoid a contract of sale. The ordinary praise or commendation, for example, bestowed by a vendor on the wares he sells, though embodying statements of fact known by the party making them to be not strictly true, does not vitiate the contract of sale.

637. A misrepresentation, moreover, to enable a purchaser to avoid a sale on the ground of deceit and fraud, must be made concerning some matter very material to the value of the contract, so that there may be fair ground for thinking that the contract would never have been entered into if the false statement had not been made. De minimis non curat lex, and, therefore, if a man represents his house to be in good repair, and a few tiles are off the roof, or two or three of the joists under the floor near the ground are rotted with the damp, or a pane of glass is broken in a garret window, such trifling defects, to use the language of Lord KENYON, " are mere bagatelles," and afford no evidence of mala fides. (*o*)   To all trifling and unimportant representations, not seriously affecting the value of the contract, and to all affirmations of matters of opinion and judgment, not amounting to positive assertions of fact with knowledge of their falsehood, the maxim of caveat emptor must apply; (*p*) for, whilst we ought not, on the one hand, to suffer plain dealing, simplicity, and good faith to become a prey to double dealing and treachery, so, on the other hand, we ought not readily to annul contracts, because

(*o*) Geddes v. Pennington, 5 Dow. 163, 164.

(*p*) Lowndes v. Lane, 2 Cox, 363. Benham v. Un. Guar. &c., 7 Exch. 744.

everything has not been conducted within the bounds of a perfect sincerity. (*q*) " Nothing but what is plainly injurious to good faith ought to be considered as a fraud sufficient to impeach a contract; dolum non nisi perspicuis indiciis probari convenit." (*r*)

638. *Fraudulent concealment.*—If a vendor has resorted to any contrivance for the purpose of concealing any defect in the subject-matter of a contract of sale, the purchaser may avoid the contract on the ground of fraud; but the vendor is not bound to point out defects which may be seen on examination. (*s*) It has been held that there was a .fraudulent concealment vitiating a contract of sale in the following cases : —where a partner who had the exclusive management and control of the partnership business, agreed to purchase the share of his co-partner, but kept back from the knowledge of the latter the true state of the accounts and of the amount of profit realized, and by that means effected the purchase for a less sum than would have been taken if the state of the partnership had been fully disclosed and fairly stated;—(*t*) where the purchaser of a policy of insurance, having secret information of the alarming illness and imminent danger of death of the party on whose life the policy had been effected, treated with an assignee of the policy for the purchase of it without disclosing the condition and state of health of the assured;—(*u*) where the vendor of a mare stated, at the time of sale, that he believed the mare to be sound but would not warrant, and the mare was at the time unsound to his

(*q*) Domat. liv. 1, tit. 18, s. 3, § 2.

(*r*) Poth. OBLIGATIONS, No. 30. As to the avoidance of contracts on the ground of fraudulent misrepresentation, see *ante.*

(*s*) Horsfall v. Thomas, 1 H. & C. 98 ; 31 L. J., Ex. 322.

(*t*) Maddeford v. Austwick, 1 Sim. 89.

(*u*) Jones v. Keene, 2 Mood. & Rob. 350.

knowledge ;—(v) where the vendor of pimento, knowing it to be sea-damaged, sold it without disclosing
the fact to the purchaser ;—(y) where the agent of
the vendor of a picture, knowing that he had induced
the purchaser to labor under a delusion with respect
to the picture, which materially influenced his judgment as to the value of it, permitted him to purchase
without removing the delusion. (z)[1]   But the vendor

(v) Wood v. Smith, 5 M. & R. 124.   the observations on this case by
(y) Jones v. Bowden, 4 Taunt. 847.   JERVIS, C. J., Keates v. Earl Cadogan,
(z) Hill v. Gray, 1 Stark. 434. See 20 L. J., C. P. 78.

[1] As to concealment of a material fact which it was a vend-
or's duty to reveal, see Otlis v. Raymond, 3 Conn. 413 ; Brown
v. Montgomery, 20 N. Y. 287 ; Van Arsdale v. Howard, 5 Ala.
596; Castleman v. Griffin, 13 Wis. 535 ; Hagee v. Grossman, 31
Ind. 223; Irvine v. Kirkpatrick, 7 Bell S. C. App. 186 ; Matthews
v. Bliss,22 Pick. 48; Paddock v. Strobridge, 29 Vt. 470; Sides v.
Hilleary, 6 Harr. & J. 86 ; Nickley v. Thomas, 22 Barb. 652 ;
Hanson v. Edgerly, 29 N. H. 343.   If the vendor use any de-
vice calculated to induce the other party to refrain from inquiring into a material fact, upon which the former has information (although such information be not exclusively
within his reach), in order to induce the sale, such transaction is voidable; Prentiss v. Russ, 16 Me. 30; Smith v.
Richards, 13 Peters, 26; Howell v. Biddlecom, 62 Barb. 131;
Coddington v. Goddard, 16 Gray, 436 ; silence on the part of
the vendor, as to a known defect, has been held to amount to
a fraud.   So, where one sold part of a lot of hay on which he
knew white lead to have been spilt without informing the
purchaser, who bought the hay for the purpose of feeding it to
a cow, and the cow dies from eating the hay, the vendor of
the hay is liable for the loss of the cow, even though he care-
fully endeavored to separate and remove the damaged hay,
and thought that he had succeeded; French v. Vining, 102
Mass. 135 ; and see Hoitt v. Holcomb, 32 N. H. 185; Veasey
v. Doton, 3 Allen, 380; Brown v. Castles, 11 Cush. 350;
Aberaman Iron Works v. Wickens, L. R. 4 Ch. Ap. 101 ; S.
C. L. R. 5 Eq. 485 ; Stephens v. Orman, 10 Florida, 9 ; Dickenson v. Lee, 106 Mass. 556.   Where an action was brought on
notes given for guano sold, and the defense set up was that
the article was worthless and not reasonably suited to the use

is not bound to inform the purchaser that the latter is under a mistake, when such mistake is not induced by the act of the vendor. Thus where the plaintiff offered to sell some oats to the defendant, and the defendant agreed to buy them supposing them to be old oats, but the plaintiff did nothing to induce the defendant, to suppose so, it was held that the sale was valid. (*a*) [1]

(*a*) Smith v. Hughes, L. R. 6 Q. B. 597 ; 40 L. J., Q. B. 221.

intended, upon which point the evidence was conflicting, and it appeared that at the time of the sale plaintiffs' agent de-- livered to defendants a jar containing some of said guano, telling them to keep it until the crop matured, and if dissatisfied they might select any chemist in the United States to analyze the sample, and if it did not come up to plaintiffs' published analysis they need not pay for the same, but the jar was lost and its contents never were analyzed : Held, that it was error in the court to refuse to charge the jury " that to entitle the defendants to a verdict in their favor they must show clearly that their bad crop resulted from the worthlessness of the guano ;" Wilcox v. Howard, 51 Ga. 298.

[1] The fraud must be successful in procuring the purchase in order to be actionable; Taylor v. Fleet, 1 Barb. 471 ; Doggett v. Emerson, 3 Story, 732, 733 ; Bowman v. Carithers, 40 Ind. 90; Hagee v. Grossman, 31 Ind. 223; Mason v. Crosby, 1 Wood. & M. 342; Clark v. Everhart, 63 Penn. St. 347; Vandewalker v. Osmer, 65 Barb. 556; Phipps v. Buckman, 30 Penn. St. 402; Morris Canal Co. v. Everett, 9 Paige, 168; Stebbins v. Eddy, 4 Mason, 414. Though it need not be the sole inducement; Shaw v. Stone, 8 Bosw. 157; the presumption, however, in such a case is that false representations of the vendor were relied on by the purchaser; Holbrook v. Burt, 22 Pick. 546 ; he has a right to rely on the vendor's representations; Young v. Harris, 2 Ala. 108; Clapton v. Cogart, 3 Sm. & M. 363; Bean v. Herrick, 12 Me. 262 ; Vandewalker v. Osmer, 65 Barb. 556; Rose v. Hurley, 39 Ind. 82, 83; Mead v. Bunn, 32 N. Y. 275; but as to where the vendor honestly believed his representations to be true, see French v. Vining, 102 Mass. 132; Beach v. Bemiss, 107 Mass. 491 ; Russell v. Clark, 7 Cranch, 69; Young v. Covell, 8 Johns. 25; Boyd v. Browne, 6 Barr, 310 ; Lord v. Goddard, 13 How.

In sales of manufactured articles and provisions, if the vendor is cognizant, at the time he sells the articles, of latent defects materially lowering their value, (U. S.) 196; Weeks v. Burton, 7 Vt. 67; Cooper v. Lovering, 106 Mass. 78, 79; Brown v. Castles, 11 Cush. 348, 351; McDonald v. Trafton, 15 Me. 225; King v. Eagle Mills, 10 Allen, 548; Stone v. Denny, 4 Met. 151; Stevens v. Fuller, 8 N. H. 463. Akin to these are actions for sales of dangerous or poisonous articles, where the vendor, either through carelessness or willfulness, neglects to give notice of its character. So a druggist who sells poison so labelled as to give the idea that it is harmless, is liable for any damage done by it, if there is no negligence on the part of others contributing. Norton v. Sewell, 106 Mass. 143; Thomas v. Winchester, 2 Selden, 397; Davidson v. Nichols, 11 Allen, 519, 520; McDonald v. Snelling, 14 Allen, 290, 295. And so, one who sells inflammable oil for illuminating purposes, is liable for the consequences, if not too remote; Wellington v. Downer Kerosene, &c. Co., 104 Mass. 64; or gunpowder to one too young to know how to use it; though in a case where it appeared that the child's parents had permitted him to use it, the defendant might not be liable for a result to which their own negligence contributed; Carter v. Towne, 103 Mass. 507.

Another kind of misrepresentation avoiding a contract was examined in Holtz v. Schmidt (59 N. Y 253). There defendants agreed that if plaintiff would purchase from them such goods as he should, from time to time, require in his business, they would sell as low as they sold the same description of goods to any other dealer. With this understanding, plaintiff made various cash purchases from time to time, the prices being fixed by reference to defendants' printed price lists which they represented to be as low as they sold to any other dealer. Defendants were at the time of the purchases selling the same kind of goods at lower prices. *Held* (GROVER, J., dissenting), that plaintiff, upon a subsequent discovery of this fact, could maintain an action ex contractu, to recover the difference between the prices paid and what the goods were sold for to others; that although the agreement created no valid obligation at the time it was made, it having been acted upon and purchases made in reference thereto, became as to such purchases a material part of the contract between the parties; and that the assent of plaintiff to pay the prices named, relying upon defendants' assurance, did not preclude him from resorting to the contract.

and rendering them totally unfit for the purpose for
which they are known to be required, and neglects to
disclose such defects to the purchaser, he is guilty of
a fraudulent concealment. (*b*)   But, in a general sale
of a horse, the vendor is not bound to disclose any
unsoundness in the animal, although he may be aware
of its existence ; and, if the purchaser makes no
inquiries as to its soundness or qualities, and the
vendor has said or done nothing to throw the purchaser off his guard or to conceal a defect, there is no
fraudulent concealment on the part of the vendor. (*c*)
The purchaser has an opportunity of inspecting and
judging of the animal himself; and the principle of
caveat emptor applies.[1]

(*b*) *Ante.* Fitz. N. B. 94, C.   175. Fitz. N. B. 94, C. Hill v. Balls.
(*c*) Jones v. Bright, 3 Moo. & P,   27 L. J., Ex. 48.

[1] Where the vendor of cattle made declarations of opinion
as to their weight, which he knew to be false, and the vendee
was induced by those declarations to purchase the cattle at a
certain price per head ; and he was not aware that the vendor
knew (approximately) their true weight ; and it was in his
power, without any great difficulty, to have had them weighed
before agreeing to purchase ; and in an action upon a note given
for a part of the purchase price of the cattle, the jury having
found the sale to have been effected by fraud and deceit, and
having awarded a certain sum to defendant by way of recoup-
ment for his damages resulting from such fraud, a judgment
pursuant to the verdict is here affirmed, and the fact that the
vendee weighed the cattle before making any payment thereon,
will not prevent his recouping damages for the vendor's
fraud, it appearing that he was not aware, when such payment was made and the note given, that the plaintiff had
actual knowledge that the statements made by him were
false.   The cattle having been purchased by defendant at
Chicago, the measure of his damages is the difference between
their actual value in the Chicago market at the time of the
purchase, and the value which they would have had in the
same market if their weight had been as represented.   Bird-
sey v. Butterfield, 34 Wis. 52.

639. *Sales " with all faults."*—If it be made a term of the contract that the subject-matter of the sale is to be taken with all faults, the stipulation will release the vendor from the obligation of disclosing all such defects as are susceptible of discovery by a rigid examination of the subject-matter of the sale. (*d*) If the vendor is not to be responsible for any defect or " error," the stipulation will protect him from all unintentional misdescription and mis-statement. Therefore, where a shipowner advertised for sale " the fine teak-built barque, *Intrepid*, A 1, as she now lies in dock, well adapted for a passenger-ship," but stipulated that the vessel was to be taken with all faults, without any allowance for any defect or error whatever, and it turned out that the barque was not teak-built, nor of class A 1, nor adapted for a passenger-ship, it was held that, as the defendant distinctly stated that he would warrant nothing, the advertisement must be taken as a mere description of the vessel, and that the real meaning of the contract was this—There is the vessel in dock; I describe her as A 1, and call her a teak-built barque ; I do not mean to warrant anything. Go and look at her, and examine and judge for yourself; and if you take her, you take her with all her faults, without any allowance for any error or misdescription on my part. (*c*)

But an agreement " to take a thing with all faults does not mean that it is to be taken with all frauds;" and the stipulation will be of no avail to the vendor, if he has knowingly and willfully misled the purchaser, or thrown him off his guard by a willful and intentional false representation, or has resorted to any art or contrivance to conceal a defect. Thus, where the

(*d*) Pickering v. Dowson, 4 Taunt. 779.   (*e*) Taylor v. Bullen, 5 Exch. 779 ; 20 L. J. Exch. 21.

owners of an unseaworthy vessel, whose hull was worm-eaten and keel broken, removed the vessel from the ways where she lay dry, and where the state of her bottom and keel might easily have been discovered, and kept her afloat in deep water where her defects were completely concealed, and then issued a printed advertisement of the sale of the vessel, which described the hull as being nearly as good as when launched, but stated that it was "to be taken with all faults," it was held that as the vendors had knowingly given a false representation of the state of the vessel, and attempted to conceal the defects in the hull, and to throw the purchaser off his guard, they could not shelter themselves under the stipulation that the vessel was to be taken with all faults. (*f*)   Where the vendor of a vessel, "to be taken with all faults," knowingly represented the vessel in his handbills and advertisements as having been built in 1816, in order to get an increased price, whereas she had been launched in 1815, it was held that this was a fraud. "The vendor," observes ABBOTT, C. J., "ought to be silent or to speak the truth.   In case he spoke at all, he was bound to disclose the real fact." (*g*)   If the defect, moreover, is of such a nature that a purchaser can not, by the most diligent examination, discover it, and the defect is known to the vendor at the time of the sale, the latter ought not, according to the opinion of Lord KENYON, to be permitted to shelter himself from the consequences of a fraudulent concealment, under a stipulation that the thing is to be taken with all faults. (*h*)   According to Lord ELLENBOROUGH, however, "if an article is sold with all faults, it is

---

(*f*) Schneider v. Heath, 3 Campb. 561.
508.

(*g*) Fletcher v. Bowsher, 2 Stark. 157.

(*h*) Mellish v. Motteux, 1 Peake,

quite immaterial how many belonged to it within the knowledge of the seller, unless he used some artifice to disguise them, and to prevent their being dis- covered by the purchaser. The very object of intro- ducing such a stipulation is to put the purchaser on his guard, and to throw upon him the burthen of ex- amining all faults, both secret and apparent." (*i*) An examination, however, is useless if the defect is of such a nature that it can not be detected by any examina- tion, however careful; and a vendor who, knowing this, sells with all faults for the purpose of exonerating himself from liability to disclose the secret defect, seems to make use of the stipulation, "to be taken with all faults," in order to cover the perpetration of a fraud. (*k*)   In the case of Mellish v. Motteux, (*l*) which has been disapproved of by Lord ELLENBOROUGH, (*m*) the twenty-two broken futtocks of the vessel were concealed only by the ballast. The defect was disclosed as soon as the ballast was taken out after the sale, and might have been easily discovered before the sale by a diligent and careful examination of the vessel. It is, therefore, wrongly described as "a defect which the purchaser could not, by any attention, possibly discover." The question whether the ballast had been put there for the purpose of concealing the defect does not appear to have been raised.

640. *When the purchaser disables himself from avoiding the contract.*—When a contract of sale is voidable at the option of the party defrauded, the latter must, when he exercises his option to avoid the contract, be in a situation to restore the subject-matter

---

(*i*) Baglehole v. Walters, 3 Campb. 155, 156.

(*k*) Sugd. Vend. and Pur. 386, 387.

(*l*) Mellish v. Motteux, 1 Peake, 156. 156.

(*m*) Baglehole v. Walters, 3 Campb. 156.

of the sale to the vendor. If he has kept the article an unreasonable time, or changed the nature of it so that he can not restore it in the same state it was in when bought, he can not avoid the contract, but must resort to his cross action. (*n*)   Thus, where a log of mahogany was sold on the faith of a representation that the log was sound throughout, and the representation was fraudulently made, but the fraud was not discovered until the log had been cut through by the purchaser, it was held that the latter, by cutting the log, had made it his own property, and could not afterwards return it to the vendor. (*o*)

641. *When a vendor is prevented from avoiding a contract of sale induced by the fraud of a purchaser.*— If a vendor has parted with the possession of goods in fulfillment of a contract of sale, obtained by fraud on the part of the purchaser, he can not, after the goods have been re-sold and passed into the hands of a bona fide sub-purchaser, disaffirm the contract, and annul the title of the latter to the property ; for, where one of two innocent parties must suffer, it is considered to be more just that the burthen should fall upon the vendor who parted with his goods, rather than upon the bona fide sub-purchaser, who trusted to the actual possession of them by the party with whom he dealt. (*p*)   But if the relation of vendor and vendee does not subsist between the defendant and the person who commits the fraud, and the goods have been obtained by false pretenses, and afterwards disposed of to a bona fide purchaser by sale not in market overt, the latter does not acquire a title to

(*n*) Clarke v. Dickson, Ell. Bl. &   777.
Ell. 154.
(*o*) Udell v. Atherton, 7 Jur. N. S.

(*p*) White v. Garden, 10 C. B. 927.
Sheppard v. Shoolbred, Car. & M. 63.

the goods as against the person who has been defrauded. (*q*)

642. *Determination of the election to avoid a contract.*—When a party has a right to determine or annul a contract on the ground of fraud, or to rely upon it and treat it as a subsisting contract, he must make his election within a reasonable time, and the election when once made is final and can not be retracted. (*r*)

643. *Sales rendered nugatory from want of title —Recovery of purchase money.*—There may be no implied warranty of title on the part of a vendor, and yet the purchaser may be entitled to recover back the purchase money, on the ground of a total failure of consideration. Thus in the case of a sale of stock, scrip, or shares in joint-stock companies, the law does not imply any undertaking or warranty from the vendor that the scrip, stock, or shares he sells are genuine, but if the vendor has innocently sold forged or counterfeit stock, scrip, or shares, the purchaser is entitled, as we have seen, to a return of the purchase money, on the ground that there has been a total failure of consideration. (*s*) Where the plaintiff succeeded the defendant as the tenant of a dwelling-house, and agreed with him for the purchase of the tenant's fixtures in the house, and paid him the purchase money, and it subsequently appeared that the fixtures belonged to the landlord, and that the tenant had no right to sell them, and the plaintiff was obliged to pay the value of them to the landlord, it was held that he was entitled to recover back the money he had paid to the defendant, on the ground that there had been a total

(*q*) Higgins v. Burton, 26 L. J., Ex. 342. Kingsford v. Merry, 1 H. & N. 503.

(*r*) *Ante.*

(*s*) Westropp v. Soloman, 8 C. B. 371. *Ante.*

failure of the consideration, and that the money had been paid under a mistake, although it appeared that the defendant had himself bought the fixtures bona fide of a preceding tenant in ignorance of the title of the landlord. (*t*)

But if the vendor does not pretend himself to be the owner of the goods he sells, but sells only such a title and interest as the law gives him in the subject-matter of the sale, the purchase money can not be re-covered back on the ground of a failure of the consideration, if it turns out that the vendor had not the title or interest which he was supposed to have, unless the vendor knew of his want of title at the time of the sale, and there has been a fraudulent concealment. Where the plaintiff and defendant both attended a sheriff's sale where goods seized under a writ of execution were being sold by auction, and the defendant purchased a lot for £18, and the plaintiff offered the defendant £5 "to let him stand in his shoes," which offer the defendant accepted, and with the assent of the sheriff made over his bargain to the plaintiff, and the plaintiff paid down £23, £18 of which were handed to the sheriff as the price of the lot, and the remaining £5 were retained by the defendant as his share of the purchase money, and it was subsequently discovered that the goods had been seized by mistake, and were not the property of the debtor against whom execution had been issued, and the plaintiff was obliged to return the goods, and then brought an action against the defendant for the recovery of the £5 on the ground that there had been a total failure of consideration, it was held that the true consideration was the transfer to

(*t*) Robinson v. Anderton, 1 Peake, 129. Leeman v. Lloyd, Wilkinson v. Lloyd, 7 Q. B. 43 ; 14 L. J., Q. B. 165.

the plaintiff of the defendant's right, such as it was, to
the £18 lot ; and, having got that, the plaintiff had
got all that he had bargained for, and agreed to buy,
and the defendant to sell, and that there was no ground
for claiming a return of the purchase money.   In deciding for the defendant, observes the court, "under
the circumstances, we wish to guard against being
supposed to doubt the right to recover back money
paid upon an ordinary purchase of a chattel, where the
purchaser does not have that for which he paid. (*u*)

644. *Void sales of things not in existence.*—If the
thing intended to be bought and sold has ceased to
exist at the time of the making of the bargain, the contract is a void contract, and the purchase money is recoverable. (*v*)   Where a contract was made for the
purchase and sale of an annuity payable during the life
of a third party, who resided abroad, and the latter was
dead and the annuity was at an end at the time of the
conclusion of the bargain, but the circumstance was
not known either to the vendor or the purchaser, it
was held that the purchase money was recoverable, as
the purchaser had got nothing at all for his money,
and there was a total failure of consideration. (*y*)
Every vendor of specific ascertained chattels impliedly
undertakes that they exist and are capable of being
transferred at the time of the sale ; and, if they have
been previously sold and delivered to other parties,
and the vendor has not the power of making the transfer he professes to make, there is no consideration for
the payment of the purchase money.   Where a contract was made between two merchants, for the sale
and purchase, at a fixed price, of an ascertained cargo

(*u*) Chapman v. Speller, 14 Q. B. 621 ; 19 L. J., Q. B. 239.

(*v*) *Ante.*   Cod. Civ. Art. 1601.

Troplong, ch. 3, DE LA VENTE.

(*y*) Strickland v. Turner, 7 Exch. 208 ; 22 L. J., Ex. 115.

of corn then on board a vessel at sea on its way from
Turkey to Great Britain, and, at the time of the making of the contract, the vessel had been driven by stress
of weather into an African port, and the cargo had become heated, and had been sold by the ship-master to
prevent its total destruction, it was held that the contract of sale made between the two merchants was a
void sale, as the vendor had nothing to sell at the time
of making the bargain ; but it would have been otherwise, if the cargo had been in existence on board the
ship at the time of making the contract, and had been
subsequently damaged and sold. (*z*)

645. *Effect of avoiding the contract.*—If the
purchaser is entitled to treat the contract of sale as a
void contract, by reason of the fraud or deceit of the
vendor, he may return the article and bring an action
for the recovery of the money paid under the void
contract, or, treating the contract as a subsisting contract, he may retain the thing sold in his own hands,
or re-sell it, and sue to recover the damages he has
sustained. (*a*) If the purchaser elects to treat the
sale as a nullity, he must forthwith return or tender
the subject-matter of the sale, or give notice to the
vendor to take it back ; for, if the purchaser keeps it
an unreasonable time, or uses it and exercises the
dominion of an owner over it, he can not afterwards
treat the sale as a void sale, and recover the purchase
money on the ground of a failure of consideration.
(*b*) If a purchaser, having a right to return the
goods sold to him, offers to return them, and the
vendor refuses to accept them, the goods remain at

(*z*) Hastie v. Couturier, 9 Exch.
102 ; 22 L. J., Ex. 299. Barr v. Gib-
son, 3 M. & W. 400.   .
     (*a*) *Ante.*   Fielder v. Starkin, 1 H.
Bl. 19. Poulton v. Lattimore, 9 B.
& C. 265.
     (*b*) Fisher v. Samuda, 1 Camp. 193.
Adam v. Richards, 2 H. Bl. 573.
Hunt v. Silk, 5 East, 452.

the risk of the vendor; and, if they are destroyed by accident, without any want of reasonable care for their preservation, the loss will be the loss of the vendor. (*c*) It does not follow that the contract is rescinded and put an end to by the return of the thing sold, although its return and acceptance are circumstances from which a jury would be at liberty to infer that the contract had been dissolved by the mutual agreement of the parties. (*d*)

646. *Breach of warranty.*—If a vendor sells property absolutely as owner, and warrants his title and right of possession to the purchaser, and the purchase money is paid, and after that the warranty is broken and the purchaser evicted and deprived of the possession and enjoyment of the thing sold, the measure of damages is the highest marketable value of the article between the time of eviction and the day of trial. If the purchaser brings his action against the vendor for a breach of warranty of the quality or soundness of the thing sold, expressly or impliedly made at the time the contract of sale was entered into, and the goods have been received back by the vendor,[1] the measure of damages is the marketable value which the goods would have possessed in the hands of the purchaser at the time of the delivery, if they had corresponded with the warranty given. If they have not been returned by the purchaser, the measure of damages is then the difference between their marketable value to the purchaser in their defective state at the time of delivery, and the value they would have possessed, had

(*c*) Okell v. Smith, 1 Stark. 107.   (*d*) Long v. Preston, 2 Moo. & P. 262.

[1] See *ante*, § 630.

they answered the warranty; and if they have been re-sold by the purchaser without delay, and before any considerable fluctuations in the market have taken place, it is the difference between the price realized on the re-sale, after deducting the costs and expenses of the re-sale, and the price they would have fetched if they had answered the warranty.

Where goods have been purchased with a warranty in England, to be exported and re-sold in China, and the goods, on their arrival in Canton, were found not to answer the warranty, the measure of damages was held to be, not the difference between the agreed price and the price realized on the re-sale in China, but between the last-named price and what they would have sold for in the Chinese market had they corresponded with the warranty. (e) And where a horse-dealer purchased horses in Wales with a warranty of soundness, with a view of re-selling them at a profit in the London market, and the horses on their arrival in London were found to be unsound, the fair measure of damages was held to be the difference between their marketable value in London as unsound horses, and what would have been their marketable value if they had been sound, and had corresponded with the warranty : and it was also held that, if any of them had been re-sold in London with a warranty before the unsoundness was discovered, the price realized on such re-sale would be evidence of their marketable value in a sound condition corresponding with the warranty; and, if they were subsequently returned and sold a third time as unsound horses, without a warranty, the price realized on such third sale would be evidence of their actual marketable value in an

---

(e) Bridge v. Wain, 1 Stark. 504. Chesterman v. Lamb, 2 Ad. & E. 129.

unsound state; and the difference between the price
realized on the two sales would be the measure of the
damages fairly recoverable from the original vendor as
resulting from his breach of warranty. If the purchaser estimated his damages according to the last-
named standard, he would not, of course, be entitled to
recover the costs, charges, and expenses of bringing
the animals up from Wales; but if he recovered only
the difference between the price paid in Wales and
the actual value of the horses in their unsound condition, he would be entitled to recover the costs and expenses of bringing them up to market. The expenses
of obtaining a certificate of unsoundness from the
Veterinary College can not be recovered from the
vendor; nor can any legal expenses which were not
the necessary result of the defendant's breach of contract. (*f*) If the purchaser, as soon as he has discovered the unsoundness of a horse and consequent
breach of warranty, tenders back the horse to the
vendor, he may recover the expense of the keep
during the time that he is preparing to re-sell the
animal to the best advantage. (*g*)

647. *Special damages—Re-sale with a warranty
—Costs of legal proceedings.*—If special damages have
been sustained by the purchaser, they may be recovered from the vendor. [1]　Thus, where the plaintiff,
having bought of the defendant a horse warranted
sound, re-sold the horse with a like warranty, and was
sued for a breach thereof by the second purchaser, and
then gave the defendant notice of the action, and

(*f*) Clare v. Maynard, 7 C. & P.
741; 6 Ad. & E. 523. Cox v. Walker,
7 C. & P. 744, cited 6 Ad. & E. 523.
Curtis v. Hannay, 3 Esp. 82.

(*g*) Caswell v. Coare, 1 Taunt. 566.
Cross v. Bartlett, 3 M. & P. 543.
Mackenzie v. Hancock, R. & M. 436.
Ante.

[1] *Ante,* vol. 1, § 488.

offered him the option of defending it, but the defendant gave no answer, and the plaintiff failed in the action and had to pay damages and £88 costs, it was held that he was entitled to recover these costs, in addition to the damages he had been compelled to pay to his immediate purchaser. (*h*) So, where the defendant sold the plaintiff a picture warranted to be painted by Claude, and the plaintiff afterwards re-sold the picture with a like warranty, and the picture turned out not to be a Claude, and the second purchaser sued the plaintiff for the breach of warranty, and recovered a certain sum for damages and costs, and the plaintiff then sued the defendant, it was held that he was entitled to recover the amount of the damages and costs paid to the second purchaser, and also his own costs incurred in defending the action brought by the latter. (*i*) But if the plaintiff has made a rash and improvident defense, if, for instance, he has had an opportunity of testing the thing purchased, and might have ascertained by examination whether it did or did not correspond with the warranty, and has neglected so to do, and runs his chance of an action, he will not be permitted to recover the cost of his defense. (*k*) But where the purchaser is justified in defending the action brought against him by a subpurchaser, it would seem that he is entitled to recover his costs as between attorney and client, and not merely as between party and party. (*l*)

648. *Of the title to ships and shares in ships.—* The ownership and right of property in ships and

(*h*) Lewis v. Peake, 7 Taunt. 153.

(*i*) Pennell v. Woodburn, 7 C. & P. 118. Dingle v. Hare, 7 C. B., N. S. 157 ; 29 L J., C. P. 143. Randall v. Raper, *ante.* Hughes v. Grœme, *ante.*

(*k*) Wrightup v. Chamberlain, 7 Sc. 598.

(*l*) Howard v. Lovegrove, L. R., 6 Ex. 43 ; 40 L. J., Ex. 13, commenting on Grace v. Morgan, 2 Sc. 793 ; 2 Bing. N. C. 534.

shares in vessels are authenticated and regulated by
the Merchant Shipping Act, 1854 (17 & 18 Vict. c.
104), part 2, and the Acts amending it. (*m.*) Whenever there is more than one owner, the right of property in the vessel is required to be divided into shares,
and the number of shares held by each owner to be
registered. But partners in any house, or co-partnership, may hold any vessel, or any shares therein, in the
name of such house or co-partnership as joint-owners,
without distinguishing the proportionate interest of
each. No greater number than thirty-two persons,
however, are entitled to be legal owners, at one and
the same time, of any ship or vessel as tenants in
common, or to be registered as such ; but any number
of persons may hold or enjoy equitable interests, and
have an equitable claim or title, as against the registered legal owners. Joint-stock companies also,
formed for the purpose of owning ships or vessels,
may appoint any number of their members, not being
less than three, to be trustees of the property in such
ships or vessels, who are to subscribe the declaration
of ownership required before registry, stating the name
and description of the company to which the vessels
belong. If a person who has no title as owner, gets
his name put upon the register, the court will rectify
the error and cause the ship to be registered in the
name of the legal owner. (*n*) After all the particulars necessary to ascertain the ownership, build, and
description of the vessel have been duly declared and
registered, a certificate of such registry embodying
such particulars is to be granted, and on the back of
this certificate is to be indorsed the names of the

(*m*) 18 & 19 Vict. c. 91.   25 & 26   (*n*) Holderness v. Lamport, 30 L.
Vict. c. 63.   34 & 35 Vict. c. 110.   35   J. Ch. 489.
& 36 Vict. c. 73.

owners and the number of shares they hold. If this certificate is lost, mislaid, or detained, the vessel may be registered de novo. Copies of the declaration of ownership, and of the ship's register, are made evidence without production of the originals ; and provision is made for registration de novo, in certain cases where the bill of sale or instrument of transfer can not be produced. Examined copies of the register or copies purporting to be certified under the hand of the person having the custody of the original, and all certificates of registry purporting to be signed as required by law, are prima facie evidence of all matters contained or recited in the registers, or indorsed on the certificates. (*o.*) The certificate of registry, therefore, affords evidence of the ownership and right of property of every registered vessel, and should be produced to every intended purchaser of the vessel, or of any share or shares therein, and be compared with the register. If the vendor of a vessel is not himself the builder or the original owner, but derives his title by purchase after registry, the bill of sale or instrument of transfer under which he claims should be produced, as well as the certificate of registry.

The master of a vessel has no authority to sell the vessel, except under very special circumstances of urgent necessity. (*p*)[1]

649. *Transfers of ships and shares in ships* must be made by bill of sale containing such description of the ship as is contained in the certificate of the surveyor, or such other description as may be sufficient

---

(*o*) 17 & 18 Vict. c. 104, part 2. Maude & Pollock on Shipping.

(*p*) The Eliza Cornish, 17 Jur. 738. The Bonita and the Charlotte, 1

Lush. 252; 30 L. J., Ad. 145. Lapraik *v.* Burrows, 13 Moo. P. C. 132. The Bonita, 30 L. J., Ad. 145.

[1] *Ante*, vol. 1, § 71, *et seq.*

to identify the ship to the satisfaction of the registrar, according to the form given in the Merchant Shipping Act, 1854. The provisions of this statute extend to an executory contract for the transfer of a ship at a future day as well as to the immediate instrument of transfer itself, so that, if the directions of the Act with regard to the form of the writing and the registration thereof are not complied with, the executory contract will not support an action for specific performance or for damages. (*q*) The duty of registering a transfer of ownership rests with the vendee; and immediately on the execution of the bill of sale the vendee becomes entitled to all the benefits and liabilities of ownership. (*r*) A ship is not like an ordinary chattel which passes by delivery; and there is no market overt for ships. The purchaser of a foreign ship is, therefore, bound to make inquiries as to the title, and will take subject to existing rights and equities. (*s*) [1]

650. *Sale and transfer of tenants' fixtures and trade fixtures.*—If an article affixed to the freehold is sold with a view to its immediate severance therefrom, the contract is simply a contract for the purchase and sale of a chattel. If it is not purchased with a view to immediate severance, the contract is then a contract for the sale and purchase of a fixture. A contract for the sale and fixing up in a dwelling-house of a copper

---

(*q*) Liverpool Borough Bank v. Turner, 29 L. J., Ch. 827; 30 L. J., Ch. 379. Chapman v. Callis, 30 L. J., C. P. 241. Hughes v. Morris, 21 L. J., Ch. 761. Duncan v. Tindal, 22 L. J., C. P. 137; 13 C. B. 258

(*r*) The Spirit of the Ocean, 34 L. J., Ad. 74. Stapleton v. Haymen, 2 H. & C. 918; 33 L. J., Ex. 170.

(*s*) Hooper v. Gumm, L. R., 2 Ch. 282; 36 L. J., Ch. 282.

---

[1] And see as to ship-building contracts; Sanford v. Wiggins Ferry Co., 27 Ind. 522; Elliot v. Edwards, 6 Vroom, 265; Williams v. Jackman, 16 Gray, 514; Andrews v. Durant, 1 Kernan, 35; Briggs v. A Light Boat, 7 Allen, 287.

or a stove is not a contract for the sale of fixtures, but of goods and chattels, and for the performance of work and labor. If a contract is made for the erection upon the soil, or in a dwelling-house, of machinery, presses, &c., the contract is properly a contract for work and labor and the supply of materials. It is a contract for the erection, and not for the sale, of a fixture, and is the same in principle as a contract to erect a pillar or build a house. (*t*).

We have already seen that, by the grant of land, all fixtures attached to the soil and freehold and belonging to the grantor, pass with the land as accessorial thereto ; and that, by the grant of a house, all things incident and accessorial to the building, pass, such as window-frames, windows, doors, and wainscots attached to the house, and furnaces, coppers, vats, and tables fastened to the walls or to the ground in the middle of the house, and all fixtures of every description annexed to the building and belonging to the grantor or landlord. (*u*) But tenants' fixtures and trade fixtures, which were put up by the tenant or occupier, and which the latter has a right to remove at the expiration of his tenancy or occupation, do not, of course, pass by the grant of the fee, unless the grantor is himself the occupier of the house and owner of the fixtures. The question as to what are and what are not tenants' or trade fixtures, removable by the occupier, and not forming part of the freehold and inheritance, principally arises between three classes of persons : 1st ;—between different descriptions of

---

(*t*) Pinner v. Arnold, 2 Cr. M. & R. 616.

(*u*) Longstaff v. Meagoe, 2 Ad. & E. 167. Birch v. Dawson, ib. 37. Hare v. Horton, 2 N. & M. 428 ; 5 B. & Ad. 715. Hitchman v. Walton, 4 M. & W. 414, 416. Mather v. Fraser, 2 Kay & J. 536 ; 25 L. J., Ch. 361.

representatives of the same owner of the inheritance,
viz., between his heir and executor. In this first case,
the rule as to severance obtains with the most rigor
in favor of the inheritance and against the right to
disannex therefrom anything which has been affixed
thereto. (*v*) 2ndly ;—between the executors of tenant
for life or in tail and the remainderman or reversioner ;
in which case the right to fixtures is considered more
favorably for executors than in the preceding case between heir and executor. The 3rd case, and that in
which the greatest latitude and indulgence have
always been allowed in favor of the claim of severance, as against the claim in respect of freehold
or inheritance, is the case between landlord and
tenant. (*w*) [1]

(*v*) Fisher v. Dixon, 12 Cl. & Fin.   (*w*) Elwes v. Maw, 3 East. 53.   14
312.   .   & 15 Vict. c. 25.

[1] The question as to what are fixtures is always a mixed
question of fact and law; Campbell v. O'Neil, 64 Pa. St. 290;
as to the principles governing the question as to what will be
a fixture see Flanders v. Wood, 24 Wis. 527 ; Meigs' Appeal,
62 Pa. St. 28 ; Richardson v. Borden, 42 Miss. 71 ; Weathersby
v. Sleeper, Id. 732 ; Perkins v. Swank, 43 Id. 349; Barthole-
mew v. Hamilton, 105 Mass. 239 ; Lampton v. Preston, 1 J. J.
Marsh, 454; English v. Foote, 16 Miss. (18 Smedes & M.) 444 ;
Wadleigh v. Janvrin, 41 N. H. 403; Potts v. New Jersey Arms
&c. Co., 14 N. J. (2 Greenl.) 395 Ford v. Cobb, 20 N. Y.
344; Hill v. Wentworth, 28 Vt. 428; Teaff v. Hewitt, 1 Ohio,
St. 511 ; Pickerell v. Carson, 8 Iowa, 544; State v. Bonham,
18 Ind. 231; Prescott v. Wells, 3 Nev. 82; Heaton v. Findlay,
12 Pa. St. 304; Gardner v. Finley, 19 Barb. 317 ; Providence
Gas Co. v. Thurber, 2 R. I. 15; McClintock v. Graham, 3
McCord, 553; Hensley v. Brodie, 16 Ark. 511 ; a fixture,
when lawfully severed, becomes personal property, and may
be sued for in replevin; Heaton v. Findlay, 12 Pa. St. 304.
What particular things are fixtures, is a question of mixed
law and fact, and when one for the jury, they should be
enabled to decide it by a clear explanation of the legal
meaning of the word. Grand Lodge, &c. v. Knox, 27 Mo.

651. *Authentication of contracts for the sale of fixtures.*—We have already seen that a contract for the sale of fixtures is not a contract for the sale of an

315. The tests usually to be applied are well stated in Voorhees v. McGinnis, 48 N. Y. 278, to be as follows: 1. Actual annexation of a permanent character, except in case of those articles not themselves annexed, but deemed to be of the freehold, from their use. 2. Adaptability to the use of the freehold. 3. The intention of the parties at the time of making the annexation; and, to the same effect, see Pea v. Pea, 35 Ind. 387; Eaves v. Estes, 10 Kan. 314; Funk v. Brigaldi, 4 Daly (N. Y.) 359. Subjoined is a catalogue of articles as to which the question has arisen or may arise, drawn principally from American reported cases. Addition to a House—see Buildings, House. Agricultural Erections—Dubois v. Kelly, 10 Barb. 496. Barn—Landon v. Platt, 34 Conn. 517. Bars—Farrar v. Stackpole, 6 Greenl. 154. Bell—Alvord, &c. M'f'g Co. v. Gleason, 36 Conn. 86. Boards —Whiting v. Barstow, 4 Pick. 310. Blower Pipe—Alvord, &c. M'f'g Co. v. Gleason, 36 Conn. 86. Boilers—Hill v. Hill, 43 Pa. St. 521. Bowling Alley—Hanrahan v. O'Reilly, 102 Mass. 201. Bricks—Lampton v. Preston, 1 J. J. Marsh, 454. Bridge Piers—Wagner v. Cleveland, &c. R. R. Co., 22 Ohio St.; Cowan v. Cowan, 12 Ohio St. 629; Northern, &c. R. R. Co. v. Canton, &c. R. R. Co. 30 Md. 347. Building—Kelly v. Austin, 46 Ill. 156; Richtmyer v. Moss, 4 Abb. App. Dec. (N. Y.) 55; Welgen v. Gettings, 21 Iowa, 177; see house, barn, mill. Building materials—Beard v. Durald, 22 La. Ann. 289. Carding machine—Graves v. Pierce, 53 Mo. 423; Taffe v. Warwick, 3 Blackf. 111; Walker v. Sherman, 20 Wend. 636; see Machinery. Chain—Farrar v. Stackpole, 6 Greenl. 154. Chandeliers —Rodgers v. Crow, 40 Mo. 91. Chimney pieces; Peck v. Batchelder, 40 Vt. 233. Cisterns—Bletkin v. Towle, 40 Me. 310; Bainway v. Cobb, 99 Mass. 457; Wall v. Hinds, 4 Gray, 256. Coffee mills—Hill on Fixtures, 34. Cotton gin—Fairis v. Walker, 1 Bailey (S. C.) 540; McKenna v. Hammond, 3 Hill (S. C.) 331; Degraffenried v. Scruggs, 4 Humph. 231; Latham v. Blakeley, 70 N. C. 369; Bratton v. Classon, 2 Strobh. 478. Crops—Whipple v. Foot, 2 Johns. 418; Newcomb v. Raner, Id. 421 (note). Counters—Pope v. Garrard, 39 Ga. 471. Cupboards—Kempton v. Eve, 2 Ves. & B. 349. " Dogs "—Farrar v. Stackpole, 6 Greenl. 154. Doors—Philbrick v. Ewing, 97 Mass. 133. Door-step—Woodman v. Pease, 17 N. H. 282.

interest in land, nor for the sale of goods and chattels.
A signed writing, consequently, is not necessary, as
between vendor and purchaser, for the authentication

Engines—Rice v. Adams, 4 Har. 332; Sparks v. State Bank,
7 Blackf. 469; Trull v. Fuller, 28 Me. 545; Corliss v. Med-
agin, 29 Id. 115; Parsons v. Copeland, 38 Id. 537; Symonds.
v. Harris, 51 Id. 14; Sweetzer v. Jones, 35 Vt. 314; Witmer's
Appeal, 45 Pa. St. 507; Murdock v. Harris, 20 Barb. 407;
Union Bank v. Emerson, 15 Mass. 159; Richardson v. Copeland,
6 Gray, 536; Phillipson v. Mallanphy, 1 Mo. 620; Baker v.
Davis, 19 N. H. 325; Buckley v. Buckley, 11 Barb. 43; Pyle
v. Pennock, 2 Watts & S. 390; Voorhees v. Freeman, Id. 116;
Oves v. Oglesby, 7 Watts, 106; Harlan v. Harlan, 15 Pa. St.
507; Roberts v. Dauphin Bank, 19 Id. 71; Christian v. Dripps,
28 Id. 271; Hull v. Alexander, 20 Id. 303; Leland v. Gassett,
17 Vt. 403. Evergreens—Empson v. Sodden, 4 B. & Ad. 655;
Fences; Hines v. Ament, 43 Mo. 298; Gibson v. Vaughan, 2
Bailey (S. C.) 389; Smith v. Carrol, 4 Greene (Iowa) 146;
Boon v. Orr, Id. 304; Glidden v. Bennett, 43 N. H. 306;
Wentz v. Fincher, 12 Ired. 297; Robertson v. Phillips, 3 Iowa,
220; see rails. Fire Frames—Gaffield v. Hapgood, 17 Pick.
192. Fire Place Frames—Gaffield v. Hopgood, 17 Pick. 192.
Floors—Philbrick v. Ewing, 97 Mass. 133. Flowers—Empson
v. Sodden, 4 B. & Ad. 655. Fruit—Warren v. Leland, 2 Barb.
613; Kain v. Fisher, 2 Seld. 597; Bank of Lansingburgh v.
Crary, 1 Barb. 542. Furnaces; Main v. Schwarzwaelder, 4 E.
D. Smith, 273; Squier v. Mayer, Freem. Ch. 249. Gas fixtures—Montague v. Dent, 10 Rich. 135; Hays v. Doane, 10 N.
J. Eq. (3 Stoct.) 84; Lawrence v. Kemp, 1 Duer, 363; Vaughen
v. Haldeman, 33 Pa. St. 522; Philbrick v. Ewing, 97 Mass.
133; Rogers v. Crow, 40 Mo. 91; Gas Co. v. Thurber, 2 R. I.
15; Guthrie v. Jones, 108 Mass. 191. Gin House—Hancock v.
Jordan, 7 Ala. 448; McDaniel v. Moody, 3 Stew. (Ala.) 314.
Greenhouses—Penton v. Roberts, 2 East, 90. Grist Mill—
Potter v. Cromwell, 40 N. Y. 287. Grass—Bank of Lansingburgh v. Crary, 1 Barb. 542; Warren v. Leland, 2 Id. 613; Kain
v. Fisher, 2 Seld. 597. Gin Stands—Richardson v. Borden, 42
Miss. 71; Cole v. Roach, 37 Tex. 413. Grates—Hill on Fixtures, 34. Hangings—Peck v. Batchelder, 40 Vt. 233. House—
Gibbs v. Estey, 15 Gray ,587; Foy v. Reddick, 31 Ind. 414; Bol-
ling v. Whittle, 1 Ala. (Sel. Cas.) 268; Rogers v. Gillinger, 30
Pa. St. 185; Powers v. Dennison, 30 Vt. 752; Tyler v. Decker,
10 Cal. 435; Goff v. O'Connor, 16 Ill. 247; Reese v. Jared, 15.

of the contract. Where fixtures have been sold at a price to be ascertained by valuation, if, after the valuation has been made and delivered to the purchaser,

Ind. 142; Leland v. Gassett, 17 Vt. 403; Clark v. Rayburn, 1 Kans. 281; Higgins v. Riddell, 12 Wis. 587; Pullen v. Bell, 40 Me. 314; Hemminway v. Cutler, 51 Id. 407; Schemmer v. North, 32 Mo. 206; Wells v. Banister, 4 Mass. 514; Taylor v. Townsend, 8 Id. 411; Washburn v. Sprout, 16 Id. 449; Fuller v. Taylor, 39 Me. 519; Washburn v. Shroat, 16 Mass. 449; Stillman v. Hamer, 8 Miss. (7 How.) 421; Fisher v. Saffer, 1 E. D. Smith, 611; Reid v. Kirk, 12 Rich. 54; Curtis v. Riddle, 7 Allen, 185; Howard v. Fessenden, 14 Id. 124; Lacy v. Gibboney, 36 Mo. 320; Dame v. Dame, 38 N. H. 429; White's Appeal, 10 Pa. St. 252; Curtiss v. Hoyt, 19 Conn. 154; Burnside v. Twitchell, 43 N. H. 390; Sturgis v. Warren, 11 Vt. 433; Taffe v. Warwick, 3 Blackf. 111. Hop Poles—Bishop v. Bishop, 1 Kern. 123. Hospital (Military)—Meigs' Appeal, 62 Pa. St. 28. Ice Chest—Park v. Baker, 7 Allen, 78. Keys—Walker v. Sherman, 20 Wend. 636. Kettles—Hunt v. Mullanphy, 1 Mo. 508. Locks—Walker v. Sherman, 20 Wend. 636. Looms—Murdock v. Harris, 20 Barb. 407. Machinery—Hatchman's Appeal, 27 Pa. St. 209; Cape v. Romeyne, 4 McLean, 384; Tibbetts v. Moore, 23 Cal. 208; Swift v. Thompson, 9 Conn. 63; Murdock v. Gifford, 18 N. Y. 28; Hovey v. Smith, 1 Barb. 372; Bartlett v. Wood, 32 Vt. 373; Vanderpoel v. Van Allen, 10 Barb. 157; Goddard v. Gould, 14 Id. 662; Voorhees v. McGinnis, 46 Id. 157; Childress v. Wright, 2 Coldw. 350; Fullam v. Stearns, 30 Vt. 443. Manure—Daniels v. Pond, 21 Pick. 367; Middlebrook v. Corwin, 15 Wend. 169; Lassell v. Reed, 6 Greenl. 222; Sawyer v. Twiss, 6 Foster (N. H.) 345; Staples v. Emery, 7 Greenl. 201. Materials—see Building Materials. Mills—Burnside v. Twitchell, 43 N. H. 390; Martin v. Cope, 28 N Y. 180. Organs—Rogers v. Crow, 40 Me. 91; Coolis v. McLagin, 29 Me. 115. Ornaments—Peck v. Batchelder, 40 Vt. 233. Out-houses—Dubois v. Kelly, 10 Barb. 496. Partitions—Hill on Fixtures, 34. Pipe—see Blower Pipe. Poles—see Hop Poles. Pumps—McKracken v. Hall, 7 Port. (Ind.) 30; Ex-parte Quincey, 1 Atk. 447; Grymes v. Boweren, 6 Bing. 437. Rails—see Fences; Robertson v. Phillips, 3 Iowa, 220. Railroads—Farmers' Loan, &c. Co. v. Creditors, &c., 20 Law Rep. 678; Coe v. Pennock, cited Red. on Railw. § 235 (n); Palmer v. Forkes, 23 Ill. 300. Rolls—Johnson v. Mehaffey, 43 Pa. St. 308. Safes—Folger v.

the latter takes possession of the fixtures, or exercises
dominion over them, he will be deemed to have
adopted the valuation and assented to the price as
ascertained by the brokers. (x)　Where the owner of
a lease of a house, and of certain fixtures in the house,
gave a memorandum to the plaintiff to the following
effect:—" In consideration of W. T. (the plaintiff)
discounting for me a bill of exchange for £80, I have
assigned to him the whole of the fixtures, as per in-
ventory," &c., it was held that the property in the
fixtures passed by this note to the plaintiff. (y)

(x) Salmon v. Watson, 4 Moore, 73.　　(y) Thompson v. Pettitt, 10 Q. B.
101.

SECTION III.

THE SALE OF INCORPOREALS.

652. *Grants and transfers of incorporeal rights and incorporeal hereditaments,* such as rights of common, rights of way or water-course, advowsons, tithes, rents, annuities, and profits issuing out of land, must, in order to be valid and irrevocable at common law, be made by deed. (*z*)   Thus a right to take tolls for the passage of a ferry or a bridge must be trans- ferred by deed. (*a*) [1]   A right to go upon another man's land, as to remove fixtures, (*b*) or to shoot and sport over a manor, or to fish in the waters thereof, whether it be a mere license of pleasure authorizing the licensee to take, but not to carry away, or a license of profit authorizing him both to take and carry off, the game or the fish, is an incorporeal right lying in grant, and can only be created by deed. (*c*)   A parol license or permis- sion will, so long as it has not been countermanded, jus- tify an entry upon the land ; (*d*) but it can confer no indefeasible right, and may be recalled at the pleasure of the grantor, unless a valuable consideration has been given and received for it, so as to give the licensee a right to the enjoyment of the privilege.   But, although the right itself can not be created at common

(*z*) Bac. Abr. Grants, E. Co. Litt. 9 a, 42 a.   14 Vin. Abr. Grant G. (a). 2 Roll. Abr. Grant (G).   Jones v. Robin, 12 Jur. 308.

(*a*) Reg. v. Marquis of Salisbury, 8 Ad. & E. 739.

(*b*) Ruffey v. Henderson, 21 L. J., Q. B. 51.

(*c*) Duke of Somerset v. Fogwell, 5 B. & C. 875 ; 8 D. & R. 747.   Bird v. Higginson, 2 Ad. & E. 696.   Thomas v. Fredericks, 16 L. J., Q. B. 393. Ewart v. Graham, 7 H. L. C. 331 ; 29 L. J. Ex. 88.

(*d*) Feltham v. Cartwright, 7 Sc 695.

[1] Washburn on Real Property, vol. 2, p. 21.*

law, so as to be indefeasible, without deed, yet a land-owner may, by a writing satisfying the Statute of Frauds,[1] agree to allow another to come upon his land and take a profit from the soil, or to exercise and enjoy thereon certain privileges, and will be responsible in damages, if he interrupt such enjoyment. (*e*)   And, if a landowner gives a parol license or permission to another to enjoy some profit or privilege on the land of the licensor necessarily involving the expenditure of money for its enjoyment, and the licensor stands by and allows the licensee to expend his money on the land in reliance on the promised enjoyment of the privilege, the license can not afterwards be withdrawn without tendering the licensee compensation for his expenditure. (*f*)   Where a colliery proprietor, wanting to construct a railway across the defendant's land, wrote a letter to the defendant, offering him a fair price for the land, and, getting no answer to his letter, and supposing that he had a right, under the powers of a local Act, to make the railway, entered upon the defendant's land, and constructed earthworks and formed a railway, and used it for three or four years with the acquiescence of the defendant, and the parties afterwards met to settle the price that was to be paid for the land, and, not being able to agree upon it, the defendant brought an action of ejectment, the Court of Chancery granted an injunction to restrain the defendant from obstructing or interfering with the plaintiff's use of the railway, on such a sum of money being paid into court as would constitute a sufficient security to the defendant for the price of the land. (*g*)

(*e*) Smart v. Jones, 15 C. B., N. S. 717; 33 L. J., C. P. 154.

(*f*) Ramsden v. Dyson, L. R., 1 H. L. 170, Clavering's Case, 5 Ves. 690.

(*g*) Powell v. Thomas, 6 Hare, 300. Laird v. Birkenhead Railway Company, 1 Johns. 500 ; 29 L. J., Ch. 218.

Ante, vol. 1, p. 296, *et seq.*

So, also, when a party has agreed to pay a certain sum for a license of profit, and has had the benefit and enjoyment of the license, it is no answer, in an action for the money agreed to be paid, to say that the license was not under seal. Therefore, where an action was brought for a sum of money agreed to be paid for the use and enjoyment of a license to fish, it was held that the defendant could not resist the action on the ground that the license was not under seal. (*h*) And where the defendant by memorandum in writing agreed with the plaintiff, for a valuable consideration, to permit the plaintiff to enter upon the defendant's land for the purpose of gathering cinders, it was held to be no answer to an action for a breach of this agreement, to set up that it was not under seal. (*i*) A parol license to enjoy an easement over or upon the soil and freehold of another, is at once determined by a transfer of the property; and the grantee of the license is consequently a trespasser, if he afterwards enters upon the land in the exercise and enjoyment of his supposed right, although he has received no notice of the transfer. (*j*)

A mere license of pleasure amounts only to a personal contract, or to an ordinary covenant between the parties, and does not transfer to the licensee or his heirs any right over, or interest in, the soil and freehold of the licenser. " If one license me and my heirs to come and hunt in his park, I must have a writing (that is a deed) of that license; for a thing passes by the license which endures in perpetuity; but if he license me one time to hunt, this is good without

---

(*h*) Holford v. Pritchard, 3 Exch. 793.

(*i*) Smart v. Jones, *ante.*

(*j*) Wallis v. Harrison, 4 M. & W.

539. Russell v. Harford, L. R., 2 Eq. 507. Roberts v. Rose, L. R., 2 Ex. 82; 35 L. J. Ex. 62.

deed; for no inheritance passes." (*k*) If the license be a mere personal license of pleasure, the licensee can not take away to his own use the game killed, or go with servants upon the land, still less send servants to kill for him, or assign his license to another. A license under seal to convey coals or timber in carts, or water in drains or channels, through or across the land of the licensor, is a license of profit and not of pleasure, and would amount to a grant of a right of way, or of a water-course. A license under seal may be of such a nature as to operate in respect of some things as a license of pleasure merely, and as to others as a grant of an incorporeal hereditament, and a direct transfer of an estate or interest in the land.

653. *Reservation of privileges and easements amounting to an express grant.*—Reservations, properly so called, are only of rents and services; and a reservation of an easement or privilege, whether to a stranger or not, operates as a fresh grant. When, therefore, in a deed of conveyance or an indenture of lease, there are words of exception and reservation of an easement or profit à prendre, they will operate as an express grant, which may be made to enure either in favor of the conveying party, his heirs and assigns, or in favor of a stranger who was no party to the deed of conveyance. Thus, where a lord of a manor conveyed to one N. and his heirs certain lands and premises, parcel of the demesne of the manor, excepting and reserving to himself and another, who was not a conveying party to the deed, their heirs and assigns, free liberty, with servants or otherwise, to come into and upon the lands so conveyed, and there to hawk, hunt, fish, and fowl, at any time thereafter, at their will and pleasure, it was held that the words of

(*k*) Ye r Book 11 Hen. VII., fol 3., cited by Parke, B., 7 M. & W. 79.

the reservation or exception so used operated as an express grant of an incorporeal hereditament, that the liberty of hawking, hunting, fowling, and fishing, granted to a person, his heirs, executors and assigns, amounted to a profit à prendre, authorizing the grantee to take and to carry away the fowl and the fish, and not to a mere license of pleasure, and that it conferred upon the grantee a right to send his servants to hawk, hunt, fish, and fowl for him in his absence. (*l*)

A right of way or of watercourse can not in strictness be made the subject either of exception or reservation. It is neither parcel of the thing granted, nor is it issuing out of the thing granted, the former being essential to an exception, and the latter to a reservation.[1] A right of way, therefore, reserved to a lessor on the making of a lease, is in strictness of law an easement newly created by way of grant from the grantee or lessee, in the same manner as a right of sporting or of fishing.

654. *Transfer of incorporeal hereditaments.*—An incorporeal hereditament in the nature of a profit à prendre is an estate capable of being inherited by the heir, and assigned to a purchaser, or otherwise conveyed away. It is a tenement within the definition of Lord Coke, who says that the word "tenement" includeth not only corporate inheritances, but also all inheritances issuing out of them, or concerning, or annexed to, or exercisable within them, as rent,

---

(*l*) Wickham v. Hawker, 7 M. & W. 63. Doe v. Lock, 2 Ad. & E. 743. Pannell v. Mill, 3 C. B. 636. Touch. 100–116. See, as to implied reservations, Suffield v. Brown, 33 L. J., Ch. 249. Shep.

[1] And see Kent v. Waite, 10 Pick. 138; Perley v. Langley, 7 N. H. 233; Coolidge v. Learned, 8 Pick. 503.

estovers, common, or other profits whatever granted
out of land. (*m*)   If, therefore, a landowner grants to
a man and his heirs a right to dig for and carry away
stone, clay, or minerals, the incorporeal right may be
demised by the grantee for years or for life, or conveyed away to another and his heirs. (*n.*) [1] Where
the Lord Mountjoy, by deed inrolled, bargained, and
sold the Manor of Camford to one Brown in fee, and
by the same indenture Brown granted to the Lord
Mountjoy, his heirs and assigns, a right to dig for ore
in the waste land of the Manor, and also to dig turf
there, and the Lord Mountjoy demised this interest
to one Laicot for twenty-one years, and Laicot assigned the same over to two other men, it was held
that the assignment was good, but that the two
assignees could not work severally, but together, with
one stock and such workmen as belonged to them
both ; and that the assignee had no exclusive right to
dig for ore, but that the land-owner himself, or the
grantor of the privilege, might also dig for ore without
derogating from the grant. (*o*)   But grants of profits
issuing out of land carrying an assignable interest can
only be made in gross, and can only be assigned by
the grantees by the ordinary conveyances known to
the law ; and it is not because the grantee may happen

(*m*) Co. Litt. 20, a.

(*n*) Muskett v. Hill, 5 Bing. N. C.
707.   Martyn v. Williams, 1 H. & N.

827 ; 26 L. J., Ex. 117.

(*o*) Mountjoy's Case, Godb. 17.
Chetham v. Williamson, 4 East, 476.

[1] Perley v. Langley, 7 N. H. 233 ; Thomas v. Marshfield
10 Pick. 364 ; Sale v. Pratt, 19 Pick. 191, 197 ; Green v. Putnam, 8 Cush. 21 ; Commonwealth v. Law, 3 Pick. 408, 413 ;
Boston Water Power Co. v. Boston & Worcester R. R. Co., 16
Id. 512 ; Waters v. Lilley, 4 Id. 145 ; Washburn on Easements,
76 ; Green v. Chelsea, 24 Pick. 71.   As to the rule laid down
in some of the States, making a grant of the uses of and dominion over land a grant of the land itself see Clement v.
Youngman, 40 Pa. St. 344 ; Caldwell v. Fulton, 31 Id. 484.

to be the owner of a close at the time the grant is made to him, that such a conveyance can be dispensed with in favor of the persons who, from time to time, may succeed him in the ownership of that close. (*p*)

655. *Grants of rights of way.*—A mere personal privilege or easement, such as a right of way in gross, not annexed or appurtenant to a tenement, can not be assigned or granted over. (*q*)   A license of pleasure can not, as we have seen,[1] be assigned.   Thus, if license be granted to me to walk in another man's garden, or to go through another man's grounds, I may not give or grant this to another. (*r*)   We have seen that a mere parol executory license is a simple authority, ex-cusing trespasses on the close of the grantor as long as it is his, and the license is not countermanded, but ceasing the moment the property passes to another.[2]

656. *Contracts for the sale of growing crops.*— We have already seen that fructus industriales, such as growing crops of turnips, potatoes, and corn, and the annual productions of the soil raised each year from fresh plants and seeds, are goods and chattels ; also growing timber, sold at so much per foot, with a view to its immediate severance and removal from the soil ; but that contracts for the sale of growing grass, grow-ing timber, underwood, growing fruit or hops, not made with a view to immediate severance and removal, are contracts for the sale of an interest in land.[3]   If a a man by deed " grants to another and his heirs the vesture or herbage of his land, by this grant do pass

---

(*p*) Wil,es, J., Bailey v. Stevens, 31 L. J., C. P. 228.
(*q*) Ackroyd v. Smith, 10 C. B. 186.

(*r*) Wingate's Maxims, 379, cited Shep. Touch. 239.

[1] *Ante*, § 651.
[2] Id.
[3] *Ante*, vol. 1, p. 301, 302, *et seq.*

the corn, grass, underwood, sweepage, and the like."
" He that hath the land also may grant all fruits that
may arise upon it after; and the property shall pass as
soon as the fruits are extant. And though the words
are not words of gift of the corn, but words of license
that it shall be lawful for the grantee to take it to his
own use, it is good to transfer the property." (*s*)
Where the lessee of a farm, being indebted to his landlord, assigned to the latter, by a bill of sale under seal,
all his hay and corn in stock and growing upon the
farm, and all his tenant right and interest to come and
unexpired in the farm, in trust to sell and pay the debt,
and hand over the surplus to such lessee, and full
power was given to the landlord to enter upon the farm
at any time thereafter, and take and carry away the
said corn and hay, it was held that growing crops, not
sown at the time of the execution of the deed, passed
under the assignment of the " tenant right" to the
grantee. (*t*)   But the general rule of law is that things
not in existence at the time of the grant can not pass
thereby ; but the grant may operate as a license to
seize and sell after acquired property. (*u*)   Although
the land itself does not pass by the grant, the grantee
has a right when the grant is under seal, to the use of
the soil for the crop to grow in until it arrives at maturity, and a right to enter upon the land to secure and
carry away the crop. (*x*) [1]

(*s*) Grantham v. Hawley, Hob. 132.   (*u*) Carr v. Allatt, and Allatt v. Carr
(*t*) Petch v. Tutin, 15 M. & W. 115.   27 L. J., Ex. 385.
(*x*) Noy's Maxim's, 55,   Plowd. 16.

[1] A contract for the sale of growing trees, where the property in the trees is intended to pass before they are severed
from the soil, is within the Statute of Frauds ; White v. Foster,
102 Mass. 378; and see Drake v. Wells, 11 Allen, 143;
Giles v. Simonds, 15 Gray, 444; Whitmarsh v. Walker, 1 Metc.
316. But in New Hampshire the rule prevailing is that an

657. *Sale of copyright.*—It is now held that copyright in a published work only exists by statute. (*y*)[1] The 5 & 6 Vict. c. 45, s. 2, enacts that the word copy-

(*y*) Reade v. Conquest, 30 L. J,. C. P. 213.

agreement for the sale of growing trees, with the right at any time in the future to enter upon the land and remove them, conveys such an interest in land as is within the Statute of Frauds. But the distinction is made between contracts made with the intention that the trees shall be immediately removed, and those where the trees are to remain upon the land for a certain period of time; Howe v. Batchelder, 49 N. H. 204; Kingsley v. Holbrook, 45 Id. 313; Putney v. Day, 6 Id. 430; Olmstead v. Niles, 7 Id. 522; Ochington v. Richey, 41 Id. 275. So in Vermont, Buck v. Pickwell, 27 Vt. 157, the rule was held established as to executory contracts; and see McGregor v. Brown, 6 Seld. 114; Vanebeck v. Roe, 50 Barb. 302; Bryant v. Crosby, 40 Me. 9, 21–23; Cutler v. Pope, 13 Id. 377; Bricker v. Hughes, 4 Ind. 146; Sherry v. Picken, 10 Id. 375; Marshall v. Ferguson, 23 Cal. 65; Austin v. Sawyer, 9 Cow. 39; Whipple v. Foot, 2 Johns. 422; Stewart v. Doughty, 9 Id. 112; Miller v. State, 39 Ind. 267; Britain v. McKay, 1 Ired. 265; Bull v. Griswold, 19 Ill. 631; Ross v. Welch, 11 Gray, 235; Green v. Armstrong, 1 Denio, 550; Warren v. Leland, 2 Barb. 614; Dubois v. Kelly, 10 Id. 496; Pierrepont v. Barnard, 5 Id. 364; Yeakle v. Jacob, 33 Pa. St. 376; Huff v. McCauley, 53 Id. 206; Pattison's Appeal, 61 Id. 294; Ellison v. Brigham, 38 Vt. 64; Sterling v. Baldwin, 42 Id. 306; Harrell v. Miller, 35 Miss. 700; Byasse v. Reese, 4 Metc. (Ky.) 372; Huff v. McCauley, 53 Pa. St. 206. If the contract has been executed by the vendee by actually severing the trees from the freehold under the contract, and was made for a valuable consideration, the property in the trees would, when cut, vest in the vendee. Buck v. Pickwell, 27 Vt. 157; Yale v. Seely, 15 Id. 221. Sales of growing timber have been, and are construed to be mere executory contracts for the sale of chattels, without the statute in several states, otherwise in others; consult Heath v. Randall, 4 Cush. 195; Russell v. Richards, 1 Fairf. 429; S. C., 2 Id. 371; McNeil v. Emerson, 15 Gray, 384; Smith v. Benson, 1 Hill (N. Y.) 176; Barnes v. Barnes, 6 Vt. 388; Mumford v. Whitney, 15 Wend. 380; Pierrpont v. Barnard, 5 Barb. 364· Bostwick v. Leach, 3 Day, ; Erskine v. Plummer, 7 Greenl. 447; Byasse v. Reese, 4 Metc. (Ky.) 372; Cain v. M'Guire, 13

[1] See Morgan's Law of Literature, vol. 2, § 234, *et seq.*

right as used in that Act shall be construed to mean "the sole and exclusive liberty or otherwise of multiplying copies" (z) of any book, sheet of letterpress, sheet of music, dramatic piece, map, chart, &c., or any subject to which the word is therein applied, and (s. 3) that the copyright in books published after the passing of the Act, (1st July, 1842) in the lifetime of the author, shall endure for the author's life, and for seven years after his death ; but if the seven years expire before the end of forty-two years from the first publication, the copyright is to last for forty-two years.[1] If the book is published after the author's death, the copyright is to endure for forty-two years from the first publication thereof.[2] Authors and proprietors of books in which there was an existing copyright at the time of the passing of the Act may (s. 4) by arrange-

(z) Novello v. Sudlow, 12 C. B. 177.   Millar v. Taylor, 4 Burr. 2303.

B. Monr. 340 ; Edwards v. Grand Trunk R. R., 54 Me. 105 ; Mumford v. Whitney, 15 Wend. 380 ; White v. Foster, 102 Mass. 375, 378 ; Wilde, J., in Claflin v. Carpenter, 4 Metc. 583 ; Drake v. Wells, 11 Allen, 14 ; Giles v. Simonds, 15 Gray, 441 ; Nettleton v. Sikes, 8 Metc. 34 ; Delaney v. Root, 99 Mass. 546 ; Parsons v. Smith, 5 Allen, 578 ; Nelson v. Nelson, 6 Gray, 385 ; Douglass v. Shumway, 13 Id. 498 ; Whitmath v. Walker, 1 Metc. 313 ; Giles v. Simonds, 15 Gray, 441 ; Killmore v. Howlett, 48 N. Y. 569.   It is for the jury to say whether an oral agreement to raise three acres of potatoes, to be delivered to plaintiffs, at a certain price per bushel, is a contract for labor and materials, or a sale of certain potatoes to be delivered, but it is not a sale of growing crops.   Prescott v. Locke, 51 N. H. 97.   A written transfer of growing grass, to be cut at the proper time by the vendor, is not so delivered, by plucking and delivering a handful of it, as to make the sale good as against third persons.   Lawson v. Patch, 5 Allen, 586.

[1] The duration of copyright is at present practically the same in the United States ; *i. e.*, twenty-eight years, with a privilege of renewal for fourteen years more.

[2] As to posthumous works, see Morgan's Law of Literature, vol. 2, § 491.

ment between themselves extend the benefit of the
Act to such existing copyright. All copyright is
(s. 25) personal property, and transmissible as such.[1]
Other shorter periods are by various statutes limited
for the duration of copyright in prints, engravings,
ornamental and useful designs, sculpture, paintings,
drawings, and photographs. (a)[2] The proprietor of
the copyright in books, if he wishes to sell and transfer the copyright, must (s. 13) make an entry in the
register of the Stationers' Company of the title of such
book, the time of its first publication, and the name
and place of abode of the publisher and proprietor of
the copyright, in the form given in the schedule ; and
every such registered proprietor may assign his interest
or any portion thereof, by making an entry in the register of the assignment, and of the name and place of
abode of the assignee, in the form given in the schedule
to the Act ; and the assignment so entered is expressly
exempted from stamp duty, and is of the same force
and effect as if it had been made by deed. (b) If the
assignment is made abroad, it must be a valid transfer
according to the law of the country in which it is
made, to constitute the transferee "an assign" of the
author within the meaning of the statute of Victoria.
(c) The assignment of the copyright of a book con-

(a) 25 & 26 Vict. c. 68. Burke's
Sup. to Godson on Patents. Burke's
International Copyright.

(b) See, as to the requisites of regis-

tration, Wood v. Boosey, L. R. 2 Q.
B. 340; Id. 3 Q. B. 423 ; 36 L. J., Q.
B. 103 ; 37 L. J., Q. B. 84.

(c) Cocks v. Purday, 5 C. B. 860.

[1] See Morgan's Law of Literature, vol. 2, chapter "Of
Contracts concerning Literary Property," § 414, *et seq.*, where
all the reported cases relating to Assignments and Transfers
of Literary Property, before and after publication, contracts
with printers, publishers, executors, administrators, assignees,
and creditors, under execution, bankruptcy, and insolvency
proceedings, are cited and discussed.

[2] Id. vol. 2, p. 108, *et seq.*

sisting of or containing a dramatic piece, does not, in the absence of an expressed intention that it should do so, pass the right of representing or performing it, which may be the subject of a subsequent assignment to a third person. (*d*)   In the absence of any contract to the contrary, the assignor of the copyright is still entitled to sell copies of the work printed before assignment. (*e*)   The assignee of the sole right of representing a dramatic piece may sue for penalties under the 3 & 4 Will. 4, c. 15, s. 2, notwithstanding the assignment is not by deed or registered under the 5 & 6 Vict. c. 45. (*f*)

An assignment of copyright by a foreigner resident abroad to another foreigner resident abroad, valid according to the law of the country where it is made, will not give the assignee a title in this country to copyright in the unpublished work of which he is assignee, so that he can transfer it by assignment to an Englishman ; but, if a foreigner having composed, but not having published, a work abroad, comes to this country and prints and publishes his work here, he will be within the protection of the Copyright Acts. (*g*) [1]

Where an agreement in writing was entered into between an author and a publisher, whereby the publisher was to publish at his own expense and risk a certain work written by the author, and, after deduct-

(*d*) Marsh v. Conquest, 17 C. B., N. S. 418 ; 33 L. J., C. P. 319.

(*e*) Taylor v. Pillow, L. R., 7 Eq. 418.

(*f*) Marsh v. Conquest, 17 C. B,. N. S. 418 ; 33 L. J., C. P. 319. Lacy v. Rhys, 4 B. & S. 873 ; 33 L. J., Q. B. 157.

(*g*) Jeffreys v. Boosey, 24 L. J., Exch. 81 ; 4 H. L. C. 815. Low v. Routledge, L. R., 1 Ch. 42 ; 35 L. j., Ch. 114. As to copyright in works and dramatic pieces published abroad, and afterwards published in this country, see Boucicault v. Delafield, 33 L. J., Ch. 38,

[1] See Morgan's Law of Literature, volume 2, chapter " On Contracts."

ing from the produce of the sale of the work the charges for printing, paper, advertisements, and other incidental expenses, and the publisher's commission, the profits remaining of any edition that should be printed were to be divided equally between the author and the publisher, it was held that this did not amount to an agreement for the sale of the copyright, but that it was a mere personal contract, a kind of special agency which could not be assigned so as to give the benefit of it to any other publisher. (*h*) ¹ So long, however, as the publisher performed his part of the contract, he would be entitled to prevent the author from publishing a fresh edition, which might interfere with the sale of an edition on hand, or from putting an end to the agency without recompensing the publisher all the expenses he had incurred. (*i*) ²

658. *Sale and assignment of patent right.*—A person who discovers some new process of manufacture, or some novelty in the useful arts, has no right at common law to the exclusive use of his discovery (*k*) But, in order to encourage persons to make useful discoveries, it is customary for the Crown to grant to the discoverer, by letters patent under the great seal, a monopoly of the use of the invention for a certain period, and to extend the grant to the "executors, administrators, and assigns" of the grantee, so as to give an assignable quality to the patent privilege. A right of this nature, created by grant under the great seal enrolled in Chancery, is matter of public record. It is an incorporeal right, termed by some writers an

(*h*) Stevens v. Benning, 1 K. & J. 174.   (*k*) Duvergier v. Fellows, 10 B. & C.
(*i*) Reade v. Bentley, 3 K. & J, 278.   829.

¹ See Morgan's Law of Literature, volume 2, chapter "On Contracts."
² Id.

incorporeal chattel, and can only be assigned by deed, in accordance with the ancient rule of law that "a thing which of its own nature can not be created without deed can not be assigned without deed." (*l*) The letters patent generally enable the grantee and his assigns to grant licenses under seal for the use of the patent privilege by other parties with whom he or they may contract or agree for the use thereof. But, if a party, by agreement with the grantee, has used and exercised the patent privilege, he can not escape from liability to pay the money he agreed to pay by showing that there was no license under seal. (*m*) The assignment may be made absolute, conditional, or defeasible on the happening of a given event ; (*n*) but, if the patent right is dealt with contrary to a condition upon which it may happen to have been granted, the right is extinguished and gone for ever. It is no ground of objection to the title of an assignee of a patent that the assignors, the executors of the grantee, had omitted to register the probate until after the date of assignment, though possibly it might be an obstacle to the maintenance of an action by the assignee for an infringement, if commenced before the registration of the probate. (*o*) [1]

(*l*) Lincoln College's case, 3 Coke, 63, a.

(*m*) Chanter v. Dewhurst, 12 M. & W. 823.

(*n*) Cartwright v. Amatt, 2 B. & P.

43. Hindmarch on Patents. Coryton on Patent Privileges.

(*o*) Elwood v. Christy, 17 C. B., N. S. 754 ; 34 L. J., C. P. 130.

[1] An inventor may so assign his invention before a patent obtained as to entitle his assignee to a patent. Herbert v. Adams, 4 Mason, 15. And such right to a patent will pass to his executor or administrator. Revision of U. S. Statutes, § 4896, title lx. § 4898 of that title (revision of 1873–4) providing that "every patent or any interest therein shall be assignable in law by an instrument in writing, and the patentee or his assigns or legal representatives may, in like manner, grant and convey an exclusive right, under his patent, to the whole

In a contract for the sale and purchase of a patent right, the vendor does not profess to sell a good and indefeasible patent right, but merely such a right as he actually possesses under the patent. (*p*) If, therefore, subsequently to the sale, the patent turns out to be invalid, without any fraud on the part of the vendor, the purchaser has no ground for claiming back his purchase money. (*q*) A contract for the sale of a patent right may be specifically enforced. (*r*)

659. *Of the title to shares in mining companies.*— The shareholders in joint-stock companies possessed of land are entitled to no direct interest in the land. No part of the realty is held in trust for them ; but all they are entitled to is, that the real and personal property held by the company should be used by the company for their benefit. (*s*) A purchaser of shares in a mining company is not entitled to a regular deduction of the title of the vendor of the share as on the sale of real estate. The vendor may establish his title by the cost-book or register of the mine. (*t*)

(*p*) Hall v. Conder, 2 C. B., N. S. 41 ; 26 L. J., C. P. 138.

(*q*) Lawes v. Purser, 6 Ell. & Bl. 935 ; 26 L. J., Q. B. 25.

(*r*) Cogent v. Gibson, 33 Beav. 557.

(*s*) Watson v. Spratley, 10 Exch.

244. Powell v. Jessop, 18 C. B. 336. Walker v. Bartlett, Id. 845. Edwards v. Hall, 25 L. J., Ch. 82. Caddick v. Skidmore, 3 Jur. N. S. 1185.

(*t*) Curling v. Flight, 5 Hare, 242.

or any specified part of the United States. An assignment, grant, or conveyance shall be void as against any subsequent purchaser or mortgagee for a valuable consideration, without notice, unless it is recorded in the patent office within three months from the date thereof." And see Woodworth v. Wilson, 4 How. 712. Such an assignment without the record required by the statute (*ante,* § 4898) is still good against the grantor, and the limitation of three months is merely directory. And excepting as to intermediate bona fide purchasers, without notice, any subsequent recording of an assignment will be sufficient to pass the title. Brooks v. Byam, 2 Story, 542 ; Curtis on Patents, § 182. As to assignments of patents in bankruptcy, see Curtis on Patents, § 175.

The partners, in whom the legal right in the mine or
minerals is vested by deed of grant, hold the mine
and the partnership joint-stock plant and machinery,
in trust to exercise the right to search for and obtain
minerals, and make a profit for the benefit of the co-
adventurers; and it has been held that the shares of
this profit, and consequently the shares in the mine,
are personal property, which may be bargained for and
transferred without note in writing, no interest in the
soil passing by the transfer, but only a right to participate in the profits of the mine. When mining
shares are sold in the share market, it is the practice
for each party to make a memorandum of the sale in
his own book, in the same manner as is made by
brokers and jobbers on the Stock Exchange. The
vendor afterwards hands a certificate of the sale to the
captain or purser of the mine, authorizing him to
transfer the shares to the purchaser in the usual way ;
and the purchaser signs an acceptance of the shares
written underneath the certificate of sale, which being
presented to the captain or purser of the mine, the
name of the purchaser is substituted in the place of
the vendor in the cost-book, and the transfer is complete. (*u*)   And as soon as the share or interest in the
profits of the concern is transferred by the outgoing
shareholder, the latter is released from all liability
upon contracts subsequently entered into by the purser or managers of the company. (*v*)

660. *Title to shares, scrip, and letters of allotment.*—The mere possession of letters of allotment of
shares or of scrip certificates of shares in projected
railway companies is prima facie evidence of ownership, and of the power of disposition over them. But

(*u*) Watson v. Spratley, 24 L. J.,   (*v*) Harvey v. Kay, 9 B. & C. 356.
Ex. 53.

in the case of registered joint-stock companies, or companies incorporated by Act of Parliament, the title to shares is evidenced by production of a certificate of proprietorship, and by reference to the register of the shareholders of the company.[1] The directors of every registered joint-stock company and incorporated railway company are directed (25 & 26 Vict. c. 89, s. 25, and 8 & 9 Vict. c. 16) to cause books to be kept, to be called the register of shareholders, and to enter from time to time therein the names, addresses, and occupations of the shareholders in the company; the shares held by them, distinguishing each share by its number; the amount paid on such shares; the date at which the name of any person was entered in the register as a shareholder; and the date at which any person ceased to be a shareholder in respect of any share. (*y*) Provision is made by the Companies Act, 1862, (*z*) and by the Railway Acts, for establishing the title to shares in case of the death or bankruptcy or insolvency of shareholders, or the marriage of female shareholders.

Any person entitled to a share in a registered joint-stock company in consequence of the death, bankruptcy, or insolvency of any shareholder, or in consequence of the marriage of any female shareholder, or in any way other than by transfer, may be registered as a shareholder upon such evidence being produced

(*y*) There is a similar provision as to debenture holders contained in the 26 & 27 Vict. c. 118.

(*z*) Sched. Table A.

[1] A sale of stock unaccompanied by a transfer upon the company's books, is good between the parties themselves; and the buyer obtains the legal ownership, with a merely equitable title against the company; Grymes v. Hore, 49 N. Y. 17. See Isham v. Buckingham, 47 N. Y. 216; Weaver v. Barden, 49 N. Y. 286; Bank of Commerce's Appeal, 73 Pa. St. 59.

as may from time to time be required by the company; and any person who has become entitled to a share in any way other than by transfer, may, instead of being registered himself, elect to have some person to be named by him registered as a holder of such share, by executing to his nominee a deed of transfer of such share, which must be presented to the company with such evidence as they may require of the title of the transferror. (*a*)　Under the Companies' Act, 1862, a certificate under the common seal of the company (s. 31), or the register (s. 37), is prima facie evidence of the ownership of a share. (*b*)

661. *Executory contracts for the sale of shares* are generally effected by brokers on the Stock Exchange, who enter the transaction in their books, and transmit bought and sold notes to their principals, specifying the number and value of the shares, and the price to be paid for them.　Executory contracts for the sale of letters of allotment, scrip, and shares in railway companies, or shares in mining companies, or registered joint-stock companies, do not, as we have already seen, come within the operation of the Statute of Frauds, as they "are neither an interest in land, (*c*) nor are they goods and merchandises," (*d*) within the meaning of that Act.　But by the 30 Vict. c. 29, contracts for the sale or transfer of any shares, stock, or other interest in a joint-stock banking company constituted under or regulated by any Act of Parliament, royal charter, or letters patent, issuing shares or stock, transferable by any deed or written instrument (except

(*a*) 25 & 26 Vict. c. 89, Table A, No. 12–16. Copeland v. North Eastern Railway Company, 6 Ell. & Bl. 284.

(*b*) Cornwall, &c., Mining Company v. Bennett, 5 H. & N. 423; 29 L. J.,

Ex. 157.

(*c*) Humble v. Mitchell, 11 Ad. & E. 205. Bradley v. Holdsworth, 3 M. & W. 422.

(*d*) Knight v. Barber, 16 M. & W. 66; 16 L. J., Ex. 18.

by the Banks of England or Ireland), are null and void, unless they set forth and designate in writing such shares, stock, or interest by the respective numbers by which the same are distinguished on the register or books of the company. Where there is no register of shares or stock by distinguishing numbers, the contract must set forth the person in whose name such shares, stock, or interest stand as the registered proprietor in the books of the company. When a bargain has been made for the sale of a certain number of ascertained shares in a particular railway company or a registered joint-stock company, the property in the shares passes by the bargain to the purchaser, and the latter becomes the equitable owner of the shares, and is entitled to a decree for specific performance, when the time for the making of the transfer arrives. (*e*) This transfer of the equitable ownership is naturally accompanied with a transfer of the benefit and the burden incident to the holding of the shares, as in the case of the transfer of the equitable ownership of lands and tenements, so that, if a call is made on the shares between the time of the making of the bargain and the time appointed for the transfer of the shares, the purchaser will be bound to pay the call, and the Court will compel him to accept and register a transfer of the shares, and clothe himself with the legal title to them, and do all proper acts to relieve the vendor from liability as the registered legal owner. (*f*) If, after the making of a bargain for the sale of shares, a dividend is declared, the dividend will belong to the purchaser; for by the custom of the Stock Exchange, the dividend until it becomes payable is included in

---

(*e*) Duncuft v. Albrecht, 12 Sim. 199. 206. Wynne v. Price, 3 De G. & S. 310. New Brunswick Company v. Muggeridge, 4 Drew. 686.

Ross v. Moses, 1 C. B. 227.

(*f*) *Ex parte* Straffon, 22 L. J., Ch.

the price of the share ; and if the vendor receives it, he will hold it as a trustee for the purchaser. If, on the other hand, before the transfer is executed, a peti-tion is presented for winding up the company under the Companies Act, 1862, (*g*) the contract is not ren-dered void by the 153rd section of that Act ; and if the broker has, in accordance with the rules and regu-lations of the Stock Exchange, been compelled to pay the price of the shares to the vendor, he will be en-titled to recover back from his principle the money so paid. (*h*)

662. *Agreements for the transfer of shares.*—If the owner of shares subject to liabilities which deprive them of all marketable value, wishes to divest himself of the shares and the attendant liabilities, and another person is willing to accept the shares, and take the chances of the speculation, and they enter into an agreement for the purpose, the contract will be specifi-cally enforced. (*i*)   But the court will not enforce an agreement to purchase, made after the presentation of a petition to wind up a company, but before advertise-ment, by making the purchaser a contributory, when both parties were ignorant of the pending petition at the time of the agreement. (*k*)   A transfer of shares which is otherwise bona fide, can not be set aside at the instance of the company, either because the ven-dor paid money to the purchaser to take the shares, or because the certificate of transfer contains false repre-sentations as to the consideration paid. (*l*)

663. *Mode of performance.*—Where shares are

(*g*) 25 & 26 Vict. c. 89.

(*h*) Chapman v. Shepherd, L. R., 2 C. P. 228 ; 36 L. J., C. P. 113.

(*i*) Cheale v. Kenward, 3 De G. & J. 27 ; 26 L. J., Ch. 784.

(*k*) *In re* London, Hamburg, and Continental Exchange Bank, *ex parte* Emmerson, L. R., 1 Ch. 433 ; 36 L. J., Ch. 177.

(*l*) Hafod Lead Mining Company, *in re, ex parte* Slater, 35 L. J., Ch. 304.

bought or sold through a broker on the Stock Exchange, the principal enters into an implied contract to sell or buy according to the customs and usages prevalent in that body. (*m*) According to the practice of the Stock Exchange, the broker who buys shares prepares the transfer deed and tenders it to the selling broker for execution, (*n*) and pays the price on the transfer being returned to him executed by the vendor and accompanied by the vendor's certificates of proprietorship. Generally there are intermediate sales, and in that case the first purchaser on a day before the selling day, called the name-day, gives to the vendor's broker the name of an ultimate purchaser to whom the shares are to be transferred. The vendor's broker thereupon prepares a deed of transfer to the ultimate purchaser, gets it executed by the vendor, and on the selling-day hands it and the share certificates to the broker of the ultimate purchaser, who pays the price agreed upon between the ultimate purchaser and the jobber, the vendor's broker paying the balance to or receiving it from the broker as the case may require. When this has been done, the liability of the first purchaser ceases, if the ultimate purchaser is a person to whom no reasonable objection can be made. (*o*) In order to relieve the jobber from liability, the ultimate purchaser whose name is given on the name-day must be a person who is willing to accept and pay for the shares; (*p*) but such purchaser is bound by the acceptance of the transfer, and payment of the

(*m*) Kelly v. Hodgkinson, L. R., 6 Eq. 496.

(*n*) Stephens v. De Medina, 4 Q. B. 428.

(*o*) Paine v. Hutchinson, L. R., 3 Ch. 388 ; 37 L. J., Ch. 485. Coles v. Bristowe, L. R., 4 Ch. 3 ; 38 L. J., Ch.

81. Grissell v. Bristowe, L. R., 4 C. P. 36 ; 38 L. J., C. P. 10. Maxted v. Paine, L. R., 6 Ex. 132 ; 40 L. J., Ex. 57.

(*p*) Maxted v. Paine, L. R., 4 Ex. 81 ; 38 L. J., Ex. 41.

price by his brokers on his behalf. (*q*) The jobber may, however, agree to guarantee that the ultimate purchaser shall register the transfer; and if he does so, and the transfer is not registered, he will be liable to indemnify the vendor against the consequences of such want of registration. (*r*) It is not the duty of the vendor or of the selling broker to get the transfer registered. All he has to do. is to execute the transfer-deed and return it to the purchaser. (*s*) It is then the duty of the latter to execute it and leave it, with the certificates of proprietorship, at the office of the company for registration, and for new certificates of proprietorship to be granted to him in his own name. Until this is done, and the transfer has been registered, and the new certificates granted, the purchaser's title to the shares is incomplete. (*t*) A contract to deliver shares in a projected company does not require the actual delivery of scrip certificates, which are the mere indicia of property; but the party contracting to deliver sufficiently performs his engagement when he places the other in the position of being the legal owner of them. (*u*) It is not incumbent on the vendor to obtain the consent of the directors to the transfer, unless the deed of settlement, or articles of association of the company, make the approval of the directors a condition precedent to the right of the shareholder to transfer his shares. (*v*) A clause in a deed of settlement, that no shareholder shall transfer his shares except in such manner as the directors shall approve, does not prevent a shareholder from entering

(*q*) Bowring v. Shepherd, L. R., 6 Q. B. 309; 40 L. J., Q. B. 129.

(*r*) Cruse v. Paine, L. R., 4 Ch. 441; 38 L. J., Ch. 225.

(*s*) Taylor v. Stray, 2 C. B., N. S. 195.

(*t*) Stray v. Russell, 28 L. J., Q. B. 287.

(*u*) Hunt v. Gunn, 13 C. B., N. S. 226.

(*v*) Wilkinson v. Lloyd, 7 Q. B. 27. Stray v. Russell, 29 L. J., Q. B. 115.

into a contract for the sale of his shares; and, if such a contract has been entered into, it will be enforced as between the vendor and purchaser, and the latter will be compelled to do all that is necessary to be done by him to obtain the consent of the directors of the registration of the transfer. (y) But the court will not compel the directors to assent; nor will specific performance be decreed where they refuse to do so. (z)

Executory contracts for the sale and purchase of shares in railway and parliamentary works' companies are fulfilled on the part of the vendor by a tender of letters of allotment of shares, if there are no shares in the market; and the letters of allotment are commonly bought and received as shares upon the Stock Exchange. (a) In the case of the sale of scrip or letters of allotment of shares in projected companies which can be lawfully bought and sold, no right of property in any particular scrip or shares passes to the purchaser until actual delivery; and the vendor will fulfill his contract by procuring and tendering to the purchaser any scrip that may be in the market. (b) But a purchaser is not, of course, bound to accept shares or scrip, or any securities, of a different kind from those he bargained for and agreed to buy. (c) [1]

(y) Poole v. Middleton, 9 W. R. 758.

(z) Bermingham v. Sheridan, 33 Beav. 660; 33 L. J., Ch. 751.

(a) Stray v. Russell, 28 L. J., Q. B. 284. Mitchell v. Newhall, 15 M & W. 309; 15 L. J., Ex. 292. Tempest v. Kilner, 3 C. B. 240; 15 L. J.. C. P. 10.

Lambert v. Heath, 15 M. & W. 486; 15 L. J., Ex. 297.

(b) Heseltine v. Siggers, 18 L. J., Exch. 166. And see Hunt v. Gunn, *ante.*

(c) Keele v. Wheeler, 7 M. & Gr. 665.

[1] An executory contract for the sale of stock, which fixes no time for its performance, does not pass any title to the stock, but is a valid contract which a party, not in default himself, can enforce; Bruce v. Smith, 44 Ind. 1; and see as to sales of stocks, Smith v. Gear, 59 Ill. 381; Leaming v. Wise, 73 Pa. St. 173.

664. *Time of performance.*—The time for the completion of an executory contract for the sale of shares is regulated by the custom of the Stock Exchange. If particular days are set apart for the settlement of accounts between brokers and their customers, and for the delivery and transfer of shares that have been agreed to be bought and sold in the intervening period, all contracts for the sale and purchase of shares to be completed on a particular day will be deemed to be made for the next settling day that will arrive after the time so appointed. (*d*) When no time is specified for the completion of the contract, the printed rules and customs of the Stock Exchange are admissible in evidence to show what is a reasonable time under all the circumstances of the case for the fulfillment of the bargain. (*e*) Where a written contract for the sale of mining shares was silent as to the time of the delivery of the shares, but fixed the time for payment of the price, it was held that evidence was admissible to show that, by a custom amongst brokers, the vendor under such a contract was not bound to deliver the shares until he had received or was offered payment of the price. (*f*)

665. *Implied undertakings and indemnities annexed to contracts for the sale and purchase of shares. —Payment of calls.*—Where the plaintiff sold mining shares to the defendant, and delivered to him a document addressed to the secretary of the mine, by which the plaintiff requested him to enter a transfer of the shares from his name into that of a transferee, whose name was left in blank that it might be filled up by the

---

(*d*) Fletcher v. Marshall, 15 M. & W. 755. Bayliffe v. Butterworth, 17 L. J., Ex. 79.

(*e*) Stewart v. Cauty, 8 M. & W. 160.

(*f*) Field v. Lelean, 30 L. J., Ex. 169; 9 W. R. 387; overruling Spartali v. Benecke, 10 C. B. 212.

holder of the document, and the blank was left in order that the defendant might insert either his own name, or that of any other person to whom he might sell the shares, and the plaintiff by delivering this document to the defendant had done all that it was incumbent on him to do to pass the property in the shares to the defendant, who, upon the receipt of it, became potentially the owner of the shares, and might have made his title perfect at any time, it was held that there was an implied contract or undertaking on the part of the defendant to indemnify the plaintiff in respect of all calls that might lawfully be made on the shares whilst they remained untransferred in the books of the company. (*g*) But, if the shares are again sold, there is no implied contract of indemnity between the original vendor and those who buy from the first purchaser. The privity of contract, and the attendant liabilities, are confined to those who deal together as vendors and purchasers, and do not extend to parties who are strangers to each other and have never come together in any way. (*h*) Such an implied indemnity does, however, exist where there have been intermediate sales in the manner above described, but the transfer is made by the original vendor direct to the ultimate purchaser, whose duty it then becomes to execute the deed and register the transfer, (*i*) a duty which he may be compelled specifically to perform. (*k*) Where the ultimate purchaser gave the name of one of his workmen as the person to whom the shares were to be transferred, and the transfer was executed to the workman, it was

(*g*) Walker v. Bartlett, 18 C. B. 863; 25 L. J., C. P. 263. Wynne v. Price, 3 De G. & S. 310.

(*h*) Sayles v. Blane, 14 Q. B. 205; 19 L. J., Q. B. 19.

(*i*) Hawkins v. Maltby, L. R., 4 Ch. 200; 38 L. J., Ch. 313.

(*k*) *In re* Overend, Gurney & Co., Musgrave and Hart's case, L. R., 5 Eq. 193; 37 L. J., Ch. 161.

held that the master, as the real purchaser and equitable owner, was bound to indemnify the vendor
against all subsequent calls in respect of the shares.
(*l*) The vendee does not become relieved from his
obligation to indemnify his vendor by re-selling and
transferring the shares to some third person. (*m*)

666. *Rights of scripholders.*—Where a defendant
had signed the subscription contract of a projected
railway company, and had received an allotment of
shares with scrip certificates, which he sold before the
special Act of incorporation of the company had
been obtained, and the shares passed through several
hands, and the holder neglected to send the scrip for
registration, and the company entered the name of
the original allottee in the register as the proprietor
of the shares, and the latter, apprehending that a call
would be made upon him, again sold the shares, it
was held that he was bound to pay over to the scrip-
holder the amount of the purchase money. (*n*) [1]

667. *Transfer deeds.*—It is essential to the validity of a deed of transfer of shares that it be duly
stamped with the proper ad valorem stamp imposed
on transfers made upon a sale (*post*, bk. 4,) also that

(*l*) Castellan v. Hobson, L. R., 10   Q. B. 458 ; 42 L. J., Q. B. 174.
Eq., 47 ; 39 L. J., Ch. 490.   (*n*) Beckitt v. Bilbrough, 19 L. J.,
(*m*) Kellock v. Enthoven, L. R., 8   Ch. 522.

[1] The right to dispose of personal property being an incident of ownership thereof, a by-law of a corporation prohibit-
ing the alienation of its stock, or restricting the same, is void,
as in restraint of trade ; Moore v. Bank of Commerce, 52 Mo.
377 ; nor will a by-law of a corporation which provides that
no shareholder shall convey any shares of its stock, except to
his legal heirs, without first offering them to the corporation
at par, avoid a contract to deliver the earnings of certain
shares of stocks ; see Price v. Minot, 107 Mass. 49.   But see
Germantown, &c., R. Co. v. Fitter, 60 Pa. St. 124, as to a
corporation's right to declare stock forfeited.

the name of the purchaser or party to whom the transfer is to be made, the number and distinguishing marks of the shares, and the price to be paid for them, be inserted in the deed before the execution thereof by the vendor; for material blanks in a deed can not, as we have seen, be afterwards filled up in the absence of the vendor. The rule of law upon this subject can not be altered or affected by the practice or custom of the Stock Exchange. (*o*) But an error in the transfer in distinguishing the numbers is immaterial, if the transferrer has at the time a sufficient number of shares. (*p*) Where a vendor of shares executed printed forms of deeds of transfer, in which the number of shares to be sold, the distinguishing marks of those shares, and the names of the transferees, were left in blank, but the stamps which the transfer bore were sufficient in value to cover a transfer of all the vendor's shares, and the broker, after the transfer deed had been delivered to him, fraudulently filled up the blanks with the whole of the vendor's shares, when he had been authorized to sell only a portion, and absconded with the purchase money, and the fraud was discovered before the transfers had been registered, it was held that the transfers were void; and the Court of Chancery granted an injunction to restrain the registration of the transfers, and prevent any steps being taken to complete the title of the purchaser. (*q*) Where a broker employed by the plaintiff to purchase shares which the plaintiff paid for, procured the instrument of transfer to the plain-

---

(*o*) Hibblewhite v. M'Morine. 6 M. & W. 200. Taylor v. Great Indian Peninsular Company, 4 De G. & J. 559; 28 L. J., Ch. 289. Swan, *ex parte*, 7 C. B., N. S. 448.

(*p*) Ind's case, L. R., 7 Ch. 485; 41 L. J., Ch. 564.

(*q*) Tayler v. Great Indian Peninsular Railway Company, *supra*. Swan, *ex parte*, *supra*. Swan v. North British Australian Company, 2 H. & C. 175; 32 L. J., Ex. 273.

tiff and the plaintiff's signature thereto, and received
from the plaintiff the certificate and transfer for the
purpose of registration, and soon afterwards, having
fraudulently procured the plaintiff to cancel his signature to the transfer, by means of the cancelled
transfer and the certificates, induced the vendor to
execute a fresh transfer to himself, and thereupon
procured the shares to be registered in his own name,
and then mortgaged them, it was held that the effect
of the first transfer was not destroyed by the cancellation fraudulently proved, and the registration in
the name of the broker and the transfers to his
mortgagee were decreed to be set aside. (*r*)

Where the previous consent of the company is made
essential to the validity of a transfer of shares, such consent may be presumed from the conduct and acts of
the company, and they may be estopped from disputing it. (*s*)   Transfer deeds of shares generally contain an agreement on the part of the purchaser to take
and hold the shares subject to the conditions on which
the transferrer himself held them, or to hold them subject to the regulations of the particular company.   One
of these rules generally is that the registered owner
shall pay calls.   If, therefore, a purchaser of shares,
after he has executed a deed of transfer, and had the
deed delivered to him or to his agent for the purpose
of registration, omits to get the deed registered, and
the vendor is compelled to pay calls by reason of his
name being left on the register, he is entitled to be
indemnified by the transferree. (*t*)   A transfer of shares
to an infant is not void but only voidable ; and if the
infant after arriving at full age affirms the transaction,

(*r*) Donaldson v. Gillot, L. R., 3 Eq.
274.

(*s*) Lane, *in re*, 33 L. J., Ch. 84.

(*t*) Walker v. Bartlett, 18 C. B.
863, overruling Humble v. Langston,
7 M. & W. 517.

he can not afterwards avoid it on the ground of his infancy. (*u*)

668. *Transfers of shares in registered joint-stock companies* must be in the form given in the schedule to the 25 & 26 Vict. c. 89, Table A, No. 8, and must be executed both by the transferrer and transferree. By this form of transfer the transferree takes the shares subject to the conditions on which the transferrer held them at the time of the execution of the transfer. The transferrer remains the holder of the shares until the name of the transferee is entered in the register; but if the company makes default, or is guilty of unnecessary delay in registering any transfer of shares, it is responsible in damages to the party injured. In the case of a company other than a limited company, every transferee of shares is, in a degree proportioned to the shares transferred, to indemnify the transferrer against all existing and future debts of the company ; and in case of a limited company, every transferee is to indemnify the transferrer against all calls made, or accrued due, on the shares transferred subsequently to the transfer. By the 25 Vict. c. 89, s. 131, it is provided that, whenever a company is wound up voluntarily, the company shall from the date of the commencement of such winding up, cease to carry on its business, and that all transfers of shares, except transfers made to or with the sanction of the liquidator, taking place after the commencement of such winding up, shall be void. This enactment does not justify the vendor in refusing to execute a transfer, and thereby casting on his broker the liability to furnish other shares to the purchaser. (*v*) By sect. 153 of the same Act

---

(*u*) In re Blakely Ordnance Company, Lumsden's case, L. R., 4 Ch. 31 ; 39 L. J., Ch. 124.

(*v*) Biederman v. Stone, L. R. 2 C. P. 504 ; 36 L. J., C. P. 198.

every transfer of shares made between the commencement of winding up and the order for winding up, is
void, unless the Court otherwise orders. But an agreement for the sale of shares in the specified interval is
not void ; and the transfer may be executed after the
winding up order has been made. (y)

669. *Registration of transfers—Payment of calls.*
—The Companies Clauses Consolidation Act, 8 Vict.
c. 16, enacts, (s. 16) that no shareholder shall be entitled to transfer any share after any call shall have been
made in respect thereof, until he shall have paid such
call, nor until he shall have paid all calls for the time
being due on every share held by him; (z) and by
the 25 & 26 Vict. c. 89, schedule, Table A, No. 10, the
company may decline to register any transfer of shares
made by a member who is indebted to them. When
a call has been made between the time of the making
of the executory contract of sale and the time appointed for making the transfer, it is the duty of the
purchaser to clear the way for the registration of the
transfer deed and the completion of the transfer by
payment of the intervening call. (a) Where the a ticles of association of a joint-stock company provided
that the directors might decline to register any transfer of shares made by a shareholder who was indebted
to them, it was held that a shareholder could not be
considered indebted to the company, in respect of a
call made by the directors, until he had received a notice of the call, specifying the person to whom the call
was to paid, and the time and place of payment. (b)
But a shareholder may be indebted to the company so

(y) Rudge v. Bowman, L. R. 3 Q.
B. 689; 37 L. J., Q. B. 193.

(z) Hall v. Norfolk Estuary Company, 21 L. J., Q. B. 94.

(a) Shaw v. Rowley, 16 M. & W.
815.

(b) Rudolphe, ex parte, 32 L. J., Q.
B. 369 ; 37 L. J., Q. B. 1 3.

as to be unable to transfer his shares, although he may have accepted a bill of exchange and handed it to the company by way of payment of the debt. (*c*)　Under the 8 Vict, c. 16, s. 16, the company is bound to register a transfer of shares on which no call can be made, as, for instance, fully paid up shares, although the transferrer be the holder of other shares on which there are calls unpaid. (*d*)　If the vendor of the shares has done all that the deed of settlement or the Act of Parliament under which the company is established, requires him to do to entitle him to transfer his shares, it becomes the duty of the directors to enter a memorial of any transfer deed that may be duly executed by him in the register of transfers, and to do all that 's necessary to be done to constitute the purchaser the holder of the shares in the place and stead of the vendor; and, if they neglect or refuse so to do they are responsible in damages to such purchaser. (*e*)　But the directors must, of course, be furnished with all the materials necessary to enable them to make the registry. (*f*)　By the 30 & 31 Vict. c. 131, s. 26, the transfer must be registered on the application of the transferrer, in the same manner and subject to the same conditions as if the application were made by the transferee. The same Act provides for the issue of share-warrants to bearer transferable by delivery. The directors of a company have no discretionary power, independently of powers expressly given to them by the articles of association, to refuse to register a transfer which has been bona fide made. There-

---

(*c*) Re London. Birmingham, &c., Bank, 34 I . J., Ch. 418.

(*d*) H bbersty v. The Manchester, Sheffield, and Lincolnshire Railway Company, L. R., 2 Q. B. 59, 471 ; 36 L. J., Q. B. 198.

(*e*) Catchpole v. Amberg., &c., 1 Ell. & Bl. 111.

(*f*) Gregory v. East India Company, 7 Q. B. 199.

fore, where a transferee gave an address at which he was only an occasional visitor, it was held that the directors were bound to register the transfer, although the company was at the time in difficulties, and the shares were sold by the transferrer in order to get rid of his responsibility. (*g*)   But if, by the deed of settlement, the acceptance of the transferee is made dependent upon the approval of the directors, they need not give their reasons for refusing to approve ; and in the absence of evidence to the contrary the court will presume that they have acted reasonably and bona fide. (*h*)[1]

670. *Compulsory registration by mandamus.*— Whenever a company, incorporated by royal charter or by act of Parliament, has imposed upon it the duty of keeping a register and inserting therein the names of the proprietors or shareholders, the court will grant a mandamus to enforce performance of the duty. (*i*) A company is not bound to register a transfer not in accordance with the statutable form. The ordinary form of transfer is by a deed simply informing the company who goes out as a shareholder, who comes in, and who is in future liable to calls; and if the transfer is incumbered with any trust, or is made by way of mortgage, or embraces other property, the company is not bound to receive and register the transfer. (*k*)   The proper course, when shares in a

---

(*g*) In re Smith, Knight & Co., Weston's case, L. R., 4 Ch. 20 ; 38 L. J., Ch. 49, 673.

(*h*) Ex parte, Penny, L. R. 8 Ch. 446 ; 42 L. J., Ch. 183.

(*i*) Norris v. Irish Land Company, 8 Ell. & Bl. 525.

(*k*) Reg. v. General Cemetery Company, 6 Ell. & Bl. 415 ; 25 L. J., Q. B. 342.

---

[1] As to payment of calls, see Wilson v. Wills Valley R. R. Co., 33 Ga. 446 ; Germantown, &c., R. Co. v. Filter, 60 Pa. St. 124.

company are made the subject of a settlement in trust, is for the settler to execute the ordinary deed of transfer in the simple form given in the statute, transferring the shares for a nominal pecuniary consideration to the trustees, and to take at the same time a separate declaration of trust. The transfer deed is then left with the secretary, and the trustee is registered as absolute owner. (*l*) By s. 30 of the Companies' Act, 1862, it is expressly enacted that no notice of any trust expressed, implied, or constructive, shall be entered on the register or be receivable by the registrar.

671. *Rectification of the register of the shareholders in registered joint-stock companies.*—By the 25 & 26 Vict. c. 89, s. 35, it is enacted that if the name of any person is without sufficient cause entered or omitted to be entered on the register of shareholders, or if default is made or unnecessary delay (*m*) takes place in entering on the register the fact of any person having ceased to be a member of the company, such person, or any member of the company, or the company itself, may by motion in any of the superior courts of law or equity, or by application to a judge sitting at chambers, apply for an order that the register may be rectified ; and the court may, if satisfied, make the order. The court may decide on any question relating to the title of any person who is a party to such proceeding to have his name entered in, or omitted from, the register, and may in any such proceeding decide any question that it may be necessary or expedient to decide for the rectification of the register. (*n*)

(*l*) Copeland v. North Eastern Railway Company, 6 Ell. & Bl. 277.

(*m*) In re Joint Stock Discount Company, Shepherd's case, L. R., 2 Eq. 564 ; Ib. 2 Ch. 16 ; 36 L. J., Ch. 32.

(*n*) Re Bank of Hindustan, &c., 34 L. J., Ch. 609. Russian (Vyksounsky)

A party may be precluded from availing himself of the jurisdiction of the court for the rectification of the register by his delay, (*o*) or if the error he seeks to rectify has been occasioned by his own misconduct and negligence (*p*) in executing stamped transfers in blank, and handing such transfers with the certificates of his proprietorship to a third party, and thereby enabling the latter to commit frauds upon innocent purchasers. (*q*) But the negligence must be the immediate and proximate cause of the fraud. (*r*) Where an action for calls was pending between a company and an applicant for an order under this section, the court refused to make an order for the rectification of the register by removing one name and inserting another. (*s*)

In cases of fraud, forgery or mistake, a company may be justified in removing the names of shareholders from their register; but when once a person has been put on the register, and has acquired the status of a proprietor, the company can not take upon themselves to deprive the party of his status and strike him off the register by their own movement in the matter, and without any claim being put forward by some one having a better title. (*t*) If, therefore,

Ironworks Company, ex parte Stewart, L. R., 1 Ch. 574; 36 L. J., Ch. 738. London, Hamburgh and Continental Exchange Bank, ex parte Ward, L. R. 2 Ch. 431; 36 L. J., Ch. 462. Ibid. Kincaid's case, L. R. 2 Ch. 412; 36 L. J., Ch. 499. Overend, Gurney, and Company, Ward and Garfit's case, L. R. 4 Eq. 189; 36 L. J., Ch. 416. The Imperial Mercantile Credit Association, Marino's case, L. R., 2 Ch. 596; 36 L. J., Ch. 468. National and Provincial Marine Insurance Company, ex parte Parker, L. R., 2 Ch. 685.

(*o*) Taite's case, L. R., 3 Eq. 795 ; 36 L. J., Ch. 475. But see, in re Bowron, Baily & Co., Bailey's case, L. R., 5 Eq. 428 ; Ib. 3 Ch. 592; 37 L. J., Ch 670.

(*p*) Ireland, Bank of, v. Trustees Evans' Charities, 5 H. L. C. 410.

(*q*) Ex parte Swan, 7 C. B., N. S. 400. 39 L. J., C. P. 113.

(*r*) Swan v. The North British Australian Company, *ante.*

(*s*) Harris, ex parte, 29 L. J., Ex. 364.

(*t*) Martin, ex parte, 2 H. & M. 669.

the company put on their register a person having only an equitable title to certain shares, they can not take his name off again, except at the instance of the party having the legal title; for it could never be permitted that a company, on discovering a flaw in a shareholder's title, should be at liberty to remove his name from the register, and treat his shares as nobody's, and appropriate them and the dividends to their own use. The position of the company in respect of their registered shares is analogous to that of a bailee, who must be taken to hold for the person whose title he has recognized, until the shares are claimed by a party showing a better title. (*u*) But, if a party has got himself placed on the register by means of forgery, misrepresentation, or fraud, and has no title at all, either legal or equitable, to the shares standing against his name, the company may remove his name from the register. (*v*)

Public companies have been termed the parliamentary book-keepers of the fund entrusted to their management; and it is a duty they owe to all persons interested in the fund, so to keep the account as that it may distinctly appear at all times what transfers and assignments have been made; and, if a stockholder can show that on a given day stock stood in his name, and that it does not now stand in his name, and that he has not authorized the transfer of it, he may require the company to replace the stock. (*y*)

672. *Registration of forged transfers.*—If a transfer of shares has been forged, and the forged transfer entered in the company's books, and the

(*u*) Ward v. South Eastern Railway Company, 29 L. J., Q. B. 177.

(*v*) Cockburn, C. J., Ward v. South Eastern Railway Company, 29 L. J., Q. B. 182. Hare v. London and North Western Railway Company, 8 W. R. 352.

(*y*) Sloman v. Bank of England, 14 Sim. 486.

name of the shareholder expunged from the registry
on the strength of the forged document, the shareholder does not thereby lose one iota of his rights
against the company ; he can compel them to restore
his name, and may enforce payment of the dividends
due to him, whether his name has been restored or
net. And, if both the shareholder and the party
claiming under the forged transfer bring actions
against the company for the recovery of the dividends
declared on the shares, the court will not compel
them to interplead to establish their rights, as the
dispute arises out of an alleged negligent act of the
company. If the company has registered a forged
transfer, it has been guilty of negligence, not having
employed a proper secretary, and is answerable to a
purchaser under the forged transfer for the value of
the shares. (*z*) Where trust-money was invested in
railway debentures made payable to three trustees, and
the debentures were left in the hands of one of the
trustees, who received the interest upon them, and
subsequently sold the debentures to a bona fide
purchaser, and forged the names of his co-trustees to
a transfer of the debentures, and the purchaser presented the debentures at the transfer-office of the
railway company, and got them transferred into his
own name, it was held that the transfer was null and
void, and that the trustees were still entitled to the
debentures ; and the Court of Chancery ordered them
to be delivered up to the trustees, and directed the
transfer and entry thereof in the company's books to

(z) Dalton v. Midland Railway
Company, 12 C. B. 458 ; 13 C. B. 474.
Hildyard v. South Sea Company, 2 P.
Wms. 75. In re Bahia and San Fran-
cisco Railway Company, in re Trittin,
L. R., 3 Q. B. 584 ; 37 L. J., Q. B.
176. Hart v. Frontino and Bolivia,
&c., Co., L. R., 5 Ex. 111 ; 39 L. J.,
Ex. 93 Johnston v. Renton, L. R., 9
Eq. 181.

be cancelled. "No laches," it was observed, "could be imputed to the trustees for suffering one of their number to hold the debentures; for some one of them must hold them, unless they are deposited with bankers, or placed in a box secured by a number of different locks of which each trustee shall hold one of the keys, and negligence can not be imputed to trustees for not taking such precautions as these." (*a*)

Where stock in a railway company stood in the names of two proprietors, and the one sold the stock and signed a transfer of the shares, and forged the signature of his co-proprietor, and the company registered the forged transfer and paid the purchaser the dividends, and the forgery was not discovered for many years, it was held that the company was nevertheless bound to replace the stock. (*b*) If the forgery has been occasioned by the plaintiff's gross negligence and misconduct, amounting to an estoppel or a ratification, (*c*) or if he has acted so as to be particeps criminis, he will be precluded from setting up or relying upon the forgery; (*d*) but the negligence or misconduct must be the proximate cause of the forgery and the direct means of effecting it. (*e*) [1]

(*a*) Cottam v. Eastern Counties Railway Company, 1 John & H. 247; 30 L. J., Ch. 217.

(*b*) Taylor v. Midland Railway Company, 28 Beav. 287; 29 L. J., Ch. 733. Sloman v. Bank of England, 14 Sim. 475.

(*c*) Ireland, Bank of, v. Evans' Charities, 5 H. L. C. 413.

(*d*) Swan ex parte, 7 C. B., N. S. 434; 30 L. J., C. P. 113.

(*e*) Swan v. North British Australian Company, *ante.*

[1] As to transfers of stock, see Sprague v. Cocheco Mfg. Co., 10 Blatchf. 173; Keeney v. Globe Mill Co., 39 Conn. 145; Smith v. American Case Co., 7 Lans. 307; State v. New Orleans Gas, &c. Co., 25 La. An. 213; Bruce v. Smith, 44 Ind. 1; Upton v. Burnham, 3 Biss. 431; Ellison v. Schneider, 25 La. An. 485; Lowry v. Commercial, &c. Bank, Taney, 310; Weiser v. Smith, 22 La. An. 156; State v. Rombauer, 46 Mo. 155.

673. *Transfers of stock in the public funds* are regulated by the 33 & 34 Vict. c. 71, which also provides for the issue of stock certificates transferable by delivery.   Persons to whom transfers of stock are made in the books of the Bank of England are re-quired to underwrite their acceptance of the transfer; but their neglect so to do does not enable the trans-ferer to treat the transfer as a nullity. (*f*) [1]

674. *Specific performance of contracts for the purchase and sale of stock and shares.*—The court will not decree specific performance of a contract for the sale of stock in the public funds generally, as one portion of stock is as good as another, and it must be the same thing to the purchaser, whether he receives the stock agreed to be sold to him, or the money that will purchase it in the market.   The purchaser, there-fore, is left to his remedy by way of action for dama-ges. (*g*)   But if the contract is for certain specific stock or shares in a particular railway company or joint-stock company, the Court will decree a specific performance as against the vendor, provided the rights of third parties have not in the meantime intervened. (*h*)   A sale of an annuity payable out of the divi-dends of particular stock, (*i*) and of the right to divi-dends upon a bankrupt's estate, have been enforced in

---

(*f*) Foster v. Bank of England, 8 Q. B. 705. As to the ordinary mode of transferring stock, see Keyser's Law of the Stock Exchange.

(*g*) Cud v. Rutter, 20 Vin. Abr. tit.

"Stocks," pl. 9.   1 P. Wms. 570.

(*h*) Doloret v. Rothschild, 1 Sim. & Stu. 598.

(*i*) Withy v. Cottle, Id. 174; 1 Turn. & Russ. 78.

---

[1] Where defendant contracted to deliver to C, plaintiff's assignor, $10,000 current funds of the United States, at 15 cents on the dollar in ten months from date; held that the contract was to deliver $10,000 legal tender notes for $1,500 in specie, and was a valid contract, for a breach, of which de-fendant must answer.   Cook v. Davis, 53 N. Y. 318.

specie. (*k*) There is no analogy, it has been observed, between a contract for the purchase and sale of a quantity of three per cent. consols, or any other stock generally, which is always to be had by any person who chooses to apply for it in the market, and where the vendor fulfils his contract by tendering any stock of the description bargained for, and a contract for certain specific numbered railway shares, mining shares, or scrip. (*l*) Where certain numbered railway shares were sold by auction, and the purchaser paid his purchase-money, but did not take a transfer of the shares, and then sold to a third party who refused to register himself as owner of the shares, and calls were made on the shares which were left unpaid, it was held that the original vendor was entitled to·a decree for specific performance against the original purchaser. (*m*) The court will not enforce performance of a contract for the purchase of scrip certificates in projected companies, and will not, when the company has been completely registered or incorporated, compel the purchaser to take a transfer of the corresponding shares from his vendor, or to indemnify the latter from calls subsequently made. (*n*) Nor will specific performance be decreed, where the directors, under the

---

(*k*) Adderley v. Dixon, 1 Sim. & Stu. 610.

(*l*) Duncuft v. Albrecht, 12 Sim. 199.

(*m*) Shaw v. Fisher, 12 Jur. Chan. 152. And see Paine v. Hutchinson, L. R., 3 Eq., 257; Id. 3 Ch. 388 ; 36 L. J., Ch. 169; 37 Id. 485. But doubts have been raised whether the original vendor is entitled to specific performance against the ultimate purchaser, where, in accordance with the practice of the Stock Exchange, there have been intermediate sales without the execution of any transfer, and the

name of the ultimate purchaser has been supplied to the broker of the original vendor, for the purpose of being inserted in the transfer deed to be executed by the latter. Hawkins v. Maltby, L. R., 4 Eq. 572 ; 37 L. J., Ch. 58. But it would seem that specific performance will be decreed in such a case. *In re* Overend, Gurney & Co., Musgrave and Hart's case, L. R., 5 Eq. 193 ; 37 L. J., Ch. 161.

(*n*) Jackson v. Cocker, 4 Beav. 59. Columbine v. Chichester, 2 Phil. Ch. C. 2.

II.—20

powers conferred by the deed of association, refuse to
assent to the transfer. (*v*)   If a party has signed an
application for shares in a registered joint-stock company, and shares have been allotted to him in consequence of his application, the Court of Chancery will
compel him to sign the written acceptance of the
transfer, and pay the calls due on the shares. (*p*)'

(*o*) Bermingham v. Sheridan, 33   (*p*) New Brunswick, &c., Company
Beav. 660.   v. Muggeridge, 4 Drew, 686.

' In an action by a purchaser of stock, induced by fraudulent representations as to its value, the measure of damages
is the difference between the real and the represented value of
such stock.   But if the stock were absolutely worthless, the
market value is of no weight upon the question of value.   A
purchaser of worthless stock, after discovering its worthlessness, is not bound to mitigate the loss of the fraudulent seller
of the stock, by himself, by fraudulent representations, selling to
an innocent purchaser; Hubbell v. Meiggs, 50 N. Y. 480; and
see Hager v. Thompson, 1 Black. 80.   Stocks are articles of
commerce passing from hand to hand like commercial paper,
and the doctrine of constructive notice by lis pendens is not
applicable to them.   Leitch v. Wells, 48 N. Y. 585 ; and see
Currie v. White, 45 N. Y. 822 ; Field v. Montmollin, 5 Bush.
(Ky.) 455.   They are in the nature of choses in action.   Arnold
v. Ruggles, 1 R. I. 165 ; Albert v. Savings Bank of Baltimore,
1 Md. Ch. 407.   A sale of corporate stock carries dividends
not yet payable.   Burroughs v. North Carolina R. R. Co., 67
N. C. 376 ; March v. Eastern R. R. Co., 43 N. H. 515 ; Kane
v. Bloodgood, 7 Johns. Ch. 90.   But one selling such stock before his certificate therefor is issued, agreeing to give the buyer
his certificate when he gets it, is not bound to pay assessments upon the shares after the sale, but before receiving the
certificate; Brigham v. Meade, 10 Allen, 245 ; Merrimac
Mining Co. v. Levy, 54 Pa. St. 227.   In Sampson v. Shaw, 101
Mass. 145, the rule as to wagers was construed to apply to an
agreement concerted to create a " corner " in a certain stock.
Under such an agreement the parties are not partners, and
one can only recover from the other an unexpended
balance of monies advanced, in an action for money had and
received; and see Boynton v. Woodbury, Id. 346 ; Central R.
R. Co. v. Collins, 40 Ga. 582 ; Stapples v. Gould, 5 Seld

520. As to when a contract for the sale of certain stocks enumerated in the New York statute relative to stock-jobbing was absolutely void; see Stebbins v. Leowolf, 3 Cush. 137. Such act does not apply to sales of distributive shares in the effects of a corporation that has been dissolved. James v. Woodruff, 10 Paige, 541. This act was repealed, however, by the act of 1858, 2 R. S. 5th ed. 980, which provides that such sale or transfer of stocks shall not be void or voidable for want or non-payment of any consideration, nor because the holder was not the owner of the same at the time the contract of sale was made. As to a contract to pay for goods in a certain kind of stock, see Eastern R. R. Co. v. Benedict, 15 Gray, 289. Stock-brokers, when ordered to purchase shares of a certain stock, have no right to purchase from themselves, or if ordered to sell, to sell it to themselves, without disclosing to their principal the fact that they are so dealing with him. New York, &c., Ins. Co. v. National, &c., Ins. Co., 14 N. Y. 85. A mere order to a broker to buy stock, means to buy it according to the rules or customs of the market. Horton v. Morgan, 19 N. Y. 170. If he is to buy on a margin, he may take a transfer of the stock to himself without separating it from similar stock standing in his own name, and hold it as a pledge for the advance he has made upon it; Id.; but in an action against a broker for a wrongful sale of stock purchased by him for the plaintiff, under an agreement that the plaintiff should keep a margin of ten per cent. upon the par value, above the market rate of the shares in the broker's hands, which plaintiff failed to do, it appearing that the shares fell in price, upon which plaintiff was notified and required by defendant to furnish money sufficient to make his margin good, upon his failing to do which, defendants sold out the stock at the stock exchange without further notice to plaintiff, held, that the parties were not bound as pledgor and pledgee, and that the plaintiff having failed to keep his contract, the defendants had a right to sell the stock; Hawks v. Drake, 49 Barb. 186; Markham v. Jaudon, Id. 462. And as to pledges of stock, see Seaman v. Reeve, 15 Barb. 424.

CHAPTER II.

THE CONTRACT OF LETTING.

SECTION I.

LANDLORD AND TENANT.

675. *Leases.*—A lease is a contract whereby the temporary use and possession of a house or land are granted by the owner to another for a stipulated or implied remuneration. He who grants the possession and use of the property to be enjoyed for hire is called the lessor or landlord; and he who has the enjoyment of it, paying the rent or hire, is called the lessee or tenant. In the Roman law the former was called "locator," the latter "conductor;" and the contract itself, "locatio rei." In the French law it is termed " bail a loyer," or a bailment for hire; the lessor is called the " bailleur," or bailor, and the hirer the " preneur," or " locataire." (*a*) If the land or realty is granted by deed to be enjoyed for a term without any payment of rent by the grantee, the grant amounts to a commodatum or gratuitous loan of the use of the land, and does not create a contract of letting and hiring between the parties. On the other hand a demise for a term of years, if it is by deed, and for the whole term which the lessor has in the premises, operates as an assignment. (*b*)[1]

(*a*) Encyc. du Droit, tit. BAIL.   (*b*) Beardmore v. Wilson, L. R., 4 C. P. 57; 38 L. J., C. P. 91.

[1] No particular form of words is necessary to constitute a

676. *Agreements for leases.*—We have already seen that all agreements for leases must be authenticated by some note or memorandum, signed according to the provisions of the Statute of Frauds.[1] We have also seen that all leases exceeding three years in duration, required by the Statute of Frauds to be evidenced by a signed writing, must now be authenticated by deed. Every lease, therefore, in writing, not under seal, for a term exceeding three years in duration, amounts only to an agreement to grant a lease for the term specified. (*c*) But, if an oral agreement for a lease has been entered into, and the intended lessee, relying on the promise of the lessor to grant the lease, takes possession of the land, and expends money in building, draining, and improving, and there is, therefore, a part performance of the contract, the court will enforce the oral contract, and compel the lessor to grant the lease agreed upon, on the ground that, by refusing to grant the lease and give the party possession in execution of the contract, he is guilty of a direct fraud, which ought to be relieved against. (*d*) But,

---

(*c*) Bond v. Rosling, Parker v. Taswell, Tidey v. Mollett, *ante.* Burton v. Reevell, 16 M. & W. 307; 16 L. J., Ex. 85. Rollason v. Leon, 7 H. & N. 73; 31 L. J., Ex. 96.

(*d*) Morphett v. Jones, 1 Swanst. 172. Gregory v. Mighell, 18 Ves. 328. Mundy v. joliffe, 5 Myl. & Cr. 167. Parker v. Smith, 1 Coll. Ch. C. 608.

lease, but when the parties are not together, the acceptance must be manifested by some appropriate act, and the manifestation put in the proper way of reaching the proposer; a mere mental determination to accept, not indicated or sought to be indicated by speech or act, is not such an acceptance. White v. Corlies, 46 N. Y. 467. A lease is a contract for the possession and profits of land and tenements on the one side, and a recompense of rent or other income on the other, and there may be a lease without any reservation of rent. Failing v. Schenck, 3 Hill, 344; Hunt v. Comstock, 15 Wend. 667.

[1] *Ante*, vol. 1, § 201.

if there is nothing more than an oral agreement for a
lease and a taking of possession by an intended lessee
without any improvement made on the land, the oral
contract can not be enforced.[1] When, however, a
party has actually been let into possession under an
oral contract of demise, and rent has been paid to and
received by the landlord, a tenancy from year to year

[1] An agreement to give a lease is not a lease ; to constitute
a lease it must be accompanied by actual possession. Becker
v. De Forest, 1 Sweeney, 528. But words of demise in a writing will constitute a lease, even if it also contain a covenant
for a further lease, if accompanied by possession. Jackson v.
Kisselbrack, 10 Johns. 336 ; Jackson v. Van Hoesen, 4 Cow.
325 ; Hallett v. Wylie, 3 Johns. 44. But see Jackson v. Moncrief, 5 Wend. 26. It has been held that an agreement to
construct a wharf, to be occupied when finished by grantee, at
a stipulated rent, accompanied by words of present demise,
will operate as a lease. People v. Kelsey, 14 Abb. Pr. 372.
As to whether mere receipts will operate as leases, see Ryan v.
Ward, 48 N. Y. 203 ; Niles v. Culver, 8 Barb. 205 ; Berrian v.
The Mayor, &c., 48 Rob. 539 ; Coon v. Knapp, 8 N. Y. 402 ;
Graves v. Friend, 5 Sandf. 568; Kellogg v. Richards, 14 Wend.
116. In Gibbons v. Dayton, 4 Hun. 451, the following receipt—
" New York, Sept. 1st, 1871. Received from Mrs. Mary Merriam the sum of sixty dollars, for one month's rent only, in
advance, for second floor rooms in house No. 165 Bleecker-
street, ending October 1, 1871, at noon. It being expressly
understood between us, the tenant and agent, or landlord
mentioned in this receipt, that this term of hiring and letting
is for one month only, and will expire as aforesaid. $60.
Thomas J. Gibbons"—was held to indicate a tenancy from
month to month. In Gartside v. Outley, 58 Ill. 211, an instrument conveying premises to the grantee for the purpose of
mining coal " so long as there is coal to mine thereon," em-
bracing also provisions as to back rents, forfeitures, &c., &c.,
was held to be a lease and not a servitude. In Shaw v.
Farnsworth, 108 Mass. 358, a proposition by a tenant at will
to " take the house for three years from " a certain day in the
future (if the owner would make certain alterations, additions
or repairs, specified), was construed to be a present demise to
commence in the future, and not a mere agreement to execute
a lease at a future time.

between the parties arises by implication of law. From every contract to grant a lease there is an implied agreement by the party contracting to grant the lease that he has a good right and title so to do. (*e*)

677. *Present demises.*—No precise words or technical form of language are requisite to constitute a present demise. An estate or term of years in the land may be created and vested in a third party, by giving him a license to enjoy a house, or making an agreement with him that he "shall reside" therein, provided some certain rent or specified service is reserved, or something is given as the consideration of the contract, and possession is given and accepted under the contract. (*f*) If there are any words showing a present intention that one is to give and the other to have possession for a determinate term, a tenancy is created; and this intention may be manifested by expressions contained in a series of letters as well as by the formal words of a single instrument. (*g*) And on the other hand, although there be precise and formal words of present demise, yet, if there appears from the face of the entire contract a contrary intention, the instrument will be considered only an agreement for a future lease, and will not operate as a present demise. (*h*)

It is a rule of law that, whatever words are sufficient to explain the intent of the parties that the one shall divest himself of the possession and profits of the land, and the other come into them for such a determinate time, for a certain hire or rent, such words,

---

(*e*) Stranks v. St. john, L. R., 2 C. P. 376; 36 L. J., C. P. 118.

(*f*) Co. Litt. 45 b. Bac. Ab. Leases (K.) Right v. Proctor, 4 Burr. 2209.

(*g*) Chapman v. Bluck, 5 Sc. 531; 4 Bing. N. C. 187. jones v. Reynolds,

1 Q. B. 506.

(*h*) Morgan v. Bissell, 3 Taunt. 72. Doe v. Powell. 8 Sc. N. R. 687. Gore v. Lloyd, 12 M. & W. 478. Doe v. Clark, 7 Q. B. 211. Taylor v. Caldwell, 3 B. & S. 826.

whether they run in the form of an assignment, or of a license, covenant or agreement, are of themselves sufficient, and will in construction of law amount to a lease for years, as effectually as if the most proper and pertinent words had been made use of for that purpose. (*i*) A lease may be made either for life, or for years,' or at will ; and a contract for letting and hiring of land will, if it can not operate as an assignment, be supported as a lease, although it was intended to pass all the lessor's interest. (*k*) Whenever the house or land of one man has been occupied and used by another, the prima facie presumption is that the use and occupation are to be paid for; and the landlord is entitled to maintain an action to recover a reasonable hire and reward for the use of the land, unless the tenant can show that he entered into possession of the property under circumstances fairly leading to an opposite conclusion. A landlord, on the other hand, who has permitted a tenant to occupy property, and has received rent from the latter for such use and occupation, will be bound by his own acts, and can not afterwards treat such tenant as a trespasser and turn him out of possession without a proper notice to quit. But if the tenant is a pauper who has been provided with a dwelling-house by the parish, or an old servant who has been accommodated with a cottage and garden by his master, or the son or other near relation of the owner, the possession and occupation do not raise a presumption of a contract of letting

---

(*i*) Bac. Abr. Leases (K.) Shep. 143.
Touch. ch. 14, 272. Bro. Abr. (Lease), (*k*) Pollock v. Stacey, 9 Q. B. 1035 ; pl. 60. Cottee v. Richardson, 7 Exch. 16 L. J., Q. B. 132.

' Leases for years, although chattels real, are no longer deemed terms as at common law, but estates. Averill v. Taylor, 8 N. Y. 44.

and hiring between the parties. The transaction amounts only to a commodatum, or gratuitous loan of the property for use. The possession of the tenant is the possession of the landlord or owner; and the former may at any time be removed at the will and pleasure of the latter. (*l*)

678. *Proof of the terms of holding.*—If a tenancy is actually created by entry on the land and payment of rent, the terms of the tenancy may be proved by oral testimony. Where land was about to be let, and printed papers of the terms of holding were distributed among parties, who assented verbally to the printed terms, and subsequently became tenants, it was held that a witness might look at the printed paper to refresh his memory when he was asked to prove the terms of the holding from recollection. (*m*) '

679. *Lease by estoppel.*—We have already seen that no man is permitted to allege or prove anything in contradiction or contravention of his own deed. Where, therefore, a man grants a lease under seal, he is not permitted to avoid his own grant by proving that he had no interest in the demised premises, unless he is a trustee for the public, deriving his authority from an Act of Parliament. (*n*) As between him and his lessee the lease operates by way of estoppel. "And if one makes a lease for years, by indenture, of lands wherein he hath nothing at the time of such lease made, and after purchases those very lands, this shall make good and unavoidable his lease, as well as if

---

(*l*) *Post.* s. 3. Bertie v. Beaumont, 16 East, 33. Hunt v. Colson, 3 M. & Sc. 791. Doe v. Stanton, 2 B. & Ald. 373.

(*m*) Lord Bolton v. Tomlin, 5 Ad. & E. 856.

(*n*) Fairtitle v. Gilbert, 2 T. R. 169.

' Wolf v. Mitchell, 24 La. Ann. 433; Lammon v. Douglas, 50 Mo. 434.

he had been in the actual possession and seisin thereof at the time of such lease made, because he having by indenture expressly demised those lands, is, by his own act, estopped and concluded to say he did not demise them ; and if he can not aver that he did not demise them, then there is nothing to take off or impeach the validity of the indenture, which expressly affirms that he did demise them ; and consequently the lessee may take advantage thereof, whenever the lessor comes to such an estate in those lands as is capable to sustain and support that lease." (*o*) And when the estoppel becomes good in point of interest, the heir of the lessor, and all persons claiming under the lessor by assignment or otherwise, are bound by the estoppel. (*p*) Upon the execution of the lease there is created, in contemplation of law, a reversion in fee simple by estoppel in the lessor, which passes by descent to his heir, and by purchase to an assignee or devisee. So long, therefore, as a lessee enjoys everything which his lease purports to grant, he has no concern with the title of the lessor, or the heir or assignee of the lessor. (*q*) If, however, it appears by the recitals of the lease that the lessor had no interest in the land, or that he had only an equitable interest, at the time of the demise, there will be no estoppel. (*r*) The lessee is also in like manner estopped from denying the lessor's title to grant the lease, and setting up such want of title as an answer to an action for the

(*o*) Bac. Abr. Lease (O).

(*p*) Trevivan v. Lawrence, 1 Salk. 276 ; 2 Smith's L. C. 5th ed. 640. Goodtitle v. Morse, 3 T. R. 371. 2 Wms. Saund. 418, a. Doe v. Thompson, 9 Q. B. 1043.

(*q*) Cuthbertson v Irving, 4 H. & N.

758 ; 6 H. & N. 135 ; 28 L. J., Ex. 306 ; 29 Id. 485.

(*r*) Pargeter v. Harris, 7 Q. B. 708 ; 15 L. J., Q. B. 117. Greenaway v. Hart, 14 C. B. 340. But see Morton v. Woods, L. R., 3 Q. B., 658 ; 4 Q. B. 293 ; 37 L. J., Q. B. 242 ; 38 Id. 81.

rent by the lessor or his assignee; (*s*) for the law will
not suffer the tenant to abuse a possession gained by
the act and confidence of the landlord, and turn it to
the injury of the latter. (*t*)[1] But he may show that

(*s*) Cuthbertson v. Irving, 6 H. & N. Phipps v. Sculthorpe, 1 B. & Ald. 50.
135; 29 L. J., Ex. 485. Levy v. Lewis, 28 L. J., C. P. 144; 30
   (*t*) Dolby v. Iles, 11 Ad. & E. 335. L. J., C. P. 142.

[1] And see Blakemore v. Tuber, 22 Ind. 466; Walrath v.
Redfield, 18 N. Y. 457. But a lessee is not estopped by the
acceptance of a deed by his lessor, to deny the title of the
grantor in such deed. In this case it did not appear that possession had been taken under the deed. Schuman v. Garratt,
16 Cal. 100. A tenant acquiring his landlord's title, by a purchase under a judgment subsequent to the demise, may set it
up against him; Nellis v. Lathrop, 22 Wend. 121; and if the
lessor's interest is sold, and the lessee attorns to the purchaser,
who acquires the title, the lessee may set up the divesting of
the title in an action by the lessor for rent accruing after.
Evertson v. Sawyer, 2 Wend. 507; Gautwell v. Miller, 1 Sandf.
516; Jackson v. Rowland, 6 Wend. 666. Where a person entered into possession of land under one landlord,
and was then induced to attorn to another under the belief and upon the claim and representation of such other
person that he had the title to the premises, and when
sued in ejectment permitted his second landlord to defend in his name, under an agreement to indemnify him
against costs, and held possession for him until evicted
in the suit, whereupon he paid rent to the original landlord,
who was plaintiff in the ejectment suit, *held*, that a recovery
for rent in a suit against the tenant by the heirs of the second
landlord, was erroneous, and that to sanction such recovery
would be giving a premium to falsehood and subject a tenant,
who had done no wrong, to a double payment of rent.
Anderson v. Smith, 63 Ill. 126. The maxim that a tenant shall
not dispute the title of his landlord, has no just application
to such a case. A person having entered into possession of
land under one, and who was induced to attorn to another
under the belief and upon the claim of the latter that he has
title, when sued for the rent by the heirs of such second
landlord, may show in defense that his attornment had been
procured by a false claim of title, and that the rent had been
demanded and paid to the landlord from whom he derived his

the lessor's title has expired ; (*u*)¹ and if he is evicted
and deprived of the use and enjoyment of the demised
premises by some person claiming by title paramount,

(*u*) Claridge v. Mackenzie, 4 Sc. E. 157. Downs v. Cooper, 2 Q. B.
N. R. 811. Doe v. Skirrow, 7 Ad. & 263.

possession, as the rightful owner. Stobie v. Dills, 62 Ill.
432.
¹ He may show that it has expired by reason, by limitation,
or by conveyance, or by judgment or other operation of law ;
and this although the tenant does not claim under that title,
and though the title be outstanding in the trustee of the lessor. Hoag v. Hoag, 35 N. Y. 469. In order that a defendant,
who has taken a lease from the plaintiff, may avail himself of
the rule that a tenant who did not enter under the lease, but
was in possession at the time it was made, is not estopped
from disputing his landlord's title, he must prove paramount
title in himself, or those under whom he claims. It is not
enough to dispute the title by averment. The production of
a lease which is valid as a contract between the parties makes
out a prima facie case for the landlord. Peralta v. Ginochio,
47 Cal. 459. A tenant is estopped by a lease which he takes
when in possession, unless he proves paramount title in himself or another, under whom he claims. Holloway v. Galliac,
Id. 474. A person in possession of land who takes a lease
from another who has bought and claims the land leased, is
estopped from denying the title of such other person, or
showing that such person was but trustee of the land for him.
Lucas v. Brooks, 18 Wall. 436. The tenant can not, during
the term of a lease, hold adverse possession against the landlord by the mere intention so to hold, and without the doing
of some act which would amount to adverse possession by a
tenant who enters under a lease. Abbey Homestead Ass'n v.
Willard, 48 Cal. 614. It was contended that a new trial was
taken in the ejectment suit after the eviction of the tenant,
which the record failed to show. But it seems that such fact
would not affect the merits of the case. Upon eviction in the
suit, the tenant was liable for mesne profits, and having no
guaranty of protection against such liability, and the landlord having failed to establish his claim by which he procured
the attornment, the tenant was justified in regarding it as
groundless, and protecting himself from a prosecution for
mesne profits. Id. 126. It seems that a tenant may show, in
defense of a suit by his landlord for rent, that the landlord's

the eviction is pleadable in bar to a demand of the rent; but it must be an actual, and not a mere constructive eviction. (*v*) An attornment to a receiver appointed by the court constitutes a tenancy by estoppel between the tenant and the receiver which the court applies for the purpose of collecting the rents till a decree can be pronounced, taking care that the tenant shall be protected both while the receiver continues to act and when he is withdrawn. (*y*) [1]

680. *Demises by agents.*—If the steward of a person not named says to an occupier, "I let you into possession in the name of the landlord," he may afterwards show by parol evidence who that landlord is, and it is not open to the tenant to dispute the title of the unnamed landlord. (*z*) Where an agreement was entered into by an agent in his own name for the letting of a house, and the rent was made payable to the agent in his own name, but at the commencement of the agreement he described himself as agent for the proprietors, it was held that he might show who were the proprietors at the time the agreement

(*v*) Delaney v. Fox, 2 C. B. N. S.   602.
768.
(*z*) Tindal, C. J., Fleming v. Good-
(*y*) Evans v. Mathias, 7 Ell. & Bl.   ing, 10 Bing. 550.

title has expired, or that a claim had been made on the tenant by one who has the real title, and can enforce payment of the rents from him in an action for use and occupation, if there has been a fresh demise, or an arrangement equivalent to one, or in a proceeding to recover mesne profits, and the tenant has submitted to such claim. But in such cases the burden of proof is on the tenant. Anderson v. Smith, 63 Ill. 126.

[1] And see Phillips v. Robertson, 2 Overt. 399; Robinson v. Hathaway, 1 Brayt. 151; Moore v. Beasley, 3 Ham. 294; Hamel v. Lawrence, 1 A. K. Marsh, 330; Reed v. Sharpley, 6 Vt. 602; Moshier v. Reding, 3 Fairf. 478; Drane v. Gregory, 3 B. Mon. 619; Shelton v. Doe, 6 Ala. 230.

was signed, and that the tenant was estopped from disputing their title. (*a*)   A land-agent, or collector of rents, has, as such, no implied authority to grant leases. (*b*)[1]

681. *Ascertainment and identification of the subject-matter of the demise.*—It may always be shown by parol evidence what was, and what was not, parcel of the demise, and intended to pass to the lessee by the deed. (*c*)[2] If a general and comprehensive term and description be used in a lease, all the things usually comprehended under such general term and description will pass to the lessee, unless the surrounding circumstances and the relative situation and interests of the contracting parties plainly show that such could not have been their intention.   By parol evidence of extrinsic circumstances, a general and comprehensive term may be controlled and restricted so as to pass much less than is ordinarily comprised under the common legal acceptance of the term, and, on the other hand, a particular and limited term and description may be extended and enlarged, so as to comprehend and include much more than it generally comprises, in order to effectuate the plain and obvious meaning of the parties.

(*a*) Per Mellor, J., Prescott v. Ingram, June 23rd, 1864.   Fleming v. Gooding, 4 M. & Sc. 455.

(*b*) Collen v. Gardner, 21 Beav. 540.
(*c*) Skipwith v. Green, 8 Mod. 311.

[1] In New York the agent's authority must be in writing. Post v. Martens, 2 Rob. 437 ; Porter v. Bleiler, 17 Barb. 149; and see Worrell v. Munn, 5 N. Y. 229 ; Wilson v. Lester, 64 Barb. 431 ; Dean v. Roesler, 1 Hilt. 420 ; see as to ratification, Commercial Bank v. Warren, 15 N. Y. 577.

[2] In Cary v. Thompson, 1 Daly 35, where plaintiff, by a sealed lease, rented to defendant two houses, describing them as " Nos. 162 and 164 Seventh avenue," parol evidence was admitted to show that a certain rear yard or lot passed with the demise of the two houses.

A lessor demised a messuage and piece of ground with the appurtenances to the defendant; and the latter, after he had taken possession, laid claim to a cellar under the messuage, on the ground that it had passed to him under the general description contained in his lease ; and it was held that the lessor might show, through the medium of parol evidence, that, at the time of the demise, and previous thereto, the cellar had been severed from the messuage, and used as a wine cellar by a wine merchant under a separate and distinct lease, at a separate rent, which was known to the defendant at the time of his acceptance of the lease, and, therefore, that it could not have been the intention of the parties that the cellar so occupied by a third party should pass to him under the general description of the messuage and ground thereunto adjoining. (*d*) Under the word " cottage " or " house," on the other hand, land may pass, if it can be shown that the land has for a length of time been used and occupied with the cottage or house at one entire rent, and has been commonly reputed to be part and parcel thereof. "Being found to be all one, it passeth well by the lease." Divers things that, by continual enjoyment with the principal thing demised, have by common reputation been deemed to belong to it, may well pass as part and parcel of the principal thing demised, if extrinsic circumstances show that such must have been the intention of the parties. (*e*) "Whenever there is a sufficient description to ascertain the thing demised, a part of the description which is inaccurate may be rejected." (*f*)

(*d*) Doe v. Burt, 1 T. R. 703. Bryan v. Wetherhead, 3 Cro. 18. Kerslake v. White, 2 Stark. 508. Martyr v. Lawrence, 10 Jur. N. S. 859.

(*e*) Gennings v. Lake, 3 Cro. 169.

Ongley v. Chambers, 1 Bing. 496–499. But see Jones v. Whelan, 16 Ir. C. L. R. 495.

(*f*) Doe v. Callow y, 5 B. & Ad. 4); 2 N. & M. 241.

682. *Things appurtenant.*—When a man grants a thing to be used for hire, he grants it with all such appurtenances and accompaniments as properly belong to it, and with all such rights of way as are necessary to enable the hirer to have that use and enjoyment of the thing demised for which the hire is agreed to be paid. (*g*) But a grant of realty, to be used and enjoyed by the grantee for a term for rent or hire, transfers to the latter a right only, as we shall presently see, to use the subject-matter of the demise in the way in which it has been previously used and enjoyed. Many things, therefore, which pass by a grant in fee, so as to give the grantee an absolute dominion over them, do not pass by a lease so as to give the lessee a right to use and enjoy them as part of the proceeds and profits of the subject-matter of the demise. The lessee, for example, has a right only to the casual profits of trees; he has no right to cut them down and sever them from the freehold and inheritance. He has a right to the profits of mines and quarries opened at the time of the demise, but has no right to open fresh mines and quarries where none before existed.

683. *Commencement and duration of leases.*—Leases for lives, as well as leases for terms of years, may now be made to commence from a day that is passed, or from a day to come, as well as from the day of the making of the lease. If the lease is limited to commence " from the date," or " from the day of the date," the words are either inclusive or exclusive, according to the context and subject-matter of the written instrument, and the apparent intention of the

(*g*) Morris v. Edgington, 3 Taunt. 290; 2 B. & C. 96. Maitland v. Mackinnon, 1 H. & C. 607; 32 L. J., Ex. 31. Kooystra v. Lucas, 5 B. & Ald. 834.   Harding v. Wilson, 3 D. & R. 49.

contracting parties. (*h*)[1]   A lease "from the day of
the date," and "from henceforth," is the same thing;
if, therefore, a lease be dated the 1st of December, and
be granted to commence "from henceforth," and be
sealed and delivered on the 12th of December, the
lease commences in contemplation of law from the
1st of December. (*i*)   If no time is mentioned for the
commencement of the lease, or if the date is an impossible date, the term will be deemed to begin from
the day of the delivery of the deed, or of the making
of the demise, if extrinsic circumstances do not rebut
such a presumption. (*k*)[2]   The commencement of the
term is necessarily controlled and regulated by extrinsic circumstances (such as the occupied or unoccupied
state of the demised premises, the surrender or determination of previous leases, and the period of the
termination of an existing tenancy), as well as by the
express terms and language of the deed.   Where a
lease was dated the 25th of March, 1783, and the term
was granted to commence "from the 25th of
March now last past," and it was proved that the
deed was not executed until some time after the
day on which it was dated, it was held that the term
commenced on the 25th of March, 1783, and not on
the 25th of March, 1782. (*l*)   If the land is demised
"for a year, and so on from year to year," or "for a
year and afterwards from year to year," this is a lease for

(*h*) Pugh v. Leeds, Duke of, 2 Cowp.
714. And see *ante*.

(*i*) Llewelyn v. Williams, Cro. Jac.
258.

(*k*) Styles v. Wardle, 4 B. & C. 908;

7 D. & R. 507. Higham v. Cookes, 4
Leon. 144. Co. Lit. 46, b.

(*l*) Steele v. Mart, 6 D. & R. 392; 4
B. & C. 272.

[1] Keyes v. Dearborn, 12 N. H. 52.
[2] Trustees v. Robinson, Wright, 436.

two years certain at lease. (*m*) But if the demise is from year to year, so long as both parties please, it is a lease only for a year certain, and is determinable at the end of the first as well as of any subsequent year. (*n*) If the demise is for "one year certain," and six months' notice afterwards, the lease is only a lease for a year. (*o*) If the land is expressed to be demised for years generally, the lease is said to be good for two years at the least. (*p*) A house and land were demised for the term of six months, and so on from six months to six months, until one of the parties should give the other six calendar months' notice of his intention to determine the tenancy, and it was held that this was a lease for one year at least. (*q*) [1]

If a lease is granted for seven, fourteen, or twenty-one years, and the lessee enters and takes possession of the demised premises, the legal construction of the lease is that the lessee is entitled at his option to take that term which is most beneficial to himself. The lessee therefore has the option, at the expiration of the first seven years, of continuing the lease on for

(*m*) Bac. Abr. Leases (L), 838. Legg v. Strudwick, 2 Salk. 414.　18 Hen. 8, 15, b.　Denn v. Cartwright, 4 East. 29.　Doe v. Green, 9 Ad. & E. 658 ; 1 P. & D. 454.

(*n*) Doe v. Smaridge, 7 Q. B. 957.

(*o*) Thompson v. Maberly, 2 Camp. 573.　Jones v. Nixon, 1 H. & C. 48 ; 31 L. J., C. P. 66.

(*p*) Bro. Abr. Lease, 13.　6 Co. 35,. 36.

(*q*) Reg. v. Chawton, 1 Q. B. 247.

[1] In the state of New York, by statute (1 Edmond's Stats. p. 563, § 3), "whenever the word 'year' or 'years' is or shall be used in any statute, deed, verbal or written contract, or any public or private instrument, the year intended to be taken shall be taken to consist of 365 days; a half year of 182 days ; and a quarter of a year of 91 days ; and the added day of a leap year, and the day immediately preceding, if they shall occur in any period so to be computed, shall be reckoned together as one day ; and the word 'month' shall be construed to mean a calendar, and not a lunar, month, unless otherwise expressed" (Id. § 4).

another seven years, and after that term has expired, for the full period of twenty-one years if he chooses so to do, the courts leaning in favor of that construction which is the most favorable to the lessee. (*r*)   Where the lessor agreed not to raise the rent nor turn the tenant out of possession so long as the rent was duly paid .quarterly, it was held that this operated as an agreément for a tenancy from year to year. If in a lease under seal the lessor covenants not to raise the rent, nor turn out the tenant, so long as the rent is duly paid, this is a lease for life. If the undertaking is contained in a lease not under seal, it operates only as a simple contract or agreement, for a breach of which the tenant may recover damages from the lessor, but it does not prevent the latter from ejecting the tenant after the ordinary notice to quit. (*s*)   If the full extent and duration of the term are uncertain, but there is a certainty for some specific portion of time, the lease will be good for such term or portion of time, and void as to the residue. (*t*)   If no time at all is mentioned for the duration of the term, and there has been ˙no entry upon the land nor payment of rent, there is no lease at all; but if the lessee has actually entered and taken possession, the duration of the term of hiring will be regulated by the nature of the subject-matter of the demise, the times limited for the payment of the rent, and the custom of the country where the property is situate.

684. *Leases from year to year.*—In the case of a general demise of farms or lands, no term or time of holding being mentioned, the presumption is by cus-

---

(*r*, Dann v. Spurrier, 3 B. & P. 404. Doe v. Dixon, 9 East, 15. Goodright v. Richardson, 3 T. R. 462.

(*s*) Doe v. Browne, 8 East, 165.
(*t*) Gwynne v. Mainstone, 3 C. & P. 302.

tom in favor of a yearly hiring (*u*) in the absence of
an express limitation of the term.[1]   If a corn-field or
an orchard is demised at a customary and ordinary
rent, the hiring will be deemed to be for a year, and so
on from year to year, in order that the tenant may
reap the harvest and gather the fruits and produce of
the soil when they come to perfection, as the rent is
reasonably presumed to be paid for the enjoyment
thereof, and not for the barren occupation of the land
itself.   " If the produce of the demised lands requires
two years to come to perfection, as if it be liquorice,
madder, &c., a general holding will, it seems, enure as
a tenancy from two years to two years, and can not be
determined by a notice to quit at the end of the first
or third year." (*v*)   Where lands were demised to J.
H., his heirs, executors, and assigns forever, at a yearly
rent, with a proviso for re-entry in case of non-payment
of rent, it was held that the deed created only a tenancy from year to year. (*y*)[2]   If an intended lessee

---

(*u*) 13 Hen. 8, 15 b.   Doe v. Watts,   Poth LOUAGE, part 1, ch. 2, art. 4, 28.
7 T. R. 85.   (*y*) Doe v. Gardiner, 12 C. B. 319.
(*v*) Adams on Eject. 4th Ed. 99.

---

[1] Said to be from the presumption that the enjoyment of
the yearly harvest was the consideration for the rent; see
Hanchett v. Whitney, 2 Ark. 240; Fowke v. Beck, 1 Spiers,
291; Ellis v. Page, 1 Pick 4; Fronty v. Wood, 2 Hill. 367;
Hall v. Hall, 8 Gill & J. 386; Moore v. Beasley, 3 Ham. 294;
and a tenant holding over, after the expiration of a term,
takes by the year upon the same conditions of letting; Dorrill
v. Stevens, 4 McCord, 59; Diller v. Roberts, 13 Serg. & R. 60;
Bacon v. Brown, 9 Conn. 334.

[2] Vrooman v. M'Kaig, 4 Md. 450; Hart v. Finney,
1 Strobh. 250; People v. Reckert, 8 Cow. 226; Thomas v.
Light, 9 Sergt. & R. 87; Lesley v. Randolph, 21 Rawle, 123;
McDowell v. Simpson, 3 Watts, 129; Schuyler v. Leggett, 2
Cow. 660; Brewer v. Knapp, 1 Pick. 332; Danforth v. Sar-
gent, 14 Mass. 491.

enters into possession of realty under an agreement for a lease, he is tenant at will or tenant by sufferance until the lease is made ; but if he remains in
possession and pays rent, he becomes tenant from year
to year until the lease is duly executed according to
the agreement. (*z*)   And if he holds over after the
expiration of the term, and the landlord receives from
him rent which has accrued due subsequently to the
expiration of the lease, he becomes a tenant from year
to year. (*a*)

If a man takes possession of premises under an invalid lease from a tenant for life, and the remainderman accepts rent, or does any act recognizing the party
in possession as his tenant, the latter forthwith becomes
a lessee from year to year. (*b*)   So, if a man enters
into possession as an intended purchaser, and agrees
"to pay and allow" to the vendor "at the rate of £100
per annum from the time of taking possession of the
premises until the completion of the purchase in equal
half-yearly payments," he becomes tenant to the intended vendor "at a fixed rent of £100 per annum,
payable half-yearly." (*c*)   A tenancy from year to year
is ordinarily implied from the payment and acceptance
of rent ; but this prima facie presumption may be rebutted by showing that the money was paid or received
by mistake.   It is entirely repugnant to the notion of
a tenancy from year to year that the option of determining it should rest solely with the tenant.   The
notion of a tenancy from year to year, the lessor binding himself not to give notice to quit, has long been

(*z*) Mann v. Lovejoy, R. & M. 355.   10 M. & W. 497.
Doe v. Pullen, 3 Sc. 276.   Doe v.   (*a*) Bishop v. Howard, 3 D. & R.
Smith, 1 M. & R. 137.   Knight v.   297 ; 2 B. & C. 100.
Benett, 11 Moore, 225 ; 3 Bing. 361.   (*b*) Doe v. Morse, 1 B. & Ad. 369.
Doe v. Amey, 12 Ad. & E. 476 ; 4 P.   (*c*) Saunders v. Musgrave 5 B. & C.
& D. 177.   Braythwayte v. Hitchcock,   524 ; 9 D. & R. 533.

exploded. (*d*)   A tenancy from year to year re-commences every year. (*e*)   A demise by a tenant from year to year to another, also to hold from year to year is, in contemplation of law, a demise from year to year during the continuance of the original demise to the intermediate landlord. (*f*)

685. *Half-yearly, quarterly, monthly, and weekly hirings.*—If an annual rent is reserved, the holding is from year to year, although the contract of demise provides that the tenant shall quit at a quarter's notice. Such a contract differs only from the usual letting from year to year in the agreement by the parties to reduce the ordinary six months' notice to quit to three months.   But if it is expressly agreed that the tenant is always to be subject to quit at six months' notice given him at any time, this constitutes a half-yearly tenancy, and the lessee will be presumed to hold from six months to six months from the time that he entered as tenant.   If he is to hold until one of the parties shall give unto the other three months' notice to quit at the expiration of such notice, the tenancy will be a quarterly tenancy. (*g*)   In the case of a demise of an unfurnished mansion at an annual rent, payable half-yearly or quarterly, the hiring is a hiring from year to year.   In the case of cottages or unfurnished apartments in a house demised at a monthly or weekly rent, the presumption is in favor of a monthly or a weekly tenancy.   Where a wharf, warehouse, and buildings, were let on the terms that a quarter's rent should be paid down on the day of the commencement of the tenancy, and should be continued to be

(*d*) Doe v. Browne, 8 East, 167
(*e*) Tomkins v. Lawrance, 8 C. & P. 731.   Gandy v. Jubber, 33 L. J., Q. B. 151.   Doe v. Dobeil, 1 G. & Dav. 213.

But this has been doubted, see Bartlett v. Baker, 34 L. J., Ex. 11.
(*f*) Pike v. Eyre, 9 B. & C. 909.
(*g*) Doe v. Grafton, 21 L. J., Q. B. 276.   Kemp v. Derrett, 3 Camp 510.

paid in advance during the continuance of the hiring, it was held that this was a quarterly, and not a yearly, hiring. (*h*) There is no objection in law to a tenancy determinable by a week's notice to quit, and a reasonable time being allowed after the expiration of the notice for the tenant to remove his goods. (*i*)

686. *Tenancy at will.*—If the lessor reserves to himself a right of re-entry at his own will and pleasure, or the lease contains an express stipulation to the effect that the tenancy may be put an end to at the will of either party, the holding is a tenancy at will. (*k*) The reservation of a yearly or quarterly rent is not inconsistent with a tenancy at will. (*l*) A mere permission to occupy creates a tenancy at will. If a tenant for years holds over after the expiration of his lease, or continues in possession pending a treaty for a further lease, (*m*) or is admitted into possession pending a treaty for a purchase, (*n*) he is strictly a tenant at the will of the landlord, and may be turned out of possession without notice to quit; but if, during the continuance of such tenancy at will, the tenant has offered, and the landlord has accepted, rent for the use of the property, the law infers that a yearly tenancy was meant to be created between them. (*o*) A minister of a dissenting congregation, placed in the possession of a chapel and dwelling-house by trustees in whom the property is vested in trust to permit the chapel and dwelling-house to be used for the purpose of religious worship, is a mere tenant at will to those

(*h*) Wilkinson v. Hall, 4 Sc. 301. Towne v. Campbell, 3 C. B. 921.

(*i*) Cornish v. Stubbs, L. R., 5 C. P. 334; 39 L. J. C. P. 202.

(*k*) Richardson v. Langridge, 4 Taunt. 131. Cudlip v. Rundal, 4 Mod. 12; 3 Salk. 156. Bayley v. Fitzmaurice, 8 Ell. & Bl. 679.

(*l*) Litt. sec. 72. Doe v. Davies, 7 Exch. 91; 21 L. J., Ex. 60. Doe v. Cox, 11 Q. B. 122; 17 L. J., Q. B. 3.

(*m*) Com. Dig. tit. Estates (H. 1). Doe v. Stennet, 2 Esp. 717.

(*n*) Doe v. Chamberlaine, 5 M. & W. 14.

(*o*) Clayton v. Blakey, 8 T. R. 3.

trustees; and his tenancy is determined instanter by a demand of possession. (*p*) A tenant at will is entitled to retain possession of the land he holds until the lessor has made a demand of possession, (*q*) or has intimated, either by express words or by his conduct and actions, his determination to put an end to the tenancy. The holding may be determined by a letter, stating that, unless the tenant pays the lessor what he owes him, he will, without delay, take measures for recovering possession of the property, (*r*) or by a demand of possession on the part of the landlord, (*s*) or by his entry on the land without the tenant's consent and making livery of seisin to another, (*t*) or exercising acts of ownership ; also by his alienation of the reversion ; by the tenant's quitting the premises; by the death of either of the parties ; by the bankruptcy of the lessor ; and, in short, by the doing of any act which amounts to the determination of the will on either side. But a tenant at will can not determine his tenancy by transferring his interest to a third party without notice to his landlord. (*u*) If the will is determined, and the landlord's consent to the occupation is withdrawn, so as to create an adverse possession, and the landlord afterwards does any act fairly leading to the presumption that he has renewed his consent to the holding, a fresh tenancy at will is created between the parties. (*v*) [1]

(*p*) Doe v. M'Kaeg, 10 B. & C. 721; 5 M. & R. 620. Doe v. Jones, 10 B. & C. 718 ; 5 M. & R. 616, 752. Revett v. Brown, 2 Moo. & P. 12 ; 5 Bing. 7.

(*q*) Right v. Beard, 13 East, 210.

(*r*) Doe v. Price, 2 M & Sc. 464 ; 9 Bing. 356.

(*s*) Locke v. Matthews, 13 C. B. N. S. 753.

(*t*) Ball v. Cullimore, 2 C. M. & R. 120.

(*u*) Pinhorn v. Souster, 8 Exch. 772.

(*v*) Doe v. Turner, 7 M. & W. 232. Turner v. Doe, 9 M. & W. 644. Doe v. Thomas, 6 Exch. 854. Randall v. Stephens, 23 L. T. R. 211.

[1] See Jones v. Jones, 2 Rich. 542 ; Campbell v. Proctor, 6 Greenl. 12; Rising v. Stannard, 17 Mass. 282 ; Phillips v.

687 *Tenancy by sufferance.*—When the landlord has demanded possession, or has done any act which is tantamount to a determination of the will, or when the tenant holds over at the expiration of a lease against the will of the lord, or after the expiration of a notice to quit, the tenant is said to be a tenant at sufferance in contradistinction to a tenant at will. (y) '

(*y*) Co. Litt. 57, b.

Court, 7 Johns. 1; Moore v. Boyd, 11 Shep. 242; Cheever v. Pearson, 16 Pick. 266; Nichols v. Williams, 8 Cow. 13; Squires v. Huffs, 3 A. K. Marsh, 17; Ellis v. Page, 1 Pick. 43; Proprietors v. McFarland, 12 Mass. 325. A tenancy at will can hardly exist in the city of New York; People v. Gallet, 64 Barb. 481; unless the intention to create such a tenancy is expressly declared in the words of the demise; Post v. Post, 14 Barb. 253. Tenancies by sufferance are guarded against in that state by a statute which provides that where a lease does not state particularly the date or time at which the tenancy shall expire, it shall be understood to expire on the first day of May next ensuing (Witt v. Mayor, 5 Rob. 248; Hunt v. Wolf, 2 Daly); and in that state as well as others.

¹ Any tenant continuing in his possession without agreement, after a particular estate is ended, is a tenant at sufferance. Livingston v. Tanner, 12 Barb. 481. But this estate can only exist by the laches of the landlord, and only attaches where a landlord negligently omits to put out the overholding tenant within a reasonable time after the termination of his lease. Rowan v. Lynde, 11 Wend. 617. But see Conway v. Starkweather, 1 Den. 113, which holds that where a tenant under a demise for a year or more holds over after the end of the term, without any new agreement with the landlord, he may, at the election of the landlord, be treated either as a trespasser or a tenant holding upon the terms of the original lease, and that distraining for rent payable after the expiration of the original term, is such an election by the landlord to consider him a tenant; an overholding tenant, being a wrongdoer, has no such election, nor is he at liberty to deny that he is in possession as tenant, if the landlord chose to hold him to that relation; and it has been held that where a tenant holds over after the expiration of his term, the law will, at the landlord's option, imply a new hiring upon the terms and

The expression, however, is not calculated to give a correct idea of the nature of the holding, and does not seem to have been very happily chosen. Although termed tenant by sufferance, he is understood to hold wrongfully and against the will, and contrary to the permission, of the landlord. He has, consequently, no estate or interest at all in the land ; and an action of ejectment may at any time be brought against him without notice or demand of possession ; and, if the lord can get possession peaceably, he is entled to take and retain possession, and so oust the wrongdoer. (*z*)   The difference, therefore, between a tenancy at will and what is called a tenancy by sufferance is that, in the one case the tenant holds by right, and has an estate or term in the land, precarious though it be, and the relationship of lessor and lessee subsists between the parties ; in the other, the tenant holds wrongfully and against the will and permission of the lord, and has no estate at all in the occupied premises. When a tenancy at sufferance has existed for twenty years, the landlord's right of entry is barred by statute, and the tenant becomes the absolute and complete owner of the property. (*a*)

688. *Leases under power.*—If a lease granted in the intended exercise of a power of leasing is invalid

(*z*) Fox v. Oakley, Peake's Ad. Ca.   (*a*) Doe v. Gower, 21 L. J,. Q. B. 57. 214.

conditions specified in the former lease. Bacon v. Bacon, 9 Conn. 334; Brewer v. Knapp, 1 Pick. 332; Ellis v. Paige, Id. 43; Fronty v. Wood, 2 Hill, 367 ; Moore v. Beasley, 3 Ham. 294; Smith v. Littlefield, 51 N. Y. 539; Diller v. Roberts, 13 S. & R. 60 ; Bacon v. Brown, 9 Conn. 334; Dorrill v. Stevens, 4 McC. 59.   And see as to tenancy at sufferance as distinguished from a tenancy at will; Stedman v. Gassett, 18 Vt. 346; Hildreth v. Conant, 10 Metc. 298; Jackson v. McCord, 12 Johns. 182; Keay v. Goodwin, 16 Mass. 1 ; Kinsley v. Ames, 2 Metc. 29; Hollis v. Poole. 3 Id. 350.

by reason of the non-observance of the terms of the power, such lease, if made bona fide, and if the lessee has entered thereunder, is deemed a contract or agreement to grant the lease, and all persons who would have been bound by the lease if lawfully granted under the power, will be bound by such contract. Acceptance of rent under such invalid lease is a confirmation of the lease as against the person so accepting rent. Leases, also, invalid at the time of the grant thereof, may become valid, if the grantor subsequently acquires the requisite power of leasing. (*b*)

689. *Demise of tolls.*—The 8 & 9 Vict. c. 106, s. 3, which provides that a lease required by law to be in writing of any tenements, &c., shall be void, unless made by deed, does not apply to agreements for letting tolls under the 3 Geo. 4, c. 126. (*c*)

690. *Rights and liabilities of lessor and lessee.*— Every lessor binds himself to give possession, and not to give the party to whom he demises a mere right to take possession from a wrong-doer by an action of ejectment; (*d*) and every lessee binds himself to accept possession and pay rent. (*e*) If a party has agreed to take a house from a particular day, provided certain things are before then done by the landlord, and the things are not done, he may decline to go on with the contract, and may refuse to take possession. (*f*) A lessee who has contracted orally for the hire of realty, and who neglects or refuses to accept posses-

(*b*) 12 & 13 Vict. c. 26. 13 Vict. c. 7.

(*c*) Shepherd v. Hodsman, 18 Q. B. 216; 21 L. J., Q. B. 263.

(*d*) Coe v. Clay, 3 Moo. & P. 59; 5 Bing. 440. Jinks v. Edwards, 11 Exch. 775. Neale v. Mackenzie, 1 M. & W.

747. Bract. lib. 2, c. 28, fol. 62. As to agreements for a lease, see Drury v. Macnamara, 5 El. & Bl. 616; 25 L. J., Q. B. 5.

(*e*) Stanley v. Hayes, 3 Q. B. 105.

(*f*) Tidey v. Mollett, *ante*.

sion of the demised premises, can not, as we have seen,
be sued upon such oral agreement for damages for not
taking possession, nor upon any oral promise to pay
rent, nor for use and occupation.   In the case of leases
under seal, the law implies from the words " yielding
and paying," or any equivalent words amounting to a
reservation of rent, a covenant on the part of the
lessee to pay the rent so reserved, and in the case of
parol leases, a promise to the like effect. (*g*)   But the
liability of a lessee upon all express and implied covenants and agreements for the payment of rent is dependent upon his being put into possession, or being
tendered and offered and afforded the power and opportunity of taking possession of the demised premises. (*h*)[1]   The quiet enjoyment also by the lessee, as
against the lessor and all that come in under him by
title, and against others claiming by title paramount,
during the time in respect of which the rent is claimed
to have accrued due, is a condition precedent to the
tenant's liability for the payment of such rent.   But
the tenant is not released from liability by reason of a
mere constructive eviction, (*i*) or a disturbance and
interruption from a mere wrong-doer.

691. *Covenants for quiet enjoyment.*—From the
use by a grantor of certain words having a known
legal operation in the creation of an estate, the law
infers a covenant on the part of such grantor to protect and preserve the estate so created ; as, if a man

(*g*) Bac. Abr. LEASES, 633 ; COVE-   (*h*) Holgate v. Kay, 1 C. & Kirw.
NANT (B.), 342.   341.

(*i*) Delaney v. Fox, *ante.*

[1] Lovering v. Lovering, 13 N. H. 513 ; MacKeebin v.
Whelcroft, 4 Har. & McHen. 135 ; Lewis v. Payn, 4 Wend.
432 ; Dexter v. Manly, 4 Cush. 14 ; Maule v. Ashmead, 8 Harris, 484.

by deed demises land for years, the word " demise "
imports or makes a covenant in law for quiet enjoyment. (*k*) If by the terms of a lease the lessor
" warrants " the demised premises to the lessee, this
amounts to an express covenant for quiet enjoyment
during the whole term granted by the lease. (*l*) Covenants for quiet enjoyment are broken, if the lessor
builds on his own adjoining land so as to darken the
lessee's windows, or does anything thereon which
creates a nuisance. The erection of a gate across a
lane through which the tenant has a way to the demised premises is a breach of a covenant for quiet
enjoyment; (*m*) and so is the placing of any structure
upon any part of the demised premises. (*n*) The
usual express covenant by the lessor that the lessee
shall quietly enjoy, &c., without interruption or disturbance by the lessor or any person claiming under
him, is not broken by an entry on the tenant by the
land-tax collector to distrain for arrears of land-tax
due from the lessor, the disturbance not being by a
person claiming by title from the lessor. (*o*) And
where a covenant for quiet enjoyment is accompanied
by a covenant by the lessee not to use the land for
certain purposes, the first covenant does not guarantee
to the tenant that he may lawfully use the land for
any purpose not included in the restrictions in the
lease. (*p*) Whenever a person demises the surface

(*k*) Hull v. City of London Brewery
Company, 2 B. & S. 737 ; 31 L. J.,
Q. B. 257.

(*l*) Williams v. Burrell, *ante.*

(*m*) Andrews v. Paradise, 8 Mod.
319. Morris v. Edgington, 3 Taunt.
24.

(*n*) Kidder v. West, 3 Lev. 167.

(*o*) Stanley v. Hayes, 3 Q. B. 105.
As to an implied covenant for title on
the part of the lessor, or that he has
power to grant an interest coextensive
with that which he assumes to grant,
see Line v. Stephenson, 7 Sc. 69. Ban-
dy v. Cartwright, 8 Exch. 913. Stranks
v. St. John, L. R., 2 C. P. 376 ; 36
L. J., C. P. 118.

(*p*) Dennett v. Atherton, L. R., 7
Q. B. 316 ; 41 L. J., Q. B. 165.

of land, reserving a right to win and work minerals, he can not exercise the right so as to let down or injure the surface ; for that would be derogating from his own grant, and would also be a breach of a covenant for quiet enjoyment. (*q*) Where there is a breach of a covenant for quiet enjoyment, the lessee is entitled to such damages as will fully compensate him for the injury sustained. (*r*)

692. *Covenants for the payment of rent.*—A covenant for the payment of rent at a specified time, when no place of payment is mentioned, is analogous to a covenant to pay a sum of money in gross on a day certain ; and it is accordingly incumbent on the covenantor to seek out the person to be paid, and pay or tender him the money. (*s*)[1] If the tenancy is a

---

(*q*) Proud v. Bates, 34 L. J., Ch. 406. As to what is included under the term "minerals," see Bell v. Wilson, Id. 572.

(*r*) Lock v. Furze, 19 C. B. N. S. 96; L. R., 1 C. P. 441; 35 L. J., C. P. 141.

(*s*) Haldane v. Johnson, 8 Exch. 689.

[1] McMurphy v. Mina, 4 N. H. 251 ; Walter v. Dewey, 16 Johns. 222 ; Menough's Appeal, 5 Watts & S. 432 ; Lush v. Druse, 4 Wend. 313. But the rules as to tender must be rigidly observed ; a mere offer to pay rent is not a tender, but the money must be actually produced and paid down, unless the landlord by some positive act or declaration on his part dispense with such production. Strong v. Blake, 46 Barb. 227 ; Hornby v. Cramer, 12 How. Pr. 490. An offer to draw a check is not a tender, although declined by the landlord; Dunbar v. Jackson, 6 Wend. 22 ; McIntire v. Clark, 7 Id. 330 ; if a debtor has the money in his pocket, and tells the creditor that he "is ready for him," but the creditor does not know that the debtor has the money with him, this is no tender; Bakeman v. Pooler, 15 Wend. 637 ; a tender to a clerk of a sub-agent of a creditor is insufficient, unless it is shown that such clerk had authority to receive the money; Hargous v. Lahens, 3 Sandf. 213 ; Hornby v. Cramer, 12 How. Pr. 490 ; Smith v. Smith, 2 Hill, 351 ; 25 Wend. 405 ; tender must be without any conditions or terms on the part of the debtor, or without any protest that he is not liable for the debt ; Wood

yearly tenancy, and no time is specified for the payment of the rent, the rent will be due once a year. (*t*)
If the rent is to be paid free of all outgoings, it must
be paid free of land-tax and tithe commutation rent-
charge. (*u*)   Where the lessor let his land at a rent
payable quarterly, and afterwards mortgaged it, but remained in possession, and obtained from the lessee,
who had no notice of the mortgage, a year's rent in
advance, it was held that the payment of the rent
before it became due was not a good payment as
against the mortgagee, who, before the rent became
due, gave the lessee notice to pay the rent to him. (*v*)
And the law is the same where the lessor grants away
the reversion. (*y*)

(*t*) Collett v. Curling, 10 Q. B. 785.

(*u*) Parish v. Sleeman, 1 De G. F.
& J. 326; 29 L. J., Ch. 96. Sweet v.
Seager, 2 C. B. N. S. 119.

(*v*) De Nicholls v. Saunders, L. R.,
5 C. P. 589; 39 L. J , C. P. 297.

(*y*) Cook v. Guerra, L. R., 7 C. P.
132; 41 L. J., C. .· P68

v. Hitchcock, 20 Wend. 47; a tenant can not legally demand
a receipt as a condition of paying his rent; 45 Barb. 579; 20
Wend. 47; 23 Id. 342; 21 N. Y. 581; where a party making a
tender demands a receipt or satisfaction-piece as a condition,
the tender is illegal; Roosevelt v. Bulls Head Bank, 45 Barb.
579; tender does not extinguish a debt, but only operates to
the interest; Raymond v. Bearnard, 12 Johns. 274; Hunter v.
Le Conte, 6 Cow. 728; but tender of money before it is due,
is bad; Mitchell v. Cook, 29 Barb. 243; if the landlord, or
other creditor, refuse the tender as not made in time, he can
not afterwards object that the tender was not in money; Duffy
v. O'Donovan, 46 N. Y. 223; or if the tender is refused on a
specified ground, the creditor can not afterwards raise any
other objection which, had he stated it then, might have been
obviated.   Hull v. Peters, 7 Barb. 331; 10 Abb. Pr. N. S. 484;
21 N. Y. 547.   Absolute refusal to receive the money, or to do
the act in consideration of which the money is to be paid, is
a waiver of tender; Murray v. Roosevelt, Anth. N. P. 138;
Vaupell v. Woodward, 2 Sandf. Ch. 143; Stone v. Sprague, 20
Barb. 509; Dana v. Fielder, 1 E. D. Smith, 463; Slingerland
v. Morse, 8 Johns. 474; Everett v. Saltus, 15 Wend. 474; Warren v. Mains, 7 Johns. 476.

693. *Covenants not to " let, set, or demise,"* restrain an assignment ; (*z*) and covenants not to " let or assign," (*a*) or not to "assign or otherwise part with," the demised premises, (*b*) restrain an underlease ; but a covenant not to " grant any underlease, or let, or assign, or otherwise part with the demised premises or any part thereof," is not broken by taking in a lodger who has the exclusive possession of the room he occupies. (*c*) Where a lessee took a person into partnership, and agreed that he should have the exclusive use of a back chamber and some other parts of the demised premises, and the joint use of the rest, it was held that the covenant had been broken, and that the right to re-enter had accrued. (*d*) And an assignment by one partner of his undivided moiety of the lease to the other partner is a breach of a covenant not to assign. (*e*) A covenant by a lessee that he will not let or underlet for more than a year does not prevent him from granting leases to commence at a future day. (*f*) A devise of the term to a stranger is an assignment within the meaning of the proviso or covenant, but not a devise to the lessee's own executor, (*g*) nor an assignment by act and operation of law, (*h*) or by the act of God, or an assignment by the sheriff under an execution, unless the execution has been obtained by collusion with the creditor in fraud of the covenant. (*i*) If the lessee does assign or underlet, notwithstanding his covenant, the assignment or underlease is good, and the lessee is only liable to an action on his cove-

---

(*z*) Greenaway v. Adams, 12 Ves. 395.

  (*a*) Roe v. Harrison, 2 T. R. 425.
  (*b*) Doe v. Worsley, 1 Campb. 20.
  (*c*) Doe v. Laming, 4 Campb. 77.
  (*d*) Doe v. Sales, 1 M. & S. 297.

(*e*) Varley v. Coppard, L. R., 7 C. P. 505.
  (*f*) Croft v. Lumley, 6 H. L. C. 737.
  (*g*) Bac. Abr. Lᴇᴀsᴇ, T.
  (*h*) Goring v. Warner, 7 Vin. Abr. 85, pl. 9.   Doe v. Smith, 5 Taunt. 795.
  (*i*) Doe v. Carter, 8 T. R. 57, 300.

nant, (*k*) unless there is a proviso in the original lease for re-entry in case of a breach of the covenant. (*l*)[1]

694. *Non-execution of the lease by the lessee.*—A person who has neither sealed and delivered an indenture of lease, nor entered and taken possession under it, can not be made responsible upon the covenants contained in the indenture; but if he enters and takes possession by force of the lease, he is deemed in law to have covenanted to hold upon the terms of the indenture and to observe the conditions of the lease, and the lessor, therefore, may distrain or bring an action for the arrears of rent. (*m*) For every grantor of an estate may annex his own terms and conditions to the grant, which will constitute a covenant annexed to the estate, so that whosoever accepts the estate will be bound by the covenant, although he has not sealed and delivered any deed. If land is leased to two for a term of years, and one puts his seal, and the other agrees to this lease, and enters and takes the profits with him, he shall be charged to pay the rent, though he has not put his seal to the deed; but if there is a

---

(*k*) Paul v. Nurse, 8 B. & C. 486.   Rep. 63.   Litt. sec. 374, 58.   Mayor,
(*l*) Roe v. Harrison, 2 T. R. 428.   &c., of Lyme v. Henley, 1 Bing. N. C.
(*m*) Brett v. Cumberland, 2 Roll.   237.   Gregg v. Coates, 23 Beav. 39.

[1] Where a lessee covenants not to demise, assign, transfer, or set over his lease, it has been held not to be a breach of the lease, or to work a forfeiture of the term, for the tenant to underlet, an under lease not being an assignment; Jackson v. Grout, 7 Cow. 285; Jackson v. Silvernail, 15 Johns. 278; Martin v. O'Conner, 43 Barb. 514; Davis v. Morris, 36 N. Y. 569; aff'g 35 Barb. 227; Hargrave v. King, 5 Ired. Eq. 430; nor, on the other hand, will a covenant "not to let or underlet the whole or any part" of the demised premises preclude an assignment of the whole interest. Lynde v. Hough, 27 Barb. 415. It is said that it is no breach of a covenant not to underlet any part of the premises, for a tenant to take in lodgers. McAdam's Landlord and Tenant, 71.

condition comprised in the deed which is not parcel
of the lease, but a condition in gross, if he does not
put his seal to the deed, though he is a party to the
lease, he is not a party to the condition. (*n*) Where
three were enfeoffed by deed, and there were several
covenants in the deed on the part of the feoffees, and
two of the feoffees only sealed the deed, and the third
entered and agreed to the estate conveyed by the deed,
he was held bound in a writ of covenant. (*o*) Where
three windmills were demised by letters-patent under
seal, which letters-patent contained a clause to the
effect that the lessee and his assignees should repair
and maintain the windmills during the term, and yield
them up in good condition at the expiration thereof,
and the lessee entered under the grant and took possession of the windmills, it was held that there resulted from the acceptance of the estate an express
covenant to repair, which was annexed to the term
granted, and ran with the land, and bound both the
lessee and his assignees by reason of the privity of
estate. (*p*) Where a lessee entered into possession
of a house under an agreement to repair, and paid
rent, and the lessor sold the estate and assigned all
his interest to the plaintiff, and the lessee continued to
occupy and pay rent to the plaintiff, it was held that
the lessee must be presumed, in the absence of evidence
to the contrary, to have agreed to continue to hold of
the plaintiff on the same terms as he held of the original lessor, and that he was therefore responsible to the
plaintiff for a breach of his agreement to repair. (*q*)

695. *Non-execution of the lease by the lessor.*—It

(*n*) 38 Ed. 3, p. 8.   Bro. Abr. Dett.
pl. 80.   Fitz. Abr. Dett. pl. 117.   Co.
Litt. 231, b.
(*o*) 2 Roll. Rep. 62.

(*p*) Brett v. Cumberland, 2 Roll.
Rep. 63.
(*q*) Arden v. Sullivan, 14 Q. B. 832.

is said that, " if an indenture of lease be sealed only on the part of the lessee, and not on the part of the lessor, nihil operat, neither in respect of the interest nor in respect of the covenants ; for the covenants depend upon the lease, and if there is no lease there is no covenant ; for if the lease had been made and afterwards surrendered all the covenants had been void." (*r*)   Where an indenture of demise for the term of eleven years, containing covenants to pay rent and repair, was executed by the lessee alone, and the latter entered and took possession and paid rent for several years, and the lessor assigned his reversion without ever having executed the lease, it was held that the assignee of the reversion could not sue upon any of the covenants of the lease, as the lease for eleven years to which they were annexed had never been created ; that the only reversion which could carry with it the right to sue upon the covenant was a reversion expectant upon the determination of the term for eleven years, which reversion had never been in existence, by reason of the non-execution of the lease by the lessor. (*s*)   But, as between the original parties, where a privity of contract exists between them, the lessee may, under certain circumstances, be held liable upon the covenants contained in the indenture, though the lease has not been executed by the lessor and the term created.   It has been said that every lease must be construed in connection with surrounding circumstances, and that a lessee may, by entering upon and taking possession of tenements under an indenture sealed by him, and by dispensing with the execution of the indenture by the lessor, render himself liable to be sued upon his covenants, as independent covenants, on the ground

(*r*) Soprani v. Skurro, Yelv. 18.   (*s*) Cardwell v. Lucas, 2 M. & W. 123.

that a party may waive a condition in his favor and dispense with its performance; and that, if a lessee executes his part of an indenture of lease, and enters and takes possession of the demised premises, and has the use of them, and gathers all the product and profits of the soil for the whole term intended to be granted without ever having required the lessor to execute the indenture, he ought, in justice, to be deemed to have waived his right to treat the execution of the lease by the lessor as a condition precedent to his liability upon his covenants; and the Court of Queen's Bench has held that a lessee who has executed an indenture of demise containing a covenant to repair, and has entered and enjoyed for the whole term intended to be granted, is liable on his covenant, though the lease has never been executed by the lessor, and that the covenant becomes, under such circumstances, an independent covenant within the rule laid down in Comyn's Digest, (*t*) that if one party executes his part of an indenture, it shall be his deed, though the other does not execute his part. (*u*) But the Court of Exchequer has held that the entry and taking of possession by the lessee before the execution of the lease by the lessor do not render the covenants to pay rent and repair independent covenants. (*v*)

696. *Concealment of latent defects.*—By the civil and continental law, "the lessor is bound to make known to the lessee all defects in the thing which he lets, and to explain everything that may give occasion to error or mistake." (*y*) But by our law, in con-

---

(*t*) Fait (C), 2.

(*u*) Cooch v. Goodman, 2 Q. B. 599. Littledale, J., 1 Ad. & E. 55. Hughes v. Clark. 10 C. B. 605.

(*v*) Pitman v. Woodbury, 3 Exch. 12. Swatman v. Ambler, 8 Id. 80. And see How. v. Greek, 54 L. J., Ex. 4.

(*y*) Domat. liv. 1, tit. 3, ss. 3, 10.

tracts for the letting and hiring of realty, the lessor is not bound to disclose to the lessee latent defects interfering with the use and enjoyment of the property let to hire. (*z*)   A lessor of a house, for example, who knows that the house is in a ruinous and dangerous state, and unfit for occupation, is not bound to disclose the fact to his lessee at the time that he grants the lease. (*a*)

Having executed the lease, and put the lessee into possession of the demised premises, or placed them at his disposal, and clothed him with the legal title to the possession and occupation thereof for the term granted by the lease, the lessor has done all that is necessary for him to do to entitle himself to the rent at the time that it is made due and payable ; he does not, in the case of demises of realty, warrant that the premises are, at the time of the demise, or that they shall continue to be during the term, in any particular state or condition, or fit for any particular purpose ; and the lessee, therefore, is bound to pay his rent, although the subject-matter of the demise is not fit for the purpose for which he required it, and although he may have had no beneficial use or enjoyment of it. If, indeed, the lessor has been guilty of any fraudulent concealment of defects which ought in good faith to have been disclosed, or has resorted to any misrepresentation calculated to mislead the lessee in some important particular as to the condition of the demised premises, the contract will be void, and the lessee will be discharged from the rent ; but, in the absence of all fraud and deceit, he is bound by his express covenant or contract, and must pay his rent, although he has not had that beneficial use and enjoyment of the demised

(*z*) Hart v. Windsor, 12 M. & W. 68.   (*a*) Keates v. Earl Cadogan, 10 C. B.
Cornfoot v. Fowke, 6 M. & W. 358.   591 ; 20 L. J., C. P. 76.

premises which was anticipated. Thus, there is no
implied warranty on the part of a lessor who lets land
for agricultural purposes, that no noxious plants are
growing on the demised premises. (*b*)   And where
the defendant took the eatage of a meadow from the
plaintiff, for the term of six months, at a rent of £40,
and turned fifteen head of cattle into the meadow,
eight of whom died from the poisonous effects of a
quantity of refuse paint which had been placed on a
manure heap, and had inadvertently been spread over
the grass prior to the defendant's occupation, and had
afterwards been eaten by the cattle; and the defendant then took his stock off the land, and tendered
back the possession of the meadow to the plaintiff,
which she refused to receive, it was held that the defendant was liable for the rent at the time it became
due, although the eddish at the time of the demise was
wholly unfit for the purpose for which it was taken,
and the defendant had not had any beneficial use or
enjoyment of it. (*c*)

697. *Demises of uninhabitable houses—Rooms
infested with bugs.*—Where an action was brought
for the non-payment of the rent of a house, and the
defendant pleaded that the house was demised to him
for the purpose of his inhabiting the same, and that,
at the time of the demise and of his taking possession,
and from thence until he quitted, the house was unfit
for habitation, and he could not dwell therein, or
have any beneficial use or occupation thereof, by
reason of its being greatly infested with bugs, without
any default on his part, and that, before the rent

(*b*) Erskine v. Adeane, L. R., 8 Ch.
756; 42 L. J., Ch. 835.

(*c*) Sutton v. Temple, 12 M. & W.
52. 27 Hen. 6 (Trin. Term), fol. 10,
pl. 6.   Hil. Term, 14 Hen. 4, fol. 27,
pl. 35.   Bro. Abr. (Dette), pl. 18, fol.
220.

became due, and as soon as he discovered the condition of the tenement, he quitted it, and gave notice
to the plaintiff, and tendered him the possession
thereof, it was held that the plea was no answer to
the action, inasmuch as the law, in the case of demises
of unfurnished houses, implies no warranty or engagement on the part of the lessor that the house is at the
time of the demise, or at the commencement of the
term, in a fit and proper state and condition for
habitation; and that, even if such a warranty or
engagement could be implied, the breach of it would
not give the tenant a right to abandon his lease, and
vacate the possession, and refuse to pay rent; but
that his remedy would be by a cross action to recover
compensation for the damage he might have sustained
by the breach of such implied contract. (*d*)[1]

(*d*) Hart v. Windsor, 12 M. & W.   see Smith v. Marrables, *post*, s. 2.
68.   As to bugs in furnished lodgings,

[1] The tenant must, it seems, at all events, put the lessor
back into the condition in which he would have been had the
contract of letting not been made; see as to this; Central
Bank v. Pindar, 46 Barb. 467; Little v. Martin, 3 Wend. 219;
Packard v. Dunsmore, 11 Cush. 282; Benford, v. Schell,
55 Pa. St. 393; Hall v. Western Transportation Co.,
34 N. Y. 284.   In Westlake v. DeGraw, 25 Wend. 672,
upon a tenant's having put an end to a lease upon
the ground that the premises were infested with certain
noxious smells, said NELSON, Ch.J.: "It must be assumed
that no fraud was practiced upon the tenant by the landlord,
as that has been negatived by the verdict of the jury. It
appears, also, that the alleged nuisance existed at and before
the defendant made the contract and entered into the possession; and that it arose from the carcasses of dead rats under
the steps of the house. The discovery was made by the succeeding tenants; and it seems to me that ordinary vigilance
on the part of the defendant would have enabled him to have
done the same. He not only appears to have been remiss in
this respect himself, but even refused to allow a mechanic,
sent by the plaintiff, to take the necessary steps to detect and

698. *Payment of rent.*—Although, therefore, houses become ruinous and fall down, and buildings, fences, and superstructures erected upon the soil, and crops growing thereon, be destroyed by floods, or burned by lightning or accidental fire, or be thrown down by enemies, yet is the tenant liable to pay the rent so long as the land remains to him, and his legal title to the occupation and use thereof continues. (*e*) [1] If the landlord is bound by custom, or has entered

(*e*) Carter v. Cummins, cited 1 Ch. C. 84. Pindar v. Ainsley, cited 1 T. R. 312. Bayne v. Walker, 3 Dow. 233. Leeds v. Cheetham, 1 Sim, 146. Arden v. Pullen, 10 M. & W. 321. Marquis of Bute v. Thompson, 13 M. & W. 493, 494. Lofft v. Dennis, 1 Ell. & Ell. 481 ; 28 L. J., Q. B. 168. Surplice v. Farnsworth, 7 M. & Gr. 579 ; 8 Sc. N. R. 307.

remove the cause of the nuisance. It was readily removable when discovered, and in its own nature was of but temporary duration. It is an inconvenience to which all buildings are more or less subject at times ; but which, with ordinary skill and attention, may be abated by the tenant. It would, I apprehend, be the introduction of a new principle into the law of landlord and tenant, and one liable to great abuse, to give countenance to this defense." But in Wallace v. Lent, 1 Daly, 481, where a landlord rented a dwelling-house to a tenant without disclosing a fact within his knowledge, that there was a deleterious stench in the house, proceeding from some unknown cause, which rendered it unfit for habitation, and the tenant went into possession with his family, and in a very short time all the inmates of the house experienced the injurious stench, producing vomiting, &c., it was held that the concealment was such a fraud on the part of the landlord, as justified the tenant in leaving the premises. Where A leased certain premises to B, and occupied the floor above such premises as a grocery store, and drippings from his grocery rendered the premises leased to B untenantable; *held*, an eviction, and upon abandonment of the premises, B was not liable for rent. Jackson v. Eddy, 12 Miss. 209.

[1] Valentine v. Godfrey, 9 Vt. 186; Ripley v. Wightman, 4 McC. 447 ; Hallett v. Wylie, 3 Johns. 44; Phillips v. Stevens, 16 Mass. 236; Fowler v. Bott, 6 Mass. 63; Smith v. Ankrim, 13 S. & M. 39; Wagner v. White, 4 Har. & J. 564; Bayley v. Lawrence, 1 Bay, 499.

into an express covenant to repair and uphold a house demised by him, and the lessee covenants to pay rent, the covenants are independent covenants, and the repairing and upholding of the house by the lessor is not a condition precedent to the liability of the lessee upon his covenant. (*f*)[1]

699. *Exception of damage by fire.*—If the lessee has covenanted to pay rent, "damage by fire excepted," and part of the demised premises is destroyed or injured by fire, the whole of the rent is not thereby suspended, but the tenant is entitled to a reasonable abatement. (*g*)   And, if the lessee covenants to pay rent, and also to repair, with an express exception of casualties by fire and tempest, the exception is confined to the covenant to repair, and does not qualify or affect the liability upon the covenant to pay rent, unless it has been extended thereto by express words. (*h*)[2]

700. *Extinction and suspension of the rent by eviction.*—If the tenant loses the benefit of the enjoyment of any portion of the demised premises by the act of the landlord, the rent is thereby suspended; but the act must be something of a grave and permanent character, dispossessing the tenant, and not a mere temporary trespass; (*i*) and there must be an actual dispossession of the tenant, and not a mere constructive eviction. (*k*)[3]   The tenant is not

(*f*) T. Term, 27 Hen. 6, fol. 10, pl. 6. Bro. Abr. Dette, pl. 18. Surplice v. Farnsworth, 8 Sc. N. R. 307; 7 M. & Gr. 584.

(*g*) Bennett v. Ireland, E. B. & E. 326.

(*h*) Monk v. Cooper, 2 Str. 763.

Belfour v. Weston, 1 T. R. 310.

(*i*) Upton v. Townend, 17 O. B. 64. Carpenter v. Parker, 3 C. B. N. S. 238.

(*k*) Delaney v. Fox, *ante.* Wheeler v. Steverson, 30 L. J., Ex. 46 ; 6 H. & N. 158.

[1] See *post*, § 707.
[2] Id.
[3] It is not necessary that an eviction should be a physical

released from liability by reason of an eviction by a
mere wrong-doer and trespasser who has no title at
all to the possession of the demised premises.[1]   Thus,

act; Dyett v. Pendleton, 8 Cow. 727; Cohen v. Dupont, 1
Sandf. 260.   In Jackson v. Eddy, where B leased certain
premises to A, under his (B's) grocery store, and the drippings
from the grocery store rendered A's premises untenable; it
was held to be such an eviction as would absolve A from the
payment of the rent.   When a landlord lets to two tenants
and the one of them makes his part disorderly and a nuisance,
it is no eviction, unless the landlord is instrumental in procuring it.   Nor is it his duty to proceed against the disorderly
tenant; Townsend v. Gilsey, 7 Abb. Pr. N. S. 59.   But under
certain circumstances it was held that the refusal by a landlord, occupying premises conjointly with his tenant, to permit
an under-tenant to occupy the premises, constituted an eviction; Randell v. Alburtes, 1 Hilt. 285; and see Christopher
v. Austin, 11 N. Y. 216; tearing down a partition separating
the entrance to the tenant's room from a grog shop, so as to

---

[1] The act of a stranger can not work an eviction; Howard
v. Doolittle, 3 Duer. 464; Gardner v. Keteltas, 3 Hill. 330;
Weeks v. Bowerman, 1 Daly, 100; Johnson v. Oppenheim,
34 N. Y. Superior Ct. R. 416 (affirmed 55 N. Y. 280); White v.
Mealio, 37 N. Y. Superior Ct. R. 72; Sherwood v. Seaman,
2 Bosw. 127; Kramer v. Cook, 7 Gray, 550; Pollard v. Shaffer,
1 Dallas, 210; Tunis v. Grandy, 22 Gratt. 109.   A tenant in
possession, who is evicted before the determination of his
lease, may recover as damages the difference between the value
of his lease for the unexpired term, and the stipulated rent, or
if the eviction be at a season when the expense of removing
is greater than it would have been at the end of his term, he
may recover such extra expense.   He can not recover as damages, however, any increased rent he may be compelled to
pay for other premises, and this without reference to the accommodation as compared with that he had before; Chatter-
ton v. Fox, 5 Duer, 64; Noyes v. Anderson, 1 Id. 342, and
Peck v. Hiler, 24 Barb. 178; but see, Wilson v. Raybould,
56 Ill. 417; or he may recover where unlawfully evicted from
premises he occupied as a livery stable; a tenant may recover
for loss of profits from boarding horses, for the difference in
the expense of keeping his own; Shaw v. Hoffman, 25 Mich.
162.   See as to a Michigan statute against violent eviction
and treble damages.   Id.

where an action of debt was brought for three years'
arrears of rent reserved upon a lease of a farm, and
the defendant pleaded that Price Rupert, an alien and

compel him to pass through the latter in order to reach his
own room, amounts to an eviction; Rogers v. Ostrom, 35
Barb. 523; or a continued habit of bringing lewd women
under the same roof with the leased premises; Dyett v.
Pendleton, 8 Cow. 327. Where a dentist occupying the second
floor of a house, under a lease allowing him to practise his
profession and receive patients, was annoyed by other tenants
in the house muffling the bell frequently, although the tenant
remonstrated with his landlord, who neglected or failed to
stop it, so that persons coming to visit the dentist would pull
at the bell, and wait from fifteen to twenty minutes and half
an hour, before effecting an entrance, or be compelled to
leave without seeing him, to the great and inevitable detri-
ment of his professional business; and in addition to this, plaintiff's family littered the stair-carpet with nut-shells, dirt, filth,
and sweepings from the storey above, and spilled water upon it,
and placed snow-balls in the window-sill, &c., to drip upon the
carpet; used insulting or impertinent language to tenant's
patients; were in the habit of singing and shouting on the
stairway, &c.; and on one occasion a placard was put on the
stairway to call attention, by his name, to the filthy condition of
the tenant's stairs—*held*, that these acts constituted an eviction; Cohen v. Dupont, 1 Sandf. 260. But an undermining of
tenant's walls by an adjoining proprietor; Kramer v. Cook 7,
Gray, 550; White v. Mealio, 37 N. Y. Superior Ct. 72; Howard
v. Doolittle, 3 Duer, 464; Sherwood v. Seaman, 2 Bosw. 127;
or a building erected by the landlord on an adjoining lot;
Palmer v. Wetmore, 2 Sandf. 316; Myers v. Gemmel, 9 N. Y.
Leg. Obs. 173; 10 Barb. 537; or the landlord's trespassing and
piling firewood on the demised land; Lounsberry v. Snyder,
31 N. Y. 514; and see Edgerton v. Page, 20 N. Y. 281;
Academy of Music v. Hackett, 2 Hilt. 217; or a landlord continuing to occupy a portion of the leased premises without
the intent to keep the tenant out of possession; Vanderpoel
v. Smith, 1 Daly, 311; nor an interference by the landlord
with the person of the tenant, although on the demised
premises; Vatel v. Herner, 1 Hilt. 149; nor the use of a privy
by a landlord in a passage-way leading to the demised premises, which was there at the time of the hiring, in such a way
as to be offensive to the tenant, the tenant not being actually

enemy of the king, invaded the realm, and with divers armed men did enter upon the demised premises, and expel him therefrom, and keep him out, so that he could not enjoy the lands during the terms, " it was resolved that the matter of the plea was insufficient." And this distinction was taken that, where the law creates a duty or charge, and the party is disabled to perform it without any default in him, and hath no remedy over, there the law will excuse him ; but when the party by his own contract creates a duty or charge upon himself, he is bound to make it good, notwithstanding any accident by inevitable necessity, because he might have provided against it by his contract. Another reason was added that, as the lessee is to have the advantage of casual profits, he must run the hazard of casual losses, and not lay the whole burthen of them upon his lessor. (*l*) So, where the parliament, during the civil wars, took

---

(*l*) Paradine v. Jane, Aleyn. 27 ; Sty. 47. Barrett v. Dutton, 4 Campb. 333. Maryon v. Carter, 4 C. & P. 295. Hills v. Sughrue, 15 M. & W. 253. Jervis v. Tomkinson, 1 H. & N. 195. Brown v. Royal Insurance Society, 28 L. J., Q. B. 277.

---

deprived of any part of his premises. Id. In Ogden v. Sanderson, 3 E. D. S. 166, it was said that where a tenant was present at a negotiation between his landlord and another, to re-let the premises to a third person, and did not object, but proposed a surrender on his own part, possession by such third person will not be an eviction. An eviction does not affect the landlord's right to collect arrears of rent ; McKeon v. Whitney, 3 Den. 452; Giles v. Comstock, 4 N. Y. 270; although the rent be payable in advance, and the eviction occurs before the expiration of the period; Id.; Whitney v. Meyers, 1 Duer. 266 ; an eviction only suspends the rent during the continuance of the eviction ; Ogden v. Sanderson, 3 E. D. S. 166; but see Lansing v. Van Alstyne, 2 Wend. 561; Blair v. Claxton, 18 N. Y. 529; Christopher v. Austin, 11 N. Y. 216. And see Lounsberry v. Snyder, 31 N. Y. 514; Edgerton v. Page, 20 N. Y. 281.

possession of a house which had been demised to a lessee for a term of years, and turned it into an hospital for sick and maimed soldiers, and so prevented the lessee from having any beneficial occupation thereof for several years, notwithstanding which the lessor brought an action of debt for the rent, no question appears to have been made but that the lessee was bound at common law to make good the rent; and the lessee consequently brought his bill in equity for relief, on the ground that he had no remedy over against the wrong-doer, because it was an act of force in the parliament, which had been pardoned by the act of oblivion; but it does not appear that he got relief even in equity. (*m*)

701. *Eviction by railway companies under statutory powers.*—If the tenant is lawfully evicted by a railway company under the powers of its Act, the tenant is discharged from the accruing rent, but not from rent that was due and in arrear at the time of the eviction. Where a yearly tenant received notice from a railway company to give up possession of certain land within six months from the notice, and the notice expired in the middle of a half year, and the tenant gave up possession to the company without obtaining or requiring compensation in respect of his unexpired term and interest in the premises, it was held that he was liable to his landlord for the whole of the half year's rent. (*n*) When a certain portion only of lands or tenements held by tenants or lessees has been taken by a railway company under the

(*m*) Harrison v. Lord North, 1 Ch. Ca. 84. As to proof of expulsion, see Mayor, &c., of Poole v. Whitt, 15 M. & W. 577. As to evidence of eviction, see Morrison v. Chadwick, 7 C. B. 283; 18 L. J., C. P. 193. Henderson v. Mears, 28 L. J., Q. B. 305. Wheeler v. Steverson, 6 H. & N. 158; 30 L. J., Ex. 46.

(*n*) Wainwright v. Ramsden, 5 M. & W. 602. *Post*, NOTICE TO QUIT.

powers of its Act, the rent is to be apportioned; and
the rent to be paid by the tenant for the residue of
the lands not taken by the company, must be settled
by agreement of the parties, or by two justices, or by
a jury. (*o*) ¹

If the lessor, after granting the lease, sells and
conveys all his estate and interest in the demised
premises, he has no longer any right to the accruing
rent. The rent passes with the reversion to the
lessor's grantee without any atornment on the part of
the tenant; but the tenant is not to be prejudiced or
damaged by payment of rent to the lessor, or by
breach of any condition for non-payment of rent, before notice of the transfer and conveyance has been
given to him by the grantee. (*p*)

702. *Payment of ground-rent by the tenant—Deduction thereof from the tenant's rent.*—The immediate landlord is by the common law bound to protect
his tenant from all paramount claims; and when,
therefore, the tenant is compelled, in order to protect
himself in the enjoyment of the land in respect of
which his rent is payable, to make payments which
ought, as between himself and his landlord, to have
been made by the latter, he is impliedly authorized to
make the payment on the landlord's behalf; and the
courts have held such payments to be payments in

(*o*) 8 & 9 Vict. c. 18, s. 119. Bac. (*p*) 4 Ann. c. 16, ss. 9, 10. And see
Abr. RENT, M. *In re* Ware, 9 Exch. De Nicholls v. Saunders, *ante.*
395.

¹ Where property is appropriated under the right of eminent domain, it is not such an eviction as will bar a suit for rent.
Folts v. Hautley, 7 Wend. 210; Gillilan v. Spratt, 3 Daly,
440. But the tenant may be entitled to an abatement; Gillespie v. Thomas, 15 Wend. 464; Foote v. Cincinnati, 11 Ohio,
408; Patterson v. Boston, 20 Pick. 159; Parks v. City of Boston, 15 Pick. 198; Mills v. Baehr, 24 Wend. 254.

satisfaction of rent due, or accruing due, to the immediate landlord.   Thus, a tenant who has been compelled
by a superior landlord, or other incumbrancer having
a title paramount to that of his immediate landlord, to
pay sums due for ground rent or other like charges,
may treat such payments as payments in satisfaction
or part satisfaction of rent due to his immediate landlord. (*q*)   But the tenant should deduct these payments from the next rent that becomes due, or from
the rent of the current year ; for, if he allows several
payments of rent to pass without giving his immediate
landlord notice of the payment, and claiming the
deduction, he will lose his right to deduct the money
he has paid from the rent. (*r*)   Payments of money
on account of the landlord, not charged upon the demised premises and leviable upon the chattels of the
occupier, can not be given in evidence in satisfaction
and discharge of the rent, unless they were expressly
directed or sanctioned by the landlord. (*s*)   The tithe
commutation Acts do not impose any personal
liability on the landlord to pay the tithe rent-
charges. (*t*)

703. *Deduction of income-tax, land-tax, sewers-
rate, and other out-goings from the rent.*—As regards
land-tax, paving-rates, and property and income-tax,
charged on land demised to a tenant, (*u*) the tenant
ought to deduct the tax or rate out of the next rent
that becomes due. If he fails to do this, he can not
deduct it from subsequent rent, nor can he recover it

(*q*) Graham v. Allsopp, 3 Exch. 198.
Taylor v. Zamira, 6 Taunt. 524. Jones·
v. Morris, 3 Exch. 742.

(*r*) Andrew v. Hancock, 3 Moore,
278. Spragg v. Hammond, 4 Moore,
440.

(*s*) Davies v. Stacey, 12 Ad. & E. 511.

(*t*) Griffinhoofe v. Daubuz, 4 E. & B.
235.

(*u*) 16 & 17 Vict. c. 34, s. 40. 27 &
28 Vict. c. 18, s. 15.

by action from the landlord. (*x*)   If the landlord is
entitled to be relieved from the assessment, it is his
duty to take the necessary steps for the purpose ; and,
if, before he has done this, the assessment is made on
the occupier, and the tax paid, it may be deducted
from the rent, although at the time the deduction is
made the landlord has obtained his exemption from
the tax. (*y*)   The landlord is in general liable to pay
taxes in proportion to the rent reserved, and not to
the improved value.   Where, therefore, a tenant built
on land demised to him, and raised the annual value
from £60 to £300, it was held that he was only entitled to deduct sewers-rate and land-tax upon the
original rent, and that he was himself properly chargeable in respect of the improved value. (*z*)   Where
the lessor was also the owner of the tithe rent-charge
upon the land, it was held that a covenant to pay " all
taxes and assessments whatsoever for or in respect of
the demised premises, save and except the level-tax,
property-tax, and land-tax," did not include the tithe
rent-charge, and that the lessee was not bound to pay
it. (*a*)

The Roman law, in its exposition and enforcement
of leases, was much more favorable to the tenant than
our own law.   There the enjoyment of the thing for
the use of which the rent was agreed to be paid was a
condition precedent to the lessor's right to demand
the rent.   If, for example, the tenant was evicted by
irresistible force, and kept out of possession, without
any default on his own part, he was discharged from
the rent, whether the eviction was the act of the lessor

(*x*) Andrew v. Hancock, *supra.*
Denby v. Moore, 1 B. & Ald. 129.
Cumming v. Bedborough, 15 M. & W.
438.

(*y*) Swatman v. Ambler, 24 L. J.,
Ex., 185.

(*z*) Smith v. Humble, 15 C. B. 321.

(*a*) Jeffrey v. Neale, L. R., 6 C. P.
240 ; 40 L. J., C. P. 191.

himself or of persons having title, or the act of mere wrong-doers. If a house demised to a tenant for habitation became ruinous and uninhabitable ; if the windows were blocked up or darkened, and the tenant deprived of light and air by the raising of the roof of an adjoining house, or his use and enjoyment of the property were interfered with by a nuisance which he had no means of abating, he might quit the demised premises, vacate his lease, and refuse further payment of rent. (*b*) If pasture land was demised for the purpose of feeding cattle, and poisonous herbs grew up and destroyed the beasts, the landlord lost his right to the rent. (*c*) If lands were granted to farm for the term of one year only, and the tenant by reason of some inevitable accident, such as a volcanic eruption, an earthquake, a frost, a hail-storm, an inundation, or a hostile incursion, lost the whole of the produce of the soil and reaped nothing, he was discharged from his rent. (*d*) If a partial injury only had been sustained — if, for instance, the growing crops were damaged by an extraordinary drought, or the unusual inclemency of the weather—the lessee was entitled to a proportionable abatement of his rent. But in order to sustain his claim for an abatement, he was bound to show that the loss arose from some unusual occurrence not reasonably to have been expected and contemplated by the parties at the time of the making of the contract. He was never granted an abatement of rent in respect of losses in any way attributable to his own want of diligence or skill, nor in respect of any accident which might reasonably have been foreseen

---

(*b*) Dig. lib. 19, tit. 2, lex 15, § 7, § 1 ; lex 33, lex 25, § 2. Cod. civ. 1726, 1727.

(*c*) Si saltum pascuum locasti in quo herba mala nascebatur, et pecora vel demortua sunt, vel deteriora facta, quod interest præstabitur, si scisti si ignorasti, pensionem non petes. Dig. lib. 19, tit. 2, lex 19, § 1.

(*d*) Ib. lex 15, § 1, 2.

and guarded against, nor for inconsiderable and trifling
losses. (*e*)   And in all leases for terms of years, the
good years were to be taken with the bad years, so
that the lessee could not claim to be excused from
rent in respect of the total loss of the harvest in any
one year of his tenancy, but could only claim the
abatement towards the expiration of the term, upon a
fair average of profit and loss. (*f*)

704. *Distress for rent.*—The lessor's right to enter
in person or by deputy upon the demised premises
and distrain the goods and chattels of the tenant for
rent or services in arrear, has existed in this country
from so early a period "that we have no memorial of
its original with us." (*g*)   It was doubtless derived
from the Roman law, which considered all the chattels and movables and personal property that the
tenant brought upon the demised premises, and all
the crops and fruits and produce of the soil growing
or stored upon the land, to be hypothecated to the
lessor as a security for the due payment of the rent, so
that the lessor might, if rent was due and unpaid,
enter upon the demised premises and take possession
of such goods and chattels and produce, and hold the
same as a security for the amount due. (*h*)   This
power of entering upon the land and taking corporeal
possession of the pledge is impliedly accorded to the
lessor on every demise of realty where there is an express reservation of, or an agreement by, the tenant to
pay a fixed ascertained rent or service. (*i*)   If there

(*e*) Domat (Louage), No. 4, 5, 6,
Pothier (Louage), No. 153.   Dig. lib.
19, tit. 2, lex 15. § 2.

(*f*) Ib. § 4; lex 55, § 1. Instit.
lib. 3, tit. 25, § 3.   Cod. lib. 4, tit. 66,
lex 1.

(*g*) Gilbert on Distress. 2 Bro. Abr.
Distress, fol. 252.   Bradby, 2.

(*h*) In prædiis rusticis fructus qui
ibi nascuntur tacite intelliguntur pig-
nori esse domino fundi locati, etiamsi
nominatim id non convenerit.   Dig.
lib. 20, tit. 2, 4, 7 ; Cod. lib. 8, tit. 15,
lex 3.   Bract. lib. 2, fol. 62, cap. 28.

(*i*) Litt. § 214,

has been merely a permissive occupation of the property, without any previous payment of rent referable
to some certain term of hiring, or to some definite
portion of a year, the lessor has no right of entry upon
the land nor power to distrain, but must proceed by
way of action upon the implied promise of the tenant
to pay a fair and reasonable compensation for the permissive use and enjoyment of the property. (*k*)   But
whenever there is a tenancy at will at a fixed rent,
there is a right to distrain. (*l*)   It is essential to the
lawful exercise of the power of distress that the dis-
trainor be the party entitled to the reversion of the
property on the determination of the lease. (*m*)   By
the 34 & 35 Vict. c. 79, the goods of lodgers are protected against distresses for rent due to the superior
landlord; and by the 35 & 36 Vict. c. 50, railway rolling stock is protected from distress when on the line.'

(*k*) Dunk v. Hunter, 5 B. & Ald.
325.

(*l*) Anderson v. Midland Railway
Company, 30 L. J., Q. B. 96. Yeo-

man v. Ellison, L. R., 2 C. P. 681 ; 36
L. J., C. P. 326.

(*m*) See the 8 & 9 Vict, c. 106.

¹ The remedies devised for the protection of landlords
with us are the common law action of debt; McKeon v.
Whitney, 3 Den. 452; or of covenant; Id.; or for use and
occupation, or by summary proceedings to obtain possession
of the premises, or for double rent, or for mesne profits which
are given by the statutes of the state.   He also may have a
remedy by proceedings in the nature of the old action for
waste in various states.   (In the state of New York this action
was abolished by the Code, § 450, and the wrongs remediable
thereby made the subject of a civil action.)   He also has his
action for trespass ; certain statutory remedies are also
provided in the various states for the recovery of premises
used for purposes of prostitution and for other illegal trades
and traffics.   The policy of a distress for rent has been adopted
in many of the American states.   The New England states
have substituted therefor the law of attachment on mesne process; which proceeding, however, preserves many of its fea-
tures.   In New York, distress has been abolished as an invid-

705. *Extinguishment of the right to distrain by an assignment of the reversion.*—If the lessor, after the making of the demise, conveys the property to a purchaser, he has no power to distrain for the rent that became due prior to the execution of the conveyance, as he is no longer possessed of the reversion expectant upon the determination of the lease. (*n*) Neither can the purchaser distrain for such rent ; for it was a fruit fallen from the reversion at the time of the conveyance of the demised premises to him. (*o*) If, however, the conveyance was preceded by the ordinary agreement between vendor and purchaser vesting the equitable estate in the latter prior to the rent becoming due, the purchaser would be entitled to recover the rent by action. (*p*)

706. *Apportionment of rent.*—The 4 & 5 Wm. 4 c. 22, respecting the apportionment of rent did not apply to leases created by parol. (*q*) But by the 33 & 34 Vict. c. 35, rents are to be deemed to accrue from day to day, and are apportionable in respect of time.

707. *Of compensation for the use and occupation*

(*n*) 43 Ed. 3, 4. Bro. Abr. Dette, pl. 39. Parmenter v. Webber, 8 Taunt. 593. Preece v. Corrie, 5 Bing. 24.

(*o*) Midgley v. Lovelace, Carth. 289 ; 12 Mod. 46.

(*p*) Anon. Skinn. 367. Midgley v. Lovelace, Carth. 290.

(*q*) Cattley v. Arnold, 28 L. J., Ch. 353. Plummer v. Whiteley, 29 L. J., Ch. 247.

ious distinction in favor of a particular class of creditors. (So also in Mississippi. Griff. Law Reg. 697.) And the courts of North Carolina have declared that it does not exist in that state. Dalgleist v. Grandy, Cam. & Nor. 22. South Carolina goes even to the extent of allowing distress for double rent where a tenant holds over after notice to quit. Reeves v. McKenzie, 1 Bailey, 497. In Alabama and Tennessee, there are no statutes on the subject; and in Ohio there is only a statute to secure a landlords' share of crops against execution against a tenant. Griff. Law Reg. 404. Under the Civil Code of Louisiana a landlord may follow furniture removed by the tenant for fifteen days after removal. Code, 2675.

of land.—The landlord, where there is no agreement for any specific rent, is entitled to recover a reasonable satisfaction for the lands, tenements, or hereditaments held or occupied by the tenant, without proof of any demise, on the implied promise resulting from the simple fact of the permissive use and enjoyment of the property; (*r*) but no action will lie, unless there is a promise either express or implied to pay for the use and occupation. (*s*) [1]

(*r*) 11 Geo. 2, c. 19, s. 14. Churchward v. Ford, 26 L. J,. Ex. 354; 2 H. & N. 446. Hellier v. Sillcox, 19 L. J., Q. B. 295. Levy v. Lewis, 6 C. B., N. S. 766; 9 C. B., N. S. 874; 28 L. J., C. P. 304; 30 L. J., C. P. 141.

Hardon v. Hesketh, 4 H. & N. 178.

(*s*) Turner v. Cameron's Coal, &c., 5 Exch. 937. Carmier v. Mercer, cited Birch v. Wright, 1 T. R. 387. Mayor of Newport v. Saunders, 3 B. & Ad. 412.

[1] An action for use and occupation is founded on a privity of contract between the landlord and the tenant. Bedford v. Terhune, 30 N. Y. 435; a mere title in the plaintiff and occupation by the defendant are not sufficient; Hall v. Southmayd, 15 Barb. 35; Wiggin v. Wiggin, 6 N. H. 298; Ryan v. Marsh; 2 N. & McC. 156; Stockett v. Watkins, 2 Gill & Johns. 326; Brewer v. Craig, 3 Harr. 214; Curtis v. Treat, 8 Shep. 525; Brolasky v. Ferguson, 48 Penn. St. 434; Steuart v. Fitch, 2 Broom, 17; Edmondson v. Kite, 43 Mo. 176; Wood v. Wilcox, 1 Den. 37; Croswell v. Crane, 7 Barb. 191; Sylvester v. Ralston, 31 Id. 286; Jennings v. Alexander, 1 Hilt. 154; Hurd v. Miller, 2 Id. 540; Taylor v. Bradley, 4 Abb. Ct. App. Dec. 363; 53 Barb. 258; Richey v. Hinde, 6 Ohio, 371; Butler v. Cowles, 4 Id. 205; Pierce v. Pierce, 25 Barb. 243; and see Vanderheuvil v. Storrs, 3 Conn. 203; Stacy v. Vermont, &c. R. R. Co., 32 Vt. 551; Bell v. Ellis, 1 Stew. & P. 284; Little v. Pierson, 7 Pick. 301; Jones v. Tipton, 2 Dana, 205; Bancroft v. Wardell, 13 Johns. 489. Such an action will not, therefore, lie ordinarily against an under-tenant; Jennings v. Alexander, 1 Hilt. 154; a power to occupy is sufficient; Hall v. Western Transportation Co., 34 N. Y. 284; nor would it lie against one having possession of land under a contract of sale; Bancroft v. Wardell, 13 Johns. 480; Stacy v. Vermont, &c. R. R. Co., 32 Vt. 551; Jones v. Tipton, 2 Dana, 295; Little v. Pierson, 7 Pick. 301; nor against a mere trespasser; Hurd v. Miller, 2 Hilt. 540; Weaver v. Jones, 24 Ala. 420; nor where one enters

708. *Constructive occupation.*—An actual personal occupation is not necessary to entitle the landlord to compensation, when the lessee has entered and taken possession, and the term has become vested in him. (*t*) But there must be proof of an actual entry on the land (*u*) and taking of possession, or it must be shown that "there has been an occupation by some other parties standing in such a relation to the defendant that their occupation is his and that he is personally liable for it." (*v*)   An entry by one of two joint lessees is an entry by both, so as to render both liable. (*y*) The action is maintainable, where no certain rent has been reserved, and where there is, consequently, no

---

(*t*) Baker v. Holtpzaffel, 4 Taunt. 45. Izon v. Gorton, 7 Sc. 547 ; 5 Bing. N. C. 507. Pollock v. Stacy, 9 Q. B. 1033.

(*u*) Lowe v. Ross, 5 Exch. 553 ; 19 L. J., Ex. 318. How v. Kennett, 3 Ad. & E. 665.

(*v*) Bull v. Sibbs, 8 T. R. 327.

(*y*) Glen v. Dungey, 4 Exch. 61 ; 18 L. J., Ex. 359.

---

into possession in expectation of becoming a lessee, and no lease is ever actually entered into; Greaton v. Smith, 33 N. Y. 246 ; or where the possession is tortious ; Reckey v. Hinde, 6 Ham. 371 ; Wiggin v. Wiggin, 6 N. H. 293 ; Stockett v. Walkins, 2 Gill & J. 326 ; nor where the actual lease is in another ; Bedford v. Terhune, 30 N. Y. 453 ; nor against a tenant holding over, after the expiration of his term, where proceedings have been instituted against him to turn him out of possession under a statute ; Featherstonhaugh v. Bradshaw, 1 Wend. 134 ; Crane v. Hardman, 4 E. D. Smith, 339 ; nor where there is no actual entry or possession ; Wood v. Wilcox, 1 Den. 37 ; though a mere taking a key and entry without continued possession ; Little v. Martin, 3 Wend. 220 ; or where the actual power and opportunity to occupy is given by the landlord to the tenant, so far as the landlord is concerned ; Hall v. Western Trans. Co., 34 N. Y. 284 ; Moffatt v. Smith, 4 Id. 126 ; Little v. Martin, 3 Wend. 220 ; it is sufficient to maintain such, the action ; and see Pott v. Gosher, 1 Yeates. 576 ; O'Fallon v. Boismean, 3 Miss. 405 ; McFaddin v. Rippey, 8 Id. 738 ; Eston v. Dugan, 21 Pick. 538 ; Codman v. Jenkins, 14 Mass. 93 ; Allen v. Thayer, 17 Id. 299 ; Fletcher v. McFarlane, 12 Id. 43.

right to distrain. (*z*) The compensation accrues de die in diem, so that, if there is no express contract for the payment of rent at specific periods, the lessor is entitled to be paid from day to day so long as the occupation lasts. (*a*) Very slight circumstances, such as entry on the lands, the putting up a notice or advertisement, sending a woman to clean windows or rooms, or workmen to put up paper or do repairs, will suffice to establish the fact of entry and of actual occupatiou. (*b*) '

An occupation by an under-tenant of the lessee is the lessee's own occupation, as much as if he were himself personally present upon the land. But if one of two joint lessees holds over after the expiration of his lease, without the assent of his co-lessee, the latter is not responsible in respect of the occupation of such co-lessee. (*c*) The occupation of the wife before marriage is not the occupation of the husband. (*d*) The actual possession and use by one of two executors of property holden on lease by their testator is not in law a possession and use by both, and does not render both chargeable as joint occupiers in their own right. (*e*) If a lessor sells or transfers his legal estate and interest in the demised premises to a third party, and the lessee receives notice of the transfer, and is required to pay his rent to the transferee and refuses, he is liable to an action at the suit of the latter. (*f*) The defen-

(*z*) Waring v. King, 8 M. & W. 574. Hamerton v. Stead, 5 D. & R. 211 ; 3 B. & C. 482.

(*a*) Packer v. Gibbins, 1 Q. B. 421.

(*b*) Sullivan v. Jones, 3 C. & P. 579. Smith v. Twoart, 2 M. & Gr. 841.

(*c*) Ibbs v. Richardson, 9 Ad. & E. 849 ; 1 P. & D. 618. Christy v. Tancred, 9 M. & W. 438, 448. Draper v.

Crofts, 15 M. & W. 166 ; 15 L. J., Ex. 92.

(*d*) Richardson v. Hall, 3 Moore, 307.

(*e*) Nation v. Tozer, 1 C. M. & R. 175.

(*f*) Lumley v. Hodgson, 16 East, 104. Birch v. Wright, 1 T. R. 378. Rennie v. Robinson, 7 Moore, 539.

¹ See last note.

dant may show that the plaintiff's interest in the premises has expired, or has been transferred to some third party ; but he is estopped from denying the lessor's title to grant the property to be enjoyed, and can not show that the lessor has only the equitable estate, or that he is entitled only as co-executor with others who do not join in the action. (*g*)   A tenant who has occupied land under a corporation and paid rent to the corporate body, is liable for use and occupation, although the corporation can not in general contract except by virtue of its common seal ; (*h*) and a corporation which has actually occupied and used lands, &c., may be made liable during the period of occupation, but not afterwards, unless there is a demise under seal. (*i*)

If a man is let into possession under an agreement for a lease to be granted at a future time, and occupies, and receives the profits of, the land, he is liable for a reasonable compensation to be paid to the owner for the use and enjoyment of the property. (*k*)   But, if he takes possession of property as a purchaser, under a contract of purchase and sale, and the vendor is unable to make out a title, and the bargain, consequently, goes off, the purchaser is not, in general, bound to pay any compensation or remuneration to the owner for the temporary occupation and enjoyment of the property. (*l*)   If, however, after a contract of purchase and sale has gone off or been abandoned, the intended purchaser continues to

<hr/>

(*g*) Phipps v. Sculthorpe, 1 B. & Ald. 50.

(*h*) Mayor of Stafford v. Till, 12 Moore, 260.

(*i*) Finlay v. Bristol and Exeter Railway Company, 7 Exch. 417 ; 21 L. J., Ex. 116 ; but see Lowe v. London R. R. Co., L. R., 14 Eq. R. 18.

(*k*) Mayor of Thetford v. Tyler, 8 Q. B. 100.

(*l*) Kirtland v. Pounsett, 2 Taunt. 145, Winterbottom v. Ingham, 7 Q. B. 611 ; 14 L. J., Q. B. 298.

occupy and take the rents and profits of the land, by the sufferance and permission of a party who is then entitled to the immediate possession, he is bound to pay a reasonable compensation to such party for the permissive use and occupation of the property. (*m*)   So, if the vendor of a house continues to reside in it after he has sold it, he is not liable in respect of such subsequent residence, unless it be shown that he was permitted to remain in possession upon the express or implied understanding that the occupation was to be paid for. (*n*)   If a lessor has agreed to complete a house demised by him, and the tenant enters and occupies, and the landlord neglects to fulfil his agreement, he is nevertheless entitled to recover a reasonable sum in respect of the use and occupation by the tenant of the incomplete house. (*o*)   If the tenant or occupier has entered as a trespasser and wrongdoer, and has remained in possession and used and occupied the land to the exclusion of the owner, it appears to be somewhat doubtful whether the latter may waive the tort, and consent to the occupation, and sue the tenant upon the ordinary implied promise to pay a reasonable remuneration for the occupation and enjoyment of the property.[1]   But, if the owner accepts rent from a trespasser, this is a waiver of the tort and a creation of a tenancy, with its accompanying rights, duties, and responsibilities.   If the landlord assigns his interest, and the tenant has notice of the assignment, and continues to occupy with the consent of the assignee, he may be sued by the

(*m*) Howard v. Shaw, 8 M. & W. 122.

(*n*) Tew v. Jones, 13 M. & W. 12.

(*o*) Smith v. Eldridge, 23 Law T. R. 270.

[1] See last note.

latter, (p) but not otherwise. (q) A lessee is not liable for use and occupation after he has been adjudicated a bankrupt, whether the trustees accept his interest in the premises, or disclaim it. (r)

709. *Use and occupation by one of several joint-tenants or tenants-in-common.*—By the 4 Anne, c. 16, s. 27, it is enacted that actions of account may be maintained by one joint-tenant and tenant-in-common, his executors, &c., against the other as bailiff, for receiving more than comes to his just share or proportion, and against the executor, &c., of such joint-tenant or tenant-in-common. This statute applies to cases where two or more persons are tenants-in-common of land leased to a third party at a rent payable to each, or where there is a rent-charge, or any money payment, or payment in kind, due to them from another person, and one receives the whole, or more than his proportionate share according to his interest in the subject of the tenancy, and not to cases where one has enjoyed more of the benefit of the land and made more by personal occupation of it than another. There are many cases in which a tenant-in-common may occupy and enjoy the common land solely, and have all the advantage to be derived from it, and yet not be liable to pay anything to his co-tenant-in-common. (s) '

(p) Standen v. Chrismas, 16 L. J.,
Q. B. 265 ; 10 Q. B. 142. 4 Anne, c.
16, s. 9.

(q) Cooke v. Moylan, 1 Exch. 67.

(r) Bankruptcy Act, 1869, sect. 23.

(s) Henderson v. Eason, 21 L. J.,
Q. B. 82.

---

[1] A demand on either of two joint tenants is sufficient; Geisler v. Weigand, 9 N. Y. 227 ; and one of two joint landlords may demand the whole rent, and commence proceedings for its non-payment in the name of both. Griffin v. Clark, 33 Barb. 46; and see Howard v. Doolittle, 3 Bosw. 464; De Mott v. Agerman, 8 Cow. 220.

710. *Covenants and agreements to repair dilapidations.*—There is no implied covenant or promise, either on the part of the lessor or the lessee of a house, to repair or uphold it during the term,[3] In

[1] City Council v. Moorhead, 2 Rich. 430 ; Mumford v. Brown, 6 Cow. 475 ; Long v. Fitzsimons, 1 Watts & S. 530. Such an obligation can only arise from contract ; Witty v. Matthews, 52 N. Y. 512 ; and this rule applies to a lessee out of possession, who has sublet to one in possession ; Clancy v. Byrne, 56 N. Y. 129. A tenant can not, without special agreement, make repairs at the expense of his landlord ; Munford v. Brown, 4 Cow. 475 ; McCarty v. Ely, 4 E. D. Smith, 375 ; but where the landlord is bound to repair, and repairs are needed, a tenant may make the repairs himself, and after due notice to the landlord, and after waiting a reasonable time, may recover the expense from the landlord ; or he may leave the premises unrepaired, and recover damages from the landlord for his failure to repair ; Myers v. Briggs, 35 N. Y. 269 ; Ward v. Kelsey, 38 Id. 80 ; Cook v. Soule, 56 Id. 420. In such a case the lessee's measure of damage is the difference in the value of the use of the premises as they are and as the lessor agreed to put them ; Cook v. Soule 56 N. Y. 420. A promise by a landlord to repair, made after the delivery and acceptance of the lease, requires a new consideration to render it binding. Walker v. Gilbert, 2 Robt. 214 ; Doupe v. Genin, 37 How. Pr. 5 ; affirmed in 45 N. Y. 119 ; Flynn v. Hatton, 43 How. 333 ; and see 1 E. D. S. 253 ; 2 Id. 248. A tenant from year to year, renting part of a dwelling-house, the residue of which is occupied by other tenants, is under no obligation to make repairs of so general, substantial, and lasting a nature, as the rebuilding of a chimney which has fallen down. Eagle v. Swayze, 2 Daly, 140 ; Johnson v. Dixon, 1 Id. 178. There is no implied warranty in the contract of letting, that the premises are tenantable ; Mayor v. Moller, 1 Hilt. 491 ; Academy of Music v. Hackett, 2 Hilt. 217 ; Post v. Vetter, 2 E. D. Smith, 248 ; Wallace v. Lent, 1 Daly, 481 ; and in the absence of any stipulation the lessor will be held to agree to take the house as it stands, and can not compel the landlord to put it into a condition fit for habitation ; Jaffe v. Harteau, 56 N. Y. 398. Under a written lease, parol evidence can not be given that the landlord at the time of executing it, promised to repair ; Cleves v. Willoughby, 7 Hill, 83. A landlord is under no obligation to the tenant to protect his premises from ad-

Dyer, it is said to be "reasonable law," where a lease of a house has been made without any covenant on either side to repair, " that the termor should require the lessor to do the repairs; and, if the lessor, after notice and request, be negligent, whereby the house falls, the lessee shall have an action upon the case against the lessor for not repairing it, and shall recover as much in damages as the inconvenience he suffers from the want of his house shall amount to." (*t*) But the Court of Queen's Bench has held that there is no obligation on the part of a landlord to repair, in the absence of an express

(*t*) Dyer, 36, b.

joining excavations; Sherwood v. Leaman, 2 Bosw. 127; Howard v. Doolittle, 3 Duer. 464; White v. Mealio, 37 N. Y. Superior Ct. 72. Where a building is injured by fire, the landlord can not be compelled to re-build or repair it for the benefit of his tenants, unless he has expressly covenanted to do so; nor is he liable for injuries consequent upon his delay to repair the part destroyed. Doape v. Genin, 45 N. Y. 119. Where a wharf was leased, and was destroyed by natural decay, before the lessee's entry, it was held that, although upon the lessee giving the lessor notice of the same, the latter neglected to repair it, the lessee was still liable for the rent. Hill v. Woodman, 14 Me. (2 Shepl.) 38; and see Cleves v. Willoughby, 7 Hill, 83. Where premises are leased for a first class hotel, a covenant to keep the same in repair is broken by permitting the flues to remain in such a condition that the rooms can not be used with a fire on account of the issuing of smoke from the grate in the room whenever a fire is lighted therein. Myers v. Bowers, 35 N. Y. 269.

In an action for rent, defendant may, under a covenant of the landlord to keep the premises in repair, set up, as a counter-claim, an amount expended by him in the necessary repair of the premises, and also damages sustained by the loss of the use of certain parts of the premises rendered untenantable for want of repair; and in such an action the defendant may recover for his expenses in repairs, even when they exceeded what it would have cost the landlord had he employed his own mechanics. Walker v. Swayze, 3 Abb. Pr. 138.

contract in that behalf; and, therefore, if a house demised falls, and destroys the furniture of the lessee, the
landlord will not be responsible in damages. (*u*)
Where the lessor covenants to repair, there is no
breach until after notice of want of repair. (*v*)   Every
covenant by a lessee that he will well and sufficiently
repair and maintain the demised premises during the
term, and deliver them up at the expiration thereof in
good repair and condition, will be construed in connection with surrounding circumstances ; and the
extent of the liability will depend upon the age of the
buildings, the state and condition of them at the time
of the demise, and the length of the lease.[1]   If the
house is an old house, the tenant is bound to keep it
up only as an old house, and can not be compelled to
replace old materials with new. (*y*)   " Where a very
old building is demised, and the lessee enters into a
covenant to repair, it is not meant that the old building is to be restored in a renewed form at the end of
the term, or of greater value than it was at the commencement of the term.   What the natural operation
of time flowing on effects, and all that the elements
bring about, in diminishing the value, constitute a loss
which, so far as it results from time and nature, falls upon
the landlord.   But the tenant is to take care that the
premises do not suffer more than the operation of time
and nature would effect ; he is bound by seasonable
applications of labor to keep the house as nearly as
possible in the same condition as when it was demised.
If it appears that he has made these applications, and
laid out money from time to time upon the premi-

(*u*) Gott v. Gandy, 2 E. & B. 845 ;   Ex. 25 ; 40 L. J., Ex. 33.
23 L. J., Q. B. 1.   (*y*) Harris v. Jones, 1 Mood. &
   (*v*) Makin v. Watkinson, L. R., 6   Rob. 175.

[1] Jaqueis v. Gould, 4 Cush. 384.

ses, it would not be fair to judge him very rigorously by the reports of a surveyor, who is generally sent in for the very purpose of finding fault. The jury are to say whether or not the lessee has done what was reasonably to be expected of him, looking to the age of the premises on the one hand, and to the words of the covenant which he has chosen to enter into, on the other." (z) If the lessee has covenanted to keep the demised premises in good repair during the term, and at the time of the demise they were old and in bad repair, he must put them in good repair as old premises, and not keep them in bad repair because they happened to be in that state when he took them. The age and class of the premises, however, with their general condition as to repair, must be looked at in order to measure the extent of the repairs to be done. (a) If the lessee has covenanted to repair buildings, "the same being first put into repair by the lessor," the liability of the lessee does not arise until after all the buildings have been put into repair by the lessor, (b) who is bound to repair in the first instance. (c) When the lessee has entered into an express covenant or agreement to repair, uphold, and keep in repair a house, or any other structure or building demised to him, he is bound to re-build or re-construct it, if it is burned by an accidental fire, or blown down by tempest, or destroyed by floods or by an inevitable accident; for "when the party, by his own contract, creates a duty or charge upon himself, he is bound to make it good, notwithstanding any accident by inevitable necessity, because he might have provided

---

(z) Tindal, C. J. Gutteridge v. Mumyard, 1 Mood. & Rob 336.

(a) Payne v. Haine, 16 M. & W. 545 ; 16 L. J., Ex. 130.

(b) Neale v. Ratcliff, 15 Q. B. 916 ; Coward v. Gregory, 36 L. J., C. P. 1 ; L. R., 2 C. P. 153.

(c) Cannock v. Jones, 3 Exch. 233.

against it by his contract." And, therefore, if the
lessee covenants to repair a house, or a bridge, and
the house is burned down by lightning or an accidental fire, or thrown down by enemies, or the bridge
is washed away, the lessee must rebuild. (*d*)[1] The
ordinary covenant to repair the demised tenements
and dwelling-houses does not extend (so as to create
a forfeiture under a proviso for re-entry in case of non-
performance of covenant) to an entirely new structure
erected during the term, not in existence and not
forming part of any buildings on the premises at the
time of the execution of the lease, (*e*) unless it appears that the land was demised for building purposes,
and that the erection of buildings by the lessee during
the term was contemplated by the parties, and that
the covenant was meant to extend to buildings thereafter to be erected. (*f*)

Where a lease, executed on the 9th of November,
contained a covenant on the part of the lessee to repair, and the tenant had taken possession and pulled
down buildings in the preceding month of June, it was
held that he could not be made responsible in an
action of covenant, as the lease was not then executed,
although the habendum of the lease stated that the
premises were to be holden from the preceding 22d
of June. The habendum marked only the duration
of the tenant's interest, and could not operate retro-

(*d*) 40 Ed. 3, fol. 6, pl. 11. Paradine v. jane, Aleyn, 27 ; 2 Saund.
421, a (2) ; Dyer, 33 a, pl. 10. Breck-
nock Company v. Pritchard, 6 T. R.
750. Bullock v Dommitt, ib. 650.

Chesterfield v. Bolton, 2 Com. Rep.
627.

(*e*) Cornish v. Cleife, 3 H. & C. 446 ;
34 L. J., Ex. 19.

(*f*) Dowse v. Cale, 2 Vent. 126 ; 3
Lev. 264.

[1] Stockwell v. Hunter, 11 Met. 448; White v. Molyneux,
2 Kelly, 127 ; Magau v. Lambert, 3 Barr. 444; Linn v. Ross,
10 Ohio, 412 ; Willard v. Tellman, 19 Wheat. 353.

spectively as a grant. (*g*)　If the lease is under seal, and the tenant has bound himself by covenant to repair, and the landlord assigns his interest, the assignee is entitled, as we have seen, to sue upon the covenant. (*h*)　Covenants to repair are covenants which run with the land, and are continuing covenants to the end of the term. (*i*)　They extend to all additions and enlargements of structures existing at the time of the demise, but not to detached, independent buildings erected after the making of the lease. (*k*)　If the landlord has evicted the tenant from part of the demised premises, the tenancy is not, as we have seen, thereby determined, and the tenant is not discharged from the performance of a covenant to repair. (*l*)　The landlord is entitled to recover damages for breach of a contract to yield up in repair at the end of the term, although he immediately proceeds to demolish the buildings. (*m*)

Where a party entered into possession under a lease which was void as to the duration of the term from its being an invalid execution of a power, but the lessee had the benefit of the possession of the land and the perception of the profits for the whole term purported to be granted, he was held liable upon his covenant to repair contained in the same lease. (*n*)　And where articles of agreement under seal were entered into between an intended lessor and lessee for the grant of a lease for twenty-one years, as soon as a license from the lord of the manor (the land being copyhold land)

(*g*) Shaw v. Kay, 1 Exch. 412 ; 17 L. J., Ex. 17.

(*h*) Bickford v. Parsons, 17 L. J., C. P. 192.

(*i*) Martin v. Clue, 22 L. J., Q. B. 147.

(*k*) Cornish v. Cleife, 34 L. J., Ex. 19 ; 3 H. & C. 446.

(*l*) Morrison v. Chadwick, *ante.*

(*m*) Rawlings v. Morgan, 18 C. B., N. S. 776 ; 34 L. J., C. P. 185.

(*n*) Beale v. Sanders, 3 Bing. N. C. 850 ; 5 Sc. 58.

could be obtained, and the lessee covenanted to keep the premises in repair during the term so to be granted, and subsequently entered and took possession of the land, and occupied the same under the agreement for the full term of twenty-one years, it was held that he was responsible upon his covenant to repair, although the intended lease had never been made, nor any license obtained from the lord. (*o*) If the lessee has not entered and held under the indenture of demise executed by him, and upon the terms of the covenant he has thought fit to enter into, but under a distinct parol demise, then he is not liable upon the covenants of the lease. (*p*) Where a lease made under a leasing power was void from non-compliance with the requirements of the power, but the lessee entered and took possession, and paid rent, and then assigned his interest, and the assignee entered and paid rent under the void lease, and continued in possession until the end of the term intended to have been granted, it was held that he must be taken to have promised to hold upon the terms of the lease, and that he was liable for not repairing according to the covenant therein contained. (*q*) We have already seen that, if a party assents verbally to certain printed terms of hiring, and enters and takes possession, he will be bound by the printed terms, although they are not signed either by him or by the lessor. (*r*) Where a tenant gave a written undertaking to hire a house for three years, and to pay rent and repair during the term, but there was no lease or any agreement on the part of the lessor, and the tenant entered and took

(*o*) Pistor v. Cater, 9 M. & W. 315.

(*p*) Pitman v. Woodbury, 3 Exch. 12.

(*q*) Beale v. Sanders, 5 Sc. 58 ; 3

Bing. N. C. 859.   Lee v. Smith, 23 L. J., Ex. 199.

(*r*) Lord Bolton v. Tomlin, 5 Ad. & E. 856.

possession and held the premises for more than three
years, it was held that he was responsible for neglecting to repair according to his undertaking. (*s*)

711. *Of the tenant's liability for injury or damage
done to the demised premises.*—In the absence of an
express covenant or agreement to repair, there results
from the demise and acceptance of the lease by the
lessee an implied covenant or promise, according as
the lease is by deed or by simple contract, to use the
property demised in a tenant-like and proper manner, [1]
to take reasonable care of it, and restore it, at the expiration of the term for which it is hired, in the same
state and condition as it was in when demised, subject
only to the deterioration produced by ordinary wear
and tear, and the reasonable use of it for the purpose
for which it was known to be required. [2]　The extent

(*s*) Richardson v. Gifford, 1 Ad. & E. 55.

[1] So it is held to be implied, from the letting of a farm for
agricultural purposes, that the tenant will cultivate and use
the land according to the rules of good husbandry.　Lewis
v. Jones, 5 Harris, 262.　He must not use in any other way,
for instance, he should not cut logs for the market upon a
portion of the land not intended to be cultivated.　Moons v.
Waite, 3 Wend. 104 ; Nave v. Berry, 23 Ala. 382.

[2] In the absence of express permission from the landlord, the taking down of partitions by a tenant is apparently an act of waste ; the question whether it is injurious is one of fact for a jury.　Agate v. Lowenbein, 57 N. Y.
604.　Accordingly where a lease of certain premises contained
a clause authorizing the lessee to make inside alterations as
he might think proper, provided that the same did not injure
the premises, *held*, that while the clause authorized alterations which in point of law and technically would be waste,
yet they must be such acts only as were unaccompanied with
actual injury to the premises ; and the acts of alteration must
not be wanton and capricious, but must be made with a purpose to facilitate the transaction of the lessee's business.　Id.
If under such a lease the tenant make extensive alterations,
taking down partitions, removing chandeliers, and destroying

of the liability of the tenant for the preservation of the property depends upon the duration and value of his own term and interest therein. A tenant for life, for example, is bound to watch over the interest of the reversioner, and is responsible for permissive as well as commissive waste, whilst a tenant at will, or from year to year, is responsible only for commissive waste; (*t*) but a tenant for a term of years who has been let into possession under a contract of demise, where the landlord had the power of protecting himself by taking a covenant to repair, is not bound, as previously mentioned, to make substantial repairs, if by the contract he has not taken that burden upon himself. If a dwelling-house demised to him becomes old and ruinous, and falls from the want of reparations, or is burned by enemies, or by accident, or by the folly and negligence of his own servant, or is destroyed by tempest, the termor is not bound to rebuild; (*u*) and he is punishable for waste, if he cuts down timber or digs stones or slates from the demised premises for the purpose of either rebuilding or repairing ; " for the power of the termor to make repairs is only in small repairs, as to make splents, mud walls, hedges, and ditches, but not large and principal repairs, as the principal timber and stone walls and tiles; but a covering with thatch he may make." (*x*)   If windows are broken by the

---

(*t*) Harnett v. Maitland, 16 M. & W. 256. Herne v. Bembow, 4 Taunt. 764. Jones v. Hill, 7 Taunt. 392 ; 1 Moore, 100. Torriano v. Young, 6 C. & P. 12.

(*u*) Lady Shrewsbury's case, 5 Co. 13, b. M'Kenzie v. M'Leod, 4 M. & Sc. 253 ; 10 Bing. 385. Salop v. Crompton, Cro. Eliz. 777.

(*x*) Maleverer v. Spinke, Dyer, 36, a.

---

plumbing work, &c., the questions whether such acts really caused injury to the reversion, or were reasonably required for the enjoyment of the premises, are questions of fact for the jury ; nor is the tenant, even if unimpeachable for waste, entitled to the possession of the materials severed by him.   Id

wind or hail, he is liable for the non-repair of them, if the consequence of his neglect would be damage to the building from rain   He must not suffer a roof of thatch to remain uncovered so as to let the timbers rot.   He must cleanse the drains and sewers, (*y*) and use all reasonable endeavors to keep the buildings wind and water tight.   But the extent of his liability for the preservation of the property will depend upon the age and general state and condition of the demised premises at the time he took possession of them, and the duration and value of his own term and interest. (*z*)   He is never responsible for ordinary wear and tear, and is not bound to replace old materials with new, except where the expense is of a trifling character, and the mischief, if neglected and left unrepaired, would operate to the serious and lasting injury of the inheritance.   " The landlord is the person who, when the subject of occupation perishes, is to provide a new one if he thinks fit." (*a*).[1]

(*y*) Russell v. Shenton, 3 Q. B. 449.   And see the French Cod. Civ., liv. 3,
(*z*) Ferguson v. ————, 2 Esp. 590.   tit. 8, art. 1719, 1720, 1754–6.
Auworth v. Johnson, 5 C. & P. 239.   (*a*) Wise v. Metcalfe, 10 B. & C. 314.

[1] A tenant for life must not prejudice the rights of the remainder man; Jackson v. Luquere, 5 Cow. 221 ; but a tenant may be entitled to reasonable estovers, such as wood from off the land, for fuel, fences, agricultural erections and other necessary improvements ; see Clarke v. Cummings, 5 Barb. 339 ; 26 Id. 409 ; Gardiner v. Hempstead, 1 Paige, 573 ; v.   , 3 Sandf. Ch. 601 ; but has no right to dig up and use soil for the manufacture of bricks for sale ; Livingston v. Reynolds, 26 Wend. 114; 2 Hill, 157 ; and see Hawley v. Wolverton, 5 Paige, 522; Jackson v. Andrew, 18 Johns. 431; Mooers v. Waite, 3 Wend. 104; Kidd v. Dennison, 6 Barb. 9; Coates v. Cheever, 1 Cow. 460 ; McGregor v. Brown, 10 N. Y. 114; Sarles v. Sarles, 3 Sandf. Ch. 601 ; Shipley v. Ritter, 7 Md. 408; Clement v. Wheeler, 25 N. H. 361 ; Owings v Emery, 6 Gill, 360.

A mere tenant at will, whose interest the Roman lawyers called "precarium," or a mere tenant from year to year, is not bound, as we have already seen, to expend money in repairs and improvements. "The farmer," observes Domat, "ought to use the lands he has in farm as any prudent and discreet man would use his own, and to keep them, preserve them, and cultivate them at the proper seasons, in the manner agreed on by the lease, or regulated by custom. He can not increase his profits out of the lands to the prejudice of the proprietor. He can not sow arable lands when they ought to lie fallow, nor sow wheat when he ought only to sow barley or oats, if these changes would make the lands to be in a worse condition at the end of the lease than they ought to be." (*b*) [1]

712. *Timber Trees.*—Wherever trees are excepted from a demise, there is, by implication a right in the lanldord to enter on the land and cut the trees at all reasonable times. (*c*)

713. *Of the duty of the tenant to preserve the landlord's landmarks and boundaries.*—Where a tenant for life, or for years, or at will, has land of his own adjoining to that which he holds as tenant, it is his duty to keep the boundaries between the two properties clear and distinct, so that at the expiration of the tenancy, the revisioner or remainderman may be able without difficulty to resume the possession of what belongs to him ; and, if the tenant or lessee neglects this duty, and suffers the boundaries to be confused, so that the

---

(*b*) Domat. l. i, tit. 4, s. 2.   (*c*) Hewitt v. Isham, 7 Exch. 79.

[1] A tenant pur autre vie who continues in possession without the consent of the owner after the determination of the life estate, at a common law, was considered a tenant by sufferance, but by statute in New York is held to be a trespasser. Livingston v. Tanner, 14 N. Y. 64; and see 8 Abb. N. S. 37.

reversioner or remainderman can not tell to what land he is entitled, the courts will give relief by compelling the person who has occasioned the difficulty to remove it, and restore the proper boundaries. if it can be done, or, if not, to give an equivalent. This relief is given, not only against the party guilty of the neglect, but also against all those who claim under him, either as volunteers or purchasers without notice. (*d*)

714. *Fences.*—There is no implied agreement on the part of a lessor to keep up the fences of closes which he retains in his own hands, and which abut on land demised to a tenant, so as to prevent the tenant's cattle from straying on to them. (*e*)

715. *Restrictive covenants as to the user of premises* entered into between lessor and lessee run with the land. A general covenant by the lessee that he will not do, or suffer to be done, upon the demised premises anything which may become an annoyance to the tenants of the adjoining houses may prevent him from opening a shop or coal-office, or carrying on any trade or business in a dwelling-house. (*f*)

716. *Defeasible leases.*—The lessor may reserve to himself a right to determine the lease and resume possession of the demised premises, at any time on giving notice of his intention to the lessee. (*g*) If a lease is made defeasible at the option of either of the parties, it may be determined by the lessor by a simple demand of possesion, or the tenant may quit the demised premises and release himself from his contract by tendering possession to the landlord ; but, if the lease is made determinable at the expiration of

(*d*) Attorney-General v. Stephens, 6 De G. M. & G. 111 ; 25 L. J., Ch. 888.

(*e*) Erskine v. Adeane, L. R., 8 Ch. 750 ; 42 L. J., Ch. 835.

(*f*) Wilkinson v. Rogers, 10 Jur. N. S.

(*g*) Doe v. Kennard, 12 Q. B. 244.

three, six or nine years, or any particular interval of time, reasonable notice of the intention to determine the contract must be given by the party who intends to avail himself of the power of defeasance. (*h*) If the lease is made determinable at the expiration of a certain time if the parties shall think fit, both must concur in determining the lease. (*i*) If power to determine the lease after a certain time is reserved, without saying by whom it is to be exercised, the law gives it to the lessee. (*k*) If an agreement is entered into for a yearly tenancy, with a proviso for determining it in the middle of the year, such a proviso does not prevent it from being a yearly tenancy. When the party is in, he is in of the whole estate for a year, liable to a defeasance on a particular event. So, where there is a lease for twenty-one years, determinable at the end of seven or fourteen years, the party, when he enters, is in of a term of twenty-one years, but a defeasible term, and which may determinate by matter ex post facto. (*l*) When the lease is determinable by notice, the notice may be given at any time, if no particular period for giving it is specified; (*m*) but it must be in strict conformity with the terms of the power of defeasance; and when performance of all the covenants that have been entered into by the lessee is made a condition precedent to his right to determine the lease, these covenants must be strictly fulfilled. (*n*)

717. *Disclaimer and forfeiture.*—If a tenant from year to year disclaims the title of his lessor; if he claims the land as his own, and refuses to pay rent on

(*h*) Goodright v. Richardson, 3 T. R. 462.

(*i*) Fowell v. Tranler, 34 L. J., Ex. 6.

(*k*) Dann v. Spurrier, 3 B. & P. 399.

(*l*) Rex v. Herstmonceaux, 7 B. & C.

555.

(*m*) Bridges v. Potts, 17 C. B., N. S. 314; 33 L. J., C. P. 338.

(*n*) Friar v. Grey, 15 Q. B. 899; 5 Exch. 584.

the ground that he is himself the owner, or if he
attorns or delivers up possession to a stranger, or professes to sell or grant the property to another; if he
cuts down timber, pulls down or alters dwelling-houses,
or obliterates fences, boundaries, and land-marks, or
opens and digs mines and quarries against the will of
the landlord, the tenancy is determinable by the latter,
and he has a right of re-entry upon the property, and
may forthwith recover possession of the demised premises. (*o*)¹ Acts of this description on the part of a
tenant from year to year work a forfeiture of his term
and interest, and convert the possession into an adverse possession, so that the tenant may at once be
proceeded against without any notice to quit and
without any demand of possession. (*p*)² But, if the
lessor dies, and adverse claimants to the property
appear and demand the rent of the tenant, and the
latter refuses to pay it until the conflicting claims
have been ascertained and settled, the refusal is not
such a disclaimer of the title of the real owner as will
justify the latter in treating the tenant as a trespasser.
(*q*) "To constitute a disclaimer (by words) there
must be a renunciation by the party of his character

(*o*) Jones v. Mills, 10 C. B., N. S. & R. 137. Doe v. Pittman, 2 N. & M.
788; 31 L. J., C. P. 66. 673.
(*p*) Doe v. Frowd, 1 M. & P. 480; (*q*) Doe v. Pasquali, 1 Peake, 259.
4 Bing. 557. Doe v. Flynn, 1 C. M. Swinfen v. Bacon, 6 H. & N. 846;
30 L. J., Ex. 368.

¹ See De Lancey v. Ga. Nun. 12 Barb. 120; Tuttle v. Reynolds, 1 Vt. 80; Duke v. Harper, 6 Yerg. 280; Jackson v.
French, 3 Wend. 337; Verplank v. Wright, 23 Id. 506.
² The lease becomes voidable at the lessor's option. Norman v. Wells, 17 Wend. 136; Clark v. Jones, 1 Den. 516; Baxter v. Lansing, 7 Paige, 350; Brown's Admr. v. Bragg, 22 Ind.
122. But the statute is to receive a strict construction. See
Hasbrock v. Paddock, 1 Barb. 535; Livingston v. Tompkins,
4 Johns. Ch, 415; Lindon v. Hepburn, 3 Sandf. 668; United
States v. Grundy, 3 Cranch. 337.

of tenant, either by setting up the title of a rival claimant, or by asserting a claim of ownership in himself." (*r*)   A mere refusal to pay rent, or a declaration by the tenant that he will continue to hold possession, or an omission to acknowledge the landlord as such by requesting further information as to title when the property has changed hands, does not render the tenancy an adverse tenancy and possession. (*s*)   All verbal disclaimers operating as a forfeiture of the tenant's interest in, and right of possession of, the demised premises, and dispensing with the necessity of a notice to quit, are restricted to tenancies from year to year.   A lease for a definite term of years can not be forfeited by mere words. (*t*)   And if, after a disclaimer by a tenant from year to year, the landlord puts in a distress for rent which became due subsequently to the disclaimer, such distress is a waiver of the disclaimer, and again clothes the tenant with a lawful possession. (*u*)   Forfeiture is also incurred by the breach of conditions annexed to the demise ; for the lessor, having the jus disponendi, may annex whatever conditions he pleases to his grant, provided they are not illegal or repugnant to the grant itself, and upon the breach of those conditions may avoid the lease. (*w*)   But the law does not favor forfeitures of estates ; and strict proof of a breach of a condition or covenant working a forfeiture of a lease is always required. (*y*)

718. *Provisos for re-entry.*—It is frequently made a term or condition of the demise, that the lease shall be forfeited and the lessor have a right to re-enter and

---

(*r*) Doe v. Cooper, 1 Sc. N. R. 41. Hunt v. Allgood, 30 L. J., C. P. 313 ; 10 C. B., N. S. 253.

(*s*) Doe v. Cawdor, 1 C. M. & R. 398.   Doe v. Stanton, 1 M. & W. 703.

(*t*) Due v. Wells, 10 Ad. & E. 436.

(*u*) Doe v. Williams, 7 C. & P. 322.

(*w*) Bac. Abr. LEASES, T. 2.

(*y*) 1 Wms. Saund. 287, b., 288, i 1 Mad. ch. 36.

re-possess himself of the demised premises for a breach
of particular covenants contained in a lease. The
right to take advantage of a proviso of this description
is, of course, confined to the lessor and the assignee
of the reversion or part of the reversion; (z) and the
lessee can not be permitted to set up his own breach
of contract as an avoidance of the lease; for no man
is permitted to take advantage of his own wrong. (a)
If it is provided that, in case of non-payment of rent,
it shall be lawful for the lessor " to enter upon the
premises for the same until it be fully satisfied," the
lessor will be entitled to enter and hold possession
until the arrears of rent are satisfied; but, when they
are satisfied, the lessee will be entitled to re-enter and
hold under the lease as before. (b)[1]   Provisos in leases
for re-entry in case of non-payment of rent or non-
performance of covenants are not " to be construed
with the strictness of conditions at common law; but,
being matters of contract between the parties, they
should be construed like all other contracts." (c)[2]

(z) 22 & 23 Vict. 35, s. 3.

(a) Reid v. Parsons, 2 Chit. 248.
Doe v. Birch, 1 M. & W. 402. Jones
v. Carter, 15 M. & W. 725.

(b) Co. Litt. 203.   Doe v. Bowditch,
15 L. J., Q. B. 267.

(c) Doe v. Eisam, M. & M. 191.
Hayne v. Cummings, 16 C. B., N. S.
425.

[1] A forfeiture will be waived, if, where a lease contain a
condition for re-entry of the lessor on non-payment of rent,
the rent in arrears is accepted after such formal re-entry.
Coon v. Brickett, 2 N. H. 163.

[2] As to where a re-entry by the landlord on breach of a
covenant, will not be presumed. See Ritchie v. Putnam, 13
Wend. 524; Tate v. Crowson, 6 Ired. 65; and see Jackson v.
Harrison, 17 Johns. 66; Jackson v. Kipp, 3 Wend. 230; Rem-
sen v. Conkling, 18 Johns. 447; McCormick v. Connell, 6
Serg. & R. 151; McRubin v. Whetcroft, 4 Har. & McHen. 135;
Connor v. Bradley, 1 How. 211; Spear v. Fuller, 8 N. H. 174;
Associates, &c., v. Howland, 11 Met. 99; Atkins v. Chelson, Id
112; Camp v. Pulver, 5 Barb. 91.

Where the lessee was to hold in consideration of the rent " and conditions" contained in the lease, and it was stipulated and " conditioned" that the lessee should not assign or underlet, it was held that the lease was forfeited, and that the lessor had a right to re-enter, on an assignment being made by the lessee. (*d*) An agreement to hire a messuage at a certain rent is an agreement to pay that rent ; and, therefore, if a power of re-entry is reserved " in case of breach of any of the agreements" contained in the written instrument of demise, the lessor may re-enter for non-payment of rent. (*e*) Where a lessee covenanted to pay rent and not to assign, and there was a proviso for re-entry if the rent was in arrear, or all or any of the covenants " hereinafter contained" on the part of the lessee should be broken, and there were no covenants on the part of the lessee after the proviso, but only a covenant by the lessor, that the lessee paying the rent, &c., should quietly enjoy, it was held that the lessor could not enter for breach of the covenant not to assign, as the proviso was restrained by the word " hereinafter" to subsequent covenants, and there were none such in the lease. (*f*) Where there is a proviso for re-entry in case of non-performance of covenants, and the lease contains a general covenant to repair, and also a covenant to repair within a certain time after notice, the landlord may at once enter for breach of the general covenant ; (*g*) but if he gives notice under the second covenant, this is a waiver of the forfeiture incurred by breach of the general covenant, and he can not recover possession until after the time limited by the notice has expired. (*h*) A notice to

---

(*d*) Doe v. Watt, 8 B. & C. 308.

(*e*) Doe v Kneller, 4 C. & P. 3.

(*f*) Doe v. Godwin, 4 M. & S. 265.

(*g*) Baylis v. Le Gros, 4 C. B., N. S. 537.

(*h*) Doe v. Meux, 4 B & C. 606.

repair " in accordance with the covenants," or "forthwith," will not, however, amount to a waiver of the
forfeiture incurred by a breach of the general covenant. (*i*) Where a right of re-entry for waste is reserved, the proviso is understood to mean such waste
as is injurious to the reversion. (*k*) Where there is a
proviso for re-entry for breach of a covenant to insure
and keep insured, it does not mean that the lessee
shall keep any one particular policy on foot, but that
he shall always keep the premises insured by some
one policy or another; and the breach will be a continuing breach so long as they remain uninsured. (*l*)

A power of re-entry, in case the lessee carries on
any trade or business upon the demised premises,
authorizes the lessor to re-enter if a school is established. (*m*) But when particular trades or occupations
are specified, no trade or business which does not
clearly fall within the description contained in the
lease will come within the proviso. (*n*) A proviso
for re-entry may be reserved in case the tenant should
become bankrupt or insolvent, (*o*) or the term granted
should be taken in execution by the sheriff; (*p*) and,
if the contingency provided for happens, the lessor
will be entitled to take possession, and to enjoy the
emblements. (*q*) If a proviso for re-entry is insensi-
ble, it is of course nugatory; for the court can not
find a meaning for that which has no meaning. (*r*)
If the lessor has the custody of the lease, and has in
anywise misrepresented the nature of the proviso, or

(*i*) Few v. Perkins, L. R,. 2 Ex. 92 ;
36 L. J., Ex. 54. Roe v. Paine, 2
Campb. 520.

  (*k*) Doe v. Bond, 5 B. & C. 855.
  (*l*) Doe v. Peck, 1 B. & Ad. 428.
  (*m*) Doe v. Keeling, 1 M. & S. 95.
  (*n*) Jones v. Thorne, 1 B. & C. 715.

(*o*) Roe v. Galliers, 2 T. R. 133. Doe
v. Ingleby, 15 M. & W. 465.
  (*p*) Rex v. Topping, M'Clel. & Y.
544.
  (*q*) Davis v. Eyton, 7 Bing. 154.
  (*r*) Doe v. Carew, 2 Q. B. 317.

of the covenants to be fulfilled, or has withholden any necessary information from the lessee, or done anything to entrap the latter into a forfeiture, the law will not permit the lessor to avail himself of such forfeiture; for that would be permitting him to take advantage of his own wrong. (*s*) When a party is let into possession under an agreement for a future lease, which is to contain certain covenants and a proviso for re-entry in case of the non-performance of those covenants, the tenant holds, as we have before seen, subject to all such of the terms of the intended lease as are applicable to a yearly tenancy; and if, before the lease is granted, the lessee does an act which would have worked a forfeiture of the lease had it been granted, the landlord will have a right to re-enter, and may forthwith recover possession. (*t*) [1]

719. *Effect of re-entry on the lessee's liability on his covenants.*—The forfeiture of the lease does not extinguish the liability of the lessee in respect of breaches of covenant that had accrued at the time of the forfeiture, so that the lessor, by taking advantage of the forfeiture and re-entering, does not deprive himself of his remedies upon the covenants of the lease for any breach of those covenants up to the time of the re-entry. (*u*) If the landlord does not think fit to

---

(*s*) Doe v. Rowe, Ry. & Mood. 346. v. Cumming, 16 C. B., N. S. 421.

(*t*) Doe v. Amey, 12 Ad. & E. 476. (*u*) Hartshorne v. Watson, 5 Sc. 506;
Doe v. Ekins, Ry. & M. 29. Hayne 4 Bing. N. C. 178.

---

[1] But where a lease is made of the entire premises constituting a hotel, and the land surrounding the same, and a covenant on the part of the lessee is inserted that the lessor may retain and occupy a room in the hotel, and board there, this covenant is not a reservation of the room from the operation of the lease, and for a forcible entry into this room the lessee alone can complain. Polack v. Shafer, 46 Cal. 270.

avail himself of the forfeiture, the liability of the lessee
upon the covenants of the lease remains unaffected by
the forfeiture ; but if the landlord brings an action of
ejectment, he can not, in general, sue the lessee in respect of breaches of covenant that have accrued subsequently to the commencement of the action. (*x*)

.720. *Waiver of a forfeiture—Lessor's right of
election.*—The right of entry for forfeiture of a lease
is governed by the general law that, where a man has
got a right to elect to do a thing to the injury of
another, his election, when once made, is final and conclusive, and he can not afterwards alter his determination. If, therefore, a lease has been forfeited, and there
is an election on the part of the landlord to enter and
defeat the lease or not as he pleases, and he by word or
act manifests his intention that the lease shall continue,
he waives the forfeiture, and can not afterwards annul
the lease. If, knowing of a forfeiture, he nevertheless tells his tenant, that he is still tenant, and that he
shall hold him to the covenants and stipulations of his
lease, the election is made, and the landlord can not
afterwards enter for the forfeiture. (*y*)[1]   On the other

(*x*) Jones v. Carter, 15 M. & W. 718.   13, 254 ; 4 B. & S. 337 ; 5 B. & S.
(*y*) Ward v. Day, 33 L. J., Q. B.   359.

[1] And so where a lease contains a covenant on the part of the
lessee not to assign, with a forfeiture of the lease in case of breach,
acceptance of rent by the lessor, accruing after an assignment,
with knowledge thereof, is a waiver of the forfeiture, and the
condition once dispensed with, is dispensed with forever, so that
the assignee can thereafter assign, and can transfer a good title
to the lease. Murray v. Harway, 56 N. Y. 337. And an assignee
of such lease when the forfeiture had been waived as aforesaid,
after the execution of a written contract for the sale and purchase of the lease, agreed with the purchaser to obtain from
the original lessors, or their successors, if possible so to do,
a written assent to the assignment ; such assent could not be
obtained because one of the original lessors had died leaving

hand, if he brings ejectment for the forfeiture, he une-
quivocally declares his election to determine the lease ;
and a subsequent distress, whether a trespass, or justifiable under 8 Anne, c. 14, s. 7, is no waiver of the
forfeiture. (*z*)   Acceptance of rent, or demand of rent,
or the bringing of an action for rent, or distraining for
rent, accruing due after a forfeiture, will be considered
as strong evidence of the lessor's determination to continue the lease and waive the forfeiture, if it appears
that, at the time the lessor received the rent, he had
notice of the breach of the condition. (*a*) [1]   A forfeiture for not repairing may be waived by the receipt of
rent which became due after the right of entry accrued,
but not by the receipt of rent becoming due before
the expiration of a notice to repair.   A forfeiture is
suspended, but not waived, by allowing a tenant further time to repair. (*b*)   A waiver of one forfeiture
does not prevent the lessor from availing himself of
subsequent forfeitures ; (*c*) and a receipt of rent is no
waiver of a continuing breach of a covenant to repair.
(*d*)   Where a breach of covenant has continued

(*z*) Grimwood v. Moss, L. R., 7 C. P. 360 ; 41 L. J., C. P. 239.

(*a*) Bac. Abr. Leases, tit. 2.   Ward v. Day, *supra.*   Denby v. Nicholl, 4 C. B., N. S. 376 ; 27 L. J., C. P. 220. Croft v. Lumley, 27 L. J., Q. B., 321 ; 5 E. & B. 648.   Cotesworth v. Spokes,

30 L. J., C. P. 221. Pellatt v. Boosey, 31 L. J., C. P. 281.

(*b*) Doe v. Meux, 4 B. & C. 606. And see Few v. Perkins, *ante.*

(*c*) Doe v. Bliss, 4 Taunt. 735.   23 & 24 Vict. c. 38, s. 6.

(*d*) Doe v. Jones, 5 Exch. 498 ; 19 L. J., Ex. 405.

infant heirs.   *Held*, that as the agreement was conditional and
the event upon which it was conditioned did not and could
not come to pass, the agreement was not enforcible, and that
the agreement of sale and purchase remained in force.   Id.;
and see Collins v. Hasbrouck, Id. 157.

[1] Hunter v. Osterhoudt, 11 Barb. 33; Jackson v. Brown-
son, 7 Johns. 227; Jackson v. Allen, 3 Cowen, 220; Bleecker
v. Smith, 13 Wend. 530; Garrett v. Scouton, 3 Den. 334; Norman v. Wells, 17 Wend. 136; Clark v. Jones, 1 Den. 516.

upwards of twenty years with full knowledge of it on the part of the lessor, and no attempt has been made to take advantage of it, neither the lessor nor his assignee can avail himself of the breach to work a forfeiture. (*e*)

721. *Relief against forfeiture.—Breach of covenants or conditions respecting insurance or payment of rent.*—The courts will relieve against a forfeiture for non-payment of rent or for breach of a covenant or condition to insure against loss or damage by fire, where no loss or damage by fire has happened, and the breach has been committed without fraud or gross negligence, and there is an insurance on foot in conformity with the covenant to insure. Relief will also be given, in certain cases, in favor of purchasers of leasehold estates with covenants for insurance annexed thereto and broken, where the purchaser has bought without notice. (*f*) But no relief will be granted in the case of forfeiture for the breach of any covenant other than covenants to pay rent or insure, except in the case of accident, mistake, or fraud. (*g*)

722. *Assignment after forfeiture.*—A right of entry which has accrued on a forfeiture can not be assigned ; and the assignee of the reversion, therefore, can not take advantage of any forfeiture incurred before the assignment ; but he is entitled to the benefit of the covenant, and of the condition of re-entry, in respect of any subsequent or continuing breach. (*h*)

723. *Surrender.—Deeds and agreements of surrender.*—We have already seen that a surrender in writing of an interest in any tenements or heredita-

---

(*e*) Gibson v. Doey, 2 H. & N. 615; 27 L. J., Ex. 37.

(*f*) 22 & 23 Vict. c. 35, ss. 4, 6, 8. 23 & 24 Vict. c. 126, ss. 1, 2.

(*g*) Gregory v. Wilson, 9 Hare, 689.

(*h*) Crane v. Batten, 23 Law T. R. 220.

ments, not being a copyhold interest, and not being
an interest which might by law have been created
without writing, is void, unless it is made by deed.
An estate for life or years, which can not be created
without deed, can not be surrendered without deed. (*i*)
But, if the estate may be created, and has been created,
without deed, it may be surrendered without deed. (*k*)
It is said that a surrender under seal immediately
divests the estate out of the surrenderor and vests it in
the surrenderee ; for this is a conveyance at common
law, to the perfection of which no other act is requisite but the bare grant; and though it be true that
every grant is a contract, and there must be an actus
contra actum, or a mutual consent, yet that consent
is implied.   A gift imports a benefit ; and an assump-
sit to take a benefit may well be presumed : and there
is the same reason why a surrender should vest the
estate before notice or agreement, as why a grant of
goods should vest the property. (*l*)   But this must
be understood only of surrenders of particular estates
which are manifestly beneficial to the surrenderee.   If
the benefit is equivocal, there will be no implied assent
or acceptance, and the surrender will be nugatory
without the express concurrence of the surrenderee.
If the tenant holds under a parol demise for a term
not exceeding three years, the term may be surrendered by an agreement in writing, signed by the
surrenderor and the surrenderee, provided it is intended
to have an immediate effect.   There can not be a
surrender to take place in futuro.   If anything is to
be done by either or both of the parties before the

<hr/>

(*i*) Shep. Touch. 397. DEFEAZANCE.   (*k*) Farmer v. Rogers, 2 Wils. 26.
Co. Litt. 338, a. 1 Wms. Saund, 236,   (*l*) Thompson v. Leach, 2 Salk.
a. Perkins v. Perkins, Cro. Eliz. 269.   617.
Lyon v. Reed, 13 M. & W. 310.

II.—25

estate of the termor is to be extinguished, the transaction amounts only to a covenant or agreement to surrender, and there is no actual surrender by the tenant, and no right of entry on the part of the landlord by the mere force of the contract. (*m*) An insufficient notice to quit, therefore, accepted in writing under the landlord's signature, does not of itself amount to a surrender of the term if it is to operate in futuro. (*n*) But an agreement between a landlord and a tenant holding a parol demise from year to year, that the tenancy should be determined, followed by the departure of the tenant, and an entry and taking of possession on the part of the landlord, becomes an actual surrender by act and operation of law. (*o*) Where a dispute arose between a yearly tenant and the landlord, and the tenant said to the landlord, " I shall quit," and the latter said, " You may do so, and I shall be glad to get rid of you," and the tenant then removed her furniture and sent the keys of the house to the landlord, and the latter accepted them and took possession, it was held that there was a surrender of the lease by operation of law. (*p*) But the mere delivery and acceptance of the key, without any entry on the demised premises and taking of possession by the landlord, would be no evidence of a surrender ; (*q*) and an abandonment of the demised premises by the tenant, and an entry of the landlord thereon for the purpose of repairing them, or airing or drying the rooms,

(*m*) Coupland v. Maynard, 12 East. 134. Weddall v. Capes, 1 M. & W. 51. Forquet v. Moore, 7 Exch. 870 ; 22 L. J. Ex. 35.

(*n*) Johnstone v. Huddlestone, 7 D. & R. 419 ; 4 B. & C. 922. Doe v. Milward. 3 M. & W. 332.

(*o*) Dodd v Acklom, 7 Sc. N. R.

423 ; 2 Smith's Leading Cas. 5th ed. 713–719. Furnivall v. Grove, 30 L. J., C. P. 3.

(*p*) Grimman v. Legge, 8 B. & C. 324. Phené v. Popplewell, 12 C. B., N. S. 334 ; 31 L. J., C. P. 235.

(*q*) Cannan v. Hartley, 19 L. J., C P. 323.

or letting them, and not with a view of taking possession as owner, will not of course amount to a surrender. (*r*)

724. *Surrenders by act and operation of law*
"take place where the owner of a particular estate has
been a party to some act, the validity of which he is
afterwards estopped from disputing, and which would
not be valid if his particular estate had continued to
exist.' Thus, if lessee for years accepts a new lease

(*r*) Bessell v. Landsberg, 7 Q. B. 638. Griffith v. Hodges, 1 C. & P. 419.

---

[1] " The rule of law as now settled by the recently adjudicated cases is, that any acts which are equivalent to an agreement on the part of the tenant to abandon, and on the part of
the landlord to resume, possession of the demised premises,
amount to a surrender by operation of law." If a landlord
re-lets the premises, without notice to the tenant that it is on
his account, it dispenses with a formal surrender on the part
of the tenant. Talbot v. Whipple, 14 Allen, 771. After an
original landlord has recognized under-tenants as his tenants
and as the persons responsible to him for the rent, he can not
hold the assignors of such, sub-tenants. Carter v. Hammett,
18 Barb. 608 ; Coleman v. Maberly, 3 T. B. Mon. 220 ; Abell v.
Williams, 3 Daly, 17 ; Jackson v. Gardner, 8 Johns. 394.
Where a landlord, on beng told by his tenant that the premises
are not fit to live in, and that he shall quit them, and pays
the rent up to that time, and the landlord notifies him that he
will re-let the premises on his (the tenant's) account, and does
find another tenant, from whom he receives rent, *held*, no evidence of a surrender; Bloomer v. Merrill, 29 How. 250;
Bloomer v. Merrill, 1 Daly, 485 ; neither is evidence of an
oral declaration by the landlord, that he will release the tenant from a further liability for rent. Goelet v. Ross, 15 Abb.
Pr. 251. But evidence that a tenant informed the landlord
that he should leave the premises on a certain day, and asked
permission to leave certain of his property upon the premises
leased, *held*, that evidence of such permission by the landlord
is evidence from which a surrender might be presumed;
Stantly v. Koehler, 1 Hilt. 354; and the mere acceptance by
the landlord of the key of the demised premises, from a tenant who quits possession during the term, is not an accept-

from his lessor, he is estopped from saying that his lessor had not power to make the new lease; and, as the lessor could not do this until the prior lease had been surrendered, the law says that the acceptance of such new lease is of itself a surrender of the former lease. So, if there be tenant for life, remainder to another in fee, and the remainder-man comes on the land and makes a feoffment to the tenant for life who accepts livery thereon, the tenant for life is thereby estopped from disputing the seisin in fee of the re- mainderman; and so the law says that such accept- ance of livery amounts to a surrender of his life estate. Again, if tenant for years accepts from his lessor a grant of a rent issuing out of the land, and payable during the term, he is thereby estopped from disput- ing his lessor's right to grant the rent; and, as this could not be done during his term, therefore he is deemed in law to have surrendered his term to the lessor. The acts in pais which bind parties by way of estoppel are all acts which anciently were, and in con- templation of law have always continued to be, acts of notoriety not less formal and solemn than the exe- cution of a deed, such as livery, entry, acceptance of an estate, and the•like. Whether a party had or had not concurred in an act of this sort was deemed a matter which there could be no difficulty in ascertain- ing; and then the legal consequences followed." (*s*) But, if the original lease is under seal, the acceptance by the lessee of a mere parol demise from the lessor will not amount to a surrender of such original lease; (*t*)

(*s*) Lyon v. Reid, 13 M. & W. 306, 　　(*t*) Shep. Touch. 397.
2 Smith's Lead. Cas. 5th ed. 714–720.

ance of the surrender, where the landlord states that he re- ceives the key but not the premises. Townsend v. Albers, 3 E. D. Smith, 560.

and, if the new lease is wholly or partially invalid, and does not pass an interest according to the contract and the intention of the parties, it will not operate as a surrender of the former lease. (*u*) A mere agreement for an increased rent will not have the effect of creating a new tenancy. (*v*)

725. *Substitution of a new tenant in the place of the original tenant.*—When there is an open and notorious shifting of the actual possession of corporeal property, in execution of an agreement between the lessor and lessee and a third party, to substitute such third party as the lessee in the place of the original lessee, there is a surrender by operation of law of such original lease. (*y*)[1] But a mere agreement for the substitution of a new tenant, not followed up by any actual change of possession, or a mere change of possession unaccompanied by an agreement of substitution, does not amount to a surrender. (*z*) It must be

(*u*) Doe v. Poole, 11 Q. B. 713 ; 17 L. J., Q. B. 143. Doe v. Courtney, ib. 702, 151.

(*v*) Geeckie v. Monk, 1 C. & K. 307. Doe v. Geeckie, 5 Q. B. 841. Crowley v. Vitty, 7 Exch. 319.

(*y*) Davison v. Gent, 1 H. & N. 744 ; 26 L. J., Ex. 122. Nickells or Nicholls v. Atherstone, 10 Q. B. 944 ; 16 L. J., Q. B. 371. Reeve v. Bird, 1 C. M. & R. 31. Walls v. Atcheson, 11 Moore, 379. Woodcock v. Nuth, 1 M. & Sc. 317. Thomas v. Cook, 2 B. & Ald. 120.

(*z*) Taylor v. Chapman, Peake's Add. Cas. 19. Cocking v. Ward, 1 C. B. 868. Kelley v. Webster, 12 C. B. 283 ; 21 L. J., C. P. 163.

[1] A lessor who has consented to a change of tenancy and of occupation, and received rent from the new tenant as an original and not as a sub-tenant, can not afterwards hold his original tenant for rent accruing during the new tenant's occupation. Smith v. Niven, 2 Barb. 180. And where, after a lessee had underlet the whole of the demised premises, by two written sub-leases, the landlord called on the under-tenants, produced the sub-leases, demanded of them the rent, forbade their paying any more rent to the original lessee, and afterwards collected all rent of the sub-tenants, *held*, that there was a surrender of the original lease by operation of law. Bailey v. Delaplaine, 1 Sandf. 5.

shown that the incoming tenant has been expressly
received and accepted by the landlord as his lessee, in
the place and stead of the original lessee, by the
mutual agreement of all parties; (*a*) for the mere
change of the possession is no evidence of the grant
and acceptance of a new lease, the prima facie presumption being that the incoming tenant has entered
and taken possession as the under-tenant or assignee
of the original lessee. (*b*)   The mere circumstance of
the landlord's having accepted rent from an assignee
or under-tenant in possession of the demised premises
is no evidence of an acceptance of such assignee or
under-tenant as his lessee in the place of the original
lessee, the prima facie presumption being that the rent
was paid by the latter as the agent of the original
lessee and on his behalf. (*c*) '

726. *Surrender and acceptance of surrender by
joint-tenants.*—Every act done by one joint-tenant
which is for the benefit of his companions will bind
them ; but those acts which prejudice his companions
in estate will not bind them ; and, if the benefit be
doubtful, two joint-tenants have no right to elect for
the third.   A surrender, therefore, or acceptance of a
surrender, by one of the several joint-tenants, will not,
in general, bind the others. (*d*)   If, however, one of
two joint-lessors lies by and allows the other to act
for him, and acquiesces in the acts of his co-owner, and

(*a*) Graham v. Whichelo, 1 Cr. &
M. 194.   M'Donnell v. Pope, 9 Hare,
707.   Matthews v. Sawell, 2 Moore,
262 ; 8 Taunt. 270.

(*b*) Doe v. Williams, 9 D. & R. 30 ;
6 B. & C. 41.

(*c*) Copeland v. Gubbins, 1 Stark.
96.   Doe v. Wood, 15 L. J., Ex. 41.

(*d*) Right v. Cuthell, 5 East, 498.

' The surrender, even where an agreement is made that
the lessee shall remain liable for the rent, puts an end to
the relation of landlord and tenant.   Bain v. Clark, 10 Johns.
424 ; Shepard v. Merrill, 2 Johns. Ch. 276.

intrusts the whole management of the business in which they are jointly interested to him, he will be bound by his acts. (*e*)

727. *Non-extinguishment by surrender of derivative estates.*—If a lessee from year to year grants an underlease of part of the premises demised to him, and then surrenders his term, the surrender will not destroy the estate and interest of the under-lessee, if the latter has not concurred in and been a party to the surrender. (*f*)

728. *Effect of the surrender on existing breaches of covenant.*—The mere surrender of the lease does not relieve the lessee from his liability in respect of breaches of covenant that have accrued prior to the surrender. The lessor, therefore, after a surrender, remains a specialty creditor for all arrears of rent, which became due before the surrender, upon the lessee's covenants for the payment of rent. (*g*)[1]

729. *Notice to quit, when necessary.*—"When a lease is determinable on a certain event, or at a particular period, no notice to quit is necessary, because both parties are equally apprised of the determination of the term." (*h*)   If, therefore, a lease is granted for a term of years, or for one year only, no notice to quit is necessary at the end of the term; (*i*) but, if the

---

(*e*) Dodd v. Acklom, 7 Sc. N. R. 415 ; 6 M. & Gr. 672.

(*f*) Co. Litt. 338, b.   4 Geo. 2, c. 28, s. 6.   Pleasant v. Benson, 14 East, 237.   Cousins v. Phillips, 3 H. & C. 892 ; 35 L. J., Ex. 84.

(*g*) Attorney-General v. Cox, 3 H. L. C. 240.

(*h*) Right v. Darby, 1 T. R. 162 ; ib. 54.

(*i*) Cobb v. Stokes, 8 East, 358.

[1] And a surrender of the remainder of a term will not discharge the lessee from payment of the rent already due; Sperry v. Miller, 8 N. Y. 336; Curtis v. Miller, 17 Barb. 477; though payable in advance; Learned v. Ryder, 61 Barb. 552; S. C., 5 Lans. 539.

tenancy is from year to year, a half year's notice must
be given on either side in order to determine the tenancy, and this notice may be given in the first as well
as in any subsequent year of the tenancy. (*k*) If a
man holds under an agreement for a lease, or under a
lease void by reason of its not having been made by
deed, for the full term intended to have been granted,
an ejectment may be brought against him at the expiration of such term without any notice to quit. (*l*)
In the case of a tenancy at will no notice to quit is
necessary ; but there must be a formal demand of
possession, or notice of the determination of the will,
on the part of the landlord, before any action of ejectment can be brought. (*m*) The tenant at will, too, in
order to discharge himself from his liability for rent,
or for a reasonable compensation for the use and enjoyment of the demised premises, must give notice to
the landlord of the fact of his abandonment of the
possession, and of his election to rescind the contract
and put an end to the tenancy. If the occupation is
the occupation of a servant or agent holding possession of the premises on account and on behalf of his
master or principal, the possession of the occupier is
the possession of the owner himself, and the latter
may at any time remove the tenant and resume possession of the property without any notice to quit. (*n*)
If the tenancy and possession are adverse, or if the
occupier holds over after the expiration of a lease, or
after a forfeiture, or after an agreement for a lease or a

(*k*) Doe v. Smaridge, 7 Q. B. 959.
Doe v. Nainby, 16 L. J., Q. B. 303.
Doe v. Geekie, 5 Q. B. 841.

(*l*) Doe v. Stratton, 1 M. & P. 187.
Tress v. Savage, 4 E. & B. 36 ; 23 L.
J., Q. B. 339.

(*m*) Right v. Beard, 13 East, 210.

Denn v. Rawlins, 10 East, 261. Doe
v. Cox, 11 Q. B. 122 ; 17 L. J., Q. B.
3.

(*n*) Doe v. Derry, 9 C. & P. 494.
Mayhew v. Suttle, 4 E. & B. 347 ; 24
L. J., Q. B. 54. White v. Bailey, 30
L. J., C. P. 253.

contract of sale has gone off and been abandoned, or after the tenancy has been determined by a dissolution of partnership, and continues in possession without the permission and against the will of the owner, no notice to quit is necessary; but the owner may at once proceed against the wrong-doer by action of ejectment for the recovery of the demised premises, or he may enter and take possession if the tenant leaves the demised premises vacant. (*o*)

If the lessor is only tenant at will, or has made a prior lease of the lands, or mortgaged them so as to give the mortgagee a right of entry, and to deprive himself of the power of granting a lease for the term specified, the tenant may be turned out without any previous notice to quit from the party who has title. (*p*)   But if the lessor at the time of making of the lease had full right and title to grant the demised premises to the lessee for the term, any subsequent grant, mortgage, sale, or lease, can not affect the tenant's right of possession, or in any way dispense with the ordinary notice to quit.[1]

(*o*) Doe v. Sayer, 3 Campb. 8.   Bluck, 8 C. & P. 464,
Doe v. Miles, 1 Stark. 181.   Doe v.   (*p*) Keech v. Hall, 1 Doug. 21.

[1] But there need be no notice to quit where the parties have agreed previously as to the date upon which the lease is to determine.   Allen v. Jacques, 21 Wend. 628; People v. Schackno, 48 Barb. 551; Gibbons v. Dayton, 4 Hun. 451; Rowan v. Lytle, 11 Wend. 619; Livingston v. Tanner, 14 N. Y. 64; Torrey v. Torrey, Id. 430. A tenant under a parol agreement for a lease, rent to be paid monthly, who refuses to accept the lease, becomes a common-law tenant at will or by sufferance, and is liable to be ejected immediately; but if the parol agreement was for a term exceeding one year, and, therefore, void by the statute, the tenancy after the acceptance of rent is from month to month, and the tenant is entitled to a month's notice.   Anderson v. Prindle, 23 Wend. 616. Where a tenant is in possession under a parol agreement void by

730. *How the notice may be given, and by whom.*—
A notice to quit may be given orally by the lessor, or
by his agent, (*q*) unless there has been an express
agreement or stipulation for a notice in writing. (*r*) [1]
A mere receiver of rents has no implied authority to
give a notice to quit; but an agent or receiver who is
entrusted with the general management of landed
property, and has a general authority to let lands from

(*q*) Timmins v. Rawlinson, 3 Bur.   (*r*) Legg v. Benion, Willes, 43.
1603. Doe v. Crick, 5 Esp. 196.

the statute of frauds, and has occupied for a year, paying the
rent monthly, this creates a tenancy from month to month
which can only be terminated by a month's notice to quit,
expiring with the end of some month reckoning from the
beginning of the tenancy. People v. Darling, 47 N. Y. 666;
Taggard v. Roosevelt, 2 E. D. Smith, 105.

[1] But where the conventional relation of landlord and tenant does not exist, the common law right of entry without
notice obtains, and notice to quit is not necessary. People v.
Fields, 1 Lans. 238; and see Jackson v. Wilsey, 9 Johns.
267; Jackson v. Aldrich, 13 Id. 106; Ives v. Ives, Id. 235;
No notice of any sort is necessary in case of a tenancy
at sufferance. Livingston v. Tanner, 14 N. Y. 64. Nor
in the case of a lease determinable upon any certain
event which is known equally by both parties. Murray v.
Armstrong, 11 Miss. 209; Hamit v. Lawrence, 2 A. K. Marsh,
366; Bedford v. McElherron, 2 Serg. & R. 49; Whitney v.
Gordon, 1 Cush. 266; Moshier v. Reding, 3 Fairf. 478; but
where it is uncertain, or from year to year, the notice must be
given. McGee v. Gibson, 1 B. Mon. 105; Goddard v. Railroad Co., 2 Rich. 346; Whitney v. Gordon, 1 Cush. 266; Murray v. Armstrong, 11 Miss. 209; Logan v. Heron, 4 Serg. &
R. 459; Clapp v. Paine, 6 Shep. 264; Dowell v. Johnson, 7
Pick. 263; Allen v. Jaquish, 21 Wend. 268; or if either party
change his mind under a tacit lease. Baker v. Adams, 5 Cush.
99. But notice to quit would not be necessary for a purchaser
at a sale by virtue of a surrogate's order for the payment of
debts, to one in possession under the testator's heirs. Jackson v. Robinson, 4 Wend. 436. It is sufficient if the notice
specify the end of the term, and make mention of no particular day.   v.   , 48 Barb. 551.

year to year, has also authority to determine such
tenancies by a notice to quit. (*s*)   And he may give
the notice in his own name, as it is not necessary that
his agency and the authority of his principals should
appear on the face of the document. (*t*)   The steward
of a corporation who is intrusted with the letting of
the corporate estates, may give a notice to quit, and
needs no authority under seal from the corporation
for the purpose. (*u*)   If there are several joint lessors
or joint owners of the property, a notice to quit, given
or signed by one or more of them on behalf of all, is
sufficient; (*v*) and the subsequent assent of such
joint-owners to a notice previously given by one or
more of them, on behalf of all, is equivalent to a precedent authority. (*y*)   But, if it is expressly provided
by the agreement of the parties that a written notice
shall be given by all of them, under their respective
hands, the notice must be signed by all, and a ratification given afterwards will not do. (*z*)   The notice
may also be given by an agent on their behalf; but
such notice, in order to be valid and effectual, must
be given in the names of the joint owners, the principals, and not in the name of the agent, unless the
agent has a general authority to let their lands; (*a*)
and the agent ought to have authority to give the
notice at the time it begins to operate ; for, if the
tenant could not safely have acted upon the notice at
the time it was given, no subsequent recognition of it
by the landlord will make it valid. (*b*)[1]   If one or more

(*s*) Doe v. Mizem, 2 M. & Rob. 56.   Alford v. Vickery, 1 Car & M. 280.

(*t*) Jones v. Phipps, L. R., 3 Q. B.   (*y*) Abbott, C. J., 3 B. & Ald. 692.
567 ; 37 L. J,, Q. B. 198.   (*z*) Right v. Cuthell, 5 East, 497.

(*u*) Roe v. Pierce, 2 Campb. 96.   (*a*) Jones v. Phipps, *supra*.

(*v*) Doe v. Hulme, 2 M. & R. 433 ;   (*b*) Doe v. Walters, 10 B. & C. 626 ;
Doe v. Summerset, 1 B. & Ad. 135.   5 M. & R. 357.   Doe v. Goldwin, 2

[1] White v. Bailey, 14 Conn. 271.

of several joint owners dissent from the notice, such of them as have joined in giving the notice to quit are entitled to enter into and hold possession of the demised premises, and receive the rents and profits of the land, jointly with the tenant or lessee of the others who have refused to join in such notice. (*c*)

731. *Form and effect of the notice—Alternative and peremptory notices.*—A notice to quit "all the property you hold of me," addressed to the tenant, is a sufficient description of the demised premises; and any general description applicable to the whole of the property will suffice. (*d*) But a landlord can not give a notice to quit which is intended to apply to a part only of premises which have been demised together at one entire rent. (*e*) A mere misdescription, however, of the premises comprised in the notice to quit, or a mistake in the Christian name of the tenant to whom such notice is addressed, does not invalidate the notice, provided the tenant has not been misled or prejudiced by such misdescription or mistake.[1] If the notice applies to a year that is past, but was clearly intended to apply to the coming year, and the tenant must have known what time was meant, he is bound by the notice. (*f*) If the notice is not a peremptory notice to quit, but is drawn up in the alternative, and seems to have been intended either to put an end to the lease or obtain an increased rent, the tenant may elect to remain in possession, paying an increased

Q. B. 146. Goodtitle v. Woodward, 3 B. & Ald. 689.

(*c*) Doe v. Caplin, 3 Taunt. 120.

(*d*) Doe v. Church, 3 Campb. 71.

(*e*) Doe v. Archer, 14 East, 245.

(*f*) Doe v. Roe, 4 Esp. 185; Doe v. Wilkinson, 12 Ad. & E. 743; 4 P. & D. 323. Doe v. Spiller, 6 Esp. 70. Doe v. Knightley, 7 T. R. 63.

[1] And if the tenant keep the notice in his possession, he waives the objection, and is bound by the notice. Doe v. Spiller, 6 Esp. 70.

rent; and, such an option having been accorded to him, he can not, if he chooses to occupy, be treated as a trespasser and wrongdoer and turned out of possession. If, however, the notice is a notice to quit or pay double the annual value under the statutes imposing penalties on tenants for holding over after a notice to quit, the alternative notice so given will be construed as a peremptory notice to quit, accompanied by a warning to the tenant of the penal consequences of disobedience, and not as an offer on the part of the landlord of a new bargain and a new lease at an increased rent. (*g*) [1]

732. *Length of the notice.*—We have already seen that, in the case of a tenancy from year to year, six calendar months' notice to quit is required to be given prior to the expiration of the current year of hiring, in order to determine the tenancy between the parties. (*h*) But whenever the tenancy commences and ends at any of the usual feasts, the customary half year intervening between two half-yearly feasts constitutes a sufficient half-year's notice, although the intermediate time be not exactly six calendar months. (*i*)

733. *Of the time of quitting specified in the notice.*—If the time at which the tenant is to quit is

(*g*) Doe v. Jackson, 1 Doug. 175.

(*h*) *Ante.* But see Rogers v. Kingston-upon-Hull Dock Company, 34 L. J., Ch. 165.

(*i*) Howard v. Wemsley, 6 Esp. 53 ; 4 ib. 199. Rogers v. Hull Dock Company, 34 L. J., Ch. 165.

[1] See the statute as to double rent in New York. 1 Edm. R. S., N. Y. 697, § 10 ; Hall v. Ballentine, 7 Johns. 536. Under similar statutes it has been held that if the tenant be notified by the lessor's assignee that if he hold over, he must pay an increased rent, he will be held to have assented thereto by his merely continuing to occupy after his lease expired. Despart v. Walbridge, 15 N. Y. 374; see also Hunt v. Bailey, 39 Mo. 257; Adriance v. Hatkemeyer, Id. 134; Dorril v. Stephens. 4 McCord, 59 ; McKinney v. Peck, 28 Ill. 174.

specified in the notice, care must be taken to make such time correspond with the termination of the term of hiring, unless the notice is given in the exercise of a power to determine the tenancy expressly reserved in the lease or agreement; (*k*) for, if the term expires at one period, and the notice is to quit at another, such notice is bad, and the lessor can not safely act upon it. (*l*)   If a tenant holds possession of a house as a tenant from year to year, under an agreement to quit at a quarter's notice, the tenant can not be expelled at the expiration of any quarter that the lessor may choose to select, but the notice must be a quarter's notice to quit at the expiration of the current year. (*m*)   If the hiring is from half-year to half-year, determinable by six month's notice to quit, the tenancy may be determined by notice at the expiration of any half-year. (*n*)   If it is a quarterly, a monthly, or a weekly hiring, the notice must be a notice to quit at the expiration of the current quarter, month, or week; if it breaks into the middle of the quarter, month, or week, it is not a good notice to quit.   If the hiring is from month to month, and the rent is made payable weekly, a notice to quit at the expiration of the current month must be given, and not a notice expiring at any one of the weeks without reference to the termination of the month.   The length of the notice, however, may be varied by local custom and usage, and by the agreement of the parties.   When the hiring is for one single quarter, month, or week, no notice at all is requisite. (*o*)   The term will, in the absence of

(*k*) Bridges v. Potts, 17 C. B., N. S. 314 ; 33 L. J., C. P. 338.

(*l*) Doe v. Lea, 11 East, 312.

(*m*) Doe v. Donovan, 1 Taunt. 555.

(*n*) Doe v. Grafton, 21 L. J., Q. B. 276.

(*o*) Doe v. Bayley, 5 C. & P. 67. Doe v. Raffan, 6 Esp. 4. Doe v. Hazell, 1 Esp. 94.   Kemp v. Derrett, 3 Campb. 511.   Huffell v. Armitstead, 7 C. & P. 56.

an express agreement to the contrary, be taken to commence at the time of the tenant's entering and taking possession of the demised premises.

A notice " to quit at the end of the first year of your tenancy, which expires half a year after the date of this notice," will be sufficient, and so also will a notice " to quit at the expiration of the current year of your tenancy," provided such notice was given half a year prior to the expiration of the current year of hiring. (*p*) Sometimes the notice is given in the alternative, in order to hit one of two periods on which the term is known to end, and it has been held that such a notice is a perfectly good notice, and possesses all the certainty that is reasonably requisite for the information of the tenant. (*q*)   A notice to a weekly tenant whose tenancy commenced on Wednesday, to quit on Friday, provided his tenancy commenced on Friday, or otherwise at the end of his tenancy next after one week from the date thereof, was held to be a good notice to determine the tenancy at the expira- of a week from the subsequent Wednesday. (*r*) [1]

734. *Of the application of the notice to the current term of hiring.*—If the notice is made to apply to the current term of hiring, and it is given too near the end of the current term to be a good notice for

---

(*p*) Doe v. Butler, 2 Esp. 589.   (*r*) Doe v. Scott, 4 Moo. & P. 20.
(*q*) Doe v. Wrightman, 4 Esp. 6.

---

[1] If the lease expires at one time and the notice to quit specifies another, it is bad; see Hanchet v. Whitney, 1 Vt. 315 ; Coffin v. Lunt, 2 Pick. 70 ; Morehead v. Watkyns, 5 B. Mon. 228 ; Den v. Drake, 2 Greenl. 523.   And the notice must be absolute; a notice demanding possession and stating that if not yielded upon a certain day, rent at a certain rent will be demanded, is not a good notice.   Ayres v. Draper, 11 Miss. 548.   And see Burns v. Bryant, 3 N. Y. 453.

that term, it will not apply to the next term of holding, as that is not the current term, and a fresh notice
to quit, therefore, must be given. (s)   The notice is
always understood to apply to the year in which it is
given, whether it expressly refers to the "current year"
or not ; and it will not operate as a notice to quit for
the succeeding year, unless it appears plainly to have
been the intention of the lessor that the notice, if invalid for the first year, should apply to the next year
of holding. (t)   Where a notice dated the 27th, and
served on the 28th, of September, required a tenant to
quit "at Lady Day next, or at the end of your current
year," and it appeared that the then current year of
hiring ended on Michaelmas Day (the 29th of September), two days after the day of the date, and one
day after the service of the notice to quit, it was held
that it could not be presumed that the notice was intended to apply to the year in which it was given, and
of which two days only remained, but that it must be
taken to apply to the next year. (u)   So, where the
term of hiring commenced and ended on the 2nd of
February, and the lessor, on the 22nd of October, 1833,
three months and ten days only before the expiration
of the year, gave the tenant notice to quit " at the expiration of half a year from the delivery of this notice
or at such other time as your present year's holding
shall expire after the expiration of half a year from the
delivery of this notice," it was held that the notice,
though bad for February, 1834, the succeeding February, was a good notice for February, 1835. (v)

735.   *The commencement of the current year of the
tenancy* is generally regulated by the commencement

(s) Doe v. Morphett, 7 Q. B. 577 ;   (u) Doe v. Culliford, 4 D. & R.
14 L. J., Q. B. 345.   248.

(t) Mills v. Goff, 14 M. & W. 75.   (v) Doe v. Smith, 5 Ad. & E. 353.

of the original holding. Where premises were demised by an agreement dated the " 13th of August, 1838," for the term of " one year and six months certain," at a yearly rent payable quarterly, " three calendar months' notice to be given on either side previous to the termination of the tenancy," and the tenant entered and held possession beyond the year and six months, and on the 7th of May, 1840, the lessor gave the tenant notice to quit on the 13th of August next, the notice was held to be good, as the year of hiring was to be calculated from that day, and not from the termination of the year and six months. (*y*)[1] And where a tenant

(*y*) Doe v. Dobell, 1 Q. B. 806. Doe v. Samuel, 5 Esp. 173.

[1] See Cretien v. Doney, 1 N. Y. 419, where A executed a lease for one year to B, which contained the following clause " B to have the privilege to the premises for one year, one month, and twenty days longer," but if he leaves he is to give four months' notice before the expiration of this lease. *Held*, that such lease created a term of two years, one month, and twenty days, in case no four months' notice was given prior to the expiration of the first year, and local custom may determine whether a lease from May 1, in one year, to May 1, in the succeeding year, includes or excludes the first days. Wilcox v. Woods, 9 Wend. 345. A lease for years to end on May 1, expires at noon of that day, and a lease from a day named to May 1, expires on midnight on April 30. The People ex rel. Elston v. Robinson, 39 Barb. 9. Under a lease for a specified term at the tenant's election, for a further term, at an increased rent, the election of the lessee to hold for the additional term at the increased rent, may be inferred from his continuing to occupy the premises and paying rent for two quarters at the increased rate, without proof of any formal election or notice to the lessor at the time of the expiration of the first term. The provision in the lease is not a mere covenant of the plaintiff for renewal; no formal renewal was contemplated by the parties. The agreement itself is, as to the additional term, a lease de futuro, requiring only the lapse of the preceding term and the election of the defendant to become a lease in presenti; all that is necessary to its validity is the fact of election. Kramer v. Cook, 7 Gray, 550.

entered into possession, under an agreement for a lease
for a term of five years and a half, and the lease was
never granted, but the tenant continued to occupy,
and when the five years and a half were nearly expired,
negotiations were entered into for a further lease at
an increased rent, to commence on the expiration of
the term of five years and a half, and this second lease
was never executed, but the defendant continued in
the occupation of the premises, paying the increased
rent, it was held that the current year of the tenancy
must be calculated from the original entry of the tenant upon the premises. (*z*)   Where, on the other hand,
a lessee of a term granted an under-lease for fourteen
years and a half from the 25th of December, and the
term consequently expired on the 24th of June, and
the under-lessee continued in possession, paying rent, it
was held that the subsequent tenancy commenced
from the termination of the preceding under-lease, and
that a notice given on the 24th of December, to quit
on the 24th of June, was a valid notice. (*a*)

736. *Calculation of the current year from one of
the usual feast days.*—The term of hiring is generally,
by the express or implied agreement of the parties,
calculated from some one or other of the quarterly
feasts ; and, if the tenant enters in the middle of a
customary quarter, and afterwards pays his rent for that
half-quarter, and continues then to pay from the commencement of a succeeding quarter, he is not a tenant
from the time of his coming in, but from the succeeding quarter-day. (*b*)   But, if he pays his rent at the
end of the quarter or half year from the time of his

(*z*) Berrey v. Lindley, 4 Sc. N. R.   H. & N. 594 ; 30 L. J., Ex. 173.
61 ; 3 M. & Gr. 498.   (*b*) Doe v. Johnson, 6 Esp. 10. Doe
   (*a*) Doe v. Lines, 111 Q. B. 402 ; 17   v. Stapleton, 3 C. & P. 275.
L. J., Q. B. 105.   Walker v. Gode, 6

coming in, the tenancy will commence from the day of his entry. (*c*)   If the notice be given to quit at Michaelmas generally, it is good for either Old or New Michaelmas.   Prima facie it would be for New Michaelmas ; but, if the holding was from Old Michaelmas, this notice would do for that also. (*d*)   Where a notice was given on the 27th of September "to quit at the expiration of the term for which you hold," evidence was permitted to be given of a general custom of the country to let from Lady Day, and of the fact of the rent being due at Michaelmas and Lady Day, and it was left to the jury to presume, in the absence of evidence to the contrary, that the tenancy, like other tenancies in that part of the country, was a tenancy from Lady Day to Lady Day. (*e*)   It has been held that, since the existence of the new style sanctioned by act of Parliament, a lease by deed of lands "to be holden from the feast of St. Michael" must be taken to mean New Michaelmas, and that extrinsic evidence is not admissible to show that it meant a holding from Old Michaelmas. (*f*)   But, although the oral expressions and agreements of the parties are inadmissible to alter or contradict the written contract, yet all the surrounding circumstances may be regarded ; and if it can be shown that the rent has always been paid at Old Michaelmas, or that by the custom of the country lands are always let at Old Michaelmas, the holding would be deemed to be from the latter period. (*g*)

737. *Admissions by the tenant of the commence-*

(*c*) Doe v. Matthews, 11 C. B. 675.

(*d*) Doe v. Perrin, 9 C. & P. 468. Doe v. Vince, 2 Campb. 256.

(*e*) Doe v. Lamb, Adam's Eject. 4th ed. 272.

(*f*) Doe v. Lea, 11 East, 312.

Smith v. Walton, 1 M. & Sc. 382 ; 8 Bing. 235.

(*g*) Furley v. Wood, 1 Esp. 198. Doe v. Benson, 4 B. & Ald. 589. Den v. Hopkinson, 3 D. & R. 507.

ment of the term.—The mere service upon the tenant of a notice to quit at a particular time is not prima facie evidence of the termination of the term at the time mentioned in such notice. (*h*) But, if the tenant is expressly told that he must leave after the expiration of six months, or if a written notice is served personally on the lessee, and the latter reads it, and makes no objection to it, this is prima facie evidence to go to a jury that the time of quitting is correctly stated in the notice. If he can not read, or does not read, the notice in the presence of the person who serves it upon him, it must go for nothing. (*i*) An admission by the tenant of a holding corresponding with the time mentioned in the notice may be rebutted by direct evidence of a different holding. (*k*) If the period of the commencement of the term is uncertain, and the lessor applies to the lessee to ascertain the time of the commencement of his lease, the lessee is bound by the information he gives, and can not be permitted afterwards to set up a different holding for the purpose of defeating proceedings that have been taken by the landlord upon the faith of such statement. (*l*)

738. *Different periods of entry.*—When the demised premises are entered upon at different periods, the notice to quit ought to refer to the time of tenant's entry upon and holding of the principal subject-matter of the demise. Thus, if buildings and land are let together, to be entered upon at different times, or holden from different periods, and the buildings constitute the principal subject-matter of demise, and the

---

(*h*) Doe v. Calvert, 2 Campb. 388.

(*i*) Thomas v. Thomas, 2 Campb. 647. Doe v. Forster, 13 East, 405. Doe v. Wombwell, 2 Campb. 559.

(*k*) Oakapple v. Copous, 4 T. R. 361. Brown v. Burtinshaw, 7 D. & R. 610.

(*l*) Doe v. Lambly, 2 Esp. 635.

land is merely accessorial thereto, the notice to quit should refer to the tenant's entry upon and holding of the buildings, and not the land ; and it is a question of fact which is the principal and which the accessorial subject of demise. (*m*) Though part of a farm is to be entered upon and quitted at different periods, *i. e.*, the pasture at Old Lady Day, the arable land at Old Candlemas, and the meadow at Old May Day, yet that is a letting from Lady Day to Lady Day ; for it is no more than the custom of most counties would have directed without any special words for that purpose in any taking from Old Lady Day, viz., that the arable land shall be entered upon at Candlemas to prepare it for the Lent corn, and the meadows not till May Day, when in the northern counties they are usually heyned for hay. (*n*)

Where a tenant entered into possession of a farm, under an agreement " to enter on the tillage land at Candlemas, and on the house and all other the premises on Lady Day following, and to quit the farm according to the times of entry as aforesaid," and the rent was reserved at Michaelmas and Lady Day, it was held that a notice to quit, delivered half a year before Lady Day, but less than half a year before Candlemas, was good, the taking being in substance from Lady Day, with a privilege for the incoming tenant to enter on the arable land at Candlemas for the sake of ploughing, &c. (*o*)   And, where the lessee of a dwelling-house, buildings, and bleaching manufacturies, pasture and meadow land, entered into possession under an agreement for a lease, by which it was stipulated that the term of hiring should com-

---

(*m*) Doe v. Howard, 11 East, 498. Doe v. Hughes, 7 M. & W. 141. Doe v. Rhodes, 11 M. & W. 600.

(*n*) Doe v. Snowdon, 2 W. Bl. 1224.

(*o*) Doe v. Spence, 6 East, 120.

mence, as to the meadow ground from the 25th of December last, as to the pasture from the 25th of March next, and as to the houses, out-houses, and other buildings, and all the rest of the premises from the 1st of May, and the first half-year's rent was made payable on the day of Pentecost, and the other at Martinmas, it was held that, the substantial subject of demise being the house and buildings for the purpose of the manufacture, the time limited for taking possession thereof was the substantial time of entry, to which a notice to quit ought to refer, and not the 25th of December, the time limited for the taking possession of the meadow land, which was merely auxiliary to the principal subject of demise. (*p*)

739. *Service of notice to quit.*—If the notice to quit is served upon the actual occupiers of the demised premises, proof of such service is sufficient to sustain an action of ejectment. (*q*)   Where the lessee puts another into possession or occupation of the demised premises, the party so let into possession is presumed to be the assignee of the lessee, and a notice to quit served upon such occupier will determine the term and sustain an ejectment against the lessee. Thus, where the tenant went away leaving his son-in-law in possession, and the lessor gave the son-in-law notice to quit and brought ejectment, and the lessee came forward to defend the possession, saying that he had received no notice, and that his term was not determined, it was held that the notice was sufficient. (*r*) If the party in occupation of the house is the mere servant of the lessee, the notice should be a notice to the lessee to quit, and not a notice to the servant. (*s*)

(*p*) Doe v. Watkins, 7 East, 556.

(*q*) Roe v. Street, 2 Ad. & E. 331.

(*r*) Doe v. Williams, 6 B. & C. 41 ; 9 D. & R. 31.

(*s*) Doe v. Woodman, 8 East, 228.

A delivery of the notice to the wife or servant of the lessee, at the dwelling-house of the latter, is a sufficient service. (*t*)   But a servant to whom it is delivered should be expressly told that it is a notice to quit, and should be requested, either orally, or by means of a written or printed address or direction, to deliver it to the tenant. (*u*)   If there is a personal service of the notice upon the tenant himself, no written direction or address upon the notice is necessary; (*v*) and, if the notice is directed to the tenant by a wrong Christian name and he neglects to repudiate it or send it back, he is deemed to have waived the misdirection and is bound by such notice. (*y*)   If two or more persons hold possession of the demised premises as joint-tenants or tenants-in common, notice to one of them is sufficient notice to all to determine the tenancy (*z*)

740. *Service of notice through the post-office.*— If a notice to quit properly addressed to the landlord or his authorized agent has been put into the post-office, and is delivered within the usual business hours, on the 25th of March, that will be a good notice for the 29th of December following, although the landlord does not actually receive it until the 26th. (*a*)

741. *Acceptance of informal notice—Proof of notice.*—If a tenant gives his landlord an insufficient notice to quit, and the landlord at first assents, b t ultimately refuses to accept the notice, and the tena t quits according to his notice, the tenancy is not de-

(*t*) Jones v. Marsh, 4 T. R. 464. Doe v. Dunbar, 1 M. & M. 11. Alford v. Vickery, 1 Car. & M. 283. Tanham v. Nicholson. L. R., 5 H. L. C. 561.

(*u*) Doe v. Lucas, 5 Esp. 152. Smith

v. Clark, 9 Dowl. 202.

(*v*) Doe v. Wrightman, 4 Esp. 5.

(*y*) Doe v. Spiller, 6 Esp. 70.

(*z*) Doe v. Crick, 5 Esp. 196.

(*a*) Papillon v. Brunton, 5 H. & N. 518 29 L. J., Ex. 265.

termined. (*b*) A written notice to quit may be proved by the production of a copy, although no notice has been given to produce the original. (*c*) [1]

742. *Waiver of notice to quit.*—If the tenant remains in possession after the expiration of a good and valid notice to quit, his possession then becomes an adverse tenancy and possession, and the landlord may either bring an action of ejectment against him, or proceed in the county court, or before justices of the peace, for the recovery of the possession of the demised premises. But, if he permits the tenant to remain in possession after the expiration of the notice, and demands and accepts rent in respect of the tenant's occupation of the property subsequently to the notice, this amounts to a waiver of the notice, (*d*) and to the creation of a new tendency taking effect at the expiration of the old one. (*e*) The same result follows, if the lessor distrains for rent which he claims to be due in respect of the tenant's occupation subsequently to the expiration of the notice. (*f*) [2] But, if a banker or agent of the lessor,

(*b*) Bessell v. Landesberg, 7 Q. B. 638.

(*c*) Doe v. Somerton, 7 Q. B. 58.

(*d*) Goodwright v. Cordwent, 6 T. R. 219. Doe v. Batten, Cowp. 243.

Blyth v. Dennett, 13 C. B. 178 ; 22 L. J., C. P. 79.

(*e*) Tayleur v. Wildin, L. R., 3 Ex. 203 ; 37 L. J., Ex. 173.

(*f*) Zouch v. Willingale, 1 H. Bl. 311.

[1] The question of service is one under the peculiar statute ; in general, however, the service must be on the tenant or on some person of proper age residing on the premises. In New York, if none such can be found, the service may be made by affixing the notice to some conspicuous part of the premises. 1 Edm. R. S. 696, § 8; see Roussell v. Kelly, 41 Cal. 360; People v. Goelet, 14 Abb. (N. Y.) Pr. N. S. 130. For the peculiar notice and proceedings necessary under the New York Squatter Act, see Laws of 1857, ch. 396; McAdams. Landlord and Tenant, 346.

[2] See Prindle v. Anderson, 19 Wend. 391 ; Whitney v.

without any special authority from the latter, receives rent from the tenant, the act of such unauthorized agent does not amount to a waiver of the notice. (*g*) The money, moreover, must be paid and accepted as rent, and not by way of satisfaction of the lessor's claim for double rent or double value, under the statutes for holding over. The giving of a second notice to quit before or after the expiration of the first notice does not necessarily amount to a waiver of the latter. (*h*)   Nor does a collateral promise by the lessor not to act upon the notice under certain circumstances, or in the case of the happening of a certain event, amount to a waiver of the notice. (*i*) If a tenant retains possession and receives the produce and profits of the demised premises after the expiration of a notice to quit given by him, such retention of possession will, in general, as against the tenant, amount to a waiver of the notice. (*k*)

743. *Proof and effect of holding over.*—There is no holding over by a tenant from the mere fact of his not sending the keys of a house to the landlord. It is enough if the tenant vacates the house and gives the landlord the means and opportunity of taking possession when he pleases; for possession is to be given on the land, and the landlord must come and take it. But if the tenant continues to use and occupy the premises after the term has ceased, he will be responsible for holding over.[1] And the tenant is re-

(*g*) Doe v. Calvert, 2 Campb. 387.
(*h*) Doe v. Humphreys, 2 East, 237.
Doe v. Steel, 3 Campb. 116.

(*i*) Whiteacre v. Symonds, 10 East, 13.
(*k*) Jones v. Shears, 4 Ad. & E. 832.

Swett, 2 Fost. 10 ; Collins v. Canty, 6 Cush. 415 ; Tuttle v. Beam, 13 Met. 275 ; Babcock v. Abbee, Id. 273 ; Stedman v. Mackintosh, 5 Ired. 571.

[2] The doctrine that where the lessee holds over and

sponsible, if his sub-tenant holds over; for the landlord is entitled, upon the determination of the tenancy, to receive full and complete possession from the tenant. (*l*)   But one joint-tenant is not responsible for a

(*l*) Henderson v. Squire, L. R., 4   cott v. Smythies, 7 C. & P. 808.
Q. B. 170 ; 38 L. J., Q. B 73.   Calde-

the lessor receives rent accruing after the expiration of the term, a new tenancy arises for a further term subject to the covenants and conditions of the original lease is true as a general rule; and the reason is, that the receipt of the rent is considered as an acknowledgment of a subsisting tenancy.   But it does not follow that the new term must necessarily be a year.   Where the former lease for was less than a year, as a quarter or a month, or where the term, though extending to a year or more, was composed of such periods, there is no ground for holding that the new term, presumed from the holding over of the tenant and the receipt of rent by the landlord, extends beyond one of the periods of the tenancy. The tenant who enters under a lease for a month and holds over, and during the second month pays rent, is not entitled to claim a new term of one year, but he becomes a tenant from month to month.   When the tenancy is found from the fact of the holding over of the tenant and the acknowledgment of the landlord, it is presumed to be of the same character—as annual, quarterly, monthly, &c., and upon the same covenants and conditions as in the previous tenancy. It rests upon implication alone.   But if the parties make an express agreement relating in any respect to the new tenancy, then in that respect there is no room for implication. Blumenberg v. Myres, 32 Cal. 93.   And see Rowan v. Lytle, Wend. 616 ; Conway v. Starkweather, 1 Den. 113 ; Blumenbury v. Meyers, 32 Cal. 93; Edwards v. Hall, 9 Allen, 462 ; Ackermann v. Lyman, 20 Wis. 454 ; Van Rensselaer's Heirs v. Penniman, 6 Wend. 569 ; Hunt v. Bailey, 39 Mo. 267; McKenney v. Peck, 28 Ill. 174.   Miller v. Levi, 44 N. Y. 489, *held*, that a provision in a lease that the lessor may " terminate the lease at the end of any year, by giving sixty days' previous notice, in case he should sell or desire to rebuild," is *a limita- tion*, and the term expires by force of a sale and notice in sixty days thereafter, and if the tenant retains possession after such sixty days it is a holding over which will give jurisdic- tion in summary proceedings for his removal.

holding over by the other. (*m*) Mere holding over
does not create a new tenancy ; nor is it in itself any
evidence of an agreeement to renew the previous ten-

(*m*) Tancred v. Christy, 12 M. & W. 316.

The question as to what is a holding over, came up in Gibbons v. Dayton, 4 Hun. 451 ; in that case the following receipt
was in evidence—" New York, Sept. 1st, 1871. Received from
Mrs. Mary Merriam the sum of sixty dollars, for one month's
rent only, in advance, for second floor rooms in house No.
165 Bleecker-street, ending October 1, 1871, at noon, it being
expressly understood between us, the tenant and agent, or
landlord mentioned in this receipt, that this term of hiring
and letting is for one month only, and will expire as aforesaid. $60. Thomas J. Gibbons." In which the court, DAVIS,
P. J. (DANIELS and BRADY, JJ., concurring), said : " The appellant is public administrator, and as such was appointed
administrator of the estate of one Anna Maria Merriam,
deceased. The respondent presented a claim for rent against
the estate, which being disputed, was submitted to reference
with the approval of the surrogate, in conformity to the statute in such case made and provided. Mrs. Merriam, the intestate, was the tenant of the respondent from month to month ;
she had been accustomed to receive on payment of the
monthly rent at the beginning of each month, an instrument
acknowledging the receipt of the rent and expressing the
term and nature of the tenancy. Such an instrument was
executed and delivered to her about the first of April, 1873,
on payment of the rent for that month. About the first of
May, Mrs. Merriam was taken sick and went to the house of
a friend, where she became so ill that she was unable to
return to her rooms, and she remained at her friend's till
her death, which occurred on the 6th of June, 1873. Her furniture and other personal property remained at the rooms
leased to her by respondent until about the 29th or 30th of
July, 1873. About the 28th of July, the appellant received
notice of the death of Mrs. Merriam, and was on that day
appointed her administrator, and on the 29th or 30th of July
removed all articles of any apparent value from the premises
previously occupied by her, and about the same time sent the
keys of the rooms to the place of business of respondent, and
left them with a boy in the office, with a message that they
were the keys of such rooms. The respondent, on learning
that the keys had been sent to his office, refused to receive

ancy. (*n*) There must be a payment and acceptance
of rent which accrued subsequently to the expiration
of the lease; and then the tenant holds as tenant from

(*n*) Gray v. Bompas, 11 C. B., N. S. 520. Jenner v. Clegg, 1 Mood. & Rob. 213.

them, and sent them back to the office of the appellant. The
clerk of the appellant also refused to receive them. On the
16th of February following, the respondent entered the rooms,
cleaned them out, and repaired them, removing the articles of
no value left in them, to the cellar of the building. The
referee held, that the intestate was tenant from month to
month, that there had been no lawful surrender of the premises, and that the appellant was liable for the rent down to the
time of the entry of the respondent on the 16th of February,
1874, at the rate of sixty dollars per month, and directed judgment accordingly. It is very clear that the tenancy was
from month to month. Neither party was bound to give any
notice to the other in order to terminate the tenancy at the
expiration of any month. The landlord could have removed
the tenant by summary proceedings, without notice; and so
the tenant could lawfully have left the premises at the expiration of any month, without notice, and without being bound
to pay further rent. People ex rel. Gledhill v. Schackno, 48
Barb. 551; People v. Goelet, 14 Abb. Pr. N. S. 130. The
death of Mrs. Merriam did not change the character of the
tenancy, and the appellant is not liable beyond the obligations
that rested and would have remained upon her had she continued to live and retain her possession down to the day
when appellant removed the property and sent the keys to the
respondent's office. She would in that case have been chargeable with rent for the months of May, June, and July; but
her tenancy would have terminated with the month of July.
The appellant acted promptly and with apparent good faith.
He was appointed administrator on the 28th of July, and on
the next day, or on the 30th, moved the furniture and everything of value from the premises, and sent the keys to the
landlord. This was a complete termination of the tenancy,
and full notice that the term would not be renewed for another month. A few articles were left in the rooms, but they
seem from the evidence to have been nothing more than
worthless things, which the referee finds to have been valueless.
The rooms were excessively dirty, but the litter and filth, and
worthless fragments and articles which tenants are often accustomed to leave behind them, have never been held to consti-

year to year upon all such of the terms of the original lease as are applicable to a yearly tenancy. (*o*) If, therefore, the lease contained a proviso for re-entry in case of non-payment of rent, the proviso is impliedly annexed to the yearly tenancy. (*p*) But if there is any evidence to show that the holding after the expiration of the lease was upon new and different terms, the legal presumption is rebutted, (*q*) and the nature of the holding becomes a question of fact. Whether any particular covenant is applicable to a yearly ten-

---

(*o*) Torriano v. Young, 6 C. & P. 11. Thomas v. Packer, 1 H. & N. 671. Bishop v. Howard, 3 D. & R. 298. Buckworth v. Simpson, 1 C. M. & R. 843. Arden v. Sullivan, 14 Q. B. 839; 19 L. J., Q. B. 271. Beale v. Sanders, 3 Bing. N. C. 850.

(*p*) Williams, J., Doe v. Amey, 12 Ad. & E. 480. Hutton v. Warren, 1 M. & W. 466.

(*q*) Mayor of Thetford v. Tyler, 8 Q. B. 95.

---

tute a continuance of the tenancy. The landlord's remedy, if any, for such an injury, is quite different from treating the tenancy as renewed by the omission to carry everything away, whether valuable or not. The referee has charged the administrator with rent after the month of July, on the ground that there was no formal surrender by him of the premises to the landlord. No form was necessary under the facts of the case, beyond a removal at or before the expiration of the month, and the restoration of the keys to the landlord so that he could enter upon possession. The case is not like that of Pugsley v. Aiken (11 N. Y. 494), where the lease was for ' one year and an indefinite period thereafter,' for in this case the express terms of the lease are 'that this term of letting and hiring is for one month only, and will expire' at noon on the first day of the following month. There should have been a recovery, therefore, only for the rent of the months of May, June, and July, with interest on each month's rent from the time it was payable. The judgment should be reversed, and a new trial granted, with costs of the appeal to the appellant, unless the respondent shall stipulate to modify the judgment by reducing it to the rent for the months above named and interest, in which case it may be affirmed as modified, without costs to either party on this appeal as against the other."

ancy is in some cases a question of fact. (*r*)　In other cases it will be a question of law.

744. *Double yearly value for holding over.*—Any tenant willfully holding over and retaining possession of the demised premises after the determination of his term, and after possession has been demanded, and notice in writing has been given him by the lessor, is liable to pay to the person kept out of possession double the yearly value of the lands, &c., detained. (*s*) [1] An action for the recovery of this penalty may be brought by the landlord, and the landlord alone, either before or after he has recovered possession of the land by an action of ejectment. (*t*)　But it has been held that the Act applies only to the case of a willful and contumacious holding over by the tenant after a valid notice to quit, and not to a holding over under a bona fide claim of title or right, though erroneous. (*u*)　A weekly or quarterly tenant has been held not to come within the operation of the statute. (*v*)　In the case of a tenancy from year to year, the ordinary notice to quit at the end of the current year of hiring is a sufficient demand of possession to entitle the lessor to double yearly value. (*y*)　If the tenant holds under a lease for a term of years certain, a notice to quit at

---

(*r*) Hyatt v. Griffiths, 17 Q. B. 505. Oakley v. Monck. L. R., 1 Ex. 159; 35 L J., Ex. 87.

(*s*) 4 Geo. 2, c. 28, s. 1.　As to the computation of the yearly value, see Robinson v. Learoyd, 7 M. & W. 48.

(*t*) Soulsby v. Neving, 9 East, 310. Harcourt v. Wyman, 3 Exch. 817. Swinfen v. Bacon, 6 H. & N. 846; 30

L. J., Ex. 37.

(*u*) Hirst v. Horn, 6 M. & W. 395. Page v. More, 15 Q. B. 684.　Swinfen v. Bacon, *supra*.

(*v*) Lloyd v. Rosbee, 2 Campb. 454 Sullivan v. Bishop, 2 C. & P. 359.

(*y*) Wilkinson v. Colley, 5 Burr. 2698.　Poole v. Warren, 8 Ad. & E. 582.　Lake v. Smith, 4 B. & P. 179.

[1] Hall v. Ballantine, 7 Johns. 536; Despart v. Walbridge, 15 N. Y. 374; Hunt v. Bailey, 39 Mo. 257; Adriance v. Hafkemeyer, Id. 134; Dorril v. Stephens, 4 McCord, 59; McKinney v. Peck, 28 Ill. 174.

the expiration of such term is likewise a sufficient demand of possession, and such notice may be given previous to the expiration of such term, or at any time afterwards, so long as the tenant continues to hold as a tenant at will. (*z*)   If the landlord has done any act amounting to a waiver of his notice to quit, he can not make such notice the foundation of an action for double value. (*a*)

745. *Double rent for holding over.*—By the 11 Geo. 2, c. 19, s. 18, it is enacted that, if any tenant gives notice to the lessor of his intention to quit at a particular time, and does not deliver up possession of the premises at the time mentioned, such tenant, his executors, &c., shall from thenceforth pay to the landlord or lessor double the rent which he would otherwise have paid, to be levied, sued for, and recovered at the same times and in the same manner as the single rent.   The tenant's notice to quit need not be in writing, in order to support the lessor's claim to double rent, nor need the lease which the tenant has determined by his notice to quit be a lease in writing. (*b*)   But the notice must be a good notice to quit at some fixed time, and at a period when the tenant is able by notice to put an end to the tenancy.   If the tenant merely gives notice that he will quit " as soon .as he can possibly get another location," (*c*) or gives notice to quit in the middle instead of at the termination of the current term of hiring, or a notice of too short a duration, and which does not therefore bind the lessor, the lease is not determined, and there can not, consequently, be any holding over by the tenant.

(*z*) Cutting v. Derby, 2 W. Bl. 1075. Messenger v. Armstrong, 1 T. R. 53.

(*a*) Ryal v. Rich, 10 East, 47.

(*b*) Timmins v. Rawlinson, 3 Burr. 1608.

(*c*) Farrance v. Elkington, 2 Campb. 592.

(*d*) A tenant who holds over for one year after notice to quit, paying double rent, may quit at the end of such year without fresh notice. (*e*)[1]

746. *Determination of tenancies by railway notices.*—If lands holden by tenants from year to year are required by railway companies for the making of a railway, the company may, in general, under the powers of their Act, either give the ordinary landlord's notice to quit ending with the current year of the tenancy, in which case no compensation would be payable in respect of any unexpired term, or six months' notice to be given at any time, in which case the tenant will be entitled to compensation for the value of the term between the expiration of the six months' notice and the time when a regular landlord's notice would have expired. If, after having given a notice not ending with the expiration of the current year, the company inform the tenant that he may hold on till the end of the current year, and he does so, the situation of the parties is the same as if a regular landlord's notice had been originally given. (*f*) If the tenant continues in possession after the expiration of the notice, he holds simply as a tenant at sufferance

---

(*d*) Johnstone v. Huddlestone, 4 B. & C. 922.

(*e*) Booth v. Macfarlane, 1 B. & Ad.

904.

(*f*) Reg. v. Lond. and Southamp. Ry. Co., 10 Ad. & E. 3.

[1] In an action of unlawful detainer against a tenant for holding over, the mere fact that the tenant has been in quiet and peaceable possession for one year before commencement of the action, will not defeat it. Johnson v. Chely, 43 Cal. 299. Equity will not relieve against a tenant holding over by reason of his landlord's laches, because he is a bad manager or insolvent or vicious, and disagreeable to his landlord; Blair v. Everett, 36 Md. 73; nor does a tenant by a holding over, unless to such length as to imply consent upon the landlord's part, become a tenant by sufferance, who is entitled to a notice to quit. Smith v. Littlefield, 51 N. Y. 539.

without any estate or interest at all in the premises, unless rent is received from him, or the premises are re-demised to him. (*g*)

745. *Recovery of possession.*—Possession of land can not be gained by an act of trespass which has never been acquiesced in by the landowner. Every person who trespasses upon another man's land and remains there tortiously may be expelled by main force. (*h*)   But if he has once gained a lawful possession which is determined, and he then continues unlawfully to hold the land, the landowner is punishable for a forcible entry, if he enters with a strong hand to dispossess him. (*i*)[1]   The tenant can not maintain an action for damages against the landlord for a trespass upon the realty in respect of the forcible entry ; for there is no trespass by the latter in entering on property which is his own, and on which he has a legal right to enter.   Therefore, if the tenant of a dwelling-house holds over wrongfully, and the landlord enters and pulls down the house, or stops up the chimney, or takes off the roof, and the tenant brings an action against the landlord for trespassing on the land, it is an answer that the house was the defendant's house, and therefore that he entered and pulled it down, &c. (*k*)   It has been laid down by PARKE, B., that, "where a breach of the peace is committed by a freeholder

---

(*g*) *Ex parte* Nadin, 17 L. J., Ch. 421.

(*h*) Browne v. Dawson, 12 Ad. & E. 629.

(*i*) Rex v. Bathurst, Say. 227. Rex v. Wilson, 8 T. R. 361.

(*k*) Burling v. Reed, 11 Q. B. 904. Davison v. Wilson, 17 L. J., Q. B. 196.

[1] See Pendleton v. Dyett, 4 Cow. 581 ; Bennett v. Bittle, 4 Rawle, 339 ; Page v. Parr, Styles, 432 ; Ogilvie v. Hull, 5 Hill, 52 ; Cohen v. Dupont, 1 Sandf. 260 ; Gilhooley v. Washington, 4 Comst. 217 ; Jackson v. Eddy, 12 Mo. 209 ; Christopher v. Austin, 1 Kern. 216.

who, in order to get into possession of his land, assaults
a person wrongfully holding possession of it against
his will, although the freeholder may be responsible to
the public in the shape of an indictment for a forcible
entry, he is not liable to the other party," and that "it
is a perfectly good justification to say that the plaintiff was in possession of the land against the will of
the defendant, who was owner, and that he entered
upon it accordingly, though in so doing a breach of
the peace was committed." (*l*)   TINDAL, C. J., is reported to have said that, " if the landlord in making
his entry upon the tenant has been guilty either of a
breach of a positive statute or of an offense against the
common law, such violation of the law in making the
entry causes the possession thereby obtained to be illegal." (*m*)   But this has since been decided not to
be law ; and it is now well established that at the determination of the term the landlord may enter and
take possession of the demised premises, and after civ-
illy requesting the tenant to depart, may, in case of his
refusal, gently lay hands upon him and turn him out,
subject only to the liability to be indicted for a forcible entry. (*n*)   If the landlord has no right to enter,
and he takes advantage of the temporary absence of
the tenant to fasten up the door of his apartments and
exclude him from re-entering, the tenant may recover
damages against the landlord for breaking and entering, although the landlord has never actually entered
the rooms. (*o*)

748. *License to eject.*—Where it was provided
that, in case of non-payment of rent or non-perform-

(*l*) Harvey v. Bridges, 14 M. & W.
442.

(*m*) Newton v. Harland, 1 Sc. N. R.
490.

(*n*) Davis v. Burrell, 10 C. B. 822.

Harvey v. Bridges, 14 M. & W. 437 ;
1 Exch. 261. Jones v. Chapman, 2
Exch. 803, 821.   Pollen v. Brewer, 7
C. B., N. S. 371.

(*o*) Lane v. Dixon, 3 C. B. 776.

ance of covenants, it should be lawful for the lessor and his agents immediately to enter upon and take possession of the demised premises, and to expel the lessee and all persons claiming under him, without any legal process, as effectually as any sheriff might do in case the lessor had obtained judgment in ejectment for the recovery of possession, and a writ had issued thereon to the sheriff in due form of law, and that the leave and license of the lessee might be pleaded in any action brought by the latter for such entry and ouster, and the agreement be used as conclusive evidence of such leave and license, it was held that the lessor had a right, as between himself and the lessee, under this agreement to eject the lessee by main force, and might plead such license in bar of an action of trespass brought by the latter. (*p*) [1]

749. *Ejectment under provisos for re-entry.*— When the lessor has a right to re-enter in case of non-payment of rent, and brings an action of ejectment, he must show that demand was made of the rent upon the demised premises, unless there is no one there on whom demand can be made, and the demand has been made on the party liable to pay, (*q*) and that the same or some part thereof has not been paid, (*r*) unless the proviso is for re-entry without any demand of the rent. (*s*)   The demand must be of the precise sum due, and must be made on the day when the rent was due and payable by the terms of the lease, and at a convenient time (which ought to be an hour) before

(*p*) Kavanagh v. Gudge, 7 Sc. N. R. 1025 ; 7 M. & Gr. 316.

(*q*) Manser v. Dix, 8 De G. M. & G. 703.

(*r*) Bro. Abr. DEMANDE, 19. Kidwelly v. Brand, Plowd. 70, a, b.

(*s*) Doe v. Masters, 2 B. & C. 490.

[1] See Fifty Associates v. Howland, 5 Cush. 214 ; Dennison v. Read, 3 Dana, 586.

sunset. (*t*)   Where the proviso is for re-entry in case
of non-payment of rent for the space of ten, fifteen, or
any other number of days after it has become due, the
demand must be made on the tenth or last day. (*u*)
Where rent was payable quarterly, and two quarters
were in arrear and were demanded together, it was
held that the lessor could not avail himself of the proviso for re-entry in case of non-payment for twenty-
one days, as the first quarter ought to have been
demanded on the twenty-first day after it had become
due. (*v*)

750. *Where there is no sufficient distress* and one
half year's rent is due and in arrear, and the lessor has
a right to re-enter for non-payment thereof, proceedings may be taken under the 15 & 16 Vict. c. 76, s.
210. (*y*)   The operation of the statute appears to be
confined to cases where the tenant was six months in
arrear at the very time when the landlord had recourse
to the statutory remedy.   If the landlord distrains for
the rent due, he waives any breach of the condition of
re-entry which had accrued prior to the taking of the
distress. (*z*)   Proof of no sufficient distress at the time
the right to re-enter accrued, is prima facie proof of
there being no sufficient distress at the time of the
service of process. (*a*)   If more than half a year's rent
is in arrear, the case is within the statute ; (*b*) but, if
more than half a year's rent is due, and there is sufficient distress on the premises to satisfy one half-year,
the landlord can not proceed under the statute, but

(*t*) Fabian's Case, Cro. Eliz. 209;
Co. Litt. 202, a. ; 1 Saund. 287, n. 16.
Doe v. Brydges, 2 D. & R. 29. Acocks
v. Phillips, 5 H. & N. 183.

(*u*) Hill v. Grange, Plowd. 172, a,
173. Clun's Case, 10 Co. 129, a.
Wood and Chiver, 4 Leon. 180. Doe
v. Wandlass, 7 T. R. 117.

(*v*) Doe v. Paul, 3 C. & P. 613.
(*y*) Doe v. Franks, 2 C. & K. 678.
(*z*) Cotesworth v. Spokes, 30 L. J.
C. P. 222.

(*a*) Doe v. Fuchau, 15 East, 286.
(*b*) Doe v. Alexander, 2 M. & S.
525.

must make his demand and entry at common law. (*c*)
But the distress must be available ; and, therefore, if
the tenant locks up the premises, so that the landlord
can not get at the goods which may happen to be
upon them, he may proceed under the statute. (*d*)
The right of re-entry must be absolute and unqualified.
If he has a right only to re-enter and hold until arrears
of rent are satisfied, and not to avoid the lease altogether, he can not avail himself of the statute. (*e*)
The tenant or his assignee or sub-lessee (*f*) may, at
any time before trial (s. 212) stay all further proceedings by paying or tendering to the lessor, or bringing
into court, the rent and arrears with costs. (*g*) [1]

(*c*) Doe v. Roe, 9 Dowl. 548,

(*d*) Doe v. Dyson, M. & M. 77.

(*e*) Doe v. Bowditch, 8 Q. B. 973.

(*f*) Doe v. Byron, 1 C. B. 623.

(*g*) Roe v. Davis, 7 East, 363.

[1] See *ante*, note 1, § 692.   Prepayment of rent with intent to
prevent a purchaser at an execution sale of the premises from
obtaining the proportion due him under the Delaware Rev.
Code, §§ 28, 398–9, after sale, will entitle the purchaser to
distrain therefor, after confirmation of the sale.   Baker v.
Burton, 3 Houst. 10.   The goods of a principal in the store of
his commission-merchant, for sale, are not liable to distress
for rent.   McCrury v. Claffin, 37 Md. 435.   A distress warrant will lie in Georgia to enforce a contract for rent, to the
effect that the tenant should pay to the landlord, for rent,
"four and one-half bales of first-class cotton, each of the
weight of five hundred pounds, the half bale to weigh two
hundred and fifty pounds, and in addition to fix that part of
the kitchen on said place that has been injured by fire,"
proper affidavit being made as to the value of the cotton, and
the cost of fixing the kitchen.   Wilkins v. Taliafero, 52 Ga.
208; and see Urguhart v. Urguhart, 46 Id. 415.   In Maryland an action of trespass will not lie against a landlord for
distress for more rent than is due.   Hamilton v. Wendolf, 36
Md. 301.   A lease was for ten years, with a stipulation that
the improvements erected might be removed at the end of the
term ; a brick malt-house was erected ; the malt-house was
personal property liable to be distrained for rent.   Spencer v.
Darlington, 74 Pa. 286.   The term could not be sold under

751. *Recovery of possession where the demised premises are deserted.*—The 11 Geo. 2, c. 19, s. 16, and the 57 Geo. 3, c. 52, give a summary remedy by proceedings before justices for recovery of demised premises, when the tenant has deserted them, and left them uncultivated or unoccupied, so that no sufficient distress can be had. And by the 3 & 4 Vict. c. 84, police magistrates and police constables within the metropolitan police district are enabled to put the lessor into possession, and determine the lease. But this power is not by any of the provisions of the last-named statute, or by the 11 & 12 Vict. c. 43, s. 34, vested in the Lord Mayor or alderman sitting in the justice room at the Mansion House or Guildhall. (*h*) The record of the proceedings need not show that any complaint or inquiry was made before the justices upon oath, nor state that the landlord had a right of re-entry. (*i*) Where a bankrupt lessee of a dwelling-house went away, leaving a person in the house whose possession was merely colorable, it was held that the justices were warranted in finding that the lessee had deserted the premises. (*k*) But where the tenant left his wife and children

(*h*) Edwards v. Hodges, 15 C. B. 477.

(*i*) Basten v. Carew, 5 D. & R. 558.

(*k*) *Ex parte* Pilton, 1 B. & Ald. 369.

a distress for rent. Id. Bidders at a sale under a distress for rent agreed that one should buy and sell to the other at the price at which he should buy; after the sale the constable gave a receipt for the purchase-money of "a lease" and the receiver of the tenant, an insolvent, in consideration of the purchase-money beyond the rent and costs, conveyed all "his interest in the lease" to the purchaser at the sale; *held,* that this conveyance did not affect the contract between the two bidders. Id. The lease stipulated that a transfer of the lease without the written consent of the lessors should be a forfeiture. The receiver of the lessee could not transfer it without the written assent of the lessor. In Georgia a tenant may have a distress warrant against a sub-tenant. Harrison v. Guill, 46 Ga. 427.

in the house, but took away his furniture and went away himself, it was held that there was no desertion ; and the judges of assize, on appeal, ordered restitution of the demised premises with costs. (*l*)   Where the justices go the first time and find the premises deserted, then, unless some one appears and pays the rent, when they go the second time they are to deliver possession to the lessor.   The proceedings of the justices are examinable in a summary way by the judges (s. 17).

752. *Recovery of possession of houses and small tenements.*—The statute 1 & 2 Vict. c. 74, enables justices of the peace to give possession to the landlord of houses and land held for a term not exceeding seven years, rent free or at a rent not exceeding £20 per annum, upon which no fine is payable, provided the tenancy has been duly determined, and notice has been given as therein provided. (*m*)   If under this statute a tenancy is proved before the justices, and a determination of that tenancy, and a refusal on the part of the tenant to quit, it is not competent to the tenant to set up the title of any third party, or raise any question of title before the magistrate. (*n*)   If the term or interest of the tenant in any house, land or corporeal hereditament, where the value of the premises or the rent does not exceed £50 by the year, (*o*) and on which no fine has been paid, has been duly determined, and the tenant or (if he does not occupy or only occupies part) any person by whom the premises or part of them are then actually occupied, neglects

(*l*) Ashcroft v. Bourne, 3 B. & Ad. 684.

(*m*) Delaney v. Fox, 1 C. B., N. S. 166.

(*n*) Rees v. Davies, 4 C. B., N. S. 62.

(*o*) If the rent does not exceed £50, the County Court has jurisdiction, though the premises are of greater annual value. Harrington, Earl of, v. Ramsey, 8 Exch. 881 ; 2 E. & B. 669 ; 22 L. J., Q. B. 460.

or refuses to deliver up possession, the landlord or his
agent may, by proper proceedings in the county court,
obtain a warrant of possession. (*p*)   The plaint must
be brought in the district where the tenements are
situate ; and the court will have jurisdiction, even
though a bona fide question of title is raised, where
neither the annual value of the lands nor the rent payable in respect thereof exceed £20. (*q*)   If, however,
the annual value or rent exceed that sum, the jurisdiction of the court will be ousted if a bonâ fide question
of title is raised ; and, even if neither rent nor value
exceed £20, yet the defendant may have the action
tried in a superior court if he can satisfy a judge that
the title to lands of greater annual value than £20 will
be affected by the decision. (*r*)   A tenant is, in general, estopped from disputing his landlord's title ; but
he may show that it has expired ; and, if there is some
evidence to support the defense, and it is not a mere
illusory claim, and the rent or annual value of the
premises exceed £20, the judge of the county court
should refrain from trying the question. (*s*)

Where on the hearing of a plaint it appeared that
one of the matters seriously in dispute was whether
the whole or part of a house had been demised, it was
held that the inquiry involved a question of title, and
that the county court had no jurisdiction in the matter.
(*t*)   A decision of a county court judge, that the title
is not in question, is by no means conclusive of the
fact.   The question may be brought before the superior courts on motion for a prohibition by affidavit ;
and, if the court directs that the party should declare,

(*p*) 19 & 20 Vict. c. 108, s. 50.

(*q*) 30 & 31 Vict. c. 142, s. 12.

(*r*) 30 & 31 Vict. c. 142, s. 13.

(*s*) Mountnoy v. Collier, 1 E. & B.
630 ; 22 L. J., Q. B. 126.   Marsh v.

Dewes, 17 Jur. 558. Kerkin v. Kerkin,
3 E. & B. 399.   Latham v. Spedding,
17 Q. B. 440.

(*t*) Chew v. Holroyd, 8 Exch. 249 ;
22 L. J., Ex. 95.

the question becomes one of evidence. (*u*)   Neither the tenant nor any one claiming through him, nor any one put into possession by him, can, during the demise, controvert the landlord's title in an action of ejectment ; but he may show that the title has expired (*x*).   If a tenancy is sought to be established through the medium of payment of rent to the plaintiff or to his agent, it must be shown that the rent was either paid by the defendant himself, or by some person through whom he claims, or by his authorized agent ; for an unauthorized payment of rent by a stranger will not be binding on the defendant, or in any way affect his rights.   Where a party distrained for rent, and the lessee paid the rent due under the distress without protest or objection, it was held that he could not after that controvert the title of the plaintiff. (*y*)

753. *Rights of out-going and incoming tenants— Away-going crops, allowances for tillage, manure, &c.*—All tenants who held by an uncertain tenure, and whose interest might at any time be determined by the will of the lord, were by the common law entitled to emblements and the crops and annual produce of the soil which had been sown or planted by them, and which had not come to maturity at the period of the determination of their interest. (*z*)   In all farming leases, the custom of the country, with respect to the mode of cultivation and the right to the away-going crop, is impliedly annexed to the terms of the lease, unless it is excluded by express provisions and stipulations. (*a*)   The general rule in

(*u*) Thompson v. Ingham, 14 Q. B. 710.

(*x*) *Ante.*   Doe v. Smythe, 4 M. & S. 347.   Doe v. Mills, 2 Ad. & E. 20. Doe v. Baytup, 3 ib. 190.

(*y*) Doe v. Mitchell, 3 Moore, 229. Hitchings v. Thompson, 5 Exch. 50.

(*z*) Litt. ss. 68, 69.

(*a*) Wigglesworth v. Dallison, 1 Doug. 201 ; 1 Smith's L. C., 5th ed., 520.

the case of farm leases is that the tenant is bound to
leave the land, when he quits, in the same state as he
found it on taking possession. If he has taken the
farm under a custom by which the outgoing tenant is
bound to leave a certain quantity of clover and grass
seeds or fallows, or a certain number of acres of growing wheat, or turnips, or other produce, or a certain
quantity of hay and straw, or manure, on the demised
premises, he must in his turn, when he quits the land,
leave it in the same state and condition, and with the
same privileges and advantages for the benefit of his
successor, that he himself enjoyed when he entered
upon it.

By the custom of some counties, the outgoing
tenant takes two-thirds of particular crops, leaving
one-third to the incoming tenant. (*b*)   In some districts all the hay and straw must be left to be consumed on the farm ; whilst in others the tenant is
entitled to take it away with him. Sometimes the
landlord or the incoming tenant has a right, and in
some instances he is bound by custom, to take the
away-going crops, and also the straw and hay, and
sometimes the manure, from the outgoing tenant at a
valuation ; and, when such a custom exists, the tenant
has a right, after the expiration of his lease, and after
he has quitted the premises, to enter upon the land as
occasion may require to improve and tend the crop.
If the landlord or the incoming tenant does not take
the crop at a valuation, the tenant has impliedly accorded to him, by general custom and usage, all
such rights and privileges as are necessary to enable
him to gather it in, and secure it, and sell or turn it to
profit and advantage when arrived at maturity, such as
free ingress and egress into and from the demised

(*b*) Holding v. Pigott, 5 Moo. & P. 427.   Griffiths v. Tombs, 7 C. & P. 810.

premises, the temporary use of the barns to thrash it out, and yard-room for the straw ; and he has a right, moreover, to the possession of the field for a reasonable time for the carrying away as well as the cutting of his corn. (*c*)   If no custom exists giving the tenant a right to the away-going crop, the landlord is, as we have before seen, entitled thereto.   The tenant, therefore, must in all cases make out and establish the custom. (*d*)   When no such custom exists, the natural consequence is that the tenant does not till or sow the ground at the close of his term of hiring ; and a custom therefore appears to prevail, in all places where the outgoing tenant is not entitled to the away-going crop, for the incoming tenant or the landlord to enter to manure and till the land, and plant the spring corn, and prepare for the harvest, prior to the termination of the lease and the commencement of his own term and interest. (*e*)

Whatever custom regulates the tenant's rights on entering, the same custom regulates his rights on leaving ; and the custom may be given in evidence, although there is a lease under seal, or a written contract of demise between the parties.   All customary allowances, also, as between outgoing tenant and the landlord or the incoming tenant, are impliedly annexed to the express terms of the lease, such as allowances for expenses incurred in draining lands that required draining according to good husbandry, though the drainage was done without the landlord's

---

(*c*) Boraston v. Green, 16 East, 81. Beaty v. Gibbons, Id. 118.   Strickland v. Maxwell, 2 Cr. & M. 539.   Griffiths v. Puleston, 13 M. & W. 358.   As to the right of the grantee of growing crops after the landlord has resumed possession, see Hayling v. Okey, 8 Exch. 545.

(*d*) Caldecott v. Smythies, 7 C. & P. 808.

(*e*) Kennedy and Granger on Tenancy Customs.

knowledge or consent; (*f*) also for manuring, tilling
fallowing, half-fallowing, and sowing the land, for seeds,
and labor, foldage, and manure. (*g*) The tenant's
rights to growing crops and produce are in all cases
strictly confined to annual crops, or the first year's
produce of seeds and roots sown or planted by him
during the last year of his tenancy, and do not extend
to trees, shrubs, and plants of a perennial character
(excepting the fruit-trees, plants, and shrubs of seeds-
men and nursery gardeners, an exception introduced
for the benefit of trade.) (*h*) Thus a border of box,
planted by a tenant in a garden demised to him, can
not be taken up and removed at the expiration of his
term, (*i*) nor a strawberry bed, (*k*) nor hedges, nor
fruit trees. (*l*)

The person primarily liable to the outgoing tenant
is the landlord; but it is usual by agreement between
the outgoing tenant, the landlord, and the incoming
tenant, for the valuation to be made between the outgoing tenant and the incoming tenant, and for the
latter to pay the former. In order, however, to make
the incoming tenant liable, there must be the consent
of all three parties; for the outgoing and incoming
tenants can not by agreement between themselves deprive the landlord of his right to set off the arrears of
rent against the valuation of the tillages. (*m*) [1]

(*f*) Mousley v. Ludlam, 21 L. J.,
Q. B. 64.

(*g*) Dalby v. Hirst, 3 Moore, 536.
Hutton v. Warren, 1 M. & W. 477.
Wilkins v. Wood, 12 Jur. Q. B. 583.
Favill v. Gaskoin, 7 Exch. 273.

(*h*) Wardell v. Usher, 3 Sc. N. R.
508.

(*i*) Empson v. Soden, 4 B. & Ad.
655.

(*k*) Watherell v. Howells, 1 Campb.
227.

(*l*) Wyndham v. Way, 4 Taunt. 316.

(*m*) Stafford v. Gardner, L. R., 7 C.
P. 242.

[1] Tenants whose estates are terminated by an uncertain
event which they can neither foresee nor control, are entitled
to the annual crop sowed by them while their estate continued;

Where the lease determines by the death of any landlord entitled for his life, or for any other uncertain interest, the tenant, instead of claims to emblements, may continue to hold and occupy such farm or lands until the expiration of the then current year of his tenancy ; (*n*) and the succeeding landlord is entitled to receive of the tenant the proper proportion of the rent for the period which may have elapsed from the day of the death of such lessor to the time of the tenant's quitting, and may distrain for such proportion. (*o*)

(*n*) 14 & 15 Vict. c. 25, s. 1. If there are, from the nature of the case, no claims to emblements, the section will not apply. Haines *v.* Welch, *infra.*

(*o*) Haines v. Welch, L. R., 4 C. P. 91 ; 38 L. J., C. P. 118.

and a tenant for years, who knows when his lease will expire, has usually some right to the crop he sowed, and to so much possession of the land as may be necessary to getting in the crop; dependent either on agreement or on usage. 1 Parsons on Contracts, 510. In Pennsylvania, the tenant's right for a definite term to his away-going crops seems to be well established.   Diffedorffer v. Jones, cited in Carson v. Blazer, 2 Binn. 487, and in Stultz v. Dickey, 5 Id. 289 ; Comfert v. Duncan, 1 Miles, 229; Demi v. Bossler, 1 Penn. 224. Such is the rule also in New Jersey. Van Doren v. Everitt, 2 Southard, 460; Templeman v. Biddle, 1 Harr. (Del.) 522. Says Parsons on Contracts, *supra :* " The local usages of this country, in this respect, vary very much, and are not often distinctly defined or well established. Thus, there is some uncertainty as to the property in the manure of a farm. Generally, in this country, the outgoing tenant can not sell or take away the manure." See Lassell v. Reed, 6 Greenl. 222 ; Staples v. Emery, 7 Id. 201 ; Daniels v. Pond, 21 Pick. 367, 371 ; Lewis v. Lyman, 22 Id. 437, 442 ; Middlebrook v. Corwin, 15 Wend. 169; Lewis v. Jones, 17 Pa. St. 262 ; Kittredge v. Woods, 3 N. H. 503; Van Doren v. Everett, 2 South. 460 ; Stultz v. Dickey, 5 Binn. 285. And this, even if the manure is lying in heaps in the farm yard, and was made by his own cattle and from his own fodder. Lassell v. Reed, 6 Greenl. 222; Middlebrook v. Corwin, 15 Wend. 169.

754. *Sale of straw off the land.*—If by the terms of the lease the hay and straw are to be consumed by the tenant on the land, and the lessee sells the crop, and the purchaser removes it, the landlord may maintain an action against the purchaser for the value of the hay or straw, &c., so removed. (*p*) It is no answer to such an action to show that the tenant has brought back an equivalent in the shape of manure. (*q*) If the value of straw sold off is to be returned in manure, the manure value, and not the market price of the straw sold, would seem to be the proper criterion of expenditure upon the land. (*r*) According to the custom of the country in some districts, the incoming tenant, in the absence of a special agreement, pays the outgoing tenant a consuming price, or two-thirds the market-price for the straw ; but if the outgoing tenant is bound to consume all the manure on the farm, the allowance in respect of straw, as between him and the incoming tenant, would be only half the market price, called a fodder price. And, where there is no special agreement to the contrary, the tenant is often by custom entitled to go out as he came in. (*s*) An outgoing tenant, therefore, who on coming in has paid for straw in accordance with the custom, is entitled to be paid for straw on going out ; and a stipulation in a lease binding the tenant " to consume with stock on the farm all the hay, straw, and clover grown thereon, which manure shall be used on the said farm," is in nowise inconsistent with the tenant's customary

(*p*) 56 Geo. 3, c. 50, s. 11. Wilmot v. Rose, 3 E. & B. 563 ; 23 L. J., Q. B. 281.

(*q*) Legh v. Lillie, 6 H. & N. 171 ; 30 L. J., Ex. 25.

(*r*) Lowndes v. Fountain, 11 Exch. 491.

(*s*) Clarke v. Westrope, 18 C. B. 774 ; 25 L. J., C. P. 287.

right to receive payment for the unconsumed straw on his going out. (*t*)[1]

755. *Removal of superstructures and :fixtures.*— Buildings and constructions of a permanent character, erected upon the demised premises by the tenant, and attached to the freehold, are irremovable by him at common law, unless they have been erected for trading purposes; but by the 14 & 15 Vict. c. 25, s. 3, provision is made for the removal of farm-buildings, and buildings, engines, or machinery, erected by the tenant with the consent in writing of the landlord, either for agricultural purposes, or for the purposes of trade and agriculture. [1]

756. *Abandonment of the right of removal.*—A covenant in a lease to yield up the demised premises, together with all fixtures thereunto belonging, is confined to fixtures which belonged to the demised premises at the time of the execution of the lease; but a covenant to yield up fixtures that may belong to the demised premises extends to fixtures that are afterwards put up by the tenant. (*u*)   Whenever the tenant

(*t*) Muncey v. Dennis, 1 H. & N. 220.

(*u*) Hitchman v. Walton, 4 M. & W. 414, Naylor v. Collinge, 1 Taunt.

19. Thresher v. E. L. Water Co., 2 B. & C. 608; 4 D. & R. 62.   Martyr v. Bradley, 2 M. & C. 25; 9 Bing. 24. West v. Blakeway, 3 Sc. N. R. 218.

[1] Where the rent reserved is one-half the crop, this entitles the landlord to one-half the straw.   Rank v. Rank, 5 Barr. 211.

[2] The rules concerning fixtures are to be construed with the greatest liberality in favor of the tenant, being the converse of the rule as between vendor and vendee, mortgagor and mortgagee, heir and executor; Tate v. Blackburn, 48 Miss. 1; and see as between landlord and tenant; Morgan v. Negley, 3 Pittsb. (Pa.) 33; Beckwith v. Boyce, 9 Miss. 560.   Where a landlord covenants that a tenant may remove the improvements made by him on the land, provided the rent is paid to the expiration of the lease, such payment is a condition precede..t to the tenant's right of removal; Mathinet v. Giddings, 10 Ohio, 364; as to what may be fixtures, see *ante*, note 1, p. 262.

has a right of removal, he must exercise such right prior to the determination of his tenancy ; he can not, after he has once quitted the demised premises, re-enter for the purpose of severing and removing fixtures. (*v*) If the tenant holds over wrongfully he loses his right to sever and remove fixtures; (*y*) but if a lease becomes forfeited, the tenant may, before the landlord re-enters, or before the forfeiture is established by the judgment of a court of law, remove his fixtures, and can not, it seems, be made responsible for so doing, (*z*) but not afterwards. (*a*) If the landlord gives the lessee permission to leave the fixtures on the premises, and makes the best terms he can for them with the incoming tenant, and the latter enters and takes possession of the fixtures, but refuses to pay for them, the lessee can not enter to remove them, nor can he recover the value of them. (*b*)   When it is provided by the terms of a lease that the lessee, at the expiration or other sooner determination of the term, is to have certain fixtures, and the lease becomes forfeited, the lessee has a reasonable time from the date of the forfeiture for the removal of his fixtures. (*c*)

757. *Right of a purchaser or mortgagee to enter and remove fixtures after a surrender of the term.*— If a lessee, possessed of tenant's fixtures removable at the expiration of his term, assigns them to a purchaser, and afterwards surrenders his lease, the purchaser has

(*v*) Lee v. Risdon, 7 Taunt. 191. Quincy, *Ex parte*, 1 Atk. 477. Dudley v. Warde, Amb. 113.

(*y*) Leader v. Homewood, 27 L. J., C. P. 316.

(*z*) Stansfeld v. Mayor of Portsmouth, 4 C. B., N. S. 131 ; 27 L. J., C. P. 124.   Storer v. Hunter, 3 B. & C. 368.

(*a*) Heap v. Barton, 12 C. B. 274. Pugh v. Aston, L. R., 8 Eq. 626 ; 38 L. J., Ch. 619.

(*b*) Roffey v. Henderson, 17 Q. B. 574 ; 21 L. J., Q. B. 49.

(*c*) Stansfeld v. Mayor, &c., of Portsmouth, 4 C. B., N. S., 133 ; 27 L. J., C. P. 124.

a right to enter and sever the fixtures, notwithstanding that the lessee himself would have forfeited his right to remove them; for an estate surrendered hath, in consideration of law, a continuance, having regard to strangers who were not parties or privies to the surrender, "lest, by a voluntary surrender, they may receive prejudice touching any right or interest they had before the surrender." (*d*) Where, therefore, a lessee mortgaged his severable tenants' and trade fixtures, and then surrendered his lease to the lessor, who granted a fresh term to the defendant, it was held that the mortgagees had a right to enter and sever the fixtures, and that they might maintain an action against the lessor for preventing them from exercising their right to sever, and in such action were entitled to recover the value of the fixtures as severed. (*e*)

758. *Non-payment of tithe rent-charge by an outgoing tenant.*—If any occupying tenant quits, leaving unpaid any tithe rent-charge (14 & 15 Vict. c. 25, s. 4), and the tithe owner gives notice of proceeding by distress for its recovery, the landlord or succeeding tenant may pay the tithe rent and any expenses incident thereto, and may recover the amount from the outgoing tenant or his legal representatives, in the same manner as if the same were a debt by simple contract due to the landlord or tenant making such payment.

759. *Inclosures of waste land by tenants.*—If the tenant during the demise has enclosed land from the adjoining waste, and used it in common with the demised premises, the title of the lessor will, as between him and the lessee, prevail over the whole, whether the tenant made the inclosure with or without the

(*d*) Co. Litt. 338, b. Co. v. Drake, 6 C. B., N. S. 798; 28
(*e*) The London Loan & Discount L. J., C. P. 297.

assent of the lessor; (*f*) and, in either case, the Statute of Limitations will not begin to run against the lessor until the termination of the lease. (*g*)

760. *Leases obtained by misrepresentation.*—An estate or interest in land once vested can not afterwards be divested in a court of law, on the ground that the deed creating the estate has been obtained by a fraudulent misrepresentation respecting some matter collateral to the contract. Where, therefore, a lessor has been induced to execute a lease by reason of a fraudulent representation on the part of the lessee as to the use to which he intended to apply the premises it was held that the lease was not thereby avoided and the term gone, but that the lessor must seek his remedy by injunction; (*h*) but, where the lease is granted for the express purpose of carrying into effect an illegal act, the courts will not lend their aid for the enforcement of any of the provisions of the illegal contract. (*i*)

761. *The cancellation of a lease* by mutual consent of the parties, discharges the covenants and promises therein contained, but does not divest the estate created by the lease, or destroy the lessor's right of action for the rent founded on the privity of estate. Arrears of rent, therefore, which accrue due prior to the cancellation of a lease may be recovered by the landlord in an action founded on the privity of estate. (*k*)

(*f*) Andrews v. Hailes, 22 L. J., Q. B. 409.   Kingsmill v. Millard, 11 Exch. 319.

(*g*) Whitmore v. Humphries, L. R,. 7 C. P. 1 ; 41 L. J., C. P. 43. A short form of lease has been provided by the 8 & 9 Vict. c. 124.

(*h*) Feret v. Hill, 15 C. B. 226.

(*i*) Ritchie v. Smith, 6 C. B. 462. Gas Light Company v. Turner, 7 Sc. 779 ; 8 Id. 609.

(*k*) Ward v. Lumley, 5 H. & N. 94 ; 29 L. J., Ex. 322.   Bolton v. Bishop of Carlisle, 2 H. Bl. 264 ; 4 B. & A. 677.

762. *Equitable assignees.*—The equitable assignee of a legal term is not liable to the lessor for rent, or for damages in respect of breaches of covenants, even though he may have been in possession. (*l*)

763. *Breach of contract to grant a lease.*—The rule which governs sales of real property, that, if the vendor fails to make a good title, the purchaser is only entitled to recover the amount of his deposit and the expenses to which he has been put, does not apply to the case of a lease granted by a lessor in excess of his leasing powers, and containing a covenant for quiet enjoyment; and, if the lease is repudiated by a person claiming under the assumed lessor, having a good title so to do, the lessee is entitled to recover the full value of the lease ; and it makes no difference that the lease was a reversionary lease, and that it was repudiated before the lessee had entered into possession under it. In such a case it was held that the lessee was entitled to recover the expense of the lease so repudiated, but not the expense of a lease of the demised premises which he took from the person really entitled to grant one after the repudiation of the first lease, nor to a £10 per cent. compensation given by the jury, on a supposed analogy to the case of a compulsory sale to a railway company under an act of parliament. (*m*) If a man contracts to grant a good and valid lease, without having any color of title to the premises intended to be demised, the intended lessee may recover all the damages he has sustained by reason of the non-performance of the contract, including the

---

(*l*) Cox v. Bishop, 8 De G. M. & G.   96 ; 34 L. J., C. P. 201 ; 35 Id. 141 ;
815.   L. R., 1 C. P. 441.
(*m*) Locke v. Furze, 19 C. B., N. S.

loss of the lease, (*n*) but not damages and costs arising out of the re-sale of the lease to a third person. (*o*) [1]

764. *Actions by landlords for use and occupation of premises.*—If lands and houses have been occupied by a tenant under a lease void as to the duration of the term by the statute of frauds, the rent reserved in the lease will be the measure of damages resulting from the breach of the implied contract to pay for the actual use and occupation of the property. (*p*) But, when no rent has been fixed upon or ascertained by the agreement of the parties, or the contract has been so far departed from that the stipulated rent forms no just criterion of value, the actual pecuniary value of the occupation will constitute the damage recoverable by the plaintiff. In case of an eviction from part of the premises, the jury must ascertain, independently of any agreement, what ought to be paid. (*q*) [2]

765. *Damages for breach of covenants for quiet enjoyment.*—A lessee under a void lease who has been ejected by the successor of the lessor has a right, in an action against the executors of the lessor for breach of a covenant for quiet enjoyment contained in his lease, to recover the value of the term. (*r*) The value of

---

(*n*) Robinson v. Harman, 18 L. J., Ex. 202.

(*o*) Spedding v. Nevill, L. R., 4 C. P. 212; 38 L. J., C. P. 133.

(*p*) *Ante.* De Medina v. Polson, Holt, 47.

(*q*) Tomlinson v. Day, 2 B. & B. 681.

(*r*) Williams v. Burrell, 1 C. B. 428.

---

[1] See Wolf v. Mitchell, 24 La. Ann. 433; Gartside v. Outley, 58 Ill. 211; Buck v. Rodgers, 39 Ind. 222. A proposal by a tenant at will to "take the house for three years from " a certain future day if the owner would put in a new furnace, which proposition is accepted by the landlord, is a present demise to commence in the future, and not an agreement to execute a lease at a future time. Shaw v. Farnsworth, 108 Mass. 358.

[2] See *ante*, note 3, § 700.

the term also is recoverable by a plaintiff who has never had possession of the demised premises, but who is clothed with an interesse termini, which is a valuable and assignable interest. (*s*)

766. *Damages for breach of covenant not to assign.*—The measure of damages for a breach by an assignee of the lease of a covenant not to assign, is such a sum as will, as far as money can, put the plaintiff in the same position as if he had still the defendant's liability, instead of the liability of another of inferior pecuniary ability, for breaches both past and future. (*t*)

767. *Damages for breach of covenant to repair.*— In an action for breach of a covenant to repair, the proper measure of damages is the amount that it will take to put the premises into repair; (*u*) but, in estimating the damages to be recovered, the age and general state and condition of the property at the time of the demise must, as we have already seen, be taken into consideration. (*v*)   If buildings fall to the ground by reason of the neglect of the covenantor to repair them, or if they are blown down by the wind, or burned by an accidental fire, the proper measure of damages is the amount that it will take to rebuild, deducting the difference in value between old materials and new, as the landlord is not entitled to be put in a better position than he was in before the fire took place, and can not have the value of a new house when the one he has lost was an old house. (*y*)   If there be both a covenant to repair and a covenant to

(*s*) Locke v. Furze, *ante.* And see Rolph v. Crouch, L. R., 3 Ex. 44 ; 37 L. J., Ex. 8.

(*t*) Williams v. Earle, I., R., 3 Q. B. 739.

(*u*) Vivian v. Champion, 2 Raym. 1125. Davies v. Underwood, 2 H. &

N. 571 ; 27 L. J., Ex. 113. Bell v. Hayden, 9 Ir. C. L. R. 301.

(*v*) *Ante.* Burdett v. Withers, 2 N. & P. 123. Paine v. Hayne, 16 M. & W. 541 ; 16 L. J., Ex. 130.

(*y*) Yates v. Dunster, 11 Exch. 15 ; 24 L. J., Ex. 226.

insure against loss from fire for a specific sum, the liability of the covenantor in respect of the cost of re-building in case the premises are burned down is not limited to the amount of the sum covenanted to be insured. (z)   If the party suing upon the covenant is only tenant for life, with remainder in tail and a reversion in fee, he can only recover such damages as are commensurate with his life estate. (a)   Where a defendant held premises under a lease with a covenant to keep and yield them up in repair, and at the expiration of the lease the premises were dilapidated to an amount fixed by the jury at £22, and the plaintiff had, before this time, made a verbal agreement with a third person to grant him a lease for a long term, and at once proceeded to pull down the premises, it was held that the plaintiff was, notwithstanding, entitled to recover substantial damages. (b)

If a lessor has covenanted to repair a dwelling-house demised by him, and the building is destroyed by fire or becomes ruinous and uninhabitable, the lessee may re-build, if the lessor neglects so to do within a reasonable period after request; and the measure of damages to be recovered by the lessee in such a case will be the costs and expenses of the re-building.[1]   We have already seen that covenants to

(z) Digby v. Atkinson, 4 Campb.   Bedingfield v. Onslow, 3 Lev. 209.
275.   (b) Rawlings v. Morgan, 18 C. B.,
(a) Evelyn v. Raddish, Holt, 543.   N. S. 776; 34 L. J., C. P. 185.

[1] If the premises are in good repair when demised, but afterwards become ruinous and dangerous, the landlord is not responsible therefor either to the occupant or the public, during the continuance of the lease, unless he has expressly agreed to repair or has renewed the lease after the need of repair has shown itself; and this rule applies to a lessee out of possession, who has sub-let to another who is in possession. Clancy v. Byrne, 56 N. Y. 129, and see Lockrow v. Horgan, 58 Id. 635.

pay rent and covenants to repair, contained in a lease,
are independent covenants, and that the lessee is not
exonerated from his liability to pay rent under his
covenant so to do by reason of the non-performance
of the lessor's covenant to repair. If, therefore, the
lessor neglects to fulfill his covenant, and delays making the repairs, he is responsible in damages for expenses incurred by the lessee in procuring a suitable
residence to reside in whilst he is prevented from having the use and enjoyment of the house during the
period of delay or neglect to fulfill the covenant. [1] But,
if the lessor fulfills his covenant by repairing as soon as
he reasonably can, he will not then be responsible for
the rent of a house which the lessee may be obliged
to take for a residence whilst the repairs are being ex-

---

[1] But he is not liable, it seems, in damages to third persons.
Such a lessee, therefore, is not liable for an injury to the
property of a person lawfully upon the premises therewith,
resulting from a neglect to keep them in repair; and this is so
although, by his covenant with his landlord, he is bound to
make all ordinary repairs. The covenant does not give a
right of action to or impose a liability in favor of a stranger.
Clancy v. Byrne, 56 N. Y. 129. The obligation of a landlord
to repair demised premises rests solely upon express contract;
a covenant to repair will not be implied, nor will an express
covenant be enlarged by construction; Witty v. Matthews, 52
N. Y. 312; nor do voluntary repairs by a landlord raise a
presumption of a covenant to repair; Moore v. Weber, 71 Pa.
St. 429; nor can a tenant make permanent repairs without
the landlord's consent, and recover for them from the landlord; Kline v. Jacobs, 68 Pa. St. 57. Where a lease contains
a condition that, in case the demised premises are so damaged
by fire, as to be untenable, the rent shall cease until they are
put in good repair, the fact that a tenant or sub-tenant continues to occupy a portion of the premises after the fire, is
not conclusive evidence that the premises are tenantable: but
other evidence as of the circumstances which induced the
tenant to remain, is proper. Kip v. Merwin, 52 N. Y. 542. In
Moore v. Weber, 71 Pa. St. 429, it was held that the maxim

ecuted. (*c*)   If an action is brought against an assignee of a lease for damages for a breach of covenant to repair, in respect of dilapidations that accrued during the time he was assignee, the criterion of damage is the loss which the landlord would sustain by the non-repair if he went into the market to sell the reversion. (*d*)   If an under-lessee refuses to repair according to his agreement, and his immediate lessor (the mesne landlord), who is himself a lessee, and bound under pain of forfeiture to keep the premises in repair, enters and repairs them, the measure of damages is the sum necessarily expended in putting them into repair, and not the costs of an action brought by the original lessor against the mesne landlord for non-repair, unless the under-lease contains a covenant to indemnify. (*e*) [1]

(*c*) Green v. Eales, 2 Q. B. 225.

(*d*) Martin, B., Smith v. Peat, 9 Exch. 161 ; 23 L. J., Ex. 85.   Doe v. Rowlands, 9 C. & P. 739.   Bell v. Hayden, 9 Ir. Com. Law Rep. 301.

(*e*) Logan v. Hall, 4 C. B. 598. Smith v. Howell, 6 Exch. 737.   Walker v. Hatton, 10 M. & W. 249.   Colley v. Streeton, 2 B. & C. 273.   Clow v. Brogden, 2 Sc. N. R. 303.

---

caveat emptor applied to a lease where an adjoining owner took down his house, leaving the tenant's goods exposed to the weather.

[1] Plaintiffs entered into a written agreement with D, by which they agreed to demise to him " stores Nos. 87 and 89," L. street, New York, for three years, D agreeing to lease or to procure responsible persons to take the lease.   Plaintiffs further agreed, if the lessees should desire, to put in a steam hoisting apparatus, they receiving, as additional rent, after its completion, twelve per cent. on its cost.   The premises were arranged to be used as one store, with a stairway at one side, communicating with the upper stories.   In the entrance-way, at the foot of the stairs, was a hand hoisting apparatus.   D leased to the defendants the upper stories of the building, giving to them therein the benefit of the agreement as to the hoisting apparatus.   Subsequently he leased the first floor to other parties, reserving no right to use any portion for a new

768. *Breach of covenants to consume hay and straw on a farm.*—If a tenant who has covenanted not to carry away hay or straw from the demised premises nevertheless sells it off the land, the proper measure of damages is not the value of the hay or straw, which is the property of the tenant, but the value of it to the land in the shape of manure, if it had been eaten and consumed by cattle and deposited on the soil. Where the landlord had agreed to purchase the outgoing tenant's straw at a valuation, and the tenant by the terms of the lease was to return the manure value of straw sold off, it was held that the landlord must pay a fodder price, which is one-half the market price; (*f*) and where the tenant was not to sell straw off the land without returning the value of it in manure, it was held that the tenant was not

(*f*) Clarke v. Westrope, *ante.*

entrance to the upper stories. Defendants notified plaintiffs that they desired the steam hoisting apparatus, which plaintiffs were proceeding to put in place of the old hand apparatus, when they were restrained by injunction, at the suit of defendants. An agreement was thereupon made between the parties that the work should be discontinued until a new entrance should be made, and, if done in a reasonable time, that defendants then would pay the extra rent, from a specified date. Several months elapsed before plaintiffs obtained permission of the lessees of the first floor to put in a new entrance, upon obtaining which a new entrance was made, and the hoisting apparatus completed. D assigned his interest in the lease to plaintiffs. In an action to recover rent, defendants set up, as a counter-claim, damages for the delay in completing the apparatus. *Held*, that the original agreement contemplated that the new apparatus should be placed in the existing stairway; that plaintiffs performed, except as prevented by defendants; that the new agreement imposed no further obligations upon plaintiffs, and that, therefore, defendant was not entitled to recoup his damages. Ayer v. Kobbe, 59 N. Y. 454.

bound to return the marketable value, but the manure value of the straw to the premises. (*g*)

769. *Damages for holding over.*—If the tenant holds over, the landlord may, in some cases, as we have seen, recover double the yearly value, or he may recover the damages and costs he has incurred by not being able to give possession to the succeeding tenant, (*h*) and also the costs incurred in ejecting the person in possession. (*i*)

770. *Of contracts for the lettiug and hiring of furnished houses and lodgings.*—Contracts for the letting and hiring of ready-furnished houses and apartments are contracts of a mixed nature, partaking partly of the nature of a demise of realty, and partly of a contract for the letting and hiring of moveable chattels (*post*, sect. 2) ; and the lessor, therefore, in contracts of this description, is clothed with the duties and responsibilities resulting from contracts for the letting and hiring of chattels in addition to those which have been previously described as flowing from demises of realty simply.

771. *Implied warranties on the part of lessors of furnished apartments.*—If a man furnishes a dwelling-house, or an apartment in a house, and offers it to be let ready-furnished, he impliedly holds it out as fit for immediate habitation and use, and the contract for the letting and hiring of it is analogous to a contract for the letting and hiring of a ship rigged and manned and prepared for sea, or of a carriage horsed and equipped and made ready for a journey on land ; and there is, consequently, an implied warranty on the part of the lessor that such ready-furnished house or

(*g*) Lowndes v. Fountain, *ante.*

(*h*) Bramley v. Chesterton, 2 C. B., N. S. 592 ; 27 L. J., C. P. 23.

(*i*) Henderson v. Squire, L. R., 4 Q. B. 170 ; 38 L. J., Q. B. 73.

lodging is reasonably fit for habitation and occupation by a tenant. If apartments have been taken on condition that they were reasonably fit for habitation and the furniture for use, and the furniture is unfit for use or is encumbered with a nuisance of so serious a nature as to deprive the tenant of all beneficial enjoyment of it, the latter is entitled to throw up both house and furniture, and bring an action against the landlord for a breach of contract. Thus, where the beds of a ready-furnished house, let to a tenant at a rent of eight guineas per week, were so infested and overrun with bugs that they could not be slept in, it was held that the tenant was justified in leaving the house and resisting the landlord's demand for the rent. (*k*) " In the case of a contract for the hire of a ready-furnished house," observes Lord ABINGER, "the letting of the goods and chattels as well as the house implies that the party who lets the house so furnished is under an obligation to supply the other contracting party with whatever goods and chattels may be fit for the use and occupation of such a house, according to its particular description, and suitable in every respect for his use." (*l*) [1]

(*k*) Smith v. Marrable, 11 M. & W. 5. cited 12 M. & W. 60, 65, 87. Campbell v. Lord Wenlock, 4 F. & F. 716.

(*l*) Sutton v. Temple, 12 M. & W. 60.

[1] In New York the law of summary proceedings does not apply to agreements for board and rooms; Wilson v. Martin, 1 Den. 602 ; otherwise it seems that lodgers are entitled to all the privileges of tenants, and enjoy the same protection as to payment of rent and of notice to quit, terminable according to the terms of the letting. If a man takes lodgings on the first or second floor of a house, he has a right to the use of the door-bell, the knocker, the skylight, the staircase, and the water-closet, unless it is otherwise stipulated at the time of taking lodgings ; and if the landlord deprives him of the use of these, an action lies ; § 67, Taylor's L. & T. 5th

772. *Rights and liabilities of lodging-house keepers
and lodgers.*—It has been held that a contract for
board and lodging, where the lodging-house keeper
undertakes generally to provide food and shelter
for man and beast, and does not agree to let any
particular room, is not a contract for an interest
in land. (*m*) A tenant of lodgings is not always
entitled to the exclusive possession of his rooms.
He may sometimes have "a mere easement of
sleeping in one room and eating and drinking in
another;" and the landlord and his servants may have
a right to enter at all times. (*n*) When a man lets
apartments in a house, he impliedly demises them
with all their proper accompaniments, and warrants to
the hirer the use of all such accessorial things as are
necessary to enable him to enjoy the principal subject-
matter of the demise in the manner intended. He
impliedly grants to the tenant the use of the door-bell,
the knocker, the skylights or windows of the staircase,
and the use of the water-closet, unless it be otherwise
stipulated at the time of the taking of the lodgings;
and, if the landlord deprives him of the use of either,
he forthwith subjects himself to an action for a breach
of contract. (*o*) The lodging-house keeper, moreover,
who remains in the general possession of the house, is
bound to exercise all ordinary and reasonable care for
the protection of the persons and property of his
tenants and lodgers; to see that the outer door is
fastened at night, and that strangers or suspected or

(*m*) *Ante,* vol. 1, p. 299.　　　　(*o*) Underwood v, Burrows, 7 C. &
(*n*) Maule, J., 3 C. B. 784.　　　　P. 28.

ed. citing Underhill v. Burrows, 7 C. & P. 26; and the doctrine of caveat emptor has no application to a demise of ready
furnished lodgings; Smith v. Marrable, 1 Carr & Marshm. 479;
and see *ante,* vol. 1, p. 299.

doubtful characters are not permitted, unknown to the lodger, to congregate in the house at unseasonable hours of the night.   He is bound, moreover, to exercise ordinary care and vigilance in the selection and appointment of the servants and domestics within the house, and to take all such precautions as a prudent householder may be expected to take to guard against robbery and fire ; but he is not responsible for the safe keeping of the property of his lodgers, (*p*) unless it has been delivered into his hands to be safely kept.[1] If, after having taken ordinary care in the selection of his servants, a theft is committed on the property of a lodger, in consequence of the front door having been incautiously left open by one of the servants who has been sent out on an errand by the guest, the lodging-house keeper is not responsible for the loss. (*q*)   Nor is he responsible for the loss of things stolen from the lodgers by his own servants. (*r*)

The lodger on the other hand, may be sued for use and occupation ;[2] and, if he brings goods and chattels of his own upon the premises, they may be distrained for the rent of the lodgings as in the ordinary cases of demises of pure realty. (*s*)   If the possession as well as the use of the furniture is granted to the lessee, the latter is bound to deliver up the furniture at the expiration of the term in good order and condition, deteriorated only by ordinary wear and tear and the reasonable use of it.   If he received linen, plate, and household utensils clean and fit for use, and

(*p*) Holder v. Soulby, 8 C. B., N. S. 254; 29 L. J., C. P, 246.

(*q*) Dansey v. Richardson, 3 E. & B. 144; 23 L. J., Q. B. 217.

(*r*) Holder v. Soulby, *supra.*

(*s*) Newman v. Anderton, 5 B. & P. 227.

[1] *Post*, ch. 3.
[2] *Ante*, § 707.

agreed "to leave them as he found them," he is bound to render the things back to the lessor in a clean state. (*t*)

773. *Destruction of buildings by fire.*—Where a contract is entered into for the use of a furnished saloon for the giving of a concert, and the saloon is destroyed by fire before the time appointed for the concert, the parties to the contract are excused from performance of it. (*u*)

774. *Proof of the duration of the term of hiring.* —Lodgings and ready-furnished apartments are rarely the subject of a yearly hiring; and there is no presumption, from a general holding thereof, in favor of a hiring for a year, and from year to year, as in the case of a demise of land. (*v*) The duration of the term corresponds, in general, with the time limited for the payment of the rent. If the rent is payable quarterly, the presumption is in favor of a hiring by the quarter; if, on the other hand, it is payable monthly or weekly, there is a hiring by the month or week. The same rules prevail in the French law. (*y*) Where a tenant agreed to pay for the occupation of furnished apartments, "from March the 4th to September the 4th, the sum of £52 10*s*." also "to occupy the rooms from the 4th of September to the 4th of December on the same terms, viz., £26 5*s*. for the three months, or to take them unfurnished at the rate of £84 per annum," it was held that this was a lease for six months and for a further period of three months, and not a lease from year to year. (*z*)

775. *Notice to quit.*—If the tenancy is for one

(*t*) Stanley v. Agnew, 12 M. & W. 827.

(*u*) Taylor v. Caldwell, 32 L. J., Q. B. 165. *Ante.*

(*v*) Wilson v. Abbott, 4 D. & R. 694.

(*y*) Pothier, Louage, No. 30.

(*z*) Atherstone v. Bostock, 2 Sc. N. R. 643.

single quarter, month or week, no notice to quit is requisite, as the duration of the holding is fixed and determined; but, if the hiring be from half-year to half-year, half-a-year's notice to quit must be given; if from quarter to quarter, a quarter's notice; if from month to month, a month's notice, and if from week to week, a week's notice to quit is, in general, requisite by custom and usage. (*a*)   If there is no custom, a reasonable notice is requisite; (*b*) and, if the lodger quits his apartments without giving such notice, he is liable to the payment of a quarter's, a month's, or a week's rent according to the term of hiring; and the lodging-house keeper may recover such rent, although he has put a bill in the windows advertising the apartments to be let, or has lighted fires in and used the rooms. (*c*)   The length of the notice may be otherwise regulated by the express agreement of the parties, and also by the custom and usage of the district.   It must, however, in all cases, expire at the end of the current term of hiring.   If a tenant remains in possession of lodgings after the termination of his term of hiring, or after the expiration of a notice to quit, the landlord may, as we have seen, assert his rights by force.

776. *Letting and hiring of stowage and places of deposit.*—A contract for the letting and hiring of a vault, or store, or place of deposit in a warehouse, is a contract analogous to the letting and hiring of an apartment in a house for the occupation of a tenant or lodger.   But the landlord only contracts that the place is fit for use so far as reasonable care can make

---

(*a*) But the custom must be proved. Huffel v. Armistead, 7 C. & P. 56.

(*b*) Jones v. Mills, 10 C. B., N. S. 788; 31 L. J., C. P. 66.

(*c*) Redpath v. Roberts, 3 Esp. 225. Griffith v. Hodges, 1 C. & P. 419. *Ante.*

it so ; and, therefore, where a tenant hired the ground-
floor of a warehouse, the upper part of which was occupied by the landlord himself, and the water from the
roof was collected by gutters into a box, from which
it was discharged by a pipe into the drains, and a hole
was made in the box by rats, through which the water
entered the warehouse and wetted the tenant's goods,
but the landlord had exercised reasonable care in examining and seeing to the security of the gutters and
box, it was held that he was not liable for the damage
so caused. (*d*)   In the civil law, a man who let out a
store or place of deposit for corn, wine, oil, or merchandise of a perishable character, impliedly warranted his
store-house to be fit for the purpose for which it was
known to be required.   If the hirer had inspected it,
and approved it prior to the contract, the store-keeper
was not responsible for patent defects which the
hirer might by the exercise of ordinary vigilance have
made himself acquainted with ; but for all latent defects causing injury to the property deposited he was
responsible.   If the store-room was in a roofed building, he was bound to keep the roof water-tight.   If
the places of deposit were upon or below the surface
of the ground, he was bound to keep them properly
drained and free from water.   If he remained in the
general possession of the premises, it was his duty to
see that the outer gates were fastened at a proper hour
of the night, that suspicious characters were not permitted to lurk about the spot, and that the rooms
and stores were watched with proper and reasonable
care. (*e*)   He was bound, in short, to take all ordinary
precautions to secure his store-house from attacks

(*d*) Carstairs v. Taylor, L. R., 6 Ex.   (*e*) Pandect. ed. Poth., lib. 19, tit. 2,
217; 40 L. J., Ex. 129.   s. 3, art. 3, 71.

from without, and from dangers within, from damage by fire and damp, and from all things hurtful to the property deposited beneath his roof.

777. *Room or standing-places in factories.*—An agreement for the use of room in a factory for the purpose of working machines will or will not amount to a demise, according to the terms of the agreement and the circumstances of the case. (*f*)

778. *Lodgings in common inns—Who may be said to be a common innkeeper.*—Every person who makes it his business to entertain travelers and passengers, and provide lodging and necessaries for them and their horses and attendants, is a common innkeeper; and it is in no way material whether he have any sign before his door or not. (*g*)[1] A London "coffee-house," where beds and provisions are furnished by the day, or for the night, or for a longer period, to all persons who may think fit to apply for them, is a common inn; and all persons who are willing and able to pay, the customary hire, are entitled to be received as guests at an inn, whether they are wayfarers or travelers, or merely residents in the locality. (*h*)   But, if a man merely opens a house for the sale of provisions and refreshments, and does not profess to furnish beds and lodging for the night, he is not a common innkeeper. (*i*)   And, if he professes to let only private

---

(*f*) See Selby v. Greares, L. R., 3 C. P. 594, where it was held there was a demise, and Hardwick v. Austin, 14 C. B., N. S. 429 ; 32 L. J., C. P. 252, where the contrary was held.

(*g*) Bac. Abr. INNS (B.)   Parker v Flint, 12 Mod. 255.

(*h*) Thompson v. Lacy, 3 B. & Ald. 283.

(*i*) Doe v. Laming, 4 Campb. 77.

[1] See State v. Mathews, 7 Dev. & Bat. 424 ; Lyon v. Smith, 1 Morris (Iowa) 184 ; Bonner v. Wilborn, 7 Geo. 296 ; Wintermute v. Clark, 5 Sandf. 247 ; Dickerson v. Rogers, 4 Humph. 170.

lodgings, and does not offer his house to the public as
a place of reception and entertainment and lodging
for all comers who are able and willing to pay for the
accommodation offered, he can not be said to keep
a common inn.[1]

779. *Duties of innkeepers.*—Every man who
opens an inn by the wayside, and professes to exercise the business and employment of a common innkeeper, is by the custom of the realm, bound to afford
such shelter and accommodation as he possesses to
all who apply and tender, or are able and ready to pay,
the customary hire, and are not drunk or disorderly,
or laboring under contagious or infectious diseases.
And, if he neglects or refuses so to do, he is liable to
an action for the recovery of any damages that may
have been sustained by reason of such refusal, and also
to an indictment at common law. (*k*)　The innkeeper

(*k*) Hawthorn v. Hammond, 1 C. & 725. Rex v. Ivens, 7 C. & P. 219.
K. 404. Howell v. jackson, 6 C. & P.

[1] One who entertains strangers occasionally, although he
receives compensation for such entertainment, is not an innkeeper.　State v. Mathews, 1 Dev. & Bat. 424; Lyon v. Smith,
1 Morris (Iowa), 184.　In order to charge a party as an innkeeper, it is only necessary to prove that all persons coming
to his house were received as guests without any previous
agreement as to the times or terms of their stay; "a public
house of entertainment to all who choose to visit it," is the
true definition of an inn.　Wintermute v. Clark, 5 Sandf. 247.
One making a special contract with an innkeeper for his
lodging, may thereby virtually relieve him from his legal
character of innkeeper.　See this question discussed in Berkshire Woolen Co. v. Proctor, 4 Cush. 417; and see Chamberlin v. Masterson, 26 Ala. 371.　The question as to whether if
one carries or sends his property to an inn, but does not go
there to eat or drink, he is a guest so far as to charge the
innkeeper as such, has been decided both in the affirmative
and the negative.　Mason v. Thompson, 9 Pick. 280; Peek v.
McGraw, 25 Wend. 653: *contra*, Grinnell v. Cook, 3 Hill (N.
Y.), 485; Thickstun v. Howard, 8 Blackf. 535.

is bound, moreover, if he has room in his stables, to receive and provide for the horses of travelers who alight at his inn, intending to become guests and to lodge there; but he is not bound to receive horses from parties who merely intend to make use of his stables as livery and bait stables, resorting elsewhere for lodging and entertainment; nor is he bound to receive the goods of a person who professes merely to make use of the inn as a place of deposit, and not to lodge there as a guest. (*l*)　Neither is he bound to provide for his guest the precise room that the latter may choose to select, nor to provide him with a bed-room, if he declares it to be his intention to sit up all night.　All that he is required to do is to find reasonable and proper accommodation for his guests; and, if he tenders such accommodation, and the guest refuses it, he may compel the latter to quit the inn, and seek for accommodation and lodging elsewhere. (*m*) [1]

780. *Of the protection of the guest from robbery and theft*—To the duties and obligations which attach to innkeepers in common with all lodging-house keepers and lessors of furnished rooms and apartments for immediate occupation, the law has superadded the duty of protecting the goods of their guests from robbery. (*n*)　But the innkeeper will not be liable, if the loss would probably not have happened had the guest used the care which a prudent man might reasonably have been expected to take under the circumstances. (*o*) [2]

(*l*) Smith v. Dearlove, 6 C. B. 132. Binns v. Pigot, 9 C. & P. 209. But see Day v. Bather, 2 H. & C. 14.

(*m*) Fell v. Knight, 8 M. & W. 276.

(*n*) Morgan v. Ravey, 6 H. & N.

265; 30 L. J., Ex. 131.　But see now the 26 & 27 Vict c. 41.

(*o*) Oppenheim v. White Lion Hotel Company, L. R., 6 C. P. 515; 40 L. J., C. P. 93.

[1] See last note.

[2] The innkeeper is an insurer of his guest's goods against

781. *Exemption of the guest's property from distress for rent.*—The carriages and horses, goods and chattels of guests sojourning at public inns, can not be

everything except the act of God or the public enemies, or the negligence or fraud of the guest himself. Mowers v. Feathers, 6 Lans. 112; Mason v. Thompson, 9 Pick. 280; Piper v. Manny, 21 Wend. 282; Grinnell v. Cook, 3 Hill (N. Y.) 485; Manning v. Wells, 9 Humph. 746; Thickstun v. Howard, 8 Blackf. 535; Mateer v. Brown, 1 Cal. 221. And this, even if the guest intrust his property to some other in the house than the inn keeper himself; Sneider v. Geiss, 1 Yeates, 34; and an inn keeper has been held liable for an injury to the plaintiff's horse while at the defendant's stable. Where the horse was placed at the stable in the evening, and the next morning one of his hind legs was found to have been broken above the gambrel joint, even though the evidence tended to show that he was treated with care and faithfulness; that he was placed in a safe and suitable stall, with sufficient and suitable bedding; and that the injury happened without the fault of any one. Shaw v. Berry, 31 Me. 478; but see Mc-Daniels v. Robinson, 26 Vt. 337; Metcalf v. Hess, 14 Ill. 129. The presumption, in case of the loss of the guest's goods, is that they were lost through the innkeeper's negligence. Kisten v. Hildebrand, 9 B. Mon. 72; McDonald v. Edgerton, 5 Barb. 560; Bennett v. Mellor, 5 T. R. 273; Berkshire Woollen Co. v. Proctor, 7 Cush. 417; Thickston v. Howard, 8 Blackf. 535; Shaw v. Berry, 31 Me. 478; Matur v. Brown, 1 Cal. 221; Manning v. Wells, 9 Humph. 746; Mason v. Thompson, 9 Pick. 280; Piper v. Manny, 21 Wend. 282; Grinnell v. Cook, 3 Hill, 485; Merritt v. Claghorn, 23 Vt. 177; Sibley v. Aldrich, 33 N. H. 553. And this will extend a loss in a free carriage sent by an innkeeper to a station to convey the guest to his house; see Dickinson v. Winchester, 4 Cush. 114; Grinnell v. Cook, 3 Hill, 486. But see Fox v. McGregor, 11 Barb. 41. A modification of the rule stated in the text appears to be laid down in Colquett v. Kirkman, which holds that, although as against the actual bailor of a horse, the livery stable keeper had a lien upon the horse for his whole account for feed and keeping, yet if the depositor was not the true owner, or if there were any prior legal incumbrance, the lien of the stable keeper was good against the true owner or prior incumbrance for the expense of feeding or taking care of the thing bailed. If the shed belong

distrained by the landlord for the rent of the premises. (*p*)

782. *Innkeeper's lien.*—An innkeeper has a lien upon goods belonging to the guest, and brought by him to the inn, for his charges for board and lodging supplied to the guest; (*q*) and it has been held that the lien attaches even when the goods do not belong to the guest, if the innkeeper receives them in the belief that they do so belong. (*r*) But he can not detain the person of his guest, or take off his clothing in order to obtain payment of his bill. (*s*)

783. *Gratuitous loans of realty.*—The gratuitously permitting a person to use a shed, by himself or his servant, for a particular purpose, is a mere revocable license, and has no analogy to a bailment of personal property, and the only duty imposed on such person is that there shall not be negligence in the use of the shed; and he is not responsible for the negligence of his servant not within the scope of his employment. (*t*)

(*p*) Bro. Abr. Distress, pl. 57, 71. 1 Roll. Abr. 68, pl. 12.

(*q*) Thompson v. Lacy, 3 B. & A. 283.

(*r*) Threlfall v. Borwick, L. R., 7

Q. B. 711; 41 L. J., Q. B. 266.

(*s*) Sunbolf v. Alford, 3 M. & W. 248.

(*t*) Williams v. Jones, 33 L. J., Ex. 297.

to one who is an innkeeper, the question of his liability will depend upon his knowledge. In Albin v. Presby, 8 N. H. 408, a traveler put his horse and loaded wagon in an open shed near the highway, without the inn keeper's knowledge; *held*, that the latter was not liable for the loss, although it was usual for guests to put their horses and wagons under such shed. Under different circumstances; see Piper v. Manny, 21 Wend. 282; Clute v. Wiggins, 14 Johns. 175.

SECTION II.

THE LETTING OF CHATTELS.

784. *Of bailments for hire.*—The term bailment, derived from the French word bail or bailler, to deliver, denotes, in the common law, a delivery or transfer of a chattel from one person to another, in order that something may be done with it, either for the benefit of the owner, or of the party who receives it as the temporary possessor, or of the mutual benefit of both of them, and is applied to contracts for the letting and hiring of chattels, as well as to contracts for the delivery of them to persons for safe custody, or to workmen to be worked upon or dealt with in the course of their employment. The term is also equally applicable to contracts for the letting and hiring of realty, although it is not used in the common law to denote that class of contracts. In the French law, the term bail a loyer, or bail for hire, anciently denoted a contract for the letting and hiring of a house, or farm, or immovable property; but in modern times it has been applied by the French jurists to contracts for the letting and hiring of personalty as well as of realty. In this class of contracts, the person who delivers the chattel for the purposes of the contract is called the bailleur or bailor, and the party who receives it the bailee.

If one man bails or delivers a chattel to another to be used for hire upon the express or implied understanding that the chattel is to be put into a serviceable state and made ready for immediate use by the hirer, there is no implied warranty or undertaking on the

part of the bailor that the chattel is in any particular
state or condition, or fit for any particular purpose.
But if he expressly or impliedly represents it to be fit
for immediate use, or to be applicable to any particular purpose, he impliedly warrants the use for which
he receives the hire. If a man, for example, lets out
the naked hull or the mere fabric of a vessel, upon the
terms that the hirer is to man and equip her, and get
her ready for sea, there is no implied warranty or undertaking on the part of the shipowner that the vessel
is in any particular state and condition at the time of
the making of the contract. But if he mans and provisions and equips the vessel himself, and holds her
out as fit for immediate use, there is an implied promise
or undertaking on his part that she is seaworthy and
fit for use, and properly found and provided with stores
and provisions, seamen and officers, and all things
needful to the due prosecution of the voyage. (*a*) So,
if a man lets out the mere fabric of a coach or carriage
upon the understanding that the hirer is to provide
the horses, harness, servants, and equipments, and prepare the vehicle for use, there is no implied warranty
or undertaking on his part that the chattel is in any
particular state or condition at the time that he
parts with the possession of it ; but if he gets it
ready for the road, he impliedly warrants the vehicle
to be road-worthy and fit for the performance of the
journey for which it is known to be required; and this
implied warranty extends to the coachman, horses, and
harness, and all the other necessary equipments for
the journey. And if a man lets out furniture for immediate use, there is an implied warranty on his part
that it is fit for use, and free from all defects inconsist-

(*a*) Lyon v. Mells, 5 East, 437. Bur- Stanton v. Richardson, L. R., 7 C. P.
gess v. Wickham, 33 L. J., Q. B. 17. 521 ; 41 L. J., C. P. 180.

ent with the reasonable and beneficial enjoyment of it.
(*b*) " If he lets out vessels for holding oil or wine,
and furnishes to the hirer vessels that are not in good
condition, he shall be responsible for the damages that
may accrue ; for he who lets out a thing for use ought
to know whether it is fit for use, and to warrant the
use for which he takes the hire." (*c*)   If he lets out a
horse bridled and saddled, and prepared for immediate
use by an equestrian, he impliedly warrants the equipments to be road-worthy and fit for use, and the horse
itself to be well shod, (*d*) and free from such vices
and defects as render it dangerous and unfit to ride.[1]

(*b*) Sutton *v.* Temple, 12 M. & W. 60.

(*c*) Domat, l. 1, tit. 4, s. 3, 8.   Dig. lib. 10, tit. 2, 19, § 1.

(*d*) Pothier (LOUAGE), No. 54. Blackmore *v.* Brist. & Exeter Rail. Co., 8 Ell. & Bl. 1051 ; 27 L. J., Q. B. 167.

The authorities in the United States as to the bailor's
warranty of fitness for use are not numerous.   Parsons on
Contracts, 179, states the rule substantially as laid down in
the text, namely, that the one letting the chattels for hire warrants them to be serviceable for the purpose loaned ; as to
whether he is bound to maintain them in a serviceable condition, there seems to be some conflict of opinion.   The case of
Isbell v. Norvell, 4 Gratt. 176, held, that where the hirer of a
slave pays a physician for attending on the slave while he is
hired, he is entitled to have the amount repaid him by the
owner of the slave.   But in the case of Redding v. Hall, 1
Bibb, 536, the same question was decided the other way, after
a careful examination of the authorities.   It is impossible to
say with certainty what the true rule of law is, until we have
further adjudication.   It was held in Harrington v. Snyder, 3
Barb. 380, that where a horse hired to perform a certain journey and back, becomes disabled by lameness, without any
fault of the hirer, so that the hirer is compelled to incur expense, in order to return by other means, these expenses
may be recouped from the bailor in his action for hire of the
horse, and if they exceed the value of the horse's services,
the bailor can not recover at all ; otherwise if the horses are
immoderately driven.   Hughes v. Boyer, 9 Watts, 556 ; and
Buford v. Tucker, 44 Ala. 89, holds that where a slave was

785. *Of the duties and responsibilities of the hirers of chattels.*—If a coach-proprietor lets his coach and horses for a journey, and the coach is driven by the coachman, and is under the direction and management of the servants of the owner, the latter is bound to keep the horses properly shod, and the carriage in good traveling order;[1] but, if the possession thereof is transferred to the hirer, and the carriage is driven and managed by the hirer's servants, this duty then falls upon the hirer, although the owner or letter of the chattel may, under certain circumstances, be obliged, as we shall presently see, to repay to the hirer the money expended by him in repairs. (e) Whenever a chattel bailed or delivered to a hirer to be used for hire has sustained a partial injury through an inherent defect in the article itself, or by reason of some inevitable accident which threatens its total and immediate destruction, and the effects of such partial injury may be obviated and the chattel preserved for future use by repairs and remedies promptly provided, there is an implied authority from the owner to the hirer to undertake the necessary repairs and apply the remedies, and incur all such expenses as a prudent

(e) Pothier (LOUAGE), No. 117, 129.

hired for a fixed and definite period, and emancipated during that term, the hirer was not bound to make a deduction from the hire on account of such emancipation. If the bailor of a chattel slave (in this case) for hire, fraudulently conceal his unsoundness, the bailment is at an end and the bailee may return him. James v. Neal, 3 T. B. Mon. 370; see Thompson v. Harlow, 31 Ga. 348. So the owner of a slave let out to a steamer, could not recover his value when he was lost overboard without the lessee's fault. Downey v. Stacey, 1 La. Ann. 426; Huntington v. Ricard, 6 Id. 806; but see Wilkes v. Hughes, 37 Ga. 361; Muldrow v. Wellington, &c. R. R. Co., 13 Rich. 69; and see Graves v. Moses, 13 Minn. 335.

[1] See cases cited in last note.

man would, under the circumstances, incur for the preservation of his own property.[1] In order to establish a claim for the payment of expenses of this description, in the Scottish law, it is necessary, observes MR. BELL, to show in the first place that the occasion of the expense was not ascribable to the hirer; secondly, that the expense was indispensably necessary; and, thirdly, that the owner had notice of it as soon as circumstances permitted. (*f*)

786. *Of the use of chattels let to hire.—Losses from negligence.*—Every hirer of a chattel is bound to use the thing let in a proper and reasonable manner, to take the same care of it that a prudent and cautious man ordinarily takes of his own property, and to return it to the bailor or owner at the time appointed for its return[2] (or within a reasonable period after request,[3] if no such time has been agreed upon), in as good condition as it was in at the time of the bailment, subject only to the deterioration produced by ordinary wear and tear and reasonable use, and by injuries caused by accidents which have happened without any fault or neglect on the part of the hirer.[4]

(*f*) 1 Bell's Com. 453.

[1] See Whitlock v. Heard, 13 Ala. 676 ; Redding v. Hall, 1 Bibb, 536.

[2] The bailor's remedy to regain possession of his chattel is an action of trover; he can not resort to force. Rotch v. Hawes, 12 Pick. 136; Trotter v. McCall, 26 Miss. 413 ; Homer v. Ewing, 3 Pick. 492 ; Setzar v. Butler, 5 Ired. 212.

[3] And what is a reasonable time will depend on the circumstances. Esmay v. Fanning, 9 Barb. 176.

[4] The contract of bailment is said to be for the benefit of both parties, and the bailee is liable only for ordinary care. 2 Kent Com. 586, 587, and note d; Millon v. Salisbury, 13 Johns. 211; Platt v. Hibbard, 7 Cow. 497; Maynard v. Buck, 100 Mass. 40. And the bailee must restrict himself to the precise use for which the bailment was made; James v.

Where the hirer contracted to deliver up a barge at the conclusion of the hiring "in good working order, with all her rigging, gear, and implements complete," it was held that this must be construed with reference to the condition of the barge (which was an old one) at the commencement of the hiring. (*h*)

787. *Losses from piracy, robbery, theft, disease, and accident.*—If the thing let to hire perishes, or is destroyed by fire, or is stolen without any neglect or want of care on the part of the hirer, the latter will not be responsible for the loss; (*i*) but in cases of stealing, a robbery by force must be proved, or, if there has been a secret theft, it must be shown by the hirer that he had taken all such precautions as are ordinarily taken by prudent men to protect their own property from depredation.[1]   If a ship hired for a partic-

(*h*) Shroder v. Ward, 13 C. B., N. S. 410; 32 L. J., C. P. 150.

(*i*) Williams v. Lloyd, W. Jones, 179. Taylor v. Caldwell, 3 B. & S. 836; 32 L. J., Q. B. 164.

Carper, 4 Sneed, 397; Maguyer v. Hawthorn, 2 Harr. 71; Columbus v. Howard, 6 Ga. 219; Tratter v. McCall, 26 Miss. 403; Moers v. Larry, 15 Gray, 451; McLauchlin v. Lomes, 3 Strob. 85; Hooks v. Smith, 18 Ala. 338. Any other use would be a conversion of the property, as *e g.*, if a horse hired to be driven to a certain place, be driven beyond. Woodman v. Hubbard, 6 Fost. 67; and see Gregg v. Wyman, 4 Cush. 322. In the case of a pledge, however, the property can be used in any way not inconsistent with the pledgor's ultimate rights. Lawrence v. Maxwell, 53 N. Y. 19.

[1] So an agreement of a bailee for hire, to return the chattel in good order, is excused, if, without fault of his, it is destroyed by an irresistible force; so *held*, in a case where a barge was destroyed on the Mississippi. McEvers v. Steamboat Sangammon, 22 Mo. 187. A clause in a lease of furniture binding the lessee "to surrender the property in as good a condition as reasonable use and wear thereof would permit," does not vary the duty imposed by the law of bailments, and consequently a loss by fire, without fault on the part of the

ular voyage, and placed in the possession and under the control of the hirer, be captured by pirates, or be lost in a storm in the ordinary course of the voyage, the owner must bear the loss; but, if the hirer has deviated from the ordinary course, and sailed unnecessarily through dangerous channels, or into seas infested with pirates, and needlessly encountered risks not contemplated by the owner at the time of the hiring, and which would probably not have been run by him except for a greatly increased rate of remuneration, the hirer is liable for the loss.

An owner of a chattel which is out on hire for an unexpired term may maintain an action against a third person for a permanent injury thereto. (*k*) [1]

788. *Determination of the bailment.*—If chattels have been bailed or let to hire for a certain term, and the bailee does an act which is equivalent to the destruction of the chattels, or which is entirely inconsistent with the terms of the bailment; if he sells, or attempts to sell, the chattels, or to dispose of them in such a way as to put it out of his power to return them, the act operates like a disclaimer of tenancy,

---

(*k*) Mears v. London & South-West. Ry. Co., 11 C. B., N. S. 850; 31 L. J., C. P. 220. And see Lancashire Wagon Co. v. Fitzhugh, 6 H. & N. 502; 30 L. J., Ex. 231.

---

hirer, falls on the owner. Hyland v. Paul, 33 Barb. 241. But the burden has been held to be on the bailee in such cases to prove absence of negligence on his part. Logan v. Matthews, 6 Pa. St. 417.

[1] Nor will the bailee be liable even if at the time of the injury, the person injuring them was in his employ, unless acting within the scope of the bailee's employment. Story on Contracts, § 884. But if the servant's action be not malicious, but in the scope of his employment, although without the express assent of his master, the bailee, the latter will be liable. Sinclair v. Pearson, 7 N. H. 219.

the bailment is at an end, and the possessory title re-verts to the bailor, and entitles him to maintain an action for the value of the chattels. (*l*)

789. *Loans of money to be used for hire.*—The lending of money for hire is ordinarily denominated a loan at interest, as distinguished from a commoda-tum or gratuitous loan, where the sum advanced only is paid back, without any interest or fruits of increase. A loan of money to be used for hire is a loan for use and consumption, the identical thing lent not being intended to be returned, but its equivalent in value and kind. The absolute property, therefore, in the subject-matter of the loan passes together with the transfer of the possession to the hirer or borrower; and the latter becomes indebted to the lender in an equiva-lent in value and amount, with interest, which must be paid and rendered to the latter at the time agreed upon or within a reasonable period after demand made, in case no time for its return has been limited. The liability of the hirer or borrower, consequently, to repay the equivalent amount is not discharged by the loss of the money from robbery, fire, or inevitable accident.[1]

(*l*) Fenn v. Bittlestone, 7 Exch. 159 ; 21 L. J., Ex. 41.

[1] And so the placing of a deposit in a bank is simply a loan of that sum of money to the bank, and, if thereafter followed only by the ordinary transactions of depositing and withdraw-ing of sums of money, raises only the simple relation of debtor and creditor, upon loans and repayments. The depositor can not charge banks as trustees, agents, or factors. Cur-tis v. Leavitt, 15 N. Y. 9; National Bank v. Eliot Bank, 20 L. R. 138; Commercial Bank v. Hughes, 17 Wend. 94; Bullard v. Randall, 1 Gray, 605; Chapman v. White, 2 Seld. 212; Downes v. Phœnix Bank, 6 Hill, 297; Foster v. Essex Bank, 17 Mass. 479; Marsh v. Oneida Central Bank, 34 Barb. 298; Bank of Northern Liberties v. Jones, 42 Pa. St. 536. All sums paid into the bank on gen-eral deposits form one fund, which money belongs thereafter

790. *Of commodatum and mutuum or gratuitous loan.*—If the bailee is to have the use and enjoyment of the subject-matter of the bailment for his own benefit and advantage, without payment of hire or reward to the bailor, then the bailment becomes a gratuitous loan. There are, in the civil law, two kinds of gratuitous loans, the one called a mutuum, which is a loan for use and consumption, the thing being bailed to be consumed and an equivalent in kind subse-

to the bank, and the depositor has only a debt owing him from the bank ; see the English case of Foley v. Hill, 2 H. L. Cas. 39 ; his property in his bank account, therefore, is in the nature of property in a chose in action ; he certainly has nothing tangible to which he has a right ; there is no specific money in the bank belonging to him ; nor has he a right, however inchoate, to any specific money in its vaults. The deposit once made, the roll of bills or check, or bag of coin, in which if passed from the depositor's hands into the bank, may be stolen by thieves, or embezzled by officers of the bank, or lost, or misapplied, but neither the bank nor the depositor can follow the particular roll or check, or coin, in order to affect their relations with each other. The bank owes the depositor a sum of money equal to the sum he deposited ; it must pay him on his requisition, and nothing more. See as to these views, Concord v. Concord Bank, 16 N. H. 26 ; Commercial Bank of Albany v. Hughes, 17 Wend. 94. The case of a special deposit is different. Where a bank received bonds on special deposit for safety from one of its customers and at his risk, and placed them in a safe with similar deposits from others, and its own securities. The bonds were stolen by a teller. The theft by the teller was not connected with his employment, and there was no liability on the bank unless they knew or had reason to suspect he was not trustworthy. Scott v. Bank of Chester Valley, 72 Pa. St. 478. In that case the bank teller had absconded and it was then discovered that his accounts were false and that he had robbed the bank during two years. *Held*, that the bank was not bound to examine the teller's accounts for the benefit of a depositor who was a gratitous bailee. And that negligence as a ground of liability must be such as enters into the cause of loss. Scott v. National Bank, &c., 79 Id. 471.

quently returned; and the other, a commodatum, which is a loan of a specific chattel to be used by the bailee and returned in individuo. In the loan by way of mutuum the bailor is called the creditor, by reason of the credit given by him to the promise of the bailee, and the latter the debtor, because he owes an equivalent to be paid back. (*m*) In the loan by way of commodatum, the parties are known in law by the ordinary appellation of borrower and lender. "The Latin language," observes GIBBON, "very happily expresses the fundamental differences between the commodatum and the mutuum which our poverty is reduced to confound under the vague and common appellation of a loan. In the former, the borrower was obliged to restore the same individual thing with which he had been accommodated for the temporary supply of his wants; in the latter, it was destined for his use and consumption, and he discharged this mutual engagement by substituting the same specific value according to a just estimation of number, of weight, and of measure." (*n*) [1]

If corn or potatoes, wine or brandy, coals or oil, be borrowed, they are borrowed to be consumed, the corn being eaten, the wine drunk, and the coals and oil burned and consumed. A loan of this description, therefore, is necessarily a mutuum; for the identical thing lent can not be returned, but an equivalent in kind must be rendered back. If money is lent to be

(*m*) Dig. lib. 50, tit. 16, lex 11; lib. 12, tit. 1, lex 2, §§ 1, 3.

(*n*) Gibbon's Roman Empire, ch. 44, 3, 2.

[1] See under the Louisiana Civil Code, Lockhart v. Wyatt, 10 Ala. 231; Waterman v. Gibson, 5 La. Ann. 672; Succession of Fowler, 7 Id. 207; Dunbar v. Hughes, 6 Id. 466; Woodworth v. Wilson, 11 Id. 402; Lafourche Navigation Co. v. Collins, 12 Id. 119; Devalcourt, 12 Id. 672; Wilson v. Wilson, 16 Id. 155.

used, the money is necessarily mixed with other coin
of a similar denomination ; it passes into other hands;
its identity and individuality are destroyed ; and the
specific pieces of coin can not be rendered back.[1]   A
loan of money, therefore, is a mutuum, the borrower
being bound to restore, not the identical money lent,
but an equivalent in the shape of money of the same
denomination and value. (*o*)   But if a horse or a book
be lent for use, the identity and individuality of the
chattel are not destroyed or in any way affected by the
use ; the same horse and the same book remain, though
the one may have been ridden and the other read; the
loan, therefore, is a commodatum ; and the borrower
does not fulfill his engagement by rendering an equivalent in the shape of a different horse or a different book
of equal value, but is bound to return the identical
thing lent. (*p*)   It is of the very essence of a commodatum that the subject-matter of the bailment be
granted to be used free of reward ; for if anything
be paid for the use of the chattel, the contract is a
contract of letting and hiring, and belongs to the class
locatio rei. (*q*)[2]

791. *Liabilities of the borrower—Of the care to
be taken of things borrowed—Negligence and misconduct of the borrower.*—In a bailment by way of
mutuum, the chattel bailed becomes the absolute
property of the bailee to do what he pleases with it,

(*o*) Et, quoniam nobis non eædem
res sed aliæ ejusdem naturæ et quali-
tatis redduntur, inde etiam mutuum
appellatum est quia ita a me tibi datur,
ut ex meo tuum fiat.   Inst. lib. 3, tit.
15.   Dig. lib. 13, tit. 6, l. 3, § 6.
    (*p*) Doct. & Stud. Dial. 2, ch. 38.
    (*q*) Inst. lib. 3, tit. 15, § 2.   Dig.
lib. 13, tit. 6.

[1] See *ante*, note 1, to § 786.
[2] Mooers v. Larry 15 Gray, 451 ; Eastman v. Sanborn, 3
Allen, 594 ; Banfield v. Whipple, 10 Id. 27 ; Graves v. Moses.
13 Minn. 335 ; Harrington v. Snyder, 3 Barb. 780.

and use it in any way he thinks fit; (*r*) but, in a bailment by way of commodatum, the temporary right of possession and user only are transferred, the right of property remaining in the lender; (*s*) and the borrower, consequently, is obliged to render back the identical thing lent in as good a condition as it was in when borrowed, subject only to the deterioration resulting from inherent defects or produced by ordinary wear and tear and the reasonable use of it for the purpose for which it was known to be required. (*t*) " If I lend a piece of plate, and covenant by deed that the party to whom it is lent shall have the use of it, and the plate be worn out by ordinary use and without any fault, I shall have no remedy for the loss. (*u*) But the borrower is bound," observes HOLT, C. J., "to the strictest care and diligence to keep the goods so as to restore them back again to the lender, because the bailee has a benefit by the use of them, so that, if the bailee be guilty of the least neglect, he will be answerable ; as if a man should lend another a horse to go westward, and the bailee go northward, if any accident happen to the horse on the northern journey, the bailee will be chargeable, because he has made use of the horse contrary to the trust he was lent to him under; and it may be, if the horse had been used no otherwise than as he was lent, that accident would not have happened to him." (*v*) If a horse is lent for the performance of an ordinary journey, and the borrower leaves the high road and travels unnecessarily through

(*r*) Appellata est autem mutui datio ab eo, quod de meo tuum fit : et ideo, sinon fiat tuum, non nascitur obligatio. Dig. lib. 12 tit. 1, § 2. Instit. lib. 3, tit. 15.

(*s*) Nemo enim commodando rem facit ejus cui commodat. Dig. lib. 9.

(*t*) Handford v. Palmer, 5 Moore, 76.

(*u*) Hale, C. B., Pomfret v. Ricroft, 1 Saund. 323, b.

(*v*) Coggs v. Bernard, 2 Raym. 915. Bract. lib. 3, ch. 2, § 1, pp. 99, 100.

by-paths or dangerous roads, and the horse falls, and is injured, he will be responsible to the lender ; but, if the horse is lent for the purpose of hunting, then the borrower is justified in using it in by-paths and dangerous places, and may expose it to all the ordinary risks of the chase, because those risks are necessarily incident to the use for which the horse was borrowed, and were known to and must have been contemplated by the lender. The gratuitously permitting a person to use a shed, by himself or his servant, for a particular purpose, is a mere revocable license, and has no analogy to a bailment of personal property ; and the only duty imposed on such person is that there shall not be negligence in the use of the shed; and he is not liable for the negligence of his servant not within the scope of his employment. (y)

792. *Losses from ordinary casualties.*—The measure of care and diligence to be exercised for the protection and preservation of a thing bailed by way of commodatum, whilst it remains in the possession of the borrower, is that amount of care, prudence, and foresight which the most diligent and careful of men exercise for the preservation and protection of their own property. The foundation for this increased liability on the part of the borrower, in comparison with the hirer of a chattel, arises from the fact that the lender himself derives no benefit from the contract, but in making the bailment performs a gratuitous act of kindness dictated by his confidence in the bailee. The borrower can not be made responsible for inevitable accidents, or casualties which could not have been foreseen, and which no human prudence could have guarded against ; but he will be answerable for the " least neglect." If the borrower of a horse put

(y) Williams v. Jones, 33 L. J., Ex. 297.

the horse in his stable, and the horse is stolen from thence, the borrower will not be answerable for him. But, if the borrower or his servant leave the stable-doors open at night, and thieves take the opportunity of that and steal the horse, he will be chargeable for the loss; for the neglect to lock the door may have encouraged the thieves, and been the occasion of the robbery. (z)

793. *Misuser by the borrower—Want of skill.*—If the borrower takes the horse off the high road against the will of the lender, and rides him into wet and slippery ground, and the horse slips and is injured, the borrower must make good the loss. It has been said that every lender of a horse for riding impliedly bargains, at the time he makes the loan, for the exercise on the part of the borrower of competent skill in riding and the management of a horse; (a) but, if the bailor chooses, without making any previous inquiry, to entrust a fiery and high-spirited horse to a stranger, of whose skill in horsemanship he knows nothing, he has no right to expect the management and dexterity of an experienced rider. Neither, if he lends valuable property to a notorious drunkard or a notoriously wild and reckless character, has he any right to expect the care and attention of a very vigilant and painstaking person. (b) By the civil law, the borrower is responsible for all losses and injuries to the thing borrowed occasioned by the private enmity of persons hostile to him, if he has by some fault or misconduct on his part provoked that enmity. (c) The loan of the use, more-

---

(z) Cloggs v. Bernard, 2 Raym. 916. Dig. lib. 44, tit. 7, l. § 4. Bract. lib. 3, ch. 2, p. 99. Instit. lib. 2, tit. 15, § 2. Doctor and Student, Dial. 2, ch. 38.

(a) Jones's Bailments, 65. Wilson v.

Brett, 11 M. & W. 115.

(b) Pothier, Pret à Usage, ch. 2, § 2, art. 2, No. 49. Bract. lib. 3, tit. 2. § 1, 99 b.

(c) Dig. lib. 19, tit. 2, lex. 27, § 4.

over, is strictly personal to the borrower, founded on the confidence reposed in him, and does not, in general, warrant a user by his servants. (*d*)

794. *Restoration of the thing borrowed or its equivalent—Loss by robbery, fire, or inevitable accident.*—In the case of a loan by way of mutuum, the borrower is bound to restore, at the time agreed upon, or within a reasonable period after request, an article of the same kind and quality as the one originally lent to him. If, by the agreement of the parties, an article of a different character is to be returned, the contract is not a mutuum, but an exchange or sale. (*e*) All such things, say the civilians, as are ordinarily regulated by number, weight, or measure, such as wine, corn, oil, money, brass, silver, or gold, may properly be made the subject of a mutuum, as they can readily be repaid in kind of the same quantity and quality; but a horse, a greyhound, a fowling-piece, and all chattels whose value depends upon the intrinsic qualities of each in particular, and not upon the general attributes of the genus, can not properly be made the subject of mutuum, because, although they are of the same kind, yet each one of the kind differs so much from another in quality and attributes, that the creditor can not be compelled against his will to take one for another.

795. As the right of property in the thing bailed is transferred to the bailee by a bailment by way of mutuum, so also is the risk of loss. If, therefore, the bailee is robbed before he reaches home, or the thing bailed is destroyed by wreck, fire, or inevitable accident before it can be used, the bailee must, neverthe-

---

(*d*) Bringloe v. Morrice, 1 Mod. 210.

(*e*) Dig. lib. 12, tit. 1, 2, 3. South

Australian Insurance Co. v. Randell, L. R., 3 P. C. 101.

less, pay the equivalent which he owes to the bailor at the time appointed. (*f*) "If money, corn, wine, or any other such thing which can not be re-delivered be borrowed, and it perish, it is at the peril of the borrower. But if a horse, or a cart, or such other things as may be used and delivered again, be used according to the purpose for which they were lent, if they perish, he who owns them shall bear the loss, if they perish not through the default of him who borrowed them, or of him who made a promise at the time of the delivery to re-deliver them safe again. If they be used in any other manner than according to the lending, in whatever manner they may perish, if it be not by default of the owner, he who borrowed them shall be charged with them in law and conscience." (*g*) When the loan is made by way of commodatum, the borrower must return the specific thing lent within a reasonable period after request, and if he neglects so to do, he is responsible for all accidents that afterwards happen to it. He has no right to detain the thing borrowed for any antecedent debt due to him. "The plain reason is that it would be a departure from the tacit obligations of the contract. No intention to give a lien for a debt can be implied from the grant of a mere favor." Neither can the borrower set up a right to detain the chattel for the payment of necessary expenses incurred by him in the keeping and preserving it. (*h*)

796. *Implied obligations and duties of the lender.*— There is an implied undertaking on the part of the

---

(*f*) Instit. lib. 3, tit. 15, § 2. Doct. & Stud. Dial. 2, ch. 38. Bract. 99, a, b.

(*g*) Noy's Maxims, ch. 43.

(*h*) Turner v. Ford, 16 M. & W. 212. Adverse claimants' eviction by title paramount, *post,* § 807.

lender to the borrower of a chattel not to conceal from the borrower secret defects in the chattel known to the lender, which may make the use of the chattel perilous to the borrower. Thus, if one man lends a gun to another, and the lender knows at the time he lends the gun that it is unsafe and dangerous to use, and neglects to disclose the fact to the borrower, he will be responsible in damages to the latter if the gun bursts and injures him. (*i*) But a gratuitous lender of an article is not liable for injury resulting to the borrower or his servant, while using it, from a defect not known to the lender. (*k*)

797. *Loans of money to one of several partners.*— Where one of several partners, who was traveling for orders, called upon the plaintiff in the country, and, after transacting business with him on account of the firm, borrowed a sum of money to defray his expenses back to London, Lord KENYON held that, as the money was lent to the partner while employed on the partnership business, the partnership was responsible for the payment of the debt. (*l*) But if the partner professes to borrow money for the firm, and misapplies it, and there be proof that the plaintiff lent it under circumstances of negligence, and out of the ordinary course of business, he can not recover the amount from the other partners. (*m*) And, if the creditor lending the money advances it at the request of one of the partners, for the known private purposes and private accommodation of the latter, and not for the trading purposes of the co-partnership, such credi-

---

(*i*) Blakemore v. Brist. & Ex. Rail. Co., 8 Ell. & Bl. 1051 ; 27 L. J. Q. B. 167.

(*k*) MacCarthy v. Young, 6 H. & N.

329 ; 37 L. J., Ex. 227.

(*l*) Rothwell v. Humphreys, 1 Esp 405.

(*m*) Loyd v. Freshfield, 9 D. & R. 19.

tor can not make the firm responsible for the repayment of the money. (*n*)   If money is lent on the individual security and credit of one partner alone, the firm at large can not be charged with the repayment of it, although it may in fact be subsequently applied, to the use of the partnership.   Thus, where one partner was in the habit of drawing bills in his own name and getting them discounted by the plaintiff, and using the proceeds of such bills in the business of the firm, and applying them to the general purposes of the partnership, it was held that the plaintiff could not treat the money advanced by way of discount on the bills accepted by the partner in his own name only as a loan to the firm. (*o*)   But, where a member of a partnership was in the habit of drawing bills in his own name upon the firm, and getting them discounted, and applying the proceeds to the general purposes of the partnership, and the firm regularly accepted and paid the bills so drawn until it became bankrupt, it was held that the members of the firm must be taken to have given their co-partner authority to raise money for the use of the firm upon the bills in question, and that the money advanced by way of discount upon them might be treated as a loan to the partnership. (*p*) There is no implication of law from the mere existence of a trade partnership, that one partner has authority to bind the firm by opening a banking account on its behalf in his own name. (*q*)

798. *Loans to registered companies.*—There is nothing illegal in a registered company commencing business, and proceeding to raise money in the exer-

(*n*) Bishop v. Countess of Jersey, 23 L. J., Ch. 483.

(*o*) Emly v. Lye, 15 East, 11. Smith v. Craven, 1 Cr. & J. 500. Bevan v. Lewis. 1 Sim. 376.

(*p*) Denton v. Rodie, 3 Campb. 493. *Ex parte* Bolitho, Buck, 100.

(*q*) The Alliance Bank v. Kearsley, L. R. 6 C. P. 433; 40 L. J., C. P. 249.

cise of their borrowing powers, before the whole of the nominal capital has been subscribed. (*r*) Many of the requirements inserted in articles of association regulating the conduct and management of the contracts of registered companies have been very properly held to be operative only as between the members and shareholders inter se, and intended for the guidance of the directors, so that the non-observance of them may constitute a breach of trust on the part of the directors towards the shareholders, but will not have the effect of annulling the contract altogether. (*s*) Thus, if the directors of a registered joint-stock company are empowered to borrow money, the power to be exercised in accordance with certain prescribed formalities, and the directors borrow money without complying with the formalities, this is a matter between them and the shareholders, and does not deprive the lender of his rights against the company. (*t*) And, although the managers of the company are raising money for purposes unauthorized by the deed of settlement or articles of association, yet, if the shareholders, with full knowledge of these transactions, take no steps to ascertain whether the capital has been properly increased or not, but reap the benefit derived from the increase, they can not be afterwards heard to say that the money was not advanced for the general use and purposes of the partnership. (*u*) And, whenever money has been borrowed by directors and has been expended in furtherance of the general purposes of the company, and the shareholders have had

---

(*r*) M'Dougall v. Jersey Imp. Hotel Co. (Limited), 34 L. J., Ch. 28.

(*s*) Bill v. Darenth Rail. Co., 1 H. & N. 306. Prince of Wales Ins. Co. v. Harding, Ell. Bl. & Ell. 183, qualifying the dicta in Earnest v. Nicholls,

6 H. L. C. 422.

(*t*) Agar v. Athenæum Assur. Co., 3 C. B. N. S. 753. Royal British Bank v. Turquand, 6 Ell. & Bl. 332.

(*u*) Re Magdalena St. Nav. Co., 29 L. J., Ch. 667.

the benefit of the loan, they will not, in general, be allowed to repudiate the transaction on the ground that the directors had no power to borrow. They can not keep the money, and repudiate the agency by which it was obtained. (*v*) Debentures issued by a company under a general power of borrowing, in part discharge of existing debts, are valid. (*w*)

799. *Damages in actions for not replacing stock.*—In an action for not replacing stock lent on a given day, the measure of damages is the value of the stock in the market on the day on which it ought to have been replaced, or at the time of trial, at the option of the plaintiff. (*x*) Where, however, a stock mortgage was made for a term of years, for securing the re-transfer of stock at the end of the term, and payment in the meantime of interest calculated on the proceeds of the stock sold to raise the loan, and, the mortgage having been allowed to run after the end of the term, the stock fell in price, it was held that the mortgagee was not entitled to the market value of the stock at the end of the term, but that the mortgagor could redeem on replacing the specific amount of stock originally sold. (*y*) If dividends are to be paid in the intermediate time, interest may be given upon the value of the capital stock. (*z*)

(*v*) Elect. Tel. Co., *In re*, 30 Beav. 225. Troup, *In re*, 29 Beav. 353.

(*w*) Inns of Court Hotel Co., *In re*, L. R. 6 Eq. 82.

(*x*) Shepherd v. Johnson, 2 East, 211. M'Arthur v. Ld. Seaforth, 2 Taunt. 257. Downes v. Back, 1 Stark. 318. Owen v. Routh, 14 C. B. 327.

(*y*) Blyth v. Carpenter, L. R. 2 Eq. 501 ; 35 L. J., Ch. 823.

(*z*) Dwyer v. Gurry, 7 Taunt. 14.

CHAPTER III.

CONTRACTS FOR SERVICES.

SECTION I.

WORK AND LABOR.

800. *Deposit or simple bailment,* styled by the Roman lawyers depositum, may be defined to be a delivery or bailment of goods in trust to be kept for the bailor and re-delivered on demand. (*a*)[1] It is of the very essence of a deposit that it be gratuitous; for, if anything is to be paid for the care and custody of the article, it immediately becomes a contract for the letting and hiring of labor and services and care to be employed upon the chattel, and belongs to the class locatio operis et custodiæ. Where shares were deposited with bankers who were to receive the dividends, charging a commission thereon, it was held that they were bailees for reward. (*b*)

In the Roman law the term depositum is applied to the delivery of realty to be kept for the owner as

---

(*a*) Dig. lib. 16, tit. 3, 1. §§ 45, 46.　　(*b*) Johnston's Claim, L. R., 6 Ch. 212. 40 L. J., Ch. 286.

[1] 2 Kent Com. § 40, p. 560, 4th ed. The Latin depositum is compounded, says ALPIAN, of de and positum. Depositum est, quod custodiendum alicui datum est. Dictum ex eo quod ponitur; prepositio enim, de, auget depositumut ostendat, totum fidei ejus commissum, quod ad coseodeam rei pertinet. Dig. Lib. 50, tit. 16, § 186.

well as to a delivery of personalty. Thus, when a man
during his absence from home committed his house,
and all that was in it, to the keeping of a friend, this
was called a deposit by the civilians. In the absence
of an express contract between the parties, the nature
of the bailment must be determined by the nature of
the thing bailed, and upon what is required to be done
for its preservation and safe keeping. When passive
custody in some secure place of deposit alone is required, as in the case of most bailments of inanimate
chattels, the bailment is a naked deposit or simple
bailment, whilst, if work and labor, services and skill,
are necessarily required for its preservation, as in the
case of bailments of living animals or perishable chattels, then the bailment becomes, as presently mentioned,
a mandate.

801. *What is necessary to constitute a deposit—
Executory and executed promises.*—To constitute a
deposit, the subject-matter of the bailment must be
either actually or constructively delivered to the bailee,
or it must be in his possession or under his control at
the time he undertakes the charge of it. A mere
promise to take charge of a thing which has never
either actually or constructively come into the possession of the promisor can not constitute a deposit. But
a delivery to the servant of the promisor, or to a person whom he has appointed to receive the chattel, and
who has consented to hold it on his behalf, or any acts
on the part of the promisor manifesting a clear intention to take charge of a thing which is not capable of
manual delivery, but which has been placed at his disposal and under his control, will constitute a deposit
in contemplation of law. Thus in the Roman law, if
a man went from home leaving the keys of his house
with his neighbor, the bailee of the keys was consid-

ered to be the depositary of the house.[1]   If a creditor holding a pledge receives payment of the debt, but continues to hold the pledge, he becomes a depositary thereof for his former debtor.   If a tradesman sells any specific chattel, but neglects to deliver it, he becomes a depositary for the purchaser.   But a man can not be made a depositary without his knowledge and consent ; he can not have the possession of another man's property with its accompanying duties and responsibilities forced upon him against his will.   Thus, if a tradesman anxious to sell his wares and merchandise sends them to my house without any previous communication with me, and without having obtained my previous consent, and they are taken in by my servant in my absence, or without my knowledge, I do not by reason thereof become the depositary of the goods, and clothe myself with the care of them. (*c*)

802. *Liabilities of the depositary—Negligent keeping—Ordinary casualties.*—A depositary is only bound to take the ordinary care of things accepted by him to keep which a reasonably prudent man takes of his own property of a like description. (*d*)[2] He will be

---

(*c*) Lethbridge v. Phillips, 2 Stark. 544.

(*d*) Giblin v. McMullen, L. R., 2 P. C. 317 ; 38 L. J., P. C. 25.

[1] The civil law divides deposits into necessary and voluntary ; the former is a deposit such as is made upon a sudden emergency, as where one upon being overwhelmed by fire, shipwreck, or any other calamity, confides his goods to the first person at hand, in the emergency of the moment—this is called miserabile depositum.   Pothier, Traite de Dépôt, n. 75 ; 1 Domat. B. 1, tit. 7, § 5, art. 1, 2.   The latter appears to have been the simple deposit by consent and agreement of the parties mentioned in the text (Dig. Lib. 16, tit. 3, § 2 ; 1 Pothier, Pand. Lib. 16, tit. 3, n. 1).   This distinction was necessary in the civil law on account of the remedy under the former, such remedy being by an action in duplum ; under the latter by an action in simplum.

[2] Spooner v. Mattoon, 40 Vt. 300 ; Dunn v. Branner, 13

liable to make compensation to the owner, if the goods
are stolen, damaged, or lost by reason of gross negligence in the keeping of them ; but he is not responsible for slight neglect or ordinary casualties. (*e*)   " He
shall stand charged or not charged, according as default or no default shall be in him." (*f*)   If a man
takes charge of money, and leaves it upon a shelf, or
in an open drawer in a place of public resort, when he
might have placed it under lock and key, this is a
want of care inconsistent with good faith, and amounts,
consequently, to gross negligence. If a package or a
box, sealed or locked, be deposited, and the depositary
is not made acquainted with the contents, he is bound
only to take that care of the article which its general
appearance seems to require ; and in case it should be
lost or destroyed through gross neglect, he will only
be liable to the extent of the apparent value of the
article without reference to the contents ; but if he is
made acquainted with the contents—if he is told that
the box contains gold or jewels, glass or china, of
great value—he is then bound to exercise a degree of
care proportioned to the proper keeping of such articles ; and if he then exposes the box in unsafe places,
or subjects it to improper treatment, and the contents

(*e*) Coggs v. Bernard, 2 Raym. 913. 50, tit. 16, 223. Jones v. Lewis, 2
Lane v. Cotton, 1 ib. 655. Southcote's Ves. sen. 240. Taylor v. Caldwell,
Case, 4 Co. 83 b. ; 1 Smith's L. C. *ante.*
5th ed. 175. Dig. lib. 16, tit. 3, 32.   (*f*) Doct. & Stud. ch. 38.
Domat. lex 1, tit. 7, s. 3, 4. Dig. lib.

La. Ann. 452 ; Chase v. Maberry, 3 Har. 266 ; Dougherty v.
Posegate, 3 Iowa, 88 ; Green v. Hollingsworth, 5 Dana, 173 ;
Mechanics' Bank v. Gordon, 5 La. Ann. 607 ; Hills v. Daniels,
15 Id. 280 ; Foster v. Essex Bank, 17 Mass. 500 ; Edson v. Weston, 17 Cow. 278 ; Sodowsky v. McFarland, 3 Dana (Ky.), 205
Whitney v. Lee, 8 Metc. 91 ; McKay v. Hamblin, 40 Miss.
472 ; Montieth v. Bissell, Wright, 411.

are damaged or destroyed, he must make compensation to the owner to the full extent of the injury sustained. (*g*) If the depositary has been guilty of
gross neglect, he can not excuse himself from liability
by showing that he lost his own goods at the same
time that he lost his neighbor's.   Thus, where a coffee-
house keeper took charge of a sum of money, and put
it with a larger sum of money of his own into his
cash-box, which he left in the public tap-room of his
coffee-house, from whence it was stolen, it was held
that the circumstance of his having lost his own money
together with the deposit would not exculpate him
from the charge of gross negligence. (*h*)

803. *Carelessness on the part of the depositor in
selecting a person notoriously unfit to be trusted.*—
The law, however, expects a depositor to exercise a
reasonable amount of vigilance in the protection of
his own interests; and, if he will blindly deposit goods
in the hands of a person of weak intellect, or a child,
or a minor without experience, or a notoriously idle
and careless, or drunken, fellow, he can not expect the
same care from them as from a prudent and cautious
housekeeper.   If the goods are injured or lost by the
gross negligence of such depositaries, he must bear
the consequence of his own rashness and folly, and
put up with the loss. (*i*) '

804. *Theft by the servant of the depositary.*—If

(*g*) Bonion's Case, Pasch. 8 Edw.
2 ; Mayn, Year Book, 275.   Fitz. Abr.
Detinue, 59.   Erst. Inst. B. 3, tit. 1,
§ 27, p. 493.   Domat. dep. 1, 17. Dig.
lib. 16, lex 1, s. 41.

(*h*) Dorman v. Jenkins, 2 Ad. & E.
258 ; 4 N. & M. 170.

(*i*) Quia, qui negligenti amico rem
custodiendam tradit, sibi ipsi et pro-
priæ fatuitati hoc debet imputare
Brac. lib. 3, 99, b. Inst. lib. 3, tit. 16,
§ 2.   Big. lib. 16, tit. 3, 32.   Holt,
C. J., Coggs v. Bernard, 2 Raym. 914,
915.

' 2 Parsons on Contracts, p. 91, 5th ed.

a servant steps out of the course of his employment to do a wrong, either fraudulently or feloniously, towards another, the master is no more answerable than any stranger. Thus, if I employ a servant to work in my house, and he carries off the property of a visitor or guest, I am not answerable for the loss. "If one man desire to lodge with another that is no common hostler, and one that is servant to him that he lodgeth with robbeth his chamber, the master shall not be charged with the robbery." (*k*)   If the servant of the depositary negligently leaves the door of a house or warehouse open, and thieves avail themselves of the opportunity thus afforded them to enter the house and steal the deposit, the depositary is not responsible for the theft. (*l*)   It is laid down by HOLT, C.J., that "no master is chargeable with the act of his servant, but when he acts in execution of the authority given by his master; and then the acts of the servant is the act of the master." (*m*)   If, therefore, a servant "quits sight of the object for which he is employed, and, without having in view his master's orders, pursues that which his own malice suggests, he no longer acts in pursuance of the authority given him, and his master will not be answerable for such act." (*n*)   It is the custom of bankers to receive and keep for the accommodation of their customers, boxes of plate and jewels, wills, deeds, and securities ; and, as no charge is made for the keeping of these things, they are gratuitous deposits. The bankers, therefore, are only bound to take ordinary care of them ; and,

(*k*) Doct. & Stud. ch. 42. Gayford v. Nicholls, 9 Exch. 702.

(*l*) Dansey v. Richardson, 3 Ell. & Bl. 169.

(*m*) Middleton v. Fowler, 1 Salk. 282.

(*n*) Lord Kenyon, M'Manus v. Crickett, 1 East, 107. Reedie v. Lond. & North West. Rail. Co., 4 Exch. 244. Peachey v. Rowland, 13 C. B. 182.

if tney are stolen by a clerk or servant employed about the bank, the bankers are not responsible, unless they have knowingly hired or kept in their service a dishonest servant. Where a large quantity of doubloons locked up in a chest was deposited in the vaults of an American bank, and the bankers, who received the chest to keep as depositaries without reward, gave the owner a receipt acknowledging that the chest had been "left at the bank for safe keeping," and a clerk in the bank opened the chest and abstracted 32,000 doubloons, and then absconded, having also robbed and defrauded the bank, it was held by the American court that the bankers were not responsible for the theft. (*o*) [1]

(*o*) Foster v. Essex Bank, 17 Massach. 479. Giblin v. McMullen, L. R.   2 P. C. 318; 38 L. J. P. C. 25; *ante.*

[1] As to special deposits, see Moody v. Keener, 7 Port. (Ala.) 218; Curtis v. Leavitt, 15 N. Y. 9; Barnes v. Ontario Bank, 19 Id. 152; State Bank v. Kain, 1 Breese, 45; State Bank v. Lock, 4 Dev. 533. A special deposit in a bank is, perhaps, the purest example of a naked bailment. The deposit is taken solely for the depositor's accommodation, the bank receiving no benefit whatever from the act, and an express stipulation or acknowledgment given in writing by an officer of the bank, does not change the character of the bailment; Foster v. Essex Bank, 17 Mass. 479; and see Dawson v. Real Estate Bank, 5 Pick. 283; Marine Bank v. Chandler, 27 Ill. 525. A depositary who sells such a deposit commits a theft. McGregor v. Ball, 4 La. Ann. 289; and see *post*, § 818; Dustin v. Hagden, 38 Ill. 352. On a deposit or bailment of money to be kept without recompense, if the bailee, without authority, attempt to transmit the money to the bailor at a distant point, and it is lost, the bailor is liable. Stewart v. Frazier, 5 Ala. 114. But an agreement between bailor and bailee that the former shall draw interest upon a special deposit, turns such special deposit into an open account. Howard v. Roeber, 33 Cal. 399; Hathaway v. Brady, 26 Id. 581. Unless under very peculiar circumstances, a bank will not be held liable for the consequences of unwarrantable, unusual, or unlawful acts of their

805. *Of the use and enjoyment by the depositary of the subject-matter of the deposit.*—A depositary has no right to make use of the deposit for his own benefit and advantage; if he does so, and the thing is lost or injured, or deteriorated in value, through such user, the depositary must make good the loss. (*p*) If, however, the subject-matter of the bailment is a living animal, such as a hound or a horse, which requires air and exercise, the bailee has an implied authority from the owner to use it to a reasonable extent, and is under an implied engagement to give it proper air and exercise. If a sum of money is bailed by one man to another under circumstances fairly leading to the presumption that the bailee has authority from the bailor to use it or not as he may think fit, the bailee will stand in the position of a mere depositary, or he will be clothed with the increased duties and liabilities of a borrower, according as he may or may not have thought fit to avail himself of the privilege of user impliedly accorded to him. If he puts the money into a coffer or bag, and refrains from using it, and so preserves its identity with the intention of restoring it in individuo to the bailor, he undertakes the duty of a mere depositary, (*q*) and is bound only to take the same care of the deposit that he is in the habit of bestowing upon his own money, and will not be re-

---

(*p*) In the Roman law the unauthorized use of the deposit amounted to a gross breach of trust. Instit. lib. 4, tit. 1, § 6. Cod. lib. 4, tit. 34, 3. Dig. lib. 16, tit. 3, 29.

(*q*) Dig. lib. 16, tit. 3, 1, § 34.

officers in relation to such special deposits; and so if the cashier or other officer steal the deposit. Foster v. Essex Bank, 17 Mass. 479; see Mechanics' Bank v. Bank of Columbia, 5 Wheat. 326. The undertaking of banking corporations with respect to their officers, is that they shall be skillful and faithful in their employments; they do not warrant their general honesty and uprightness. Morse on Banking, p. 83.

sponsible for loss by robbery, fire, or any other casualty. But if he were to mix the sum deposited with his own money with the intention of restoring an equivalent, and so to destroy the identity and individuality of the subject-matter of the bailment, this would be a user of the money which would at once alter the nature and character of the bailment, converting it into a loan for use and consumption with its increased duties and responsibilities. (*r*)   Where corn was deposited by a farmer with a miller, to be used as part of the miller's current consumable stock, subject to the right of the farmer to claim at any time an equal quantity of wheat of similar quality, or, in lieu thereof, the market price of such quantity, it was held that this was a sale and not a bailment. (*s*)

806. *Transfer of the deposit to a stranger—Remedy of the depositor.*—If a depositary commits a breach of trust, and sells or wastes the deposit, the depositor may maintain an action against the purchaser for the recovery of the value of the deposit if the latter neglects to yield it up on demand, (*t*) unless the thing has been purchased in market overt.   If the goods are bailed by A to B, to be kept by the latter, and B bails them to C, who uses and wastes the goods, C is liable to an action at the suit of A for the recovery of compensation for the damages sustained. (*u*)   Where a depositary has wrongfully sold the goods deposited with him, the bailor may sue him immediately for the conversion.   If he does not discover the conversion until after the lapse of six years, he is, nevertheless,

---

(*r*) Dig. lib. 12, tit. 1, 4.   Inst. lib. 3, tit. 15, § 2.

(*s*) South Australian Ins. Co. v. Randall, L. R., 3 C. P. 101.

(*t*) Cooper v. Willomat, 1 C. B. 672.

Fenn v. Bittlestone, 7 Exch. 159. White v. Spettigue, 13 M. & W. 603.

(*u*) 12 Ed. 4, fol. 13, pl. 9 ; fol. 9, pl. 5.   Loeschman v. Machin, 2 Stark. 311.

entitled to sue the depositary for refusing to deliver up the goods, and the statute of limitations will run only from the refusal to deliver on request, and not from the sale. (*v*)

807. *Restoration of the deposit.*—The depositary is bound to deliver up the deposit to the owner on demand, although the latter may be an entire stranger to him. Where a pony-chaise was bailed to a workman to be painted, and the latter deposited it in the hands of a party who refused to deliver it up to the owner unless the latter produced either the person who actually deposited the chaise in his hands, or an order from him for its delivery, it was held that the owner was entitled to the possession of his property without doing either the one or the other. (*y*) The bailee has no better title than the bailor; and, consequently, if a person entitled to the property as against the bailor, claims it, the bailee must give it up to him. (*z*)

808. *Joint and several deposits.*—Where goods and chattels are deposited in the hands of a bailee by the concurring will of several joint owners, one of them has no right to demand them back without the authority of all the joint depositors. If some of them ask the bailee to return the property, and others desire him to keep it, the bailee is not liable to an action at the suit of those who require him to return it. (*a*) If goods and chattels, deeds or securities, are deposited by two persons jointly in the hands of a third, to be kept, it is not in the power of one of them alone, without the concurrence of the other, to take them

---

(*v*) Wilkinson v. Verity, L. R., 6 C. P. 206 ; 40 L. J. C. P. 141.

(*y*) Buxton v. Baughan, 6 C. & P. 674.

(*z*) Biddle v. Bond, 6 B. & S. 325 ; 34 L. J., Q. B. 137.

(*a*) Attwood v. Ernest, 13 C. B. 889 ; 22 L. J., C. P. 225.

out of the hands of the bailee. (*b*)　If the bailee is bound by his contract to deliver the goods to the two jointly, his refusal to deliver them on the demand of one party alone is not a conversion, nor is his detention from such one party an unlawful detainer.　But if an action is brought by several joint bailors against the bailee for non-delivery of the goods, it is a good defense to the action that the goods have been delivered up to one of them. (*c*)　When the deposit is not a joint deposit founded on a joint contract, but is made by one of several joint owners, the depositor may sue alone, "as, if a charter be made to four, and one of them bails the charter to keep, he alone, without the others, may bring detinue." (*d*)　And, wherever several joint owners allow one of them to deal with their property, and place it in the hands of a bailee, the latter is accountable to the owner with whom he deals. (*e*) [1]

(*b*) May v. Harvey, 13 East. 197. Thel. Dig. lib. 11, cap. 47. Jones Bailments, 50. Noy's Life, appended to Noy's Maxims, 8th ed. 1821.

(*c*) Burke v. Bryant. Addison on Torts, p. 350. Brandon v. Scott, 7 Ell. & Bl. 237 ; 26 L. J., Q. B. 163. Wat-

son v. Evans, 1 H. & C. 664 ; 32 L. J., Ex. 137.

(*d*) Thel. Dig. lib. 11, cap. 47, s. 8. Broadbent v. Ledward, 11 Ad. & E. 211.

(*e*) Martin, B., Walshe v. Provnn, 8 Exch. 852.

[1] The civil law divides all deposits into simple deposits and sequestrations ; a simple deposit is one made by one or more persons having a common interest.　Pothier, Traité de Dépôt, 1.　A sequestration is where the deposit is made by one or more persons, of whom each has a different and adverse interest from or against the other depositors.　Proprie autem in sequestre est depositum quod a pluribus in solidum certâ conditione custodiendum reddendum que traditur.　Dig. Lib. 10, tit. 3, l. 6 ; Pothier, Pand. lib. 16, tit. 3, n. 58 ; 1 Domat, B. 1, tit. 7 ; Prelim. Obs. ; Pothier, Traité de Dépôt, n. 1, 84 ; Sequestre dicitur, apud quem plures eandem rem de quâ controversia est, deposuerunt ; Id. ; Dig. Lib. 50, tit. 16, l. 110 ; these sequestrations, again, are of two sorts, conventional and judicial, the first being made by contract or agreement between

809. *Transfers of the subject-matter of the bailment—Adverse claimants.*—When chattels have been bailed, to be holden by the bailee at the disposal of the bailor, a question often arises as to the nature and extent of the liabilities of the bailee to persons who claim to be the owners of the chattels by sale or mortgage from the bailor. If the bailee has received the chattels upon the terms that he is to deliver them to the bailor, or to any person authorized by him to receive them, a bona fide purchaser or mortgagee, who is in possession of a bill of sale, or assignment, or mortgage, executed by the bailor, transferring all the bailor's interest in the chattels to such purchaser or mortgagee, may, on presenting such bill of sale or mortgage to the bailee, lawfully demand possession of the chattels, and in case of the refusal of the latter to deliver them to him, may maintain an action for their recovery, the bill of sale or mortgage signed by the bailor being an authority or direction to the bailee to deliver up the chattels to the purchaser or mortgagee.

810. *Eviction by title paramount.*—Where the plaintiff brought an action against the defendant for a breach of his promise to return a horse sent to him by the plaintiff, and the defense was that S was the owner of the horse and had forcibly taken it away from the defendant, it was held that this was a discharge of the

parties, the second by order of a court in a proceeding before it.   Pothier, Traité de Dépôt, n. 84, 85, 90–100 ; Civil Code of Louisiana, of 1825, art. 2941, 2948; 1 Domat, B. 1, tit. 7, § 4, art. 1.   In a sequestration, of whatever sort, the depositary or bailee is a mere stakeholder, and is bound to deliver the things deposited to him who is ultimately adjudged to be entitled to them.   Dig. Lib. 16, tit. 3, l. 5, § 1, 2 ; Id. l. 7 ; 1 Domat, B.1, tit. 7; Prelim. Obs.; Id. tit. 7, § 4, art. 5 ; Ayleffe, Pand. B. 4, tit. 17, p. 519–520; Pothier, Traité de Dépôt, n. 1 ; Civil Code of Louisana (1825), art. 2946; Lafarge v. Morgan, 11 Martin R. 462, 522.

defendant's promise, it being analogous to an eviction of a lessee by title paramount. (*f*) So where a bailor mortgages a chattel bailed, and the mortgagee has a right to demand possession from the bailee, and does demand it, the latter may refuse to give the chattel up to the bailor. (*g*)

811. *Stakes in the hands of stakeholders to abide the event of a lawful game.*—If money has been deposited in the hands of a stakeholder to abide the event of a lawful game or race, and then to be paid over to the winner, the stakeholder holds the money as agent of the winner, and is bound on demand to pay it over to him. (*h*) But if the party is not strictly a stakeholder holding money in that character, but receives it as agent for a known principal, he is accountable only to the latter for the money. (*i*) If the deposit has been made by two persons jointly, it can not, as we have seen, be revoked and the thing deposited be demanded back by one of them alone. If a valid and binding contract is made between A and B for the performance of some act or duty by B by an appointed day, or within a reasonable time after the making of the contract, and for the payment of money by A to B on the act being done, and the sum to be paid is, by the mutual agreement of the parties, deposited by A in the hands of C, to be paid over to B on the performance of his contract, and in default to be returned to A, the deposit can not be revoked and the money demanded back from the stakeholder by A without

---

(*f*) Shelbury v. Scotsford, Yelv. 23. Littledale, J,. Wilson v. Anderson, 1 B. & Ad. 457. Biddle v. Bond, 34 L. J., Q. B. 137 ; 6 B. & S. 225.

(*g*) European & Australian Royal Mail Co. v. Royal Mail Steam Packet Co., 30 L. J., C. P. 247.

(*h*) Applegarth v. Colley, 10 M. & W. 733.

(*i*) Bamford v. Shuttleworth, 11 Ad. & E. 926. Edgell v. Day, L. R., 1 C. P. 80 ; 35 L. J.. C. P. 7.

the consent of B, (*k*) unless the transaction is illegal.
(*l*) As soon as the stakeholder has received the deposit, he is bound to hold it to abide the event, and must not pay it over to either party until the condition upon which it was made payable or returnable has been accomplished. Thus, where an auctioneer has received a deposit from the purchaser of an estate, to be paid over to the vendor if a good title to the property is made out by the latter, and in default thereof, to be returned to the intended purchaser, the latter has no right to demand back the deposit, and the auctioneer is not justified in returning it, without the consent of the vendor. But if the vendor is not able to establish his title, or the contract is rescinded or abandoned by the mutual consent of the contracting parties, the auctioneer then holds the deposit for the use, and at the disposal, of the party from whom he received it, and is bound to return it on the request of the latter. (*m*) So long as the contract between the parties interested in the deposit remains open, and the event is undetermined, the right to the deposit remains in suspension, and each of the parties has an equal interest in the due fulfillment of the trust by the stakeholder. Stewards of a horse-race do not stand in the position of arbitrators between the persons who have horses in the race ; and it is not necessary that they should meet together and come to a joint decision as to which horse has won, to enable the winner to recover the stakes. (*n*)

If the deposit has been made to abide the event of

(*k*) Marryat v. Broderick, 2 M. & W. 372 ; Emery v. Richards, 14 M. & W. 728 ; 15 L. J., Ex. 49.

(*l*) Eltham v. Kingsman, 1 B. & Ald. 683. Batty v. Marriott, 5 C. B. 818 ; 17 L. J., C. P. 215.

(*m*) Burrough v. Skinner, 5 Burr. 2639. Edwards v. Hodding, 5 Taunt. 815. Gray v. Gutteridge, 1 M. & R. 614. Duncan v. Cafe, 2 M. & W. 246.

(*n*) Parr v. Winteringham, 1 Ell. & Ell. 394 ; 28 Law J., Q. B. 123.

a wager, or for the purpose of carrying into effect an
unlawful transaction, the depositor may, as we have
seen, at any time before the event has happened or
the deposit has been paid over, demand it back and
maintain an action for its recovery. (*o*)

812. *Power of the depositary to compel rival claimants to establish their title by interpleader.*—If the
event, when it does transpire, is not of a decisive character, and both parties set up a title to the deposit, the
depositary may compel them to interplead, and so
establish the right. This may be done when the depositary claims no interest in the deposit, and is not
colluding with either party. (*p*)　A stakeholder may
also pay money into court under the Trustee Relief
Act. (*q*)

813. *Liabilities of the depositary when he holds
possession wrongfully.*—If the depositary is in default
in neglecting to return the chattel on demand, he is
responsible for the subsequent loss or destruction of
the article, and for all injuries that may afterwards
happen to it, by whatever means occasioned. He
must restore it, moreover, with all its increase and
profits. Thus, he who has taken charge of a flock of
sheep must restore the wool shorn from their backs
and the lambs they have produced, together with the
sheep themselves ; and, if the profits, produce, and increase are of a perishable nature, such as milk, eggs,
and butter, and have been necessarily sold, the produce
of the sale must be paid to the depositor. The depositary, however, can not be called upon to deliver

---

(*o*) Holmes v. Sixsmith, 7 Exch. 802;
21 L. J. Ex. 312.

(*p*) Crawshay v. Thornton, 7 Sim.
398. Pearson v. Cardon, 2 Russ. &
M. 606. Tanner v. The European
Bank, L. R. 1 Ex. 261 ; 35 L. J., Ex.

151. Nelson v. Baxter, 23 L. J., Ch.
705 ; 2 H. & M. 334. 23 & 24 Vict. c.
126, s. 12.

(*q*) United Kingdom Life Assurance
Co., *In re*, 34 L. J. Ch. 554.

up the accessary without the principal. If the depositor turns out to be a thief and to have stolen the things deposited, and the true owner appears, the depositary must restore them to the latter. (*r*)

814. *Liabilities resulting from the taking possession of goods by finding.*—A man may clothe himself with the ordinary obligations and liabilities of a depositary by finding and taking possession of the lost property of another as well as by receiving property direct from the hands of the owner. In Noy's Maxims, it is observed (ch. 43), " If one man finds goods of another, and they be hurt or lost by the negligence of him who found them, he shall be liable to make them good to the owner." So in Doctor and Student, it is said, " If one man finds goods of another, and they be after hurt or lost by willful negligence, he shall be charged to the owner. But, if they be lost by other casualty, as if they be laid in a house that by chance is burned, or if he deliver them to another to keep, that runneth away with them, I think he be discharged." (*s*)   " When a man doth find goods," further observes Lord Coke, " it hath been said, and so commonly held, that, if he doth dispossess himself of them by this he shall be discharged ; but this is not so, as appears by the 12 E. 4, fo. 13. For he who finds goods is bound to answer for them to him who hath the property ; and, if he deliver them over to any one, unless it be to the right owner, he shall be charged for them ; for at the first it is in his election whether he will take them or not into his custody ; but, when he hath them, he ought to keep them safely ; and, if he be wise, he will search out the right owner of them, and deliver them to him. An action on the case

(*r*) Domat (du depot), s. 4, § 2 ; s.1,   (*s*) Dial. 2, ch. 38. Story. 64, 65,
§ 5. Dig. lib. 16, tit. 3.

lieth against him for ill and negligent keeping." (*t*)
So by the civil law, if the finder of a lost article took
the thing lost into his possession, he was obliged to
take care of it and preserve it for the owner.   He was
deemed, moreover, to be guilty of a theft, if he made
no attempt to discover the owner and restore the lost
property, or if, knowing the owner, he kept the property without any intention to restore it. (*u*)

815. *Liabilities of the depositor.*—The depositor
is by the Roman law bound to reimburse the bailee
all extraordinary expenses incurred by him in the
preservation of the thing committed to his keeping;
and such a liability may, under certain circumstances,
exist in our own law.   The French law, moreover,
concedes to the depositary a right to detain the chattel
until he has received payment of such expenses. (*v*)
But no such right exists in the common law; and no
depositary is ever permitted in this country to set up
a right of lien upon the chattel for the mere expenses
he has incurred in keeping and preserving it.

816. *Deposits of money with one of several partners.*—A receipt of money by one partner on account
of the firm, in the ordinary course of the business of
the co-partnership, is the receipt of the co-partnership
at large; and all the partners are individually responsible for the proper application of the money deposited. (*y*)   If two attorneys in partnership together are
in the habit of receiving money to place out on securities, and one of them receives a sum of money to be
laid out on security, the other is responsible for the

(*t*) Izaack v. Clark, 2 Bulst. 312.

(*u*) Dig. lib. 47, tit. 2, lex. 43, § 4.
As to recovering the halves of bank
notes, see Smith v. Mundy, 29 L. J.,
Q. B. 172.

(*v*) Pothier (Depot) No. 59; (OBLI-

GATIONS) No. 625.   Cod. Civ. art.
1948

(*y*) Dundonald v. Masterman, L. R.
7 Eq. 504; 38 L. J., Ch. 350.   St.
Aubyn v, Smart, L. R. 3 Ch. 646.

proper application of the money, although the party receiving it gives his own separate receipt for it, making himself individually accountable for the amount on demand. (*z*)   But it must be proved that the client relied on the joint judgment and joint security of the firm, and that it was part of the ordinary course of business of the firm to receive and hold money until a good mortgage security offered, and then invest it; for it is no part of the ordinary business or duties of attorneys to receive and hold money for general purposes of investment. (*a*)   Where one of a firm of solicitors received from a client a sum of money, for which a receipt was given in the name of the firm, stating that part of the money was in payment of certain costs due to the firm, and that the residue was to make arrangements with the client's creditors, and the solicitor misappropriated the money, it was held that the transaction with the client was within the scope of the partnership business, and that the partners in the firm were jointly and severally liable to make good the amount. (*b*)   If one of several partners in trade obtains money in the ordinary course of dealing of the co-partnership, but by means of false and fraudulent representations, and converts the money, when received, to his own use in fraud of his partners, the partnership is nevertheless responsible for the moneys so received in the name of the firm; and an innocent partner may, consequently, be as much bound by such fraudulent acts and transactions as if he himself had personally been a party to them. (*c*)

(*z*) Willet v. Chambers, 2 Cowp. 814.

(*a*) Harman v. Johnson, 2 Ell. & Bl. 61; 22 L. J., Q. B. 297.

(*b*) Atkinson v. Macreth, L. R., 2 Eq. 570; 35 L. J., Ch. 624.

(*c*) Rapp v. Latham, 2 B. & Ald. 795. Stone v. Marsh, R. & M. 368; 6 B. & C. 551. Keating v. Marsh, 1 Mont. & Ayr, 582.

But if the fraud has not been committed in the course of the partnership dealings, but in the private and separate transactions of the single partner himself with third parties, the innocent partner can not be made responsible to those who have been defrauded in the course of such transactions. Thus, if a partner who holds money in his hands as a trustee for third parties, brings that money into the partnership account, and employs it in the business as his own money, the other partners can not be made responsible for the repayment of the money so employed in the business, unless they knew at the time that the money was trust money, and not the property of their co-partner. (*d*) But if money is deposited in the hands of one of several partners of a banking firm at the bank, to be held temporarily by the bank, and subsequently applied in the purchase of some particular security, and the partner absconds with the money, the firm is responsible for the repayment of the amount, although they had given no authority to their partner to receive money for investment, and the transaction, so far as it related to the application of the money when received, was not in the ordinary course of business. (*e*) And, where the senior partner of a firm of stock-brokers bought transferable bonds for the plaintiff, and kept the bonds for him, and afterwards sold them, and made away with the money, it was held that the firm was responsible to the plaintiffs for the value of the bonds, although the junior partners were entirely ignorant of the transaction. (*'f*)

817. *Deposits of money with bankers.*—Money d :-

(*d*) *Ex parte* Heaton, Buck, 386. Smith v. Jameson, 5 T. R. 601.

(*e*) Thompson v. Bell, 10 Exch 10; 23 L. J. Ex. 321.

(*f*) La Marquise de Ribeyre v. Barclay, 23 Beav. 125; 26 L. J., Ch. 747.

posited in the hands of bankers in the ordinary course of business is money lent to the banker by the depositor, with a superadded obligation that it is to be repaid when called for by cheque. If interest is to be paid by the banker, the transaction amounts to a letting and hiring of the money or a loan at interest; if no interest is to be paid on the deposit, it is a commodatum or gratuitous loan; and in this last case, if the money remains for six years in the banker's hands without any payment by him of any part of the principal, or any acknowledgment by him in writing of the existence of the loan and of the debt, the statute of limitations will be a bar to its recovery by action. (*g*) In ordinary cases of deposits of money with bankers the transaction amounts to a mutuum or loan for use and consumption, it being understood that the banker is to have the use of the money in return for his consent to take charge of it. (*h*) [1] " Money, when paid into a bank, ceases altogether to be the money of the depositor; it is then the money of the banker, who is bound to return an equivalent by paying a

---

(*g*) Pott v. Clegg, 16 M. & W. 321; 16 L. J. Ex. 210. Howard v. Danbury, 2 C. B. 806.

(*h*) Alderson, B., Robarts v. Tucker

16 Q. B 575. Pott v. Clagg, 16 M. & W. 321; 16 L. J., Ex. 210. Sims v. Bond, 2 N. & M. 608.

---

[1] See *ante*, note 1, p. 461. Banks and banking companies are not public servants, and no duty exists on their part, corresponding to the duty of common carriers or innkeepers, to receive all persons offering themselves as customers. A bank may select arbitrarily its customers from among those offering themselves as such, and are not accountable to anybody for their selection or refusal. Thatcher v. Bank, &c., of New York, 5 Sandf. 121. Neither does the acceptance of a customer's deposit bind the bank to continue keeping his account; nor on the customer's part is there any implied contract that he will continue to deposit. Morse on Banking, 25.

similar sum to that deposited with him when he is asked for it or ordered to pay it. It is the banker's money; he deals with it as his own; he makes what profit he can of it, which profit he retains to himself, paying back only the principal sum, according to the custom of bankers in some places, or the principal and a small rate of interest, according to the custom of bankers in other places." The money, therefore, being his own, he is guilty of no breach of trust in employing it. He is not answerable to the principal if he puts it in jeopardy by engaging in hazardous speculations; but he is, of course, answerable for an equivalent amount to be paid to his customer when demanded. (*i*) [1]

818. *Deposit of bills, notes, and securities in the hands of bankers.*—But bills deposited in the hands of a banker remain the property of the customer, unless there be a special agreement transferring the property in them to the banker, so that, upon the death or failure of the banker, the customer has a right to the bills so long as they remain in specie; [2] but the banker has a lien upon them, if the customer has overdrawn his account. [3] Where a customer was in the habit of depositing bills with his bankers, which bills were indorsed by him, and were entered in the bank books to his credit as bills, not as cash, and after such entry the customer was allowed to draw to the full amount of such bills by cheques, and the bankers became bankrupt, it was held that the customer, who had a cash balance in his favor at the time

---

(*i*) Foley v. Hill, 2 H. L. C. 36. *Ante.*

[1] See last note.

[2] This is what is called a special deposit, which is usually the simplest form of depositum, see note 1, *ante*, p. 480.

[3] *Post*, § 832.

of the bankruptcy, was entitled to the bills, there being no evidence that he had agreed that, when the bills were deposited, they were to become the property. of the bankers. (*k*)   And, where a customer paid a bank-note into the bank after the ordinary hours of business, and the bankers, having previously resolved to stop payment, did not carry the amount of the note to the customer's account, but placed it aside in a separate place of deposit, taking care not to mix it with the general assets of the house, it was held that the note still remained the property of the customer. (*l*)[1]   If bank-notes deposited by a customer turn out to be worthless paper, by reason of the insolvency of the bank which issued the notes, the loss falls upon the customer, if there has been no laches on the part of the banker with whom the notes were deposited.   If the banker gives a receipt for the notes

---

(*k*) Thompson v. Giles, 3 D. & R.   (*l*) Sadler v. Belcher, 2 Mood. &
763 ; 2 B. & C. 442.   Rob. 489. *Ante ; post.*

---

[1] So if a deposit be stolen before it has been mingled with the funds of the bank, or if it be embezzled or fraudulently misapplied by an officer of the bank, the bank is, none the less, liable for the deposit.   Concord v. Concord Bank, 16 N. H. 26 ; Commercial Bank of Albany v. Hughes, 17 Wend. 94.   In Georgia, &c. Banking Co. v. Dabney, it appeared that the deposits were in Confederate notes, which were rapidly depreciating in value, and which ultimately became worthless. Accordingly a notice was given in 1862, by a bank to its depositors, to withdraw their deposits, though repeated in February, 1864, with the further notice, that on failing to withdraw, the deposits would be sealed up in packages and held at their risk. *Held*, that such notices, without proof of any further action on the part either of the bank or its customers, in relation to such deposits, does not, in law, discharge the bank from all liability, under the ordinance of 1865, on account of the total failure of Confederate money.   Such facts are proper for the consideration to the jury in adjusting the equities between the parties.   52 Ga. 515.

as cash, he is not precluded by such receipt from sub-sequently showing that what he received was not cash, but spurious paper. (*m*)

819. *Receipt of cheques by bankers on account of their customers.*—When a cheque is paid into a bank to be placed to the account of a customer, the banker is bound to use due diligence in getting the cheque paid, and must give prompt notice to his customer in case it is not paid; and, if he omits to do either of these things, he makes the cheque his own and must bear the loss, if loss there be. Where the plaintiff received a cheque drawn upon his own bankers, [1] and took it to their bank, and handed it to a clerk, with directions to place it to his account, and the clerk received the cheque without any observation, and the bankers, finding that the drawer of the cheque had overdrawn his account and was keeping out of the way, gave the plaintiff notice on the following day that the cheque would not be honored by them, and that the amount of it would not be placed to his credit, it was held that the bankers were not precluded, by their having received the cheque with-

---

(*m*) Timmins v. Gibbins, 18 Q. B. 722; 21 L. J., Q. B. 403.

[1] Ivory v. Bank of State of Missouri, 36 Miss. 475; State Bank v. Bank of the Capitol, 41 Barb. 343; and this independently of whether the customer's name is on the check or not. McKinster v. Bank of Utica, 9 Wend. 46; 11 Id. 473. And the measure of damages will be the actual loss sustained. Tyson v. State Bank, 6 Blackf. 225; Bank of Washington v. Triplett, 1 Pet. 25; McKinster v. Bank of Utica, 9 Wend. 46. "Where a bank demands and receives payment of a dishonored note from an indorser, and he, seeking in his turn to recover from a prior indorser, fails to do so by reason of a default by the bank in not making a proper demand upon the maker, which in sufficiency was unknown to the paying indorser, when he made the payment, he shall recover back the amount of his payment from the bank." Morse on Banking, 342.

out comment in the first instance, from subsequently
refusing to credit the plaintiff with the amount; but
that, if the plaintiff, at the time he deposited the
cheque, had asked the bankers whether they would
pay it, he would have been entitled to an answer, and
that the bankers would have been bound by such
answer. (*n*) It is often impossible to ascertain till
the close of the day, at the clearing-house, what sums
of money may be paid in to each particular account,
and what are the drafts upon it; and bankers, therefore, may receive cheques drawn upon them by their
customers, and may reserve to themselves the right of
honoring them, or not honoring them, according to
the result of the day's transactions at the clearing-
house.   Where bankers, at the time of receiving a
cheque drawn upon them by one customer, and presented by another, stated that they were not then in
funds, but that they would keep the cheque in the hope
of being furnished with money to pay it, in the course
of the day, it was held that they were bound to appropriate the first money they received from their customer, the drawer, in satisfaction and discharge of
such cheque. (*o*) [1]

(*n*) Boyd v. Emmerson, 2 Ad. & E.   (*o*) Kilsby v. Williams, 5 B. & Ald.
202.   919.

[1] It seems that a bank is liable for frauds or mistakes of
the cashier or clerks in their entries in its books, or for false
accounts of deposits, &c.   Salem Bank v. Gloucester Bank, 17
Mass. 1 ; Id. 33 ; Andrews v. President, &c. of Suffolk Bank,
12 Gray, 461.   Where plaintiff, to the knowledge of defendant, a customer, employed in its bank a paying and a receiving teller, the general duty of the latter being to receive
moneys paid or deposited.   In his absence other officers or
clerks acted in his place.   Defendant, having overdrawn his
account by mistake, received a letter from the paying teller
requesting him to call; he went to the bank, and at the request of the paying teller paid him, over the counter, the

820. *Of the duty of bankers to honor the drafts of their customers—Payment of cheques.*—It is the duty of the banker to pay the debt due to the customer pursuant to the order, cheque, or draft of the latter. The customer may order the debt to be paid to himself or anybody else, or he may order it to be carried over or transferred from his own account to the account of any other person he pleases. He may do so by written instrument or verbal direction; but the banker is entitled to require some written evidence of the order of the transfer. (p)[1] The banker is bound by law to honor the cheques and drafts of his customers, provided they are presented within banking hours, and provided he has in his hands sufficient funds for the purpose belonging to

(*b*) Watts v. Christie, 11 Beav. 546 ;   18 L. J., Ch. 173.   Walker v. Rostron, 9 M. & W. 4e1.

amount required to rectify the error; this was not entered on the books of the bank. It did not appear that the receiving teller was in the bank. In an action to recover the amount overdrawn, *held*, that the bank was bound by the payment. East River, &c. Bank v. Gove, 57 N. Y. 459.

[1] Watson v. Phœnix Bank, 8 Met. 217 ; Downes v. Phœnix Bank, 6 Hill, 297. The bank has the right to pay out money on a verbal order, if it will, but it is likewise entitled to demand a written order or voucher. Coffin v. Henshaw, 10 Ind. 277.

There is no rule as to the amount for which a depositor may draw his check. The rule of law forbidding a creditor to split up his demand does not affect this principle, which is based upon a custom of the banking business so ancient, unquestioned, and well known that courts will take judicial notice of it without proof. Munn v. Birch, 25 Ill. 35 ; Chicago Ins. Co. v. Stanford, 28 Id. 168. But a customer will not be allowed to vex unnecessarily a bank. Chicago Ins. Co. v. Stanford, Id. It was held, in True v. Thomas, 16 Me. 36, that the drawing of a check for a larger sum than the depositor's balance, or for a sum larger than he had reasonable grounds to expect funds to meet, in the absence of any explanation, is a fraud.

the customer; (*q*) and, if he refuses, he is liable to an action by the customer for substantial damages without proof of actual damage; for it is a discredit to the customer to have his cheque refused payment. (*r*) Where the plaintiff paid a sum of money to a banker in London, and directed him to forward the money to certain country bankers to the plaintiff's credit by a particular day, and the London banker received the money and neglected to forward it, it was held that he was responsible for all damages sustained by the plaintiff by reason of his not having the money at the time and place appointed. (*s*) The acceptance by a customer of a bill of exchange payable at his bankers is tantamount to an order from him to his banker to pay the bill to the person who, according to the law merchant, is capable of giving a good discharge for it, *i. e.*, to a person who becomes the holder by a genuine indorsement, or, if the bill is originally payable to bearer, or if there is afterwards a genuine indorsement in blank, to the person who seems to be the holder. (*t*) [1] If bankers have indorsed a bill of exchange accepted by a customer, and the bill is presented to them when

(*q*) Agra Bank, &c., v. Hoffman, 34 L. J., Ch. 285.

(*r*) Marzetti v. Williams, *ante.* Rolin v. Steward, 14 C. B. 595; 23 L. J., C. P. 148. Boyd v. Emmerson, 2 Ad. & E. 184. Whitaker v. Bank of Eng., 1 C. M. & R. 744. Cumming v. Shand, 5 H. & N. 95; 29 L. J,. Ex.

129. As to orders on bankers operating by way of NOVATION AND SUBSTITUTION, see *ante.*

(*s*) Shillibeer v. Glyn, 2 M. & W. 143. Wheatley v. Low, Cro. Jac. 668 Loe's Case, Palm. 281.

(*t*) Kymer v. Laurie, 18 L. J., Q. B. 218. Robarts v. Tucker, *post.*

[1] It is likewise the duty of the bank to pay his customer's notes, bills, and acceptances, if made payable by it; it is the presumption of law that these are, like checks, a customer's order to pay which he meant to have obeyed; Morse on Banking, 30; and if not paid, the drawer has his action against the bank for the non-payment. In case of an acceptance, the right of action for such refusal is in the acceptor, and not in the drawer. 3 Pick. 96.

it arrives at maturity, and they pay it on the day it
becomes due, the bankers so paying may reserve to
themselves the right to examine into the state of the
accounts between them and the acceptor, their customer, and determine whether they honor the bill for
the acceptor, or take it up on their own account as
indorsers. (*u*)

821. *Payment of cheques under suspicious circumstances—Negligence.*—If bankers pay a cheque under
circumstances of suspicion which ought to have put
them on their guard, and induced them to make
inquiry before paying it, they can not debit their customer with the amount, if the cheque was never
uttered or put into circulation by the customer. Thus,
where the customer, finding that he had drawn a
cheque for a wrong sum, tore it into four pieces and
threw them away, and these four pieces were picked
up, and neatly pasted together, and presented at the
bank by a stranger for payment, but the rents and the
pasting of the paper were quite visible, and the face
of the cheque was soiled and dirty, and the cashier,
nevertheless, paid it without demur or inquiry, it was
held that the bankers had been guilty of a neglect of
duty, and could not, under the circumstances, debit
their customer with the payment. (*x*)   But, if the
tearing is done in such a way that it is reasonable to
presume it to have been done for the purpose of trans-
mitting the cheque through the post, there will then
be no neglect of duty on the part of those who pay
the cheque in ignorance of its having been torn up
with the intention of cancelling it. (*y*)[1]

(*u*) Pollard v. Ogden, 2 Ell. & Bl.   Campb. 485.
464 ; 22 L. J., Q. B. 439.   (*y*) Ingham v. Primrose, 28 L. J.,
(*x*) Scholey v. Ramsbottom,   2   C. P. 294.

[1] And so in the case of stale checks.   Although there is no

822. *Joint accounts and joint deposits with bankers.*—Where money is paid into a bank to the joint account of several persons nominatim, it can not

rule of law fixing the time that shall be conclusive against a check, yet it is said to be a sound and ordinary rule of business that a bank must not pay an old check without inquiry. Morse on Banking, 262. But one who is not a sufferer by delay in presenting his check, is liable upon it until the statute of limitations has run against it. Harbeck v. Craft, 4 Duer, 122; Cruger v. Armstrong, 3 Johns. Cas. 5; Conroy v. Warren, Id. 259; Murray v. Judah, 6 Cow. 490; Mohawk Bank v. Broderick, 10 Wend. 306; 13 Id. 133; Tuttle v. Phœnix Bank, 2 Hill, 425. It is suggested that an old check may reasonably be regarded with suspicion; and the bank may reasonably defer payment until it shall have time to make inquiries. Morse on Banking, 263. The holder of a bank check is bound to present it within a reasonable time; otherwise the delay is at his own peril. Woodruff v. Plant, 41 Conn. 344. But what is a reasonable time must depend upon the particular circumstances of the case. Id. Where a plaintiff, desiring to make a remittance to a creditor at a distance, and there being no bank in the place where he lived, asked the defendant, who had an account with a banker in a neighboring city, to take the amount of him in bank bills and give him his check therefor, and the defendant, fully understanding the object, took the bank bills and gave the plaintiff his check upon the banker, payable to the plaintiff's order, the defendant the same day depositing the bills with the banker. The plaintiff at once endorsed the check to his creditor, and sent it by the next mail. It was three days before the check reached the place where the banker resided, and was presented for payment, at which time the banker had failed, and payment was refused. The plaintiff, having taken up the check, sued the defendant thereon. *Held*, that the check was presented within a reasonable time in the circumstances, and that the defendant was liable. Id. But it is said that a check on a bank is never due until presented, and therefore never overdue until it has been presented and dishonored. Cruger v. Armstrong, 3 Johns. Cas. 5; Story on Promissory Notes, Sharswood's Ed., 678–679. In Gale v. Miller, 54 N. Y. 536, it was held that the check is of no vitality whatever until transferred to some person other than the drawer or the bank. And whether a check is so old that the bank, in a particular case, was justified in

be drawn out by one of them alone; for the bankers
are not discharged from liability by payment to one
of the depositors without the authority of the others.
(z) But, when one dies, the money may be drawn
out by the survivor. Such is the case with money
deposited in a bank in the joint names of husband
and wife. (a) [1]

823. *Deposits and accounts with bankers in the
names of trustees, agents, and receivers.*—In a banking
account of the ordinary kind between a banker and
his customers, it is not competent to any third party
to interpose and to say that the customer was his
agent and that the banker has contracted with such
third party through the medium of such customer, his
agent. All cheques and money paid into the bank by

(z) Innes v. Stephenson, 1 Mood. &   Ad. 375.
Rob. 147.   Sims v. Brittain, 4 B. &   (a) Williams v. Davies, 33 L. J., P.
& M. 127.

refusal to cash it upon demand, is a question for the jury. See
Morse on Banking, 264; Lancaster Bank v. Woodward, 18
Pa. St. 357. In the last-named case, a check was drawn upon
a bank in which the drawer had no funds; but a year after the
date of its making, it happened that the drawer did have funds
in the bank, and upon presentation of the check it was paid.
The drawer in the meantime had discharged the original debt
for which the check had been drawn, considering that the
check was no longer good. *Held*, that payment by the bank
of so old a check, under the suspicious circumstances of a continued omission to deposit funds to meet it, which were sufficient to put the bank on inquiry, constituted a degree of negligence on the part of the bank so great that the court felt justified in taking the case from the jury and holding, as matter of
law, that the bank could not recover the amount so paid. So
the fact that a draft or check was presented at a bank at such
a distance from the place where it was drawn that it could not
have reached there in the ordinary course of the mails, or of
a messenger, would be sufficient to put a bank on its guard.
[1] Morse on Banking, p. 266.

the customer are, as between the banker and the customer, the cheques and money of the customer, whoever may be the real owner of them. If the owner of the cash allows his agent to deal with it as his own, and pay it into the bank in his own name, he has no power over it after it has reached the banker's hands. On the other hand, it is not competent to the banker, after he has placed the money to the credit of the customer, to deny the title of the latter to the money, and to set up a jus tertii, or to revoke the credit. (*b*) If several joint owners of a sum of money allow one of them to deal with their money and place it in the hands of a banker to his separate account, the banker must treat that as a contract with the one individual dealing with him, and the latter can not impose upon the banker as many contracts as there are owners of the money. (*c*)

824. *Separate accounts opened by the same person in different capacities.*—Generally, as between banker and customer, the banker looks only to the customer in respect of the account opened in that customer's name, and whatever cheques that customer chooses to draw, the banker is to honor, and is not to inquire what the moneys are that are paid into that account, or for what purpose they are drawn out. But, when the customer opens two separate accounts, the one being a private account of his own, and the other an account as trustee or receiver of the moneys of a known third party, the bankers are bound to take

---

(*b*) Tassell v. Cooper, 9 C. B. 533.   (*c*) Sims v. Brittain, 4 B. & Ad. 375.
Pinto v. Santos, 5 Taunt. 447.

[1] Morse on Banking, 266; and so in the case of deposits by an assignee in bankruptcy. Id. But the signature of one of several co-administrators or executors to a check is a sufficient authority to the bank to pay it. Id. 267.

notice that the moneys placed to the last named account are not the moneys of their customer, and they can not make an arrangement with the latter for an appropriation of the balance in their hands on the fiduciary account to liquidate a balance due to them from their customer upon his own private account. They have no right to combine with the receiver for the appropriation of his principal's money to discharge the private debt due to them from the receiver; for no person dealing with another, and knowing him to have in his hands or under his control money belonging to a third person, can deal with the individual holding that money for his own private benefit, when the effect of the transaction is that a fraud is necessarily committed upon such third party. (*d*).

825. *Loss of trust-money in the hands of bankers.*—If an agent or trustee who has received a sum of money for the use of his principal or beneficiary, pays the money into a bank in the name of the principal or beneficiary, and places it to the account of the latter, the amount then remains in the bank at the risk of the principal; and, if the banker fails, the principal mnst bear the loss. But, if the agent or trustee pays in the money to his own account and of his own credit, this is a user of the money for which he will be responsible. If he had an implied authority to use the money, and has so exercised it, then he stands, as before-mentioned, in the position of a borrower for use and consumption. In either case he is bound to make good the loss. (*e*)

826. *Payment of forged cheques, drafts, and*

(*d*) Bodenham v. Hoskins, 21 L. J., Ch. 864; 16 Jur. 721. Bridgman v. Gill, 24 Beav. 302. Kingston, *Ex parte*, L. R., 6 Ch. 632. Per Blackburn, J., Bailey v. Finch, L. R., 7 Q. B. 42 ; 41 L. J., Q. B. 83.

(*e*) Robinson v. Ward, R. & M. 276. Wren v. Kirton, 11 Ves. 377. Rocke v. Hart, Id. 61. Massey v. Banner, 4 Mad. 418, 419 ; 1 Jac. & Walk. 241.

orders on bankers—Forgery facilitated by the negligence of the customer.—If money is drawn out of the bank by means of a forged order purporting to have been made by the customer, the banker must sustain the loss. Where a cheque drawn by a customer on his banker for a sum of money described in the body of the cheque in words and figures was afterwards altered by the holder, who substituted in a different handwriting a larger sum than that mentioned in the cheque, in such a manner that no one, in the ordinary course of business, would have observed it, and the banker paid the larger sum to the holder, it was held that he could not lawfully debit the customer with the over-payment. (f)[1] But, if the banker has been defrauded through the carelessness or negligence of the customer in drawing the cheque, the loss must be borne by the customer. Where the customer signed several blank cheques, and left them in the hands of his wife to be filled up, and she handed a cheque to a clerk to be filled up for £50 2s. 3d., and the clerk filled up the cheque for the specified amount, and showed it to the wife, but the "fifty" was commenced

(f) Hall v. Fuller, 5 B. & C. 750; 8 D. & R. 464. As to advances by bankers, at the request of their customers, on forged securities, see Woods v. Thiedemann, 1 H. & C. 478; or on securities fraudulently obtained, *Re* Carew's Estate, 31 Beav. 39; 31 L. J., Ch. 214.

[1] A bank is bound to know its customer's handwriting (that is to say, his signature; for it is not matter of suspicion that the body of the check be not in his own writing), and must suffer the whole loss from a payment upon a check forged in his name; Levy v. Bank of the United States, 4 Dall. 234; Weisser v. Denison, 6 Seld. 68; Bank of the United States v. Bank of Georgia, 10 Wheat. 333; Bank of Commerce v. Union Bank, 3 Const. 230; Goddard v. Merchants' Bank, 4 Id. 147; and a fraudulent alteration in the body of a check or bill, after signature, renders the check a technical forgery. Goodman v. Eastman, 4 N. H. 455; Sewall v. Boston Water Power Co., 4 Allen, 277.

in the middle of the line, so that the words "three hundred and" could easily be written before it, and space was left at the bottom of the cheque for the insertion of the figure 3 between the £ and the figures 50, and the clerk on his way to the bank altered the cheque to £350, and got that amount from the bankers and absconded, it was held that the customer must bear the loss, as it had been occasioned by his own negligence and the negligence of his agent in dealing with the blank cheque. (*g*) [1]

827. *Forged indorsements.*—We have seen that

(*g*) Young v. Grote, 12 Moore, 489 ; 4 Bing. 257.

[1] It is well that the American student should bear in mind that the English cases are to be used with great caution in cases arising upon checks payable to order, since in England this matter has been always more or less controlled by statute. It was originally enacted that all checks should be drawn "to bearer," or to "A. or bearer;" and all instruments drawn payable to order were regarded as inland bills of exchange, and required to be stamped as such. By 16 & 17 Vict. 59, s. 19, this was changed; but the act provided that "any draft or order drawn upon a banker for a sum of money payable to order on demand, which shall, when presented for payment, purport to be endorsed by the person to whom the same shall be drawn payable, shall be a sufficient authority to such banker to pay the amount of such draft or order to the bearer thereof; and it shall not be incumbent on such banker to prove that such endorsement, or any subsequent endorsement, was made by or under the direction or authority of the person to whom the said draft or order was or is made payable, either by the drawer or any endorser thereof;" which provision, it is apparent, changes the English custom, if at all, very slightly, since a check payable to order, when the banker is under no obligation to assure himself of the endorsement, is practically a check payable to bearer. With us, where such checks are in use, it would seem to be the duty of every drawer of a check to so preface it as to guard against an alteration of the amount of its face; and if he do not so reasonably guard against it, or if the alteration be rendered possible by his own carelessness, he, and not the bank, is liable. It is not an unfrequent case that a

if a bill of exchange has been accepted by a customer
payable to order at his bankers, the acceptance of the
bill is an authority to the bankers to pay the bill only
to a person who becomes the holder by a genuine
indorsement from such customer.   If bankers wish to
avoid the responsibility of deciding on the genuineness of the indorsement, they must require their customer to make his bills payable at his own offices, and
to honor the bills by giving a cheque on them ; for
they can not debit a customer with a payment made
to a party who claims through a forged indorsement
and so can not give a valid discharge for the bill,
unless there are circumstances amounting to a direction from the customer to the bankers to pay the bill
without reference to the genuineness of the indorsement, or a subsequent admission on the part of the
customer of the genuineness of the indorsement
inducing the bankers to alter their position, so as
to preclude the customer from showing it to be
forged. (*h*) [1]

(*h*) Robarts v. Tucker, 16 Q. B. 578.

bank, after payment of a check, may have reason to suspect it a
forgery of the drawer's signature, and exhibit it to him. In such
cases, if the forgery, either from its skillfulness or from the drawer's imperfect vision, or haste, or other cause, be himself deceived
it has been unanimously held that his declaration that the
writing of the signature is his, will not estop him from afterwards proving the contrary; Weisser v. Denison, 6 Seld. 68;
so held in case of a note; Hall v. Huse, 10 Mass. 40; and in
case of bank bills, Salem Bank v. Gloucester Bank, 17
Mass. 1.   This appears to be the tendency of modern decisions.
Consult Coggell v. American Exchange Bank, 1 Comst. 113;
Weisser v. Denison, 6 Seld. 68; Morgan v. Bank of New
York, 1 Kern. 404; Belknap v. Bank of North America,
    ; Mahaiwe Bank v. Douglas, 31 Conn. 170; Wade v.
Withington, 1 Allen, 561; Morse on Banking, p. 301. The
alteration of a check in a part not material may be disregarded.
Smith v. Smith, 1 R. I. 398.
    [1] Where a check is drawn payable to the order of any

828. *Cheques paid by mistake.*—If a banker pays
the cheque of a customer, supposing that he has funds,
and afterwards finds that the customer has overdrawn

actual person or corporation, the bank is liable for its payment to any one else. Smith v. Smith, 1 R. I. 398; Boston v.
Benson, 12 Cush. 61; Wheelock v. Freeman, 13 Pick. 165.
Checks made payable to words or initials, or intended or supposed to refer to a fictitious name, or to figures, will be considered as payable to bearer, and subject to all the rules relating
to such checks. Story on Promissory Notes, § 480; Willetts
v. Phœnix Bank, 2 Duer. 121 ; Mechanics' Bank v. Stratton, 3
Keyes, 365 ; Morse on Banking, 239.   So strictly is the
bank's risk of paying checks to order enforced, that it was
held, in Graves v. American Exchange Bank, 17 N. Y. 205,
that payment to a person of precisely the same name or initials
did not relieve the bank from liability.   To this decision, however, Roosevelt, J., dissented.   Acceptance and payment, or
either, concludes the drawees, as against the payees, only as to
the genuineness of the drawer's signature.   Canal Bank v.
Bank of Albany, 1 Hill, 287.   "If anywhere in the chain of
orders or endorsements there is a forgery, the bank may recover
back, even though a considerable time has elapsed since payment ; provided that it acts with due promptitude and dispatch
so soon as the discovery is made."   Morse on Banking, 309.
A mere clerical error in a check may be disregarded.   Id.
293–294. A check was drawn to Cook ; Barnes endorsed Cook's
name without his authority, and received the money; the
bank deducted the check from the drawer's account, and settled with him on that basis.   *Held*, that Cook could recover
the amount of the check from the bank.   The conduct of the
bank was an acceptance, and bound it as a certified check
would.   Seventh National Bank v. Cook, 73 Pa. St. 483.   A
bank is not bound to know the handwriting or the genuineness of the filling up of a check drawn upon and paid by it.
It is legally concluded only as to the signature of the drawer
and its own certification.   National, &c., Bank v. National, &c.,.
Bank, 55 N. Y. 211.   Where, therefore, a bank has paid by
mistake to a *bona fide* holder a certified check, which, after certification, had been fraudulently altered by raising the amount,
it can recover back the sum thus paid, unless such holder has
suffered loss in consequence of the mistake.   Id.   And the sum
as written will control the sum as expressed in figures.   The
figures in the margin are only an index for convenience of

his account, and that he has no funds, the banker can not recover the money from the party who presented the cheque ; (*i*) but, if the cheque was not drawn on the banker, and the latter does not pay the cheque as a banker honoring the draft of his customer, but in the same way as if he were giving change for a bank note all parties believing the cheque to be genuine, he can recover back the money he has paid, if it turns out to be forged and worthless. (*k*) [1]

(*i*) Chambers v. Miller. 13 C. B., N. S. 125 ; 32 L. J., C. P. 30.

(*k*) Woodland v. Fear, 7 Ell. & Bl. 522.

reference, and are no part of the bill. So held in Smith v. Smith, 1 R. I. 398, which goes to the further extent, in a case where the figures were altered by the holder to conform to the sum as expressed in the writing, of declaring that not only did not such alteration vitiate the bill, but that it was not competent to show that the bill was in fact negotiated for the amount as expressed by the figures, instead of that expressed by the writing.

[1] See last note. A bank, by certifying a check in the usual form, simply certifies to the genuineness of the signature of the drawer, and that he has funds sufficient to meet it, and engages that those funds will not be withdrawn from the bank by him; it does not warrant the genuineness of the body of the check as to the payee or amount. Marine, &c. Bank v. National, &c. Bank, 59 N. Y. 67. Accordingly *held*, where plaintiff certified a check which had been altered, by changing the date, name of payee, and raising the amount, and subsequently paid the same to defendant, that the amount could be recovered back as for money paid by mistake. Id. Where money is paid on a "raised" check by mistake, neither party being in fault, the general rule is that it may be recovered back as paid without consideration. Espy v. Bank of Cincinnati, 18 Wall. 604. Where a party to whom such a check is offered sends it to the bank on which it is drawn, for information, the law presumes that the bank has knowledge of the drawer's signature and of the state of his account, and it is responsible for what may be replied on these points, and unless there is something in the terms in which information is asked that points the attention of the bank officer beyond these two matters, his verbal response that the check is "good" or

829. *Payment of cheques at branch banks.*—The different branch banks of a banking company are, as regards their separate customers, separate companies, so that a customer who keeps an account with one branch has no right to draw cheques upon, and have them cashed by, another branch. They are also separate and distinct for many other purposes. (*l*)   But, where a customer had an account with two branches of a bank, it was held that in the absence of any special agreement with their customer the bank had a right to consider the two accounts as one, and to refuse the customer's cheque when, on adding the two accounts together, the balance was against him. (*m*) [1]

830. *Crossed cheques.*—By the 21 & 22 Vict. c. 79, it is enacted (s. 1), that whenever a cheque or draft on any banker, payable to bearer or to order on demand, shall be issued crossed with the name of a banker, or with two transverse lines with the words "and company," or any abbreviation thereof, such crossing shall be deemed a material part of the cheque or draft, and, except as thereafter mentioned, shall not be obliterated, or added to, or altered, by any person whomsoever after the issuing thereof ; and the banker upon whom such cheque or draft shall be drawn shall not pay such cheque or draft to any other than the banker with

---

(*l*) Woodland v. Fear, 7 Ell. & Bl. 521 ; 26 L. J., Q. B. 202.

(*m*) Garnett v. M'Kewan, L. R., 8 Ex. 10 ; 42 L. J., Ex. 1.

"all right," will be limited to them, and will not extend the genuineness of the filling-in of the check as to payee or amount.   Id.

[1] The establishment of branch banks is discouraged in the United States, and must be authorized by the legislature. City Bank of Columbus v. Beach, 1 Blatchf. C. C. 425; Bank of Augusta v. Earle, 13 Pet. 519 ; People v. Oakland, &c., Bank, 1 Dougl. 284; Tombigbee R. R. Co. v. Kneeland, 4 How. (U. S.) 16.

whose name such cheque or draft shall be so crossed, or, if the same be crossed as aforesaid without a banker's name, to any other than a banker.   By sect. 2, whenever any such cheque or draft shall have been issued uncrossed, or shall be crossed with the words " and company," or any abbreviation thereof, and without the name of any banker, any lawful holder of such cheque or draft while the same remains so uncrossed, or crossed with the words "and company," or any abbreviation thereof, without the name of any banker, may cross the same with the name of a banker ; and, whenever any such cheque or draft shall be uncrossed, any such lawful holder may cross the same with the words "and company," or any abbreviation thereof, with or without the name of a banker; and any such crossing shall be deemed a material part of the cheque or draft, and shall not be obliterated, or added to, or altered by any person whomsoever after the making thereof; and the banker upon whom such cheque or draft shall be drawn shall not pay such cheque or draft to any other than the banker with whose name such check or draft shall be so crossed.   But it is provided (sect. 4), that no banker paying a cheque or draft which does not, at the time when it is presented for payment, plainly appear to be, or to have been, crossed, or to have been obliterated, added to, or altered, shall be in any way responsible, or incur any liability, nor shall such payment be questioned by reason of such cheque having been so crossed, or having been so obliterated, added to, or altered, and of his having paid the same to a person other than a banker, or other than a banker with whose name such cheque or draft shall have been so crossed, unless such banker shall have acted malâ fide, or been guilty of negligence in

so paying such cheque. (*n*)   By sect. 5, in the construction of the Act, the word "banker" shall include
any person or persons, or corporation, or joint-stock
company, acting as a banker or bankers.[1]

(*n*) See Simmons v. Taylor (4 C. B.,   Vict. c. 25, which differs in its pro-
N. S. 463 ; 27 L. J., C. P. 248), which,   visions from the 21 & 22 Vict. c. 79.
however, was decided on the 19 & 20

[1] There is no custom or usage in the United States,
sufficiently old or universal to be regarded as a legal usage.
"Supposing the direction to be properly given, however," says
Morse on Banking, 333, "the collecting and the paying
bank must both respect it. . . . It would amount to an
express designation by the drawer of the manner in which
alone he authorized payment to be demanded or made, and
assuredly he could be released from no liability or obligation
by any circumstances naturally occurring in the ordinary
process of carrying out his own bidding.   There seems to be
no authority for supposing that anything short of this un-
mistakable action on the part of the drawer would be held to
operate as a waiver by him of his customary privileges. . . .
Of late the germ of a similar custom has begun to manifest
itself.   Occasionally checks have stamped or written upon
them some form of words which is intended to secure their
payment exclusively through the clearing house.   No especial
form has as yet been generally accepted, and the legal effect
of none of those in use has ever been passed upon.   It is
safe to say, however, that there is no question but that the
drawer could embody in his order a direction to his bank to
pay only upon presentation of the instrument in the usual
course through the clearing house, and that such a direction
would be valid and as binding upon the bank as a direction
to pay only to the order of a particular person.   Probably
the drawer of the check is the only person who could legally
impose this duty upon the drawee bank, for he is the only
person who has a right to give to the bank any orders in the
premises.   Though, if the check be payable to the order of A
B, it is barely possible that the privilege of including this
matter in his order when indorsing over might be accorded
to A B also.   In all cases it may be laid down that the words
used should be intelligible, which is certainly not the case
with many of the forms hitherto adopted.   The mere crossing
with the name of the banker is a species of mark which derives

831. *Lien of bankers.*—Bankers have a lien upon all the securities of their customers in their hands for advances made by them to their customers in the ordinary course of business, unless such securities have been received under some special arrangement inconsistent with the exercise of the right, (*o*) or for some special purpose. (*p*)[1]

832. *Damages for non-payment of cheques by bankers.*—If a banker refuses to pay a cheque drawn upon him by a trader who keeps an account with him, and who has sufficient assets in the hands of the banker to meet the cheque at the time it is presented for payment, such trader is entitled, as we have seen, to recover substantial damages without proof of any actual damage, since the dishonoring of cheques is likely to be very injurious to the credit of persons in trade. (*q*)[2]

833. *Of a mandate or gratuitous commission.*—If

(*o*) Jones v. Peppercorn, 28 L. J., Ch. 158. Meadows, *In re*, 28 L. J., Ch. 891. City Bank, *Ex parte*, 3 Law T. R. N. S. 792. *Ex parte* National Bank, L. R., 14 Eq. 507. *In re* European Bank, L. R., 8 Ch. 41.

(*p*) Brandao v. Barnett, 12 Cl. & Fin. 787. Wylde v. Radford, 33 L. J., Ch. 51.

(*q*) Rolin v. Steward, 14 C. B. 595 ; 23 L. J., C. P. 148.

its meaning through the interpretation of usage. But if words which assume to have a signification are used, they must succeed in expressing with some degree of clearness, that meaning which is desired, or they will not be construed to import it."

[1] The effect of crossing a check is, practically, to make it payable through the clearing-house. Marsh v. Oneida Bank, 34 Barb. 298 ; Beckwith v. Union Bank, 4 Sandf. 604 ; Ford v. Thornton, 3 Leigh. 695 ; United States v. Malcalester, 9 Burr. 475 ; McDowell v. Bank of Wilmington, 1 Harring, 369 ; State Bank v. Armstrong, 4 Dev. 519 ; Commercial Bank of Albany v. Hughes, 17 Wend. 94 ; Dawson v. Real Estate Bank, 5 Pike, 282, but none are special deposits. Morse on Banking, 35.

[2] Matter of Brown, 2 Story, 512.

the bailee or depositary expressly or impliedly undertakes for something more than the mere passive custody of the thing bailed, the bailment advances from a mere naked deposit or simple bailment to a mandate, and the bailee becomes clothed with the duties and implied engagements of a mandatary, in addition to those of a mere depositary for keeping. If money is bailed to a man upon the faith of a promise made by him to take and deliver it to a banker, or to invest it in the public funds, or lay it out in the purchase of lands, this is an express mandate. An implied mandate arises when the bailee takes charge of living animals or perishable chattels, for whose preservation and safe keeping a certain amount of work and labor, attention and skill, is necessarily requisite, and which the bailee, by accepting the trust and duty, impliedly undertakes to furnish. It is essential to the existence of a mandate that it be gratuitous ; for, if anything is to be paid for what is expressly or impliedly agreed to be done, the contract immediately becomes a contract of letting and hiring of labor and skill to be performed and exercised upon the thing bailed. (*r*)

The term mandatum or mandate was applied in the Roman law to all gratuitous agencies and procurations, whether made concerning land or realty or chattels, and whether accompanied or unaccompanied by any transfer or delivery of property. (*s*) In the common law, the term is generally restricted to express or implied promises made on bailments of chattels that something shall be done with them gratuitously for the benefit of the bailor. The bailor who makes the request and gives the directions as to the disposal of the

---

(*r*) In summâ sciendum est, mandatum nisi gratuitum sit in aliam formam negotii cadere ; nam, mercede consti-tutâ, incipit locatio et conductio esse. Instit. lib. 3, tit. 27, § 13.

(*s*) Instit. lib. 3, tit. 27.

chattel is called the mandator; and the bailee who receives the chattel upon the terms expressed or implied, and assents to the directions, and undertakes the trust to be performed, is called the mandatary. So long as there has been no actual bailment by the delivery and acceptance of the chattel, there is no binding contract of mandate. A promise to do something with a thing that has never been put into the actual or constructive possession of the promisor is a mere nudum pactum, which may be revoked; but when the bailment has been made upon the faith of the promise, and the promisor has obtained possession of the chattel in execution of the mandate, the contract is complete, and he is bound faithfully to discharge the trust he has undertaken.[1]

834. *Non-feazance and mis-feazance.*—It has been said, in reference to gratuitous undertakings to perform work, that, if the promisor does not proceed on the

---

[1] Being liable for gross negligence only, but see Thorne v. Deas, 4 Johns. 84; McGee v. Bast, 6 J. J. Marsh. 455; Foster v. Essex Bank, 17 Mass. 479; Tracy v. Wood, 3 Mason, 132; McNabb v. Lockhart, 18 Ga. 495; Skelley v. Kuhn, 17 Ill. 170; Fulton v. Alexander, 21 Tex. 148; Kemp v. Farlow, 5 Ind. 462; Lampley v. Scott, 24 Miss. 528; Stover v. Gowen, 18 Me. 174; and see *ante*, note 2, p. 99, § 56, vol. 1; Anderson v. Foresman, Wright, 598; Connor v. Winton, 8 Ind. 315; Jourdan v. Reed, 1 Iowa, 135; McLean v. Rutherford, 8 Mo. 109; Stanton v. Bell, 2 Hawks, 145; Sodowsky v. McFarland, 3 Dana, 205; Tompkins v. Saltmarsh, 14 Sergt. & R. 275; Bland v. Wormuck, 2 Murph. 373; Beardsley v. Richardson, 16 Wend. 25. Under the Louisiana Civil Code, which has modified the Roman law, it is not of the essence of mandate that it be gratuitous. The agent's right to compensation may be inferred from the relations of the parties, or the nature of the services. Waterman v. Gibson, 5 La. Ann. 672; Succession of Fowler, 7 Id. 207; and see Lafourche Navigation Co. v. Collins, 12 Id. 119; Dunbar v. Hughes, 6 Id. 466; Devalcourt v. Dillon, 12 Id. 672; Wilson v. Wilson, 16 Id. 155.

work, no action will lie against him for the non-feazance; but, "if he proceeds on the employment, he
makes himself liable for any misfeazance in the course
of that work." But when a man promises to perform
work upon, or to do something with, the chattel of
another, and the chattel is bailed to him for the purpose expressed, his acceptance of the possession of the
chattel in execution of his engagement is an "entering
on the work and employment;" and, if, after having
accepted such possession and taken the chattel away
with him, he neglects to do that which he promised
to perform, this neglect is a misfeazance, for which he
shall be responsible. (*t*) "A bare being trusted," observes HOLT, C. J., "with another man's goods must be
taken to be a sufficient consideration, if the bailee once
enter upon the trust and take the goods into his possession." (*u*) Where a sum of money was bailed to a
party upon the faith of an undertaking made by him
to cause the sum to be paid to the bailor or his order
at a distant place, it was held that the bailment of the
money was a sufficient consideration for the undertaking, and that the mandatary was responsible for the
non-fulfillment of his engagement. (*v*) So, where certain boilers were delivered to a man upon the faith of
an undertaking made by him to weigh them gratuitously and return them to the bailor in as perfect and
complete condition as they were in at the time of the
making of the bailment, and the mandatary took the
boilers to pieces in order to weigh them, but refused
to put them together again, it was held that he was
responsible for his breach of contract, and must make
good the damage that had been sustained by the man-

(*t*) Holt, C. J., Coggs v. Bernard, C. P. 175 ; 13 C. B. 466.
2 Raym. 919, 920. Elsee v. Gatward, (*u*) Coggs v. Bernard, 2 Raym. 912.
5 T. R. 149. Balfe v. West, 22 L. J., (*v*) Shillibeer v. Glynn, 2 M. & W.
143.

dator. The mandatary may, indeed, revoke his promise and return the chattel, if he does it without delay, and before his acceptance of the trust and omission to fulfill it have occasioned loss or damage to the mandator ; but he can not, if the revocation will place the latter in a worse position than he was in at the time the mandate was accepted and the promise made, lawfully withdraw such promise, and refuse to execute the trust. " Every man is at liberty," it is observed in the Institutes, " to refuse a mandate ; but when once accepted and undertaken, it must be performed or renounced as soon as possible, that the mandator may transact the business himself or through another." (*y*) If, therefore, a party undertakes to procure an insurance for another, and proceeds to carry his undertaking into effect by getting a policy underwritten, but deals so negligently with the policy that the benefit of the insurance is totally lost to the party for whom he promised to effect it, he is liable to an action ; (*z*) but if, after having made the promise, he simply neglects to get the insurance effected, he does not incur any legal liability for the default. (*a*) [1]

835. *Bailment of money and chattels to be carried gratuitously—Loss or damage from negligence.*—A bailee who has undertaken gratuitously to convey money or goods from one place to another, and has entered upon the trust by accepting possession of the money or the goods, is bound to exercise the same

(*y*) Inst. lib. 3, tit. 27, § 11.

(*z*) Wallace v. Tellfair, cited Wilkinson v. Coverdale, 1 Esp. 76.

(*a*) Thorne v. Deas, 4 Johns. (U. S.) 84.

[1] The distinction made in the text between liability for non-feazance and misfeazance, is treated by Parsons on Contracts as the liability of the bailee in mandatum, ex contractu and ex delictu (vol. 2, p. 101), Salem Bank v. Gloucester Bank, 67 Mass. 1.

care and diligence in the execution of the task as a person of ordinary care and prudence might be expected to exercise in the conveyance of his own property. If by negligence and mismanagement in the accomplishment of his undertaking the money or the goods are lost or stolen, injured or spoiled, he will be responsible for the loss. But he is not responsible for the loss of the money, if he is forcibly robbed without any default on his part.[1]

836. *Bailments of chattels to be mended or repaired gratuitously—Employment of unskillful persons.*—If a chattel is bailed to a workman or artificer in some particular art, craft, or profession, upon the faith of an undertaking made by the bailee to mend, repair, or improve it gratuitously for the benefit of the mandator, the mandatary must complete the work within a reasonable period, and must be especially mindful that the article is not injured in his hands during the performance of the work through a want of that knowledge and skill which every workman and artificer in his particular art or craft is bound to possess.[2] But, if a person, known to be unskilled in the particular work or employment he gratuitously undertakes, does the work at the solicitation of a friend with such ability as he possesses, he stands excused, although it is unskillfully done; for it is the mandator's own folly to trust him, and the party engages for no more than a reasonable exertion of his capacity. Thus, where a mandatary undertook to get some articles that had

---

[1] See Eddy v. Livingston, 35 Mo. 487; Graves v. Ticknor, 6 N. H. 537; Beardsley v. Richardson, 11 Wend. 25; Bland v. Wormack, 2 Murph. 373; Delaware Bank v. Smith, 1 Edm. (N. Y.) Sel. Cas. 351; Anderson v. Foresman, Wright, 593; Lloyd v. Barden, 2 Strobh. 343; Jenkins v. Morton, 1 Sneed. 248; Colyar v. Taylor, 1 Coldw. 372.

[2] *Post*, § 877, 878.

been bailed to him entered at the Custom House, and gave by mistake a wrong description, but appeared to have acted bonâ fide and to the best of his ability, it was held that he was not responsible for a seizure of the goods by the Custom-House officers. " Had the situation or profession of the bailee," observes Lord LOUGHBOROUGH, "been such as to imply skill, an omission of that skill would have been imputable to him as gross negligence. If, in this case, a shipbroker or a clerk in the Custom House had undertaken to enter the goods, a wrong entry would in him be gross negligence, because the situation and employment necessarily imply a competent degree of knowledge in making such entries." (*b*)

837. *In respect of the custody and safe keeping of the chattel*, the mandatary is clothed with the ordinary liabilities and responsibilities of a depositary.

838. *Bailment of money for investment.*—If money is bailed to a man upon the faith of a promise or assurance made by him to place it out at interest, or to purchase an annuity with it for the benefit of the bailor, the mandatary who accepts the money and enters upon the execution of the trust impliedly promises to be diligent and careful in the fulfillment of his undertaking, and to exercise common and ordinary care in the selection of a safe investment ; and, if the money is lost by his miscarriage and neglect, an action will lie against him for the loss. (*c*) But the mandatary is not responsible (if he does not exercise any trade or profession denoting that he has peculiar skill in money matters) for the exercise of more than ordinary care and caution ; and he is not liable for the

(*b*) Shiells v. Blackburne, 1 H. Bl. 159. Moore v. Mourgue, 2 Cowp. 479.

(*c*) Coggs v. Bernard, 2 Raym. 910. Whitehead v. Greetham, 10 Moore, 194 ; 2 Bing. 464.

failure of the investment, if he has used such skill and
knowledge as he possessed, and has acted with uprightness and honesty of purpose in the transaction of
the business confided to him. " The only duty that is
imposed upon him under such a retainer and employment is a duty to act faithfully and honestly, and not
to be guilty of any gross or corrupt neglect in the
discharge of that which he undertakes to do." (*d*)
But an attorney, whose profession and employment
naturally lead him to have some knowledge of securities for money and pecuniary investments, is responsible for the exercise of a reasonable amount of professional knowledge and skill in the selection of a safe
investment, although he acts gratuitously. (*e*)   His
office, profession, and employment imply skill and
invite confidence; and an omission of that skill is
imputable to him as gross negligence. (*f*) [1]   If a sum
of money is entrusted to a man to be transmitted to
some distant part, or to be laid out by him in some
purchase or investment for the benefit of the mandator, and with an express or implied authority or permission to use the money himself until the purpose
for which it was bailed can be accomplished, and the
mandatary accordingly spends the money with the
intention of replacing it when necessary with other
money, or pays it into his bankers to his own account,
and not to the separate account of the mandator, the
bailment of the money becomes a loan for use and

(*d*) Dartnall v. Howard, 4 B. & C.
350, 351.
  (*e*) Donaldson v. Haldane, 7 Cl. &
Fin. 762. Bourne v. Diggles, 2 Chitt.

311. Craig v. Watson, 8 Beav. 427.
Smith v. Pococke, 23 L. J., Ch. 545;
18 Jur. 478.
  (*f*) Shiells v. Blackburne, *supra*.

[1] Tracy v. Wood, 3 Mason, 132; Ulmer v. Ulmer, 2 Nott.
& McC. 489; Foster v. Essex Bank, 17 Mass. 479.

consumption, and the bailee is clothed with the duties and liabilities and implied engagements of a borrower by way of mutuum, in addition to those of a mandatary.[1]   In these cases the money is payable, as we have seen, absolutely and at all events; and the bailee cannot excuse himself from the obligation to repay the amount by showing a loss by robbery or from inevitable accident.

839. *Bailments of living animals—Negligent management.*—If the subject-matter of the bailment consists of living animals, such as horses, oxen, cattle or sheep, the mandatary is bound to furnish them with suitable food and nourishment, and to give them a proper and reasonable amount of exercise and fresh air. If a man takes charge of cattle or sheep, and afterwards takes no heed of them, but lets them stray away on a common, and get drowned or lost, this is a breach of trust, and he is responsible for the loss. (*g*) If he turns a horse, of which he has consented gratuit-

---

(*g*) Hil. Term, 2 Hen. 7, 9 b. Coggs v. Bernard, 2 Raym. 913.

[1] See *ante*, note 1, p. 493. We have already considered the peculiar liabilities of banks; it is said, further, that where bills and notes are deposited with a bank for collection, the bank is an agent to collect, and not merely to transmit for collection, and is liable for the neglect of any of its agents, however proper its selection of such agents may have been. Allen v. Merchants' Bank, 22 Wend. 215; Bank of Orleans v. Smith, 3 Hill, 560; Montgomery Co. Bank v. Albany City Bank, 3 Seld. 459; Van Wart v. Wooley, 3 B. & C. 439; Thomson v. Bank of South Carolina, 3 Hill, 77; Mechanics' Bank v. Earp, 4 Rawle, 384; Taber v. Penett, 2 Gallison, 565; Fabens v. Mercantile Bank, 23 Pick. 330; Dorchester & Milton Bank v. New England Bank, 1 Cush. 177; Warren Bank v. Suffolk Bank, 10 Cush. 583; East Haddam Bank v. Scovil, 12 Conn. 303; Jackson v. Union Bank, 6 Har. & J. 146; Baldwin v. Bank of Louisiana, 1 La. Ann. 15; Bellemire v. Bank of U. S., 4 Whart. 105; Bank of Washington v. Neale, 1 Pet. 25.

ously to take charge, into a dangerous pasture after
dark, and the horse falls into a pit or well, or into the
shaft of a mine, this is a gross neglect and breach of
trust, and he shall be responsible for the loss. (*h*)   If
he places a horse in a pasture surrounded by rotten
and very defective fences, and the horse, by reason
thereof, strays away and is lost, this also is a breach of
trust, for which he shall be answerable; but, if the
horse was a wild, ungovernable animal, and got away
through its own impatience of restraint as much as by
reason of the defective fences, then the bailee will not
be responsible for the loss. (*i*)   What is, and what is
not, gross negligence amounting to a breach of trust
is often a mixed question of law and fact, but more
generally a pure question of fact.   It must be judged
of by the actual state of society, the general usages of
life, and the dangers peculiar to the times, as well as
by the apparent nature and value of the subject-matter
of the bailment and the degree of care it seems to require. (*k*)   Where a man proved to be conversant
with, and skilled in, horses was commissioned to ride
a horse to a neighboring village, for the purpose of
showing it for sale, and on his arrival he rode the
horse into the race-ground, which was wet and slippery, and the horse slipped and fell several times,
and at last in falling broke one of its knees, it was
held that the bailee had been guilty of a culpable neglect and breach of trust, and was answerable for the
damage. (*l*)   If a farrier undertakes to treat a living
animal for some disorder gratuitously, he is nevertheless bound to exercise the ordinary knowledge and
skill of his art or profession in the course of his treat-

(*h*) Rooth v. Wilson, 1 B. & Ald. 61,
62.

(*i*) Domat. (Depot), s. 3, 6.

(*k*) Story on Bailments, 9, 10.

(*l*) Wilson v. Brett, 11 M. & W. 113.

ment, and will be responsible for injuries resulting from his neglect to do so. (*m*) [1]

840. *Bailments of perishable commodities.* —If the subject-matter of the bailment is a perishable commodity, the bailee is bound to bestow such an amount of labor and vigilance for its preservation as would ordinarily be bestowed by a prudent owner. If the mandatary of a valuable painting lets it lie on the damp ground, or places it in a kitchen, or against a damp wall in a room where there is no fire, when he might have placed it in a dry situation and in perfect security, this is an act of gross negligence. (*n*)

841. *Of the use of the subject-matter of the mandate.*—A mandatary has no right to make use of the

(*m*) Shiells v. Blackburne, 1 H. Bl.   (*n*) Mytton v. Cock, 2 Str. 1099.
162.

[1] The gratuitous bailee is liable only for such negligence as he is guilty of in spite of the better skill or knowledge which he either actually had or undertook to have. Hanover on the Law of Horses, p. 231. "In cases of mere gratuitous loans, the use is to be deemed strictly a personal favor, and confined to the borrower, unless a more extensive use can be implied from other circumstances, such as, for instances, lending a horse on trial. In general, it may be said, in the absence of all controlling circumstances, that the use intended by the parties is the natural and ordinary use for which the thing is adapted;" Id. 232; Howard v. Babcock, 21 Ill. 259; Bennet v. O'Brien, 37 Id. 250; Phillips v. Condon, 14 Id. 84; Scranton v. Baxter, 4 Sandf. 8; Wood v. McClure, 7 Ind. 155; Carpenter v. Branch, 13 Vt. 161; Eastman v. Sanborn, 3 Allen, 594; and the animal must be used as stipulated; if loaned to the master to ride, his servant should not ride him; Scranton v. Baxter, 4 Sandf. 8; if loaned to be driven to Boston, it should not be driven in an opposite direction, if loaned for a week, it must not be kept a month, &c. ; Wheelslock v. Wheelright, 5 Mass. 104; Booth v. Terrell, 16 Ga. 25. But if the animal be borrowed, to be redelivered on request, and it dies before the request, the bailee is not liable; Hanover on the Law of Horses, p. 223; nor where it dies on his hands from a disease; Id. See Rey v. Toney, 24 Mo. 600.

subject-matter of the bailment for his own gain and advantage; if he does so, and it is lost, or in any way injured or deteriorated in value by reason of the user, he must, in common with a depositary, make good the loss. The moderate exercise of a horse, or a hound, or a living animal, is necessary for its health and safe preservation, and is, consequently, a user for the benefit of the owner. A mandatary who has charge of a milch-cow or of sheep is bound to milk the cow and shear the sheep, and must account for the produce to the mandator; if he sells the milk or the wool, and refuses to pay over the money, this is a conversion of it to his own use, and a breach of trust, for which he shall be held responsible. If the bailment is made under circumstances leading to the conclusion that the bailee was to have the use of the thing in return for his labor and pains in the keeping of it, as if he were to have the milk of the cow, the wool of the sheep, or the young of animals bearing increase, for his own benefit and advantage, then the bailment would amount to a contract of borrowing and lending, and not to a mandate.

842. *Theft and negligence by servants of the mandatary.*—If the mandatary has given express directions to his servant to take into his custody money, or chattels, or securities, and do with them that which he himself has undertaken to perform, the negligence of the servant in carrying into execution the orders of the master is the negligence of the master, and the latter will be responsible accordingly; but, if the servant deals with the property of his own will, and without the warrant or authority of the master, the latter is not responsible, unless there be a default in him in knowingly employing a drunken, negligent, or dishonest servant.

843. *Payment of expenses.*—By the Roman law the mandator was bound to re-imburse the mandatary all expenses that he had necessarily and unavoidably incurred in the safe keeping and preservation of a chattel entrusted to his care and management; for it was considered that a gratuitous commission executed for the behoof of the mandator ought not to be made a subject of expense and charge to the mandatary. (*o*) In the common law, if the mandatary must necessarily incur expense in the execution of the commission entrusted to him, he is clothed with an implied authority from the mandator to defray such expenses. (*p*) The French law accords to the mandatary a right to detain the chattel until he has received payment of the expenses he has incurred in the execution of the trust concerning it. In our own law no such right exists; and no lien is permitted to be claimed by one man upon the property of another for the expenses attendant upon the execution of a gratuitous commission. [1]

(*o*) Dig. lib. 16, tit. 3, l. 12, § 23.　　(*p*) Story's Bailments, § 197.
Domat. lib. 1, tit. 15, s. 2, § 6.

[1] A contract of mandate is terminated either: 1. By the death of the mandatory, if the mandate be wholly unexecuted; for, if partially executed, his personal representatives, under certain circumstances, will be bound to complete it. In the case of joint mandatories, if the mandate be of such a nature as to require the joint services of all, the death of one dissolves it, but not otherwise. 2. By the death of the mandator, if the mandate be wholly unexecuted; since, if partially executed, it may be an injury to the mandatory to have it cease, in which case the mandator's representatives may be bound to complete it. 3. By incapacity of the parties, such as marriage (in the case of a female), insanity, or the like. 4. By a notice of renunciation of his agreement by the mandatory to the mandator, before the execution of the mandate has begun.　5. By a revocation by the mandator, express or implied, before execution begun.　6. By the mandator's bank-

845. *Task-work.*—A contract for the letting out and hiring of "work by the great," or, as it is more commonly called, job or task-work, is a contract for the doing of work in the lump or the job, for a stipulated or implied remuneration, such as a contract to build a house, or dig a well, or make a canal, or to construct a ship or a carriage out of materials furnished by the employer, or to sell goods for a commission on the sale. A contract of this description was styled by the civilians locatio operis faciendi, or the letting out of work to be done. The employer was called locator operis, or the letter-out of the work ; and the workman who undertook the task, and bestowed his labor and skill in its completion, for a reward to be paid to him, was called conductor operis, or the hirer of the work. The terms letter and hirer, however, are applicable, in different senses, to each of the contracting parties. Thus the locator operis, or letter-out of the work, is also conductor operarum, or hirer of the labor and services; and the conductor operis, or hirer of the work, is also locator operarum, or the letter-out of the labor and services. (*q*) When chattels are delivered to a warehouseman or storekeeper to be taken care of or kept for hire, the contract is a contract for the letting and hiring of care and custody, termed locatio operis et custodiæ.

845. *Of the distinction between contracts for work*

(*q*) Sed dicendum est in hâc specie locationis diverso respectu eundem et locatorem et conductorem videri. Nam qui operam locare dicitur, ille idem dicitur conducere opus faciendum ; et ex contrario qui operam dicitur conducere, idem dicitur locare aliquid faciendum ; ut conductor operis idem sit operæ locator, et locator operis idem operæ conductor. Vin. Com. lib. 3, tit. 25, p. 758. Poth. Louage, No. 392.

ruptcy. 7. By the mandatary's bankruptcy, in case the execution of the mandate involve the payment of money on his part See Story on Contracts, § 857.

and services and contracts of sale.—There is a great analogy, as before mentioned, between contracts for working up materials and the contract of sale ; for, if the materials for the work, as well as the work itself, have been furnished by the workman, then the contract is in general a contract of sale ; while, on the other hand, if the employer has furnished the materials, and the undertaker of the work contributes his labor merely, the contract is a contract of letting and hiring of labor. If the groundwork of the labor or the principal material entering into its composition has been provided by the employer, the contract is a contract for the letting and hiring of work, although the undertaker of the work may have furnished the accessorial materials necessary for its completion. If a man, for instance, sends his own cloth to a tailor to be made into a coat, and the tailor furnishes the buttons, the thread, and the trimmings, the contract is nevertheless a letting and hiring of work, and not a contract of buying and selling. (*r*) In the case of works of art, the work and skill of the workman constitute, in general, the essence of the contract, the materials being merely accessorial ; and, whenever the skill and labor are of the highest description, and the materials of small comparative value, the contract is a contract for work, labor, and materials, and not a contract of sale. (*s*) A contract, for example, for the printing of a book is a contract for the letting and hiring of work and services, although the printer supplies both the paper and the ink, and not a contract of sale. (*t*) But a contract by a dentist to make a set of artificial teeth,

(*r*) Pothier, Louage d'ouvrage, No. 394.

(*s*) See, however, the remarks of Crompton, J., and Blackburn, J., n: Lee v. Griffin, 1 B. L. S. 278.

(*t*) Clay v. Yates, 1 H. & N. 73 ; 25 L. J., Ex. 237.

to fit the mouth of the employer, is a contract for the sale of a chattel and not a contract for work and labor. (*u*) When a contract has been entered into for the building of a house on the land of the employer, and the builder furnishes the timber, stone, and materials for the construction of the building, the contract is not a contract of sale, although it appears as if the builder sold the materials, but a contract of letting and hiring, because the land which is the principal material for the labor, and to which the building is merely an accessory, has been provided by the employer. (*z*) If, indeed, the builder is, by the contract, to provide the ground as well as the accessorial materials for the house, then the contract is a contract of purchase and sale.

846. *Executory and executed contracts for work.* —Contracts for work and services, like all other contracts of letting and hiring, are perfected by the bare consent of the parties, so that as soon as the mutual promises are exchanged, the right to the benefit of work passes to the workman or hirer of the job, and the right to the labor to the employer or letter of the work. (*a*) If a mutual misunderstanding has arisen without any fault or want of good faith on either side, as if the workman has mistaken the meaning of the employer, and made one thing when another was ordered, the contract is void, as no valid and effectual consent to bind the parties has ever been given. If there is no mutual engagement between the parties for the one to do the work, and the other to provide it and pay for its execution, there is, as we have before seen, no binding contract at all, unless the engage-

---

(*u*) Lee v. Griffin, *supra.*　　(*a*) Lara v. Gen. Apoth. Co., 26
(*z*) Dig. lib. 19, tit. 2, lex. 22, § 2.　　L. J,. Ex. 225. *Ante.*

ment is under seal. The workman in such a case is not bound to enter upon his task; nor is the other party bound to provide the work and pay the hire. But, when the work has been actually done, the person at whose request and by whose orders it was executed must pay for it, although the workman was originally under no legal obligation to do the work, nor the employer to employ him. The law generally implies a promise from the employer to pay a reasonable compensation for services rendered, unless it appears that the services were to be gratuitous, or that the workman relied for payment upon a particular fund, and not upon the personal responsibility of the employer. (*b*) When a person has, by fraud, induced another to perform a service for him, intending not to pay for the performance of it, still there is a liability implied by the law, which may be enforced in the same way as an obligation arising out of an express contract. (*c*)

847. *Work and services in preserving a lost chattel, and restoring it to the owner.*—Doubts have at different times been expressed as to whether a person who has voluntarily bestowed his own labor and services, and incurred expense, in the recovery and restoration of a lost chattel to the owner, is entitled to an action to recover compensation and remuneration therefor. (*d*) In the case of the recovery and restoration of shipwrecked property he is clearly entitled to such a compensation; and there seems to be no valid reason for confining this right of reward to cases of salvage from shipwreck.

(*b*) *Ante.* Poucher v. Norman, 3 B. & C. 744. Parke, B., Higgins v. Hopkins, 3 Exch. 166. Hingeston v. Kelly, 18 L. J., Ex. 360. Alexander v. Worman, 6 H. & N. 100 ; 30 L J.,

(*c*) Rumsey v. N. E. Ry. Co., 14 C. B. N. S. 641 ; 32 L. J., C. P. 244.

(*d*) Lampleigh v. Braithwaite, 1 Smith's L. C. 5th ed., 135.

Ex. 198.

" In the French law," observes DOMAT, " he who receives back a thing which he had lost is obliged, on his part, to reimburse the finder the expenses incurred by him in the preservation and restoration of the thing lost, such as the expense of feeding a strayed beast which required nourishment, or the carriage and conveyance of the thing lost to some place of safety, or the expense of advertisements, or the publication of printed notices, in order to give information to the owner." (*e*)   If the owner is present and cognizant of the exertions made to recover his lost property, it will be a question of fact whether there was or was not an implied request on his part for the performance of the service actually rendered, and a tacit understanding between the parties that the person doing the work should be rewarded for his pains.

848. *Salvage services.*—In order to encourage persons to lend their aid and assistance for the protection and preservation of property and life from shipwreck, the law gives to the parties by whose labor and assistance the property or lives have been saved from impending peril, a claim to a fair and reasonable compensation for their services, and a right to retain the property until they have received it. (*f*) This compensation is called salvage, a term derived from the French word salver, or sauver, to save.   The amount of salvage payable in the case of the recovery of property lost by shipwreck or abandoned at sea (*g*) depends upon the value of the thing saved, the degree of danger of loss, and the

(*e*) Domat, liv. 2, tit. 9, s. 2, No. 2. Dig. lib. 47, tit. 2, lex 43, § 8.

(*f*) Hartford v. Jones, 1 Raym. 393 ; Salk. 654, pl. 2.   17 & 18 Vict. c 104, s. 458–470.   24 Vict. c. 10, s.

9.   25 & 26 Vict. c. 63, s. 59.   The Fusilier, 2 Moo. P. C. N. S. 51 ; 34 L. J., Adm. 25.   The Phantom, L. R. 1 Adm. 58.

(*g*) The Genessee, 12 Jur. 401.

amount of labor and skill employed in saving it.
Some maritime codes have proportioned the amount
to the value of the thing saved, without reference to
the surrounding circumstances of the case; but this is
obviously unjust; and our own law, therefore, merely
directs as a general principle that a fair and reasonable
compensation shall be made. (*h*). If the salvors are
guilty of misconduct, and occasion injury to the ship
and cargo by rescuing the vessel from one danger only
to run her into another, the claim for salvage will be
lost. (*i*)   But if success is finally obtained, no mere
mistake or error of judgment in the manner of procuring it, and no misconduct short of that which is willful
and may be considered criminal on the part of the
salvors, will work an entire forfeiture of the salvage.
Mistake or misconduct, not willful, but diminishing the
value of the property salved, or occasioning expense to
the owners, will, however, be considered in estimating
the amount of compensation to be awarded. (*k*)   There
can be no claim to salvage where the efforts to salve
have not been attended with success. (*l*) [1]   A man can

(*h*) The Otto Hermann, 33 L. J.,
Adm. 189, The Thomas Fielden, 32
L. J., Adm. 61.

(*i*) The Dosseitei, 10 Jur. 855.

(*k*) The Atlas, 15 Moo. P. C. 329.

(*l*) The Edward Hawkins, 31 L. J.,
Adm. 46.   The Atlas, 31 L. J., Adm.
210.

[1] The three elements necessary to obtain salvage are:
1. Marine peril. 2. Voluntary service. 3. Success. 11 Parsons on Contracts, 315.   The peril or danger must be extraordinary, or must have appeared so to the exercise of a sound
discretion.   The Charlotte, 3 W. Rob. 71.   If a ship-master,
with his crew, might have saved the ship, interference of salvors
will be presumed to be unnecessary; Hand v. The Elvira, Gil-
pin, 67; the salvors may, however, introduce proof that the
master would not have saved it.   It would be equally a salvage
service whether it were rendered at sea or upon property
wrecked at sea but then on the land.   Stevens v. Bales of
Cotton, Bee. 170; and in case of a service by landsmen; Id.
The salvage service most liberally rewarded is that of saving

not entitle himself to salvage in respect of services
which have been rendered contrary to the express
wishes and directions of the owner, and has no right
to interfere with persons employed by the owner to
save the property. (*m*) And if one set of men have
taken possession of a vessel abandoned at sea, and are
endeavoring to preserve it, another set have no right
to molest them and become participators in the salvage,
unless it appears that the first would not have been
able to effect the purpose without the aid of the others.
(*n*) A passenger is not entitled to claim salvage in
respect of that ordinary assistance to a vessel in distress
which it is the interest of all persons on board to give
for the purpose of avoiding the common danger. (*o*)

(*m*) Sutton v. Buck, 2 Taunt. 312.   (*o*) The Branston, 2 Hag. 3.   The
(*n*) Abbott, 495.   Vrede, 1 Lush. 322 ; 30 L. J., Adm.
                                       209.

" derelict" property. To constitute derelict, there must be a
vessel or cargo abandoned and deserted by the master and
crew, with no purpose of returning to it, and no hope of saving or recovering it themselves. The Minerva, 1 Spinks,
Adm. 271 ; The Watt, 2 W. Rob. 70 ; Rowe v. Brig ——, 1
Mason, 372 ; The Amethyst, Davies, 20 ; Mason v. Ship Blai-
reau, 2 Cranch, 240. If the master and crew remain on board,
although they give up the possession and control to the salvors,
it is not derelict ; 2 Parsons on Contracts, 315 ; though, if the
master and crew have left the vessel, a mere intention to send
assistance to her would not prevent the ship from being derelict ; Id. ; and if the vessel be deserted, it will be presumed to
be derelict, unless an intention to return be proved on the
part of those who left her, or some of them ; Id. ; The Bark
Island City, 1 Black. 121 ; The Bee, Ware, 332 ; Tyson v.
Prior, 1 Gallis, 133 ; Clarke v. Brig Dodge Healy, 4 Wash.
C. C. 651 ; The Schooner Emulous, 1 Sumner, 207 ; The John
Perkins, 21 Law Rep. 94. A ship or a cargo sunk is considered derelict ; but not if the owner had not lost the hope and
purpose of recovering his property, and had not ceased his
efforts for that purpose. So are goods floating from the vessel
out to sea ; not, however, if the goods are on the water, and
the master is endeavoring to save them. 2 Parsons on Contracts, 315.

But for extraordinary services rendered and dangers incurred for the preservation of the vessel, the passenger is as much entitled to salvage as a mere stranger. (*p*) And salvage service may be performed, even by the seamen of the ship salved, when an abandonment of her has put an end to their original contract. (*q*) Where salvage services are performed by one ship to another, both ships belonging to the same owner, the master and crew of the ship which has performed the salvage services are entitled to salvage remuneration, provided the services performed are not within the contract which they originally entered into with the owners, and for which they would be paid by their ordinary wages. (*r*) And the owners of a salving vessel are entitled to remuneration, although some of them are also owners of the vessel which did the mischief. (*s*) An agreement for salvage which is reasonable and equitable at the time it is made, is valid, notwithstanding circumstances may render the salvage services more expensive or hazardous than was anticipated. (*t*) By the 17 & 18 Vict. c. 104, s. 182, every stipulation by which any seaman consents to abandon any righ⁴ which he may have or obtain in the nature of salvage, is wholly inoperative; but by the 25 & 26 Vict. c. 63, s. 18, this is not to apply to the case of any agreement made by the seamen belonging to any ship which by the terms of the agreement is to be employed on salvage service. Persons who merely furnish boats, sails, and tackle, or other articles of use for salvage purposes, are not entitled to be paid as salvors, but for the use

(*p*) Newman v. Walters, 3 B. & P. 612.

(*q*) The Vrede, 30 L. J., Adm. 209. The Le Jouet, L. R., 3 A. & E. 556; 41 L. J., Adm. 95.

(*r*) The Sappho, L. R., 3 P. C. 690;

40 L. J., P. C. 48. The Scout, L. R., 3 A. & E. 512; 41 L. J., Adm. 42.

(*s*) The Glengabeer, L. R., 3 A. & E. 534; 41 L. J., Adm. 84.

(*t*) The Waverley, 40 L. J., Adm. 42.

of the articles they have supplied. (*u*) There is no distinction between river salvage and sea salvage, the danger and meritorious nature of the services in either case being the ground on which the compensation is awarded. (*x*)

849. *Services by trustees.*—The law raises no implied promise of remuneration in respect of services of a fiduciary character. (*y*) If, therefore, a solicitor consents to act as a trustee of property, and renders professional services in matters relating to the trust estate confided to him, he is not entitled to charge for such services, whether he acts for himself alone, being sole trustee, or for himself and others who are his cotrustees, unless there is a provision in the deed or will creating the trust enabling him to receive remuneration for the transaction of such business ; but he is entitled to charge the trust estate with costs out of pocket. (*z*) A trustee, moreover, is not allowed to make the execution of the trust a source of profit to himself, and can not sue upon an express contract between him and his co-trustees for payment for his services to the trust ; for each trustee is to be a check and control upon each and all the co-trustees; and one of them can not authorize another to make professional charges to be paid out of the trust fund. Where, therefore, a number of trustees appointed one of their own body, who was a lawyer, " factor to the trust," with an allowance for his necessary charges and expenses and a " reasonable gratification," and the factor sued his co-trustees for his professional charges

---

(*u*) The Charlotte, 12 Jur. 568.

(*v*) The Carrier Dove, 2 Moo. P.C., ? . S. 243. And see Nicholson v. Chapman, 2 H. Bl. 258.

(*y*) Barrett v. Hartley, L. R., 2 Eq. ; 89.

(*z*) Moore v. Frowd, 3 Myl. & Cr. 45. Christophers v. White, 10 Beav. 523. Manson v. Baillie, 2 Macq. H. L. C So, over-ruling Cradock v. Piper 1 Mac. & Gord. 664.

"by reason of their having employed him as their commissioner, factor, cashier, and attorney in the aforesaid trust," it was held that he was not entitled to recover these charges either from them or from the trust estate. (*a*) Where one of several solicitors in partnership has taken upon himself the office of trustee, the firm of which he is a member can not charge for professional services rendered by them in the execution of the trust. (*b*)

In a recent case where it was proved that the partner of a trustee had, as solicitor to the trust, transacted the whole trust business entirely on his own account and for his own exclusive benefit, under an arrangement which had been made between him and his partner, that they should not be partners in any matters relating to the trust property, but that the partner who was not a trustee, should, in all matters relating to the trust, act as sole solicitor to the trust, and be entitled to receive, for his own exclusive benefit, all costs and charges which might be incurred in the execution of the trust. the professional charges of the partner were allowed to be paid out of the trust estate. (*c*)

850. *Promises of presents in return for services.* —If services have been rendered and benefits conferred on the express understanding that the person rendering the services is to trust entirely to the generosity of the party benefitted, and not to look for payment as a right, there is no contract. (*d*) But, if a person promises to make a present in return for ser-

---

(*a*) Manson v. Baillie, 2 Macq. H. L. C. 80, questioning Cradock v. Piper, *supra.* Aberdeen Rail. Co. v. Blaikie, 1 Macq. H. L. C. 461.

(*b*) Collins v. Carey, 2 Beav. 128.

Broughton v. Broughton, 5 De G. M. & G. 160.

(*c*) Clack v. Carlon, 30 L. J., Ch. 639.

(*d*) Roberts v. Smith, 4 H. & N. 321; 28 L. J., Ex. 164.

vices rendered, there is evidence of a contract to pay a reasonable sum. (*e*)

851. *Honorary and gratuitous services.*—If the employment is by custom and usage of a purely honorary and gratuitous character, the prima facie presumption of a letting and hiring of the services is. rebutted as soon as the custom is proved and established. The office of an arbitrator is deemed to be an honorary office ; and a person who acts as such can not charge for his services, unless it appears from the terms of the submission or the surrounding circumstances of the transaction that it was the intention of the parties that the arbitrator should be .paid for his time and trouble, or unless there is an express promise to pay him for his services. (*f*)   Barristers likewise exercise an office and profession of an honorary character.   They are presumed in law not to afford their professional services with any mercenary view, and can not, therefore, maintain an action for remuneration for advice or advocacy in matter of litigation, or for services ancillary to the service of an advocate, although there be an express contract to pay them a stipulated sum for such service ; (*g*) but in cases unconnected with advocacy, and for services not of a professional character, a barrister may, it seems, contract for remuneration, A physician may sue for his services, if he is registered as a physician under the medical Act, and is not prohibited by the college to which he belongs from bringing an action for his

(*e*) Jewry v. Busk, 5 Taunt. 302; Bryant v. Flight, 5 M. & W. 114. Bird v. M'Gaheg, 2 C. & K. 708.

(*f*) Virany v. Warne, 4 Esp. 47. Hoggins v. Gordon, 3 Q. B. 474.

(*g*) Kennedy v. Broun, 13 C. B. N. S. 677 ; 32 L. J., C. P. 137. Broun v. Kennedy, 33 L. J., Ch. 71, 342 ; 33

Beav. 133. Hobart v. Butler, 9 Ir. C. L. R. 157. Morris v. Hunt, 1 Chitt. 551. Veitch v. Russell, 3 Q. B. 928. Egan v. Guard. Kens. Un., Id. 935, n. Att.-Gen. v. The Royal College of Physicians, 1 Johns. & H. 561, 591 ; 30 L. J., Ch. 757. Mostyn v. Mostyn, L. R., 5 Ch. 457 ; 39 L. J., Ch. 780.

charges. (*h*)   If the service appears to have been rendered as a gratuitous act of kindness, or in discharge of a public duty, the prima facie presumption of a contract of letting and hiring is repelled.   Thus, if a man undertakes a journey to become bail for his friend, (*i*) or attend as a witness in a court of justice, he is not entitled to be paid for his trouble.   In the last case, as the attendance to give evidence is a duty of a public nature, an express promise to remunerate the witness for so doing is invalid ; but the witness is entitled to compensation according to the scale framed by the judges under the Common Law Procedure Acts. (*k*)

852. *Rights and liabilities of employer and workman.*—A person who employs another by the piece or by the job, or who lets out task work to be done for an express or implied remuneration, is, in general, bound to do every thing that is necessary to be done on his part to enable the hirer of the work to execute his engagement, and earn the hire or reward.   He impliedly undertakes to resort to no misrepresentation or concealment calculated to mislead the servant or undertaker of the work and give him a false estimate of the nature and extent of it, to accept the work when completed, and to pay the customary hire, in case no specific rate of remuneration has been agreed upon. When there is an absolute and unqualified refusal on the part of the employer to permit the workman to perform his task, or the employer does an act absolutely incapacitating himself from performing his part of the engagement, the undertaker of the work has a right, if he has done anything under the contract, to

---

(*h*) 21 & 22 Vict. c. 90, s. 31. Gibbon v. Budd, 2 H. & C. 92 ; 32 L. J., Ex. 182.

(*i*) Reason v. Wirdnam, 1 C. & P. 434.

(*k*) Nokes v. Gibbon, 26 L. J., Ch. 208.

sue immediately, for remuneration on a quantum
meruit if the contract is defeasible, or, if not, for compensation for the damage he has sustained in being
prevented from earning the stipulated hire. (*l*) [1]

853. *Defeasible contracts for work and services.*—
If a laborer is employed to dig potatoes at so much
an acre, or to cut turf at so much a load, or to make
excavations of earthwork at so much per cubic foot,
the employer may, if there is no determinate term or
employment, dispense, at any time, with the future
services of the workman, paying him for the work
actually done. If a party employs a factor or agent to
collect his rents, or transact his business for him, for
certain commission or reward, the employment is determinable at the will of the employer, unless it is
coupled with an interest, and the party employed is
something more than an agent in the transaction. If
an agent is employed to sell property on commission,
it is competent to the employer, at any time before a
sale has been actually effected, to revoke the authority
and deprive the agent of the expected commission ;
(*m*) but if expenses have been incurred by the agent
in executing the authority intrusted to him, he will be
entitled to recover such expenses from the employer,
and also a reasonable compensation for any labor or
trouble he may have undertaken in endeavoring to
execute his commission, unless it appears to have been
the understanding of the parties that nothing was to
be paid unless the act authorized to be done was fully

(*l*) Planche v. Colburn, 1 M. & Sc. Co., 17 C. B. N. S. 733 ; 34 L. J., C.
51. Emmens v. Elderton, *post.* Prick- P. 15.
ett v. Badger, 1 C. B. N. S. 304.   (*m*) Simpson v. Lamb, 17 C. B 603;
Inchbald v. Western Neilgherry Coffee 25 L. J., C. P. 113.

[1] See *post*, § 2.   Master and Servant.

accomplished. (*n*)   If a commission agent employed to sell property has found a purchaser and affected the authorized contract of sale, he will be entitled to his commission, although the employer may refuse to fulfill the contract; and, if he has found a party willing to buy, and the employer is then unable or unwilling to sell, the agent will be entitled to remuneration for his services. (*o*)

854. *Time of performance.*—Time is frequently of the essence of the contract as regards the commencement of the work, but not so with regard to its completion.   If it is made a positive term of the contract that the work shall be commenced on a day named, the employer may refuse the services of the workman, and decline to employ him, if he does not tender his services or commence the work at the appointed period; but when the work has been commenced, the completion of it by a day named will not in general be a condition precedent to the workman's right to the stipulated hire.   When the materials for the work, for example, have been furnished by the employer, and the produce of the labor becomes, consequently, the property of the latter as the work proceeds, the non-performance of the work by an appointed time does not release the employer from his obligation to pay the contract price.   He must in such a case perform his part of the engagement, and bring a cross action against the undertaker of the work to recover compensation for any damage he may have sustained by reason of the non-completion of the work at the appointed period. (*p*)   If after the time of completion the employer urges the

(*n*) Moffatt v. Laurie, 15 C. B. 583. De Bernardy v. Harding, 8 Exch. 822. Camponari v. Woodburn, 15 C. B. 400.

(*o*) Prickett v. Badger, 1 C. B. N. S. 296.

(*p*) Lucas v. Godwin, 4 Sc. 509.

continuance of the work, or encourages the workman to proceed, he waives the condition as to time. (*q*)

855. *Entire performance of a contract for work is often a condition precedent to payment.*—Thus, if a coachman agrees to convey a passenger from London to York for a certain stipulated remuneration, and carries him only half the distance, he is not entitled to any payment, the precedent act to be performed being entire and indivisible. Where the plaintiff undertook to make "complete" certain dilapidated chandeliers for the sum of £19, and returned them in an incomplete state, it was held that he could not maintain an action for the work actually done. (*r*) And, where an attorney covenanted to pay his clerk 2*s.* for every quire of paper he copied out, it was held that this was an entire covenant, of which no apportionment could be made pro ratâ, and that the clerk, consequently, could not maintain an action to recover remuneration for copying out any number of sheets less than a quire. (*s*) So, where the plaintiff offered to cure a flock of sheep and lambs of a disease called the scab at so much per head for the sheep, and so much for the lambs, and stated that he did not expect to be paid unless he cured all the sheep and lambs, whereupon the defendant accepted his offer, and agreed to employ him ; and the plaintiff, after he had materially checked the complaint, but before he had cured the whole of the flock, brought his action for the money, it was held that he was not entitled to recover anything for his pains. (*t*)

856. *Divisible and apportionable work.*—But, if the work is in its nature divisible and apportionable,

(*q*) Burn v. Miller, 4 Taunt, 748.
(*r*) Sinclair v. Bowles, 4 M. & R. 3 ;
9 B. & C. 94.
(*s*) Needler v. Gnest, Aleyn, 9.
(*t*) Bates v. Hudson, 6 D. & R. 3.

and there is nothing in the terms of the contract which, either by express stipulation or necessary intendment, precludes the plaintiff from recovering in respect of a partial execution of it, the plaintiff may, on performing a part only of his engagement, require a corresponding part performance on the part of the defendant. (*u*)   Thus, where a ship, being damaged at sea, put into a harbor to receive some repairs, and an agreement was made with a shipwright to put her " into thorough repair," but nothing was said as to the amount, or time, or mode of payment, and, before the repairs were completed, the shipwright demanded payment for what he had done, it was held that the contract was not an entire contract to do the whole of the repairs and make no demand for payment until they were completed, but that the shipwright might from time to time, in the course of the work, demand payment for what he had done, before proceeding to complete the residue. (*a*)   And if, in a contract of this description, the defendant is deprived, by accident, of the benefit of the work before it is finished, the workman is not, by reason of such accident, deprived of his right to remuneration. (*b*)

857. *Building contracts.*—If a contract has been entered into to build a house for a specific sum, to be paid on the completion of the building, the contract is entire and indivisible, and the employer is not bound to pay for a half or a quarter of a house; for the court and jury can have no right to apportion that which the parties themselves have treated as entire.   But, where a builder engages to build a house, to be paid for his work and labor, and the materials

(*u*) Taylor v. Laird, 1 H. & N. 266.   (*b*) Menetone v. Athawes, 3 Burr.
(*a*) Roberts v. Havelock, 3 B. & Ad.   1592.
404.

supplied by measure and value, or according to the customary rate of remuneration, he is entitled to demand payment from time to time as the work proceeds. Every builder who contracts for the building of a house impliedly undertakes to furnish everything reasonably necessary for its completion. (*c*) Where an action was brought by a builder against his employer upon a special contract for the building of a house for a certain sum, and the builder had omitted to put into the building certain joists according to his contract, it was contended that, as the employer had got the benefit of the house, he was bound to pay what it was fairly worth; but, per MANSFIELD, C. J., " The defendant made no such agreement. He says, ' I agreed to pay you, if you would build my house in a certain manner, which you have not done.' The plaintiff can not now be permitted to turn round and say, ' I will be paid by a measure and value price instead of the contract price.'" (*d*) If an architect, employed to prepare plans and specifications for a house, and to procure a builder to erect it, takes out the quantities, and represents to a builder that they are correct, and the builder thereupon makes a tender which is accepted, the builder can not recover more than the contract price from the employer, although it turns out that the quantities are wrong, and the builder has expended upon the building a much larger amount of material than he contemplated. (*e*)

858. *Work to be approved of before payment.*—If a tailor undertakes to make me a coat, or a coach-builder to build me a carriage, upon the terms that I am not to take and pay for it, if, on inspection, I dis-

---

(*c*) Williams v. Fitzmaurice, 3 H. & N. 844.

(*d*) Ellis v. Hamlen, 3 Taunt. 52.

(*e*) Scrivener v. Pash, L. R., 1 C. P. 715.

approve of the style and workmanship, I am at liberty
to return the coat or the carriage, and refuse payment
of the price, .if I think fit so to do. But if I engage
an artist to work up my own materials, or to paint a
ceiling in my house, and I have, consequently, no opportunity or power of returning him the produce of
his labor, I can not make my approval of the work a
condition precedent to his right to demand some
remuneration for what he has done. (*f*) If a contract for the building or repairing of a house provides
for the inspection and approval of the work by the
employer before payment of the contract price, the
employer must be afforded an opportunity of inspection before he can be called upon to pay ; but he can
not, by withholding his approval unreasonably and
mala fide, after an opportunity of inspection has been
afforded him, deprive the workman of his hire. (*g*)
The employer has, indeed, a right in all cases to inspect the work before he pays for it ; but his approval
of a builder's work is by no means essential to the
maintenance of an action by the builder. It will
always be a question for the jury to determine, whether
the employer has acted bonâ fide, and ought reasonably to have been satisfied with the work done. (*h*)
But, where the workman works up his own materials
in the manufacture of a chattel, the employer may
reserve to himself a right to rescind the contract and
reject the chattel, if he finds, on trial or inspection
that it does not suit him, either on the score of work-

(*f*) Andrews v. Belfield, 2 C. B. N.
S. 779.

(*g*) Dallman v. King, 5 S. C. 382.
" Ces termes, si je suis content de
l'ouvrage, ne doivent pas etre entendus
en ce sens, que le locateur puisse etre
admis indistinctement à dire qu'il
n'est pas content de l'ouvrage, pour se
dispenser de payer la gratification
promise, ce qui rendrait cette clause
nulle et illusoire." Poth. Louage,
No. 417.

(*h*) Parsons v. Sexton, 4 C. B. 899 ;
16 L. J., C. P. 184. Hughes v. Lenny
5 M. & W. 193. '

manship, or of convenience, or taste. (*i*) If his acceptance of an engine, or machine, and payment of the contract price, are made dependent upon his approval of the strength and soundness of the workmanship, and he rejects the machine because it does not work well, or does not answer his purpose, and not because it is deficient either in strength or soundness, he will be held responsible for the price. (*k*)

859. *When the right to receive payment is made dependent upon the approval of an architect or surveyor*, or the production of a certificate that the work has been done according to contract, no right can arise which can be enforced until the approval has been given or the certificate has been obtained. (*l*) Work, therefore, which has been done, but not to the satisfaction of the surveyor or architect, can not be charged for; (*m*) but, if the certificate is fraudulently or corruptly withheld, the court will give relief; and an action may, in certain cases, be maintained for the wrongful or fraudulent withholding of the certificate both against the architect and against the employer. (*n*) If the certificate is not, by the express terms of the contract, required to be in writing, the architect's approbation, testified by word of mouth, is sufficient. (*o*) When the certificate has been granted, the architect is functus officio, and can not vary or alter it. (*p*)

(*i*) Andrews v. Belfield, 2 C. B. N. S. 779.

(*k*) Ripley v. Lordan, 6 Jur. N. S. 1078.

(*l*) Scott v. Liverpool Corp., 25 L. J., Ch. 230. Morgan v. Birnie, 3 M. & Sc. 76 ; 9 Bing. 672. Mayor, &c., of Salford v. Ackers, 16 L. J., Ex. 6. Moffat v. Dickson, 22 ib. C. P. 268 ; 13 C. B. 543.

(*m*) Dobson v. Hudson, 1 C. B. N. S. 659 ; 26 L. J., C. P. 153.

(*n*) Milner v. Field, 5 Exch. 829 ; 20 L. J., Ex. 68. Batterbury v. Vyse, 2 H. & C. 42 ; 32 L. J., Ex. 177. Stadhard v. Lee, 3 B. & S. 364; 32 L. J., Q. B. 75.

(*o*) Roberts v. Watkins, 32 L. J., C. P. 291 ; 14 C. B. N. S. 592.

(*p*) Jones v. Jones, 17 L. J., Q. B. 170.

860. *Relief against biassed or corrupt decisions of architects and surveyors.*—If an architect's certificate is wrongfully or fraudulently withheld, the court will give relief, not only against the parties who are bound to pay, but also against the architect, surveyor, or engineer; and any stipulation in the contract, placing the latter in the position of an arbitrator between the employer and the workman, and making his decision final, and purporting to exclude the jurisdiction of any court with reference to his conduct, will be nugatory and of no effect. (*q*)   If questions arising between the contractor for works and the employer are, by the contract, left to the determination of the architect, and the latter has a personal interest unknown to the contractor, and adverse to him, (*r*) or does not act fairly between the parties, or manifest any undue leaning, bias, partiality, or corruption, the Court of Chancery will review his decision and interfere to give relief, however strenuously the parties may by their contract have endeavored to exclude the jurisdiction of the court. (*s*)

861. *Actions for wrongfully withholding the certificate* may be maintained both against the architect and the employer, if it can be proved that the builder has fulfilled his contract and done all things necessary to be done by him to entitle him to the certificate, and that the architect had full knowledge thereof, and nevertheless neglected to certify in collusion with and by the procurement of the employer. (*t*)   But the

---

(*q*) Scott v. Liv. Corp., 25 L. J., Ch. 227.

(*r*) Kimberley v. Dick, L. R., 13 Eq. 1; 41 L. J., Ch. 38.

(*s*) Kemp v. Rose, 1 Giff. 258. Scott v. Liv. Corp., *supra*, Ormes v. Beadel, 2 Giff. 166; 30 L. J.. Ch. 1. Pawley v. Turnbull, 3 Giff. 70. Bliss v. Smith, 34 Beav. 508.

(*t*) Batterbury v. Vyse, 2 H. & C. 42; 32 L. J,. Ex. 177. Milner v. Field, 5 Exch. 829; 20 L. J., Ex. 68. Scott v. Liv. Corp. 25 L. J., Ch. 230,

employer is not responsible for any misconduct of his architect or surveyor in refusing to certify not brought about by his instrumentality or interference. (*u*)

862. *Effect of the employer's taking possession and making use of the unfinished work.*—A landowner who by a building-contract provides a site for the erection of a house and delivers the ground to the builder, does not thereby part with the possession of his land. The builder has the mere temporary custody of it, and may be turned off at any time by the employer. (*v*) Where by a building contract it was stipulated that certain houses should be built on the land of the employer for a certain sum by a specified day to the satisfaction of a surveyor, upon whose approval payment was to be made, and the builder became bankrupt and was unable to complete the houses, and the employer then took possession of them and finished them, it was held that his taking possession of the unfinished houses did not amount to a waiver of the contract or of any of the terms or conditions thereof, and afforded no evidence that he accepted the benefit of the work actually done under an implied contract to pay for it according to measure and value. (*y*)

863. *Defective work accepted by the employer.*— Whenever the employer has accepted and retains the benefit of work done for him under a special contract, which has been abandoned or rescinded, and remains no longer a subsisting contract, he is liable to pay a reasonable remuneration in respect thereof. If the workman undertakes to repair a chattel, the property of the employer, and the new work and materials are

(*u*) Clarke v. Watson, 18 C. B. N. S. 278 ; 34 L. J., C. P. 148.

(*v*) The Marquis Camden v. Batterbury, 7 C. B. N. S. 878 ; 28 L. J., C.

P. 335.

(*y*) Munro v. Butt, 8 Ell. & Bl. 738. Ranger v. Gt. West. Rail. Co., 5 H. L. C. 118.

so intermixed with the old work, that the one can not be separated from the other without injury to the chattel, so that the employer must of necessity accept the work, his liability to pay for it, in case it has been negligently and unskillfully executed, depends upon the utility or inutility of the work. If the chattel has been benefitted and rendered more valuable by what has been done, the employer must pay the fair value of the workmanship; if it is in no wise improved, and the work done has been so negligently executed as to be worth nothing, the employer can not be called upon for payment. If the contract is an entire and indivisible contract for the completion of certain work, such as the contract to "make complete" the dilapidated chandeliers for the sum of £10 previously mentioned, and the chattel is returned in an unfinished state, the employer may require the undertaker of the work to complete and perfect the article, and refuse payment of the money until it is done. The retention by the employer of his own unfinished chattel does not, in such a case, raise any inference of a waiver of any of the terms or conditions of the special contract or of the entering into a new contract to pay upon a quantum meruit. (z)

864. *Substantial performance of building contracts.*—When a contract has been entered into for the building of a house for a certain sum of money to be paid on the completion of the building in accordance with certain plans and specifications, it is not essential to the maintenance of an action upon the contract that there should be an exact performance of the contract in every minute particular; for, wherever divers acts and things of different degrees of importance are

(z) Munro v. Butt, 8 Ell. & Bl. 752.   Ellis v. Hamden, *ante.*

to be done on one side in return for a stipulated remuneration on the other, the performance of all the things in every minute particular is not, in general, a condition precedent to the liability to make some remuneration ; but, if the contract has been substantially fulfilled the plaintiff is entitled to maintain an action upon it, (*a*) the defendant being entitled to such a deduction from the contract price as will enable him to complete the work in exact accordance with the contract. In every contract for work there is a condition implied by law that the work shall be done in a proper and workmanlike manner ; but this is not a condition going to the essence of the contract. " If it were a condition precedent to the plaintiff's remuneration," observes TINDAL, C. J., "a little deficiency of any sort would deprive the plaintiff of all claim for payment ; but under such circumstances a jury may say what the plaintiff really deserves to have." (*b*)

A building contract, with all its specifications and details, may be broken to the letter with trifling damage to the employer ; and, if performance in every minute particular were made a condition precedent to the builder's right to sue upon the contract for work done, "a trifling injury to the one party might occasion the loss of all remuneration to the other for a long and laborious service." (*c*) But where it appears from the whole tenor of the agreement, that the parties thereto intended, the one to insist upon, and the other to submit to, conditions, however unreasonable and oppressive, the court will in such case give effect to them. (*d*)

Where a party engages to do certain work on cer-

(*a*) *Ante.*

(*b*) Lucas v. Godwin, 3 Bing. N. C. 744 ; 4 Sc. 509.

(*c*) Tindall, C. J., Stavers v. Curl-ing, 3 Sc. 755.

(*d*) Stadhard or Stannard v. Lee, 3 B. & S. 364 ; 32 L. J., Q. B. 75.

tain specified terms and in a certain specified manner, but does not perform the work so as to correspond with the specification, he is not entitled to recover the price agreed upon in the specification, nor can he recover according to the actual value of the work done as if there had been no special contract. What the plaintiff is entitled to recover is the price agreed upon in the specification, subject to a deduction ; and the measure of that deduction is the sum which it would take to alter the work to make it correspond with the specification. (*e*)   And the defendant is not, by reason of his having given evidence of such breach of contract on the part of the plaintiff, and obtained a reduction of the agreed price, according to the difference between the value of the work actually done and that which ought to have been done according to the contract, precluded from bringing his cross action to recover compensation for any special damage he may have sustained by reason of the non-compliance by the plaintiff with the strict terms of the engagement. (*f*) Care, however, must be taken to mark the distinction between an action on the special contract itself for the agreed price of the work, and an action upon a bill of exchange or promissory note given by way of payment of the amount.   In the former the value of the work only can be recovered ; in the latter the party holding bills given for the price of the work done can recover on them, unless there has been a total failure of the consideration.   If the consideration fails partially, as by the inferiority of the work, the buyer must seek his remedy by a cross action.   The contract may be divisible ; but the security is entire. (*g*)

(*e*) Thornton v. Place, 1 Mood & Rob. 218.

(*f*) *Ante.* Mondel v. Steel, 8 M.

& W. 858. Rigge v. Burbridge, 15 M. & W. 599.

(*g*) Tye v. Gwynne, 2 Campb. 347.

865. *Abatement of the contract price.*—Whenever a contract for work and services on the one side, and payment on the other, has been so far executed as to give rise to a cause of action in respect of the work done, but has not been fully performed, it is competent to the defendant to show, in reduction of the price agreed to be paid, that the subject-matter of the contract is diminished in value by reason of the incomplete and inefficient execution of the work by the plaintiff. Thus, where the plaintiff agreed to erect a powerful warm-air apparatus in a chapel, and the defendant agreed to pay him the sum of £70 for so doing, and the claim for the money was resisted on the ground that the apparatus was imperfect and did not answer, it was held by TINDAL, C. J., that, if the apparatus was altogether unfit for the purpose, and did not at all answer the end for which it was intended, the defendant was not bound to pay for it; but that, if the apparatus was in the main effective, but not quite so complete as it ought to have been according to the contract, the action was maintainable for the price, and that the jury might deduct from the full price such a sum as would enable the defendant to do that which was required to make it complete and perfectly effective. (*h*)

866. *Effect of non-performance of building contracts by the time specified.*—In the case of a contract to build a house, where the employer furnishes the land, which is the principal material for the work, if the house is not built by the time specified in the contract, but is afterwards completed, the employer who has got the house, and has had the value of his land increased by its erection thereon, can never be permitted to free himself from his obligation to pay

(*h*) Cutler v. Close, 5 C. & P. 338. Chapel v. Hickes, 2 Cr. & M. 214.

for it by alleging that the work was not done by the time appointed. The stipulation as to time is not, in such a case, "a condition going to the essence of the contract. The parties never could have contemplated that, if the house were not completed by the day named, the builder should have no remuneration; at all events, if an engagement so unreasonable was contemplated, the parties should have. expressed themselves with a precision that could not be mistaken." (*i*)

867. *Penalties for non-performance of building contracts by a time specified.*—Where, by articles of agreement for the altering and repairing of a warehouse for a fixed sum, it was stipulated that, in the event of the work not being fully completed in three months, the builder should "forfeit and pay" to the employer £5 every week he should be engaged in such work beyond the three months, such penalty or forfeiture to be deducted from the amount which might remain owing on the completion of the work, it was held, in an action brought for extra work, that the employer was entitled to set off the penalty against the price of such extra work, and that he had a double remedy, either to set it off as a payment, or to deduct it from the contract price. (*k*)   If performance by the time specified has been prevented by the ordering of extra work, or by the interference of the employer or his agent, the claim to the penalties can not be enforced. (*l*)

868. *Of the giving of security for the due per-*

(*i*) Tindall, C. J., Lucas v. Godwin, 4 Sc. 509; 3 Bing. N. C. 744.   Littler v. Holland, 3 T. R. 590.   Maryon v. Carter, 4 C. & P. 295.   Kingdom v. Cox, 2 C. B. 661; 15 L. J., C. P. 95.

(*k*) Duckworth v. Alison, 1 M. & W. 412.   Fletcher v. Dyche, 2 T. R. 32.

Legge v. Harlock, 12 Q. B. 1015.

(*l*) Westwood v. Secret. Ind., 11 W. R. 261; 7 L. T. R. N. S. 736.   Russell v. Sa Da Bandiera, 13 C. B. N. S. 149; 32 L. J., C. P. 68.   Roberts v. Bury Commissioners, L. R., 5 C. P. 310; 39 L. J., C. P. 129.

formance of the contract.—If security is to be given
by the workman for the due performance of his contract, the giving of the security is a condition precedent to any liability on the part of the employer upon
the contract, unless the condition has been waived by
the workman's being required to proceed with the
work, or the work having been executed, without
security. (*m*)

869. *Destruction of work before payment—Loss
of materials, and loss of the price of the work.*—If
the contract is entire for the performance of a specific
work for a specified sum, so that the performance of
the whole of the work bargained for and agreed to be
done is a condition precedent to the right to payment
for any part of it, the workman will be deprived of all
legal right to remuneration if the work is destroyed
by accident before it has been completed ; (*n*) but, if
the workman is entitled to payment from time to time
as the work proceeds, the destruction of the work
before its completion will not deprive the workman of
his hire. Thus, if the contract is an entire and indivisible contract for the building of a house for a specific
sum to be paid on its completion, and the edifice is
destroyed by lightning, fire, or tempest, during the
progress of the work, the contractor must stand to the
loss, and be himself at the expense of repairing the
damage. But, if the contract price of the building is
to be paid by installments on the completion of certain
specified portions of the work, each installment becomes a debt due to the builder, as the particular
portion specified is completed ; and if the house is
destroyed by accident, the employer would be bound

(*m*) Roberts v. Brett, 6 C. B. N. S.   (*n*) Appleby v. Myers, L. R. 2 C. P.
635. Kingston v. Preston, cited 2   651 ; 36 L. J., C. P. 331.
Doug. 689.

to pay the installments then due, but would not be responsible for the intermediate work and labor and materials. (*o*)

In the Roman law, if a builder was employed to build a house on the land of the employer, and the building was overthrown by an earthquake, or destroyed by lightning, during the progress of the work, the employer was accountable both for the materials which the undertaker of the work had furnished and for what was due on account of the workmanship, inasmuch as the materials and the produce of the labor became the property of the employer as soon as they were fixed on the land ; but, if, by an express contract between the parties, the payment of the money was made conditional on the completion and approval of the building, so that nothing was due until the whole of the work had been performed, then the builder lost both the value of his materials and of his workmanship, and was bound to re-construct the building before he called upon the employer for payment. (*m*)

When the contract is entire and indivisible for the manufacture out of materials furnished by the employer of a particular chattel for a specific sum, to be paid on the completion and delivery of the chattel to the employer, and the chattel is destroyed by inevitable accident whilst it remains unfinished in the hands of the workman, the employer must stand to the loss of his materials, and the workman to the loss of the price and value of his labor. Thus if a printer is employed to print a book at so much per sheet, the price and value of the printing to be paid for on the completion of the work, and before the whole impression has been

(*o*) Menetone v. Athawes, 3 Burr.   (*m*) Dig. lib. 19, tit. 3, lex 59. Dig.
1592. Tripp v. Armitage, 4 M. & W.   lib. 6, tit. 1, lex 39.
699. *Ante*

worked off and made ready for delivery, an accidental fire breaks out upon the printer's premises and consumes the work, the employer must stand to the loss of his paper, and the printer to the loss of the price and value of his labor and skill. (*n*)   But if the work has been completed, and the copies have been printed and made ready for delivery, and placed at the disposal of the employer, they remain at his risk ; and, if an accidental fire then breaks out and consumes them, he must stand to the loss, and pay the printer his hire. (*o*)

If a shipwright is employed to repair a ship, the accessorial materials supplied by him for the work become, as we have previously seen, the property of the employer, as soon as they are attached to the vessel under repair, upon the principle that omne accessorium sequitur suum principale ; and if the completion of the work is not made, either by agreement or by custom, a condition precedent to the payment, and the ship is accidentally burnt, the loss of such materials, as well as of the value of the work and labor employed upon them, is the loss of the employer and not of the workman, and the employer, consequently, must pay the fair value of the labor and materials, although he can reap no benefit from what has been done. (*p*)   But, where a man contracts to expend materials and labor on buildings belonging to and in the occupation of the employer, to be paid for on completion of the whole, and before completion the buildings are destroyed by accidental fire, the contractor is excused from completing the work, but is not entitled to any compensation for the work already done

---

(*n*) Gillett v. Mawman, 1 Taunt. 140.

(*o*) Adlard v. Booth, 7 C. & P. 108.

(*p*) Menetone v. Athawes, 3 Burr. 1592.

which has perished without any default of the employer. (*q*)

Where a contract for the building of a ship vests the general property in the ship in the employer as the materials are put together and fashioned, (*r*) and the ship is destroyed by fire, the loss of the materials and workmanship will fall on the employer; but if the property in the thing destroyed remains with the workman, the loss will fall upon the latter.

870. *Deviations from building contracts—Extras.* —If work has been agreed to be done, and materials supplied, under a building contract for certain estimated prices, and there has subsequently been a deviation from the original plan by consent of the parties, the contract and estimate are not on that account excluded, but are to be the rule of payment, as far as the contract can be traced to have been followed, and the excess only is to be paid for according to the usual rates of charging; but if the original plan has been so entirely abandoned that it is impossible to trace the contract, and to say to what part of it the work shall be applied, the workman may charge for the whole work by measure and value, as if no contract at all had ever been made. But there must be a total deviation, so that the terms of the original contract are not applicable to the new work. (*s*) For all work done beyond the contract, under subsequent or antecedent directions, the plaintiff may recover, just as if no special contract had ever been made. (*t*) But the mere fact of the defendant having assented to certain alterations is not sufficient to make him liable to pay for them as extras

(*q*) Appleby v. Myers, L. R., 2 C. P. 651 ; 36 L. J., C. P. 331.

(*r*) Clarke v. Spence, *ante.* , Wood v. Bell, 25 L. J., Q. B. 153, 321.

(*s*) Pepper v. Burland, Peake, 139.

Robson v. Godfrey, Holt, N. P. C. 236. Ellis v. Hamlen, 3 Taunt. 52.

(*t*) Thornton v. Place, 1 Mood. & Rob. 219. Fletcher v. Gillespie, 3 Bing. 637.

not covered by the contract, unless the alterations are
of such a nature that he can not fail to be aware that
they must increase the expense, and can not be done
for the contract price. (*u*)   If extras have been done
by the plaintiff without any authority from the defendant, the latter is not bound to pay for them. (*v*)   If
they are to be done only on the direction in writing
of the architect, a direction in writing must be obtained. (*y*)   In cases of variation set up by way of
defense, the courts look to the subsequent conduct of
the parties, for this obvious reason, that, as the parties
intend the contract to remain in force, so far as it is
not varied, it is only by comparing the conduct of the
parties subsequently to the making of the alleged variation with the terms originally agreed upon that the
court can determine with certainty upon oral evidence
that such variations were mutually intended to take
effect.

871. *Prevention of performance of building contracts.*—Where an agreement was entered into between
the plaintiff and defendant that the plaintiff should
pull down the walls of three houses, and erect for the
defendant, on the site thereof, a malt-house and other
buildings, and the plaintiff was ready and offered to
do the work, but the defendant prevented him, it was
held that the plaintiff had done all that was necessary
to be done to enable him to sue the defendant for a
breach of contract. (*z*)   The builder or workman is
not in such a case entitled to recover the full stipulated
remuneration as if the buildings had been actually

(*u*) Lovelock v. King, 1 Mood. &
Rob. 60.

(*v*) Dobson v. Hudson, 1 C. B. N.
S. 659 ; 26 L. J., C. P. 153.

(*y*) Myers v. Sarl, 30 L. J., Q. B.

9. Russell v. Sa Da Bandiera, 13 C.
B. N. S. 149 ; 32 L. J., C. P. 68.

(*z*) Peters v. Opie, 1 Ventr. 177 ; 2
Saund. 350. Collins v. Price, 5 Bing.
132. Ferry v. Williams, 8 Taunt. 70 ;
1 Moore, 498.

erected. A fair deduction must be made from the contract price in respect of the value of materials which have never been supplied and wages which have never been paid; and the damages must be confined to the actual pecuniary loss sustained by the plaintiff. (*a*)

872. *Of the right of lien of workmen and artificers.*—Every workman to whom a chattel has been delivered by the owner to be mended, repaired, or altered for hire, and who has bestowed his labor upon it, has a lien upon the chattel for his hire. This right of lien is a mere right of retainer until the pecuniary claim has been satisfied, and carries with it no right of sale. (*b*) A workman who has detained a chattel in the exercise of a right of lien is not entitled, in the absence of any usage of trade, to charge warehouse rent or the expense of keeping the chattel. (*c*)

873. *Liabilities of task-workmen.*—Every person who has entered into a contract for the performance of a particular task or job is bound to enter upon his employment without delay; to be active, industrious, careful, and diligent in the performance of the work; to do it according to orders given and assented to; (*d*) to complete it within a reasonable period, if no precise time has been agreed upon for its fulfillment; and to exercise a reasonable amount of care and skill in its execution. If the work is to be performed under the direction of a surveyor to be appointed by the employer, the appointment of such surveyor is a condition precedent to the liability of the workman to commence his task; and, if the surveyor is not ap-

(*a*) *Post.* Masterton v. Mayor, &c., of Brooketyre, 7 Hill. N. Y. Rep. 61.

(*b*) Thames Iron Works, &c., v. Patent Derrick Co., 29 L. J., Ch. 714.

(*c*) Somes v. Brit. Emp., &c., 30 L. J., Q. B. 229; 28 ib. 221; E. B. & E. 353.

(*d*) Streeter v. Horlock, 7 Moore, 287.

pointed within a reasonable period, the workman is released from his engagement to do the work. (*e*)   In ordinary cases, the workman may accomplish the work through the medium of inferior agents and workmen ; but, if the work is a work of art and genius, and the contract is founded upon the personal talent and capacity of the artist, he impliedly undertakes to perform the work himself, and may not intrust it to an inferior agent of less skill and reputation. (*f*)

874. *Of the implied obligation to do the work well—Skilled workmen.*—Every person who professes to be a skilled workman impliedly undertakes to do his work well and in a workmanlike manner, and according to the rules and principles of his trade or art.   " When a person is employed in a work of skill, the employer buys both his labor and his judgment ; he ought not to undertake the work if he can not succeed ; and he should know whether he will or not." (*g*)   The public profession of an art is a representation and undertaking, to all who require and make use of the services of the professed artisan, that the latter is possessed of, and will exercise, the ordinary amount of skill and knowledge incident to his particular craft, art, or profession. (*h*)   If, therefore, an accountant is employed to make out an account, and he miscalculates the amounts and carries wrong

---

(*e*) Coombe v. Greene, 11 M. & W. 483.

(*f*) Le principe, que le conducteur peut faire l'ouvrage par un autre, reçoit exception à l'égard des ouvrages de génie dans lequels on considère le talent personnel de celui à qui on le donne à faire ; comme, lorsque j'ai fait marché avec un peintre pour peindre un plafond, il ne lui est pas permis de la faire faire par un autre

sans mon consentement. Poth. Louage No. 421.   Robson v. Drummond, 2 B. & Ad. 308.

(*g*) Bayley, J., Duncan v. Blundell, 3 Stark. 7, cited 5 M. & P. 548.   C'est de sa parte une faute de se charger d'une chose qui surpasse ses forces. Pothier, Louage, 404, No. 525.

(*h*) Harmer v. Cornelius, 5 C. B. N. S. 246 ; [28] L. J., C. P. 85.

balances to the injury of the employer, he is responsible in damages to the latter. (*i*) If a carpenter undertakes to roof a barn, and employs defective materials, or does his work so negligently and unskillfully that the thatch sinks and lets in the wet, he is liable for the injury to the building so occasioned. (*k*) Where a carpenter undertook to build a booth on a race-course, and the booth fell down in the middle of the races from bad materials and bad workmanship, it was held that the carpenter was responsible for the damage that had been sustained. (*l*) The degree of skill and diligence which is required from the workman rises in proportion to the value, the delicacy, and the beauty of the work, and the fragility and brittleness of the materials. The Roman law required the exercise of greater skill and diligence from workmen who undertook the delicate work of raising or removing pillars of granite and porphyry, than from those who were employed upon common materials; and greater care from a person who undertook to remove a column, than from a man who was employed in the transport of a rude block of stone. (*m*)

875. *Work rendered useless by the negligence or incompetence of the workman.*—Whenever the work contracted to be done is a work of art and skill, and the undertaker, being charged with the bare work, executes it so negligently and unskillfully as to render it utterly useless to the employer, he can not call upon the latter for payment of it. Thus, where a builder contracted with the defendant to re-build the front of his house, and built it out of the perpendicular, so that

(*i*) Story v. Richardson, 8 Sc. 291 ; 5 Bing. N. C. 123.

(*k*) Basten v. Butter, 7 East, 479. Moneypenny v. Hartland, 2 C. & P.

378. Pothier, Louage, No. 427 ; Tr. des Oblig., 163.

(*l*) Broom v. Davis, 7 East, 480, n. (*a*).

(*m*) Dig. lib. 19, tit. 2, lex 25, § 7.

it was in danger of falling, and required to be taken down, it was held that the builder could not maintain an action in respect of such defective execution of the work. "If there has been no beneficial service," observes Lord ELLENBOROUGH, "there shall be no pay." (n) And where a man undertook to erect a stove in a shop, and to lay a tube under the floor, which would carry off the smoke, and the plan entirely failed, and the stove could not be used, it was held that he was not entitled to an action in respect of his work and labor in the erection of the stove. (o) "If a man has contracted with another to build him a house for a certain sum, it would not be sufficient for him to show that he had put together such a quantity of brick and mortar; he ought to be prepared to show that he had done the stipulated work according to the contract." (p) When a building is so negligently constructed as to be dangerous and unfit for use, the employer may require the builder to take down the structure, and rebuild it; and if the builder neglects so to do, and refuses to fulfill his part of the contract, the employer may give him notice to remove his materials from off the land, and may resist payment of any portion of the price of the work. If he retains the materials, and makes use of them, he will be bound to pay their fair value; but if the materials are altogether useless, or the employer has suffered from the breach of contract on the part of the workman more damage and injury than they are worth, he is not bound to pay anything. (q)

(n) Farnsworth v. Garrard, 1 Campb. 38. Denew v. Daverell, 3 Campb. 451.

(o) Duncan v. Blundell, 3 Stark. 6. Hayselden v. Stuff, 5 Ad. & E. 161.

(p) Le Blance, J., Basten v. Butter, 7 East, 484.

(q) Tindall, C. J., Hill v. Featherstonehaugh, 5 M. & P. 544, 548. Farnsworth v. Gerrard, 1 Campb. 38. Pothier, Louage d'ouvrage, No. 434.

876. *Useless and unskillful professional services.*
—If a surgeon requires his patient to undergo an operation which turns out to have been altogether useless
or unnecessary, he can not make it the subject of a
pecuniary claim or charge on such patient. If a medical man ignorantly and unskillfully administers improper medicines, and the patient, consequently, derives
no benefit from his attendance, the medical man is not
entitled to any remuneration for what he has done ;
but if he has employed the ordinary amount of skill in
his profession, and has applied remedies fitted to the
complaint, and calculated to do good in general, he is
entitled to his hire and reward, although they may
have failed in the particular instance, such failure being
then attributable to some peculiarity in the constitu-
tion of the patient, for which the medical man is not
responsible. (*r*)   If a surveyor, engineer, or architect,
from negligence or want of skill, gives his employers
a grossly incorrect estimate of the cost of certain works,
and thereby leads them into unnecessary expenses, he is
not entitled to be paid for his plans, estimates, and
specifications. (*s*)   But if the incorrectness of the estimate arises from inherent difficulties in the work itself,
the employer will not be relieved from the obligation
of payment.   If a solicitor conducting a suit is guilty
of misconduct and negligence, by reason whereof all
the previous steps taken in the cause become useless,
he can not recover his charges for any part of the business he has done ; but if the suit fails from causes over
which the solicitor has no control, the case is otherwise. (*t*)   If a solicitor issues a writ, and proceeds

(*r*) Kannen v. McMullen, Peake, 83.
Hupe v. Phelps, 2 Stark. 480.

(*s*) Moneypenny v. Hartland, 2 C.
& P. 378.

(*t*) Bracey v. Carter, 12 Ad. & E.

373.   Long v. Orsi, 13 C. B. 615 ; 26
L. J., C. P. 127.   Stokes v. Trumper,
2 Kay & J. 232.   Chapman v. Van
Toll, 8 Ell. & Bl. 396 ; 37 L. J., Q.
B. 1.

thereon in a court of special and peculiar jurisdiction, he is bound to acquaint himself with the machinery and practice of the court, and to see that it is adequate for the purposes of the suit; and if the suit fails from the ignorance of the solicitor in this respect, he can not recover his costs and charges of the abortive proceedings. (*v*)   If a parliamentary agent employed to obtain an act of parliament draws the clauses of the bill himself, and frames them so negligently and carelessly that one of the main objects of the statute can not be accomplished, the negligence may deprive him of all right to remuneration, or it may go merely in reduction of the value of his services. (*y*)

877. *Actions against solicitors, surgeons, valuers, &c., for negligence.*—Every solicitor employed by a purchaser of freehold or leasehold property impliedly undertakes to exercise reasonable care and skill in the investigation of the title of the vendor.   If his client has purchased leasehold property under conditions that he is to have no abstract of the vendor's title, and that the lessor's title is not to be objected to, or gone into, this will not exonerate the solicitor from the duty of investigating the vendor's title so far as to ascertain that there is a lease to him creating the interest he professes to sell, and that it has been duly registered where registration is necessary. (*z*)   But a solicitor is not liable to an action for negligence, at the suit of one between whom and himself the relation of solicitor and client does not exist, for giving, in answer to a casual enquiry, erroneous information as to the contents of a deed. (*a*)   A solicitor retained to defend an

---

(*v*) Cox v. Leech, 1 C. B. N. S. 617; 26 L. J., C. P. 125.

(*y*) Baker v. Milward, 8 Ir. C. L. R. 514.

(*z*) Allen v. Clark, 11 W. R. 304.

As to the receipt of money for investment by one of several solicitors in partnership, see *ante.*

(*a*) Fish v. Kelly, 17 C. B., N. S. 194.

action is not guilty of actionable negligence if he enters into a compromise without the consent of his client, provided he acts bonâ fide, and with reasonable care and skill, and the compromise is for the benefit of the client, and is not made in defiance of his express prohibition. (*b*)   But, if a solicitor, having express directions from the client to the contrary, nevertheless enters into a compromise, he is liable to an action for damages, though the damage actually sustained is nominal, and though the compromise is reasonable and bonâ fide and for the benefit of the client. (*c*)   By the 33 & 34 Vict. c. 28, agreements may be made between solicitors and their clients with respect to the remuneration of the former ; but, by sect. 7, a provision in any agreement that the solicitor shall not be liable for negligence, or that he shall be relieved from any responsibility to which he would otherwise be subject as such solicitor, is wholly void.

To render a medical man liable for negligence or want of due care or skill, it is not enough that there has been a less degree of skill than some other medical men might have shown, or a less degree of care than even he himself might have bestowed ; nor is it enough that he has himself acknowledged some degree of want of care ; there must have been a want of competent and ordinary care and skill, and to such a degree as to have led to a bad result. (*d*)

(*b*) Chown v. Parrtt, 14 C. B., N. S. 74; 32 L. J., C. P. 197.   Prestwich v. Poley, 18 C. B., N. S. 806 ; 44 L. J., C. P. 189.

(*c*) Fray v. Voules, 1 El. & El. 839 ; 28 L. J., Q. B. 232.

(*d*) Rich v. Pierpont, 3 F. & E. 35.

[1] A physician and surgeon, in the performance of his professional duties, is liable for injuries resulting from want of ordinary diligence, care, and skill.   McNevins v. Lowe, 40 Ill. 209 ; Landon v. Humphrey, 9 Conn. 209; Ritchey v. West, 23 Ill. 385 ; Graham v. Gautier, 21 Tex. 111; Howard v, Grover, 28 Me. 777; Patten v. Wiggin, 51 Id. 594; Leighton v. Sagent, 27

If I hire the labor and services and skill of a surgeon, an apothecary, a farrier, a solicitor, or any other
professional person, he impliedly undertakes for the

N. H. 760; Bellinger v. Craigue, 31 Barb. 534; Gallaher v.
Thompson, Wright, 466; Craig v. Chambers, 17 Ohio St. 253;
McCandless v. McWha, 22 Pa. St. 261; Scudder v. Crossan,
43 Ind. 343. But if the patient's own negligence contributes
to the injury or the damage, he can not recover against the
physician. Hubbard v. Thompson, 109 Mass. 286; Scudder v.
Crossan, 43 Ind. 343. The law requires the use of ordinary
skill and diligence, and it is erroneous to charge the jury that
the law requires "such reasonable skill and diligence as are
ordinarily exercised in the profession by thoroughly educated
surgeons, having regard to the improvements and advanced
state of the profession at the time;" the true measure is that
degree of skill ordinarily exercised by the profession as a
whole—not that exercised by the thoroughly educated, nor
merely of the well educated, but of the average. Smothers v.
Hanks, 34 Iowa, 286; Almond v. Nugent, Id. 300; and see
Chamberlin v. Morgan, 68 Pa. St. 168; Wood v. Clapp, 4 Sneed,
65; Young v. Morrison 14 Ind. 595; Teft v. Wilcox, 6 Kan. 46;
Heath v. Glisan, 3 Oreg. 64; Boydston v. Gillner Id. 118;
Williams v. Poppleton, Id. 139; West v. Martin, 31. Mo. 375;
Carpenter v. Blake, 60 Barb. 488. And it is wholly immaterial whether the physician has shown greater skill in treating
other persons. Id. It is the patient's duty to conform to the necessary prescriptions and treatment of the physician, if they be
such as a surgeon or physician of ordinary skill and care
would adopt or sanction, and, if he will not, or, under the press-
ure of pain, can not, the surgeon or physician is not responsible for injury resulting therefrom. Haire v. Reese, 7 Phil.
138. No presumption of the absence of proper care or
skill on the part of a surgeon or physician arises from the
fact that a patient under his care does not recover, or that a
complete cure was not effected. Id. And where a surgeon's
want of skill and care was set up in defense to his action for
the value of his services, the burden is on the defendant to
show that no want of care on his own part tended to prevent
a cure, or to consummate the injury of which he complains.
Baird v. Morford, 29 Iowa, 521. A surgeon is entitled to compensation for services which are beneficial to the patient, even
if more skillful services might have been rendered by others.
Alder v. Buckley, 1 Swan. 69. The law requires that a dentist

possession and exercise of ordinary skill and knowledge in the practice of his art or profession, and is responsible for any injury I may sustain from his neg-

should use a reasonable degree of skill and care in his professional operations, not that he is capable of the highest attainments of his profession. Simonds v. Henry, 39 Me. 155. And a dentist using chloroform is only required to look to the natural and probable effects of such agent, and can not be held liable for results arising from the peculiar temperament or condition of the person, of which he had no knowledge. Boyle v. Winslow, 5 Phil. (Pa.) 136. In actions for malpractice against physicians and surgeons, evidence of the following facts has been held admissible, " that the point of amputation was too high " and that " the danger of death was increased by choosing that point " (Wright v. Hardy, 22 Wis. 348), the circumstances in life of the parties (Fowler v. Sergeant, 1 Grant's Cas. 355), that the surgeon had received a good surgical and medical education, and was " regularly educated " and " skillful " (Leighton v. Sargent, 27 N. H. 460), that defendant's treatment of the case was " according to the botanic system of practise and medicine which he professed and was known to follow " (Bowman v. Woods, Greene, Iowa 441). But, without peculiar allegations to render it admissible, it is inadmissible to show facts " as to the weakness of the bones of plaintiff's family;" West v. Martin, 31 Me. 375; nor the opinion of the physician (he being sworn for the purpose) with whom defendant studied, as to his professional skill; Leighton v. Sargent, 31 N. H. 119; nor his general reputation among the profession; Id.; nor is the testimony of other physicians as to their opinion of the course pursued by defendant, as drawn from the defendant's declarations as to cases alleged to have been treated by him, or from the witness's own observation of the symptoms; Id.; nor evidence of defendant's treatment of other surgical cases, years after the treatment in question; Id.; nor that the physican abandoned his patient, or refused to prescribe for him; Bemus v. Howard, 3 Watts. 55. Evidence is permitted, in cases of malpractice, where it appears that other medical men were called in, as to the custom of physicians in regard to consultations, but a medical witness for the plaintiff can not be asked as to the measure of the defendant's responsibility for his patient. Mertz v. Detweiler, 8 Watts and S. 376. In such an action it is not, however, improper to exhibit the injured limb to the jury. Fow-

lect to exercise such skill. (*e*) A person who holds
himself out as a valuer of ecclesiastical property is
bound to bring to the performance of the duty he
undertakes a knowledge of the general rules applicable to the subject and of the proper mode of valuing
ecclesiastical dilapidations. (*f*) But, where the selling broker was selected by both buyer and seller to
determine whether goods sold were of a fair average
quality, it was held that he was not liable for want of
skill. (*g*) Every solicitor is responsible for gross
ignorance, or gross negligence, (*h*)[1] but not for erro-

(*e*) Seare v. Prentice, 8 East, 352.
Slater v. Baker, 2 Wils. 359. Hancke
v. Hooper, 7 C. & P. 84. Lanphier
v. Phipos, 8 C. & P. 479.

(*f*) Jenkins v. Betham, 15 C. B.
168.

(*g*) Pappa v. Rose, L. R., 6 C. P.
626; ib., 7 C. P. 525; 41 L. J., C. P.
11, 187.

(*h*) Pitt v. Yalden. 4 Burr. 2060.
Cooper v. Stephenson, 21 L. J., Q. B.
229.

ler v. Sargent, 1 Grant Cas. 355; and see as to these actions
generally, Twombly v. Leach 11 Cash. 397; Chamberlin v.
Porter, 9 Minn. 260; Wilmot v. Howard, 37 Vt. 447; Gran-
nis v. Brander, 5 Day, 260; Raynolds v. Graves, 3 Wis.
416.

[1] And it seems that if he excuse himself for such neglect
upon the ground that he was not satisfied of the expediency of
taking the proceeding, and doubtful if it were to his client's best
interests, he should so inform his client, and request specific instructions. Dearborn v. Dearborn, 15 Mass. 316. But see
Crooker v. Hutchinson, 2 D. Chip. (Vt.) 117, which holds that if
not specially directed to prosecute, he is justified in refraining, if
he be influenced by a prudent regard for his client's interest. It
was held in Cox v. Livingston, 2 Watts and S. 103, that if an
attorney is instructed to bring suit upon a note, it is not discretionary with him to do so or not, but he must follow his instructions, even though he acts in good faith, and, as he judge
for the best interests of his client; but see Hogg v. Martin
Riley, 156. No universal rule as to the amount of skill required of lawyers in conducting proceedings for their clients
is deducible from the cases; but the question of negligence
will be one for the jury. Hogg v. Martin, Riley, 256; Evans v.
Watrous, 2 Porter, 205. He would not, for instance be liable for negligence in refraining from bringing a suit against

neous advice and mistakes not amounting to evidence
of positive incompetency for the discharge of his professional duties. (i) [1]

(i) Purves v. Landell, 12 Cl. & Fin.   98. Shilcock v. Passman, 7 C. & P.
                                         289.

persons whom he knew to be insolvent, where he was given a
demand against such persons, and told to do the best he could
with it; and a judgment obtained against him at law on that
ground was restrained by injunction in Wright v. Ligon, 1
Harp. Eq. (S. C.) 166. Nor is he liable to an action for negligence where he acts honestly and to the best of his ability.
Lynch v. Commonwealth, 16 Serg. and R. 368. There is no
implied agreement in the relation of counsel and client that
the proceedings undertaken will terminate successfully, or
that the counsel's opinion will be ultmately sustained by a
court of last resort; counsel only undertakes to avoid errors
which no member of the profession, of ordinary prudence, diligence, or skill would commit. Bowman v. Tallman, 27 How.
Pr. 212; Gallaher v. Thompson, Wright, 466; and see Weima
v. Sloane, 6 McLean, 259; Ex parte Gibberson, 4 Cranch, 503.
An attorney is not bound to be personally present at the
proceedings in which he is employed. Williams v. Reed, 3
Mass. 405; Cox v. Sullivan, 7 Ga. 44. Nor is it negligence in
an attorney to unite secured with unsecured debts in a single
suit. Williams v. Reed, 3 Mass. 405. An attorney was held
liable where he filled up a blank writ with the words "twelve
dollars" instead of "twelve hundred dollars," whereby his
client sustained a loss. Varnum v. Martin, 15 Pick. 450. It is
negligence in an attorney to disobey the instructions of his client.
Gilbert v. Williams, 8 Mass. 51; and see *post*, note to § 920;

[1] Bowman v. Tallman, 40 How. Pr. 1. An attorney can not
be charged with negligence when he accepts as a correct exposition of the law a decision of the supreme court of his
state, upon the question of the liability of stockholders of corporations of the state in advance of any decision thereon by the
supreme court of the United States. Marsh v. Whitmore, 21
Wall. 178; but an attorney was held responsible for the damage
resulting to his client from the effects of his instructing him not
to answer a certain question; Gihon v. Albert, 7 Paige, 278.
An attorney must disclose to his client the fact of his holding
an adverse retainer; though concealment of the fact will
not necessarily imply fraud; Williams v. Reed, 3 Mass. 405.

878. *Willful selection of unqualified persons.*—
The employer himself is bound to exercise ordinary
caution and discrimination in the choice and selection

or having attached goods, which were replevied, to omit
to defend the replevin suit. Smallwood v. Norton, 20 Me.
83; or to disregard a well known and clearly defined rule of
law. Goodman v. Walker, 30 Ala. 482. But a declaration
against an attorney for negligence, must aver the payment of
his fees. Caviland v. Gale. 3 Cal. 108.

An attorney employed by trustees appointed by a public act
of the legislature is bound to know the extent of the authority
of the trustees who employ him. Butler v. Mitchell, 15 Wis. 355.
It is an attorney's duty, having undertaken to collect a debt, to
take the necessary proceedings to do it, and, if he neglect to take
such proceedings, he is liable to his client for any injury sustained
by reason of such neglect. Dearborn v. Dearborn, 15 Mass. 316;
Walpole v. Carlisle, 32 Ind. 415; Crooker v. Hutchinson,
1 D. Chip. (Vt.) 117; and so as to other proceedings in his
client's interest; Stubbs v. Beene, 37 Ala. 627; Hughes v.
Boyce, 2 La. Ann. 803; Walker v. Goodman, 21 Ala. 647;
Odlin v. Stetson, 17 Me. 244; Phillips v. Bridge, 11 Mass. 246;
Dearborn v. Dearborn, 15 Mass. 316; Crooker v. Hutchinson,
1 Vt. 73; McWilliams v. Hopkins, 4 Rawle, 382. Only reasonable diligence is required in the case of an attorney, as in all
other cases; Riddle v. Poorman, 3 Pa. 224; Watson v. Muirhead, 57 Pa. St. 161; and he is only liable for gross negligence;
Pennington v. Gell, 11 Ark. 212; but see Cox v. Sullivan, 7 Ga.
144; O'Barr v. Alexander, 37 Ga. 175; Holmes v. Peck, 1 R.
T. 242; Wilson v. Russ, 19 Me. 421; which hold that he would
be liable for ordinary neglect, to be determined by a reference
to the peculiar proceedings in which he is employed, and he
is entitled to the ordinary presumption in his favor; Id.;
Holmes v. Peck, 1 R. T. 242. Unless the actual amount of loss
by his negligence is shown, an attorney is only liable for nominal damages, and he is only liable for the actual results of his
negligence at the most. Cox v. Sullivan, 7 Ga. 44; Wilcox
v. Plummer, 4 Pet. 172; Suydam v. Vance, 2 McLean, 99;
Grayson v. Wilkinson, 13 Miss. (5 Sm. & M.) 268; O'Hara
v. Brophy, 24 How. Pr. 379; Miller v. Wilson, 24 Pa. St. 114;
Stephens v. White, 2 Wash. (Va.) 203; Oldham v. Sparks, 28
Tex. 425; Reilly v. Cavanaugh, 29 Ind. 435; Eccles v. Stephenson, 3 Bibb, 517; Rootes v. Stone, 2 Leigh, 650; but he
is not liable for interest on the debt lost through his negligence; Rootes v. Stone. 2 Leigh, 650; nor for the loss of

of the party he employs. If he selects a common quack or an unauthorized practitioner, the latter is responsible only for a reasonable and bonâ fide exertion of his capacity. He is bound to exercise such skill as he actually possesses ; and, if he has done his best and failed, he can not be made responsible for a want of skill ; for it was the employer's own fault to trust an unlearned and unskillful person, known not to be regularly and properly qualified. If the employer "voluntarily employs in one art a man who openly exercises another, his folly," observes Sir WILLIAM JONES, "has no claim to indulgence; and, unless the latter makes false pretensions or a special undertaking, no more can be fairly demanded of him than the best of his ability. The case which Sadi relates with elegance and humor in his Gulistan, or Rose Garden, is not inapplicable to the present subject. 'A man who had a disorder in his eyes called on a farrier for a remedy ; and he applied to them a medicine commonly used for his patients. The man lost his sight, and brought an action for the damages ;' but the judge said, 'No action lies; for, if the complainant had not himself been an ass, he would never have employed a farrier.' And Sadi proceeds to intimate that, 'if a person will employ a common mat-maker to weave or embroider a fine carpet, he must impute the bad workmanship to his own folly.' " (*k*)

879. *Bailment of materials to workmen to be manufactured or repaired for hire.*—When chattels or materials for work have been bailed or delivered to a workman to be repaired, made up, or dealt with by

(*k*) Bailments, citing Rosar. Polit. c. 7.

evidence of a debt. Huntington v. Rumril, 3 Day, 390 ; nor for the loss of papers stolen from his office ; Hill v. Barney, 18 N. H. 607.

him in the way of his trade, he is bound to take all reasonable and ordinary forethought and precaution for their protection and preservation; and, if a loss has occurred from robbery, or from fire or inundation, or from waste or decay, he must show that he had taken all such precautions as are ordinarily taken by prudent men to guard against the mischief.

880. *Re-delivery of materials furnished by the employer.*—If the bailor, before the work has been done, countermands the order for it, he has a right to the immediate return of the chattel, although, by his having countermanded the order, he may render himself liable to an action for a breach of contract. (*l*) If the bailee by mistake, or in obedience to a forged order, returns the chattel to the wrong person, and the article is lost, he is responsible for the loss. (*m*)

881. *Contracts for the performance of work— Building contracts—Prevention of performance— Damages.*—Where a contract has been entered into for the building of a house, and the owner refuses to permit the building to be completed, and prevents the workman from earning the stipulated remuneration, the measure of damages in respect of so much of the contract as remains unperformed is the difference between what the performance would have cost the plaintiff and the price which the defendant agreed to pay. (*n*) And in all cases of prevention of performance, where the plaintiff has been deprived by the defendant of the benefit of the contract, the plaintiff is entitled to recover what he has lost by the act of the defendant. (*o*)

(*l*) Lilley v. Barnsley, 1 C. & K. 344.

(*m*) Wilson v. Powis, 11 Moore, 543. Lubbock v. Inglis, 1 Stark. 104.

(*n*) Masterton v. Mayor, &c., Brooketyre, *ante.*

(*o*) Planché v. Colburn, 1 M. & Sc. 51. Inchbald v. West, &c., Coffee Co., *ante.*

When a contract for the performance of work and labor has not been fully carried out by the workman, but the employer has, and retains, the benefit of a part performance, and the contract is divisible and apportionable, or the plaintiff has been discharged from his liability to complete the portion unperformed, the measure of the damages is the residue of the full sum agreed to be paid, after deducting such an amount as will enable the defendant to get the contract completed and carried out according to the original intention of the contracting parties. (*p*)   If the plaintiff has contracted to do the work and supply materials for a fixed sum, and the defendant afterwards finds some of the materials, the defendant is entitled to deduct the fair value of his materials from the contract price. (*q*)   Where a judgment had been recovered by the plaintiff against a relation of the defendant, and the latter promised the plaintiff that, if he would forbear to issue execution upon the judgment, the defendant would erect and finish a substantial house, and cause a lease thereof to be granted to the plaintiff, and the plaintiff promised that such lease, when granted, should be in full satisfaction of the judgment, it was held that the measure of damages from the breach of the defendant's promise was the value of the house, if it had been erected, and of the lease thereof and not the difference between the value of the judgment and the value of the house and lease. (*r*)

(*p*) *Ante.* Cutler v. Close, 5 C. & P. 339.

(*q*) Newton v. Forster, 12 M. & W.

772.

(*r*) Strutt v. Farlar, 16 M. & W. 249; 16 L. J., Ex. 84.

SECTION II.

MASTER AND SERVANT.

882. *Of contracts of hiring and service.*—The contract of letting and hiring relates as frequently to human labor and skill, care, and attention, as to moveable and immoveable property, realty, and personalty ; the labor and services of workmen and artificers being daily hired to be employed in domestic affairs, in the cultivation of land, in the building of houses, in the manufacture of materials furnished to be worked up, and upon chattels which have been bailed or delivered to the workman to be mended or repaired. (*a*)   In order to constitute a contract of hiring and service, there must be either an express or an implied mutual engagement binding one party to employ and remunerate, and the other to serve, for some determinate term or period.   It has been said that, if the employer merely covenants to pay so long as the servant continues to serve, leaving it optional, either with the servant to serve, or with the employer to employ, there is no contract of hiring and service. (*b*)   But this decision has been doubted; (*c*) and, if the servant binds himself to serve for some determinate term, and the employer expressly or impliedly covenants or promises to retain the servant in his service for the term, there is a contract of hiring and service.

Where the plaintiff covenanted that his son should serve and continue with the defendant as his assistant in the art of a surgeon-dentist for five years, and should

(*a*) Ostendit definitio, duo esse genera locationis, rerum unam, alteram operarum seu factorum. Vin. Com. lib. 3, tit. 25, 757. Pandect. Pothier, lib. 19, tit. 2, Art. 1.

(*b*) Williamson v. Taylor, 5 Q. B. 175.

(*c*) Emmens v. Elderton, 4 H. L. C. 624 ; 13 C. B. 495. Whittle v. Frankland, 2 B. & S. 49 ; 31 L. J. M. C. 81.

execute and perform such work and service in the art as the defendant should direct, and the defendant covenanted with the plaintiff that he would, during the term of five years, in case the son should well and faithfully serve, &c., pay him certain weekly wages, it was held that, as there was no express covenant on the part of the defendant to employ or retain the son in the defendant's service for five years, the defendant was at liberty to dismiss him whenever he pleased, and discontinue the payment of the weekly wages. (*d*) But this decision is not reconcileable with other authorities; and it is apprehended that, wherever one party covenants to serve for a particular period, and the other covenants to pay him a salary or wages for the service during the term, there is an implied covenant on the part of the latter to retain the servant in his service during the term, provided the latter serves faithfully, and is guilty of no misconduct warranting a dismissal. Where it was agreed between the plaintiff and a joint-stock company that the plaintiff should be the permanent attorney of the company, and should receive and accept a salary of £100 a year in lieu of his annual bill of costs, and should for such salary advise and act for the company on all occasions, it was held that there was an implied contract on the part of the company to retain the attorney in their service for one year at least, and pay him the salary he had agreed to accept, but that the word "permanent" did not confer any durable appointment beyond the year, so as to prevent the employer from withdrawing the retainer. (*e*) [1]

(*d*) Dunn v. Sayles, 5 Q. B. 685.

(*e*) Emmens v. Elderton, 13 C. B. 495; 4 H. L. C. 645. Reg. v. Welch, 2 Ell. & Bl. 362. Rust v. Nottidge, 1 Ell. & Bl. 99. Hartley v. Cummings, 17 L. J., C.' P. 84. Pilkington v. Scott, 15 M. & W. 660. M'Intyre v. Belcher, 32 L. J., C. P. 254.

[1] The term " employee" in its ordinary and usual sense in-

Whenever one party agrees to retain or hire, and
another agrees to serve for a certain term, at a specified
salary, there is a contract of hiring and service, although the servant may never be called upon or required to do any work.   There are many cases of hiring and employment of parties to serve in some particular character or capacity where the servant is
bound to serve if called upon, and is entitled to his
salary by holding himself in readiness to serve, although his services are not called into requisition by
the employer.   In these cases there is a continuous
hiring or retainer ; and the readiness and willingness
to serve on the part of the servant are equivalent to
actual service.[1]

883. *Authentication and proof of the contract.—*
A contract of hiring and service need not be authenticated by writing, unless the hiring exceeds a year in
duration ;[2] and if reduced into writing, it need not be

cludes all whose services are rendered for another; it is not
restricted to any kind of employment or service, but includes
as well the professional man as the common laborer. Gurney v.
Atlantic, &c., Ry. Co., 58 N. Y. 358. An order appointing a receiver of a railroad company directed him, among other things,
to pay debts " owing to the laborers and employees" of the company " for labor and services actually done in connection with
that company's railways." Held, that it included a claim of
counsel for professional services rendered by him on employment of the company in litigations relating to the railway, its
interests, and business. Id. A police officer is not a servant of
the city appointing him in any such sense as to take away his
right of action against it for damages sustained by him by
reason of its defective highway; Kimball v. Boston 1 Allen,
417; nor is a fireman ; Palmer v. Portsmouth, 413 N. H. 265;
nor does the relation exist between one who employs a contractor to do certain work, and the servant of such contractor
engaged in the work ; Bartlett v. Singer Mfg. Co., 1 Sweeny,
595 ; West v. St. Louis, &c. R. R., 63 Ill. 545.

[1] Parsons on Contracts, 95.

[2] *Ante*, vol. i. § 212, p. 317.

stamped, if it is a contract for the hire of "laborers, artificers, manufacturers, or menial servants," and not a contract of apprenticeship.[1] In the absence of an express contract between the parties, a hiring may be presumed from the mere fact of the service, unless the service has been with near relations. If a man, for example, serves a stranger in the capacity of a clerk, or of a menial servant, or servant in husbandry, for a continued period, the law presumes that the service has been rendered in fulfillment of a contract of hiring and service ; and if the party has. served without anything being said as to wages, the law presumes that there was a contract for customary and reasonable wages. (*f*)[2] But if the service has been with the parent or uncle, or other near relation of the party serving, a hiring can not be implied or presumed from it, but an express hiring mnst be proved in order to support a claim for wages ; for the law regards services rendered by near relations to one another as gratuitous acts of kindness and charity, and does not presume that they are to be paid for, unless there is an express contract to that effect. (*g*) And if a poor person is taken out of charity and provided with food, lodging, clothes, and necessaries, and set to work, no contract of hiring and service is implied therefrom, however long the party may continue to serve. (*h*)

884. *Yearly hirings—Domestic servants.*—When

(*f*) Lord Ellenborough, C. J., 15 East, 454. Phillips v. Jones, 1 Ad. & E. 333.

(*g*) Davies v. Davies, 9 C. & P. 87. Gregory Stoke v. Pitminster, 2 Bott.

P. L. C. 206, case 269. R. v. Sow, 1 B. & Ald. 181. R. v. St. Mary Guildford, 2 Bott. 209, c. 273 ; Cald. 521. R. v. Stokesley, 6 T. R. 757.

(*h*) R. v. Weyhill, 1 W. Bl. 206 ; 2 Bott. 207, case 271.

[1] *Post*, § 906.
[2] See Woodward v. Washburn, 3 Den. 369 ; Moore v. Tickee, 3 Dev. L. 244.

the employment of a servant is of a permanent nature, and annual wages are reserved, the hiring is a yearly hiring ; and when the servant is not a household or domestic servant, the hiring can not be put an end to by either party without the consent of the other, before the termination of the current year. (*i*)[1] A hiring of a servant in husbandry, for example, is an indefeasible yearly hiring, analogous to a yearly tenancy. At the end of each year a new contract arises to serve for the year commencing, which will continue as long as the parties may please, and can only be terminated at the end of the current year, unless the servant is guilty of misconduct. (*k*) A general hiring of a clerk, foreman, journeyman, or traveler, at annual wages, "with board in the house," is, in general, a yearly hiring, which can only be put an end to by consent, or at the expiration of the current year; (*l*) and so also is a general hiring of a governess at annual wages, with board in the house; (*m*) but the duration of the term of hiring will be regulated and controlled by custom and usage and

(*i*) Emmens v. Elderton, *ante.*

(*k*) R. v. Lyth, 5 T. R. 337 ; 3 ib. 76.

(*l*) Beeston v. Collyer, 12 Moore, 552. R. v. Batheaston, Burr. Set. Cas. 823, No. 257. Turner v. Robinson, 5 B. & Ad. 789 ; 2 N. & M. 829. Davis v. Marshall, 9 W. R. 520.

(*m*) Todd v. Kerrich, 8 Exch. 151 ; 22 L. J., Ex. 1.

[1] A hiring of personal service for which payment is made quarterly is not necessarily a hiring by the quarter, or terminable by a quarter's notice. Tatterson v. Suffolk Mfg. Co., 106 Mass. 56. A and B agreed orally that B should hire his services to A at a yearly rate. B served a year, and began the second year without a new bargain. Held, in an action by B for his wages during his second year, that the original negotiations between the parties were competent evidence to show the terms of the contract, express or implied, under which the parties continued their relation ; and that the statute of frauds was no bar to the action. Ib. ; and see Jordan v. Foxworth, 48 Miss. 607 ; Beach v. Mullin, 34 N. J. L. 343.

the surrounding circumstances of the case. (*n*) A general hiring of postilions and ostlers, upon the terms that they are to receive board and lodging in the house, and the vails or perquisites of the stables in lieu of wages, is a yearly hiring; (*o*) and so also is a general hiring of a warehouseman, " the employer engaging to pay £12 10*s.* per month for the first year, and advance £10 per annum until the salary should be £180;" (*p*) also a general hiring of editors, sub-editors, reporters, and other persons regularly employed upon old-standing and permanently-established newspapers and periodicals. (*q*) Reservations of quarterly, monthly, or weekly wages are not inconsistent with a yearly hiring. " Whether the wages be to be paid by the week or the year can not make any alteration in the duration of the service, if the contract were for a year ;" (*r*) but if there has been no continued service for a lengthened period, and there is nothing in the nature of the employment, and no particular custom or usage leading necessarily to the conclusion that the hiring was for a year, the payment of weekly or monthly wages raises a presumption in favor of a weekly or monthly hiring. (*s*) A " hiring for twelve months certain, and to continue from time to time until three months' notice in writing be given by either party to determine the same," is a hiring for a year certain only ; and either party is at liberty to put an end to it at the expiration of the year, by giving three months' previous notice. (*t*)

(*n*) Fairman v. Oakford, 5 H. & N. 636 ; 29 L. J., Ex. 459.

(*o*) Burr. Set. Cas. 759, No. 232. 2 Bott. 229, 230, pl. 294, 297.

(*p*) Fawcett v. Cash, 5 B. & Ad. 908.

(*q*) Holcroft v. Barber, 1 Car. & Kirw. 4. Baxter v. Nurse, ib. 10.

Williams v. Byrne, 2 N. & P. 139.

(*r*) Kenyon, C. J., 4 T. R. 246. R. v. Seaton, Cald. 440.

(*s*) R. v. Pucklechurch, 5 East, 384. Baxter v. Nurse, 7 Sc. N. R. 801 ; 6 M. & Gr. 935.

(*t*) Brown v. Symons, 8 C. B. N. S. 208 ; 29 L. J., C. P. 251.

885. *Indefeasible and defeasible yearly hirings—Month's warning or a month's wages.*—If by the custom or usage of trade the hiring may be put an end to and the contract dissolved, by notice given by either of the parties, the hiring is a conditional or defeasible yearly hiring, determinable by giving the customary notice at any time during the term. By the custom of particular trades a general hiring of a commercial traveler is a hiring for a year, subject to an implied understanding that either party may determine the engagement by giving three months' notice. (*u*)   A general hiring of menial or household servants, such as cooks, scullions, housemaids, footmen, butlers, coachmen, grooms, where no time is mentioned for the duration of the service, is a hiring for a year, and so on from year to year, defeasible by custom and usage, at the option of either of the parties, on giving a month's warning, or paying or tendering a month's wages.   If the contract is put into writing, the customary power of defeasance is impliedly annexed to the express terms of the written agreement, unless the custom is excluded by express words. (*v*) A servant may be a menial servant, and as such clothed with this implied power of defeasance, although he does not reside within the walls of the master's house.   This has been held to be the case with a head gardener hired for a year at £100 wages, with a house in the master's grounds, and the privilege of taking in apprentices for a year at £15 premium ; (*y*) also with a huntsman engaged at a salary of £100 a year, with a house to live in and perquisites. (*z*)

(*u*) Metzner v. Bolton, 9 Exch. 518 ; 23 L. J., Ex. 130.

(*v*) Johnson v. Blenkensop, 5 Jur. 870.

(*y*) Nowlan v. Ablett, 2 C. M. & R. 57.

(*z*) Nicoll v. Greaves, 17 C. B., N. S. 27 ; 33 L. J., C. P. 259.

When a power of defeasance is vested in the parties either by custom or special agreement, or the contract is made defeasible upon the happening of a given event, the hiring is nevertheless a yearly hiring; so that, if the power of defeasance is not exercised, and the contract is permitted to run on, and the service to continue for a year, there is a year's hiring and service, which will gain a settlement under the poor laws. (*a*) "It is a yearly hiring, notwithstanding the power of determining it, if that is not exercised before the expiration of the year. The contingency not having happened, and the contract not having been defeated during the year, it enures after the year's service as a yearly hiring." (*b*)   A servant may engage himself to serve for a certain determinate period, but may give the employer the option of determining the contract and dismissing him at any period of the service. Where the engagement of a clerk or a superintendent was to be for three years, "at the option" of the employer, at a yearly salary, it was held that this was a contract binding the servant to serve three years, and giving the employer the option of determining the contract at the end of each year by a proper notice, but not of dismissing the servant at any time; that the option to be exercised by the employer was whether the servant was to remain for one, two, or three years, and that, if he was dismissed in the middle of a current year, he was entitled to compensation. (*c*)

886. *Hiring by the month and week.*—Where a

(*a*) R. v. Atherton, Burr. Set. Cas. 203, No. 71. R. v. Birdbrooke, 4 T. R. 246.   R. v. Farleigh Wallop, 1 B. & Ad. 340, 342.   R. v. New Windsor, Burr. Set. Cas. 22, No. 7.   R. v. Gt. Yarmouth, 5 M. & S. 114. R. v. Northwold, 2 D. & R. 792.

(*b*) R. v. Sandhurst, 7 B. & C. 562 ; 1 M. & R. 101.   R. v. Byker, 3 D. & R. 336 ; 2 B. & C. 119.   R. v. Lidney, Burr. Set. Cas. 1.

(*c*) Down v. Pinto, 9 Exch. 327 ; 23 L. J. Ex. 103.

journeyman miller was hired " at monthly wages, with
liberty to depart at a month's wages or a month's
warning," the hiring was held to be a hiring by the
month ; (*d*) but, when the wages are reserved weekly
with a proviso for a month's warning, the presumption
is in favor of a conditional and defeasible yearly hiring.
If there be anything in the contract to show that the
hiring was intended to be for a year, then a reservation of weekly wages will not control that hiring.
But, if the payment of weekly wages be the only circumstance from which the duration of the contract is
to be collected, it must be taken to be only a weekly
hiring. (*e*) " The mere arrangement," observes BAYLEY,
J., " that the wages shall be at one rate in the summer
and at another in the winter does not show that the
parties contemplated a service to endure through the
summer and winter, and therefor that they intended a
hiring for a year ; but shows only that they intended
that, if the servant, being hired at weekly wages,
should remain till the summer, he should then have
so much per week. The true meaning of such an
arrangement is merely this : that the servant's wages
as a weekly servant are to be regulated by the
seasons." (*f*) But, if the nature of the employment or the terms of the contract are inconsistent
with a weekly hiring, the reservation of weekly
wages will be regarded merely as a mode of payment,
and not as an indication of the duration of the

(*d*) R. v. Clare, 2 Bott, 229, pl.
295.

(*e*) Ellenborough, C. J., R. v. Dodderhill, 3 M. & S. 245. Burr. Set.
Cas. 280, No. 98. R. v. Pucklechurch,
5 East, 384. R. v. Hanbury, 2 East,
425. R. v. Mitcham, 12 East, 352.
Ashurst, J., R. v. Newton Toney, 2
T. R. 455. R. v. Odiham, ib. 622.

Baxter v. Nurse, 7 Sc. N. R. 801 ; 6
M. & Gr. 935. R. v. Elstack, 2 Bott.
227, pl. 292. R. v. Dedham, 2 Bott.
227, pl. 292. R. v. Warminster, 9 D.
& R. 70. Evans v. Roe, L. R., 7 C.
P. 138.

(*f*) R. v. Rolvenden, 1 M. & R.
691. R. v. Dodderhill, 3 M. & S.
243. R. v. Lambeth, 4 ib. 315.

contract. (*g*)   Thus, the presumption of a weekly hiring resulting from a reservation of weekly wages is rebutted by a stipulation for a fortnight's or a month's notice to quit. (*h*) [1]

887. *Service at will.*—A boy was employed to work "for meat, drink, and clothes, as long as he had a mind to stop," and served for two years upon these terms; and the service was held to be a mere service at will. (*i*)   So, where an assistant workman was "to come and go as he liked," and an ostler and his master were "to be at liberty to separate when they pleased," the service was held to be a service at will. (*k*)   In these cases there is in truth no contract of hiring at all. (*l*)   The transaction amounts merely to an authority to serve upon certain terms.   If the work is actually performed and accepted, the law raises an implied promise of remuneration from the employer to the workman; but the former is not bound to provide the work; nor is the latter bound to execute it.

888. *Rights and liabilities of master and servant.* —It is the first duty of the master, after the contract of hiring and service has been entered into, to take the servant into his employ and enable him to earn the hire or reward agreed to be paid; [2] and, if he neg-

---

(*g*) Davis v. Marshall, 9 W. R. 520.

(*h*) R. v. Hampreston, 5 T. R. 208. R. v. St. Andrew, Pershore, 8 B. & C. 679.   R. v. Birdbrooke, 4 T. R. 246. R. v. Gt. Yarmouth, 5 M. & S. 117.

(*i*) R. v. Christ's Parish, York, 3 B. & C. 459; 5 D. & R. 314.

(*k*) R. v. Gt. Bowden, 7 B. & C. 249.

(*l*) R. v. St. Matthew's, Ipswich, 3 T. R. 449.

---

[1] Where a person of full age is hired by the year as a clerk by a merchant, the relation of master and servant is thereby created.   Woodward v. Washburn, 3 Den. 369.

[2] Where an employer has printed rules and regulations hung up in his workshop, requiring workmen to give notice a certain number of days before leaving, and to work out the time, or else to forfeit the wages due, if a workman does not

lects so to do, he renders himself liable forthwith to an action for a breach of contract. "The master is bound to provide for the safety of his servant in the course of his employment to the best of his judgment, information, and belief; but the law does not imply, from the mere relation of master and servant, an obligation on the part of the master to take more care of the servant than he may reasonably be expected to take of himself." (*m*) If the servant sustains injury in the course of his employment from the negigence of the master, the latter will be responsible in damages, (*n*) [1] although there is no implied agreement

(*m*) Riley v. Baxendale, 30 L. J., Ex. 87. Priestly v. Fowler, 3 M. & W. 5. Patterson v. Wallace, 1 Macq. H. L. C. 748. Davies v. England, 33 L. J., Q. B. 321. As to injuries from unfenced machinery, see Holmes v. Clarke, 30 L. J. Ex. 135 ; 31 L. J. Ex. 356 ; 7 H. & N. 937.

(*n*) Ashworth v. Stanwix, 30 L. J., Q. B. 183. Clarke v. Holmes, 7 H. and N. 937; 31 L. J., Ex. 356. Weems v. Mathieson, 4 Macq. H. L. C. 215. Mellors v. Shaw, 1 B. & S. 437 ; 30 L. J., Q. B. 333.

know of such rules when he begins work, the fact that he is afterwards informed of them, and continues to work without objection, does not, as a matter of law, show that he assented to the rules as a part of his contract. Collins v. New England Iron Co., 115 Mass. 23.

[1] And this negligence may consist in the employment by him of unfit and incompetent co-servants; Sizer v. Syracuse, 7 Lans. 61; or in furnishing for work to be done, or for the use of the servant, machinery. or other improper implements or things—improper and unsafe for the purposes to which they are to be applied; Id. ; West v. St. Louis, &c. R. R. Co., 63 Ill. 545. In the latter case, a railway company chartered by the legislature, contracted with certain parties to construct its road and its appurtenances. These contractors, through their superintendent, hired the plaintiff to work upon a freight-house they were building for the company. A poisonous mixture, in which corrosive sublimate was an ingredient, was applied to the timber to prevent decay. The plaintiff was injured by breathing the exhalations of this substance, and by handling the timber to which it had been applied. Held, that the railway company was not liable to the plaintiff for the in-

by the master in an ordinary contract of hiring and service not to expose the servant to extraordinary risks in the course of his employment; (*o*) but the

(*o*) Riley v. Baxendale, 6 H. & N. 445 ; 80 L. J., Ex. 87.

jury he received, but that the contractors were solely responsible, and were not, in this respect, the servants of the company. West v. St. Louis, Vandalia, and Terre Haute Railroad Co. — Ill. 545. Where the wrongful act is done by contractors or lessees of a chartered company in pursuance of the special powers and privileges conferred upon the company by its charter, and but for such charter they would have no right to prosecute the particular business, such contractors or lessees, as to third parties who may be injured by their acts, will be regarded as the servants of the company acting under its discretion, and the company will be held liable for any abuse of such of its privileges by its contractors or lessees. But it seems the contractors themselves are servants of the company. Chicago, &c., R. R. Co. v. McCarthy, 20 Ill. 385; Stone v. Cheshire R. R. Co., 19 N. H. 427 ; Carman v. Steub., &c., R. R. Co., 4 Ohio, St. § 399 ; Hofnagle v. New York, &c., R. R. Co., — N. Y. 608; Cleghorn v. New York, &c., R. R. Co., 56 Id. 44. But the master is not liable to his servant for damages sustained by the negligent act of a fellow-servant while engaged in the same general employment, unless the master was negligent in the selection of the servant at fault. Hogan v. Central P. R. R. Co., 49 Cal. 128; and see Gibson v. Pacific R. R. Co., 46 Mo. 163 ; Wonder v. Baltimore, &c., R. R. Co., 32 Md. 411 ; and whether the injury from the fellow-servant's act is the result of the master's negligence in employing an incompetent servant is a question for the jury ; Ardesco Oil Co. v. Gilson, 63 Pa. St. 146; and see Connolly v. Davidson, 15 Minn. 519; Harper v. Indianapolis, &c., R. R. Co., 47 Mo. 567; Davis v. Detroit, &c., R. R. Co., 2 Mich. 105 ; and if the servant's negligence contribute to the injury, he can not recover; Johnson v. Bruner, 61 Pa. St. 58; and see Spelman v. Fisher, &c., Works, 56 Barb. 151. Where an employee was injured by the falling of a hoisting apparatus, *held*, that the liability of the defendant depended upon three facts: 1. That the method of attaching the hoisting rope was defective and unsafe, and that the injury was caused by the defect. 2. That the defendant knew or ought to have known of the defect

master is not liable for surgical attendance and medicine rendered to a servant who has been injured in
the execution of the master's service, unless the surgeon has been called in by the master's orders; (p) [1]

(p) Wannell v. Adney, 3 B. & P. 247.　Cooper v. Phillips, 4 C. & P. 581.

3. That the plaintiff did not know of it, and had not equal
means of knowledge.　Malone v. Hawley, 46 Cal. 409.

It is competent for a jury in assessing damages to an employee resulting from negligence of the employer, to consider
what, before the injury, was the health and physical ability of
the plaintiff to maintain himself and family, as compared with
his condition in such particulars afterwards ; his loss of time,
and how far the injury was permanent in its character and
results, as well as the physical and mental suffering he sustained by reason of the injury ; and they should allow such
damages as they think will fairly and justly compensate him
for all loss and injury sustained.　But the jury can not consider the plaintiff's " condition in life," whether he is rich or
poor.　Id.　Plaintiff, while employed upon a barge, which was
being used in lightering a steamship, was injured through the
negligence of one engaged upon the steamship in discharging
her cargo.　In an action to recover for the injury, defendant's
answer admitted that at the time of the accident, defendant
owned and had the control and management of the steamer ;
the barge was not owned by defendant, and plaintiff was employed and paid by its master.　*Held*, that the proof, together
with the admission in the answer, was sufficient to authorize
the jury to find that the man who caused the injury was a servant of defendant, and working for it at the time ; that he and
plaintiff were not fellow servants within the meaning of the
rule exempting an employer from liability for an injury to
one employee by the act of another ; and that said rule, therefore, furnished no objection to the maintenance of the action.
Svenson v. Atlantic, &c., M. Steamship Co., 57 N. Y. 108.　In an
action brought by a servant against his master to recover for
personal injuries received by him in breaking and falling
through a floor in his master's shop, over which it was his
duty to pass, it appeared that he knew that the floor was de-
cayed, and that there were holes in it ; but it did not appear
that he could have ascertained that the place where he broke

---

[1] But a master was held liable for similar charges in Rice
v. Borehenny, 2 Houst. 74.

nor for injuries sustained from the unseaworthiness of a vessel in which the servant is employed; (*q*) nor for injuries which one servant has sustained through the negligence of another servant of the same employer, provided the master provides proper machinery, (*r*) and takes care that his servants are persons of competent skill and ordinary carefulness; (*s*) for a servant, when he engages to serve a master, undertakes as between him and his master to run all the ordinary

(*q*) Couch v. Steel, 23 L. J., Q. B. 121.

(*r*) Searle v. Lindsay, 11 C. B. N. S. 429; 31 L. J., C. P. 106.

(*s*) Potter v. Faulkner, 1 B. & S. 800: 31 L. J., Q. B. 30. Senior v. Ward, 1 El. & El. 385.

through was dangerous without examining parts of the floor not open to his inspection. *Held*, that the court could not say that he was guilty of negligence, and that the question was for the jury. Huddleston v. Lowell Machine Shop, 282. While a master is liable to a servant for injuries resulting from the negligence of a fellow servant who has been charged with the performance, in place of the master, of duties owed by the master to the servant, where the negligence relates to the performance of those duties, he is not liable for the negligence of a competent fellow-servant who does not thus stand in the place of the master, although he may have some authority and power of direction over the injured servant. Hoffnagle v. New York, &c., R. R. Co., — N. Y. 608. Where the servants of a railroad company, while in the discharge of their duties, pervert the appliances of the company to wanton and malicious purposes to the injury of others, the company is liable for such injuries. Chicago, Burlington, and Quincy Railroad Co. v. Dickson, — Ill. 151. If a servant of a railroad company be injured through the incompetency and unskillfulness of a fellow-servant, or in consequence of defects in machinery or track, and the company be guilty of negligence in the employment and retention of such agent, or in the construction and repair of its machinery and track, it is liable in damages. Chicago and Alton Railroad Co. v. Sullivan, Admx. Id. 293; and habitual intemperance of a conductor, under circumstances bringing knowledge thereof to his employers, is sufficient to render them liable for injury resulting therefrom; Id; but see Chapman v. Erie R'y, — N. Y. 579.

risks of the service. (*t*) [1] Every servant, on the other hand, impliedly undertakes to obey the just and reasonable commands of the master, and to be careful,

(*t*) Hutchinson v. York, Newc. & Berw. Rail. Co., 5 Exch. 343 ; 19 L. J., Ex. 296. Wigmore v. Jay, ib. 300 ; 5 Exch. 354. Seymour *v.* Maddox, 20 L. J., Q. B. 327 ; 16 Q. B. 326. Lovegrove v. L. B. & S. C. Ry. Co., 16 C. B. N. S. 669 ; 33 L. J., C. P. 329. Morgan *v.* Vale of Neath Ry. Co., 5 B. & S. 736 ; 33 L. J., Q, B. 260. Waller v. The S. E. Ry. Co., 3 H. & C. 102 ; 32 L. J., Ex. 205. Murphy v. Caralli, 3 H. & C. 462 ; 34 L. J., Ex. 14. Tunney v. Midland Ry. Co., L. R., 1 C. P. 291. As to who are fellow-servants, see Hall v. Johnson. 3 H. & C., 589 ; 34 L. J., Ex. 222. Feltham v. England, L. R., 2 Q. B. 33 ; 36 L. J., Q. B. 14. Warburton v. Great Western Ry. Co., L. R., 2 Ex. 30 ; 36 L. J., Ex. 9.

[1] For the negligence, however gross or culpable, of a servant while engaged in the business of the master, the latter is not liable in punitive damages, unless he is also chargeable with gross misconduct. Ordinary negligence will not suffice to impose such a liability; it must be reckless, and of a criminal nature, and must be clearly established. Such misconduct may be established, however, by showing that the act of the servant was authorized or ratified, or that the master employed or retained the servant knowing that he was incompetent, or, from bad habits, unfit for the position he occupied. Cleghorn v. N. Y. C. and H. R. R. R. Co., 56 N. Y. 44. A master is not liable, in exemplary damages, for the act of his servant, where the plaintiff would not have been entitled to recover such damages had the suit been against the servant; Townsend v. N. Y. C. and H. R. R. R. Co., Id. 295 ; nor where he would not be liable if he had done the act himself; Russell v. Irley, 13 Ala. 131 ; or where he did not authorize the act ; Harris v. Nicholas, 4 Munf. 483 ; Thames Steamboat Co. v. Housatonic R. R. Co., 24 Conn. 40 ; Church v. Mansfield, 20 Id. 20 ; Id. 284 ; Evansville, &c., R. R. Co. v. Baum, 26 Ind. 70 ; McCoy v. McKowen, 26 Miss. 487 ; Wesson v. Seaboard, &c., R. R. Co., 4 Jones (N. C.) L. 379 ; Yerger v. Warren, 31 Pa. St. 319 ; nor will the master be liable for acts of his servant, who departs from his master's instructions; Oxford v. Peter, 28 Ill. 434 ; unless he is aware of such departure; Elder v. Bemis, 2 Metc. 599 ; or out of the course of his employment; Foster v. Essex Bank, 17 Mass. 479 ; Kerns v. Piper, 4 Watts 222 ; Wilson v. Peverly, 2 N. H. 548 ; Aycrigg v. New York, &c., R. R. Co., 30 N. J. L. 460. The principle as stated above has not prevented considerable confusion in the cases. In

diligent, and industrious in the performance of the work intrusted to him to execute. A servant who professes to be capable of undertaking an office of

Laning v. New York Central R. R. Co., 49 N. Y. 521, it was held that the duty of the master to the servant, and the implied contract between them, is, that the master shall furnish proper, perfect, and adequate machinery or other materials and appliances necessary for the work which the servant is to do; and that he shall employ competent and skillful fellow-servants, or shall use all due and reasonable care to employ such; and that this duty and contract must be affirmatively and positively fulfilled by the master. And the court of appeals sustained, with one judge dissenting, a verdict for the plaintiff upon the following facts: Plaintiff was an employee of the defendant's railroad company. He worked, with others, under the directions of Westman, defendant's foreman. Westman directed Foreman and Churchill, two lads, to erect a scaffold, and they did so, unskillfully, and of poor materials. Plaintiff, while working on this scaffold, sustained injuries by its fall. The foreman, Westman, was originally competent and skillful, but during his employment by defendant, had acquired habits of intemperance in strong drink, which became known to Coleby, defendant's hiring agent; the plaintiff himself knew the same fact, but he did not know who built the scaffold, or how it was built. There was plenty of good material furnished by defendant for building scaffolds. The question of contributory negligence on the servant's part, said the opinion, was one for the jury, with which the court could not have to do. As to the intemperance of Westman, the court said: "The testimony does not show directly, though it is an inference which a jury might make fairly, that his condition in that respect was a cause of injury to the plaintiff; for they might well infer that if his faculties had been without confusion from strong drink, he would not have put these lads, deficient in judgment and strength, to a work requiring discretion and power, or would have inspected the result of their work before using it." Previously, the same court, in Wright v. New York Central R. R., 25 N. Y. 565, had substantially held that the injuries must positively appear to have resulted from the unskillfulness, incompetency, or imprudence of the servant, and rejected the idea of an inference in the absence of such positive proof. In Flike v. Boston and Albany R. R. Co., 53 Id. 549, plaintiff's intestate was a fireman upon a freight train on the defendant's

skill impliedly represents himself to be possessed of
the skill requisite for the due discharge of the functions
of the office ; and if he does not possess that skill, or

road ; his train was run into by some cars which became detached from another freight train ahead of his, and he was
killed. The first train had but two brakemen, when it should
have had three, the third one oversleeping and failing to accompany the train, and the train being sent out by the train-
dispatcher with only two brakemen ; the lack of the third
brakeman caused the accident. A verdict for the plaintiff was
sustained by one vote. The ground of dissent of the minority is
stated by Judge Folger (in Malone v. Hathaway, referred to below) to have been, that the train-dispatcher was not (as the ma-
jority held) such an agent of the company as to make the latter
responsible for his negligence. Again, in Corcoran v. Holbrook,
59 N. Y. 518, the defendants operated a cotton mill, to the
management of which they gave no personal attention, but
intrusted it entirely to a general agent, who had full power.
In the mill was an elevator, which for upwards of thirty years
had been used by the superintendents, bosses, and employees
of the mill in passing from one floor to another of the mill
while engaged in work there, and this to the knowledge of
their superiors and bosses, and that the plaintiff had been accustomed so to ride. The right of the plaintiff to use the elevator to pass to the upper floor is conceded in the opinion of
the supreme court, and the conclusion of the referee that she
was not guilty of any negligence in so doing is undisturbed.
The sole ground of reversal was, that the defendants were not
liable for the negligence of their general agent in omitting to
repair the broken chain, after notice to him that it was unsafe,
and that unless repaired some of the employees would get
hurt. The defendants, who operated the mill at the time of
the injury ; gave no personal attention to conducting the mill,
but it was managed by a general agent, who had general
charge of the mill, machinery, and operatives, with power to
purchase all supplies, and hire and discharge operatives. Said
the court : It is evident that this general agent was not a mere
fellow-servant of the plaintiff, who was a common hand in the
mill, but that he was charged with the performance of the duties which the defendants owed to the hands employed in the
mill. There was no other person to discharge those duties,
and the defendants could not, by absenting themselves from

if, possessing it, he fails to exercise it, he is responsible
for a breach of contract. A servant, in the service of
a tradesman, impliedly promises to do no act know-

the mill and refraining from giving any personal attention to
its conduct, but committing the entire charge of it to an agent,
exonerate themselves from those duties, or from the consequences of a failure to perform them. It was the duty of the
defendants toward their employees to keep the elevator in a
safe condition, and to repair any injury to it which would en-
danger the lives or limbs of their employees, who were lawfully and properly, and in the performance of their functions,
in the habit of using it. That duty they delegated to their
general agent. As to acts which a master or principal is
bound as such to perform toward his employees, if he dele-
gates the performance of them to an agent, the agent occupies the place of the master, and the latter is deemed present,
and liable for the manner in which they are performed. This
rule is as applicable to individuals as to corporations, and requires us to sustain the conclusion of the referee, that the defendants were responsible for the neglect of their general
agent, he having the means and power to keep the elevator in
repair, and that notice to such general agent was notice to the
defendants that the elevator was out of repair, and the defendants were consequently guilty of gross negligence in
omitting to repair it. In Malone v. Hathaway, not yet reported,
but referred to in the Albany Law Journal, vol. 13, p. 174,
the same court reversed a verdict for plaintiff where deceased,
an employee in defendant's brewery, was killed by the fall of
a mash-tub, which was proved to have been substantially re-
built and perfectly safe when deceased entered the employment,
and about eleven months before; and where the failure to
look to the supports afterward was the fault of Bagley, a co-
servant, foreman of carpenters, against whose competency and
skill nothing was alleged. Distinguishing the case from
Laning v. New York Central R. R. Co., and Flike v. Boston
and Albany R. R. Co. cases (cited *supra*), on the ground that
those were cases of corporations, which can only act by and
through servants, and from the case of Corcoran v. Holbrook,
59 N. Y. 517, on the ground that in the latter the defendants
were absent, and had delegated all their powers and devolved
all their duties upon a general agent or superintendent. And
see Brickner v. New York, &c., R. R. Co., 49 N. Y. 672;
Holmes v. Clark, 10 Wend. 405 ; Hoey v. D. & B. R. R. Co,

ingly and willfully which may injure his master's trade or undermine his business. He must not attempt to draw away his master's customers ; but there is no law which prevents him from soliciting prospective custom from them at some future period when he hopes to be able to set up in business for himself. (*u*) His possession of the master's property is, as we have already seen, the master's possession. He has in contemplation of law the mere custody of it, so that, if he is provided with a house or a lodging by the master, he may be turned out of it at any moment without any notice to quit. (*v*)

(*u*) Nichol v. Martin, 2 Esp. 734.   (*v*) Mayhew v. Suttle, *ante*

8 Id. 930 ; Hoffman v. New York, &c., R. R. Co., 55 N. Y. 608 ; Keegan v. West. R. R. Co., 8 Id. 175 ; Noyes v. Smith, 28 Vt. 59 ; Ford v. Fitchburg R. R. Co., 110 Mass. —; Snow v. Housatonic R. R. Co., 8 Allen, 441. As to when the negligence of an agent of the master, is not negligence of the master, see Faulkner v. Erie Ry. Co., 49 Barb. 328 ; Albro v. Agawam Canal Co., 6 Cush. 75 ; Hart v. Vermont, &c., Ry. Co., 32 Vt. 473 ; Wright v. New York, &c., R. R. Co., 25 N. Y. 562 ; Warner v. Erie Ry. Co., 39 Id. 468. As to contributory negligence on the part of the servant, see Spooner v. Brooklyn City R. R. Co., 31 Barb. 419 ; Nicholson v. Erie Ry. Co., 41 N. Y. 528 ; Russell v. Hudson River R. R. Co., 17 Id. 137 ; Sprong v. Boston, &c., R. R. Co., 60 Barb. 30 ; Dougan v. Champ., &c., Co., 6 Lans. 430 ; Stewart v. President, &c., 12 Allen, 58 ; Connolly v. Davidson, 15 Minn. 519 ; Wonder v. Baltimore, &c., R. R. Co., 32 Md. 411 ; Harper v. Indianapolis, &c., R. R. Co., 47 Mo. 567 ; Davis v. Detroit, &c., R. R. Co., 20 Mich. 105 ; Lalor v. Chicago, &c., R. R. Co., 52 Ill. 401 ; Chicago, &c., R. R. Co. v. Murphy, 53 Id. 336 ; and generally, Perry v. March, 25 Ala. 657 ; McGlynn v. Brodie, 31 Cal. 376 ; Corbin v. American Mills, 27 Conn. 274 ; Hayden v. Smithville, &c., Co., 29 Conn. 548 ; Pensacola, &c., R. R. Co. v. Nash, 12 Fla. 497 ; Indianapolis, &c., R. R. Co. v. Love, 10 Ind. 554, Carey v. Courcelle, 17 La. Ann. 108 ; Buzzell v. Laconia Co., 48 Me. 113 ; Harrison v. Central R. R. Co., 31 N. J. L. 293 ; Johnson v. Bruner, 6 Phil. (Pa.) 554 ; Haines v. East Tennessee, &c., R. R. Co., 3 Coldw. 222.

889. *Dismissal of skilled servants for incompetency.*—If a laborer, servant, or artisan professes to be skilled in some particular art, craft, or mystery, and has been hired as a skilled servant, and is found to be utterly incompetent to do what he has expressly or impliedly undertaken to perform, the employer is not bound to go on employing him to the end of the term, but may at once dismiss him. (*y*)

890. *Dismissal for misconduct.*—If a servant willfully disobeys or habitually neglects the just and reasonable orders of the master; if he absents himself repeatedly from the service, or refuse to perform his work, or to submit to the domestic regulations of the house, or is guilty of gross moral misconduct, or of fraudulent misrepresentation and deceit in the discharge of his duties, to the injury of his employer, (*z*) the contract may be dissolved by the master, and the servant dismissed. The following instances of misconduct and disobedience have been held to warrant a dismissal of the servant and a dissolution of the contract by the master:—Being frequently absent and often sleeping out without leave ; (*a*) pregnancy ; (*b*) assaulting a fellow maid-servant with intent to ravish her ; (*c*) refusing to work during the customary hours of labor ; (*d*) habitually neglecting to perform the duties he had undertaken to discharge; (*e*) refusing to conform to the hour of dinner; (*f*) abusing and insulting the master and disturbing the peace of his family ; (*g*) trespassing unlawfully in game preserves, after

(*y*) Horton v. McMurtry, 5 H. & N. 667 ; 29 L. J., Ex. 260.

(*z*) Harmer v. Cornelius, 5 C. B. N. S. 246 ; 28 L. J., C. P. 85.

(*a*) Robinson v. Hindman, 3 Esp. 235. As to pleading misconduct, see Burgess v. Beaumont, 7 M. & Gr. 962. Lush v. Russell, 5 Exch. 203.

(*b*) R. v. Brampton, Cald. 14, 16, 17.

(*c*) Atkin v. Acton, 4 C. & P. 208.

(*d*) Lilley v. Elwin, 11 Q. B. 742 ; 17 L. J., Q. B. 132.

(*e*) Arding v. Lomax, 24 L. J,. Ex. 80.

(*f*) Spain v. Arnott, 2 Stark. 256.

(*g*) Shaw v. Chairitie, 3 C. & K. 25.

having been cautioned and ordered not to enter them;
(*h*) enticing away the master's servants; (*i*) becoming
the father of a bastard; (*k*) seducing the master's
maid-servant; repeatedly coming home intoxicated;
(*l*) making fraudulent or grossly inaccurate entries in
account-books; (*m*) absence from the master's dwelling-house for a night to visit a sick mother against
the will of the master, and after leave of absence had
been asked for and refused; (*n*) the setting up of a
claim inconsistent with the relation of master and servant, such as a claim to be a partner; (*o*) or the assertion of rights and privileges not warranted by the contract or the nature of the service, and injurious to the
interests of the master. (*p*)   And it is apprehended
that the entertaining of guests at the master's expense,
without his knowledge and without any express or implied permission so to do, would be a good ground of
dismissal.   If a justifying cause for the dismissal exists,
the master may avail himself of it as a defense to an
action, although it may not have formed the ground
of dismissal, and although the master may not have
known of its existence at the time he discharged the
servant. (*q*)

The following instances of misconduct and disobedience of orders have been held not to constitute a
sufficient ground of dismissal and dissolution of the
contract of hiring and service without notice:—
Temporary absence without leave, producing no serious
inconvenience to the employer; (*r*) occasional inso-

(*h*) Read v. Dunsmore, 9 C. & P.
588.

(*i*) Lumley v. Gye, 2 Ell. & Bl. 216.

(*k*) R. v. Welford, Cald. 57.

(*l*) Wise v. Wilson, 1 C. & K. 662.

(*m*) Baillie v. Kell, 6 Sc. 379; 4
Bing. N. C. 638.

(*n*) Turner v. Mason, 14 M. & W.

112; 14 L. J., Ex. 311.

(*o*) Amor v. Fearon, 1 P. & D. 398.

(*p*) Lacy v. Osbaldiston, 8 C. & P.
80.

(*q*) Spotswood v. Barrow, 5 Exch.
110; 19 L. J., Ex. 226.

(*r*) Fillieul v. Armstrong, 7 Ad. &
E. 557.

lence of manners and sulkiness; occasional disobedience in matters of trifling moment, such as neglecting to come on one or two occasions when the bell rang; stopping at one hotel when ordered to stop at another; (*s*) temporary absence on customary holidays, (*t*) or for the purpose of having a severe hurt attended to (*u*) or for the purpose of procuring another situation, such absence being warranted by custom. (*v*)

891. *Discharge by order of justices.*—Servants in husbandry, laborers, miners, artificers, handycraftsmen, and workmen in various branches of trade and manufactures, are liable to be summoned by their masters before justices for absenting themselves without lawful excuse, and refusing to work and fulfill their contracts, and may, on conviction, be compelled to find security for the completion of their contract, or be fined or imprisoned. (*y*)

892. *Warning—Notice to leave.*—In the case of a yearly hiring, not made defeasible by custom or by the agreement of the parties, reasonable notice must be given on either side of the intention of determining the contract, which notice must expire with the current year of hiring, as in the case of a tenancy from year to year; but the same length of notice is not required in the case of a yearly hiring of a servant as is required in the case of a yearly hiring of land. A quarter's notice, given a quarter of a year before the expiration of the current year of hiring, would in all cases be amply sufficient; and a month's notice is often all that is required by custom and usage to de-

(*s*) Callo v. Brouncker, 4 C. & P. 518. Cussons v. Skinner, 11 M. & W. 161.

(*t*) Reg. v. Stoke, 5 Q. B. 303.

(*u*) Chandler v. Grieves, 2 H. Bl. 606 n.

(*v*) R. v. Islip, 1 Str. 423. R. v. Polesworth, 2 B. & Ald. 483.

(*y*) Re Turner, 15 L. J., M. C. 140. Burn's Justice (SERVANTS). 30 & 31 Vict. c. 141.

termine the contract and entitle the servant to
leave.

893. *Payment of wages.*—If the contract of hiring
and service leaves the amount of salary to be fixed by
a third party, an application by the clerk or servant to
such third party to fix the salary is a condition precedent to the liability of the employer. (*z*)

894. *Disability from sickness.*—If a household
servant, hired for a year or any aliquot portion of a
year, is hurt or temporarily disabled, or falls sick,
whilst doing his master's business, the master is not
entitled to make any deduction from the agreed wages
for the time that the servant was incapacitated for the
performance of his ordinary work; (*a*) but, if he has
been struck down with disease and permanently disabled, so that he can never be expected to return to his
work, the contract of hiring is dissolved, and the
master may dismiss him. (*b*)

895. *Wrongful dismissal.*—If, after having taken
the servant into his service, the master improperly
dismisses him, or prevents him by a continued system
of persecution from continuing in the service, he is
bound to make compensation to the servant for all
the damages sustained by the latter; for the law implies, from a person who contracts to pay a salary for
services for a certain term, a contract to permit those
services to be performed. (*c*)   Formerly, in certain
cases, where the servant had tendered his services, and
had been ready and willing to do his work, but had

(*z*) Owen v. Bowen, 4 C. & P. 93.

(*a*) R. v. Sudbrooke, 1 Smith, 59.
Chandler v. Grieves, 2 H. Bl. 606, n.

(*b*) Cuckson v. Stones, 1 Ell. & Ell.
248 ; 28 L. J., Q. B. 25.

(*c*) Emmens v. Elderton, *ante.* So
by the French law, Si c'est par le

fait du maître qui est le conducteur de
ces services, qu'il ne les lui rend pas,
le maître doit payer au serviteur l'année
entiere de ces services ; et il peut
même être condamné aux dammages
et intérêts du domestique.   Pothier,
Louage, No. 173, 174.

been wrongfully prevented, such tender of service and readiness and willingness to serve were considered tantamount to actual service, and he has been allowed, after the term or service has expired, to recover as for work actually done, (*d*) upon the principle stated in the Roman law, and frequently relied upon by continental jurists, that, whenever it has been agreed that one man shall do a certain act, and that another person shall pay a sum of money for the doing of it, and he who is to do the act is ready and offers to fulfill his engagement, but is prevented by the other, he has done that which is equivalent to performance, and acquires a complete right to the money. (*e*) But considerable doubt has recently been thrown on this doctrine of constructive service; and it seems to be considered that, if the servant is improperly dismissed, he ought not to keep himself in a state of readiness to serve during the residue of the term of hiring, but should endeavor to find another situation, and should sue on the special contract for the damage he has sustained by reason of the wrongful dismissal. (*f*) Where a traveler hired a courier to travel with him on the continent from the 1st of June, 1852, and the traveler renounced the contract before the time arrived, declaring that he should not go abroad, and had no occasion for the courier's services, it was held that the courier was not bound to wait for the 1st of June and

(*d*) Gandell v. Pontigny, 4 Campb. 375. Collins v. Price, 2 M. & P. 239; 5 Bing. 132. Smith v. Kingsford, 3 Sc. 279.

(*e*) 1 Dig. Lib. 50, tit. 17, l. 161. Domat. lib. 1, tit. 1, s. 4, xviii. Pothier, OBLIGATIONS, No. 212. Holt, C. J., Lancashire v. Killingworth, 1 Ld. Raym. 687. Smith v. Wilson, 8 East. 443.

(*f*) Parke, B., Emmens v. Elderton, *ante.* Fewings v. Tisdal, 1 Exch. 295. Erle, J., Goodman v. Pocock, 15 Q. B. 583. Pagani v. Gandolfi, 2 C. & P. 370. Clossman v. Lacoste, 23 L. T. R., Q. B. 91. Yelland, *ex parte*, L. R., 4 Eq. 350,

then tender his services, but that he might at once sue
for the breach of contract. (*g*)

896. *Of the month's wages in lieu of a month's
warning.*—When a defeasible yearly hiring has been
dissolved by the dismissal of the servant without
notice, the month's wages payable by custom are not,
in contemplation of law, wages for services, but a sum
to be paid as a compensation to the servant for being
turned away without notice. (*h*) [1]

897. *Damages for a wrongful dismissal—Dissolution of the contract—Wages pro ratâ.*—Whenever
one party has absolutely refused to perform his part
of the contract, he puts it in the power of the other
party, either to sue for a breach of it, or to treat the
contract as rescinded or abandoned, and sue on a
quantum meruit for the work actually done. (*i*)   If
the party elects to treat the contract as a subsisting
contract, and to sue for a breach of it he can not
afterwards go on a quantum meruit as for an abandoned contract.   If, for example, a servant hired by
the year at yearly wages, payable quarterly, brings an
action upon the contract, and recovers damages for a
wrongful dismissal, he can not afterwards maintain an
action for wages pro ratâ up to the time of his dismissal.   The damages, therefore, in the action on the
special contract should be assessed so as to include
the wages up to the time of the dismissal. (*k*)   When
the contract is for a year's service, at wages payable
yearly, the contract is entire and indivisible, and the
servant or workman can not recover from the em-

(*g*) Hochster v. De La Tour, 2 Ell. &
Bl. 678 ; 22 L. J., Q. B 455. See Frost
v. Knight, L. R., 5 Ex 322 ; ib., 7 Ex.
111 ; 39 L. J., Ex. 227 ; 41 L. J., Ex. 78.
(*h*) Fewings v. Tisdal, 1 Exch. 295 ;

17 L. J., Ex. 19.
(*i*) De Bernardy v. Harding, 8 Exch.
822. Prickett v. Badger, 1 C. B. N. S. 305.
(*k*) Goodman v. Pocock, 15 Q. B.
576 ; 19 L. J., Q. B, 410.

[1] A month's notice not necessary from the proprietor to
the carrier of a newspaper. Hallaway v. Bennett, 10 N. Y. 108.

ployer wages pro ratâ, unless the contract has been rescinded or abandoned, or has been put an end to by the exercise of a power of defeasance vested in the parties; so that, if the servant dies in the middle of the year, his personal representatives will not be entitled to recover a proportionate part of the salary in respect of the time he actually served; (*l*) and, if he is himself guilty of such misconduct as entitles the master to dissolve the contract and dismiss him from his service, he will lose all right to wages in respect of the portion of the year he has actually served. (*m*) But, if the contract is put an end to by virtue of a power of defeasance vested in either of the parties by custom or by agreement, the wages are apportionable, and the servant must be paid pro ratâ up to the time of his departure. If, however, the contract is dissolved by mutual consent, and nothing is said of by-gone services or wages not due at the time of the dissolution of the contract, no new contract arises by implication of law to pay wages pro ratâ. (*n*)

898. *Amount of wages recoverable—Deductions.* —If the amount of wages to be paid has not been settled and agreed upon by the contract, there is an implied promise on the part of the employer to pay wages according to the customary and reasonable rate of remuneration. The master can not deduct from

---

(*l*) Countess of Plymouth v. Throgmorton, Salk. 65 ; 3 Mod. 153. Cutter v. Powell. 6 T. R. 326.

(*m*) Car riens est due tanque le fin de l'an, quod nota, et le contract est entier, et ne poet ester sever. Bro. Abr. fol. 57 (LABORER), pl. 48 ; ib. fol. 170, pl. 31 ; APPORTIONMENT, 26, pl. 13. Vin. Abr. (APPORTIONMENT) 8 & 9. Spain v. Arnott. 2 Stark. N. P. 256. Huttman v. Boulnois, 2 C. & P.

512. Turner v. Robinson, 5 B. & Ad. 789. Ridgway v. Hung. M. Co., 3 Ad. & E. 171. Lilley v. Elwin, 17 L. J., Q. B. 135. Poth. Louage, No. 174.

(*n*) Lamburn v. Cruden, 2 Sc. N. R. 534 ; 2 M. & Gr. 253. Aliter, if there was no hiring for a year, or the master sends the servant away. Bailey v. Rimmell, 1 M. & W. 506. Phillips v. Jones, 1 Ad. & E. 333.

wages money paid by him to effect the servant's cure from a dangerous illness. (*o*) The wages in certain trades, moreover, can not in general be lawfully paid otherwise than in the current coin of the realm.

899. *Presumption of payment of wages.*—If a servant has left a considerable time without claiming wages, the presumption is that all the wages have been paid. (*p*) And, if it is usual, in the case of particular classes of servants and workmen, to pay the wages weekly or monthly, and many weeks or months have elapsed without any claim or demand on the part of the servant, there is a primâ facie presumption of payment. (*q*)

900. *Jurisdiction of justices.*—By the 20 Geo. 2, c. 19, the 31 Geo. 2, c. 11, the 4 Geo 4, c. 34, and the 30 & 31 Vict. c. 141, disputes between servants in husbandry, artificers, handicraftsmen, miners, colliers, pitmen, glassmen, potters, and workers in divers branches of manufacture, (*r*) and their masters, respecting the non-payment of wages, or the non-fulfillment of a contract of service, are to be heard and determined by two justices of the peace, who may examine the complainant upon oath, and make an order for the payment of such wages as shall appear to be due, provided the sum do not exceed £10 in the case of a servant, nor £5 in the case of any artificer, handicraftsman, miner, &c., (*s*) or for compensation for the non-fulfillment of the contract. (*t*) These Acts

(*o*) Sellen v. Norman, 4 C. & P. 80.

(*p*) Sellen v. Norman, 4 C. & P. 81. Evans v. Birch, 3 Campb. 10. Parke, B., Gough v. Findon, 7 Exch. 50.

(*q*) Abbott, C. J., 4 C. & P. 81 n.

(*r*) Lowther v. Radnor, Earl of, 8 East, 113. Branwell v. Penneck, 7 B. & C. 539. *Ex parte* Bailey, 23 L. J.,

M. C. 161. Domestic servants are not within these statutes, Kitchen v. Shaw, 6 Ad. & E. 729. But a dairymaid is within them, *ex parte* Hughes, 23 L. J., M. C. 138.

(*s*) Burn's Justice (SERVANTS).

(*t*) See the 30 & 31 Vict. c. 141, s. 9.

extend only to masters and servants, and not to contracts for the doing of task-work. (*u*)

901. *Dissolution of the contract by the death of the parties.*—A contract of hiring and service is dissolved by the death of the master or servant. (*v*) If the contract is made with a firm in partnership to serve the firm for a certain term, the contract is dissolved by the death of one of the partners. (*y*)

902. *Seamen's wages.*—By the 17 & 18 Vict. c. 104, a summary remedy is provided for the recovery of seamen's wages which are not to be dependent on the ship's earning freight, and, in case of the death of the seaman, are to be apportioned and paid in manner therein provided (ss. 181–204). (*z*) The master is liable, the ship is liable, and the owner is liable for the mariner's wages (*a*) When seamen enter into articles to serve for a voyage or for a certain term, a contract by the master to pay increased wages for the services they are by the articles bound to render, is nugatory and void. (*b*) A seaman's contract of service may be terminated either by final abandonment of the ship or by discharge given by the master. (*c*)

903. *Of contracts of apprenticeship.*—When the employer exercises some trade, craft or mystery, and it is made a term of the contract that he shall teach as well as employ and remunerate the servant for some specific period in return for the service rendered, the contract amounts to an apprenticeship, a term derived from the French word apprendre, to learn. Every contract to serve on the one hand, and to em-

(*u*) Lancaster v. Greaves, 9 B. & C. 628. *Ex parte* Johnson, 7 Dowl. 702. R. v. Heywood, 1 M. & S. 624.

(*v*) Farrow v. Wilson, L. R., 4 C. P. 744 ; 38 L. J., C. P. 326.

(*y*) Tasker v. Shepherd, 6 H. & N. 575 ; 30 L. J., Ex. 207.

(*z*) See also the 24 Vict. c. 10, and the 25 & 26 Vict. c. 63, s. 18, *et seq.*

(*a*) The Stephen Wright, 12 Jur. 732.

(*b*) Harris v. Carter, 23 L. J., Q. B. 295.

(*c*) The Warrior, 1 Lush. 476.

ploy and teach or instruct on the other, amounts to a
contract of apprenticeship, and must be duly stamped.
(*d*) If there is an engagement on the part of the
servant to serve and to learn, but no express or implied engagement on the part of the employer to
teach, so that no action can be maintained upon the
contract against the latter for neglecting to teach
the contract is a contract of hiring and service
only, and not a contract of apprenticeship. (*e*) It is
not necessary that the words "to learn" and "to
teach" should be used by the parties in framing their
contract ; for an agreement to take and maintain a
person "after the manner of an apprentice" will constitute an apprenticeship. Nor need the word
" apprentice " be used , for, wherever it appears to
have been the intention of the parties that the one
was to teach and the other to learn, the contract will
be a contract of apprenticeship, whatever may be the
words used to express that intention. (*f*) As the
contract is always made to last for more than one year,
it must be authenticated by writing, signed by the
party to be charged therewith. By the 5 Eliz. c. 4, s.
25, the binding of an apprentice for the purpose of
exercising trades was required to be made by indenture ; but now by the 54 Geo. 3, c. 96, s. 2, it is enacted that it shall be lawful for any person to take or
retain or become an apprentice, though not according
to the 25th, 30th, and 41st sections of the statute of
Elizabeth, and that indentures, deeds, and agreements
in writing entered into for that purpose, which would
be otherwise invalid and ineffectual, shall be valid and
effectual ; but it is provided that the enactment shall

(*d*) R. v. Nether Knutsford, 1 B. &   (*e*) R. v. Shinfield, 14 East, 541. R.
Ad. 726.   v. Burbach, 1 M. & S. 370.

(*f*) R. v. Wishford, 5 N. & M. 540

not affect the immemorial customs of towns or by-laws of corporations. It is essential to the validity of the contract that the consideration or premium be duly set forth upon the face of the instrument, in order that the proper amount of stamp duty may be secured thereon. (*g*)   An indenture of apprenticeship is sufficiently executed by the apprentice desiring a bystander to write his name for him opposite the seal, and by· his then taking the deed and delivering it to his master. (*h*)

904. *Rights and liabilities of parties to indentures of apprenticeship.*—An infant above the age of fourteen, and unmarried, is by the custom of London responsible upon covenants contained in indentures of apprenticeship executed by him just the same as if he were of full age; (*i*) but he is by the common law, where the apprenticeship is not within the city of London, exempt from all liability ex contractu, by reason of his minority.   Therefore it is that his friends ordinarily become bound for his faithful service and good conduct during the period of the apprenticeship. The parties who covenant for the continued service and good conduct of an infant apprentice are not responsible upon their covenants for trifling and pardonable instances of misconduct, such as staying out on Sunday evenings half an hour beyond the time allowed, (*k*) or for temporary absence and disobedience of orders, unattended by substantial injury to the master.   But for all gross misconduct and repeated or lengthened absence producing substantial injury to the master they will be held responsible; and, if an infant apprentice, who has executed indentures of

(*g*) R. v. ·Keynsham, 5 East, 311. Westlake v. Adams, 5 C. B. N. S. 248 ; 27 L. J., C. P. 271.

(*h*) R. v. Longnor, 4 B. & Ad. 649. (*i*) Burton v. Palmer, 2 Bulstr. 192. (*k*) Wright v. Gihon, 3 C. & P. 583.

apprenticeship, avoids the contract on his coming of age, and refuses to continue in the service of his master, they are bound to make good whatever damage is sustained by the latter by reason of such repudiation of the contract. (*l*) The sickness of the apprentice, or his incapacity to serve and to learn by reason of ill-health or an accident, does not discharge the master from his covenant to provide for him and to maintain him, inasmuch as the latter takes him for better and for worse, and must minister to his necessities in sickness as well as in health. (*m*) If the master has covenanted to teach three trades, and ceases to carry on one of them, he is guilty of a breach of contract, and the apprentice may, if he pleases, refuse to continue to serve. (*n*) [1]

905. *Misconduct of the apprentice—Dissolution of the contract.*—The same amount of misconduct which, in the case of a contract of hiring and service, would authorize the master to dissolve the contract and discharge the servant, will not release him from

---

(*l*) Cuming v. Hill, 3 B. & Ald. 59.   (*n*) Ellen v. Topp, 6 Exch. 424 ; 20
(*m*) R. v. Hales Owen, 1 Str. 99.   L. J., Ex., 241.
Reg. v. Smith, 8 C. & P. 153.

[1] See as to apprentices in the United States; Owen v. State, 48 Ala. 338; People v. New York Juvenile Asylum, 2 Thomp. & C. 775; Bardwell v. Parrington, 107 Mass. 419; Cannon v. Stuart, 3 Houst. 223; Commonwealth v. Atkinson, 8 Phil. 375; Cann v. Williams, 3 Houst. 78; Mitchell v. McElvin, 45 Ga. 558; Howry v. Calloway, 48 Miss. 587; People v. Hoster, 14 Abb. Pr. (N. S.) 414; Ford v. McVay, 55 Ill. 119; Cockran v. State, 46 Ala. 714; Maddox v. State, 32 Ind. 111; Timmins v. Lacy, 30 Dex. 115; Doane v. Covel, 56 Me. 527; Fisher v. Lunger, 33 N. J. L. (4 Vroom) 100; Briggs v. Harris, 64 N. C. 413; Mather v. Turner, 1 Abb. Pr. (N. S.) 84. A master who takes an apprentice for the purpose of instructing him in any particular art or trade, has no right to require services of him as a menial or house servant; Commonwealth v. Hemperley. 4 Pa. L. J. R. 440.

liability upon his covenant in an indenture of apprenticeship. (*o*)   But, if the apprentice is guilty of such an amount of misconduct as renders it impracticable for the master to maintain, employ, and teach him, according to the terms of the indentures, the master can not be sued for neglecting to perform his covenants in that behalf, inasmuch as the capability and willingness of the apprentice to be instructed, maintained, and provided for by the master are naturally conditions precedent to the liability of the latter upon such covenants. (*p*) If the apprentice deserts the master's service and enlists in the army, or contracts another relation which disables him from lawfully returning to his master, the latter is not bound to receive him back and instruct him if he returns. (*q*)   " By the custom of London it is a sufficient cause for a master to turn away his apprentice if he frequents gaming houses," although gaming may not be expressly prohibited by the indentures. (*r*)   If the fulfillment of the contract has not been prevented by the wrongful act of the master, the latter is not bound to refund any portion of the premium he has received. (*s*)   The indentures of apprenticeship of an infant apprentice may be avoided by the infant, so far as regards his own personal liability on the contract, on his coming of age ; and the master must trust for the continuance of the service thereunder to the covenants of those who engage for the infant, unless the binding is under the

(*o*) Winston v. Lynn, 2 D. & R. 475 ; 1 B. & C. 460.   Wise v. Wilson, 1 C. & K. 669.   Phillips v. Clift, 4 H. & N. 168 ; 28 L. J., Ex. 153.

(*p*) Mercer & Whall. 5 Q. B. 447–466 ; 14 L. J., Q. B. 267.   Rayment or Raymond v. Minton, L. R. 1 Ex.

244 ; 35 L. J., Ex. 153.   Brown v. Banks, 3 Giff. 190.

(*q*) Hughes v. Humphreys, 9 D. & R. 721 ; 6 B. & C. 680.

(*r*) Woodroffe v. Farnham, 2 Vern. 290.

(*s*) Cuff v. Brown, 5 Pr. 297.

authority of an act of parliament. (*t*)   The contract
may also be dissolved by cancelling the indentures,
or by giving them up with the consent of all parties
animo cancellandi ; likewise by the death of the master or of the apprentice, (*u*) or by the bankruptcy of the
master. (*x*)   If the master dies during the term, his
representatives are not bound to return any part of the
premium, as there is only a partial failure of consideration ; (*y*) and, if the apprentice becomes permanently
ill, the covenant that he shall serve during the term is
discharged. (*z*)

906. *Discharge by award of justices.*—The contract may also be dissolved by an award of justices at
quarter session for the county, if the master resides in
a county, or of a mayor or other head officer of a
borough, with the assent of three other of his brethren
or men of best reputation therein, if the master resides
within a borough, who may also in certain cases order
all or any portion of the premium paid with such
apprentice to be refunded. (*a*)

907. *Damages for refusing to employ and for
wrongful dismissal.*—If a master or employer renoun-
ces the contract he has made with a workman or
servant, and deprives him of the means of earning the
stipulated remuneration, or refuses to take him into
his employ, the jury, in assessing the damages, are
justified in looking to all that has happened, or is
likely to happen, to increase or mitigate the loss of
the plaintiff down to the time of trial. (*b*)   If an

(*t*) *Ex parte* Davis, 5 T. R. 715. *Ex
parte* Gill, 7 East, 376.

(*u*) Baxter v. Burfield, 2 Str. 1266.
32 Geo. 3, c. 57.

(*x*) 32 & 33 Vict. c. 71, s. 33.

(*y*) Whincup v. Hughes, L. R. 6
C. P. 78; 40 L. J., C. P. 104.

(*z*) Boast v. Firth, L. R., 4 C. P. 1 ;
38 L. J., C. P. 1.

(*a*) Finley v. Jowle, 12 East, 248.
Re Gray, 2 D. & L. 539.

(*b*) Hochster v. De La Tour, 22 L.
J., Q. B. 455. Lake v. Campbell, 4
Law T. R. N. S. 582.

action is brought by a domestic servant for a dismissal without the customary month's notice, a month's wages are recoverable as the agreed damages.[1] If the contract is not defeasible by giving a month's notice, but is for a year's service, and the defendant is improperly discharged before the end of the year, he may recover for the work actually done by him up to the time of his dismissal, and for the damage he has sustained by being prevented from continuing his services and earning the stipulated hire. (c)[2] The action may be brought as soon as the dismissal takes place; and the measure of damages is an indemnity to the plaintiff for the loss he sustains by the breach. If he has found other equally eligible employment the damages would be small; but if not, they might far exceed the salary agreed to be paid. (d)

908. *Damages against apprentices.*—Where an action was brought upon a covenant in an apprenticeship deed to recover damages for the loss of the services of the apprentice, it was held that damages were recoverable only up to the time of action brought as

(c) Cutter v. Powell, 2 Smiths' L. C. 20.

(d) Emmens v. Elderton, 4 H. L. C. 645.

[1] See *ante*, §§ 887, 900.

[2] So, too, a conspiracy to obtain from a master mechanic whose business requires the employment of workmen, money which he is under no legal liability to pay, by inducing, or threatening to induce, workmen to leave his employment, and deterring, or threatening to deter, others from entering it, so as to render him reasonably apprehensive that he can not carry on business without making the payment, is illegal; and in an action of tort he may recover the sum so paid, and damages for the injury of his business by the acts of the conspirators; but whether he can recover back the sum paid, in an action of contract, as money had and received to his use, quære. Carew v. Rutherford, 106 Mass. 1. And all the members of a society upholding a strike are guilty of conspiracy. Commonwealth v. Currea, 3 Pittsb. 143.

the contract continued in force, and the apprentice might still be compelled to serve. (*e*)[1]

SECTION III.

PRINCIPAL AND AGENT.

909. *Of agencies and commissions.*—Whenever one man undertakes the management of the business of another without hire or reward, and enters upon his task, the contract between the parties is, as we have before seen, a contract of mandate, or a gratuitous commission.[2] When the person employed is to be paid for his services, the contract is a contract for the letting and hiring of work and labor, care and attention, and belongs to the class locatio operis faciendi.[3] If the services of the party are hired for a term, the contract is a contract of hiring and service.[4] In either case the party employing is the principal, and the person employed, the agent. If a commission-agent is engaged to sell goods for the principal, he paying him a certain sum per quarter, it does not necessarily follow that there is a contract of hiring and service between the parties. (*a*)

910. *Revocation of authority.*—If no term of service has been expressly or impliedly agreed upon, the employer may at any time dispense with the future services of the agent, and revoke the authority delegated to him, so far as it relates to things to be done

(*e*) Lewis v. Peachy, 1 H. & C. 518 ; 31 L. J., Ex. 496.
(*a*) Butterfield v. Marler, 3 C. & K. 163.

[1] See cases cited *ante*, note 1, p. 602.
[2] *Ante*, §§ 789, 833, *et seq.*
[3] *Ante*, § 845½.
[4] *Ante*, § 822.

and remaining unexecuted.[1]   If a party is engaged as a "permanent attorney," the word "permanent" does not confer any durable or special appointment as attorney, and the principal is not precluded from withdrawing the retainer; but if he is retained at a yearly salary, he is, in general, entitled to damages, if he is

---

[1] Blackstone v. Buttermore, 53 Pa. St. 260. Saving the rights of third persons; Wharton's Commentaries on Agency and Agents, § 93; and the revocation may be by parol, even if the authority given were under seal; see Brookshire v. Brookshire, 8 Ired. 74; Pickler v. State, 18 Ind. 266; Spear v. Gardner, 16 La. Ann. 383; and this revocation may be implied as well as express; Torre v. Thiele, 25 La. Ann. 418. As if a principal himself perform the duties formerly entrusted to the agent, or appoint another agent for the same purpose, and in the same place, these would be facts from which a revocation might be inferred. The revocation takes effect from the time when it becomes known to the agent; Robertson v. Cloud, 47 Miss. 208; and see Jones v. Hopkins, 61 Me. 780. So if the revocation were contained in a letter, it would take effect from the date of his receipt, and not of the mailing of the letter. Robertson v. Cloud, *supra*. Notice of the death of a principal is not a notice to the agent of revocation of the agency, if the rights of third parties in any way intervene, as where the agent has executed a bona fide contract for his principal, or is engaged in directing a lawsuit, or mercantile transactions, which cannot be abruptly terminated, or where the subject-matter of the agency is to begin upon the principal's death. Wharton's Commentaries on Agency and Agents, § 101. Third parties are not bound by the revocation, until they have received notice thereof. Diversy v. Kellogg, 44 Ill. 114; Morgan v. Still, 5 Binn. 305; Tier v. Thompson, 35 Vt. 179; Weile v. United States, 7 Ct. and Cl. 535; Beard v. Kirk, 11 N. H. 397; Fellows v. Hastford, &c. Steamboat Co., 38 Conn. 197; Reed v. Latham, 40 Id. 452; Watts v. Cavanagh, 35 Vt. 34. So the Roman law provided that "Despensatori qui ignorante debitore remotus est ab actu recte solvitur ex voluntate enim domini ei salvitur, quam si nescit mutatem qui salvit liberatur; Dig. Lib. 51, D. de Sol. et. lib. XLVI. 3.   And the revocation of an agent's authority revokes all the authority of sub-agents.   Story on Agency, § 469.

dismissed before the end of the year. (*b*)   Things actually done by the agent in the execution of his commission will, of course, be binding upon the principal;
but the agent can not, after his authority has been
countermanded, enter, as between himself and the principal, into any fresh transaction.   If the principal furnishes his agent with a sum of money, to be expended
in the purchase of property, the principal may at any
time, before the purchase is made and the money expended, revoke the authority, and require the money
to be repaid to him. (*c*)   If goods are intrusted to a
commission-agent for sale, the principal may, at any
time before a sale has been made, require the goods
to be returned to him; (*d*) and the agent has no right
to sell contrary to the express directions or instructions
of his employer, for the purpose of repaying himself
his advances. (*e*)   But the right to stop money intrusted to an agent to be paid to a third party, or to
stop a sale, or revoke the orders or authority given, is
always subject to this limitation that the agent is
merely an agent, and is not himself interested in, or
responsible for, the payment of the money according
to the directions he received when it was placed in his
hands, (*f*) and has not done anything to render himself personally liable to the third party in consequence
of the orders of the principal. (*g*)   But mere advances
made by a factor do not give him any rights in dero-
gation of the right of the principal to give directions
as to the time and manner of sale, unless such rights
are conferred upon the factor by some express agree-

(*b*) Emmens v. Elderton, 13 C. B.
495; 4 H. L. C. 624.

(*c*) Fletcher v. Marshall, 15 M. &
W. 763.

(*d*) Raleigh v. Atkinson, 6 M. & W.
670.

(*e*) Smart v. Sandars, 3 C. B. 380;
16 L. J., C. P. 39.   Chinnock v Sains-
bury, 30 L. J., Ch. 409.

(*f*) Yates v. Hoppe, 9 C. B. 541.

(*g*) M'Ewen v. Woods, 11 Q. B. 13;
17 L. J., Q. B. 207.

ment, or by a known usage of trade. (*h*) If an agent agrees to act for a firm in partnership for a term of years, the contract is dissolved by the death of one of the partners during the term. (*i*)

911. *When the agent's authority is irrevocable.*— An authority coupled with an interest can not be revoked.[1] Where, therefore, a debtor handed to his creditor a power of attorney, authorizing him to sell certain lands of the debtor, and pay the debt out of the proceeds of the sale, it was held that this power of attorney could not be revoked. (*k*)[2]

912. *Accounts.*—It is the duty of an agent to keep regular accounts and vouchers; (*l*)[3] and, if he refuses to account, after demand is made, he will be responsi-

(*h*) De Comas v. Prost, 2 Moo. P. C., N. S. 158.

(*i*) Tasker v. Shepherd, 6 H. & N. 676 ; 30 L. J., Ex. 207.

(*k*) Gaussen v. Morton, 10 B. & C. 731. Clerk v. Laurie, 2 H. & N. 200.

(*l*) Romilly M. R. Stainton v. The Carron Co., 24 Beav. 353.

[1] See Hartley's Appeal, 53 Pa. St. 212 ; Marfield v. Goodhue, 3 Comst. 62 ; Hutchins v. Hibbard, 34 N. Y. 24 ; Hunt v. Ronsmaniere, 8 Wheat. 174 ; Knapp v. Alford, 10 Paige, 205 ; Manfield v. Douglass, 1 Sandf. 360 ; Smyth v. Craig, 3 Watts, & S. 14. So in case of an assignment to pay debts, the power can not be revoked until the trust is performed and satisfied. Goodwin v. Bowden, 54 Me. 424. But if the consideration for the interest fail, the power can be revoked; *Ex parte* Smither, 1 Deac. 413. The fact that the principal and agent are partners, will not, of itself, render the agency irrevocable. Travers v. Crane, 15 Cal. 127 ; Gundlach v. Fischer, 59 Ill. 172 ; Potter v. Merchants' Bank, 28 N. Y. 641 ; Blackstone v. Buttermore, 53 Pa. St. 266 ; Barr v. Schroeder, 32 Cal. 609.

[2] But see Coffin v. Landis, 46 Pa. St. 426 ; Peacock v. Cummings, Id. 434.

[3] Riley v. State, 22 Tex. 703 ; Chinn v. Chinn, 22 La. Ann. 597 ; Kerfoot v. Hyman, 52 Ill. 502 ; Hass v. Damon, 9 Iowa, 589 ; Clark v. Moody, 17 Mass. 145 ; Hart v. Ten Eyck, 2 Johns. Ch. 108 ; Peterson v. Porguard, 9 B. Mon. 309 ; Eston v. Welton, 32 N. H. 352 ; Clark v. Moody, 19 Mass. 145.

ble in damages. (*m*) [1]   If goods have been intrusted
to an agent to sell, and he renders no account of
them, it will be presumed primâ facie, that they may
have been sold and the money received. (*n*) [2]   If an
agent mixes up his principal's property with his own
he must show clearly what part of the property belongs
to him ; and, if he fails in doing so, it will be treated
as the property of the principal. (*o*) [3]

913. *Liabilities of brokers, factors, and commission-agents, to their principals.*— All persons are
brokers who contrive, make, and conclude bargains
and contracts between merchants and tradesmen for
which they have a "fee or reward." (*p*) [4]   Every

(*m*) Topham v. Braddick, 1 Taunt. 575.

(*n*) Hunter v. Welsh, 1 Stark. 224.

(*o*) Storey's Eq. Jur. § 468.

(*p*) Milford v. Hughes, 16 M. & W. 177.

[1] In Haas v. Damon, 9 Iowa, 589, it is said that, failing
upon reasonable opportunity to account, he is liable to such
suit without demand ; and if, after demand, he retain moneys
received, he is liable for such moneys, with interest, even if he
has received no interest. Dodge v. Perkins, 9 Pick. 368 ;
Reid v. Glass Factory, 3 Com. 393 ; Comegys v. State, 10 Gill
& J. 175 ; Williams v. Storr, 6 Johns. Ch. 653 ; Leake v.
Sutherland, 25 Ark. 219 ; Bedell v. Janney, 4 Gilman, 193 ;
Clemens v. Caldwell, 7 B. Mon. 171 ; Anderson v. State, 2
Kelly, 370 ; Dodge v. Perkins, 9 Peck, 368 ; Utica Co. v.
Lynch, 11 Paige, 520 ; Brown v. Ricketts, 4 Johns. Ch. 303 ;
Jacot v. Emmett, 11 Paige, 142.

[2] Wharton's Commentaries on Agency and Agents, § 301.

[3] Norris v. Hero, 22 La. Ann. 605 ; Curtwell v. Allard, 7
Bush. 482 ; Graver's Estate, 50 Pa. St. 189 ; Bartlet v. Hamilton, 46 Me. 425 ; Manning v. Manning, 1 Johns. C. 527 ; Massachusetts Ins. Co. v. Carpenter, 2 Sweeney, 734 ; De Peyster
v. Clarkson, 2 Wend. 77 ; Peyton v. Smith, 2 Dev. & Bat. Eq.
325 ; Farmer's Bank v. King, 57 Pa. St. 202 ; Pinckney v.
Dunn, 2 S. C. 314 ; Kerr v. Laird, 27 Miss. 544 ; Dyott's Estate, 2 Watts. & Serg. 565 ; Farmers' Bank v. King, 57 Pa. St.
202.

[4] See Wharton's Commentaries on Agency and Agents,
§ 700.

broker and commission-agent who is employed to make purchases, or to sell on behalf of his principal, impliedly promises to execute the commission intrusted to him in a careful, skillful, and diligent manner, and to obey the orders and directions he receives.[1] If he is ordered to purchase an article of first rate quality, and he buys an inferior commodity, he is guilty of a breach of contract, and is responsible to the principal in damages. (*q*) He is bound to exercise his judgment and discretion to the best advantage for the benefit of his principal,[2] to render just and true accounts,[3] and to keep the property of his principal unmixed with his own property, or the property of other parties. (*r*)[4] He has, in general, an implied authority to sell at such time and for such prices as he may, in the exercise of his discretion, think best for his employer; he may sell on credit, if it is customary so to do,[5] or if he acts under a del credere commission; and he

---

(*q*) Mainwaring v. Brandon 2 Moore, 125.

(*r*) Clarke v. Tipping, 9 Beav. 284.

Thom v. Bigland, 8 Exch. 725. Gray v. Haig, 20 Beav. 238.

[1] Brokers have implied authority to do whatever is necessary to the purpose or subject-matter of their appointment. The Monte Allegre, 9 Wheat. 643; Andrews v. Kneeland, 6 Cow. 354; Saladin v. Mitchell, 45 Ill. 79; but see Dodd v. Farlow, 11 Allen, 420; Pickering v. Demerrett, 100 Mass. 416; Day v. Holmes, 103 Id. 306; State v. Delafield, 8 Paige, 524; Bank of the State v. Bugbee, 1 Abb. App. Dec. (N. Y.) 86; Parsons v. Martin, 11 Gray, 111.

[2] A broker can not act by substitute, but, like an attorney, is selected for some cause of preference, as confidence in his skill or sagacity; but the mechanical part of his duties may be performed by a clerk or employee. Lock's Appeal, 72 Pa. St. 491.

[3] See *ante*, note ——

[4] See Evans v. Wahn, 71 Pa. St. 69.

[5] See *ante*,

must account for the produce of all sales effected by him when called upon so to do. (*s*) He can not himself become the purchaser of the property entrusted to him to sell, unless he deals for it with the principal, openly and fairly "at arm's length," and after a full disclosure of everything he knows concerning it; (*t*)' nor can he purchase his own goods for his principal (*u*)² Where an agent employed to sell land sold it to a company in which he was interested as a shareholder and director, it was held that he was entitled to no commission from his employer in respect of the sale. (*x*)

If money has been paid by a principal to his brokers to enable them to carry out a contract which he had authorized, and which, at the time of such payment, he believed them to have entered into on his account, whereas, in truth, the authorized contract had never been made, the principal may recover the money from the agents. (*y*)

A mere forwarding agent is not bound to see whether the quality of goods, which he is employed to ship or to forward, corresponds with a contract

(*s*) Crosskey v. Mills, 1 C. M. & R. 298. Boorman v. Brown, 3 Q. B. 515, 527. Boden v. French, 10 C. B. 886.

(*t*) Murphy v. O'Shea, 2 Jones & Lat. 422. Trevelyan v. Charter, 9 Beav. 140.

(*u*) Bentley v. Craven, 18 Beav. 76.

(*v*) Salomans v. Pender, 3 H. & C. 639; 34 L. J., Ex. 95.

(*y*) Bostock v. Jardine, 3 H. & C. 700; 34 L. J. Ex. 142.

¹ See *ante*, ——

² Id. And see Taussig v. Hart, 58 N. Y. 425. It has been held, however, that where a principal agrees with his agent to pay him a specified sum for a piece of land, the agent may make the best bargain he can for the land, if there be no fraud. Anderson v. Wieser, 24 Iowa, 428. But, as a general rule, any usage by which an agent claims to appropriate the profts of his principal, is forbidden, and fraudulent on the agent's part.

which he has been instrumental in negotiat-
ing. (*z*)

914. *Del credere commissions.*—When the agent,
in consideration of an addition commission, guarantees to his principal, the payment of all debts that
become due through his agency to the principal, he is
said to act under a del credere commission, a phrase
derived from the Italian word credere, to trust. (*a*)
Every person accepting and acting under a commission of this sort for the sale of goods makes himself
responsible for the solvency of his vendees, and becomes absolutely liable to the principal for the payment of the price of the goods he sells. (*b*)   Factors
and commission-agents for sale, who receive and sell
goods for foreign principals, or for parties residing
at a distance, usually conduct their agency under a
del credere commission, guaranteeing the solvency of
the buyers, or undertaking for the due payment of the
price realized on sales effected by them.   Their contract, however, is not a contract or promise, as we
have seen, to answer for the debt or default of another
within the meaning of the statute of frauds, but an
original independent contract, and only another form
of selling goods. (*c*)   Where a factor having a del
credere commission has made advances to his principal, and has sold goods on account of the latter, he
can not, whether he has received the proceeds of the
sale or not, recover from the principal so much of the
advances as is covered by the price of the goods,
unless there is an express agreement between them,
making the advances payable immediately, and post--

(*z*) Zuilchenbart v. Alexander, 1 B.
B. & S. 234 ; 29 L. J., Q. B. 236 ; 30
ib., Q. B. 254.

(*a*) Grove v. Dubois, 1 T. R. 12.

(*b*) Mackenzie v. Scott, 6 Bro. P. C.
291.

(*c*) Couturier v. Hastie, 8 Exch. 40.
Wickham v. Wickham, 2 Kay & J.
478.

poning the time of payment of the price of the goods,
(*d*) A person to whom goods are sent to be sold
and who is at liberty to sell them at any price he
pleases, he paying a fixed price for them to the owner,
is not an agent. (*e*)[1]

(*d*) Graham v. Ackroyd, 10 Hare,   (*e*) White, *ex parte*, L. R. 6 Ch. 397.
202.

[1] The effect of a del credere commission is to render the factor responsible to his principal, in the first instance, and when
the principal employs a factor or broker to sell for him, under
a del credere commission, he wishes it to be understood that he
looks to him for payment, and that he has no objection to recovering the price from the vendee. The rules of law, as
they regard principal and factor, are for the benefit of the
principal and, provided he appears before payment, he comes
into his full rights to receive the price, and the vendee will
not be justified in afterwards paying the factor; but after the
principal has dealt with the factor as the real purchaser of the
goods, which, by the del credere commission, he may be considered to have done, the factor then stands in the situation
of a principal, and, in that character, he sells to the buyer on
his own account. The commission del credere is an authority
to the factor to receive the price, and so long as the principal
does not interfere and countermand that authority, the factor
has a right to treat the vendee as his debtor, and is the person
warranted to receive the price from the vendee. If it were
otherwise, in what a situation would the factor be placed; he
would still be liable, under his del credere commission, to his
employer, and yet not have the means of getting the money
into his own hands, by calling on the buyer. And it is the
same thing whether the factor acts under a commission del
credere, or is in advance of his principal by actual payments.
Livermore on Prin. & Agent, 227.

   " In this country, the guaranty of a del credere agent," said
MITCHEL, J., in Sherwood v. Stone, 14 N. Y. (4 Kernan)
267, " is understood to be a contract directly with the principal to pay him on the expiration of the time of credit,
whether the purchaser be solvent or not; that is, the whole
contract between the factor and his principal, and it is an
original undertaking, without any relation to the debt or liability of another. The law (not the contract of the parties)
then adds a quality to such a transaction, that, although the

915. *Liabilities of insurance-brokers to their principals.*—If an insurance-broker neglects to attend to the orders of his principal, or is guilty of miscon-

---

factor may sue the purchaser in his own name, the principal has also the right to sue. This however, does not convert an express original undertaking of the factor with his principal, absolutely to pay the debt at maturity, into a collateral and conditional agreement to pay it if the purchaser does not. A guaranty by a factor differs very especially from a promise to pay the debt at maturity, into a collateral and conditional agreement to pay it if the purchaser does not. A guaranty by a factor differs very especially from a promise to pay the debt of another, in another particular ; the principal transfers a right (although not the exclusive right) to the factor to sue for and recover the money in his own name, and to collect the debt and hold the money, accounting only for the net balance of account between the parties. Thus the debt of the purchaser is, to some extent, made the property of the factor, and he, to that extent, becomes the purchaser of it, and so far substitutes his liability in place of that of the purchaser. The effect of this generally is to make the factor practically the owner of the debt, and this is almost invariably so, if he remains solvent and on just terms with his principal. In that case, the principal is unknown to the purchaser."

A del credere factor guarantees the solvency of the purchaser only, and if they pay the price to him, his contract does not extend further to a guarantee of the remittance. Leverick v. Meigs, 1 Cow. 645; Heubach v. Mollman, 2 Duer, 227; Colton v. Dunham, Paige, 267; Swan v. Nesmith, 7 Pick. (Mass.) 220.

It is a general rule of law that a sale by a factor creates a contract between the principal and the purchaser, and that the debt created by the sale is a debt due from the purchaser to the principal. The exception to this rule seems to arise in the case of factors under a del credere commission ; that commission giving rise to, and being, in effect, a contract of guaranty between the factor as guarantor, and the principal as guarantee, which guarantee becomes binding upon the factor, of course, upon default, absolute; or the inability or incapacity to pay upon the part of the purchaser. The consideration of this contract of guaranty is usually an increased commission to the factor, or it perhaps might be other good or valuable interest.

duct and negligence in effecting an insurance, he will be responsible for all the damage that has been sustained by his employer, and may be clothed with all the re-

The effect of the commission is, however, limited to this contract of guaranty to the principal himself. It in no sense operates to extinguish the ordinary relation between principal and agent, being matter in addition thereto, and not in variation thereof, or subtraction therefrom. The peculiar obligation of the del credere factor to his principal is therefore not primary, but secondary. He is a surety only, and not a debtor. (See this questioned, however, in Edwards on Bailments, 280, 281; Dunlap's Paley on Agency, 110, note; Hurlbut v. Pacific Ins. Co., 2 Sumn. 480.) Punctual payment by the purchaser discharges him from all liability. Neither is his engagement regarded as a collateral promise to pay the debt of another under the statute of frauds. Nor is his obligation so contingent as to require legal measures to be exhausted against the purchaser, before the factor is bound. It amounts to, and is, an engagement to see that the principal receives his money upon the day it becomes due. And this not merely by the receipt of acceptances from the buyer, but by the absolute payment in money or other medium authorized by or satisfactory to the principal. Story on Agency, §§ 98, 215; McKenzie v. Scott, 6 Bro. Parl. Cas. 280; Paley on Agency, by Lloyd, 41, 42; Muller v. Bohlens, 2 Wash. C. C. 378; Tompkins v. Perkins, 3 Mason, 232; Holbrook v. Wight, 24 Wend. 169; 2 Kent's Com. [12th ed.] 625, note (g).

But if the money is once received from the purchaser by the factor, any peculiarity in his position and responsibility ceases, and he becomes an ordinary factor, liable only for due diligence in remitting to his principal. Story on Agency, § 215; Leverick v. Meigs, 1 Cow. (N. Y.) 645; Mackenzie v. Scott, *ubi supra;* Livermore on Agency, 408-411 (ed. 1818); Smith on Merc. Law, 52 (2d ed), Id. ch. 5, § 2, p. 98 (3d ed. 1843); Russel on Factors, art. Del Credere Commission; Sherwood v. Stone, 14 N. Y. 267; Bradley v. Richardson, 23 Vt. 720, 731.

A factor del credere may sue the debtor in his own name. Sherwood v. Stone, *ubi supra;* though see Bramble v. Spiller, 18 W. R. 316; see Dunlap's Paley, note, p. 110,—but if he elect so to do, the principal may, in spite of the del credere commission, sue the purchaser himself. Wolff v. Koppel, 5

sponsibilities which would have devolved upon the underwriter had the insurance been regularly effected.[1] He may be compelled to pay to his principal the full sum ordered to be insured, or a total or average loss, as the case may be; but, when he is proceeded against for losses by perils which he ought to have insured against, he is, of course, entitled to every benefit and objection which the underwriter himself could have taken advantage of if the insurance had been duly effected, such as fraud, deviation, non-compliance with warranties, or the like. (*f*) He is bound, moreover, to exercise a reasonable and proper amount of care, skill and judgment in the execution of his duty. (*g*) If a merchant abroad has effects in the hands of his correspondent here, he has a right to expect that the latter will obey an order to insure, because he is entitled to call his money out of the other's hands when and in what manner he pleases; and, although he has no effects, yet, if the course of dealing between them be such that the one has been used to send orders for insurance, and the other to comply with them, the former has a right to expect that his orders for insurance will still be obeyed

(*f*) Park v. Hammond, 2 Marsh. 191.   Mallough v. Barber, 4 Campb. 150.   Turpin v. Bilton, 6 Sc. N. R. 447.

(*g*) Chapman v. Walton, 10 Bing. 57; 3 M. & Sc. 389.   Cahill v. Dawson, 26 L. J., C. P. 253.

Hill. (N. Y.), 458; Holbrook v. Wight, 24 Wend. 169; Thompson v. Parkins, 3 Mason, 232; Gall v. Comber, 7 Taunt, 558; Peele v. Northcote, 7 Taunt. 478; Morris v. Cleasby, 4 M. & Selwyn, 566.

[1] French v. Reed, 6 Binn. 308. But not if he has merely made a loose gratuitous promise to insure. Thorn v. Deas, 4 Johns. R. 84; McGee v. Bast, 6 J. J. Marsh, 456. Insurance brokers have the same implied authority with others to do whatever is necessary to their employment, so they may abandon in case of loss. Chesapeake Ins. v. Stark, 6 Cranch. 268.

unless he receives notice to the contrary. If the merchant abroad sends bills of lading to his correspondent here, he may ingraft on them an order to insure, as the implied condition on which the bills of lading shall be accepted, which the other must obey if he accept them, for it is one entire transaction. (*h*) If the broker finds that he is unable to effect an insurance upon the terms offered by the principal, it is his duty to give the latter notice of the fact. If he makes the insurance on terms different from those prescribed he will be responsible to the principal. (*i*) But, if insufficient orders are sent, and the agent or broker does all that is usual to get the insurance effected, that is sufficient. (*k*) The insurance-broker is agent for both parties; first, for the assured, in effecting the policy, and in everything that is to be done in consequence of it; then he is agent for the underwriter as to the premium, but for nothing else. If he neglects to pay the premium to the underwriter, the latter may maintain an action for its recovery, unless circumstances have occurred entitling the insured to a return of the premium, in which case it is the duty of the broker, if he has notice thereof, to retain the money and return it to the insurer. (*l*) If he has acted as the agent of the underwriter in paying the loss upon the policy, the payment by the broker is a payment by the underwriter himself. (*m*) It is the usage, amongst merchants, insurance-brokers, and underwriters, in the city of London, to set off the general balance of accounts between the broker and the underwriter, at the time of the loss, against the loss,

---

(*h*) Smith v. Lascelles, 2 T. R. 189. Corlett v. Gordon, 3 Campb. 472.

(*i*) Callander v. Oelrichs, 6 Sc. 761.

(*k*) Smith v. Cologan, 2 T. R. 188, n.

(*l*) Shee v. Clarkson, 12 East, 507.

(*m*) Edgar v. Bumstead, 1 Campb. 410. Jamison v. Swainstone, 2 ib. 547, n.

and for the broker then to debit himself to that amount in his account with the assured, and the underwriter is then considered to be discharged of his debt to the assured ; and, when the assured is cognizant of this course of dealing, and assents to it, the passing of the accounts between the broker, the underwriter, and the assured, operates as a payment to the latter, and as an extinguishment of the.underwriter's debt. (*n*)   The broker now keeps two accounts with underwriters, called the credit and the cash accounts, into which the premiums received from the principals of the broker go, and the balance on which is due from the broker to the underwriter, and in no way from the individual assured, whose particular premium has gone into that account. (*o*)   The authority given to a broker when he is to effect a policy of insurance does not extend to warrant him in cancelling it. (*p*) [1]

916. *Share-brokers and stock-brokers.*—If a share-

(*n*) Stewart v. Aberdein, 4 M. & W. 211.

(*o*) As to brokers accounts, see Beckwith v. Bullen, 8 El. & Bl. 683 ; 27 L. J., Q. B. 162.   Blackburn, J., Xenos v. Wickham, 33 L. J., C. P. 19.

(*p*) Xenos v. Wickham, L. R., 2 H. L. 296 ; 36 L. J., C. P. 316.

---

[1] It is the rule with us that one travelling and soliciting insurance—in the event of insuring—is the agent of the company, and not of the insured.   Coe v. Wilkinson, 13 Wall. 222 ; Franklin v. Ins. Co., 42 Mo. 456 ; Winnesheik Ins. Co. v. Holzgrape, 53 Ill. 516 ; Woodbury v. Charter Oak Co., 31 Conn. 526 ; Pierce v. Ins. Co., 50 N. H. 297 ; North American Ins. Co. v. Throop, 22 Mich. 456 ; Wass v. Maine, &c., Ins. Co., 61 Me. 537 ; American, &c., Ins. Co. v. McLanthan, 11 Kan. 533.   An insurance broker is bound to exercise the diligence customary with good and prudent experts, in his department of business.   He must take the usual methods of ascertaining that the insurers are sound ; Wharton's Commentaries on Agency and Agents, § 205 ; and see that their principal, in case of adjustment, does not suffer.   Rundle v. Moore, 3 Johns. Cas. 36.

broker, directed to buy shares, buys what is ordinarily bought and sold in the stock market as shares, he has fulfilled his commission, and can not be made responsible for the fraud or misconduct of parties who may have issued the shares without authority. There is no warranty or undertaking, either on the part of a broker employed to buy shares or scrip, or on the part of the principal who employs him, that the article, which merely passes through the broker's or the principal's hands, is anything more than what it purports on the face of it to be, and what it is generally understood to be in the market. (*q*) Every principal who employs a stock-broker or share-broker to transact business for him in the stock or share market is bound by the rules of the Stock Exchange and the established mode of transacting business, whether he knew of the usage or not. (*r*) If a share-broker, employed to effect a sale of shares or scrip, sells pursuant to his authority, and the principal neglects to deliver the shares, and the broker is consequently obliged to buy other shares in the market, at an advanced rate, for the fulfillment of the contract of sale, such share-broker is entitled to recover from the principal, his employer, all the damages he has sustained, and all the costs and expenses incurred by him in the execution of the commission, besides the customary remuneration for his trouble and loss of time. (*s*) And, generally, whenever the share-broker has been compelled by the custom of the Stock Exchange to make good the default of the principal, he has a remedy over against the latter. Therefore, if he pays calls on shares which

(*q*) Lamert v. Heath, 15 M. & W. 486 ; 15 L. J., Ex. 298. Mitchell v. Newhall, 15 M. & W. 308 ; 15 L. J., Ex. 292. Westropp v. Solomon, 8 C. B. 373.

(*r*) Sutton v. Totham, 10 Ad. & E. 27. Bowlby v. Bell, 3 C. B. 284. Pollock v. Stables, 12 Q. B. 774.

(*s*) Bayliffe v. Butterworth, 1 Exch. 425.

he has purchased for his principal, he may recover the amount from the latter. (*t*)

917. *Solicitors* are, as we have already seen, bound, in common with all professional men, to act faithfully and diligently, and exercise a reasonable degree of care and skill in the conduct and management of the business intrusted to them to execute.[1]   Gifts and

---

(*t*) Bayley v. Wilkins, 7 C. B. 899.   Taylor v. Stray, 2 C. B. N. S. 175;
26 L. J., C. P. 287.

[1] See *ante*, § 877, note on p. 566.   An attorney with us, by which general term may be included all grades of lawyers, has a presumption of authority in his favor, and upon appearing for his client in court, will be presumed to have an authority to do so.   Thomas v. Steele, 22 Wis. 207; Pillsbury v. Dugan, 9 Ohio, 117.   Leslie v. Fischer, 62 Ill. 118;   Hamilton v. Wright, 37 N Y. 502; Proprietors v. Bishop, 2 Vt. 231; Osborn v. Bk. U. S., 9 Wheat. 231; Post v. Haight, 1 How. Pr. 171.   But the fiction is, that every attorney so appearing has his formal warrant of attorney from the client; Leslie v. Fischer, 62 Ill, 118; and although, under the above presumption, such is very rarely the fact, the opposite party has a right to call upon the attorney to produce his warrant. O'Flynn v. Eagle, 7 Mich. 306; Gillespie's case, 3 Yerg. 325; Silkman v Boiger, 4 E. D. Smith, 236; Lynch v. Commonwealth, 16 S & R. 358; Campbell v. Galbreath, 5 Watts, 423; O'Flynn v. Eagle, 7 Mich. 306; McAlexander v. Wright, 3 T. B. Monr. 194; Clark v. Willett, 35 Cal. 534.   See Knowlton v. Plantation No. 4, 14 Me. 20; Savery v. Savery, 8 Iowa, 217; Hellman v. Whennie, 3 Rich. (S. C.) 364; Barnes v. Profilet, 5 La. Ann. 117.   But if the court be satisfied by the attorney's declaration or by other parol evidence of the attorney's authority, it will be sufficient.   Hardin v. Ho-yo-po-nubby, 27 Miss. 567; Bogardus v. Livingston, 2 Hilt. (N. Y.) 236; Manchester Bk. v. Fellows, 28 N. H. 302; Farrington v. Wright, 1 Minn. 241; Field v. Proprietors, 1 Cush. 11. Bridgton v. Bennett, 23 Me. 420; Henck v. Todhunter, 7 Har. & J. 275; Cartwell v. Manifee, 2 Ark. 355; Commis. v. Purdey, 36 Barb. 266; Boutlier v. Johnson, 2 Browne, Pa. 17; Allen v. Green, 1 Bailey, 448; West v. Houston, 3 Harr. (Del.) 15; Bush v. Miller, 13 Barb. 481; Farm. & Mech. Bk. v. Troy Bk., 1 Dougl. (Mich.) 457.   See, however, under North Carolina

purchases by a solicitor from his client are, as we have
seen, invalid, unless the confidential relationship has
been determined as regards the particular transaction,

act, Day v. Adams, 63 N. C. 254; Ninety Nine Plaintiffs v.
Vanderbilt, 4 Duer, 632 ; Hirshfield v. Landman, 2 E. D. Smith,
208 ; Rogers v. Park, 4 Humph. 480 ; King of Spain v. Oliver,
2 Wash. 429. If it appear that the attorney has no authority
to appear, proceedings taken by him will be set aside upon
motion. Hess v. Cole, 23 N. J. L. (3 Zab.) 116; Handely v.
Statelor, 6 Litt. (Ky.) 186 ; Boykin v. Holden, 6 La. Ann. 120 ;
Frye v. Calhoun Co., 14 Ill. 132 ; Crichfield v. Porter, 3 Ohio,
518; Powell v. Spaulding, 3 Iowa, 443. An attorney is an
officer of the court, and proceedings to disbar him must be upon
an order to show cause why he should not be suspended or removed, from his office or in the nature of an attachment as for a
contempt. Ex parte Brown, 2 Miss. 303 ; Ex parte Mills, 1 Mich.
392 ; In re Percy, 36 N. Y. 651 ; Paul v. Percell, 1 Browne (Pa.)
348 ; U. S. v. Porter, 2 Cranch, 60; Perry v. State, 3 Iowa,
550 ; Rice v. Com., 18 B. Monr. 472 ; State v. Start, 7 Iowa,
499 ; State v. Watkins, 3 Mo. 388; Beene v. State, 22 Ark.
149 ; Ex parte Bryant, 24 N. H. 149 ; Com. v. Newton, 1 Grant,
453 ; Fisher's case, 6 Leigh, 619 ; Saxton v. Stowell, 11 Paige,
526 ; People v. Harvey, 41 Ill. 277 ; State v. Holding, 1 Mc-
Cord (S. C.) 379 ; Smith v. State, 1 Yerg. 228 ; Baker v. Com.,
10 Bush, 592 ; Gehrke v. Jod, 59 Mo. 522; Withers v. State,
36 Ala. 252. There was no cause shown why the attorney
should be disbarred in Jackson v. State, 21 Tex. 668 ; Fletcher
v. Dangerfield, 20 Cal. 427 ; State v. Kirke, 12 Fla. 278 ; Perry
v. State, 3 Iowa, 550; State v. Foreman, 3 Mo. 602; State v.
Chapman, 11 Ohio, 430. An unauthorized appearance by which
an innocent defendant is made to suffer, may collaterally impeach such appearance. Henck v. Todhunter, 7 Har. & J.
275 ; Turner v. Carruthers, 17 Cal. 431 ; Hayes v. Shattuck,
21 Cal. 51 ; Dalton v. Dalton, 33 Ga. 243 ; Jackson v. Stewart,
6 Johns. 34 ; Beckley v. Newcomb, 24 N. H. 359 ; Mexico v.
De Arargoix, 5 Duer, 643 ; Tally v. Reynolds, 1 Ark. 99 ;
Kent v. Richards, 3 Md. Ch. 392 ; Conrey v. Brenham, 1 La.
Ann. 397 ; Bank Com. v. Bank of Buffalo, 6 Paige, 497 ; Fowler v. Morrill, 8 Tex. 153 ; Cox v. Hill, 3 Ohio, 411 ; Pillsbury
v. Dugan, 9 Ohio, 117 ; Hill v. Mendenhall, 21 Wall. 453 ;
Norris v. Douglass, 5 N. J. L. 317 ; Williams v. Butler, 35 Ill.
544. But the defendant must be guilty of no laches in so
doing; Am. Ins. Co. v. Oakley, 9 Paige, 496 ; Legree v. Rich-

and some disinterested advice has been taken and acted upon by the client; (*u*) but the validity of the purchase can not be impeached by a stranger. (*v*)   If

(*u*) Holman v. Loynes, 18 Jur. 839.   (*v*) Knight v. Bowyer, 26 L. J., Ch
Simpson v. Lamb, 7 Ell. & Bl. 84.   769.
Gibbs v. Daniel, 4 Giff. 1.

ard, 10 La. Ann. 669; if he be, the judgment may be continued, and the defendant remitted to his remedy against the attorney. See Denton v. Noyes, 5 Johns. (N. Y.) 296; Blodget v. Conklin, 9 How. (N. Y.) Pr. 442; Cyphert v. McClune, 22 Pa. St. 195; Walworth v. Henderson, 9 La Ann. 339. But not if the attorney is irresponsible. Campbell v. Bristol, 19 Wend. 101. An attorney employed by an agent is the attorney of the principal; Porter v. Peckham, 44 Cal. 204; and the agent is liable for wrongfully instructing them, but not for their own negligence. Wilson v. Smith, 3 How. 763; Buckland v. Conway, 16 Mass. 366; see Harrold v. Gillespie, 7 Humph. 59; Hobbs v. Duff, 43 Cal. 485; Watson v. Muirhead, 57 Penn. St. 247; the attorney himself may not employ a substitute or substitutes, although he may employ subordinates to assist him. See In re Bleakly, 5 Paige, (N. Y.) 311; Hitchcock v. McGehee, 7 Port. 556; Johnson v. Cunningham, 1 Ala. 249; Kellogg v. Norris, 10 Ark. 18; Ratcliff v. Baird, 14 Tex. 43; Polland v. Rowland, 2 Blackf. 22; Power v. Kent, 1 Cow. 211; Birkbeck v. Stafford, 14 Abb. Pr. 285; 23 How. Pr. 236; McEwen v. Mazyck, 3 Rich. (S. C.) 210; Cook v. Ritter, 4 E. D. Smith, 253. The question of the attorney's negligence has been considered, *ante*, note 1, p. 566. The rule is generally stated, that he is liable only for his own negligence, and for that of his clerks and subordinates; Whitney v. Corporation, 104 Mass. 152; Lewis v. Peck, 10 Ala. 142; Bradstreet v. Everson, 72 Pa. St. 124; Pollard v. Rowland, 2 Blackf. 22; Wilkinson v. Griswold, 12 Sm. & M. 669; Power v. Kent, 1 Cowen, 211; Birkbeck v. Stafford, 14 Abb. Pr. 285; 23 How. Pr. 236; and he is also held liable for the negligence of his partners; Smyth v. Harvie, 31 Ill. 62; Dwight v. Simon, 4 La Ann. 490; Poole v. Gist, 4 McCord, 250; Norton v. Cooper, 3 Sm. & G. 375; Warner v. Griswold, 8 Wend. 665; Livingston v. Cox, 6 Penn. St. 360; Mardis v. Shackleford, 4 Ala. 493; Morgan v. Roberts, 38 Ill. 65; but no liability will attach to him for negligence of his associates, counsel, or for the negligence of any expert or specialist employed by him in matters entrusted to their own particular discretion and skill. Watson v. Muir-

a solicitor discontinues proceedings in an action which he has commenced by direction of his client, he is bound to show a reasonable and satisfactory ground

head, 57 Penn. St. 247; Porter v. Peckham, 44 Cal. 204. The attorney who has once engaged in a case, can not accept engagements adversely to the client engaging his services, even if the engagements are to do merely formal and perfunctory acts. Spinks v. Davis, 32 Miss. 152; Taylor v. Bank, 14 Ala. 633; Howell v. Baker, 4 Johns. Ch. 118; McArthur v. Fry, 10 Kansas, 231; Warren v. Sprague, 4 Edw. 416; Commonwealth v. Gibbs, 4 Gray, 146; Price v. Grand Rapids R. R., 18 Ind. 139; Gaulden v. State, 11 Ga. 47; Wilson v. State, 16 Ind. 392; Herrick v. Catley, 1 Daly, 512; 30 How. Pr. 208; Sherwood v. R. R., 15 Barb. 650; nor can an attorney represent both sides of a case, even though the proceeding is an amicable one; Valentine v. Stewart, 15 Cal. 387; Sherwood v. Saratoga R. R. Co., 15 Barb. 650; though a case might properly be referred to the opposite party's counsel as a sort of umpire. Per contra, Joslin v. Cowee, 56 N. Y. 626. It has been said that the attorney can not use information once received from a client, adversely to him, but see as to the extent to which this rule will be carried. Price v. Railroad, 18 Ind. 137; Henry v. Raman, 25 Pa. St. 354; Porter v. Peckham, 44 Cal. 204. The relation of attorney and client may terminate by a revocation of authority, as in the case of any agent without interest; Gibbons v. Gibbons, 4 Harring. 105; Carver v. United States, 7 Ct. of Cl. 499; Hunt's Estate, 1 Tucker, 55; In re Paschal, 10 Wall. 483; Wells v. Hatch, 43 N. H. 246; Hazlett v. Gill, 5 Rob. 611; Faust v. Repoor, 15 How, 570; but this must be done by formal leave of the court, if the attorney be of record, and by service of the order of substitution upon the opposite party. Krekeler v. Thaule, 46 How. Pr. 138; Robertson v. M'Clellin, 7 How. Pr. 90; Dalon v. Lewis, 7 How. Pr. 132; Given v. Driggs, 3 Caines, 300; Hildreth v. Harvey, 3 Johns. Ca. 300; Dorlon v. Lewis, 7 How. (N. Y.) Pr. 132; Bogardus v. Richtmeyer, 3 Abb. (N. Y.) Pr. 179; Grant v. White, 6 Cal. 55; 55; Roussin v. Stuart, 33 Cal. 208; otherwise the new attorney's acts will be disregarded; Jerome v. Bowman, 1 Wend. 393; though this rule will not be oppressively enforced against parties acting in good faith; State v. Gulick 7 N. J. L. 435; Fuller v. Brown, 10 La. Ann. 350; McLaren v. Charrier, 5 Paige, 530; Thorp v. Fowler, 5 Cow. 446. But

for such discontinuance; and he must, in general, give due notice to his client of his intentions to discontinue; and, if he improperly throws up a cause, he has

the court will not direct a substitution unless the attorney's fees are paid; Supervisors v. Broadhead, 44 How. Pr. 411; Carver v. U. S., 7 Ct. of Cl. 499; Pleasants v. Kortrecht, 5 Heisk. 694; Walton v. Sugg, Phill. (N. C.) 98. See Paschal, in re, 10 Wall. 483; Sloo v. Law, 4 Blatch. 268; Mumford v. Murray, Hopk. N. Y. 369; Hoffman v. Van Nostrand 14 Abb. N. Y. 336; Stevenson v. Stevenson, 3 Edw. (N. Y.) 340; Gardner v. Tayler, 5 Abb. (N. Y.) N. S. 83; S. C., 36 How. Pr. 63. The right of an attorney to his fees in the United States, is the same as the right of any other person to compensation for services rendered upon employment, and may be recovered in the same way by a suit at law. Richardson v. Rowland, 40 Conn. 565; Harland v. Lilienthal, 53 N. Y. 438; Brady v. Mayor, 1 Sandf. 559; Brackett v. Sears, 15 Mich. 244; Nichols v. Scott, 12 Vt. 47; Clendinen v. Black, 2 Bailey (S. C.) 488; Miller v. Beal, 26 Ind. 234; Webb v. Browning, 14 Mo. 353; Daw v. Ewell, 2 Cranch, C. C. 144; Wylie v. Coxe, 15 How. (U. S.) 416; Smith v. Davis, 45 N. H. 566; Sanford v. Ruckman, 24 How. N. Y. Pr. 521; Stevens v. Monges, 1 Harr. (Del.) 124; Van Atta v. McKinney, 16 N. J. L., 1 Harr. 235; Foster v. Jack, 4 Watts, 339. But the attorney's compensation is more or less under the direction of the court, and it has been said that if a lawyer take advantage of his relation to his client to elicit extortionate and oppressive fees or gifts, they may be recovered back by the client, and the attorney punished by the court. See Lecatt v. Sallee, 3 Porter, 115; Phillips v. Overton, 4 Hayw. 291; Rose v. Mynett, 7 Yerg. 30; Thurston v. Percival, 1 Pick, 415; Rust v. Larue, 4 Lett. (Ky.) 416. Courts will discourage arrangements between attorneys and clients to prosecute causes on shares. Elliott v. McClelland, 17 Ala. 206; Halloway v. Lowe, 7 Port. 488; Merritt v. Lambert, 10 Paige 352; Satterlee v. Frazer, 2 Sandf. 241; Boardman v. Thompson, 25 Iowa, 487. This is the traditional spirit of the law; the Roman law divided contingent fees into pactum de quota litis, by which the attorney was to share the proceeds of the suit, and the palmarium victoriæ, or agreement, in case of success, for an extra remuneration. The first was absolutely null, and was held so reprehensible as to be a ground for disbarring the attorney. Decree of Constantianus, L. 5, c. d., *post* 2, 6. The

no right to be paid pro ratâ for his work and labor.
(*w*) If a cause which he is retained to conduct fails
through his negligence, he can not recover from his

(*w*) Nicholls v. Wilson, 11 M. & W. 106.

palmarium victoriæ was not considered dishonorable, but the
agreement to pay such a reward was only a natural obligation, and not efficacious unless ratified after termination
of the process. It was held, at the same time, that such
fee should not, with other payments, exceed a hundred
gold pieces for each process; L. J, § 12 D., de ex. cog. 50, 13.
And Ulpian holds in disfavor unliquidated contingent fees; Id.
But an attorney may make and sustain a special agreement
with his client. Jenkins v. Williams, 2 How. (N. Y.) Pr. 261;
Lander v. Caldwell, 4 Kans. 339; Major v. Gibson, 1 Patt. &
H. Va. 48; Lecat v.Sallee, 3 Port. (Ala.) 115; Wallis v. Loubat,
2 Den. 607; Eastern v. Smith, 1 E. D. Smith, 318. If this
special agreement be set aside by the court, or by the parties,
the attorney may still recover for his services on a quantum
meriut. Greaves v. Lockwood, 30 Conn. 276; Roselins v.
Delachaise, 5 La. Ann. 482; Michen v. Gravier, 11 La. Ann.
596; Savings Bk. v. Benton, 2 Metc. (Ky.) 240; Hood v.
Ware, 34 Ga. 328; Brewer v. Cook, 11 La. Ann. 637; Vilas
v. Downer, 21 Vt. 419; Phelps v. Hunt, 40 Conn. 97; Macarty's
Succession, 3 Id. 518; Lee's Succession, 4 Id. 578;
Virgin's Succession, 18 Id. 42; Turner v. Myers, 23
Iowa, 391; Barker v. York, 3 La. Ann. 90; Burghart v. Gard-
ner, 3 Barb. 64; Chicago R. R. Co. v. Larned, 26 Ill. 216;
Goodal v. Bedel, 20 N. H. 205; Bogardus v. Livingston, 7
Abb. (N. Y.) Pr. 428; Fore v. Chandler, 24 Tex. 146; see Seely
v. North, 16 Conn. 92; Briggs v. Georgia, 15 Vt. 61; Smith
v. Dougherty, 37 Vt. 530; Stow v. Hamlin, 1 How. (N. Y.)
Pr. 452; Planters' Bank v. Heinberger, 4 Cold. 578; McMa-
hon v. Smith, 6 Heisk. 167; Hotchkins v. Le Roy, 9 Johns
R. 142; Bowman v. Tallman, 27 How. (N. Y.) 212; Kentucky
Bk. v. Cowles, 7 Penn. St. 543; Duncan v. Yancy, 1 McCord,
(S. C.) 149. The success of the attorney's services will make no
difference as to his right to remuneration, unless their failure
be due to his own negligence. See Maynard v. Briggs, 26
Vt. 94; Nixon v. Phelps, 29 Id. 198; Bredin v. Kingland, 4
Watts, 420; Gleason v. Clark, 9 Cowen, 57; Runyan v.
Nichols, 11 Johns. R. 547; Hopping v. Quin, 12 Wend. 517;
Wills v. Kane, 2 Grant (Pa.) 60; Brackett v. Norton, 4
Conn. 517; Porter v. Ruckman, 38 N. Y. 210. If the attor-

client money expended by him subsequently to such
negligence. "If he is not entitled to charge for his
labor, he can not charge for his money." (*x*)   A solic-

(*x*) Lewis v. Samuel, 8 Q. B. 685.

ney's services be immoral or illegal he can not recover any
more than any other agent or servant. Treat v. Jones, 28
Conn. 334; Hallett v. Oakes, 1 Cush. 296; Trist v. Child, 21
Wall, 441; Arrington v. Sneed. 18 Tex. 135. The attorney's
lien for fees is recognized by the present civil law (Glüch.
Commis. V., § 372), and this attaches not only to the papers
in the case, which would be on the general principle upon
which one has a lien for his compensation upon a thing upon
which he has bestowed lawful labor. Dennett v. Cutts, 11
N. H. 163; Howard v. Osceola, 22 Wis. 453; Stewart v.
Flowers, 44 Miss. 513; White v. Harlow, 5 Gray, 463; but see
Walton v. Dickerson, 7 Penn. St. 376; Dubois's Appeal, 38
Penn. St. 231; Newton v. Porter, 5 Lansing, 416; and it is
said that the papers can not be held under a lien, except for
services relating to them; Bowling Green, &c., Institution v.
Todd, 52 N. Y. 489; but to funds of the client in his hands
('n re Paschal, 10 Wall. 483), or to be recovered by his exertions. Wylie v. Coxe, 15 How. 415; Hutchinson v. Howard,
15 Vt. 544; Stratton v. Hussey, 62 Me. 286 (qualifying Potter v. Mayo, 3 Greenl. 34; Newbert v. Cunningham, 50 Me.
231; Cooley v. Patterson, 52 Id. 472); Andrews v. Morse, 12
Conn. 444; Benjamin v. Benjamin, 17 Id. 110; Walker v.
Sargeant, 14 Vt. 247; Hutchinson v. Pettes, 18 Id. 616; Power
v. Kent, 1 Cowen, 172; Martin v. Hawks, 15 Johns. 405;
Rooney v. R. R., 18 N. Y. 368; Bowling Green Bank v. Todd,
52 Id. 489; Sexton v. Pike, 13 Ark. 193; Waters v. Grace,
23 Id. 118; Carter v. Davis, 8 Fla. 183. It is said, in some
states, that the lien does not attach until judgment; see Sweet
v. Bartlett, 4 Sandf. 661; Henchey v. Chicago, 41 Ill. 136;
Potter v. Mayo, 3 Green. 34; Hobson v. Watson, 34 Me. 20;
Getchell v. Clark, 5 Mass. 309; Foot v. Tewksbury, 2 Vt. 97;
Hutchinson v. Howard, 15 Id. 247; Hutchinson v. Pettes, 18
Id. 616; and in some the lien is matter of statute. In Massachusetts the attorney has such lien only when he is lawfully
possessed of an execution, or has prosecuted a suit to final
judgment in favor of his client, and not then, as against a
payment to the judgment creditor without notice of the lien.
Simmons v. Almy, 103 Mass. 33; and see Baker v. Cook, 11
Id. 236; Getchell v. Clark, 5 Id. 309; so in Vermont (Citi-

itor is responsible to the client for all sums received
by him in the conduct of the business entrusted to
him, and must render a true and faithful account

zens, &c., Bank v. Culver, 54 N. H. 327; and the statutory lien must be enforced according to the law of the state
giving it. Id.   Some states hold that this lien, however, only
extends to costs and disbursements; see Cozzens v. Whitney,
3 R. I. 79; McDonald v. Napier, 14 Ga. 89; Humphrey v.
Browning, 46 Ill. 476; Elwood v. Wilson, 21 Iowa, 523;
ex parte Kyle, 1 Cal. 331; Mansfield v. Dorland, 2 Id. 507;
Young v. Dearborn, 27 N. H. 324; Currier v. R. R., 37 Id.
223; Wells v. Hatch, 43 Id. 246; Dennett v. Cutts, 11 Id.
163; Citizens' Nat. Bank v. Culver, 54 Id.   327; while
many cases deny the existence of the lien at all, but give him
. mere right to deduct from the client's funds in his hands.
Walton v. Dickerson, 7 Pa. St. 376; Hill v. Brinkley, 10 Ind.
102; Frissel v. Haile, 18 Mo. 18; Irwin v. Workman, 3 Watts.
357 : Dubois's Appeal, 38 Penn. St. 231; Newbaker v. Alricks,
5 Watts. 183.   It was said, in Patten v. Wilson, 34 Pa. St. 299,
that such claims by the attorney are not liens, but equitable
assignments, which the courts will protect; and see generally
as to the attorney's lien; Marshall v. Meech, 51 N. Y. 140;
Forsyth v. Beveridge, 52 Ill. 268; Mansfield v. Dorland, 2
Cal. 230; Rooney v. Railroad, 18 N. Y. 368; Warfield v.
Campbell, 38 Ala. 527; Ward v. Syme, 9 How. Pr. 16; as
to whether a set off against a judgment obtained will affect
the lien; see Stratton v. Hussey, 62 Me. 288; Currier v. R. R,
37 N. H. 223; Boyer v. Clark, 3 Neb. 161; Carter v. Davis, 8
Fla. 183; Walker v. Sargeant, 14 Vt. 247; Porter v. Lane, 8
Johns. 357; Mohawk Bank v. Burrows, 6 Johns. Ch. 357;
Johnson v. Bullard, 44 Ind. 270.

The relation of attorney and client can also be determined,
II., by the termination of the particular suit in which he
was engaged; Love v. Hall, 3 Yerg. 408; Adams v. Bank,
23 How. (N. Y.) Pr. 45; Bathgate v. Haskin, 59 N. Y. 533;
Langdon v. Castleton, 30 Vt. 285; Jackson v. Bartlett, 8
Johns. R. 361; Richardson v. Talbot, 2 Bibb. 382; Gray v.
Wass, 1 Greenl. 257.   But the attorney must not withdraw
upon an adverse judgment, if his client is at such a distance
that he can not be   consulted, and it is to the latter's
interest to have the judgment reviewed.   See Bathgate v. Haskin, 59 N. Y. 533;   Bach v. Ballard, 13 La. Ann. 487.
Or, III., by leave to the attorney to withdraw from the

thereof when called upon so to do. Where, on a sale of real estate, the solicitor of the vendor receives the deposit as agent of the vendor, he has not, in the case, given him by the court. United States v. Curry, 9 How. 100; and see Boyd v. Stone, 5 Wis. 240; Martinis v. Johnson, 31 N. J. L. 1 Zab. 239; Bach v. Bullard, 19 La. Ann. 487; or, IV., by the client's death; Balbi v. Duvet, 3 Edw. (N. Y.) 418; Risley v. Fellows, 10 Ill. 531; Judson v. Love, 35 Cal. 463; Whitehead v. Lord, 7 Exch. 691; Gleason v. Dodd, 4 Metc. 333; Putnam v. Van Buren, 7 How. (N. Y.) Pr. 31; Beach v. Gregory, 2 Abb. (N. Y.) Pr. 206. See this question discussed, *ante*, note, p. 699; or, V., by the attorney's incapacity; as, for instance, his insanity, disbarment, promotion to the bench (Given v. Driggs, 3 Caines, 150), or death. Vielie v. Bennett, 3 Johns. Cas. 557; Hildreth v. Harvey, Id. 300. And the opposite party must serve the other with notice to appoint a new attorney; a mere knowledge of his attorney's death in the party, or personal service on him of papers, or a posting of the notice of the attorney's death in the clerk's office, will not be valid. The attorney's liability to his client is to notify him of every circumstance affecting his interest, or requiring action on his part to exhibit ordinary and usual diligence and skill in his profession. See as to the amount of skill required; Marsh v Whitman, 21 Wall. 178; Morrill v. Graham, 27 Tex. 646; Holmes v. Peck, 1 R. I. 242; O'Barr v. Alexander, 37 Ga. 195; Cox v. Sullivan, 7 Id. 144; Wilson v. Russ, 20 Me. 421; Goodman v. Walker, 30 Ala. 482; Walpole v. Carlisle, 32 Ind. 415; Stephens v. Walker, 55 Ill. 151; Pidgeon v. Williams, 21. Grat. 251; Bowman v. Tallman, 27 How. (N. Y.) Pr. 212; Lynch v. Commonwealth, 16 S. & R. 368; and see as to the diligence required, Nisbet v. Lawson, 1 Ga. 275; O'Barr v. Alexander. 37 Id. 195; Stubbs v. Beene, 37 Ala. 627; Spiller v. Davidson, 4 La. Ann. 171; Gambert v. Hunt, 44 Cal. 542; Walpole v. Carlisle, 32 Ind. 415; Hastings v. Halleck, 13 Cal. 203; Stevens v. Walker, 55 Ill. 151; Wilson v. Coffin, 2 Cush. 316; Harter v. Morris, 88 Ohio St. 492; Pidgeon v. Williams, 21 Grat. 251; Goodman v. Walker, 30 Ala. (N. S.) 482; Cox v. Sullivan, 7 Ga. 144; Wilson v. Russell, 20 Me. 421; Holmes v. Peck, 1 R. I. 242; Walson v. Muirhead, 57 Penn. St. 161; Lynch v. Commonwealth, 16 S. & R. 368; Bowman v. Tallman, 27 How. (N. Y.) Pr. 212; and see *ante*, note   He can not defend himself from the consequences of his negligence on the ground that his services were gratuitous. Wharton on Negligence, § 436. And he is

absence of any stipulation to that effect, any duty, like
that of an auctioneer, to the vendee, but must pay it
over to his principal, the vendor, on demand. (*y*)   He

(*y*) Edgell *v.* Day, L. R., 1. C. P. 80; 35 L. J., C. P. 7.

liable for damages arising from his officious intermeddling
with a case. O'Hara v. Brophy, 24 How Pr. 279; Bradt v.
Walton, 8 Johns R. 298.   While his relation as the attorney
of his employer exists, he has power to bind his client by his
acts within the case in which he is retained.   See generally
as to this, Nave v. Bairs, 22 Ind. 318; Chambers v. Hodges,
23 Tex. 104; Russel v. Lane, 1 Barb. 519; Jenny v. Delesdernier, 20 Me. 183; Fairbanks v. Stanley, 18 Id. 296; Lawson
v. Betteson, 20 Ark. 401; Sampson v. Obleyer, 22 Cal. 200;
Greenlee v. McDowell, 4 Ired. 481; Rice v. Wilkins, 21 Me. 558;
Bethel v. Cormack, 2 Md. ch. 143.   He has absolutely control
of the case put into his hands.   Nightingale v. Railroad, 2
Sawyer, 339; Simpson v. Lombas, 14 La. Ann. 103; Commissioners v. Younger, 29 Cal. 147; Ward v. Hollins, 14 Md.
158; Pierce v. Strickland, 2 Story, 292; Clark v. Randall,
9 Wis. 135.   And is solely responsible to his client for his
acts and proceedings therein; consult Lawson v. Betterson.
12 Ark. 401; Sampson v. Obleyer, 22 Cal. 200; Foster v.
Wiley, 27 Mich. 244; Collett v. Foster, 2 H. & N. 356; Crook
v. Wright, R. & M. 278; Beeke v. Penn. 7 C. & P 397; Greenlee v. McDowell, 4 Ired. Eq. 481; Chambers v. Hodges, 23
Tex. 194; Bethel Church v. Carmack, 2 Md. Ch. 143; Cox v.
Livingston, 2 Watts & S. 103; Miller v. Wilson, 24 Pa.
St. 114.   He may, in the exercise of such power, accept
service of papers (Hofferman v. Burt, 7 Iowa, 320) to discontinue; Gaillard v. Smart, 6 Con. 385; or appeal (Adams v.
Robinson, 1 Peck, 462) or restore (Reenhold v. Alberti, 1 Bin.
469) a suit, to waive formalities or advantages gained by him
in the course of the proceedings; Hanson v. Hoitt, 14 N. H.
56; Alton v. Gilmanton, 2 Id. 520; Pierce v. Perkins, 2
Dev. (N. C.) 250; Hart v. Spalding, 1 Cal. 213; or even verification or proof of facts or papers; Smith v. Milliken, 2 Min.
319; Lewis v. Sumner, 13 Metc. 269; Wenans v. Lindsay, 1
How. 557; Starke v. Kenan, 11 Ala. 819; Talbot v. McGee, 7
T. B. Mon. 377; Pike v. Emerson, 5 N. H. 293; Gilkeson v.
Snyder, 8 W. & S. 200; Farmers' Bank v. Sprigg, 11 Md. 389;
Smith v. Dixon, 3 Met. (Ky.) 438; La Crosse v. Robert, 11
La. Ann. 33; and he may release an attachment; Moulton
v. Bowker, 115 Mass. 36; confess judgment; though see

is responsible also, as we have already seen, for the
safe investment of all moneys intrusted to, and accepted by him for investment. (y) [1] But the town

(*y*) *Ante*, § 194.

Denton v. Noyes, 6 Johns. 296; but see People v. Sanborn, 1 Scam. (2 Ill.) 123; or (before an execution is actually issued) to stipulate as to its levy; Union Bank v.
Georgetown, 5 Pet. 99; Willand v. White, 109 Mass. 392;
or open a judgment; Clussman v. Merkel, 3 Bosw. 402;
Read v. French, 28 N. Y. 285; or submit to an arbitra-
tion; Cahill v. Benn, 6 Binney, 99; Wader v. Powell, 31
Ga. 1; Smith v. Bassard, 2 McCord, 406; Stokely v. Robinson, 34 Pa. St. 315; but see Markley v. Amos, 8 Rich.
(S. C.) 468. But he has no power to bind his client by va-
cating a judgment; Quinn v. Lloyd, 5 Abb. Pr. N. S. 281;
or to stipulate not to move for a new trial; People v. Mayor,
&c., 11 Abb. 66; or to assign his clients' suit; Mayer v. Blease,
4 S. C. 10; Weathers v. Roe, 4 Dana, 474; Head v. Gervaise,
1 Walk. Ch. 431; or to compromise. This last, however, differs in different states. See McDowell v. Second Av. R. R.,
5 Bosw. (N. Y.) 670; Mallory v. Mariner, 15 Wis. 172; Abbe
v. Rood, 6 McLean, 106; Gordon v. Coolidge, 1 Sumn. 537;
Wieland v. White, 109 Mass. 392; Peru Steel Co. v. Whipple
File Co., 109 Mass. 464; Holker v. Parker, 7 Cranch, 436;
Potter v. Parsons, 14 Iowa, 286; Fogg v. Sanborn, 48 Me. 432;
Christie v. Sawyer, 44 N. H. 298; Reinhold v. Alberti, 1 Bin-
ney, 469; North Mo. R. R. v. Stephens, 36 Mo. 150; *contra*,
Nolan v. Jackson, 16 Ill. 272; Doub v. Barnes, 1 Md. Ch. 127;
Derwort v. Loomer, 21 Conn. 245; Vail v. Jackson, 13 Vt.
314; Maddux v. Bevan, 39 Md. 485; Smith v. Dixon, 3 Met.
(Ky.) 438; Smock v. Dude, 5 Rand. (Va.) 639; Marbourg v.
Smith, 11 Kan. 562; Davidson v. Rozier, 23 Mo. 387; Falker
v. Parker, 7 Cranch, 436, 452; Dodd v. Dodds, 9 Pa. St. 315;
Maddux v. Bevan, 39 Md. 485; or to agree to or do anything
that shall bar a client's action; Marbourg v. Smith, 11 Kan.
554; Lambert v. Sandford, 2 Blackf. 137; or imperil his case;
Mitchell v. Cotten, 3 Fla. 136; Marshall v. Nagle, 1 Bailey,
308; Shores v. Caswell, 13 Met. 413; Murray v. House, 11
Johns. R. 464; East River Bank v. Kennedy, 9 Bosw. 573;

[1] See *ante*, § 794.

agent of a country solicitor is not responsible to the
clients of the latter for money received whilst conducting their causes or legal proceedings. The privity

Bowne v. Hyde, 6 Barb. 392; Springer v. Whipple, 17 Me.
351; York Bank v. Appleton, 17 Id. 55; Bell v. Bank, 8 Ala.
590; or to release indorser's; Varnum v. Bellamy, 4 McLean,
87; or garnishee's; Quarles v. Porter, 12 Mo. 76; nor can he
purchase land for his client under the latter's execution;
Beardsley v. Root, 11 Johns. 404; and see Corbin v. Mul-
ligan, 1 Bush, 297; or to settle his client's claim by the
receipt of anything but money, unless expressly or impliedly
authorized; Child v. Dwight, 1 Dev. & Bat. Eq. 171; Treas-
urers v. McDowell, 1 Hill (S. C.), 184; Patten v. Fullerton, 27
Me. 58; Baldwin v. Merrill, Humph. 132; Perkins v. Grant,
2 La. Ann. 328; Phelps v. Preston, 9 Id. 488; Campbell
v. Bailey, 19 Id. 172; Garvin v. Lowry, 15 Mass. 24;
Jeter v. Haviland, 24 Ga. 252; Huston v. Mitchell, 14 Serg.
& R. 307; West v. Ball, 12 Ala. 340; though he might
take a short note of a person of undoubted credit; Livingston v. Radcliff, 6 Barb. 201; Chapman v. Cowles, 41 Ala.
103; Davis v. Lee, 20 La. Ann. 248; Trumble v. Nicholson, 27
Ill. 189. An attorney employed to procure the assignment of
a mortgage, can not receive its payment; Williams v. Walker,
2 Sandf. Ch. 535. Nor can an attorney assign or transfer his
client's claim to a third party without his client's authority;
Child v. Eureka, 44 N. H. 354; Goodfellow v. Landis, 36 Mo.
168; Penniman v. Patchen, 5 Vt. 346; Campbell's Appeal,
29 Pa. St. 401; Rowland v. State, 58 Id. 196; Fassit v.
Middleton, 47 Id. 214; Heed v. Gervaise, Walk. Ch. 431;
Card v. Wallridge, 18 Ohio, 411; Terhune v. Colton, 10 N. J.
Eq. (2 Stock.) 21; White v. Hildreth, 13 N. H. 104. Nor will
payment to one not attorney of record (Wart v. Lee, 3 Yeates,
7) or to the late attorney of a dead man (Clark v. Richards,
3 E. D. Smith, 89) discharge the person making the payment,
if a collusive arrangement between the attorney and the
attorney on the other side is invalid; Child v. Dwight, 1 Dev.
& Bat. Eq. 171; Craig v. Ely, 5 Stew. & Port. 354; Chambers v. Miller, 7 Watts, 63. Clark v. Kingsland, 1 Smedes & M.
248 (Miss.), held, that an attorney for a foreign client had no
authority to control his client's interest in matters subsequent
to the litigation; and as a general rule, the attorney's authority
closes entirely after judgment entered, and he must have a new
authority to proceed further; see Kellogg v. Gilbert, 10 Johns,

of contract is solely between the town agent and his principal and employer, the country solicitor; he knows nothing of the clients of the latter, and is bound to account only to his principal. But the court will, as before mentioned, sometimes interfere summarily for the protection of the client. The solicitor must, in general, one month before action against his client, deliver his bill of costs, signed by him, to his client; (*z*) and, when his bill has been paid, he is bound to deliver up, if called upon, all papers and documents in his hands belonging to his client, in good order and properly arranged. (*a*)

918. *Sheriff's officers,* expressly employed by a solicitor to execute process, may maintain an action against the latter for the recovery of such fees as are usually allowed on the taxation of costs by the course and practice of the courts, and are not bound to resort to the clients of the solicitor for remuneration. (*b*)

919. *Duties of estate and house-agents.*—A house-agent employed to procure a tenant for a house is bound to use due care and caution in the letting of the house, and to make all proper and necessary en-

(*z*) Phipps v. Daubney, 16 Q. B. 514. Smith v. Pococke, 22 L. J., Ch. 545.

(*a*) North-West R. Co. v. Sharp, 18 Jur. 964.

(*b*) Foster v. Blakelock, 8 D. & R. 48.

220; Simonton v. Burrell, 21 Wend. 362; Givens v. Briscoe, 3 J. J. Marsh, 532; Jewett v. Wadleigh, 32 Me. 110; but there are many natural exceptions to this rule, arising from the circumstances of the case; see Scott v. Seiler, 5 Watts, 235; Lynch v. Com. 16 S. & R. 388; Nelson v. Cook, 19 Ill. 440; Corning v. Sutherland, 3 Hill (N. Y.), 552; Hyams v. Michel, 3 Rich. (S. C.) 303; Silvis v. Ely, 3 Watts & S. 420; Hollington, *ex parte*, 43 L. J. Ch. 99; Erwin v. Blake, 8 Pet. 18; Willard v. Goodrich, 31 Vt. 597; Day v. Welles, 31 Conn. 344; Steward v. Biddlecum, 2 N. Y.; 2 Comst. 103; Hopkins v. Willard, 14 Vt. 474; Gorham v. Gale, 7 Cowen, 739; Jenney v. Delesdernier, 20 Me. 183; Read v. French, 28 N. Y. 285.

quiries touching the respectability and solvency of the tenant. If, therefore, he lets the house to a notoriously insolvent person, or to one whom he knows to be insolvent, he will be responsible in damages to his employer. (*c*)

920. *Receipt of money and goods by agents on account of their principals.*—It is a settled rule that an agent shall not, after accounting with his principal, and receiving money in his capacity of agent, afterwards say that he did not do so, and did not receive it for the benefit of his principal, but for some other person, (*d*) unless there has been a mistake and a void payment ab initio, so that the money never was, in truth, received for the principal. But, if the agent effects a contract of sale at a high price in consequence of a fraudulent misrepresentation made by him, and receives such price, but is afterwards compelled to refund the money to the purchaser, the principal can not maintain an action for money had and received, against the agent, to recover the price, inasmuch as the sale is avoided by the fraud of the agent, and the money received under it becomes the property of the purchaser, and is not money had and received for the use of the principal. (*e*)   And, although an agent has received goods from his principal to hold on account of the latter, or although he has received goods from a third party, and has agreed to hold them for his principal, he may, under certain circumstances, set up a jus tertii. Thus, if an auctioneer has received goods for public sale from a person who is not the owner of them, and has no right to sell them, and the real

---

(*c*) Heys *v.* Tindall, 1 B. & S. 296; 30 L. J., Q. B. 362.

(*d*) Dixon v. Hamond, 2 B. & Ald. 313. Hawes v. Watson, 2 B. & C.

540. Edgell v. Day, 35 L. J., C. P. 7; L. R., 1 C. P. 80.

(*e*) Parke, B., Murray v. Mann, 17 L. J., Ex. 256. 3 Exch. 541.

owner intervenes and forbids the sale, or claims the
money realized by the sale, the auctioneer may set up
the title of such real owner against the claims of the
fictitious owner from whom he received the goods. (*f*)
So, where a wharfinger received notice that goods deposited at his wharf were marked with a fraudulent
imitation of a trademark, and that the owner of the
trade-mark was about to apply to the Court of Chancery for an injunction to prevent the sale of the goods,
and, after the injunction had been granted, but before
the wharfinger had notice that it had been granted,
he refused to deliver the goods to the owner, it was
held that he was justified in such refusal. (*g*)

Where a managing owner of a ship, or " ship's
husband," employed certain agents for general purposes, and amongst others to receive and pay moneys
on account of the ship, and kept a general account
with them, and also a separate account as managing
owner or ship's husband of the ship's disbursements and
earnings, and, in order to obtain the freight earned by
the vessel from the East India Company, it was necessary that a receipt signed by the managing owner,
and by one or more of the other owners also, should
be given for the money due, and, upon a receipt of
this description, the agents received £2,000, which
was placed by them to the credit of the managing
owner in his account with them, it was held that the
money was received by the agents as agents of the
managing owner, and that the transaction was in effect
the same as if the other joint-owners and the managing owner had received the money, and it had been
then handed over to the managing owner, who had

(*f*) Biddle v. Bond, 6 B. & S. 225 ;   (*g*) Hunt v. Maniere, 33 Beav. 157 ;
34 L. J., Q. B. 137.   Hardman v.   34 L. J., Ch. 142.
Wilcock, 9 Bing. 382.

then placed it in the hands of the agents, as his
bankers,[1] on his own account, and that the joint-owners
could not treat the agents as their debtors. (*h*)   But
where the plaintiffs were owners of a ship, and one of
them was ship's husband, and the latter instructed the
defendant at Quebec to charter the vessel from thence
to England, and the defendant effected a charter-party,
making the freight payable to himself at Quebec, and
received the freight, and claimed to retain it in liquida-
tion of a debt due to him from such ship's husband, it
was held that the contract between the ship's husband
and the ship agent with respect to the management
and chartering of the vessel was a contract which belonged to all the shipowners, and that the defendant
was bound to pay over to them the money received
under that contract. (*i*)

921. *Receipt of money by sub-agents.*—Every agent
is responsible for money received by a sub-agent employed by him for the purpose of receiving the money,
whether the principal had, or had not, reason to suppose that there was any necessity for the employment
of a sub-agent. Thus, if the customer of certain bankers
hands them a bill, in order that they may receive the
money due upon it, and they send the bill to their cor-
respondents at a distant place, and the bill is presented
by them, and the amount paid, the payment to the
sub-agent employed by the bankers for the purpose of
receiving the money is a payment to the bankers to
whom the bill was delivered by the customer, and they
are responsible to him for the money, although it never
reaches their hands and is never passed by them to

(*h*) Sims v. Brittain, 4 B. & Ad. 375.   (*i*) Walshe v. Provan, 8 Exch. 843.

[1] *Ante*, § 801.

the credit of the customer. (*k*)   The sub-agent so employed to receive money is accountable only to the agent, his employer, and can not be sued for the money by the principal. (*l*)   But if he is not strictly a sub-agent, as, for example, if he has received direct instructions from the principal, or is in any respect the agent of the latter, he will be accountable accordingly. Thus, where a creditor employs a country solicitor to recover a debt, and the country solicitor employs a London solicitor to set the legal machinery in motion and the debt is paid to the London solicitor, the latter is accountable to the client for the money, and can not retain it in satisfaction and discharge of a debt due to him from his immediate employer, the country solicitor. (*m*)

922. *Payment by one agent to another agent.*— Where an agent who receives money for his principal pays it over to another agent of that principal, he is bound to pay it in such a way as shall enable the agent to perform his duty to his principal, *i.e.,* he must pay in cash, and not merely settle it in account between that agent and himself; or, if he does so settle it, he takes it on himself to show an authority from his principal, and that there was an account between the principal and that agent, on which the principal was indebted to the latter. (*n*)

923. *Purchases by the agent with the money of the principal.*—The property of a principal intrusted to his factor or agent belongs to the principal, notwithstanding any change which the property may have undergone in point of form, so long as such property

(*k*) Mackersay v. Ramsays, 9 Cl. & Fin. 845.

(*l*) Ireland v. Thompson, 4 C. B 149; 17 L. J., C. P., 248. Stephens v. Badcock, 3 B. & A. D., 354. Cart-

wright v. Hately, Ves. jun. 292. Story's Agency, s. 203.

(*m*) Hanley v. Cassan, 11 Jur. 1088.
(*n*) Alderson, B., ib.

is capable of being identified and distinguished. Where, therefore, a draft for money was intrusted to a broker to buy exchequer bills for his principal, and the broker received the money and purchased American securities with it, and absconded, and was taken on his way to America, and surrendered the securities to his principal, it was held that the principal was entitled to the securities so purchased as against the assignees of the broker, who had become bankrupt. (o)

924. *Frauds by agents on their principals.*—Agents are in a sense trustees, and they owe to their principals a similar duty to that which trustees owe to their cestui que trust. Therefore, when two agents concur in a fraud, both are liable in equity, although one of them only has the benefit of the fraud. Where two confidential agents of a partnership conspired together to obtain for themselves the shares of the partner at an undervalue by keeping the accounts of the firm fraudulently, it was held that their misconduct might be treated as a breach of trust. (p)

925. *Payment of commission.*—If the amount of commission is named by the principal in his letter of instruction to the agent, and the agent declares that it is quite inadequate, but nevertheless acts upon the instructions, he will be bound by the specified commission. If he accepts the retainer, he must take it in its entirety, and can not adopt part and repudiate part, and sue for a reasonable remuneration for his services. (q) A commission-agent, employed to negotiate a sale upon the terms that he is to be paid a commission on the amount of purchase-money, or on the happening of a certain event, will not be entitled to

(o) Taylor v. Plumer, 3 M. & S. 562.

(p) Walsham v. Stainton, 33 L. J.,

Ch. 68.

(q) Moore v. Maxwell, 2 C. & K., 554.

SEC. III.] *PRINCIPAL AND AGENT.* 639

any commission until the purchase-money has been received, or the event has happened, unless there has been fraudulent delay or willful neglect on the part of the employer. (*r*)   In the ordinary course of commercial dealings a compensation is impliedly understood to be due to every person who undertakes the duties and services of an agent, the amount being generally governed by the usage of trade ; but parties who sell as mortgagees or trustees are not entitled to commission, in the absence of any express contract or agreement to pay them for their services.   Where a broker took an assignment of several cargoes in trust to sell on their arrival, and out of the proceeds to repay the amount of his advances, and some of the cargoes were received and sold by him under the power in the deed, whilst the rest were sold under an order made in a suit instituted by him to enforce his security, it was held that in the latter sales he was entitled to his ordinary commission, but not in the former, as he sold, as regarded them, as a trustee. (*s*)   The fact that a party has agreed to sell goods on commission may be proved by oral evidence, though the terms as to the payment of such commission have been reduced into writing. (*t*)   An authority to sell upon certain terms and for certain commission is revoked by the death of the principal before the authority has been acted upon and executed ; and if the agent sells after the death of the principal, he will not be entitled to the agreed commission, unless the personal representative has renewed the authority with knowledge of the contract. (*u*)   If the commission is to be paid on the "net pro-

---

(*r*) Bull v. Price, 5 M. & P. 2 ; 7 Bing. 237. Alder v. Boyle, 4 C. B. 635.

(*s*) Arnold v. Garner 2 Ph. 231.

(*t*) Whitfield v. Brand, 16 M. & W. 282.

(*u*) Campanari v. Woodburn, 15 C. B. 400 ; 24 L. J., C. P. 13.

ceeds," it is payable only on the actual sum which reaches the pocket of the principal after deducting all charges and expenses. (*v*)

926. *Extra work by agents.*—For all work done by the agent in discharge of his business as agent he is paid by his commission, and can make no extra charge; but for work done by order of the principal, beyond his duty as an agent, he is entitled to make an extra charge, provided the work was done under circumstances fairly giving rise to an inference that he was to receive an extra remuneration. (*y*)

927. *Right of ship-brokers to commission.*—Ship-brokers are usually entitled, by the custom and usage of trade, to £5 per cent. commission upon the freight payable upon charter-parties obtained and entered into by their aid and exertions ; and if the amount of freight is uncertain, they may, if they think fit, sue for a reasonable remuneration upon a quantum meruit. The right to the commission does not depend upon the fact of the ship's earning freight ; and the claim is not liable to be cut down by the loss of the vessel, or her failure to get a cargo. (*z*) When a ship-broker has introduced the captain of a ship and a merchant to each other, and they by his means enter into some negotiation for a voyage, the broker is, in general, by usage of trade, entitled to his commission if a charter-party is effected between them for that voyage, even though they may employ another broker to prepare the charter-party, or may write the charter-party themselves. And if a broker, authorized by both parties, and acting as the agent of each, communicates to the merchant what the ship-owner charges, and also communicates to the ship-owner what the merchant will give, and he

---

(*v*) Caine v. Horsfall, 1 Exch. 519.   658.
(*y*) Marshall v Parsons, 9 C. & P.   (*z*) Hill v. Kitching, 3 C. B. 306.

names the ship and the parties, so as to identify the transaction, and a charter-party is ultimately effected for that voyage, this broker is entitled to his commission; but if he does not mention the names, so as to identify the transaction, he does not get his commission to the exclusion of another broker who afterwards introduces the parties personally to each other ; for, if the ship and the parties are not named, the brokers might change the ship, and put in another, pending the negotiation. (*a*)

Where a ship-owner employed A, a ship-broker, to procure a charter for his ship, and A employed B, another broker, who procured the charter, evidence of a usage of trade was admitted to show that the second broker, who actually procured the charter, was entitled to his commission from the ship-owner. (*b*)   But to render the ship-owner responsible upon an implied contract with the second broker, it must be shown that the ship-owner was cognizant of the employment of the latter, and knew, at the time he accepted the charter, that it had been obtained through his instrumentality. (*c*)   A usage of trade can not be given in evidence to impose on the party who has entered into the contract another and wholly different obligation, and to show that, because he has agreed to consign the ship to the charterer's agents on the outward voyage, he is therefore liable to pay the agent's commission on the homeward cargo. (*d*)

928. *Right to commission of policy brokers.*—By the 30 Vict. c. 23, s. 16, the principal is not to be liable

---

(*a*) Burnett v. Bouch, 9 C. & P. 624.

(*b*) Smith v. Boutcher, 1 C. & K. 574.   But see Schmating v. Tomlinson, 6 Taunt. 147.   Boulton v. Jones, 2 H. & N. 564.

(*c*) Smith v. Boucher, 1 C. & K. 576.

(*d*) Phillips v. Briard, 1 H. & N. 27 ; 25 L. J., Ex. 233.

to pay the brokers commission upon effecting a policy of sea insurance, or any premium paid by the broker, unless the policy is duly stamped ; and any sums so paid are to be deemed to have been paid without consideration, and are to remain the property of the principal.

929. *Right to commission of travelers for orders.*—When a commission-agent, employed by a manufacturer to obtain orders, is to receive a commission "on all goods bought" by persons from whom he obtains orders, the commission is earned as soon as a valid bargain of purchase and sale has been made between the manufacturer and the purchaser introduced by such agent, whether the goods are at the time in existence or not in existence, and whether the contract is, or is not, ultimately carried into effect, and whether it turns out to be a bad bargain, productive of loss, or an advantageous transaction. (*e*)

930. *Commission of house-agents, estate-agents and auctioneers.*—If a man having a house or estate to sell or let, places it in the hands of several house-agents, with instructions to procure a purchaser or tenant, the successful agent is alone entitled to commission, unless instructions have been given to the other house-agents to advertise the house, or render some particular or special services in the matter, entitling them by the custom of the trade to some remuneration. (*f*) But, if the relation of buyer or seller is really brought about by the act of the agent, he is entitled to his commission, although the actual sale was not effected by him. (*g*) Where A promised to pay B a sum of money if he would procure him a tenant

(*e*) Lockwood v. Levick, 8 C. B., N. S. 603 ; 29 L. J., C. P. 340.

(*f*) Prickett v. Badger, 1 C. B., N. S. 685.

S. 296 ; 26 L. J., C. P. 33.

(*g*) Green v. Bartlett, 14 C. B., N. S. 685.

at a certain rent, it was held that B was entitled to the money as soon as a party introduced by him had been accepted by A, and a binding agreement for the tenancy had been entered into. (*h*)   In a great number of instances house-agents go to a great deal of trouble on the terms that, if they get no purchaser they shall have no claim ; and, if upon the contingencies which have happened nothing was to be paid, nothing can of course be recovered. (*i*)   Where an auctioneer was employed to sell ground-rents by auction, on the terms of receiving one per cent. commission on the sale, and, after he had advertised the sale, but before the day of sale, the employer sold the rents by private contract, it was held that a notorious custom in the trade, for the auctioneer to receive his full commission in such a case, might be engrafted upon the contract. (*k*)   But the usage must be so universal that every one in the trade must be taken to know it. (*l*)

931. *The right of the agent to be reimbursed upon the revocation of his authority* depends upon the terms of the contract by which his services were retained, and the custom and usage of the trade in which he is engaged.   When an agent is employed to sell or to let, on the terms that he is to be paid a certain percentage on the price or the rent, the general understanding is that he takes his chance of a large remuneration in case he finds a purchaser or a tenant, but gets nothing if he fails in so doing; but, if trouble and expense have been properly incurred by the agent in endeavouring to carry into effect the instructions of the principal, and the latter revokes the authority, and prevents the agent from reaping the ex-

(*h*) Horford v. Wilson, 1 Taunt. 15.   (*k*) Rainy v. Vernon, 9 C. & P.

(*i*) Green v. Mules, 30 L. J., C. P.   559.

343.   (*l*) Wood v. Wood, 1 Ib. 60.

pected reward, the principal is bound to remunerate him for his trouble and expenses in the matter. (*m*)

Where an estate-agent, employed to sell at a given price, succeeds in finding a purchaser, but the principal then declines to sell, the agent is entitled to sue for a reasonable remuneration for his services ; and the amount of his commission on the price would seem to be the sum to which he is fairly entitled ; but, if the authority is revoked before it is executed, and a purchaser has been found, it does not follow that he is entitled to sue upon an implied contract for remuneration for his work and labor in endeavoring to find a purchaser or a tenant. (*n*)   If it is the practice of house-agents to charge a fee for entering property to be let or sold in their register book, and the employer has notice of this, or it is proved to be a known custom of the trade, the employer will be bound-to pay this fee, although the authority may be revoked, or the agent may have failed to render any beneficial service.   This registration fee is all that the house-agent is entitled to charge for ordinary services, in the absence of any special instructions for advertisements. (*o*)

Where a public company employed a broker to dispose of their shares, on the terms that he should be paid £100 down, and £400 in addition upon the allotment of the whole of the shares of the company, and the broker disposed of a considerable number of shares, when the company was wound up, it was held that the broker was prevented from earning the £400

(*m*) Simpson v. Lamb, 17 C. B. 616.

(*n*) Pickett v. Badger, 1 C. B., N. S. 296 ; 26 L. J., C. P. 33.

Campanari v. Woodburn, 15 C. B. 407.

(*o*) Simpson v. Lamb, 17 C. B. 616.

by the act of the company, and was therefore entitled to sue them for damages. (*p*)

932. *Lien of factors and brokers.*—Factors and brokers to whom goods are consigned to be sold have a lien for the general balance due to them from their employers or principals in the ordinary course of their business as factors, and for their acceptances on behalf of such employers, upon the goods whilst they are in their possession, and on the moneys realised by the sale of them. (*q*) This right exists universally by the custom of the trade. It is part of the law merchant, and as such is judicially taken notice of by the courts, no proof being ever required as a matter of fact that such general lien exists. The lien does not extend to a collateral debt not growing out of the relationship of principal and factor, such as a debt due for rent, (*r*) nor to goods which have not actually reached the hands of the factor, (*s*) and come into his possession with the consent and direction of the owner ; consequently, if goods have been left at the factor's place of business by mistake or inadvertence, (*t*) or have been taken possession of by him without the authority of the owner, he can not set up a lien upon them for his balance. (*u*) And, if the party from whom he receives the goods is only an agent, he can not retain them as against the true owner of the debt that was due to him from the agent at the time the goods were put into his hands, and which was not contracted on the credit of the deposit of the goods ; but it is otherwise if he has made advances on the credit of the de-

<hr>

(*p*) Inchbald v. Western Neilgherry &c., Co., 17 C. B., N. S. 733 ; 34 L. J., C P. 15.

(*q*) Kruger v. Wilcox, Ambl. 252. Hudson v. Granger, 5 B. & Ald. 31. Hammond v. Barclay, 2 East, 227.

(*r*) Houghton v. Mathews, 3 B. & P. 485.

(*s*) Kinloch v. Craig, 3 T. R. 123.

(*t*) Lucas v. Dorrien, 7 Taunt. 278,

(*u*) Taylor v. Robinson, 2 Moore, 730.

posit, not knowing the depositor to be an agent. (*v*) The factor can only claim a lien for his general balance upon goods which come to his hands as factor. A factor, therefore, who effects a policy of insurance, not as factor but as an insurance-broker, is not entitled to a general lien on a policy in his hands for a balance due to him in his character of factor. (*y*)'

933. *Lien of insurance-brokers.*—Insurance-brokers have also, by the general usage and custom of trade, a lien for the general balance due to them from their employers upon all policies effected by them for such employers, and left in their hands, and upon all moneys received by them upon such policies from the underwriters, unless the party for whom they effected the policy was himself only an agent in the matter, in which case the extent of the lien will depend upon the disclosure or concealment of the agency, and the degree of credit they may have given to the agent, under the impression that he was the party really interested in the policy. The lien does not extend to a collateral debt not incurred in respect to brokerage business. If a policy-broker is employed by an agent, and there is no disclosure of the agency, and nothing to lead the broker to think that any third party is interested in the policy, and the assurance is accordingly

(*v*) Pultney v. Keymer, 3 Esp. 181.　　(*y*) Dixon v. Stansfield, 10 C. B. 398.

' An insurance broker may retain his principal's policy, if the latter be indebted to him on the balance of their insurance accounts; Spring v. Ins. Co., 8 Wheat, 268; Moody v. Webster, 3 Pick. 454; Cranston v. Ins. Co., 5 Bin. 538; and may apply to such balance moneys received on account of the policy, even with notice that it belongs to a third person; see Foster v. Hoyt, 3 Johns. Cas. 327; but not if he knows his principal to be the agent of another party. Shook v. David-son, 16 Pet. 1; Bank v. Bank, 17 Id. 174; and see Jarvis v. Rodgers, 15 Mass. 396.

effected in the name of the agent as owner, and a loss occurs, and the policy is allowed, after the loss, to remain in the broker's hands, and the latter then permits the agent to get into his debt, not knowing him to be an agent, the broker will have a lien as against the principal upon the policy, and upon the money he receives thereon from the underwriters, to the extent of the debt due to him from the agent as well as for his commission and charges for effecting the policy. (*z*) But, if there is the slightest indication of the agency to the broker, such as a declaration by a British subject in time of war that the property is neutral, (*a*) or a statement that the assurance is to be effected "for a correspondent in the country," (*b*) or that the property to be insured belongs to a merchant abroad, who has consigned it to the agent with full power of disposition over it, and with authority to indorse the bill of lading, (*c*) the broker will have a lien only for his commission and charges for the insurance, and not for the balance due to him from the agent.[1]

934. *Lien of solicitors.*—Solicitors also have a lien upon all money recovered by them in the actions and suits in which they are employed, and upon all the deeds and papers and other articles of their clients which come to their hands in their professsional capacity, for the purposes of business, not only for the costs of the particular cause or matter with which such deeds or papers are connected, but for the costs due to them

---

(*z*) Mann v. Forrester, 4 Campb. 61. 337.
Westwood v. Bell, ib. 355. Olive v. Smith, 5 Taunt. 56.

(*a*) Maauss v. Henderson, 1 East,

(*b*) Snook v. Davidson, 2 Campb. 218.

(*c*) Lanyon v. Blanchard, ib. 597.

See last note.

generally from their clients. (*d*)   But the lien does
not attach while the suit is still pending ; and the
parties may compromise the dispute and thus deprive
the solicitor of his lien, if the compromise is bonâ fide.
(*e*)   By the 23 & 24 Vict. c. 127, s. 28, the court may
charge property recovered through the instrumentality
of a solicitor with the payment of his costs. If
the solicitor discharges himself during the suit, he
loses his lien, so far, at any rate, as relates to papers
necessary for the successful prosecution of the suit ;
but it is otherwise if he is discharged by his client. (*f*)
A solicitor has no lien upon the will of a client for
the costs incurred in the preparation of it, and can
not therefore refuse to produce it after his client's
death until his costs have been paid. And, where
deeds are delivered for a specific purpose, the right of
lien is extinguished as soon as the particular purpose
has been accomplished; and it may be superseded
altogether by the attorney's taking from the client
security for his costs. (*g*)   A solicitor can not set up
the lien of his London agent on the papers of his client
against the claims of that client, the client having
paid his solicitor's bill. (*h*)   The town agent of a
country solicitor has a lien only upon the money recovered, and upon the papers in his hands in the particular cause in which he is engaged, for the amount
due to him by the solicitor in that particular cause.
He can not set up a claim of lien for the general balance due to him from the country solicitor who em-

(*d*) Stevenson v. Blakelock, 1 M.
& S. 535. Lambert v. Buckmaster, 2
B. & C. 616. Blunden v. Desert, 2
Dru. & W. 405. Friswell v. King, 15
Sim. 191.

(*e*) Morrison *ex parte*, L. R., 4 Q. B.
153. S. C. Sullivan v. Pearson, 38 L.

J., Q. B. 65. Mercer v. Graves, L. R.,
7 Q. B. 499 ; 41 L. J., Q. B. 212.

(*f*) Faithful, *in re*, L. R., 6 Eq.
325.

(*g*) Genges v. Genges, 18 Ves. 294.
Balch v. Lymes, Turn. & R. 92.

(*h*) *In re* Andrew, 30 L. J., Ex.
403.

ploys him, and can not retain the money or papers of the client to satisfy his general debt. (*i*) [1]

A solicitor can not set up a general lien for the balance due to him in respect of services not rendered by him as a solicitor; nor can he detain deeds and papers which do not come to him in his professional character. He has no lien, for example, where he acts or holds papers as town clerk, (*k*) or steward of a manor; (*l*) he can not set up any lien which is inconsistent with the nature of his employment, or the terms, or conditions, or express or implied trust upon which he received the papers. (*m*) His right, moreover, is dependent upon the rights of his clients; and he can not acquire more extensive powers over the papers in his hands than the client himself possessed at the time he deposited them with him. (*n*) If a solicitor transacts business for a firm in partnership collectively, and also manages the private business of the members of the firm individually, he has no lien upon the private securities, deeds, and writings of one partner in respect of the business done for the firm. (*o*)[2]

935. *Lien of shipmasters.*—An agent can not, in general, acquire a lien upon the property of his principal for work done by others whom he has employed and paid. But a shipmaster has a lien on the freight, not only for his wages, but for any expenditure which

---

(*i*) White v. R. Ex. Ass. Co., 7 Moore, 249. Moody v. Spencer, 2 D. & R. 6. Anon., 2 Dick. 802.

(*k*) Champernown v. Scott, 6 Mad. 93.

(*l*) Rex v. Sankey, 5 Ad. & E. 428.

(*m*) Lawson v. Dickenson, 8 Mod. 307.

(*n*) Hollis v. Clarige, 4 Taunt. 807. Esdaile v. Oxenham, 3 B. & C. 229. Lightfoot v. Keene, 1 M. & W. 745. Molesworth v. Robbins, 2 Jones & Lat. 358.

(*o*) Steadman v. Hockly, 15 M. & W. 553.

[1] See *ante*, § 790.

[2] Id.

he may make in the ordinary discharge of his duties as master, and which is necessary for the performance of the voyage ; (*p*) and where he makes a special contract, in itself *ultra vires*, in order to fulfill which he incurs special expenses, if the owner adopts the benefit of that contract, he must also bear its burthens. Where, therefore, the master of an ordinary seeking ship entered into a charter-party, under seal, to carry troops from the Mauritius to England, and stipulated, on his own responsibility, in the charter-party, that he would make certain alterations in the ship, in order to enable him to carry the troops, and at the Cape of Good Hope entered into another charter-party, not under seal, to a similar effect, and made the specified alterations, and paid money and drew bills to meet the expenses necessary to the making of these alterations, and the voyage was performed, it was held that, in equity, the master was first entitled out of the freight earned under these charter-parties, to be repaid the sums advanced, and to be indemnified against the bills, and that the owner (or his mortgagee) was only entitled to the nett freight after deducting these charges. (*q*) At common law the master has a possessory lien on the cargo, not only for freight, but also for general average. (*r*)

636. *Indemnification of agents.*—The principal is bound to indemnify his agent in respect of all payments which may be made by the latter in the due course of his employment. (*s*) If the agent has necessarily incurred liabilities and expenses in follow-

---

(*p*) The Feronia, L. R., 2 Adm. 65 ; 37 L. J., Adm. 60.

(*q*) Bristow v. Whitmore, 9 H. L. C. 391.

(*r*) Cleary v. M'Andrew, 2 Moo. P. C., N. S. 216.

(*s*) Risbourg v. Bruckner, 3 C. B., N. S. 823 ; 27 L. J., C. P. 90. Taylor v. Stray, 2 C. B., N. S. 175. Westropp v. Solomon, 8 C. B. 369. Johnstone v. Usborne, 11 Ad. & E. 549.

ing out his instructions bonâ fide, he may sue the principal upon an implied promise of indemnity ; (*t*) but he can not resort to the principal for an indemnity against the consequences of his own default, wrongful act, or want of skill and caution in the execution of his commission, (*u*) although a general indemnity against all charges and expenses he may be put to in executing his commission may have been given to him by his employer. (*v*) If the agent, in the execution of his commission, has been compelled to pay money on behalf of the principal, he is entitled to recover the amount from the latter, whether the principal has or has not been relieved from liability by the payment. (*y*) If A employs B as a broker to buy shares in a company, according to the rules of the Stock Exchange, for a certain account day, and B, in accordance with such rules, pays for and takes a transfer of the shares on that day, A is bound to repay B the amount so paid, although before such account-day the company is being wound up under the 25 & 26 Vict. c. 89, s. 153, which enacts that every transfer of shares shall then be void, unless the court otherwise orders. (*z*) By the Roman and continental law, it is laid down that there results from all agencies, mandates, and commissions, an implied contract on the part of the principal or employer to indemnify the agent for all his disbursements and expenses, and for all the lia-

(*t*) Adamson v. Jarris, 4 Bing. 71 ; 12 Moore, 241. Betts v. Gibbins, 2 Ad. & El. 57 ; 4 N. & M. 64. Rawlings v. Bell, 1 C. B. 960.

(*u*) Toplis v. Grane, 7 Sc. 641. Farebrother v. Ansley, 1 Camp. 347. Duncan v. Hill, L. R., 8 Ex. 242 ; 42 L. J., Ex. 179.

(*v*) Ibbett v. De la Salle, 30 L. J., Ex. 44.

(*y*) Brittain v. Lloyd, 14 M. & W. 762 ; 15 L. J., Ex. 43. Spurrier v. Elderton, 5 Esp. 1. Pettiman v. Keble, 9 C. B. 701.

(*z*) Chapman v. Shepherd, L. R., 2 C. P. 228 ; 36 L. J., C. P. 113. Biederman v. Stone, 36 L J., C. P. 198 ; L. R., 2 C. P. 504.

bilities incurred by him in the execution of his commission. (*a*)

937. *Breach of warranty of authority by agents*
Where an agent pretended to be authorized by a specified firm to purchase a ship on their behalf, and it turned out that he had no authority, and the shipowner was obliged to look out for another purchaser of the vessel, and lost £250 on the re-sale, it was held that the £250 was the measure of damage in an action against the agent for a breach of an implied undertaking or promise that the authority which he professed to have did in point of fact exist. (*b*) Where an agent pretended to be authorized to grant a lease, and it turned out that he had no such authority, it was held that the intended lessee was entitled to recover the value of the lease and all costs paid and incurred by him in endeavoring to enforce specific performance down to the time when the agent disclosed the fact of his want of authority, but not the damages and costs arising out of the re-sale by the intended lessee of his lease. (*c*) If a man puts money into the hands of another to purchase goods, and he neglects to make the purchase, and is sued for a breach of his undertaking in that behalf, the proper measure of damages is the value of the goods to the employer if they had been duly purchased, not the value of the money. (*d*)

(*a*) Dig. lib. 17, tit. 1, lex 12, § 9.
Poth. Mandat, No. 68–75. Domat. liv.
1, tit. 15, § 2.

(*b*) Simons v. Patchett, 17 Ell. &
Bl. 568 ; 26 L. J., Q. B. 195. And
see further, as to damages recoverable
for false representation of authority
by agents, Collen v. Wright, 8 Ell.
and Bl. 659; 27 L. J., Q. B. 215.

Hughes v. Græme, *ante* ; Pow v. Davis, *ante.*

(*c*) Spedding v. Nevell, L. R., 4 C.
P. 212 ; 38 L. J., C. P. 133. Godwin
v. Francis, L. R., 5 C. P. 295 ; 39 L.
J., C. P. 121.

(*d*) Ehrensperger v. Anderson, 3
Exch. 158.

SECTION IV.

CONTRACTS FOR CARRIAGE.

938. *Of contracts for the carriage of merchandise.*—Every person who accepts goods and chattels for conveyance to a particular destination for hire or reward, paid or agreed to be paid him for the carriage of them, impliedly lets out his labor and care in return for the hire or reward agreed to be paid to him. The contract, therefore, belongs to the class locatio operis. It was styled by the Roman jurists locatio operis mercium vehendarum, or the letting out of the work of carrying merchandise. The owner who delivered the goods to the carrier to be carried was the letter of the work of carrying ; and he was also at the same time the hirer of the labor and services of the carrier ; whilst the carrier, on the other hand, was both the hirer of the work of carrying and the letter of his own labor and services, care, and attention, to be employed in and about the conveyance and transport of the merchandise.

939. *Contracts of affreightment—Charter-parties.*—When goods and merchandise are carried by sea from one place to another, they are usually shipped on board a vessel under a charter-party or a bill of lading. A charter-party is a contract whereby the ship-owner or the shipmaster covenants or agrees for the use of the ship by the charterer for some specified period of time, or for a particular voyage or adventure. The contract derives its name from the Latin term charta partita, there being anciently as many divided parts of the contract as there were parties to it, each party

having his part of the contract as a security against
fraud or mistake. The customary stipulations on the
part of the shipowner or master are, that the ship shall
be tight and staunch, and well equipped and manned,
and furnished with all the necessaries for the voyage ;
that she shall be ready by a day appointed to receive
the cargo, and shall wait a certain number of days to
take it on board, and after lading, shall sail with the
first fair wind for the destined port, and there deliver
the goods in proper order and condition to the order
of the charterer ; and further, that during the continuance of the voyage the ship shall be tight and staunch,
and furnished with sufficient men and other necessaries,
to the best of the owner's endeavors. The charterer,
on the other hand, usually covenants to load the ship
after she shall be ready to receive her cargo, and unload her within a certain number of days, and to pay
freight at so much per ton according to the tonnage
of the vessel, or according to the quantity of goods
shipped on board, or according to the time of the ship's
employment. Prima facie, the law of the place where a
contract is made is that which the parties are to be
presumed to have adopted as the footing upon which
they dealt ; and such law ought to prevail in the absence of circumstances indicating a different intention.
But a contract of affreightment made between a charterer and shipowner of different nationalities in a place
where they are both foreigners may, under some circumstances, be construed by the law of the nation of
the ship. (*a*)

940. *When the contract operates as a demise or
bailment of the ship.*—Although the shipowner, by the
charter-party, expressly grants the vessel to be used

(*a*) Lloyd v. Guibert, 6 B. & S. 100 ; L. R., 1 Q. B. 115 ; 35 L. J., Q. B. 74.

by the charterer, the contract will, nevertheless, not amount in general to a demise or bailment of the ship to the charterer, so as to clothe him with the possession of the vessel, but simply to a contract for the use of the ship, together with the services of the master and crew, for the conveyance of merchandise, *i.e.*, to a contract for the letting and hiring of the work of carrying merchandise. If the end sought to be attained by a charter-party can be accomplished without a transfer of the possession of the vessel to the charterer, the courts will not give effect to the contract as a demise of the ship, although there may be express words of grant and demise. (*b*) If, however, the nature of the service and the due attainment of the object sought to be accomplished require the vessel to be absolutely under the control, and subject to the orders and directions, of the charterer; if she is to be employed in warfare, or in the fishing or coasting trade, or as a general ship for the conveyance of merchandise by the charterer for third parties, and is to be at the general disposal of the latter to sail upon any service that he may require, the courts will give effect to the contract as a demise of the ship. (*c*) In this case the contract is a contract for the letting and hiring of a chattel, and belongs to the class locatio rei. [1] The services of the master and crew pass as merely accessorial to the principal subject-matter of the contract ; they attorn, as it were, to the charterer, and become temporarily the servants of the latter, bound to obey his orders.

941. *Parties to charter-parties.*—If the parties

(*b*) Christie v. Lewis, 5 Mooer, 253 ; 2 B. & B. 410. Saville v. Campion, 2 B. & Ald. 510. Dean v. Hogg, 4 M. & Sc. 195.

(*c*) Trinity House v. Clerk, 4 M. & S. 295, 299. Hutton v. Bragg, 7 Taunt. 14.

[1] *Ante,* § 790.

have contracted by deed, the contract is with those who have executed the instrument, and covenanted therein in their own names, or by some known title or description. If the charter-party contains covenants both on the part of the owners and the master for the conveyance of the cargo, and has been executed by both, either the owners or the master are responsible at the election of the covenantee. If it has been entered into and executed by the owners alone, they alone are liable upon it ; whilst, if the master is the only executing party, the contract is with him alone, although the deed may be expressed to be made by him for and on behalf of his employers, the shipowners. If the master covenants in his own name, the contract is exclusively the contract of the master.[1] He constitutes himself in such a case the carrier of the goods, and becomes personally responsible upon the express covenants contained in the charter party, and also upon all such implied covenants and engagements as result from the contract and the nature of the employ-ment. (*d*)

When a charter-party of affreightment operates as a demise or bailment of the ship to the charterer, and the vessel is employed by the latter as a general ship

---

(*d*) Horsley v. Rush, cited 7 T. R. 209.

[1] See *ante*, vol 1, § 71, *et seq.* as to a charter party made by a master. See King v. Lennox, 19 Johns. R. 235 ; Hurry v. Assignees of Hurry, 2 Wash. R. 145 ; The Schooner Tribune, 3 Sumn. R. 144. It is said, in Dixon on the Law of Shipping, citing Pickering v. Holt, 6 Greenl. R. 160, to be well settled that "the master has no power, merely in the character of master, without a superadded agency, to bind the owners by a charter party under his hand and seal, so as to subject them to an action of covenant thereon. See 3 Kent Com. 3d ed. 204 ; Mears v. Morrison, Breese, 172 ; Deming v. Bullitt, 1 Black, 241.

for the conveyance of merchandise, the charterer becomes the carrier of the goods shipped on board, and the master is his servant and agent whilst procuring freight and contracting with third parties for the carriage of merchandise, and not the agent of the registered owners of the vessel, and the latter, consequently, can not be made responsible for the loss of, or injury to, the goods shipped on board under such contracts. (*e*) But when the charter-party operates merely as a contract between the charterer and the shipowner for the conveyance by the latter of goods and merchandise to be shipped on board by the charterer, the registered owners are then the carriers of the goods, and will be responsible to the charterer for the non-conveyance of them, according to their contract. And if the ship is put up as a general ship, without any intimation that she is under charter, and third parties ship goods and take bills of lading from the master, the owners will be responsible for the safe stowage and carriage of the goods so shipped. (*f*) If in such a case the master refuses to sign bills of lading, except " as per charter-party," the shipper can not be compelled to accept such bills, but may insist on having his goods returned. (*g*) Although the shipowners are not parties to a charter-party under seal, entered into by the master in his own name on their behalf, yet they are responsible for a breach of those duties and obligations which attach to them in their character of carriers, independently of the charter-party. Thus, where a plaintiff had shipped a cargo of oranges on board a vessel, of which the defendants were the

(*e*) James v. Jones, 3 Esp. 27. Major v. White, 7 C. & P. 41.

(*f*) Sandeman v. Scurr, L. R., 2 Q. B. 86 ; 56 L. J., Q. B. 58. The Figlia Maggiore, L. R., 2 A. & E. 106 ; 37 L. J., Adm. 52.

(*g*) Peck v. Larsen, L. R., 12 Eq. 378 ; 40 L. J., Ch. 763.

owners, to be carried for hire from St. Michael's to London, but the defendants employed an unskillful master, through whose negligence the oranges were lost, it was held that the shipowners were responsible for the loss, although the goods had been shipped on board by virtue of a charter-party of affreightment under seal executed by the master, by which the latter had covenanted to convey the cargo to its destination. (*h*) When the contract of affreightment is not under seal, the action for the breach of such contract, and of the implied promises and engagements resulting from the acceptance of goods to be carried for hire, may be brought, either against the owners who appoint the master to the command of the vessel, and constitute him their agent for the employment of the ship, or against the master who has accepted the goods to be carried, whether the contract is expressed to be made, or whether the goods have been accepted by him, in his own name only, or for and on behalf of his principals and employers; but, when the plaintiff has elected to proceed against and has sued one, the other is discharged. (*i*) An agent is not ordinarily liable, as we shall presently see, upon simple contracts entered into by him in a representative character on behalf of his principal ; but the master of a ship is considered to be something more than a mere agent, and is made responsible accordingly. (*k*) [1]

942. *Performance of the terms and conditions of the contract.*—If, by a charter-party of affreightment,

(*h*) Leslie v. Wilson, 6 Moore, 429 ; 3 B. & B. 171. Fletcher v. Braddick, 5 B. & P. 186. Fenton v. Dub. St. P. Co., 8 Ad. & E. 843.

(*i*) Priestly v. Fernie, 3 H. & C. 977 ; 34 L. J., Ex. 172.

(*k*) Ellis v. Turner, 8 T. R., 533 Boson v. Sandford, 1 Show. 104. Morse v. Slue, 1 ventr. 190, 238. Liver Alkali Co. v. Johnson, L. R., 7 Ex. 367 ; 41 L. J., Ex. 110.

[1] See *ante*, vol. 1, § 71, *et seq.*, and last note.

a shipowner agrees that his ship shall sail to a " safe port " to take in a cargo, the naming of a " safe port " is a condition precedent to the shipowner's liability to send out the vessel. (*l*) The voyage begins from the time the vessel breaks ground to proceed to her place of loading; so that if the charter-party contains the usual exception of dangers and accidents of seas, rivers, and navigation during the voyage, and the vessel is delayed or hindered by foul weather in getting there, the delay is within the exception. (*m*) If the shipowner agrees that the vessel shall leave England on or before a particular day to bring back a cargo from a foreign port, or that she shall arrive at a foreign port by a particular day and shall be ready to receive cargo, the departure or arrival of the vessel at the time specified constitute a condition precedent to the freighter's liability to provide the cargo, and use the ship, and pay freight. (*n*) Where, by charter-party, the freighter covenanted to pay freight for a vessel at so much a ton per month until her final discharge, so much of such freight as might be earned at the time of the arrival of the ship at her first destined port abroad, to be paid within ten days next after arrival there, and the remainder of the freight at specific periods, it was held that the arrival of the ship at her first destined port abroad was a condition precedent to the owner's right to recover any freight. (*o*)

943. *Representations in charter-parties.*—If a vessel is described in a charter-party as A 1, it is a war-

(*l*) Rae v. Hackett, 12 M. & W. 724; 13 L. J., Ex. 216.

(*m*) Barker v. M'Andrew, 18 C. B. N. S. 759; 34 L J., C. P. 191.

(*n*) Glaholm v. Hayes, 2 Sc. N. R. 471. Shadforth v. Higgin, 3 Campb. 385. Lovatt v. Hamilton, 5 M. & W.

644. Oliver v. Fielden, 4 Exch. 135. Croockewit v. Fletcher, 1 H. & N. 912; 26 L. J., Ex. 153. Behn v. Burness, 3 B. & S. 759; 32 L. J., Q. B. 204.

(*o*) Graves v. Legg, 9 Exch. 717; 23 L. J., Ex. 231.

ranty that she is A 1 at the time the description is given, but not that she shall continue so, or retain the same letter on her arrival at the port of loading. (*p*) A representation in a charter-party that the ship chartered is "now at sea, having sailed three weeks ago," is a warranty; (*q*) and describing her as "the steamship H," is a warranty that the principal motive power is steam; (*r*) but a representation that she is 180 tons when she is 200 is mere description and a warranty. (*s*) A statement in a charter-party that the ship is expected to be at Alexandria about the 13th of December is a warranty that she is then in such a place and under such engagement as that she may reasonably be expected to be at Alexandria about the day named. (*t*) Whenever a descriptive statement in a charter-party was intended to be a substantive part of the contract, it will be as a warranty.　Such a statement is more or less important, in proportion as the object of the contract more or less depends upon it.　In some cases, if not performed by the party making it, it will enable the other to repudiate the contract *in toto*.　In other cases it gives only a claim to compensation in damages for a breach of contract. (*u*) [1]

(*p*) Hurst v. Osborne, 18 C. B. 154; 25 L. J., C. P. 209. Ruth v. Macmillan, 33 L. J., Ex. 38 ; 2 H. & C. 750.

(*q*) Ollive v. Booker, 1 Exch. 416.

(*r*) Fraser v. The Telegraph Construction Co., L. R., 7 Q. B. 566; 41 L. J., Q. B. 249.

(*s*) Baker v. Windle, 6 El. & Bl. 674.

(*t*) Corkling v. Massey, L. R., 8 C, P. 395 ; 42 L. J., C. P., 153.

(*u*) Behn v. Burness, 3 B. & S. 753 : 32 L. J., Q. B. 204. Neill v. Whitworth, 34 ib. C. P. 155 ; 18 C. B. N. S. 435.

[1] It is always an implied warranty in the contract, that the ship he sufficient for the voyage ; and the owner, like all other common carriers, is an insurer against everything except the perils. Putnam v. Wood, 3 Mass. 481 ; Pelva v. Low, 2 J hns. C ts. 134; Elliott v. Russell, 10 Johns. 1 ; Richards v. Gil ert, 5 Day, 415 ; Emery v. Hersey, 4 Greenl. 407 ; Bell v.

944. *Substantial performance of conditions precedent.*—Where the plaintiff covenanted to let his ship to freight to the defendants, and take a cargo on board, and proceed therewith to Naples, and make delivery thereof to the agents of the defendants, and, having so done, receive on board a return cargo, and the defendants, in consideration of the premises, covenanted that they would provide a complete homeward cargo and pay freight, and the plaintiff received the cargo and proceeded with it to Naples, where it was seized by the Neapolitan Government, it was held that the material part of the covenant was the letting of the ship and the making of the voyage, and, as that

---

Reed, 4 Binn. 127; Hart v. Allen, 2 Watts, 114; Reed v. Dick, 8 Id. 480; 3 Kent Com. (5th ed.) 205. It is the duty of the owner of a ship, when he charters her or puts her up for freight, to see that she is in a suitable condition to transport her cargo in safety, and he is to keep her in that condition, unless prevented by perils of the seas or unavoidable accidents. If the goods be lost by any defects in the vessel, whether latent or visible, known or unknown, the owner is answerable to the freighter, upon the principle that he tacitly contracts that his vessel shall be fit for the purpose for which he designs her. Putnam v. Wood, 3 Mass. 481; and see Kimball v. Tucker, 10 Id. 192; Goodridge v. Lord, Id. 483. The owner's responsibility begins when the wharfinger's ends, when the goods are delivered to some responsible person upon the ship; 3 Kent (5th ed.) 206; Dixon on Shipping, § 119; and the shipowner is liable for latent defects in his ship, whose existence is unknown to himself; Backhouse v. Sneed, 1 Murphy, 173. And it is held to constitute unseaworthiness if a ship proceed without a pilot in waters where it is the custom to take a licensed pilot. Keller v. Firemens' Ins. Co., 3 Hill, 250; McMillan v. Insurance Co., 1 Rice, 248; Silva v. Low, 1 Johns. Cas. 184; Dow v. Smith, 1 Caines, 32; Bell v. Read, 4 Binn. 124; Brown v. Gerrard, 4 Yates, 115; Stocker v. Merrimack Ins. Co., 6 Mass. 220; Cleveland v. Union Ins. Co., 8 Id. 308; and this, even where a pilot refused to take out the ship; Stanwood v. Rich, cited in Dixon on Shipping, § 121.

had been performed, the defendants were bound to provide the return cargo and pay the freight. (*x*) And, where the plaintiff's let a ship to the defendants, and covenanted to take on board at Havre six pipes of brandy, with such other goods as the captain might procure on freight, and proceed therewith to Terceira, and there take a cargo on board and proceed therewith to London, and the defendants in consideration of the completion of the voyage, covenanted to pay freight, and guaranteed the ship a complete cargo home, and it appeared that the voyage to Terceira had been performed, and that the ship was ready to receive the return cargo at that place, it was held that the covenant relating to the taking on board the brandy at Havre and carrying it to Terceira was not a condition precedent to the liability of the defendants upon their covenant to provide the homeward cargo, but a distinct and independent covenant, for the breach of which the plaintiffs were liable in damages. (*y*)

945. *Time of performance.*—If the vessel is to proceed to a particular port and there load a full cargo, the loading must be completed within a reasonable time ; and, if unusual and extraordinary circumstances arise preventing the shipowner from doing what he has undertaken to do, he must make compensation in damages, as he ought to have provided against the unforeseen contingency by his contract. (*z*) If parties by advertisement hold out that they are ready to give a guarantee that a vessel shall sail on a particular day,

---

(*x*) Storer v. Gordon, 3 M & S. 308. (*y*) Fothergill v. Walton, 8 Taunt. 576 ; 2 Moore, 630. Stavers v. Curling, 3 Sc. 740. Pust v. Dowie, 33 L. J., Q. B. 172 ; 34 ib. 127 ; 5 B. & S. 20. Behn v. Burness, *ante.*

(*z*) Adams v. Royal Mail, &c., 5 C.

B. N. S. 497 ; 28 L. J., C. P. 33. Kearon v. Pearson, 7 H. & N. 386 ; 31 L. J., Ex. 1 ; and see Ford v. Cotesworth, L. R., 4 Q. B. 134 ; 39 L. J., Q. B. 188, where the charter party was silent as to the time for unloading.

and an intended passenger takes a berth on the strength of the assurance, the time named will be of the essence of the contract. (*a*) But this is not the case, if merchandise is shipped on board, and the vessel carries it to the place of destination. Where, by charter-party, the plaintiff let his vessel to freight to the defendant, and covenanted that the vessel should sail with the next wind on a voyage to Cadiz, and the defendant covenanted that, if the ship went the intended voyage and returned to the Downs, the plaintiff should have so much by way of freight for the voyage, the substance of the covenant was considered to be that the ship should perform the intended voyage, that being the primary intention of the parties, and not merely that she should sail with the next wind, which might change every hour, and that this was shown by the covenant of the defendant, who was to pay so much for the performance of the voyage, and not merely for sailing with the next wind. (*b*) And, where the covenant was that the vessel should proceed with the first convoy to Spain and Portugal, and there make a delivery of the cargo, &c., in consideration whereof the defendant covenanted to pay freight, it was held that the main object of the contract was the performance of the voyage, and that the sailing with the first convoy was not a condition precedent to the plaintiff's right to recover freight for the voyage actually performed, but a distinct covenant, for the breach of which he was liable in damages. (*c*) So, where the covenant was that the ship should sail on freight to Demerara on or before the 12th of February

---

(*a*) Cranston v. Marshall, 5 Exch. 395 ; 19 L. J., Ex. 340.

(*b*) Constable v. Cloberie, Palm. 397. Bornmann v. Tooke, 1 Campb. 377.

(*c*) Davidson v. Gwynne, 12 East, 380.

and the vessel did not sail until the 12th of March, LAWRENCE, J., held that, as the voyage had been actually performed, and the cargo conveyed to the destined port, and the profit of it gained by the defendant, there could be no foundation for saying that the defendant should not pay the freight for it according to the covenant, and that he might bring a cross action to recover damages for the not sailing in time, if he had sustained any. (*d*) And, where the plaintiff let his vessel to the defendant, and covenanted forthwith to make her tight, staunch, and strong, and well, and sufficiently manned and victualled, &c., for a twelve month's voyage, and the defendant covenanted to pay freight so much per ton per month, and the vessel was taken into the service of the defendants, who used her for several months, and then refused to fulfill their covenant to pay freight, on the ground that the plaintiff had not manned and victualled the ship, and made her tight and strong, according to his covenant, it was held that, as the defendants had not repudiated the ship because she was not forthwith made tight, staunch, and strong, but had taken her into their service and navigated her, they had no right to insist that the forthwith making her tight, &c., was a condition precedent to their own liability upon the covenant. (*e*)

946. *Reasonable time of performance.*—If a shipowner covenants generally that a ship shall sail to a particular port, and there take on board a cargo to be provided by the charterer, the sailing of the vessel direct and without any deviation or delay to the appointed port is not a condition precedent to the charterer's liability to provide and ship the cargo; but, if

---

(*d*) Hall v. Cazenove, 4 East, 477.   (*e*) Havelock v. Geddes, 10 East,

the delay has been unreasonable, and the charterer has thereby lost all the benefit of the voyage, and been prevented from procuring the cargo, he will then be released from his liability upon the contract. (*f*)

947. *Waiver of time of performance.*—If a shipowner agrees that his vessel shall leave England for a foreign port on or before a particular day to bring back a cargo, the departure of the vessel at the time specified may be so far of the essence of the contract that the charterer or freighter will not be bound to provide the cargo and use the ship and pay freight unless the vessel sails at the time appointed and proceeds by the direct and usual course to the place of destination ; (*g*) but, if the vessel sails after the time, and the charterer nevertheless ships the cargo on board and uses the ship, the time of the vessel's sailing from England is no longer of the essence of the contract, and he can not refuse to pay freight and to fulfill his part of the engagement because the vessel did not sail on the exact day specified. If it is covenanted by the shipowner that the ship shall be at a particular port by a day named ready to take a cargo on board, the charterer or freighter may not be bound by his covenant or agreement to ship a cargo on board and pay freight, if the vessel is not ready at the place appointed by the day named ; but, if, after the day has passed, the cargo is shipped on board pursuant to the covenant, the time of shipment can not be relied upon as a condition precedent to the payment of the freight.

948. *Mode of performance—Complete cargo.*—

(*f*) Clipsham v. Vertue, 5 Q. B. 265. Tarrabochia v. Hickie, 1 H. & N. 183 ; 26 L. j., Ex. 26. Hurst v. Usborne, 18 C. B. 144 ; 25 L. J., C. P. 209.

(*g*) Freeman v. Taylor, 1 M. & Sc. 182 ; 8 Bing. 124. Ollive v. Booker, 1 Exch. 421. Behn v. Burness, 3 B. & S. 760; 32 L. J, Q. B. 206.

The performance of a contract that a vessel shall sail to a foreign port, and there load a particular cargo, is to be regulated, as regards the loading of the cargo, by the custom and usage of the port where the cargo is to be taken on board. (*h*) If the charterer has agreed to load the ship with a full and complete cargo, he is bound, in certain cases to fill up interstices with broken stowage. (*i*) In some cases he may load a full cargo of the lightest commodities; and, if any ballast is then wanting, it must be put in by the master. (*k*) It is the duty of the owner of a vessel to stow the cargo with as much skill as a competent stevedore can do ; (*l*) but he is not responsible to the charterer, when the stevedore is appointed by the latter, although it is provided that he is to act under the master's orders; for such a provision only means that the master is to have a general control over the stevedore, so as to secure the proper trim and safety of the ship. (*m*)'

949. *Impossibility of performance—Contracts to procure and carry cargoes and merchandise.*—We have already seen that it is a rule of law that, whenever a party enters into an absolute and unqualified contract to do some particular act, the impossibility of

(*h*) Cuthbert v. Cumming, 11 Exch. 408 ; 24 L. J., Ex. 310. Hudson v. Clementson, 18 C. B. 213.

(*i*) Cole v. Meek, 15 C. B. N. S. 795 ; 33 L. J., C. P., 183.

(*k*) Irving v. Clegg, 1 Bing. N. C. 53. Moorson v. Page, 4 Campb. 103.

(*l*) Anglo-African Company v. Lansed, L. R., 1 C. P. 226 ; 35 L. J., C. P. 145.

(*m*) Blaikie v. Stembridge, 6 C. B. N. S. 909 ; 28 L. J., C. P. 329.

' See Taunton Copper Co. v. Merchants' Ins. Co., 22 Peck, 108 ; Stilson v. Wyman, Davies, 172 ; The Paragon Ware, 322 ; The Rebecca, Id. 188 ; The Waldo, Davies, 161 ; The Schooner Seaside, 2 Sumner, 567 ; Bartol v. Dodge, 5 Greenl. 282 ; Barber v. Brace, 3 Conn. 9 ; Smith v. Wright, 1 Caines, 43 ; Lenox v. Union Ins. Co., 3 Johns. Cas. 178 ; Vernard v. Hudson, 3 Sumner, 405 ; Creary v. Holly, 14 Wend. 26 ; Waring v. Morse,

performance occasioned by inevitable accident, or by some unforeseen occurrence over which he had no control, will not release him from the obligation of his contract. (*n*) Therefore, if a shipowner has covenanted to procure and ship on board a cargo of guano, corn, or timber, at a specified port, the circumstance that no guano, corn, or timber was to be procured at that port, (*o*) or that its exportation had been prohibited, (*p*) or that the loading of it on board was prevented by an embargo, (*q*) or by want of water, (*r*) or by the plague, (*s*) will not constitute an answer to an action for the non-performance of the contract.

950. *Implied authority of the agents of ship-charterers.*—The agent of the charterer of a ship, to whom the ship is addressed for loading under a charter-party, has no implied authority to substitute a different voyage from that which is stipulated for by the charter-party, and can not by agreement with the shipmaster substitute a different port of loading, or a different quality or description of cargo, from that prescribed by the charter-party. (*t*)

951. *Shipment and carriage of merchandise under bills of lading.*—When the use of an entire vessel, or a certain amount of stowage therein, is not contracted for, but the merchant or owner of the goods merely sends certain parcels or packages of goods on board, to be conveyed to the port of destination, the master or commander of the vessel, or some person acting for him, usually gives a receipt for them, and

(*n*) *Ante,*

(*o*) Hills v. Sughrue, 15 M. & W. 261. Kirk v. Gibbs, 1 H. & N. 815; 26 L. J., Ex. 209.

(*p*) Blight v. Page, 3 B. & P. 295, n.

(*q*) Sjoerds v. Luscombe, 16 East, 201.

(*r*) Schilizzi v. Derry, 4 Ell. & Bl. 886.

(*s*) Barker v. Hodgson, 3 M. & S. 267. Marquis of Bute v. Thompson, 13 M. & W. 487.

(*t*) Sickens v. Irving, 7 C. B., N. S, 165; 29 L. J., C. P. 25.

the master afterwards signs and delivers to the merchant sometimes two and sometimes three parts of a
bill of lading,[1] of which the merchant commonly sends
one or two to his agent, factor, or other person to
whom the goods are to be delivered at the place of
destination : that is, one on board the ship with the
goods, another by the post or other conveyance, and
one he retains for his own security. (x) The bill of
lading is a written or printed memorandum, signed by
the master, acknowledging the shipment of the goods
on board, and promising to deliver them at the port
of destination to a person named as the consignee, or
his assigns, on payment of freight, primage, and average, " the act of God, the queen's enemies, fire, and all
the every other dangers and accidents of the seas, rivers, and navigation of whatever nature and kind soever
excepted."   The master, who thus acknowledges the
receipt of the goods, and promises to carry and deliver
them is personally responsible for the fulfillment of his
engagement ; (y) and the shipowner or charterer, who
receives the fruit and earnings of the ship, is also
liable upon the bill of lading, although he is not
named therein. (z)   Delivery to the shipowner's servants alongside the vessel is equivalent to a delivery
on board. (a)   The duty to deliver the goods under a
bill of lading arises on presentment of the bill ; and, if
it is not presented to the master on the arrival of the
ship at her place of destination, the master is not
bound to keep the goods for an indefinite time on
board his ship, but may deliver them to any trust-

(x) Abbott on Shipping, by Serjt.
Shee, 279.
(y) Domat, lib. 1, tit. 16, s. 2,
(z) Cannan v. Meaburn, 8 Moore, 127.

(a) British Columbia & Vancouver
Island Spar, Lumber, and Saw-mill
Co., Lim., v. Nettleship, L. R, 3 C. P.
489 ; 37 L. J., C. P. 237.

[1] *Ante,* § 604.

worthy person to be kept until the bill of lading is presented. (*b*) A bill of lading signed by the master is not conclusive upon the shipowner as to the shipment of the goods mentioned therein; (*c*) but it is so upon the master as against the consignee or assignee under a bill of lading without notice, unless in the case of fraud. (*d*) The consignee has no right to deduct from the freight payable on delivery of goods the value of articles which, though mentioned in the bill of lading, turn out not to have been put on board. (*e*)

952. *Countermand of the shipment—Re-delivery of the goods to the consignor.*—When goods have been shipped by a charterer or consignor on board a vessel to be carried and delivered to the consignee, pursuant to a contract of sale, or under bills of lading, or under any contract by which the ownership and right of property in the goods have been transferred to the consignee or some third party, the consignor's power over the goods is gone, and he can not lawfully countermand the consignment and require the goods to be delivered back to him. He can not, after he has ceased to be the owner of them, stop them in transitu, and prevent their delivery to the consignee, unless the latter has become bankrupt.[1] But, if the goods are merely addressed to the consignor's agent for sale, or under circumstances which do not divest the consignor of his ownership and right of property in the goods, he

---

(*b*) Howard v. Shepherd, 19 L. J., C. P. 255; 9 C. B. 321. And see the 25 & 26 Vict. c. 63, s. 67, *post.*

(*c*) Grant v. Norway, 10 C. B. 688. Hubbersty v. Ward, 8 Exch. 334. Vallieri v. Boyland, L. R., 1 C. P.

382; 35 L. J., C. P. 215. Jessel v. Bath, L. R., 2 Ex. 267; 36 L. J., Ex. 149.

(*d*) 18 & 19 Vict. c. III, s. 3.

(*e*) Meyer v. Dresser, 16 C. B. N. S. 646; 33 L. J., C. P. 289

[1] *Ante.*

may countermand the consignment and require the goods to be returned to him, subject to the following qualifications and restrictions. If the ship is a general ship, carrying other goods besides those of the consignor, the goods must be demanded back a convenient time before the period appointed for the ship's sailing, and the demand must be accompanied by a tender of the freight, and of the reasonable costs and charges of the re-shipment and re-delivery of the goods, and the demand must appear to have been made at a time when it was reasonably in the power of the master to comply with it, without injury to the cargo or the property of other parties on board, and without creating delay in sailing. If the entire vessel has been chartered, the charterer may demand back the goods, on tendering all the reasonable charges and lawful claims of the shipowner and master upon them, together with the expenses of re-shipment. (*f*) By the Spanish commercial code, every person who embarks goods in a general ship may unload the goods shipped, paying half freight, the expense of loading and unloading, and all the damage to the other shippers, unless these last oppose the unloading, in which case they are entitled to the goods, and must take them upon themselves, paying the contract price. (*g*) An owner of goods shipped to proceed to a foreign port has a right to have them re-delivered to him when the vessel, having commenced her voyage, meets with a disaster, whereby the goods are damaged so much that they can not be profitably carried to their destination. (*h*)

953. *Loss of or damage to goods by the way.*—

(*f*) Thompson v. Small, 1 C. B. 328 ; 14 L. J., C. P. 157.

(*g*) Cod. de Com. 765, Art. cited 1

C. B. 355.

(*h*) Blasco v. Fletcher, 14 C. B. N. S. 147 ; 32 L. J., C. P. 284.

Whenever a party has absolutely contracted to carry cargoes or merchandise from one place to another, subject to certain express exceptions, he has impliedly contracted to carry them safely ; (*i*) and the circumstance that he had been prevented from fulfilling his contract by some casualty or inevitable accident, will constitute no answer to an action brought against him for the recovery of damages for the breach of contract, if the casualty has not been expressly provided against by the contract. Therefore, where the defendant agreed to carry the plaintiff's goods by ship from Gibraltar to London, calling at Cadiz, and the goods were seized by the revenue authorities at Cadiz, and condemned and sold, it was held that such seizure and sale formed no answer to an action for the non-delivery of the goods. (*k*) If the vessel becomes disabled, and gets to port in a sinking state, the master is bound to tranship and forward the cargo, if he has the means of transhipment at hand, (*l*) and is allowed a reasonable time to do so ; (*m*) but, if the vessel is wrecked, and the master has no means of transhipment, (*n*) and no prospect of obtaining any, or if the cargo is of a perishable nature, and can not be transhipped and forwarded to the place of destination without risk of serious injury or total destruction, he is then clothed with an implied authority from the owners of such cargo to do the best he can with it for their benefit ; and, if, being unable to communicate with the owner,

---

(*i*) Rogers v. Head, Cro. Jac. 262. Matthers v. Hopping, 1 Keb. 852.

(*k*) Spence v. Chodwick, 10 Q. B. 517 ; 16 L. J., Q. B. 313. Evans v. Hutton, 5 Sc. N. R. 670 ; 2 Dowl. N. S. 600. Gosling v. Higgins, 1 Campb. 450.

(*l*) Cannan v. Meaburn, 8 Moore, 127.

(*m*) The Soblomsten, L. R., 1 Adm. 293 ; 36 L. J., Adm. 5.

(*n*) As to the duty of the master to tranship and forward the goods, see Shipton v. Thornton, 9 Ad. & E. 337. Gibbs v. Grey, 2 H. & N. 30 ; 26 L. J., Ex. 286. Mathews v. Gibbs, 2 El. & El. 282 ; 30 L. J, Q. B. 55. But see the Hamburg, 32 L. J, Adm. 161.

he acts bonâ fide with ordinary diligence, forethought, and prudence, he exempts his employers, the shipowners, from all liability for the loss. (*o*)   But he is not entitled to carry on goods in an unfit state against the express wish of the shippers in order to earn the freight. (*p*)[1]   In such a case the accomplishment of the contract by the shipowner has been prevented by peril of the sea and the dangers and accidents of navigation.   Damage done to a cargo by rats is not a danger or accident of the seas ; and therefore, if a ship is greatly infested by rats and serious damage done to the cargo, the undertaker of the work of carrying is responsible for the injury, although he may have kept cats on board for the express purpose of destroying the rats. (*q*)[2]

(*o*) The Giatitudine, 3 Rob. 261. Ireland v. Thompson, 4 C. B. 168 ; 17 L. J., C. P. 241. The Australasian Steam Co. v. Morse, L .R., 4 P. C. 222.

(*p*) Notara v. Henderson, L. R., 5

Q. B. 246 ; ib. 7 Q. B. 225 ; 39 L. J., Q. B. 167 ; 41 ib. 158.

(*q*) Laveroni v. Drury, 8 Exch. 170 ; 22 L. J., Ex. 2.   Kay v. Wheeler, L. R., 2 C. P. 302 ; 36 L, J., C. P. 180.

[1] But see Jordan v. Warren Ins. Co., 1 Story, 342 ; The Ship Nathaniel Hooper, 3 Sumner, 554 ; Cage v. Baltimore Ins. Co., 7 Cranch, 358 ; Hunter v. Union Ins. Co., 1 Wash. C. C. 530 ; Hedfield v. Jameson, 2 Mump. 53 ; Bark v. Norton, 2 McLean, 422.   " If the goods be delivered in specie, being articles of the same sort as those shipped, and not the mere remains of its destruction or decay," says Dixon on Shipping, § 193, "freight is due, and accordingly, though the goods may be totally lost to all the purposes for which they can be available to the shipper, there is not a total loss of freight.   Hugg v. Augusta Ins. Co., 7 How. 593 ; Griswold v. New York Ins. Co., 3 Johns. 321.   But for goods which perish by the perils of the sea during the voyage, no freight is due ; as where a ship leaks owing to tempestuous weather ; and sugar, which was being carried in hogsheads properly stowed, was washed out, and had disappeared.   Frith v. Baker, 2 Johns. 327. But if the commodity is lost by decay, leakage, evaporation, or other causes than the perils of the sea, freight is still due.   Id.   Coffin v. Storer, 5 Mass. 251.

[2] Aymar v. Astor, 6 Cowen, 266 ; 3 Kent Com. 300 ; Dixon

954. *Of the implied promise to carry safely.*— Whenever goods have been bailed by one man to another upon the faith of an express or implied undertaking by the latter to carry them to a distant part, it is no answer to an action brought against him to recover damages for the breach of his engagement, to say that the goods were lost by the way, the very fact of the loss affording prima facie evidence of neglect and want of care. (*r*) If the goods have been stolen, or consumed by fire, or destroyed by accident, without fault or neglect or want of care and caution on the part of the undertaker of the work, the latter stands excused, and may avail himself of the robbery or the unavoidable accident as an answer to an action brought against him for the non-delivery of the goods to the consignee. " He is only," observes HOLT, C. J., " to do the best he can ; and if he be robbed, &c., it is a good account ; for it would be unreasonable to charge him with a trust further than the nature of the thing puts it into his power to perform it." (*s*) A loss by theft or secret purloining of goods is prima facie evidence of negligent keeping ; and the carrier must rebut this presumption by showing that he had taken all such precautions as appeared to be necessary to guard against it. In an action against the commander of a

(*r*) Parry v. Roberts, 3 Ad. & E. 120.   (*s*) Holt, C. J., 1 Smith's L. C. 5th ed. 181, 182.

on Shipping, § 264, maintains that the owner is liable for damage to the ship by rats, and that such damage is not included in "perils of the sea." And see Garrigues v. Coxe, 1 Binn. 592. But the rule as to the cargo is not laid down as broadly with us as in the text, Aymar v. Astor, cited above, holding that a damage to the cargo by rats is not one of the exceptions necessarily included under the "perils of the sea," in the bill of lading, but the question must depend upon whether there was due diligence on the part of the master and mariners to prevent it.

ship of war for the loss of two casks of dollars which had been delivered to him to be carried from the river Plate to London upon freight for hire, it appeared that on the arrival of the ship in the Thames, the two casks had been opened and plundered by the crew ; and it was held that the very occurrence of the loss was prima facie evidence of negligent keeping on the part of the defendant, and that he was responsible for the loss, (*t*)   In the contract of a shipowner to carry goods shipped on board his vessel, it has been held that there is no implied condition that the vessel shall be seaworthy, but the rule is not undisputed. (*u*) [1]

(*t*) Hodgson v. Fullarton, 4 Taunt. 787. Hatchwell v. Cooke, 6 Taunt. 577.

(*u*) Schloss v. Heriot, 14 C. B., N. S. 59; 32 L. J., C. P. 211.

[1] But the English case cited by the author was an action to recover plaintiff's proportion of average. As to the rule in the United States, see the cases cited in note 1, p. 660. But the implied warranty of seaworthiness, at the commencement of the voyage, attaches between insurer and insured; and the insured (whether on ship, freight, or cargo,) is understood to warrant impliedly that the ship is, in construction, materials, qualification of the master, competency and numbers of her crew, in equipment, tackle, rigging, stores, and general outfit, fit for the voyage or service proposed. Warren v. United Ins. Co., 2 Johns. 231 ; Prescott v. Union Ins. Co., 1 Whart. 399; Deshon v. Merchants' Ins. Co., 11 Metc. 207 ; Starbuck v. New England Ins. Co., 19 Pick, 199. And in Putnam v. Wood, 3 Mass. 48; the rule is laid down emphatically as between shipper and owner as well, the court holding that it is the duty of the owner of a ship, when he charters her, or puts her up for freight, to see that she is in a suitable condition to transport her cargo in safety; and he is to keep her in that condition, unless prevented by perils of the seas, or unavoidable accidents. If the goods are lost by any defect in the vessel, whether latent or visible, known or unknown, the owner is answerable to the freighter, upon the principle that he tacitly contracts that his vessel shall be fit for the use for which he employs her ; and there is no difference between insurers of

955. *Limitation of liability by special contract.—* There are certain cases, as we shall presently see, where a carrier contracts for the conveyance of very perishable or fragile articles, in which he may accept the goods and contract to carry them on the express terms that he shall not be responsible for damage done to them in the transit.[1] Generally speaking, however, it is not competent to a party to enter into a contract for the performance of a particular duty, and by the same contract to stipulate that he shall be exempt from all legal responsibility if he neglects to do what he has undertaken to perform. " We can not," observes Lord ELLENBOROUGH, " construe a contract for the carriage of goods between the owners of vessels carrying goods for hire and the persons putting the goods on board so as to make the owners say we will not be answerable at all for any loss occasioned by our own misconduct ; for this would in effect be saying, ' We will be at liberty to receive your goods on board a vessel, however leaky ; we will not be bound to provide a crew equal to the navigation of her ; and if through

the ship and insurers of the cargo in this respect. If the ship be not seaworthy at the commencement of the voyage, the contract of insurance is void, and the insurers, whether of ship or cargo, are discharged. Taylor v. Lowell, 3 Mass. 331. And the implied warranty of seaworthiness is, that the vessel shall be able to perform her voyage with the cargo with which she is then loaded. Abbott v. Broome, 1 Caines, 292. Nor is it sufficient to satisfy this warranty of seaworthiness that the ship has been pronounced seaworthy by skillful shipwrights, after careful examination. Brig Casco, Davies, 192 ; 5 Kent Com. 391, note. Hoxie v. Pacific Mutual Ins. Co., 7 Allen, 211. The only exception is in the case of what are known as " time policies," effected on a vessel at sea ; in these cases there is no implied warranty of seaworthiness. On a time policy on a vessel in port, the warranty is understood. Hoxie v. Pacific Ins. Co., 7 Allen, 221.

[1] See *post,* § 988.

these defaults the goods are lost, we will pay nothing.'" (*v*)

A stipulation in a bill of lading that the shipowner
is not to be accountable for leakage or breakage ab-
solves him from responsibility for leakage and breakage the result of mere accident, where no blame is imputable, or for leakage the result of bad stowage
where the shippers have themselves superintended the
stowage, (*y*) but does not exempt him from the
obligation which the law imposes upon him of taking
reasonable care of goods entrusted to him to be carried.
(*z*)   And an exception in a bill of lading of " accidents
or damage of the seas, rivers, and steam navigation of
whatever nature or kind soever," does not protect the
shipowner from liability for damage arising from a
collision caused by gross negligence of his ship's master and crew. (*a*)

956. *Loss by the act of God, dangers and accidents
of the seas, rivers, and navigation.*—From losses occasioned by the act of God, by the Queen's enemies,
and the dangers and perils of the sea and of navigation, the carrier by water is, and always has been, exempt by the common law ; but he is not exempt, nor
does the exception in the bill of lading or other contract of affreightment exempt him, from accidents occasioned by his own negligence and misconduct or
want of skill, or the negligence, misconduct, or want
of skill of the persons whom he has entrusted with the
navigation of the vessel. (*b*)   The expression " act of

(*v*) Lyon v. Mells, 5 East, 438.
Ellis v. Turner, 8 T. R. 531. See
however, The Duero, L. R., 2 A. &
E. 293 ; 38 L. J., Adm. 69.

(*y*) Ohrloff v. Briscall, L. R., 1 P.
C. 231 ; 35 L. J., P. C. 63.

(*z*) Phillips v. Clark, 2 C. B., N. S.
164. Czech v. The General Steam

Navigation Co., L. R., 3 C. P. 14 ; 37
L. J., C. P. 3.

(*a*) Lloyd v. Gen. Iron Screw Col.
Co., 3 H. & C. 284 ; 33 L. J., Ex.
269.

(*b*) Mansfield, C. J., 1 Doug. 278.
Siordet v. Hall, 1 M. & P. 561.

God " denotes natural accidents, such as lightning, earthquake, and tempest, and not accidents arising from the negligence of man. And the term " dangers and accidents of the sea and of navigation " denotes the dangers and accidents peculiar to the ocean and to navigation from port to port which no human care or skill can guard against, or surmount, such as accidents resulting from the irresistible violence of the winds and waves, and from tides and currents; (*c*) the destruction of a perishable cargo or of living animals from the rolling of a ship in a storm ; (*d*) jettison of goods from irresistible necessity to lighten the ship and save her from foundering; (*e*) the grounding of a vessel on the hard and uneven bottom of a dry harbor, in which she had been obliged to take refuge, (*f*) or on a sunken rock or sand-bank not generally known, and not marked on the ordinary charts or maps; irresistible attacks by pirates; (*g*) the accidental breaking of tackle by which the vessel is moored in port ; (*h*) or accidental collisions in fogs or storms, where no blame is imputable to either of the vessels striking together. (*i*)

(*c*) Hodgson v. Malcolm, 2 B. & P., N. R. 336.

(*d*) Lawrence v. Aberdein, 5 B. & Ald. 110.

(*e*) Bird v. Astcock, 2 Bulst, 280.

(*f*) Fletcher v. Inglis, 2 B. & Ald. 315.

(*g*) Pickering v. Barclay, Styles, 132.

(*h*) Laurie v. Douglas, 15 M. & W. 746.

(*i*) Buller v. Fisher, 3 Esp. 67.

[1] Lord Mansfield's rule was, that the act of God was " something in opposition to the act of man." The law presumes against the carrier, unless he shows it was done by the king's enemies, or by such an act as could not happen by the intervention of man. Richards v. Gilbert, 5 Day, 415 ; Mc Arthur v. Sears, 21 Wend. 190 ; Sherman v. Wells, 28 Barb. 403 ; Fergusson v. Brent, 12 Md. 9. The act of God concurring with other and human agencies will not excuse. Sprowl v. Kellar, 4 Stew. & P 382 ; but see Hill v. Sturgeon, 28 Mo. 323. So where a flood rises higher than ever it was known to before, it is an act of God, and the carrier will be relieved, unless his own

957. *When a loss occasioned by negligence or misconduct is not a loss from peril of the sea, though the sea does the mischief.*—The general rule in cases

negligence, as, for instance, his neglect to forward the goods before, has reasonably contributed to the loss by the flood. Read v. Spalding, 5 Bosw. 395; 30 N. Y 630; see Michaels v. New York, &c., R. R. Co., 30 N. Y. 564; Merritt v. Earle, 29 N. Y. 115. It must be something against which human foresight or sagacity could not have guarded. Colt v. Mc-Mechen, 6 Johns. 160; McArthur v. Sears, 21 Wend. 190; Mc-Call v. Brock, 5 Strobh. 119; Steamboat Co. v. Tiers, 4 Zab. 697. But when the rudder of a ship proved defective, although the ship had been lately completely repaired, the carrier could not escape on that plea. Backhouse v. Sneed, 1 Murph. 173. Explosion of a boiler is not an act of God, nor a conspiracy of servants to leave their master's employment. Blackstone v. New York, &c., R. R. Co., 1 Bosw. 177; but see Cox v. Peterson, 30 Ala. 608; Hibler v. McCartney, 31 Id. 501; nor a collision on river, even if it were entirely the fault of another vessel, colliding with the carrier; Converse v. Brainard, 27 Conn. 607; nor thefts by the crew or others; Schieffelin v. Harver, 6 Johns. 170; nor the shifting of a buoy at the entrance to a harbor, while the ship was absent on her voyage; Reeves v. Waterman, 2 Spears, 197; nor for delay on account of the increased dangers of navigation as winter approached; Falway v. Northern Transportation Co., 15 Wis. 129; nor by cars running over one who, having no place to stand on a train, fell from it; Golden v. Pennsylvania R. R. Co., 30 Pa. St. 242; nor a dense fog, if loss occur through want of care, as running at a high rate of speed; The Rocket, 1 Biss. 354; nor for injuries, from extreme cold, to perishable goods (as potatoes), if the carrier did not take due care to protect them. Wing v. New York, &c., R. R. Co., 1 Hilt. 263; Bulkley v. Naumkeag Cotton Co., 24 How. (U. S.) 386. Fire caused by lightning; Mershon v. Hobensack, 2 Zab. 372; or striking upon a rock not hitherto known, and not laid down in any chart; Williams v. Grant, 6 Conn. 487; Pennerville v. Cullen, 5 Harring, 238; Collier v. Valentine, 11 Mo. 299; or a snag in a river, brought there by a recent freshet, Smyrl v. Niolon, 2 Bailey, 421; Faulkner v. Wright, 1 Rice, 108; an unexpected obstruction to navigation by the freezing of a canal; Parsons v. Hardy, 14 Wend. 215; Harris v. Rand, 4 N. H. 259; and see to the same point, Crosby v. Fitch, 12 Conn. 410; Price v. Hartshorn, 44 N. Y. 94.

of insurance is, that the immediate and not the remote cause of loss is to be considered : but this rule does not apply as between the owner and the carrier of goods. Thus, if a vessel deviates from its proper course, and sails unnecessarily through dangerous straits and channels, or into seas infested with pirates, and is wrecked or plundered in consequence of such deviation, the loss, though proximately caused by what is usually termed "a peril of the sea," is deemed to have been occasioned by the misconduct of the master or commander, who had improperly gone out of his way to meet the danger. A collision arising from the negligence of the crew of the ship is not a peril of the sea within the meaning of an exception of loss arising from perils of the sea in a bill of lading. (*k*) If the cargo is seriously damaged or destroyed by rats, the loss is not the result of a danger or an accident of the seas, but of neglect and want of care on the part of the master and crew. (*l*) If a vessel becomes unseaworthy and the owner neglects to avail himself of an opportunity to repair her, and thereby causes the loss of the cargo, the loss is the result of negligence. (*m*) If the vessel at the time of the commencement of the voyage is unseaworthy—if the hull is worm-eaten or gnawed by rats, or the timbers are rotten, and the vessel is shaken to pieces and founders in a gale which a stout and seaworthy ship would have withstood in safety, the loss, though proximately caused by the violence of the winds and waves, has not, in contemplation of law, been occasioned by peril of the seas, but by the negligence and misconduct of the owner of the ship, who is responsible to the owner of the cargo for

(*k*) Grilt v. The General Iron Screw Col.Co.,L.R.,1 C. P. 600; ib.,3 C.P.476; 35 L. J., C. P. 321 ; 37 L. J., C. P. 205.

(*l*) Laveroni v. Drury, *ante.*

(*m*) Worms v. Storey, 11 Exch. 430 ; 25 L. J., Ex. 1.

the loss of the goods shipped on board. (*n*)   When,
on the other hand, from the rolling and laboring of a
ship in a storm, a number of horses, though properly
stowed and secured on board at the commencement
of the tempest, broke loose and kicked each other to
death in the hold of the vessel, the loss, though proximately caused by their own hoofs, was deemed to have
been occasioned by peril of the sea. (*o*)[1]

"If a ship perish in consequence of striking against
a rock or shallow, the circumstance under which that
event has taken place must be ascertained in order to
decide whether it happened by a peril of the sea, or by
the fault of the owner, carrier, or master.[2]   If the situation of a rock or shallow is generally known, and the
ship is not forced upon it by adverse winds, or storms
and tempests, the loss is to be imputed to the fault of
the master.   And it matters not, in such a case, whether
the loss arises from his rashness in not taking a pilot,
or from his own ignorance or unskillfulness.   On the
other hand, if the ship is forced upon such a rock or
shallow by adverse winds or tempests, or if the shallow
is occasioned by a recent and sudden collection of
sand in a place where ships could before sail with
safety, or if the rock or shallow is not generally
known; in all these cases the loss is to be attributed
to the act of God, and it is deemed a peril of the
sea." (*p*)   If the carrier by water overloads his vessel,
and so causes it to founder in a gale of wind, the loss
is occasioned by the negligence of man; but it is,
otherwise, if the boat has not been surcharged, but
sinks solely through the violence of the winds and

(*n*) Hunter v. Potts, 4 Campb. 202.   (*o*) Gabay v. Lloyd, 3 B. & C. 793.
                                                             (*p*) Abbott, by Shee, 389, 8th ed.

[1] See last note.

[2] Williams v. Grant, 16 Conn. 487; Pennerville v. Cullen,
5 Harring. 238; Collier v. Valentine. 11 Mo. 299.

waves. (*q*)   If a hoyman shoots a bridge in tempestuous weather or at a dangerous period of the tide, and
the hoy is sunk, the loss is occasioned by the negligence of the hoyman ; but, if he has shot the bridge
at a proper time and in proper weather, but the hoy
has been taken aback by a sudden gust of wind, and
has been driven against the abutments of the bridge
and sunk, and the goods on board lost, the loss is
deemed to have been occasioned by the act of God
and the carrier, consequently, is exempt from responsibility in respect thereof. (*r*)

958. *Proof that the loss was occasioned by negligence and not by a peril of the sea.*—In order to determine whether the loss has or has not been occasioned
by the negligence or want of skill of the servants of
the shipowner, " the established rules of nautical practice, the usages and regulations of particular ports and
rivers, the state of the wind, the tide, and the light,
the degree of vigilance of the master and crew, and
all other circumstances bearing upon the conduct and
management of the vessel must be considered." (*s*) [1]

959. *Loss by fire.—Limitation of the responsibility of owners and part owners of ships by statute.*—
By the 17 & 18 Vict. c. 104, s. 503, it is enacted that
no owner of any sea-going ship or share therein shall
be liable to make good any loss or damage which may
happen, without his fault or privity, to any goods or
merchandise taken on board such ship by reason of
any fire happening on board, or to any gold, silver,
diamonds, watches, jewels or precious stones taken on
board, by reason of any robbery, embezzlement, mak-

(*q*) 22 Assiz. 41. Williams v. Lloyd,   (*s*) Abbott, *ut sup.* 207. **Tuff v.**
Jones's Rep. 180.   Warman, 5 C. B. N. S. 573

(*r*) Amies v. Stevens, 1 Str. 128.

[1] See *ante*, note 1, p. 677.

ing away with, or secreting thereof, unless the owner or shipper thereof has at the time of shipping the same, inserted in his bills of lading, or otherwise declared in writing to the master or owner of such ship, the true nature and value of such articles. (*t*) And by the 25 & 26 Vict. c. 63, s. 54, the owners of any ship, whether British or foreign, (*u*) shall not in cases where all or any of the following events occur without their actual fault or privity, that is to say :— (1) where any loss of life or personal injury is caused to any person being carried in such ship ; (2) where any damage or loss is caused to any goods, merchandise, or other things whatsoever on board any such ship ; (3) where any loss of life or personal injury is by reason of the improper navigation of such ship as aforesaid caused to any person carried in any other ship or boat ; (*v*) (4) where any loss or damage is, by reason of the improper navigation of such ship as aforesaid, caused to any other ship or boat, or to any goods, merchandise, or other things whatsoever on board any other ship or boat—be answerable in damages in respect of loss of life or personal injury, either alone or together with loss or damage to ships, boats, goods, merchandise, or other things, to an aggregate amount exceeding £15 for each ton of their ship's tonnage ; nor in respect of loss or damage to ships, goods, merchandise, or other things, whether there be in addition loss of life or personal injury or not, to an aggregate amount exceeding £8 for each ton of the ship's tonnage. By the 17 & 18 Vict. c. 104, s. 516, nothing contained in the act is to take away any lia-

---

(*t*) The nature of the articles must be described, and their money value stated. Williams v. Afric. St. Ship Co., 1 H. & N. 302 ; 26 L. J., Ex. 69.

(*u*) The Amalia, 32 L. J., Adm. 191.

(*v*) As to the mode of procedure in case of loss of life or personal injury, see the 17 & 18 Vict. c. 104, ss. 507-512.

bility to which any master or seaman, being also owner
or part owner of the ship to which he belongs, is subject in his capacity of master or seaman.

The limitation of liability under the Act of 1854,
does not extend to the owner of any lighter, barge, boat
or vessel, used solely in rivers or inland navigation, or to
any ship or vessel not duly registered. (y) The Acts,
it will be seen, embrace two descriptions of losses, the
one a loss or damage to the cargo laden on board the
ship occasioned by the negligence of the master or
mariners, and rendering the shipowner liable, ex contractu, at common law to the extent of the value of
such cargo; and the other a loss or damage to the
ship or cargo of some third party, occasioned by the
negligence or misconduct of the master, in respect of
which the owner is liable ex dilicto, but not upon any
contract. To an action, ex delicto in respect of an injury to the property of a third party, both the shipowner
and the master are liable—the owner, as the employer,
responsible for the wrongful act done by the servant
in the course of his employment, and the other as the
party actually committing the injury; and it is this
liability ex delicto to which the Act of 1854 refers,
when it provides that nothing therein contained shall
lessen or take away any responsibility to which any
master or mariner might then by law be liable,
notwithstanding such master or mariner might be an
owner or part owner of his ship or vessel. If the
master be a part owner, his responsibility, if he is sued
(ex delicto) in his character of master, and not as
one of several part owners, will not be limited by the
Act; but if he is sued as one of the part owners with
the other part owners, the circumstance of the loss

(y) Morewood v. Pollok, 22 L. J., Q. B. 250; 1 Ell. & Bl. 743.

being occasioned by his fault, and with his privity, will not take away from the other part owners the protection which the statute intended to give them. (*z*) If the ship is sunk by a collision with another vessel, the shipowner is not released from liability by the loss of his vessel. (*a*) [1]

(*z*) Bayley, J., Wilson v. Dickson, 2 B. & Ald. 13.

(*a*) Brown v. Wilkinson, 15 M. & W. 391 ; 16 L. J., Ex. 34. The Mellonna, 12 Jur. 271.

[1] The act of congress of March 3, 1851, to limit the liability of shipowners, as contained in the Revised Statutes of the United States, Revision of 1873–1874, is as follows: § 4281.—If any shipper of platina, gold dust, silver bullion, or other precious metals, coins, jewelry, bills of any bank or public body, diamonds or other precious stones, or any gold or silver in a manufactured or unmanufactured state, watches, clocks, or time-pieces of any description, trinkets, orders, notes or securities for payment of money, stamps, maps, writings, title-deeds, printings, engravings, pictures, gold or silver plate or plated articles, glass, china, silks in a manufactured or unmanufactured state, and whether wrought up or not wrought up with any other material, furs, or lace, or any of them contained in any parcel or package or trunk, shall lade the same as freight or baggage on any vessel, without, at the time of such lading giving to the master, clerk, agent, or owner of such vessel receiving the same, a written notice of the true character and value thereof, and having the same entered on the bill of lading therefor, the master and owner of such vessel shall not be liable as carriers thereof in any form or manner ; nor shall any such master or owner be liable for any such goods beyond the value and according to the character thereof so notified and entered. § 4282.—No owner of any vessel shall be liable to answer for or make good to any person any loss or damage which may happen to any merchandise whatsoever, which shall be shipped, taken in, or put on board any such vessel, by reason or by means of any fire happening to or on board the vessel, unless such fire is caused by the design or neglect of such owner. § 4283.—The liability of the owner of any vessel for any embezzlement, loss, or destruction by any person of any property, goods, or merchandise shipped or put on board of such vessel, or for any loss, damage, or

960. *Losses occasioned by the negligence of licensed pilots.*—The 17 and 18 Vict. c. 104, s. 388, further exempts the owner and master of a ship from liability in

injury by collision, or for any act, matter or thing lost, damage or forfeiture done, occasioned or incurred, without the privity or knowledge of such owner or owners, shall in no case exceed the amount or value of the interest of such owner in such vessel, and her freight then pending. § 4284.—Whenever any such embezzlement, loss, or destruction is suffered by several freighters or owners of goods, wares, merchandise, or any property whatsoever on the same voyage. and the whole value of the vessel and her freight for the voyage is not sufficient to make compensation to each of them, they shall receive compensation from the owner in proportion to their respective losses; and for that purpose, the freighters and owners of the property, and the owner of the vessel, or any of them, may take the appropriate proceedings in any court for the purpose of apportioning the sum for which the owner of the vessel may be liable among the parties entitled thereto. § 4285.—It shall be deemed a sufficient compliance on the part of such owner with the requirements of this Title, relating to his liability for any embezzlement, loss, or destruction of any property, goods, or merchandise, if he shall transfer his interest in such vessel and freight for the benefit of such claimants, to a trustee to be appointed by any court of competent jurisdiction, to act as such trustee for the person who may prove to be legally entitled thereto ; from and after which transfer all claims and proceedings against the owner shall cease. § 4286.—The charterer of any vessel, in case he shall man, victual, and navigate such vessel at his own expense, or by his own procurement, shall be deemed the owner of such vessel, within the meaning of the provisions of this Title relating to the limitation of the liability of the owners of vessels; and such vessel, when so chartered, shall be liable in the same manner as if navigated by the owner thereof. § 4287.—Nothing in the five preceding sections shall be construed to take away or affect the remedy to which any party may be entitled against the master, officers, or seamen, for or on account of any embezzlement, injury, loss, or destruction of merchandise, or property put on board any vessel, or on account of any negligence, fraud, or other malversation of such master, officers, or seamen, respectively; nor to lessen or take away any

respect of losses or damage occasioned by the neglect or incapacity of a licensed pilot in charge of the
vessel. " The shipowners are not responsible when
they take a pilot by compulsion ; but in all other cases
they are responsible for the acts of the pilot." (*b*)   " It
is the duty of the master to look after the pilot in the
case of his palpable incompetency, or intoxication, or
of the loss of his faculties. The taking of a pilot
under the Act does not relieve the shipowner from the
ordinary legal consequences resulting from the negligence of the master and crew." (*c*)

(*b*) The Energy, L. R., 3 A. & E.   Jur. 298.   The Duke of Manchester,
48 ; 39 L. J., Adm. 25.   The Ocean   10 Jur. 865.   The Iron Duke, 9 Jur.
Wave, L. R., 3 P. C. 205.   The Cala-   476.   The Iona, L. R., 1 P. C. 426.
bar, L. R., 2 P. C. 238.   The Lion,   The Valasquez, L. R., 1 P. C. 494 ;
L. R., 2 P. C. 52 ; 38 L. J., P.C. 57.   36 L. J., Adm. 19.   The Queen, L.
    (*c*) Dr. Lushington, The Eden, 10   R., 2 A. & E. 354 ; 38 L. J., Adm. 39.

responsibility to which any master or seamen of any vessel
may by law be liable, notwithstanding such master or seaman
may be an owner or part owner of the vessel.   § 4288.—Any
person shipping oil of vitriol, unslacked lime, inflammable
matches, or gunpowder in a vessel taking cargo for divers
persons or freight, without delivering at the time of shipment a note in writing, expressing the nature and character
of such merchandise to the master, mate, officer, or person in
charge of the lading of the vessel, shall be liable to the
United States in a penalty of one thousand dollars.   But this
section shall not apply to any vessel of any description whatsoever used in rivers or inland navigation.   § 4289.—The
provisions of this Title relating to the limitation of the liability of the owners of vessels, shall not apply to the owners
of any canal boat, barge, or lighter, or to any vessel of any
description whatsoever used in rivers or inland navigation.
As to the liability for loss by fire under this Title, see Walker
v. Transportation Company, 3 Wall, 150.   As to the loss not
exceeding the value of the ship or the interest of the owner
therein and the transfer to a trustee, see Norwich Company v.
Wright, 13 Wall. 104; the steamboat City of Norwich, 1 Ben.
89.   As to when the charterer of a vessel will be considered
the owner, see Thorp v. Hammond, 12 Wall. 408; and as to

961. *Delivery of goods by shipowners.*—There is an implied engagement on the part of every undertaker of the work of carrying, to proceed by the usual and ordinary course to the port of destination or place of delivery without delay, and without unnecessary deviation. (*d*) If it is customary for the carrier by water to carry merely from port to port, or from wharf to wharf, and for the owner or consignee to fetch the goods from the vessel itself, or from the wharf, as soon as the arrival of the ship has been reported, the carrier must give such owner or consignee notice of the arrival of the goods on board, or at the customary place of destination, in order to discharge himself from further liability as a carrier. He can not at once discharge himself from all responsibility by immediately landing the goods without any notice to the consignee, but is bound to keep the goods on board or on the wharf, at his own risk, for a reasonable time, to enable the consignee or his assigns to come and fetch them. (*e*) The Merchant Shipping Amendment Act, 1862 (25 & 26 Vict. c 63, ss. 67, et seq.), empowers the shipowner to enter and land goods in default of entry and landing by the owner; and nowithstanding the landing, the shipowner may, by giving notice for that purpose, preserve his lien for freight. The Act also provides for the sale of the goods, if they are not claimed by the owner. (*f*)

(*d*) Davies v. Garrett, 4 M. & P. 540; 6 Bing. 716.

(*e*) Bourne v. Gatifff, 3 Sc. N. R. 44; 8 ib. 604; 11 Cl. & Fin. 45.

(*f*) Berresford v. Mongomerie, 17 C. B. N. S. 379; 34 L. J., C. P. 41. Willson v. London, Italian, and Adriatic Steam Nav. Co., 35 L. J., C. P. 9; L. R., 1 C. P. 61.

the exception of vessels employed in inland navigation, see Propeller Niagara v. Cordes, 21 How. (U. S.) 26; Moore v. Transportation Company, 24 Id. 1.

962. *Losses on board lighters conveying goods from the ship to the shore.*—When the vessel is not able to discharge at a wharf, but the goods are placed in lighters to be conveyed from the ship to the shore, and are lost on their passage through the neglect or want of skill of the lighterman, the loss will fall on the owner of the goods, if the lighterman is paid and employed by him ; (*g*) but if he is employed and paid by the shipowner or carrier, he is then the servant of the latter, expediting the goods in the further prosecution of the voyage to their place of destination, and the carrier, consequently, must make good the loss. Generally speaking, the task of discharging the cargo in the port of London is accomplished through the medium of public lightermen, whose lighters are entered at Waterman's Hall, and who are public officers employed and paid by the merchants and owners of the goods. The lightermen are responsible, in their character of common carriers, to the merchant who employs them ; and the shipowner is discharged as soon as the goods have been safely loaded on board such lighters. But he is not, by the custom of the river Thames, exonerated from liability until the loading is complete ; and he is not discharged from his obligation to guard the portion of the cargo that has been placed in the lighter, by telling the lighterman that he has not sufficient hands on board to take care of it. He is, on the other hand, bound to take care of the lighter and its contents until it is fully laden, and is ready to leave the side of the ship. (*h*) The protection afforded by the 17 & 18 Vict. c. 104, s. 503, to owners of sea-going vessels in respect of loss or

---

(*g*) Sparrow v. Caruthers, 2 Str. 1236. Strong v. Natally, 4 B. & P. 16-19.

(*h*) Catley v. Wintringham, 1 Peake, 202. Robinson v. Turpin, ib. 203 n. (a).

damage by fire to goods or merchandise shipped on ' board, does not extend to the case of a fire happening on board lighters employed by the shipowner in carrying goods from the shore to be laden on board the vessel. (*i*) Therefore, if goods are set on fire by reason of the negligence of such lightermen, the shipowners are responsible for the damage.[1]

963. *Payment of the freight or hire*—If a charter-party amounts to a demise of the ship to the charterer for a certain term at a certain hire, and the vessel is bailed to him pursuant to the contract, he is responsible for the payment of the hire at the expiration of the term of hiring, although the vessel may have been lost; but, if the shipowner merely grants the use of the vessel, retaining the possession of it through the medium of his own seamen and servants, the shipowner loses his right to the hire, at the same time that the charterer is deprived of the use and enjoyment of the vessel. When the charter-party amounts merely to a contract by the shipowner or shipmaster for the conveyance of merchandise to a specified destination, the fulfillment of the covenant or undertaking to carry the goods, or the shipowner's readiness and willingness to fulfill it, is a condition precedent to the payment of the hire, so that the plaintiff must of necessity show the work done, or that he was ready and willing to do it, and was hindered from doing it by the defendant,

(*i*) Morewood v. Pollok, 22 L. J., B. 250; ɪ Ell. & Bl. 743.

[1] In cases of general average, a loss upon lighters, used when a ship is in distress, or to save her from any calamity, is considered as though it were a jettison, and enters into the computation, but if lost upon such lighters used for purposes of sending the goods ashore, their loss gives no claim to contribution; Dixon on Shipping, § 558; and see in the case of the jettisoned goods; Whitteridge v. Norris, 6 Mass. 125; Lewis v. Williams, ɪ Hall, 430; The Nathaniel Hooper, 3 Sumner, 542.

before he can demand the money. (*k*) Ordinarily,
the right to the freight does not arise until the goods
are not only conveyed to their destination, but also
delivered ; (*l*) or, in the case of a charter-party, until
the charterers have had the full use of the ship for the
purposes for which they chartered it. (*m*) The freight
may, however, by the special contract of the parties,
be made payable on the delivery of the goods on
board, (*n*) on the sailing, (*o*) or on the final sailing of
the vessel from the port of loading (*p*) prior to the
performance of the voyage, or at any other period of
time which they may choose to appoint ; but, in all
cases of doubtful construction, the courts will adhere
to the maxim that the freight is not due until it has
been earned by the performance of the work for which
it is to be paid. (*q*) Where the freight was to be paid
"within three days after the arrival of the ship, and
before delivery of any portion of the goods," and the
ship arrived in port, but was sunk and the goods destroyed within the three days, it was held that the
freight was not payable. (*r*) If freight is paid in advance and the cargo is lost, the freight so paid can not
be recovered back, (*s*) unless the loss has been oc-

(*k*) Tate v. Meek, 2 Moore, 291.
Campion v. Colvin, 3 Sc. 350 ; 3 Bing.
N. C. 17. Pothier, Traité de la
charte-partie, part 1, s. 3, § 2. Cleary
v. M'Andrew, 2 Moo. P. C. N. S. 216.
The Soblomsten, L. R., 1 Adm. 293 ;
36 L. J., Adm. 5.

(*l*) Cato v. Irving, 5 De G. & S.
210, 224 ; 21 L. J., Ch. 675.

(*m*) Brown v. Tanner, L., R. 3 Ch.
597 ; 37 L. J. Ch. 923.

(*n*) Andrew v. Moorhouse, 5 Taunt.
438 ; 1 Marsh. 122. De Silvale v.
Kendall, 4 M. & S. 42.

(*o*) Thompson v. Gillespy, 5 Ell. &
Bl. 209 ; 24 L. J., Q. B. 340. Hudson
v. Bilton, 6 El. & Bl. 565 ; 26 L. J.,
Q. B. 27.

(*p*) Roelundts v. Harrison, 9 Exch.
444 ; 23 L. J., Ex. 169.

(*q*) Mashiter v. Buller, 1 Campb.
84. Abbott, C. J., Manfield v. Maitland, 4 B. & Ald. 585. Vlierboom v.
Chapman, 13 M. & W. 230.

(*r*) Duthie v. Hilton, L. R., 4 C. P.
138 ; 38 L. J., C. P. 93.

(*s*) Saunders v. Drew, 3 B. & Ad.
450. Byrne v. Schiller, L. R., 6 Ex.
319 ; 40 L. J., Ex. 177.

casioned by negligence, or misconduct, or want of skill in the navigation of the vessel. If by the occurrence of an accident on the voyage delay is occasioned, the master may claim a reasonable time to carry on the cargo, either in the same ship when repaired, or by transhipping it into another vessel. (*t*)

When the use of the entire vessel is bargained for, (*u*) and the charterer covenants or agrees to provide and ship a full cargo, and pay freight therefor at so much a ton, and the shipowner sends out the vessel, the circumstance that the lading has been prevented by some unforeseen cause or inevitable accident does not release the charterer from his contract. And, when the goods have been shipped on board, the charterer can not abandon them and refuse to pay the freight on the ground that they have been damaged or destroyed by perils of the sea, (*x*) or by the fault of the master and crew; (*y*) nor can he deduct from the freight the value of missing articles. (*z*) When the charterer merely covenants to pay freight at the rate of so much a ton, etc., for the goods actually shipped on board, and does not covenant to furnish any particular quantity of goods, he is only liable for the quantity of goods actually shipped ; but, if he contracts for the use of the entire ship, or part of a ship, or for a certain specified tonnage, the payment of freight must be proportioned to the amount of tonnage, space, or accommodation he has contracted for. If he covenants to ship on board a full and complete cargo, and to pay so much a ton for every ton loaded

(*t*) Cleary v. M'Andrew, 2 Moo. P. C., N. S. 216.

(*u*) As to putting cargo in the cabin, see Mitcheson v. Nicol, 7 Exch. 929 ; and on deck, see Neill v. Ridley, 9 Exch. 680.

(*x*) Abbott on Shipping, 380, 381.

(*y*) Dakin v. Oxley, 15 C. B., N. S. 646 ; 33 L. J., C. P. 115.

(*z*) Meyer v. Dresser, 16 C. B., N. S. 646. 33 L. J., C. P. 289.

on board, he is bound to put on board and to pay freight for as much as the ship will hold and safely carry, whatever may be the amount of the burthen and tonnage of the vessel mentioned in the charter-party. A misdescription of the ship's burthen does not in such a case exonerate the charterer from the liability to ship on board, and to pay freight for, a full and complete cargo, provided the charterer has had an opportunity of examining the ship, and forming his own judgment of her capacity, and there has been no fraudulent misrepresentation or concealment of the truth. (*a*)   Although the charterer has taken the whole ship, and covenanted to provide and put on board, and pay freight for, a " full and complete cargo," yet the shipowner may take on board merchandise as ballast, provided it occupies no larger space than the ballast would have done, and does not interfere with the proper shipment and carriage of the cargo. (*b*)

964. *Calculation of the freight.*—When freight is covenanted to be paid at the rate of so much per ton for the goods shipped on board, the freight is to be calculated and paid on that quantity alone which is put on board, carried throughout the whole voyage, and delivered, at the end of it, to the merchant. If, therefore, a cargo of corn increases in bulk and weight during the voyage, or after the cargo is taken out of the vessel, the freight is payable only on the quantity actually shipped on board, and not on the increased quantity delivered ; for such a cargo may be increased in bulk and deteriorated in quality by the negligence of the master and crew during the voyage. (*c*)

(*a*) Hunter v. Fry, 2 B. &. Ald. 424. Thomas v. Clarke, 2 Stark. 450. Barker v. Windle, 6 Ell. & Bl. 675.

(*b*) Towse v. Henderson, 4 Exch. 893.

(*c*) Gibson v. Sturge, 24 L. J., Ex. 121. Buckle v. Knoop, L. R., 2 Ex. 125, 333 ; 36 L. J., Ex. 49, 223.

965. *Payment pro ratâ.*—If the covenant or agreement of the shipowner or master be entire for the conveyance of a full cargo of merchandise for a specific sum, the charterer is not bound to accept and pay for half a cargo ; but, if the charterer loads less than a full cargo, or if part of the cargo is lost without any default on the part of the shipowner, the whole of the sum is payable. (*d*) And, if he agrees to pay by the bale or cask, or at the rate of so much a ton, he is bound to accept and pay for what has been actually brought and tendered to him. (*e*) He must pay, also, in all cases, for such goods as he actually accepts ; and, if he voluntarily accepts goods short of the port of destination, so as to raise an inference that further carriage of the goods was dispensed with, (*f*) he is liable upon an implied contract to pay pro ratâ itineris peracti. This apportionment usually happens when the ship, by reason of some disaster, goes into a port short of the place of destination, and is unable to prosecute and complete the voyage. (*g*)

966. *Time freight.*—When the charterer engages to pay so much per month, week, or day of the voyage, or of the ship's employment, and no time is fixed for the commencement of the computation, his liability for the freight will begin on the day that the ship breaks ground and commences the voyage, and will continue during all unavoidable delays for provisions repairs, &c., not occasioned by the negligence or misconduct of the master or owners. (*h*) The month is always understood to be a calendar, and not a lunar,

(*d*) Robinson v. Knight, L. R., 8 C. P. 465 ; 42 L. J., C. P. 211. The Norway, 3 Moo. P. C., N. S. 245.

(*e*) Christy v. Row, 1 Taunt. 314. Ritchie v. Atkinson, 10 East, 295, 310.

(*f*) The Soblomsten, L. R., 1 Adm. 293 ; 36 L. J., Adm. 5.

(*g*) Vlierboom v. Chapman, 13 M. & W. 239.

(*h*) Havelock v. Geddes, 10 East, 566. Ripley v. Scaife, 5 B. & C. 169.

month ; (*i*) and the freight becomes due in general at
the expiration of each month, or other interval of
time limited by the parties for its payment, whether
the ship does or does not ultimately arrive at her place
of destination.　But, where the freighter covenanted
to pay freight for a vessel at so much a ton per month
until her final discharge, so much of such freight as
might be earned at the time of the arrival of the ship
at her first destined port abroad to be paid within ten
days after her arrival there, and the remainder of the .
freight at specific periods, it was held that the arrival
of the ship at her first destined port abroad was a condition precedent to the owner's right to recover any
freight. (*k*)

967. *Shipowner's lien for the freight—Payment
of freight by the consignee.*—If the shipowners have
by the charter-party divested themselves of the possession of the vessel in favor of the charterer,
they have, of course, no lien upon the goods shipped
on board, and can not take possession of them and
detain them as a security for the rent or hire agreed to
be paid for the use of the vessel. (*l*)　But, if the
charter-party does not amount to a bailment of the
ship, but the shipowners keep possession of the vessel,
and contract merely to carry merchandise for the
charterer for certain freight, the delivery of the goods,
and the payment of the freight constitute mutual conditions to be performed at the same time, so that the
shipowner may retain the cargo until he is tendered
payment of the freight. (*m*)'　When, however, by the

(*i*) Jolly v. Young, 1 Esp. 186.
(*k*) Gibbon v. Mendez, 2 B. & Ald.
17. Smith v. Wilson, 1 East. 437.
(*l*) Hutton v Bragg, 7 Taunt. 14.

(*m*) Saville v. Campion, 2 B. &
Ald. 503. Campion v. Colvin, 3 Sc.
388 ; 3 Bing. N. C. 17. Tate v. Meek,
2 Moore, 293.

' Dixon on Shipping, § 174; The Eddy, 5 Wall. 493; Du-

terms of the contract, credit is given for the payment of the freight, as, for instance, if it is to be paid a month or three months after the arrival of the ship, the carrier must forthwith deliver the goods, and rely on the subsequent performance by the charterer of his contract to pay ; (*n*) and, if the latter becomes bankrupt prior to the arrival of the vessel at the port of destination, his assignees are entitled to demand the goods, and the shipowners can not claim any lien upon them for freight. (*o*) If the master does not think fit to insist on his right of detention, but delivers the goods to the consignee, and the latter afterwards refuses to pay the freight, or pays the master by a bill of exchange which turns out to be worthless, the master may resort to the consignor or shipper for payment, (*p*) unless he has for his own convenience and accom-

(*n*) Alsager v. St. Kath. Dock Co., 14 M. & W. 794 ; 15 L. J., Ex. 34.

(*o*) Tamvaco v. Simpson, L. R., 1 C. P. 363 ; 35 L. J., C. P. 196. Fry v. Chartered Mercantile Bk. of India,

&c., L. R., 1 C. P. 689 ; L. J., C. P. 306.

(*p*) Tapley v. Martens, 8 T. R. 453. Shepard v. De Bernales, 13 East, 572. Domett v. Beckford, 5 B. & Ap. 521.

pont v. Vance, 19 How. (U. S.) 168. And not only the owner has a lien, but the seamen have a lien for their wages on the freight. In Poland v. Brig Spartan (Ware, 134), it was held that the seamens' lien on the freight was not taken away by the statute which gave them process against the vessel ; and that if the vessel was chartered by persons bearing the expense of victualling and manning her, the lien would attach to cargo shipped on the charterer's account for a charge in the nature of freight ; and see Sheppard v. Taylor, 5 Pet. 675 ; Brown v. Lull, 2 Sumn. 443 ; Pittman v. Hooper, 3 Sumn. 50. So, too, the lien against the cargo will attach where the ship and cargo belong to the same person, although it has passed to assignees upon the insolvency of its owner ; Poland v Brig Spartan, Ware, 134 ; Sheppard v. Taylor, 5 Pet. 675 ; "and if the owner receives any freight, whether in full or in part of what is earned, the whole wages due attach upon it ; for as the wages are nailed to the last plank of the ship, so also they are to the last payment of the freight ;" Brown v. Lull, 2 Sumn. 443 ; Pittman v. Hooper, 3 Id. 50, 186.

modation preferred a bill when he might have had cash.
(*q*)   Payment to the shipowners on their demand is
a discharge against any claim by the master ; and, on
the other hand, payment to the master, in the absence
of any notice from the owners to withhold it, is a valid
payment as against them. (*r*)   The consignee is
primâ facie the owner of the goods, and as such, is
liable for the freight ; but, if he be not the owner, he
is not liable for freight simply as consignee, except on
a new contract to pay the freight.   If the goods have
always been delivered on payment of freight by the
defendant, that is reasonable evidence that in the particular case he agreed to pay the freight. (*s*)

968. *Of the liability for freight resulting from
the acceptance of goods under bills of lading.*—It has
been held that, if a person receives goods under a bill
of lading in which it is expressed that the goods are
to be delivered to him, he paying freight, he, by implication, agrees to pay freight. (*t*)   The law does not,
however, imply any contract for the payment of the
freight from the delivery and acceptance of less than
the whole cargo, (*u*) or from the mere fact of the acceptance of the goods ; but it is for a jury to say
whether the acceptance, coupled with the particular
terms of the bill of lading under which the goods
were received, establishes the existence of a contract
on the part of the consignee to pay the freight. (*x*)
If the consignee receives the goods without any dis-

(*q*) Strong v. Hart, 6 B. & C. 160.
(*r*) Smith v. Plummer, 1 B. & Ald.
575. Atkinson v. Cotesworth, 3 B. &
C. 648.
(*s*) Coleman v. Lambert, 5 M. &
W. 505.
(*t*) Cock v Taylor, 13 East, 403.
Wilson v. Kymer 1 M. & S. 157.

Bell v. Kymer, 5 Taunt. 477. Gumm
v. Tyrie, 33 L. J., Q. B. 97 ; 34 ib.
124 ; 6 B. & S. 299.
(*u*) Young v. Moeler, 5 Ell. & Bl.
762 ; S. C. nom. Möller v. Young,
25 L. J., Q. B. 94.
(*x*) Zwilchenbart v. Henderson, 9
Exch. 722 ; 23 L. J., Ex. 234.

claimer of his liability, and there is no reference on the face of the bill of lading to any charter-party whereby the consignor has contracted to pay the freight, the presumption is that the consignee has agreed to pay it; but when the bill of lading provides for the payment of the freight as per charter-party, and the consignor has contracted by such charter-party for the payment of the freight, it does not necessarily follow that the consignee, by accepting the goods under the bill of lading, has himself contracted to pay it, although he is generally considered so to do. The contract for the payment of the freight inserted in the charter-party does not run with the property in the goods, and is not transferred with it so as to throw the burden of performance upon the parties into whose hands the goods come by indorsement of the bill of lading. But it has been so much the practice for the indorsee of the bill of lading to pay the freight which the consignor or charterer has by the charter-party, contracted with the shipowner to pay, that the acceptance of the goods by such indorsee without any disclaimer of his liability is evidence of a new contract and a new agreement for the payment of the freight mentioned therein, the consideration for which is the delivery of the goods to him at his request ; (y) and if such new contract is established, the remedy for the freight on the bill of lading against the consignee or his assignee co-exists with the remedy against the original consignor or charterer upon the charter-party. (z)   Where a charter-party, stipulating for freight in a lump sum of £2,800 in full of all charges, contained the following clause, "The captain to sign bills of lading at any rate of freight without prejudice to this charter," it was held

(y) Sanders *v.* Vanzeller, 4 Q. B. 295. Kemp *v.* Clark, 12 Q. B. 647.   (z) Christy *v.* Row, 1 Taunt. 300. Shepard *v.* De Bernales, 13 East, 565.

that, so long as the goods shipped remained the property of the charterers or of their agents, they were liable to the lump freight, and the shipowners had a lien for it, but that the shipowners might be bound to deliver the goods to a bonâ fide holder for value of the bill of lading upon payment of the freight mentioned in the bill of lading. (*a*) The master has no authority to draw bills of lading making the freight payable otherwise than to the owner. (*b*) If the amount of the freight is specified on the face of the bill of lading, it is, in general, conclusive between the parties. (*c*) Where, therefore, a mere nominal rate of freight was provided to be paid by the bill of lading, the shipowner being also owner of the cargo, it was held that a subsequent mortgagee of the ship and freight could not charge the assignee of the bill of lading the current rate of freight, but was confined to the nominal freight specified on the face of the bill of lading. (*d*) If the receiver of the goods appears on the face of the bill of lading to be an agent acting on behalf of a known principal who is the consignee, the principal and not the agent is then liable for the freight. (*e*) But if the agency is undisclosed, and the principal has given the agent no authority to pledge his credit for the payment of the freight, and the goods never reach the hands of the principal, the latter can not be made responsible for the amount of the freight; (*f*) and the agent who actually received the goods under the bill of lading is then the party to be pro-

---

(*a*) Gledstanes v. Allen, 12 C. B., 202.

(*b*) Reynolds v. Jex, 34 L. J., Q. B. 251.

(*c*) Foster v. Colby, 3 H. & N. 715; 28 L. J., Ex. 81. Shand v. Sanderson, 4 H. & N. 389; 28 L. J., Ex. 278.

(*d*) Brown v. North, 8 Exch. 1; 22 L. J., Ex. 49.

(*e*) Amos v. Temperley, 8 M. & W. 805.

(*f*) Tobin v. Crawford, 9 M. & W. 718.

ceeded against. (*g*) Where a bill of lading represented the freight of goods to have been paid, when, in fact, it had not been paid, it was held by the court that, though such representation was, not conclusive as between the shipper of the goods and the shipowner, yet, as against an endorsee for value of the bill of lading without notice, the freight must be held to have been paid. (*h*)

Where, by the terms of the charter-party, the ship is let for a particular voyage, and the charterers are to pay the shipowners a lump freight for the whole voyage, and the master, at the request of the charterers, is to make bills of lading at any rate and payable in any manner the charterers may choose, without prejudice to the charter, this gives to the charterers the direct management as to the terms on which the bills of lading are to be signed. And, when it is once shown that the master was, in fact, acting for the charterers, and this is made known to the shippers, the charterers are entitled to recover the freight under the general authority which the shipowners have conferred upon them. (*i*)

969. *Stipulated payments in lieu of freight extinguishing the right of lien.*—When it is stipulated that a certain specified sum of money shall be paid in respect of goods shipped on board a particular vessel within a certain specified period after the sailing of the vessel, whether the goods shall then have been conveyed to their place of destination or not, or whether they shall ever be so conveyed or not, and to secure

(*g*) Dougal v. Kemble, 3 Bing. 383; 11 Moore, 250.

(*h*) Howard v. Tucker, 1 B. & Ad. 712. Kirchner v. Venus, 12 Moore, P. C. 399.

(*i*) Marquand v. Banner, 6 Ell. & Bl. 245; 25 L. J., Q. B. 313. Kern v. Deslandes, 10 C. B., N. S. 205; 30 L. J., C. P. 297.

this arrangement the amount is made payable by the shipper, the sum stipulated to be paid is not freight, but a payment in lieu of freight.   In this case there is no lien upon the goods to secure the payment, neither the consignee nor his goods being liable for the payment of the sum stipulated to be paid, which is held to be not freight, but a remuneration for receiving the goods with a qualified contract for conveying them, and not a reward for actual conveyance. (*k*)   But parties who have by special contract superseded the rights and obligations which the law attaches to freight in its legal sense, may, if they think fit, create a lien on the goods for the performance of the agreement into which they have entered ; and they may do this, either by express conditions contained in the contract itself or by agreeing that, in case of failure of performance of that agreement, the right of lien for what is due shall subsist as if there had been an agreement for freight ; and the usage of the place where the contract was made may be annexed to the contract so as to create a lien, provided both parties were cognizant of the usage at the time they made their contract. (*l*)

970. *Retainer of goods in the Queen's warehouse for freight.*—By the 22 & 23 Vict. c. 37, s. 2, any officer of the customs, having the charge or custody of any goods which shall have come to his hands under the laws relating to the customs, is authorised and empowered to refuse delivery thereof from the Queen's warehouse or other place in which the same shall be deposited, until proof shall be given to his satisfaction that the freight due upon such goods has been paid.

971. *Payment of demurrage on charter-parties and bills of lading.*—Where the charter-party is silent

<hr />

(*k*) How v. Kirchner, 11 Moore, P. C. 25.

(*l*) Kirchner v. Venus, 12 Moore, P. C. 398.

as to the time to be occupied in the discharge, the contract implied by law is that each party will use reasonable diligence in performing that part of the delivery which, by the custom of the port, falls upon him ; and there is no implied contract by the shipowner that the discharge shall be performed in the time usually taken at the port. (*m*) The charterer usually covenants or promises to load or unload the vessel within a certain time, or, if he fails so to do, to pay so much per diem during the delay. This payment, as well as the delay itself, is called in mercantile and legal phraseology, demurrage. The charterer can not escape from liability upon his express covenant or promise to pay demurrage, by showing that the delay was occasioned by some unforeseen event not provided for by the contract, such as the crowded state of the docks, the delays of Custom-house officers, or the inclemency of the weather, (*n*) or the neglect of the holders of the bill of lading to present it and claim the goods. (*o*) But, if the delay is occasioned by the wrongful and unauthorized interference of the shipowner himself with the unloading of the cargo, the detention is not then the detention of the charterer, and the shipowner can not claim demurrage in respect thereof. (*p*) The lay days count in general from the time the vessel arrives in the dock, and is in the management of the dock company's or harbor-master's officers ; (*q*) and when neither is to blame for delay, the number of days run from the time when the ship is in a dischargeable state ; and if no period is mentioned, the cargo is to be discharged in a reasonable

(*m*) Ford v. Cotesworth, L. R., 4 Q. B. 127   38 L. J., Q. B. 52.

(*n*) Blight v. Page, 3 B. & P. 295, n. Barret v. Dutton, 4 Campb. 333.

(*o*) Erichsen v. Barkworth, 3 H. & N. 894 ; 28 L. J., Ex. 95.

(*p*) Benson v. Blunt, 1 Q. B. 870.

(*q*) Tapscott v. Balfour, L. R., 8 C. P. 46 ; 42 L. J., C. P. 16.

time, to commence from the time when the ship is in
a state to begin delivering. (r) Where £5 per diem demurrage was stipulated to be paid, "to reckon from the
time of the vessel being ready to unload, and in turn
to deliver," it was held that the words "in turn to deliver" applied to the public rules and regulations of
the port of discharge, and that the charterers were not
liable for the payment of demurrage until their "turn
to deliver" had come, in conformity with the regulations of the port. (s) If, after the loading has been
completed, the vessel is detained by a sudden frost, (t)
or by foul weather and contrary winds, no right to demurrage arises by reason of such detention. (u)

The days mentioned in the clause of demurrage
are understood, it is said, by the custom of the port
of London, to be working days, and do not, consequently, include Sundays and Custom-house holidays. (v) There does not, however, appear to be any
general custom to this effect. (y) The lay days allowed
are, moreover, to be reckoned from the time of the
ship's arrival at the usual place of discharge, and not
from her arrival at the entrance of the port, although
for the purposes of navigation she may have discharged
a portion of her cargo at the entrance of the port. (z) If
the parties, by mutual consent, substitute a new port
for the port mentioned in the contract of affreightment, the freighter will be entitled to the lay days,
and the shipowner to the demurrage, stipulated for by

(r) Brown v. Johnson, 1 Car. &
Marsh. 440 ; 10 M. & W. 331.

(s) Robertson v. Jackson, 2 C. B.
412 ; 15 L. J., C. P. 28   Taylor v.
Clay, 9 Q. B. 713. Leidemann v.
Schultz, 14 C. B. 51. But see Lawson
v. Burness, 1 H. & C. 396.

(t) Pringle v. Mollett, 6 M. & W.
83.

(u) Jamieson v. Laurie, 6 Bro. P.
C. 474.

(v) Cochran v Retberg, 3 Esp. 121.

(y) Brown v. Johnson, 10 M. & W.
334.

(z) Brereton v. Chapman, 7 Bing.
559. Kell v. Anderson, 10 M. & W.
498. Bastifell v. Lloyd, 1 H. & C.
388 ; 31 L. J., Ex. 413.

the original contract. (*a*) If a consignee accepts goods under a bill of lading, at the bottom of which is a memorandum, to the effect that the ship is to be cleared within a certain time, and that demurrage, at the rate of so much per diem, is to be paid after that day, he will be liable for the payment of such demurrage, and may be sued therefor by the master ; (*b*) but he is not responsible to the master for demurrage if no such clause is contained in the bill of lading, (*c*) or if the delay is caused by the master's improperly refusing to deliver the whole cargo. (*d*) Where, by the bill of lading, the vessel is to be unloaded in her regular turn, the consignor is liable for her detention beyond her regular turn, although there is no express contract for demurrage in the bill of lading. (*e*)

972. *Primage and average.*—The freighter whose merchandise has been conveyed to the port of destination is also liable for the payment of certain customary charges called primage and average. The first is a small customary payment to the master for his trouble, and the second consists of several petty charges, such as towage, beaconage, pilotage, &c. (*f*)

973. *General average and contribution.*—By the ancient laws of the Rhodians it was provided that, if several persons had laden goods on board a ship to be carried for hire, and the goods of one of them were thrown overboard in a storm to lighten the vessel and save her from perishing, the loss incurred for the sake

(*a*) Jackson v. Galloway, 6 Sc. 792.

(*b*) Jesson v. Solly, 4 Taunt. 54. Stindt v. Roberts, 17 L. J., Q. B. 166 ; 12 Jur. 518. Wegener v. Smith, 15 C. B. 285 ; 24 L. J., C. P. 25.

(*c*) Brouncker v. Scott, 4 Taunt. 1. Smith v. Sieveking, 5 Ell. & Bl. 589 ; 24 L. J., Q. B. 257. Chappell v. Comfort, 10 C. B., N. S. 802 : 31 L. J., C. P. 58.

(*d*) Young v. Moeller, 5 Ell. & Bl. 762. S. C. nom. Möller v. Young, 25 L. J., Q. B. 94.

(*e*) Cawthron v. Trickett, 15 C. B., N. S. 754 ; 33 L. J., C. P. 182. And see Shadforth v. Cory, 32 L. J., Q. B. 379.

(*f*) Abbott, 404. Pothier (Avaries), No. 147.

of all should be made good by the contribution of
all. (*g*)   This equitable rule of law was adopted by
the Romans, and has been introduced into the maritime code of continental Europe.   It is said to have
been engrafted upon our own common law by the
Normans, and has certainly existed as a custom
amongst merchants in this country from a very early
period.   The obligation to contribute, which is deemed
by the common law to be tacitly entered into by
the shipowners and owners of the cargo, is called general or gross average ; and the parties subject thereto
are bound to contribute rateably according to the
value of their several proportions of the property
saved.   The law of contribution is thus explained by
Domat in his Treatise on the Civil Law :—" When, in
order to lighten a ship in peril of shipwreck, part of
the cargo is cast into the sea, and the ship by that
means is saved, this loss is common to all those who
have anything to lose in that peril.   Thus the master
of the ship, all those whose merchandise or effects
have been saved, and those whose goods have been
thrown overboard, will each bear their share of the
loss, in proportion to the share they had in the whole.
If, for example, the ship and the whole cargo were
worth 100,000 crowns, and that which was cast overboard was worth 20,000 crowns, the loss being a fifth,
each will contribute a fifth part of the value of what
he has saved, which will make in all 16,000 crowns ;
and by this contribution, those who lost the 20,000
crowns, in recovering 16,000, will remain losers only
of a fifth part, like the rest." (*h*)

(*g*) Dig. lib. 14, tit. 2, lex 1, De   Code de Commerce, liv. 2, tit. 11,
llege Rhodiâ. Pothier, Traité des   Des Avaries.
Avaries, Partie 2, ed. Dupin, 371.   (*h*) Domat, les Lois Civiles, liv. 2,
                        tit. 9, s. 2, 6.

Everything saved pays contribution according to its value; the shipowner contributes in proportion to the value of the ship and furniture, except the provisions of the passengers and crew, (*i*) and the passengers and owners of goods shipped on board in proportion to the value of the property they save, excepting the clothes on their backs, but not excepting their wearing apparel and jewels deposited on board. (*k*) The freight and earnings of the ship, after deducting the wages of the master and crew and other expenses of the voyage, likewise form the subject of contribution and general average; and, if a ship be chartered out and home for one entire and indivisible sum for the use of the ship out and home, the entire freight for the outward and homeward voyage must, when ultimately earned, contribute to the loss, whether the loss has occured upon the outward or the homeward voyage. (*l*) Goods stowed upon the deck of the vessel, and thrown overboard during a storm, are not excluded from the benefit of general average and contribution, unless it be shown that the lading was improper and calculated to impede the navigation of the vessel, and increase the risk of the voyage. (*m*)

To establish a claim for general average, it must be shown that the goods were thrown overboard in a moment of distress and danger, with a view of preserving the ship and cargo; if they have been washed out of the ship by the violence of the waves, or have been damaged or destroyed by lightning or tempest, or have been unnecessarily cast overboard by the mas-

(*i*) Brown v. Stapyleton, 4 Bing. 119.

(*k*) Pothier, Avaries, art 3. By the civil law, wearing apparel was made to contribute towards the general average. Dig. lib. 14, tit. 2, Lex 2, § 2.

(*l*) Williams v. Lond. A. Co., 1 M. & S. 325.

(*m*) Milward v.. Hibbert, 3 Q. B. 120, 137. Gould v. Oliver, 2 Sc. N. R. 241. Johnson v. Chapman, 19 C. B., N. S., 563; 35 L. J., C. P. 23.

ter, or crew, or passengers, the loss will not support a
claim for general average. (*n*)   If the masts and
cables of the vessel have been cut away for the purpose
of preventing shipwreck, the owners of the cargo must
contribute towards the loss of the shipowner ; but, if
they are blown away, or injured in consequence of the
necessity of carrying a great and unusual press of can-
vas to escape a threatening danger, or if the ship was
not seaworthy at the commencement of the voyage,
and the loss was occasioned by reason of such unseaworthiness, the loss is not the subject of contribution
and general average. (*o*)   If a ship accidentally runs
foul of another ship in a fog or storm, and the master
is compelled to cut away his rigging in order to preserve the ship and cargo, and is obliged to put into
port to repair and renew that which has been sacri-
ficed, the expense of re-landing and warehousing the
cargo, and of the repairs, so far as they are absolutely
necessary to enable the ship to prosecute the voyage,
form the subject of general average. (*p*)

If part of the cargo has been taken out and put
into lighters, to enable a stranded vessel to be got
afloat and sent into port for repairs, the whole expense
of the operation, which is for the common benefit of
ship, goods, and freight, forms the subject of general
average ; (*q*)[1] but not, as a general rule, expenses in-

(*n*) Mouse's case, 12 Co. 63. Dobson v. Wilson, 3 Campb. 486. Pothier,
Part 2, s. 2, art. 1.

(*o*) Birkley v. Presgrave, 1 East,
220. Covington v. Roberts, 5 B. & P.
379. Power v. Whitmore, 4 M. & S.
149. Schloss v. Heriott, 14 C. B.,
N. S. 59 ; 32 L. J., C. P. 211. Dig.
lib. 14, tit 2, lex 3, lex 5. Domat, liv.

2, tit. 19, s. 2, 11.

(*p*) Plummer v. Wildman, 3 M. &
S. 482, qualified by Hallett v. Wig-
ram, 9 C. B. 601 ; 19 L. J., C. P. 288.
Hall v. Janson, 4 Ell. & Bl. 508.
Harrison v. Bank of Australia, L. R.,
7 Ex. 39 ; 41 L. J., Ex. 36.

(*q*) Moran v. Jones, 7 Ell. & Bl.
533 , 26 L. J., Q. B. 187.

[1] Whittridge v. Norris, 6 Mass. 125 ; Lewis v. Williams, 1

curred after the cargo has been safely discharged and warehoused for the purpose of saving the ship alone. (*r*)

If it is necessary to lighten the ship to enable her to get into a port of safety, and a portion of the cargo is taken out for the purpose and put into lighters, and the lighters perish ere they reach the shore, the loss will be common, and the owners of the residue of the cargo must contribute thereto, as it was for the general benefit that the discharge was made. But, if the ship is cast away and the lighter gets safe to port, there is then, it is said, no contribution, but each must bear his own loss. If a ship that has been saved from one danger of shipwreck by throwing some of the goods overboard, is afterwards sunk in another place, and a portion of the cargo is recovered from the wreck, the owners of the cargo so recovered must contribute to make up the loss of those whose goods were thrown overboard for the purpose of avoiding the first peril, as the goods recovered might then have perished but for the sacrifice of the things thrown overboard to escape it. But, if he whose goods were thrown overboard at first, happens afterwards to recover them, he shall not contribute towards the subsequent loss, as that loss has in nowise contributed to the safety of the goods so recovered. If by reason of a jettison of goods, some portions of the residue of the cargo have been exposed and injured, this injury must, by the civil law, be made good by contribution. The owner of the damaged goods himself contributes towards the total loss ac-

(*r*) Job v. Langton, 6 Ell. & Bl. 792 ; 26 L. J., Q. B. 97. Walthew v. Mav- rojani, L. R., 5 Ex. 116 ; 39 L. J., Ex. 81.

Hall, 430; The Nathaniel Hooper, 3 Sumner, 542; Hayliger v. Fireman's Ins. Co. 11 Johns. 85.

cording to the actual value of such goods after the injury, and is then entitled to contribution in respect of his own partial loss. (*s*)   It has been held that the expenditure of ammunition in resisting capture by a privateer, the damage done to the ship in the combat, and the expense of curing the wounded, are not the subject of contribution and general average.   The correctness of this decision, however, may be doubted, opposed as it is to the opinions of some of the most eminent writers on maritime law, and to the acknowledged principle of contribution. (*t*)   By the civil law, the goods cast overboard were valued only at their invoice price or prime cost.   " A practice formerly prevailed in this country to adopt this valuation if the loss happened before half the voyage was performed ; but if it happened afterwards, then to value the goods at the clear price which they would have fetched at the place of destination.   The last valuation is now adopted in all cases where the average is adjusted after the ship's arrival at the place of destination. But if the ship is compelled to return to its port of lading, and the average is immediately adjusted, the goods only contribute according to the invoice price," (*u*) or even less, if in all probability they would have arrived in a damaged state, the general rule being that the value of goods jettisoned is to be taken to be the sum which it may fairly be assumed they would have been worth to the owner at the port of adjustment. (*x*)   As soon as the average has been calculated, and

---

(*s*) Dig. lib. 14, tit 2, lex 4, § 1, 2, 7. Domat. liv. 2, tit. 9, s. 14 (AVARIES), No. 145. Pothier, des Avaries, art. 4.

(*t*) Taylor v. Curtis, 6 Taunt. 608. Ib. 638—643. Phillips on Insurance,
337. Benecke, 280. Pothier (Avaries), s. 2, No. 144.

(*u*) Abbott, CONTRIBUTION.

(*x*) Fletcher v. Alexander, L. R., 3 C. P. 375 ; 37 L. J., C. P. 193.

the exact amount of contribution ascertained, an action may be brought for its recovery. (*y*) [1]

974. *Damages for breach of charter-parties.*—The

(*y*) Birkley v. Presgrave, 1 East, 220. See the form of declaration, Schloss v. Heriott, 14 C. B., N. S. 59; 32 L. J., C. P. 214.

[1] " The main characteristic of a general average," says Dixon on Shipping, § 546, " is that it is the intentional result of the act of man, not immediately the physical effect of the perils insured against. A storm arises; the ship is making water with every sea, or drifting in upon rocks and breakers, and in imminent peril of being lost. If goods are thrown overboard to lighten her, or masts cut away to bring her up, the damage is a general average loss. If, instead of this, the goods are washed out by the waves, or the mast snapped asunder by the wind, the loss falls entirely on the owner of the property damaged; and if he be insured, is the basis of a claim against his insurers in partial loss." And consult as to what may be proper cases for general average, the recent adjudications in McLain v. Cummings, 73 Pa. St. 98; The Milwaukee Belle, 2 Biss. 197; The Congress, 1 Id. 42; Fowler v. Rathbone, 12 Wall. 102; Bales of Cotton, 8 Blatchf. 221; Fitzpatrick v. Bales of Cotton, 3 Ben. 42; Jones v. Bridge, 2 Sweeney, 431; Star of Hope, 9 Wall. 203; Rathbone v. Fowler, 6 Blatchf. 294. When the wages, provisions, and other expenses of a voyage to a port of necessity may contribute to a general average, see Thornton v. United States Ins. Co., 12 Me. (3 Fairf.) 150; Potter v. Ocean Ins. Co., 3 Sumn. 27; Walden v. Leroy, 2 Caines, 262; Henshaw v. Marine Ins. Co., Id. 247; Parker v. Phœnix Ins. Co., 8 Johns. 307; Rogers v. Murray, 3 Bosw. 357; The Mary, 1 Sprague, 17; Leavenworth v. Delafield, 1 Caines, 573; Bedford Ins. Co. v. Parker, 2 Pick. 1. But sailor's wages and provisions are not liable for repairs and demurrage; Wightman v. McAdam, 2 Brev. 230; Dunham v. Commercial Ins. Co., 11 Johns. 315; McBride v. Marine Ins. Co., 7 Id. 431. But the expense or loss must have been intended to save and preserve the remaining property, and have been successful in so doing. Williams v. Suffolk Ins. Co., 3 Sumn. 510. Everything is to be estimated in the general average as it is at the time; Maggrath v. Church, 1 Caines, 196; whether it be exposed to the actual risk or not, so long as it has a common interest with the rest; Nelson v. Belmont, 21 N. Y. 36. And the expenses of a trial and appeal in a

measure of damages for the breach of the ordinary
contract or covenant in a charter-party to procure and
ship a cargo and pay freight[1] is to be ascertained by
calculating the freight to be earned, and deducting the
expense which the shipowner would have been put to,
but did not incur, in earning it, and also what the ship
earned (if anything) during the period which would
have been occupied in performing the voyage if the
charter-party had been fulfilled. (z)   If, subsequently
to the breach of contract, the shipmaster has been
offered a cargo and has refused it, or has neglected an
opportunity of receiving cargo and earning freight, the
measure of damages will be the amount of freight
agreed to be paid, minus what the ship-master
might have earned if he had thought fit. (a)   When
goods shipped on board have been sold at an intermediate port to defray expenses necessarily incurred
in repairing the vessel, the shipper is not entitled to
claim the price they might have realized at the port
of delivery unless the ship and cargo arrived there in
safety. (b)[2]

(z) Smith v. M'Guire, 3 H. & N.   (a) Harries v. Edmonds, 1 C. & K. 686.
567; 27 L. J., Ex. 465. Wilson v.   (b) Atkinson v, Stephens, 21 L. J,.
Hicks, 26 ib. 442.   Ex. 333.

foreign court will constitute a general average loss; Dorr v.
Union Ins. Co., 8 Mass. 494; but medical attendance for a
sailor on the ship; Reed v. Canfield, 1 Sumn. 195; Nevitt v.
Clark, Olc. Adm. 316; a master's commissions or disbursements; Dodge v. Union Ins. Co. 17 Mass. 471; or foreign exchange (Id.) may not. The question as to whether a voluntary
stranding of a vessel is a case for general average, is answered
in the negative in Meech v. Robinson, 4 Whart. (Pa.) 360; and
affirmatively in Mutual Safety Ins. Co. v. Cargo Brig George,
Olc. Adm. 89; Gray v. Waln, 2 Serg. & R. 229; Cozr v. Richards, Id. 237; and see Bradhurst v. Columbian Ins. Co., 9
Johns. 9; and cases cited at the commencement of this note.

[1] *Ante*, § 939.
[2] It is the master's duty to sell a cargo at a port of neces-

975. *Restrictions on the carriage of dangerous goods.*—By the 36 & 37 Vict. c. 85, s. 25, the master or owner of any vessel may refuse to take on board any package or parcel which he suspects to contain goods of a dangerous nature, and may require it to be opened to ascertain the fact. By s. 26, where any dangerous goods (*c*) or any goods which, in the judgment of the master or owner of the vessel, are of a dangerous nature, have been sent or brought aboard any vessel without being marked or without notice being given as required by the Act, (*d*) the master or owner of the vessel may cause such goods to be thrown overboard,

---

(*c*) That is, aquafortis, vitriol, naphtha, benzine, gunpowder, lucifer-matches, nitro-glycerine, petroleum, or any other goods of a dangerous nature, sect. 23.

(*d*) By sect. 23, the nature of the goods must be marked on the outside of the package, and written notice of their nature and of the name and address of the sender or carrier must be given at or before the time of sending the same to be shipped, or taking the same on board the vessel.

---

sity, whether this be the original port of the shipment to which the ship may have returned, or any intermediate port at which the ship arrives; and this he may do, in the absence of instructions from the shipper, even though the cargo may be in a condition to be carried in specie to the port of destination and there landed. Jordan v. Warren Ins. Co., 1 Story, 342. In case of shipwreck, the sale is on the ground that it is a legal necessity, and not that it is best for all concerned. Bryant v. Commonwealth Ins. Co., 13 Pick. 543. But see as to the sale, Searle v. Scovell, 4 Johns. Cas. 218; Saltus v. Ocean Ins. Co., 12 Johns. 107 ; American Ins. Co. v. Center, 4 Wend. 52; Hall v. Franklin Ins. Co., 9 Pick. 478; Treadwell v. Union Ins. Co., 6 Cowen, 270; Jordan v. Warren Ins. Co., 1 Story, C. C. 342. A sale is, however, the last thing that the master should think of, and is only justified by a necessity which supersedes all human laws; Dixon on Shipping, § 160; and the master has no right to sell the cargo because the whole can not be sent on; Id. § 166 The owners of the cargo so sold have a lien upon the vessel for its value. Id. § 165. And persons buying under such circumstances do not acquire a title as against the owner, but must answer to him for the

together with any package or receptacle in which they are contained; and neither the master nor the owner of the vessel will be subject to any liability in respect of such throwing overboard.[1]

976. *Carriage of passengers and merchandise by land by parties not being common carriers—Injuries to passengers and goods.*—All persons who undertake the work of carrying passengers by land for hire impliedly warrant their vehicles, horses, harness, and equipments to be roadworthy, in good traveling order, and reasonably secure and sufficient in strength for the accomplishment of the journey, so far as that condition of things can be secured by the exercise of skill and foresight; but the carrier does not warrant that they shall be perfect for their purpose; and, therefore, he is not responsible for a defect in the vehicle, the existence of which no skill, care, or foresight could have detected. (e)　As the work of driving is a work of skill, the carrier or coach-proprietor impliedly undertakes, if he drives himself, that he is possessed of, and will exercise, competent skill and knowledge of driving. If, on the other hand, he accomplishes the work through the medium of inferior agents and servants, he impliedly undertakes to provide fit and proper persons to execute the office. If the driver overloads the carriage, or drives with immoderate speed, or with defective reins, or with reins so loose

---

(e) Barns v. Cork & Bandon Rail. Co., 13 Ir. C. L. R. 546. Christie v. Griggs, 2 Campb. 81. Sharp v. Grey, 9 Bing. 457; 2 M. & Sc. 620. Read—head v. The Midland Ry. Co., L. R., 4 Q. B. 379; 38 L. J., Q. B. 169. Francis v. Cockerell, L. R., 5 Q. B. 154; 39 L. J., Q. B. 291.

value; Id. § 160; Everett v. Saltus, 15 Wend. 474; Dodge v. Union Ins. Co., 17 Mass. 478; Whitney v. Fireman's Ins. Co., 18 Johns. 208.

[1] See § 288, Revised Statutes of the United States, printed *ante*, on p. 686 of this volume.

that he can not readily command his horses, or if he passes unnecessarily along unsafe parts of the road, or through narrow gateways or dangerous passages, or takes the wrong side of the road, and a collision occurs, the proprietor of the carriage will be answerable for injuries sustained by the passengers. (*f*) And if, from the negligence or recklessness of the driver, or defects in the carriage, harness, or equipments, the passenger is placed in so perilous a situation as to render it advisable for him to leap to the ground to avoid a greater peril reasonably to be apprehended, and he sustains an injury in so doing, the coach proprietor is answerable therefor. (*g*) In determining the question of negligence in cases of collision, the law or custom of the road as to passing vehicles is to be taken into consideration; but it does not follow that a person who neglects that custom, and is on the wrong side of the road when a collision takes place, is necessarily guilty of negligence. "Circumstances may frequently arise where a deviation from what is called the law of the road would not only be justifiable, but absolutely necessary." (*h*)

Every person who receives goods to be carried from one place to another is bound to provide tarpaulins and proper "covering to protect the goods from injury by rain." (*i*)

977. *Loss of goods or money by the way.*—A person who receives things to be carried by him for hire to a certain destination can not set up a mere loss of them by the way as an answer to an action for the non-delivery of them according to his contract.[1]

(*f*) Aston *v.* Heaven, 2 Esp. 536. Bremner *v.* Williams, 1 C. & P. 414.

(*g*) Jones *v.* Boyce, 1 Stark. 493.

(*h*) Wayde *v.* Lady Carr, 2 D. & R. 256.

(*i*) Webb *v.* Page, 6 Sc. N. R. 957; 6 M. & Gr. 204. Walker *v.* Jackson, 10 M. & W. 168.

[1] *Ante*, §§ 953, 954, 958.

Where the plaintiff delivered to the defendant £3, to be carried to Southwark, for reasonable hire and reward, it was held that the law would imply a promise from the defendant " safely to convey " the money, although he was not a common carrier, and although no sum certain had been agreed to be paid him as the price of the carriage. (*k*) And, where a traveler hired a cab for the conveyance of himself and his luggage to a railway station, and the luggage was placed on the outside of the cab, it was held that the law would imply from the acceptance of the luggage by the cabman, to be carried, together with the passenger, for hire, a promise from him "safely and securely" to carry it, and that he was responsible for the loss of a portion of it by the way. (*l*) [1] This promise to carry safely, which the law implies from all persons who undertake the carriage of goods for hire, is not understood to mean that the goods shall be carried and delivered safe at all events, but that they shall be kept safe from all such hazards and contingencies as might have been foreseen and guarded against by the exercise of vigilance or skill. The contract is " a contract to carry safely and securely as far as regards the neglect of the carrier himself and his servants, but not to insure the safety of the goods;" and the carrier therefore would not be liable for losses by robbers, or any taking by force ; but he is primâ facie responsible for a secret theft of them, and can only discharge

---

(*k*) Rogers v. Head, Cro. Jac. 262.   (*l*) Ross v. Hill, 2 C. B. 877; 15
Matthews v. Hopping, 1 Keb. 852.   L. J., C. P. 182.

[1] Peixotti v. McLaughlin, 1 Strob. 468; Dickinson v. Winchester, 4 Cush. 115; and this although the consideration for the passenger's carrying was that he should put up at a certain hotel, whose proprietor was proprietor of the conveyance; Dickinson v. Winchester, *supra*.

himself from liability by proving his own care and watchfulness and blamelessness in the matter.[1]

Where the defendant received eleven boxes of gold dust, under a special contract to carry them and deliver them at the Bank of England, " robbers and dangers of the road excepted," and one of the boxes was secretly stolen, it was held that the defendant was responsible for the loss; that a secret theft or pilfering was not within the exception as to robbers, nor was it a danger of the road within the meaning of the contract. (*m*) If the owner accompanies the goods to take care of them, and loses them himself, the carrier is not responsible for the loss. (*n*) But, if the goods are actually bailed or delivered into the hands of the carrier, under a stipulation that the owner's servant shall accompany them, "the carrier accepting no responsibility," the latter will still be liable for the consequences of his own negligence. (*o*)

978. *Who is to be deemed a common carrier.*—Every person who plies with a carriage by land, or a boat or vessel by water, between different places, and professes openly to carry passengers and goods for hire, is a common carrier.[2] Such are railway companies, who

(*m*) De Rothschild v. R. M. St. P. Co., 7 Exch 734 ; 21 L. J., Ex. 273.
(*n*) Brind v. Dale, 8 C. & P. 209, 211 ; 2 M. & Rob. 80.

(*o*) Martin v. The Great Indian Pen. Ry. Co., L. R., 3 Ex. 9 ; 37 L. J., Ex. 27.

[1] *Ante*, §§ 953, 954–958.
[2] A person who undertakes, though only on that particular occasion, to carry for hire, without special contract, incurs the responsibility of a common carrier; Moss v. Bettis, 4 Heisk, 661 ; but see Fish v. Clark, 49 N. Y. 122. One who has never assumed or offered to carry chattels of a certain class, except upon special terms, is not liable, as a common carrier, for a refusal to carry such property. Lake Shore, &c., R. R. Co. v. Perkins, 25 Mich. 329. And one who contracts

profess to carry passengers, parcels, and merchandise,
stage-coach and stage-wagon proprietors, lightermen,
hoymen, barge owners, canal boatmen, and the owners
and masters of ships and steamboats employed as general ships trading regularly from port to port for the
transportation of all persons offering themselves or
their goods to be conveyed for hire to the port of
destination. (*p*)　The owner of a lighter, hoy, or flat,
which he uses regularly for carrying therein for hire
from place to place the goods of such persons as choose
to employ him, is a common carrier, although he does
not ply regularly between fixed termini. (*q*)　It is the
duty of all who hold themselves out to the world as
common carriers, to carry, for every person who tenders them the proper charge, all goods which they
have convenience for carrying, and in respect of which
they hold themselves out as carriers, without subject-
ing the person tendering the goods to any unreason-

(*p*) Robinson v. Dunmore, 2 B. &
P. 416. Laveroni v. Drury, 8 Exch.
166. Crouch v. Lond. & North-West.

Rail. Co., 23 L. J., C. P. 73.
(*q*) Liver Alkali Co. v. Johnson, L.
I., 7 Ex. 267; 41 L. J., Ex. 110.

to cut timber and transport it to a place where it is to be delivered and used, is not, while transporting it, a common carrier. Pike v. Nash, 3 Abb. N. Y. (App. Dec.) 610.　One main-
taining a ferry for his own use or for the convenience of customers, is not a common carrier; Self v. Dunn, 42 Ga. 528;
and see Fish v. Clark, 2 Lans. 176.　A tow boat company is
not a common carrier; Arctic, &c., Ins. Co. v. Austin, 54 Barb.
559; or one who carries gratuitously; Citizens' Bank v. Nan-
tucket Steamboat Co., 2 Story, 16.　As to who are private carriers, and not common, see Pennewill v. Cullen, 5 Harr. 238;
Shelden v. Robinson, 7 N. H. 157; Moriarty v. Harnden's
Express, 1 Daly, 227.　And whether one is a common carrier
or not, is a question for the jury under direction of the
court; Haynie v. Baylor, 18 Tex. 498; Gordon v. Hutchinson, 1 Watts. & S. 285; and consult generally Southern Ex.
Co. v. McVeigh, 20 Gratt. 264; Christenson v. American
Ex. Co., 15 Minn. 270; Paige v. Smith, 99 Mass. 395.

able or unusual conditions. (*r*) By many of the railway Acts it is expressly enacted that railway companies shall act as common carriers, that they shall convey passengers and goods by locomotive engines, and that they shall provide for all persons conveying and sending goods by their railway every reasonable convenience and facility for the loading and unloading of goods. (*s*)

979. *The nature and extent of the duties of the common carrier are regulated by the nature and extent of his public profession and practice.*—If he selects a particular line or description of business, he can not, so long as he adheres to it with good faith, be compelled to go beyond it. If he is a common carrier of passengers merely, he can not be compelled to carry goods. If he journeys by a particular roundabout road between one place and another, he is not bound to carry by a shorter route ; but he is bound to use reasonable despatch and to deliver within a reasonable time. (*t*) If he limits his enterprise and business to the carriage of particular classes of merchandise or chattels, he can only be compelled to carry the things he publicly professes to carry, and is in the habit of carrying. If the carriage of certain commodities is attended with inconvenience or some peculiar risk, he may refuse to receive and carry such articles as a common carrier, (*x*) but may, nevertheless, accept and carry them under a special contract throwing the risk of damage to them from ordinary accidents during

(*r*) Garton v. Brist. & Ex. Rail. Co. 1 B. & S. 162 ; 30 L. J., Q. B. 294.

(*s*) Pegler v. Monm. Rail. &c., Co., 6 H. & N. 644 ; 30 L. J., Ex. 249.

(*t*) Hales v. Lond. & N. W. R. Co.,

4 B. & S. 66 ; 32 L. J., Q. B. 292. *In re* Oxlade v. The North Eastern Ry. Co., 15 C. B., N. S. 680.

(*x*) Johnson v. Mid. R. Co., 4 Exch. 371. McManus v. Lanc. & York. R. Co., 4 H. & N. 327 ; 28 L, J., Ex. 353.

the transit upon the owner or the consignor. (y) [1] In the absence of a contract to deliver at a particular time, the duty of a common carrier is to deliver at a reasonable time, looking at all the circumstances of the case; and since his first duty is to carry safely, he is justified in incurring delay, if delay is necessary to secure the safe carriage. (z)

As regards dogs and live animals, which a common carrier is not, by his public profession and employment, bound to carry, (a) he may decline to re-

---

(y) Peek v. North Staff. Rail. Co., 32 L. J., Q. B. 241. Phillips v. Edwards, 28 L. J., Ex. 52 ; 3 H. & N. 813. Austin v. Manch. R. Co., 16 Q. B. 600 ; 10 C. B. 454. Carr v. Lanc. & York. Rail. Co., 7 Exch. 707.

(z) Great Northern Ry. Co. v. Taylor, L. R., 1 C. P. 385 ; 35 L. J., C. P. 210.

(a) See however, Willes, J., in Blower v. the Great Western Ry. Co., L. R., 7 C. P. 662 ; 41 L. J., C. P. 268.

---

[1] See the recent case of Lake Shore, &c., R. R. Co. v. Perkins, 25 Mich. 329, which held that one who was in the habit of making special contracts for the transportation of live stock, was not liable, as a common carrier, for refusing to carry such chattels. Also Roberts v. Riley, 15 La. Ann. 103; Moore v. Evans, 14 Barb. 524 ; Bingham v. Rogers, 6 Watts & S, 495; Moriarty v. Harnden's Express, 1 Daly, 227. So a common carrier of passengers may make a special agreement that a passage shall be made in one continuous trip, and within a specified time. Barker v. Coffin, 31 Barb. 556. If common carriers specially undertake to deliver safely any article carried, they will be responsible thereunder, even for a loss by unavoidable accident. Guither v. Barnet, 2 Brev. 488. When bills of lading are special contracts, see Farnham v. Camden, &c., R. R. Co., 55 Pa. St. 53. A receipt given by a common carrier must be interpreted as a whole. Butler v. Steamer Arrow, 6 McLean, 470. But carriers can not make a special contract against their own negligence; for such a contract would be against public policy. Indianapolis, &c., R. R. Co. v. Allen, 31 Ind. 394 ; Michigan &c. R. R. Co. v. Eaton, Id. 397, note, but the special contract must be express, and can not be established from custom ; Cox v. Hersley, 69 Pa. St. 243; but see Farmers', &c., Co. v. Champlain, &c., Co., 18 Vt. 131.

ceive and carry them except upon certain special conditions, and under a special contract regulating and defining the nature and extent of his liability. (*b*)[1] But in the case of a railway or canal company the conditions or special contract must be just and reasonable, must not exempt the company from liability for their own neglect or default, and must be in writing, signed by the consignor or his agent. (*c*) Where carriers by sea give public notice that they receive goods for shipment on the condition and agreement only of the ship sailing under a bill of lading in the form ordinarily adopted, they are not bound to receive and carry otherwise than in accordance with their published terms. (*d*)

The mere posting up at a particular railway station of a list of tolls taken by the company for the carriage of coals, amongst other things, will not constitute the company common carriers of coals from that particular station, if it appears that they have no accommodation there for receiving coals, and do not, in point of fact, carry them from that spot, although they carry them over other parts of their line. (*e*)

By the 29 & 30 Vict. c. 69, s. 6, no carrier is bound to receive or carry any goods which are specially dangerous. (*f*) If a carrier is employed to carry an article of such a dangerous nature as to require extraor-

---

(*b*) Harrison v. Lond. & Br. Rail. Co., 29 L. J., Q. B 218 ; 31 L. J., Q. B. 113 ; 2 B. & S. 122.

(*c*) 17 & 18 Vict. c. 31, s. 7. *Post.*
(*d*) Phillips v. Edwards, *ante*, Wilton v. Royal Atlantic Mail St. Packet Co., 10 C. B., N. S. 453 ; 30 L. J., C. P. 369.

(*e*) Oxlade v. North-E. Rail. Co., 15 C. B., N. S, 680. Johnson v. Mid. Rail. Co., 4 Exch. 372.

(*f*) Specially dangerous goods are nitro-glycerine or glonoine oil, and any other goods that may be so declared by order in council, 29 & 30 Vict. c. 69, ss. 1 and 2.

[1] See Lake Shore, &c., R. R. Co. v. Perkins, 25 Mich. 329, cited *ante*, note 1, p. 718.

dinary care in its conveyance, the fact must be communicated to him, or the consignor will be responsible for any injury that may result to the carrier or his servants from the want of such communication. (*g*)[1]

980. *Of the public profession of railway companies made through the medium of their time-tables.*—If a railway company publishes, or authorizes the publication of, a time-table, representing that a train will run at a particular hour to a particular place, the company impliedly undertakes to dispatch a train at or about the time specified, and will be responsible in damages to all who tender themselves for conveyance at the appointed time and find that no train at all has been provided ; (*h*) but railway companies do not by their time-tables guarantee the arrival of their trains at intermediate stations, or their departure from them, at the exact time fixed. All they undertake to do is to carry the passenger without any unreasonable and unnecessary delay. (*i*)

981. *Booking places in coaches.*—If four ladies, wishing to travel together, take " the whole inside of a coach," the coach-proprietor and his servants have no right to separate them, and do not fulfill their contract by furnishing a double-bodied coach, and tendering three inside places in one division and one in the other. (*k*) " If a person takes a place in a stage-coach, and pays at the time only a deposit, as half the fare, for example, and is not at the inn ready to take his place when the coach is setting off, the coach-proprietor is at liberty to fill up his place with another pas-

(*g*) Farrant v. Barnes, 11 C. B., N. S. 553 ; 31 L. J., C. P. 137.

(*h*) Denton v. Gt. North, R. Co., 5 Ell. & Bl. 868 ; 25 L. J., Q. B. 129.

(*i*) Hurst v. Gt. West. Rail. Co., 19 C. B., N. S. 310 ; 34 L. J., C. P. 264.

(*k*) Long v. Horne, 1 C. & P. 611.

[1] See *ante*, § 4288 U. S. Rev. Stat., printed on p. 686 of this vol.

senger; but, if at the time of taking his place, he pays the whole of the fare, in such case the coach-proprietor can not dispose of his place, but the passenger may take it at any stage of the journey he thinks fit." (*l*)

982. *Implied undertaking of railway companies to forward passengers without unnecessary delay.*— Every railway company also which has sold tickets to an intended passenger impliedly undertakes to provide means of conveyance and forward him to his place of destination with reasonable speed. (*m*) [1] If railways are impeded by snow, the company must use all reasonable exertions to forward their passengers and clear the line for traffic. (*n*) [2]

983. *Contracts for the carriage of passengers* by common carriers impose upon them the duty of taking the utmost care for the safe conveyance of such passengers; and, if an accident arises causing injury to

---

(*l*) Ker v. Mountain, 1 Esp. 26.   Gt. North. Ry. Co., 1 H & N. 408.

(*m*) Gt. North. Rail. Co. v. Hawcroft, 21 L. J., Q. B. 179. Hamlin v.   (*n*) Briddon v. Gt. North. Ry. Co., 28 L. J., Ex. 51.

[1] See Galena, &c., R. R. Co. v. Rae, 18 Ill. 488; Denney v. New York, &c., R. R. Co., 13 Gray, 481; Lifford v. R. R. Co., 7 Rich. 409; Lowe v. Moss, 12 Ill. 477; *contra*, Nashville, &c. R. R. Co. v. Johnson, 6 Heisk, 271; holding that he is not liable for delay by an accident not inevitable, if there be no negligence on his part. And in an action for not delivering goods in a reasonable time, the measure of damages is the value of the goods at the place and time they should have been delivered, and the loss and expense caused by the delay; Kyle v. Laurens R. R. Co., 10 Rich. 382; or, in a proper case, the value of the use of the article during the time of its detention; Priestly v. Northern, &c., R. R. Co., 26 Ill. 205; or for the loss of a market for the goods; Falway v. Northern Transportation Co., 15 Wis. 129; and the "reasonable time" is a question for the jury; Conger v. Hudson River R. R. Co., 6 Duer, 275.

[2] And when the cause of the delay, as ice or low water, is removed, the duty to transport revives. **Lowe v. Moss,** 12 Ill. 477.

any of them, a common carrier can discharge himself
from liability only by proving that the accident was
inevitable, (*o*) ¹ that is, that it did not occur from the
want of due care, not only on the part of himself and
his servants, but also on the part of any independent
contractor who may have been employed by him to
construct the means of conveyance. (*p*)   The carrier,
however, is not bound at his peril to provide a carriage roadworthy at the commencement of the journey ; and, if the carriage turns out to be defective, he
is not liable to a passenger for the consequences, if the
defect was of such a nature that it could neither be
guarded against in the process of construction nor discovered by subsequent examination. (*q*) ² But a
passenger may, by special agreement, contract to be
carried at his own risk, so as to exempt the company
from responsibility for even the gross and willful negligence of their servants. (*r*)

984. *Limitation of the liability of common carriers
by public notice.*—[Although, as we have seen, the common carrier may limit his liability, at common law, by
express contract, yet he can not do so merely by means
of printed notices, placards and posters affixed to his
conveyance, or printed upon his tickets. Every
owner or maintainer of a conveyance can not be al-

(*o*) Burns v. Cork & Bandon Ry.
Co., *post*.

(*p*) Grote v. The Chester & Holy-
head Ry. Co., 2 Ex. 251. Burns v.
The Cork & Bandon Ry. Co., 13 Ir.
C. L. R. 543. Francis v. Cockerell,
L. R., 5 Q. B. 184; 39 L. J., Q. B.

291.   John v. Bacon, L. R., 5 C. P.
437 ; 39 L. J., C. P. 365.

(*q*) Readhead   v.   The   Midland
Ry. Co., L. R., 4 Q. B. 379; 38 L.
J., Q. B. 169.

(*r*) McCawley v. Farness Ry. Co.,
L. R., 8 Q. B. 57 ; 42 L. J., Q. B. 4.

¹ See *ante*, note 1, p. 677. Where a trunk in the possession
of a common carrier is lost, the inference is that it was lost or
mislaid through the negligence of the carrier; Camden, &c.,
R. R. Co. v. Baldauff, 16 Pa. St. 67.

² See *ante*, note 1, p. 660.

lowed to change the law of the land, at his own convenience, by simply displaying a memoranda that "the
baggage of passengers is at the risk of the owners." [1]

The utmost effect of such a notice would be to
protect the carrier from the ordinary and known risks
of transportation. [2]

In order to make such a notice a special contract
binding on the passenger, such as the carrier has a
right to make, the passenger, on his part, must assent
to it. [3] But the burden of proving the passenger's
assent is, in every case, on the carrier. [4] It has been
held that a carrier may limit his liability by a general
notice if its terms are clear and explicit, and if the
party with whom the carrier deals is fully informed of
its terms and effect. [5] And where the notice was
printed in English, and the passenger was a German,
who did not understand that language, it was held
that the terms must be explained to him in order to

[1] Hollister v. Nowlen, 19 Wend. 234; Cole v. Goodwin,
Id. 234 ; Clark v. Faxton, 21 Id. 153 ; Powell v. Myers, 26 Id.
591 ; Camden Transportation Co. v. Belknap, 21 Id. 354 ;
Jones v. Voorhies, 10 Ohio, 145 ; Southern Ex. Co., v. Newby,
36 Ga. 635 ; Mosher v. Southern Ex. Co., 38 Id. 37 ; Prentice
v. Decker, 49 Barb. 21 ; Lunburger v. Westcott, Id. 285 ; Bean
v. Green, 12 Me. 422 ; Derwort v. Loomer, 21 Conn. 245 ;
Moses v. Boston, &c., R. R. Co., 32 N. H. 523.

[2] Nashville R. R. Co. v. Johnson, 6 Heisk, 271 ; Durr v.
New Jersey, &c., Co., 11 N. Y. (1 Kern.) 485 ; Rawson v. Pennsylvania R. R. Co., 2 Abb. (N. Y.) Pr., N. S. 220 ; Kimball v.
Rutland R. R. Co., 26 Vt. 247 ; Nevins v. Bay State, &c., Co.,
4 Bosw. 225.

[3] Sager v. Portsmouth, &c., R. R. Co., 31 Me. 228 ; Fille-
brown v. Grand Trunk R. R. Co., 55 Me. 462.

[4] McMillan v. Michigan, &c., R. R. Co., 16 Mich. 79 ; Farmers' &c., Bank v. Champlain Transportation Co., 23 Vt.
186 ; Bean v. Green, 12 Me. (3 Fairf.) 422 . Verner v. Sweitzer, 32 Pa. St. 208 ; Mobile, &c., R. R. Co., 4 Weiner, 49
Miss. 725.

[5] Camden, &c., R. R. Co. v. Baldauf, 16 Pa. St. 67.

relieve the carrier. · If the shipper of goods accept a
receipt containing a printed notice of restrictions upon
the carrier's liability, with full knowledge of the same,
and without objection, he will be held to consent to
the special contract as fully as if he had signed his
name thereto.' But the question of such knowledge
and assent is one of fact for the jury, to be determined
by evidence aliunde, and is not a subject of presumption from the terms of the receipt alone, or from the
naked fact of the receipt having been delivered to the
shipper.⁵ So it was held that evidence that a notice
that baggage carried in the "Telegraph Line" would
be at the risk of the owner, conspicuously placarded
in most of the stage office's on the route, and particularly where the plaintiff had resided for three years
immediately preceding the loss of his trunk, would
not authorize a jury to infer knowledge, in the plaintiff,
of the terms upon which the coaches were run.⁴ Nor
is a passenger on a steamboat chargeable with notice
of the contents of a placard posted in the boat, merely
from the fact that he had the opportunity to read it, if
he so desired.⁵

Neither will carriers be permitted, by special contract, to change the law of the land. It is against public policy, for instance, to permit common carriers to
make special contracts against their own negligence.⁶

---

¹ Camden, &c., R. R. Co. v. Baldauf, 16 Pa. St. 67.
³ Adams Ex. Co. v. Haynes, 42 Ill. 89.
³ Id. 49.
⁴ Hollister v. Nowlen, 19 Wend. 234; Cole v. Goodrich,
Id. 251.
⁵ Macklin v. New Jersey Steamboat Co., 7 Abb. (N. Y.) Pr.,
N. S. 229.
⁶ Indianapolis, &c., R. R. Co. v. Allen, 31 Ind. 394; Michigan, &c., R. R. Co. v. Heaton, Id. 397; Railroad Company v.
Lockwood, 17 Wall. 357.

985. *Carriage of gold and silver, jewelry, title-deeds, glass, silk, &c.*—As the common carrier was responsible at common law for the safe carriage of goods and merchandise, and was bound to make good losses by robbery, he was allowed to charge a rate of carriage proportioned to the risk he ran. This risk naturally depended upon the value of the articles he carried ; and, therefore, when a common carrier was required to carry a bag of gold across Hounslow Heath, it was thought that he was justly entitled to charge more than the ordinary rate of remuneration for merchandise. (*s*) "His warranty and insurance," observes Lord MANSFIELD, "are in respect to the reward he is to receive ; and the reward ought to be proportionable to the risk. If he makes a greater warranty and insurance, he will take greater care, use more caution, and be at the expense of more guards and other methods of security ; and, therefore, he ought, in reason and in justice, to have a greater reward." "A higher price ought in conscience, to be paid him for insuring the safety of money, jewels, and valuable things, than for insuring common goods of small value." (*t*) Hence, when packages were brought to common carriers for conveyance, it became usual for the latter to ask the value, and to charge accordingly, and it was held that the owner was, in all cases, bound by his representation of value, and could not give evidence of the falseness of his own statement in order to throw an increased responsibility upon the common carrier. But the owner was not bound to declare the value of the parcel unless he was asked ; if the common carrier asked no questions, and there was no fraud or intentional concealment, to give the case a

---

(*s*) Tyly v. Morrice, Carth. 486.　　　(*t*) Aston, J., 4 Burr. 2302, 2303.

false complexion, the common carrier was responsible for the safety of the parcel, whatever might be its value. (*u*)

To obviate the inconvenience of asking questions in each case, and the difficulty of proving the statements made on each occasion, common carriers resorted to the expedient of advertising in newspapers, and posting on the walls of their booking-offices, public notices, to the effect that they would not be liable for the loss of money and valuables enclosed in packages and parcels, unless they received notice of their existence, nor for the loss of ordinary goods and chattels beyond a certain amount, unless the value of such goods was declared and entered at the office, and an increased rate of remuneration paid for their conveyance. So long as these public notices and advertisements were used with the bonâ fide intention of protecting the common carrier against fraud on the part of persons sending packages of great value and small bulk for conveyance, and of securing to him a rate of remuneration proportioned to the value of the parcel and the risk he ran, they were encouraged and supported ; (*x*) but, when they were used, as they soon were, for the purpose of enabling the common carrier altogether to shake off his common law responsibility, and of concealing and favoring fraud towards his customers, and shielding him from the consequences of his own negligence and misconduct, they were condemned and discouraged. All sorts of difficulties at last arose with respect to these notices. On some occasions they were held to be inoperative, because the party bringing the goods to the office where they were posted up, was unable to read, and the notice

<hr/>

(*u*) Riley v. Horne, 2 M. A P. 340.   Harris v. Packwood, 3 Taunt. 264,
(*x*) Gibbon v. Paynton, 4 Burr. 2301.   Marsh v. Horne, 5 B. & C. 326.

consequently afforded him no information, (*y*) or being able to read, he never did read the notice; (*z*) and it was sometimes held that the attention of the consignor of the parcel ought to be drawn to the printed terms of conveyance in such a way that, if he remained in ignorance of them, such ignorance was willful or attributable to his own negligence. (*a*)[1]

The contradictory decisions upon the proof and effect of these notices, and the confused state of the law respecting them, at last rendered the interference of the legislature necessary in order to protect the common carrier, on the one hand, from fraud and concealment on the part of the consignor of parcels and packages and to protect the consignor, on the other, from fraud negligence, and misconduct on the part of the common carrier.

986. *Common Carriers' Act—Declaration of value by consignors.*—The 11 Geo. 4, and 1 Wm. 4, c. 68, commonly called the Carriers' Act, exempts common carriers by land from liability for the loss of, (*b*) or injury to, gold or silver, precious stones, jewelry watches, clocks, trinkets, bills, orders, notes, or securities for payment of money, stamps, maps, writings title deeds, paintings, engravings, pictures, (*c*) plated articles, glass, silks, (*d*) in a manufactured or unman-

---

(*y*) Davis v. Willan, 2 Stark. 280.

(*z*) Kerr v. Willan, ib. 54. Butler v. Heane, 2 Campb. 415.

(*a*) Clayton v. Hunt, 3 ib. 27. Gouger v. Jolly, Holt, 317. Walker v. Jackson, 10 M. & W. 173. Brooke v. Pickwick, 4 Bing. 222.

(*b*) Hearn v. Lond. & L. S. R. Co. 10 Exch. 801 ; 24 L. J., Ex. 180.

(*c*) Where framed pictures are sent by a carrier, the frames, as well as the pictures, are within the Act. Henderson v. London & North Western Ry. Co., L. R., 5 Ex. 90.

(*d*) Silk guards and silk dresses are included under the term silks. Bernstein v. Baxendale, 6 C. B., N. S. 259 ; 28 L. J., C. P. 265, overruling Davey v. Mason, Car. & M. 50. So, also, is elastic silk webbing, made as described in Brunt v. The Midland Ry. Co., 2 H. & C. 889 ; 33 L. J., Ex. 187.

[1] See *ante*, § 987.

ufactured state, furs, lace, (e) &c., contained in any parcel or package which shall have been delivered, either to be carried for hire or to accompany the person of any passenger in any public conveyance, when the value of such articles or property contained in such parcel or package shall exceed the sum of ten pounds, unless, at the time of the delivery thereof for the purpose of being carried or of accompanying the person of any passenger, the value and nature of such articles or property shall have been declared by the person sending or delivering the same and the increased charge thereinafter mentioned, or an engagement to pay the same, accepted by the person receiving such parcel or package.   Mere mention of the value to a station-master is no declaration of value within the meaning of the Act, if it was not intended to operate as a declaration of value. (f)   When the declaration is formally made, the carrier is entitled, if the value exceed £10, and he has a notice of the increased rate of charge for parcels exceeding the value of £10 stuck up in his office, to demand the increased rate of charge; but, if he does not think to notify the increased rate of charge, he can not demand it; and, if he has notified it, but fails to demand it, he must, be taken to have received the goods subject to his common law liability as an insurer of their safe conveyance, and will not be entitled to the protection of the statute. (g) The consignor is bound by his declaration, and can not afterwards show that the value of the goods exceeded that declared. (h)   If the journey is to be performed

---

(e) By the 28 & 29 Vict. c. 94, s. 1, the term "lace" is not to include machine-made l ce.

(f) Robinson v. S. W. Rail. Co. 19 C. B., N. S 51; 34 L. J., C. P. 235.

(g) Behrens v. Gt. North Rail. Co., 30 L. J., Ex. 153; 31 L. J., Ex. 299; 7 H. & N. 950.

(h) M'Cance v. Lond. & N. W. R. Co., 3 H. & C. 343; 34 L. J., Ex. 39.

partly by land and partly by sea, the carrier is entitled to the protection of the Merchant Shipping Acts, as far as the journey is to be performed at sea, (*i*) and to the protection of the Carriers' Act so far as it is to be performed by land ; (*k*) and he will not lose such protection by having received the goods under a special contract, unless its terms are inconsistent with the goods having been received by him in his capacity of a carrier. (*l*)

987. *Losses from robbery and theft by the common carrier's servants.*—Nothing in the Carrier's Act is (s. 8) to protect any common carrier for hire from liability to answer for loss of, or injury to, any goods or articles arising from the felonious acts of any coachman, guard, bookkeeper, porter, or other servant in the carrier's employ, nor to protect any such coachman, &c., from liability for any loss or injury occasioned by his own personal neglect or misconduct. The common carrier's liability, therefore, in respect of losses resulting from thefts committed by his own servants, or persons in his employ, remains the same as it was before the statute was passed. The statute imposes no express liability upon the common carrier. It simply relieves him from the necessity of proving a notice limiting his liability in certain cases, and then restricts that relief to losses not occasioned by the felonious acts of persons in his employ. If, therefore, a common carrier has given express notice to the consignor that he will not be responsible for parcels or packages above the value of £10, unless the value is declared, and an increased rate of remuneration paid

---

(*i*) London & S. W. Rail. Co. v. James, L. R., 8 Ch. 241 ; 42 L, J., Ch. 337.

(*k*) Le Conteur v. London & S. W. Ry. Co., 6. B. & S. 961 ; L. R., 1 Q. B. 54 ; 35 L. J., Q. B. 40.

(*l*) Baxendale v. The Great Eastern Ry. Co., L. R., 4 Q. B. 244 ; 38 L. J., Q. B. 137.

according to a printed tariff or scale of charge, and
the common carrier afterwards accepts a parcel to be
carried, knowing it to be worth more than £10, without demanding or receiving the premium for insurance, and the parcel is purloined by his own servant,
the case is not within the protection of the statute,
and the common carrier is responsible for the theft.
(*m*)   But if he receives the goods under a special contract, and not upon his customary liability as an insurer of safe conveyance, he is chargeable only for negligence and want of ordinary care. (*n*)

In order to establish the fact of theft by the common
carrier's servants, it is not enough to lay before a jury
facts from which they might infer that such a felony
had been committed.   Evidence reasonably sufficient
to obtain a conviction for the felony must be proved
by the plaintiff, in order to give him the benefit of the
exception in the statute. (*o*)

988. *Liabilities of the common carrier's servants.*
—Sect. 8 of the statute provides, that the Act shall
not protect the coachman, guard, bookkeeper, or other
servant of the common carrier, from liability for losses
or injuries occasioned by their own personal neglect
and misconduct.   This applies to liabilities ex delicto;
for the coachman, guard, or other servant is not, by
the common law, liable in any way ex contractu to
the owner of the goods for loss or damage arising from
his own personal negligence.   The contract for the
carriage of them is made with the common carrier or
coach-proprietor who carries on the business, and not
with a mere servant or agent who has no interest in

(*m*) Metcalfe v. Lond. & Br. Rail.
Co., 4 C. B., N. S. 307 ; 27 L. J., C.
P. 205.

(*n*) Butt v. Gt. West. Rail. Co., 11

C. B. 140.   Gt. West. Rail. Co. v.
Rimell, 27 L. J., C. P. 204.

(*o*) Metcalfe v. Lond. & Br. Rail.
Co., *supra*

the concern, and does not share in the profits of the trade. Thus, where an action was brought against a coach-porter for the value of a parcel lost by him, and also against the driver of a stage coach for the loss of a trunk, it was held that, as the defendant in each case had received the article as the servant and agent of the coach-proprietor, and not on his own account, he could not be sued by the owner of the goods for the loss. (*p*)

989. *Inability of common carriers to rid themselves by public notice of the duties imposed upon them by the ancient custom of the realm[1]—Limitation of the liability of common carriers by special contract.*—The fourth section of the Carrier's Act enacts, that no public notice or declaration shall be deemed or construed to limit, or in anywise affect the liability at common law of any common carriers in respect of any articles or goods to be carried or conveyed by them, but that they shall be liable, as at common law, to answer for the loss of, or injury to, any articles and goods in respect whereof they may not be entitled to the benefit of that Act, any public notice or declaration by them made and given contrary thereto, or in anywise limiting such liability, notwithstanding. But nothing contained in the Act is (s. 6) to annul or in anywise affect any special contract between common carriers and any other parties for the conveyance of goods and merchandise. This statute is confined to public notices, such as were very common before the Act—notices addressed to the public at large, raising a question in every case whether the notice was brought home to the particular person. It is not applicable to a notice

---

(*p*) Cavanagh v. Such, 1 Pr. 331. Williams v. Cranston, 2 Stark. 82.

[1] See *ante,* § 987.

specifically delivered to form the basis of a special contract with him. (*q*)   Where the common carrier is not a common carrier of the particular description of goods tendered him for conveyance, and has the option of receiving them or rejecting them at his own good will and pleasure, he may prescribe his own terms of conveyance; and, if the party delivering goods to be carried has been personally served with a notice of the terms on which the common carrier carries goods, and, after seeing the notice sends the goods, he must be taken to agree that they shall be carried on those terms, and there is then a special contract between him and the common carrier for their conveyance, (*r*) unless the carriage is by railway or canal, so as to necessitate a signed special contract under the Railway and Canal Traffic Act. (*s*)   But this is not the case with regard to such articles as the common carrier is bound by his public profession and employment to carry.   With regard to them, the owner has a right to insist that the common carrier shall receive the goods subject to all the responsibilities incident to his employment. (*t*)   " If the delivery of the goods under such circumstances authorizes an implication of any kind, the presumption is as strong, to say the least, that the owner intended to insist on his legal rights, as it is that he was willing to yield to the wishes of the carrier." (*u*)   Special contracts with railway and canal companies must, as we shall presently see, be authen-

---

(*q*) Walker v. York & North Mid. Rail. Co., 2 Ell. & Bl. 761. Van Toll v. South Eastern Rail, Co., 31 L. J., C. P. 241.

(*r*) Wightman, J., 2 Ell. & Bl. 760.

(*s*) *Post*

(*t*) Ld. Kenyon, Kirkman v. Shaw-cross, 6 T. R. 17.   Garton v. Brist. & Ex. Rail. Co., 1 B. & S. 162 ; 30 L. J., Q. B. 276.

(*u*) Hollister v. Nowlen, 19 Wend. 247, New Jersey St. Nav. Co. v. Merchts. Bank, 6 How. 344.   Crouch v. London & North West. R. Co., 23 L. J., C. P. 73.

ticated by a signed writing.[1] If the consignor of packages exceeding £10 in value, containing the valuable articles specified in the Carrier's Act, objects to pay the ad valorem rate of carriage or premium of insurance, and wishes to have the parcel carried as a parcel of ordinary value, at the ordinary rate of carriage for parcels of similar bulk and weight, the common carrier may, if he pleases, waive his right to the increased remuneration or premium of insurance, and agree to carry for a smaller sum, upon the terms that he is not then to be responsible upon the extended customary liability of a common carrier as an insurer against robbery and the dangers and accidents of the road. "This limitation," observes PARKE, B., "it is competent for a common carrier to make, because, being entitled by common law to insist on the full price of carriage being paid beforehand, he may, if such price be not paid, refuse to carry upon the terms imposed by the common law, and insist upon his own terms." (*v*)

990. *Common carriers may protect themselves by special contract from loss by fire and sea risks*, and may carry goods on the terms that they are not to be held responsible at all for such losses. (*y*)[2]

991. *Stipulations exempting common carriers by water from loss of luggage, unless a bill of lading has been signed for it.*—Where the Atlantic Mail Steam Navigation Company issued passengers' tickets on which was printed a notice or condition "that the ship will not be accountable for luggage, goods, or other descriptions of property, unless bills of lading

(*v*) Wyld v. Pickford, 8 M. & W. 458.

(*y*) Maving v. Todd, 1 Stark. 74.

Collins v. Brist. & Ex. Rail. Co., 11 Exch. 790 ; 7 H. L. C. 205.

[1] *Post*, §§ 1002, 1003.
[2] *Infra.*

have been signed therefor, each passenger allowed
twenty cubic feet of luggage free," it was held that the
company had a right to impose this condition on
their passengers provided it was imposed upon all
alike ; that the passenger, therefore, was bound to get
a bill of lading for all the luggage for which he intended to make the ship accountable, but that he had
the option of taking luggage under his own personal
control without any bill of lading, carrying it, in that
case, at his own risk. (*z*)   If the company does not
impose the same terms upon all passengers alike, or
the passenger offers to sign a bill of lading and is unable to obtain it, the company can not avail themselves of the condition as protecting them from liability. (*a*)

992. *When the carrier may by special contract
exempt himself from all responsibility for damage to
certain classes and decriptions of goods in transitu.*—
Whenever a man enters into a contract for the carriage of goods, he impliedly grants or lets out some
labor and care for the accomplishment of the work
of carrying, in return for the hire paid or agreed to be
paid him ; and it was formerly held that he could not
enter into the contract, and at the same time say that
he would bestow no labor or care at all in and about
the performance of what he had undertaken to do, and
for which he received his hire.   " It is impossible,"
justly observes Lord ELLENBOURGH, " without outrag-
ing common sense, so to construe a special contract
for the carriage of goods, as to make the carrier say,.
'We will receive your goods; but we will not be
bound to take any care of them, and will not be an-

(*z*) Wilton *v.* Royal Atl. Mail St.   (*a*) Gt. West. Rail. Co. *v.* Good-
Nav. Co., 10 C. B., N. S. 453; 30 L.   man, 12 C. B. 313.
J., C. P. 369.

swerable at all for any loss occasioned by our own misconduct, be it ever so gross and injurious.'" (*b*) "If the carrier should perchance refuse to carry the stuffe, unless promise were made unto him that he should not be charged for any misdemeanor that should be in him, the promise were void; for it were against reason and against good manners; and so it is in all other cases like." (*c*) In the case of articles of a perishable nature, such as fish, or of a very delicate and fragile nature, such as statuary, sculptured alabaster, or marble, which the common carrier does not commonly profess to carry, and which may be readily injured, nobody knows how, the common carrier may, as we have seen, refuse to receive and carry such articles, except under a special contract exonerating him from all responsibility for damage done to them in transitu not occasioned by the neglect or default of himself or his servants. (*d*) So, with regard to horses, it is said to be very reasonable that common carriers by railway should be allowed to make agreements for the purpose of protecting themselves against the peculiar risks attendant upon the carriage of horses by railway, arising from the rapid motion and strange noises, which are calculated to alarm horses and cause them to kick and break the carriage, and do themselves injury. It was, therefore, held, before the passing of the Railway and Canal Traffic Act,[1] that railway companies might, by special contract, throw the risk of the conveyance of a horse by railway upon the owner of the horse, so that, if the horse was injured in the transit from any ordinary

---

(*b*) Lyon v. Mells, 5 East, 438.

(*c*) Doct. & Stud. Dial. 2, ch. 39. Noy's Maxims, ch. 43, 92.

(*d*) Beal v. South Devon Rail. Co.,

5 H. & N. 875; 29 L. J., Ex. 441. Peek v. North Staff. Rail. Co., 32 L. J., Q. B. 241. Leeson v. Holt, 1 Stark. 186.

[1] *Post*, § 1003.

railway casualty, the owner would have no remedy against the company for the loss. (*e*)

The notices commonly given by common carriers before the passing of the Carrier's Act, that they would not be responsible for the loss of or damage to parcels above a certain value, unless the value was declared and a premium of insurance paid, were held to apply only to the responsibilities and liabilities of the carrier as an insurer of the safety of the goods, and did not and could not exempt him, in the absence of fraudulent concealment of value or risk on the part of the consignor, from the consequences of his own misconduct or negligence, or from the misconduct and negligence of his servants and persons in his employ. (*f*) " By understanding the terms of the notice in this limited sense," observes BAYLEY, J., " the common carrier will be exempt from those peculiar liabilities which attach to him only in his character of common carrier, but not from the consequence of his own misfeazance, for which every bailee is responsible." (*g*) Having, by notice or special contract, divested himself of his customary liability of an insurer against robbery and fire and the dangers and accidents of the road," he still," observes PARKE, B.," undertakes to carry from one place to another, and for some reward in respect of the carriage, and is therefore bound to use ordinary care in the custody of the goods, and their conveyance to, and delivery at, the place of destination, and in providing proper vehicles for their carriage." (*h*)   Where a cask of brandy of the value of

(*e*) Carr v. Lanc. & York. Rail. Co., 7 Exch. 714.   Harrison v. Lond. Br. & S. Co. Rail. Co., *ante*, qualified by Peek v. North Staff. Rail. Co., 32 L. J., Q. B. 241.

(*f*) Birket v. Willan, 2 B. & Ald.

356.   Duff v. Budd, 6 Moore, 477.

(*g*) Garnett v. Willan, 5 B. & Ald. 57.

(*h*) Wyld v. Pickford, 8 M. & W. 461.   Smith v. Horne, 8 Taunt. 144; 2 Moore, 18.

£70 was accepted by a common carrier to be carried
for hire, and the cask began to leak on the road, and
the carrier's servant was told that the brandy was es-
caping, but he made no attempt to stop the leak and
save the brandy at any of the stages at which he
stopped, although he might easily have done so, and
the brandy was consequently lost, it was held that the
carrier was not protected from the consequences of
the negligence of his servant by having given notice
to the consignor that he would not be answerable for
any goods of what nature or kind soever above the
value of £5, if lost, stolen, or damaged, unless a special
agreement was made and an adequate premium paid
over and above the common carriage ; for here the
goods were of large bulk and known quality, and the
value was obvious as well as the degree of care reasonably requisite for their conveyance. (*k*)

993. *Void limitations of liability.*—A person who
undertakes the public employment of a common carrier of merchandise or of passengers and luggage has
no more right, it is apprehended, to engraft upon his
contract or employment the terms that "all merchandise received by him to be carried is carried at the risk of
the owners," or that " all luggage delivered to him by his
passengers is carried at the risk of the passengers,"
and that " he will not be responsible if it is lost or
damaged by the way," than a common innkeeper has
to refuse to receive guests, except on the terms that
he shall not be responsible for the safe keeping of
their goods and luggage deposited in his inn. The
consignor of merchandise or the passenger has a right
to reject these terms, and to insist that merchandise,
such as is ordinarily carried by the common carrier, or

(*k*) Beck v. Evans, 16 East, 247.   Smith v. Horne, 8 Taunt. 144; 2
Moore, 18.

the customary allowance of luggage for a passenger,
shall be taken at the common carrier's risk, provided
the consignor makes the declaration of value, and is
ready to pay the premium of insurance, in those cases
where the declaration and payment are required by
law. "The traveller," observes an American judge,
" is under a sort of moral duress, a necessity of employing the common carrier ; and the latter shall not be
allowed to throw off his legal liability. He shall not
be privileged to make himself a common carrier for
his own benefit and a mandatary or less to his employer. He is a public servant, with certain duties
defined by law ; and, as ASHURST, J., said of the duties
of innkeepers, they are indelible."(*l*)   But in our own
law, where the carriage of particular articles is attended
with any peculiar or extraordinary risk, the common
carrier is entitled, as we have seen, to refuse to receive
and carry such articles, unless the nature and value of
the articles are declared, and an increased charge paid
for insurance ; but he may, at the same time, receive
and carry them under a special contract, providing
that they shall be carried at the risk of the owner at a
lower rate of charge. [1]   And, if he is a common carrier
of passengers merely, and does not profess to carry,
and does not receive for carriage, luggage with his passengers, but allows them to carry with them, under
their own care, a small quantity of personal luggage,
he is not responsible for the loss of it. (*m*) [2]

(*l*) Cowen, J., Cole v. Goodwin, 19   234. Angell on Carriers, App. xviii.,
Wend. 281. Hollister v. Nowlen, ib.   xxiii,

(*m*) See *infra.*

[1] *Ante,* §§ 994, 995.

[2] And so with the passenger: a common carrier, in consideration of an abatement, in whole or in part, of his legal fare,
may lawfully contract with a passenger that he will take upon
himself the risk of damage from any negligence of the carrier's

994. *Loss of passengers' luggage by railway companies.*—If a railway company starts an excursion train for passengers merely, but allows each passenger to carry with him a small quantity of luggage free at his own risk, and passengers avail themselves of the privilege, and the luggage is lost, the company is not responsible for the loss of it ; (*n*) but it is otherwise in the case of ordinary trains for passengers and luggage where the company receive luggage for carriage. (*o*) Where a railway company made a by-law to the effect that they "would not be responsible for the care of luggage, unless booked and paid for," it was held that the by-law was null and void. (*p*) Railway companies are responsible for the acts and omissions of their porters in the management and delivery of passengers' luggage. (*q*) But if a passenger packs merchandise in carpet-bags and portmanteaus, and passes it off as luggage, he can not recover for the loss of it, as he is guilty of an unfair concealment towards the company, in preventing them from making the charge they would be entitled to make for the carriage of merchandise. (*r*) A railway company is, in general,

---

(*n*) Stewart v. Lond. & N. West. Rail. Co., 33 L. J., Ex. 199 ; 3 H. & C. 135.

(*o*) As to what is "ordinary luggage," see Phelps v. Lond. & N. W. Rail. Co., 34 L. J., C. P. 259; 19 C. B., N. S. 321. Hudston v. Midland Ry. Co., L. R.. 4 Q. B. 366 ; 38 L.

J., Q. B. 213. Macrow v. Great Western Ry. Co., L. R., 6 Q. B. 612 ; 40 L. J., Q. B. 300.

(*p*) Williams v. Gt. West. Rail. Co., 10 Exch. 15.

(*q*) Mid. Rail. Co. v. Bromley, 17 C. B. 375 ; 25 L. J., C. P. 94.

(*r*) Cahill v. Lond. & North-West.

---

agents or servants, for which the carrier would otherwise be liable. Bissell v. New York, &c., R. R. Co., 25 N. Y. 442. Public policy is satisfied by holding the carrier bound to take the risk of its servants' negligence when the passenger pays the fare established by the legislature. He may voluntarily, and for any valuable consideration, waive the right to indemnity, and such a contract is binding. Id.

liable for the loss of a passenger's luggage, though carried in the carriage in which he himself is travelling. (*s*) But the passenger must take ordinary care of it ; and, therefore, where the passenger left the carriage in which his luggage was for another in the course of the journey, and his portmanteau was stolen, it was held that the company was not responsible. (*t*)

995. *Losses occasioned by the negligence of the consignor—Defective packing.*—If the loss has been occasioned by the negligence of the consignor or his servants, in not properly packing or securing the goods, the carrier is not responsible for the loss. If wine or spirits escape by reason of a defective bung in a cask, the carrier will not be answerable, (*u*) unless it be shown that the carrier had notice of the leakage, and had the means of stopping it and neglected to do so, and that by reason thereof the plaintiff sustained the injury of which he complains (*x*) If the defective packing of goods is patent and visible, and easily remedied, and the common carrier accepts the goods for conveyance, he is bound to take all reasonable means to provide for their safety. (*y*) But if the mode of packing is that in ordinary use, and the carrier is led by the sender's conduct to conclude that it is safe, the carrier will not be responsible for injury to the goods arising from such packing. (*z*)

996. *Loss arising from the nature and character*

Rail. Co., 13 C. B., N. S. 818 ; 31 L. J., C. P. 271 ; 30 ib. 294. Belfast & Ballymena Rail. Co. v. Keys, 9 H. L. C. 556. Great Northern Rail. Co. v. Shepherd, 8 Exch. 30 ; 21 L. J., Ex. 286.

(*s*) Le Conteur v. London. & South Western Ry. Co., L. R., 1 Q. B. 54 ; 6 B. & S. 961 ; 35 L. J., Q. B. 40.

(*t*) Talley v. Great West. Ry. Co., L. R., 6 C. P. 44 ; 40 L. J., C. P. 9

(*u*) Hudson v. Baxendale, 2 H. & N. 575.

(*x*) Beck v. Evans, 16 East, 244.

(*y*) Stuart v. Crawley, 2 Start. 324.

(*z*) Richardson v. North - Eastern Ry. Co., L. R., 7 C. P. 74 ; 41 L. J., C. P. 60.

of the thing carried.—A common carrier is not liable for the deterioration by ordinary wear and tear of the goods carried, (*a*) or for loss arising from their inherent tendency to decay or ignite. (*b*) Nor is he liable for injury to animals, the result of some vice which, by its own internal development, affects the animal without any default or negligence of the carrier. (*c*)

997. *Inability of railway and canal companies to exempt themselves from responsibility for negligence.*—By s. 7 of the 17 & 18 Vict. c. 31, it is enacted that every railway company shall be liable for loss of, or injury to, any horses, cattle, or other animals, or to any articles, goods, or things, in the receiving, (*d*) forwarding or delivering thereof, occasioned by the neglect or default of such company or its servants, notwithstanding any notice, condition, or declaration made and given by such company contrary thereto, or in anywise limiting such liability. And it is declared that every such notice, condition, or declaration shall be null and void; but nothing contained in the Act is to prevent railway and canal companies from making such conditions with respect to the receiving, forwarding, and delivering of horses, cattle, animals, articles, goods, or things, as shall be adjudged by the court or judge before whom any question relating thereto shall be tried, to be just and reasonable; but every notice, condition, and declaration under the statute, however reasonable, must be made in writing, and be signed in

---

(*a*) Brass v. Maitland, 6 El. & Bl. 470. Alstor v. Herring, 11 Exch. 822.

(*b*) Rohl v. Parr, 1 Esp. 444. Boyd v. Dubois, 3 Campb. 133.

(*c*) Blower v. Gt. West. Ry. Co., L. R., 7 C., P. 655; 41 L. J., C. P. 268.

Kendall v. London & North-Western Ry. Co., L. R., 7 Ex. 373; 41 L. J., Ex. 184.

(*d*) As to when a horse is received, see Hodgman v. The West Midland Ry. Co., 35 L. J., Q. B 233; 35 L. J., Q. B. 85; 5 B. & S. 173; 6 B. & S. 560.

the mode provided by the statute,[1] in order to be binding in law upon the sender. (*e*)

998. *Declaration of value.*—No greater damages than £50 are to be recovered for loss of or injury to a horse, (*f*) £15 per head for neat cattle, and £2 per head for sheep and pigs, unless the person sending or delivering the same to such company shall at the time of such delivery have declared them to be of higher value, in which case the company is entitled to demand and receive, by way of compensation for the increased risk and care thereby occasioned, a reasonable per-centage upon the excess of the value so declared above the limited sums to be paid in addition to the ordinary rate of charge ; and such per-centage or increased rate of charge is to be notified in the manner prescribed by the 11 Geo. 4 & 1 Wm. 4, c. 68, and to be binding upon the company in manner therein mentioned. (*g*)

999. *Special contracts with railway and canal companies for the carriage of goods and chattels.*—By the Railway and Canal Traffic Regulation Act (17 & 18 Vict. c. 31), it is further enacted (s. 7), that no special contract between any railway or canal company and any other parties respecting the receiving, forwarding, or delivering of any animals, articles, goods, or things, shall be binding upon or affect any such party unless the same be signed by him, or by the

(*e*) McManus v. Lanc. & York. Rail. Co., 4 H. & N. 335 ; 28 L. J. Ex. 359. Peek v. North Staff. Rail. Co., 10 H. L. C. 473 ; 32 L. J., Q. B. 241. Simons v. Gt. West. Railw. Co., 18 C. B. 805 ; 26 L. J., C. P. 25.

(*f*) McCance v. Lond. & N. W. Rail. Co., 3 H. & C. 343 34 L. J., Ex. 39.

(*g*) Hodgman v. West. Mid. Rail. Co., 5 B. & S. 173 ; 33 L. J., Q. B. 233. As to dogs, see Harrison v. Lond. &. Br. Rail Co., 2 B. & S. 122, 152 ; 29 L. J., Q. B. 214 ; 31 L. J. Q. B. 113. As to the mode of declaring the value, see Robinson v. The London & South Western Rail. Co., *ante*.

[1] See *ante*, § 987.

person delivering such animals, articles, goods, or things respectively, for carriage; but nothing therein contained is to alter or affect the rights, privileges, or liabilities of any such company, under the 11 Geo. 4, & 1 Wm. 4, c. 68, with respect to articles of the description mentioned in that Act. Special contracts with railway and canal companies, therefore, for the carriage of merchandise and chattels, are placed under the control of the judges, so that no contract signed by the customer, regulating the liability of the company in and about the safe keeping, preservation, and carriage of such chattels, can protect the company, unless the judge shall think the conditions imposed by the contract just and reasonable; and no condition, however just and reasonable, can protect the company, unless it be contained in a contract signed in accordance with the statute. (*h*)　But no special contract signed according to the statute is necessary to define the nature and extent of the public profession of the common carrier and of the duties he undertakes in favor of the public at large; (*i*) and a contract not signed is valid as against the company. (*k*)

1000. *What are unjust and unreasonable conditions in special contracts for the carriage of chattels by railway or canal.*—Whenever, in order to bring a railway or canal company within the protection of a condition or special contract, it is necessary to construe it as excluding responsibility for losses occasioned by the company's negligence and misconduct, the condition

---

(*h*) Peek v. North Staff. Rail. Co., 10 H. L. C. 473; 32 L. J., Q. B. 241. Aldridge v. Gt. West. Rail. Co., 15 C. B., N. S. 582; 33 L. J., Q. B. 161. Allday v. Gt. West. Rail. Co., 34 L. J., Q. B. 5; 5 B. & S. 903. Lond & North-West. Rail. Co. v. Dunham, 18 C. B. 829. McManus v. Lanc. & York. Rail. Co., 4 H. & N. 335; 28 L. J., Ex. 359.

(*i*) *Ante.*

(*k*) Baxendale v. Creat Eastern Ry. Co., L. R., 4 Q. B. 244, 251; 38 L. J., Q. B. 137.

or special contract is unreasonable and unjust, and therefore void. (*l*) Where a railway company ac- cepted horses for conveyance under a special contract providing that the horses were to be carried at the risk of the owner, and that the company were not to be responsible for any injury, however caused, to horses travelling upon the railway or in the company's vehi- cles, and the company provided rotten and insecure carriages, so that holes were made by the horses' feet in the bottom of the carriages, and the animals were injured, it was held that the special contract did not protect the company from responsibility for the injury, as the damage did not result from any of the risks naturally incident to railway travelling, but from their own negligence in not providing proper vehicles for the conveyance of the horses. (*m*) And, where a railway company received goods to be carried under a condition absolving them from all liability for the loss of, or damage to, goods insufficiently or improperly packed, marked, directed, or described, the condition was held to be unreasonable and unjust, as insufficient packing, marking, or directing, &c., of goods constitu- ted no sufficient ground for relieving the company from all liability respecting the performance of the duty they had undertaken to fulfill. (*n*) [1]

It is the duty of every railway or canal company setting up a condition in qualification and restriction

(*l*) Peek v. North Staff. Rail. Co., *supra.* Lloyd v. Waterford & Lim. Rail. Co., 15 Ir. Com. Law Rep., Q. B. 37. Allday v. Gt Western Ry. Co,, *supra.* Rooth v. N. East. R. Co., L. R., 2 Ex. 173; 36 L. J., Ex. 83.

(*m*) McManus v. Lanc. & York Rail. Co., 4 H. & N. 335; 28 L. J. Ex. 359. Gregory v. West. Mid. Rail.

Co., 2 H. & C. 951; 33 L. J., Ex. 155. Harrison v. Lond. Br. & S. C. Rail. Co., 29 L. J., Q. B. 214; 31 L. J., Q. B. 113.

(*n*) Simons v. Gt. West. Rail. Co., *ante,* Lond. & North-West. Rail. Co. v. Dunham, *supra.* Garton v. The Bristol & Exeter Rail. Co., 1 B. & S. 112; 30 L. J., Q. B. 273.

[1] Redfield on Carriers, § 149.

of their common law liability to make out that the condition is just and reasonable; and, if they make an extra charge for insuring the safe conveyance of live animals, they must show that the extra charge is reasonable and just. (*o*)[1]

1001. *What are just and reasonable conditions.*— It has been held that a condition that all claims for loss or damage should be made within seven days after the time when the goods have been delivered, is just and reasonable, (*p*) also a condition that a railway company will not undertake to forward goods by any particular train, or be answerable for their non-arrival in time for any particular market, (*q*) and that they will not be responsible, under any circumstances, for loss of market or other loss or injury arising from detention of trains, exposure to weather, stowage, or from any cause whatever other than gross neglect or fraud, (*r*) or that they will not be responsible for the risks attendant upon the carriage by railway of perishable articles, live animals, and chattels, such as accidents occasioned by the fright or restiveness of horses, or from the wheel of a carriage taking fire, (*s*) or loss arising from delay in forwarding fish, where it is impossible to know the exact condition of the fish at the time of its delivery to be carried, and where the slightest delay in its transmission may occasion a vast loss, (*t*) or for loss or damage to fragile materials

(*o*) Harrison v. Lond., Br. & S. C. Rail. Co., Garton v. Britt. & Ex. Ry. Co., Peek v. North Staff. &c. Co., *ante.*

(*p*) Lewis v. Gt. West. Rail. Co., 29 L. J., Ex. 425 ; 5 H. & N. 867.

(*q*) Beal v. S. Dv. R. Co., 5 H. & N. 875 ; 29 L. J., Ex. 441. White v. G. W.

R.Co., 2 C. B., N. S. 7 ; 26 L. J., C. P. 158. Lord v. Mid. R. Co., L. R., 2 C. P. 339 ; 36 L J., C. P. 170.

(*r*) Beal v. S. D. R. Co., 3 H. & C. 337.

(*s*) Austin v. Man. R. Co., 10 C. B. 475.

(*t*) Beal v. S. Dv. R. Co., *supra.* Wren v. E. Co. R. Co., 35 Law T. R., Q. B. 5.

.. [1] So a regulation by a carrier of passengers that the passenger must either pay fare or produce his ticket, is a reasonable regulation. Townshend v. N. Y., &c. R. R. Co., 6 Am. R. R. 160.

such as statuary or sculptured marbles, not occasioned by the negligence of the company or its servants. (*u*) If the company offers the consignor a bonâ fide practical choice, either to have his goods carried in the usual way, at a reasonable rate, or at his own risk at a lower rate, and he elects the latter, the condition is not unreasonable. (*x*)[1]

1002. *Liability of a railway company during sea transit.*—When a railway or canal company contracts by through booking to carry any animals, luggage, or goods from place to place, partly by railway and partly by sea, or partly by canal and partly by sea, a condition exempting the company from liability for any loss or damage which may arise during the carriage by sea of such animals, luggage, or goods from the act of God, the king's enemies, fire, accidents from machinery, boilers, and steam, and all and every other dangers and accidents of the seas, rivers, and navigation, of whatever nature and kind soever, will, if published in a conspicuous manner in the office when such through booking is effected, and if printed in a legible manner on the receipt or freight note which the company gives for such animals, luggage, or goods, be valid as part of the contract between the consignor of such animals

---

(*u*) Peek v. North Staff. R. Co., *ante.*

(*x*) Blackburne, J., ib. Stewart v. London & North-Western Ry. Co., 3 H. & C., 135 : 33 L. J., Ex. 199. See Zunz v. South-Eastern Ry. Co., L. R.,4 Q. B. 539 ; 38 L. J., Q. B. 209. Van Toll v. South-Eastern Rail. Co., 12 C. B., N. S. 75 ; 31 L. J., C. P. 241. The 17 & 18 Vict. c. 31, s. 7. is extended by the 26 & 27 Vict. c. 92, to steam vessels employed by railway companies, as auxiliary to their line of railway, and to the traffic carried on by means of such steam vessels. But it does not apply to passengers' luggage, nor to goods received by the company for safe custody, and not for carriage.

[1] See Camden, &c., R. R. Co. v. Belknap, 21 Wend. 354; Hickox v. Naugatuck R. R. Co., 31 Conn. 281.

luggage, or goods and the company, in the same manner as if the company had signed and delivered to the consignor a bill of lading containing such condition. (*a*)

Where a railway company, under a contract for carrying persons, animals, or goods by sea, procure the same to be carried in a vessel not belonging to the company, they will be answerable in damages in respect of loss of life or personal injury, or in respect of loss or damage to such animals or goods during the carriage in such vessel, in like manner, and to the same amount, as they would be answerable if the vessel had belonged to them. (*b*)[1]

1003. *Of the implied authority of the servants of a railway company to bind the company by special contract.*—"It is the duty of railway companies to have some person capable of giving directions and of dealing with everything that the exigency of the traffic may require, and of granting any reasonable demand. The persons who are said to be general superintendent and managing director have power to bind the company as to all things within the scope of the business of the company by any contract within the limits of their employment." (*c*)   If they act beyond

---

(*a*) 31 & 32 Vict. c. 119, s. 14.
(*b*) 34 & 35 Vict. c. 78, s. 12.
(*c*) Brown v Brist. & Ex. Rail. Co,

4 Law T. R., N. S., Ex. 830. Robinson v. The Great Western Railw. Co., 35 L. J., C. P. 123.

[1] So where a line of passenger transportation, by stage-coaches, was intersected by a ferry not belonging to the passenger carriers, but hired to carry their stages across, the stage company was held responsible for the negligence or misconduct of the ferry company and its servants, as being, for the time, the former's agents and servants; McLean v. Burbank, 11 Minn. 277.

the scope of their ordinary business, it must be shown, in order to bind the company, that they are acting under a special authority from the company, that is, the board of directors. (*d*) But, if there is a particular course of dealing with which the consignor is acquainted, he must be taken to know that the servants have no power to bind the company on any but the usual terms. (*e*) [1]

1004. *Acceptance of goods to be carried beyond the district traveled over by the carrier to whom they have been delivered.*—When a common carrier takes into his care a parcel directed to a particular place, and does not by positive agreement limit his responsibility to a part only of the distance, that is prima facie evidence of an undertaking on his part to carry the parcel to the place to which it is directed, although the place may be beyond the limits within which he ordinarily professes to carry on his trade. His responsibility, therefore, continues to the door of the address to which the goods are destined ; and he can not release himself from such responsibility by transferring the goods to another carrier, or sending them by another conveyance; (*f*) and it makes no difference whether part of the carriage is by land and part by water, or whether part of the distance is by railway, part by water, and part by stage coach. (*g*) If a railway company accepts goods for conveyance to a particular destination beyond the limits of its own line of railroad, and receives one entire payment for the whole journey, and the goods are lost whilst in the hands of another railway company to whom they have been delivered

(*d*) Taff Vale Rail. Co. v. Giles, 23 L. J., Q. B. 43.

(*e*) Slim v. Great Northern Rail., 23 L. J., C. P. 168.

(*f*) Garnett v. Willan, 5 B. & Ald. 53.

(*g*) Wilby v. West Corn. Rail. Co., 2 H. & N. 707.

[1] See *ante*, note 1, p. 750.

to be forwarded on their journey, the first railway company is responsible for the loss, as being the party contracting with the consignor or consignee, for the conveyance of them; (*h*) and a proviso in the contract exonerating the company from all liability in respect of loss of, or damage to, the goods occurring beyond the limits of its own line of railway, from the negligence of other companies to whom the goods have been delivered to be forwarded, is repugnant and void. (*i*) But if the company limits its public profession of a common carrier to its own line of railway, and undertakes merely to forward goods to another railway company for further transit, and expressly receives the price of such further transit for the mere purpose of conveying it to such last-named company, they may exempt themselves from liability for loss, damage, or detention, after they have been delivered to other carriers, and are no longer in their possession. (*k*) Railway companies may also enter into such arrangements with one another as to become agents for one another, and responsible for each other's acts, so that a contract to carry and deliver cattle made with one company may render the other liable for a breach occurring on the line of the latter. (*l*) If one railway company receives goods to carry part of the way, and then transfers them to another company to carry them to the place of destination, the agents of the latter company are agents of the first company for receiving notice of countermand; and if they receive

---

(*h*) Muschamp v. Lanc. and Prest. Rail. Co., 8 M. & W. 421. Webber v. Gt. West. Rail. Co., 3 H. & C. 771; 34 L. J., Ex. 170. Watson v. Ambergate Rail. Co., 15 Jur. 448. Mytton v. Mid. Rail. Co., 4 H. & N. 620; 28 L. J., Ex, 385.

(*i*) Brist. & Ex. Rail. Co. v. Collins, 7 H. L. C. 321.

(*k*) Aldridge v. Gt. West. Rail. Co., 15 C. B., N. S. 582; 33 L. J., C. P. 161.

(*l*) Gill v. Manchester, &c., Rail. Co., L. R., 8 Q. B. 186; 42 L. J., Q. B. 89.

such notice and pay no attention to it, the first company is responsible for the neglect. (m)[1] The consignor may receive the goods at any stage of the journey, and may alter their destination at his pleasure. (n)

1005. *Effect of giving the carrier a wrong direction for the delivery of the goods.*—If, after the carrier has fulfilled his part of the contract by conveying
the goods to the place to which they are directed, it
should appear that there is no such person as the one
to whom the goods are addressed, or if the consignee
refuses them, then an entirely new contract arises by
implication of law between the carrier and the consignor; the carrier holds the goods as the bailee of the
consignor, and is bound to take due and ordinary care

(m) Scothorn v. South Staff. Rail. Co., 8 Exch. 345. Crouch v. Gt. West. Rail. Co., 27 L. J., Ex. 345; 3 H. & N. 201.

(n) London & N. W. Rail. Co. v. Bartlett, 7 H. & N. 400; 31 L. J., Ex. 92. Butterworth v. Brownlow, 19 C. B., N. S 409; 34 L. J,. C. P. 266.

[1] A carrier who receives goods as a carrier, and not as a
forwarder, and forwards them to their destination from the
end of his line, in the exercise of a sound discretion, can not
be held responsible for want of notice of his action to the
owner or consignee. Cramer v. American, &c., Ex. Co., 56
Mo. 524. In Massachusetts, Connecticut, and Vermont, it is
the rule that the first carrier is not liable for the negligence
of any other, unless he has assumed such liability by special
contract. Nutting v. Connecticut, &c., R. R. Co., 1 Gray,
502; Hood v. Connecticut, &c., R. R. Co., 22 Conn. 1; Id. 502;
Farmers', &c., Bank v. Transportation Company, 33 Vt. 186.
In Connecticut it is said that the presumption is, that the first
carrier undertakes to be responsible only for his own default.
Hood v. Connecticut River R. R. Co., 22 Conn. 1; Converse
v. Norwich, &c., Co., 33 Id. 166. But in that state it has been
also held, that a carrier has no power to contract for the delivery of goods at the end of its line, and outside of the state;
Naugatuck R. R. Co. v. Waterbury Button Co., 24 Id. 168;
and in New York it is held that the fact of a carrier receiving
goods addressed to a point beyond his route, is not primâ
facie evidence of his undertaking to carry through to that
point. Fairchild v. Slocum, 19 Wend. 329; Redfield on
Carriers, ch. xv., and cases cited.

of them, and to deliver them to the consignor, on being paid his fair and reasonable charges. (*o*)

1006. *Payment of the fare or hire—Carrier's lien.*—When credit has not, by the express contract of the parties, been given for the payment of the price of the carriage of goods, the delivery of the goods to the consignee and the payment of the price of the carriage of them are concurrent acts to be performed at the same time, so that the carrier is entitled to retain possession of the things he has carried until he receives or is tendered his hire for their conveyance. If the consignee refuses to pay the sum demanded for the carriage of them, the carrier is not justified in at once sending them back to the place from whence they came, but must hold them a reasonable time, to see if the consignee will accept and pay for them. (*p*) If he still refuses, the carrier then holds them at the disposal and for the benefit of the consignor, and is entitled to look to the latter for the payment of his hire. But the carrier has no right of lien, by the common law, for anything beyond the price of the carriage of the goods conveyed. He can not detain them until he has received payment of a general balance due to him from the owners of such goods. (*q*) When goods delivered to be carried are received from the wagon of the common carrier by the consignee, and are merely carried into the warehouse to be weighed, the carrier has no right to charge for warehouse-room ; and if the goods are taken up on the road, and have never been booked, he has no right to charge for the

(*o*) Metcalfe *v.* Lond. & Br. Rail. Co., 4 C. B. N. S. 318 ; 38 L. J., C. P. 335. Heugh v. Lond. & North West. Ry. Co., L. R., 5 Ex. 51 ; 39 L. J., Ex. 48. McKean v. M'Ivor, L. R., 6 Ex. 36 ; 40 L. J., Ex. 30.

(*p*) Gt. West. Ry. Co. *v.* Crouch, 3 H. & N. 201. S. C. Crouch v. Gt. Western Ry. Co., 27 L. J., Ex. 345.
(*q*) Butler *v.* Woolcott, 2 B. & P., N. R. 64.

booking of them ; and if, after tender of the price of
the carriage, he detains them for these small charges,
the detention is unlawful, and an action may be brought
against him in respect thereof. (*r*)[1] If a railway company makes and posts at the offices and stations a by-
law to the effect that every passenger who loses his
ticket shall be liable to pay the full fare from the most
distant station on the line, the company has no power
to enforce the by-law by detaining the person of a

(*r*) Lambert v. Robinson, 1 Esp. 119.

---

[1] See Boggs v. Martin, 13 B. Mon. 239–243. The owner
may deduct the amount of injury received by goods from the
amount of the carrier's lien.   Snow v. Carruth, 19 Month.
Law Rep. 198.   The lien does not attach until the service has
been performed. Palmer v. Lorillard, 16 Johns. 348. A common carrier who innocently receives goods from a wrong-
doer, without the owner's consent, has no lien on them as
against the owner; Robinson v. Baker, 7 Cush. 137 ; even for
freight on them paid to a previous carrier; Stevens v. Boston,
&c., R. R. Co., 8 Gray, 262. A false and fraudulent promise
to pay charges upon goods, made to a carrier, for the purpose
of inducing a delivery, does not divest his lien, and he may
sue for the goods in replevin.   Bigelow v. Heaton, 6 Hill, 43 ;
Hayes v. Riddle, 1 Sandf. 248.   The last carrier may detain
the goods until all charges during the transit are paid ; Lee
v. Salter, Lalor Supp. to H. & Denio, 163 ; this lien includes
charges of warehouse men and forwarders.   See Cooper v.
Kane, 19 Wend. 386 ; Dawson v. Kettle, 4 Hill, 1007.   Carriers of passengers have a lien upon the baggage of a passenger for the amount of his fare, but not upon his person.
McDaniel v. Robinson, 26 Vt. 316 ; Root v. Great Western
R. R. Co., 45 N. Y. 524.   The carrier might, before this decision, charge himself by proof of his usage of simply delivering to the next carrier ahead of him.   Van Santvoord v.
St. John, 6 Hill, 157 ; Farmers', &c., Bank v. Transportation
Co., 23 Vt. 186.   Where a telegraph company agrees to transmit a message to its final destination, it is liable for the
negligence of connecting lines.   Shearman and Redfield on
Negligence, § 562.

passenger who has lost his ticket and refuses to pay the specified amount. (*s*)

1007. *Common carrier's charges — Railway charges—By-laws*—The statutes requiring justices of the peace to assess and fix the price of all land carriage of goods have long since been repealed; (*t*) but the hire or charge for the carriage must be fair and reasonable, and must not exceed the ordinary and customary rate of remuneration. If a person sends to a carrier's office to know his rate of charge, the carrier is bound by the representation there made by his clerks; and, if goods are sent upon the faith of such representation, the carrier can not charge more than the sum named, although the clerk may have inadvertently fallen into a mistake. (*u*) When, by a railway Act, it is enacted that the word "toll" shall include the charge for goods conveyed by the railway, whether for the use of the railway, or for the moving power, or for the use of the carriage, prima facie it includes everything that a carrier does, and for which he is entitled to charge. (*x*) By the acts of parliament under which railway companies are incorporated, it is generally provided that the charges for the carriage of goods shall be reasonable and equal to all persons. Where a railway company acted as a common carrier of goods, and issued certain scales of charge for the carriage, including the collection, loading, unloading, and delivery, and also carried goods for other carriers, to whom they have made certain allowances for collection, &c., but in their dealings with a particular carrier

---

(*s*) Chilton v. Lond. & Croyd. Rail. Co., 16 M. & W. 212 ; 16 L. J., Ex. 89.

(*t*) 7 & 8 Geo. 4, c. 39.

(*u*) Winkfield v. Packington, 2 C. & P. 600.

(*x*) Pegler v. Monm. Rail. & Can. Co., 6 H. & N. 644; 30 L. J., Ex. 249.

they refused to make these allowances, it was held that the charges to the latter were not equal or reasonable, and that he might recover from the company divers extra charges paid by him over and above what had been charged to other carriers and to the public, such payments not being voluntary, but made in order to induce the company to do that which they were by law bound to do without requiring such payments. No distinction must be made by the company between one class of persons and another. The company can not, therefore, charge a person, who is himself a common carrier, for a parcel or package, whatever may be its contents, more than it would charge one of the public. (*y*) Charges for collection and delivery of parcels can not be included in the general charge for the carriage, so as to impose upon parties who do not require these services, and do not avail themselves of them, the burthen of paying for them. (*z*) No unreasonable preference or advantage can lawfully be given to any particular person or company, or to any particular description of traffic. (*a*) But the fair interests of the railway company must be taken into consideration; and they are entitled to make a difference in their charges where it is shown that there is a difference in the cost of carriage to the company, and in the labor and expense incurred by them in the delivery of the goods. (*b*)

1008. *Carriage of packed parcels.*—A railway

(*y*) Parker v. Gt. West. Rail. Co., 7 M. & Gr. 253 ; 7 Sc. N. R. 835 ; 11 C. B. 545 ; 21 L. J., C. P. 57. Parker v. Brist. & Ex. Rail. Co., 6 Exch. 702·

(*z*) Baxendale v. Gt. West. Rail. Co., 16 C. B., N. S. 137; 33 L. J., C. P. 197. Garton v. Bristol & Exeter Rail. Co., 1 B. & S. 112 ; 30 L. J., Q. B. 273.

(*a*) 17 & 18 Vict. c. 31, s. 2.

(*b*) Ransome v. E. Co. Rail. Co,. 1 C. B., N. S. 437. Oxlade v. North-East. Rail. Co., ib. 454. Baxendale v. East. Co. Rail. Co., 4 C. B., N. S. 81 ; 27 L. J., C. P. 137. As to tonnage rates and parcel rates, see Parker v. Gt. West,. 6 Ell. & Bl. 103.

company has no right to make an increased charge for packed parcels, in order to prevent carriers from entering into competition with them in the conveyance of goods; and there is no difference between a packed parcel sent to an individual containing parcels belonging to a variety of people, and parcels sent to an individual all the contents being his own. (*c*) But in certain cases an extra charge might be made for increased risk; (*d*) and, if the company has to make separate deliveries to several different persons, they are entitled to make an additional charge in respect of the increased trouble. (*e*) When the duty of making equal charges to all persons is not imposed upon the company, they may impose a different rate of carriage for packed parcels from what they charge for ordinary packages. (*f*)

1009. *Charge for luggage by excursion trains.*— Where a passenger by an excursion train, knowing that the railway company did not allow passengers to carry luggage by such trains, nevertheless secretly put luggage into the train, it was held that the law would imply a promise from the wrongdoer to pay the company for the carriage of it. (*g*)

1010. *Notice of action to railway companies.*— When an Act of Parliament constituting and incorporating a railway company provides that no action should be brought against the company for anything

(*c*) Pickford *v.* Grand Junc. Rail. Co., 10 M. & W. 399. Crouch v. Gt. North. Rail. Co., 11 Exch. 755. Piddington v. S. E. R. Co., 5 C. B., N. S. 120; 27 L. J., C. P. 295. Baxendale v. The London and South Western Rail. Co., L. R., 1 Ex. 127; 35 L. J., Ex. 108. Garton v. Brist. & Exeter Rail. Co., *supra*. Great Western Ry. Co. v. Sutton, L. R., 4 H. L. 226; 38 L. J., Ex. 177.

(*d*) Garton v. Bristol & Ex. Rail. Co., 4 H. & N. 49; 28 L. J., Ex. 169.

(*e*) Baxendale v. East. Co. Rail. Co., *supra*.

(*f*) Branly v. S. E. Rail. Co., 30 L. J., C. P. 286; 12 C. B., N. S. 63.

(*g*) Rumsey v. N. E. R. Co., 32 L. J., C. P. 245; 14 C. B., N. S. 641.

done or omitted to be done pursuant to the Act, or in execution of the powers and authorities given by the Act, unless previous notice in writing shall have been given by the party intending to prosecute such action, or unless such action shall have been brought within a certain limited period, the enactment does not, in general, extend to actions ex contractu, and does not restrain or affect the liability of the company upon contracts entered into by it in its character of a common carrier. The omission by a plaintiff, consequently, to give such notice does not preclude him from recovering damages against the company for its negligence or misconduct, or for a breach of those duties and obligations which result from the nature of its employment as a common carrier. (*h*) But, where the parties were trying, in an action ex contractu, the right of the company to make certain charges under the particular provisions of their Act of Parliament, the action was considered to be brought for something done under the Act, and notice of action was held to be necessary. (*i*)

1011. *Of the parties to be made plaintiffs in actions against carriers for the loss of, or injury to, goods.*—The action against a carrier for the loss of goods entrusted to him for conveyance should, in the absence of an express contract for the carriage of them, be brought by the owner of the goods; for with him, as the party damnified, is the implied contract for their safe conveyance deemed to be made. When goods are delivered to a carrier in execution of a contract of sale, for the purpose of transmission to an intended purchaser, and no express contract founded

---

(*h*) Palmer v. Grand Junc. Rail. Co., 4 M. & W. 749; 7 Dowl. P. C. 232. Carpue v. Lond. & Bright. Rail. Co.,

5 Q. B. 747.

(*i*) Kent v. Gt. West. Rail. Co., 3 C. B. 714; 16 L. J., C. P. 72.

upon a pecuniary consideration moving from the consignor has been entered into between the carrier and the consignor for the carriage of them, the law raises an implied promise for their safe conveyance in favor of the party in whom the right of property in the goods is at the time vested. If, therefore, the right of property and the risk of loss have, by a previous contract of purchase and sale, or a contract to send the goods in satisfaction and discharge of a debt due from the consignor to the consignee, passed to the consignee, the latter is the only party entitled to sue the carrier for an injury to the goods, whether such carrier be a carrier by land or a carrier by water, and whether he be named by the purchaser or chosen by the vendor. (*k*) If, on the other hand, from fraud or non-compliance with the requisites of the Statute of Frauds, no actual sale has taken place so as to transfer the right of property and the risk of loss from the consignor to the consignee, the consignor is the proper party to maintain the action. (*l*) So, if a tradesman merely sends goods for approval to a particular customer, or on terms of "sale or return," or sends goods of the value of £10 and upwards pursuant to an oral order or an oral contract of sale, to a person who has not given "earnest" or made a part payment, or accepted any part of the goods, and the contract is void by reason of non-compliance with the provisions of the Statute of Frauds, then, as there has been no actual sale so as to transfer the right of property

---

(*k*) Dawes v. Peck, 8 T. R. 332. Dutton v. Solomonson, 3 B. & P. 584. Dunlop v. Lambert, 6 Cl. & Fin. 600. Brown v. Hodgson, 2 Cambp. 36. King v. Meredith, ib. 639. Fragano v. Long, 4 B. & C. 219. Coxe v. Harden, 4 East, 217. Evans v. Nichol, 4 Sc. N. R. 43.

(*l*) Coombs v. Brist. & Ex. Rail. Co., 3 H. & N. 510 ; 27 L. J., Ex. 401. Duff v. Budd, 6 Moore, 469. Stephenson v. Hart, 1 M. & P. 357 ; 4 Bing. 476.

and the risk of loss to the consignee, the consignor is the party to sue the carrier. (*m*)   But, when a special contract has been entered into between the carrier and the consignor, whereby the carrier, in consideration of a sum of money paid or agreed to be paid by the consignor as the price of the carriage of goods, agrees with him to convey them to the consignee, it is no answer to an action brought by the consignor against the carrier upon such special contract to say that he is not the owner of the goods.   In such a case the action may be brought either by the consignor with whom the express engagement was made, or by the consignee, as the owner of the goods in whose behalf it was made. (*n*)

Where the plaintiff, the consignor, having received goods from Amsterdam to be transmitted to the consignee in Surinam, shipped them on board the defendant's vessel, upon a bill of lading which stated that the goods were shipped by the plaintiff, that they were to be delivered in Surinam to the consignee or his assigns, and that the freight was paid by the plaintiff in London, it was held, by Lord ELLEN-BOROUGH, that the defendant, after having signed such a bill of lading, could not bring the ownership of the goods into question.   The consideration upon which the contract was founded moved from the plaintiff; the undertaking was made to him ; and he was therefore entitled to maintain the action to recover the value of the goods, and would hold the sum recovered as a trustee for the real owner. (*o*)   Where a laundress residing at Hammersmith, was in the habit of em-

---

(*m*) Coates v. Chaplain, 3 Q. B. 489.

(*n*) Davis v. James, 5 Burr. 2680. Bell v. Chaplain, Hard. 321.   Moore v. Wilson, 1 T. R. 659.   Dunlop v. Lambert, 6 Cl. & Fin. 600.

(*o*) Joseph v. Knox, 3 Campb. 320. Sargent v. Morris, 3 B. & Ald. 277.

ploying a carrier to convey linen from Hammersmith to the consignee at London, and the carrier was paid by the laundress, it was held that the latter was entitled to maintain an action upon the special contract against the carrier for the loss of the goods by the way, although they belonged to the consignee. (*p*) In these cases the bailee of the goods, who has a special property in them, may enforce the express contract entered into with the carrier, unless his principal interferes to prevent him. "The rule is, that either the bailor or the bailee may sue; and, whichever first obtains damages, it is a full satisfaction." (*q*) But a settlement for loss or damage, made with a person bringing the goods to the carrier, which person has no property or interest in the goods, will not be an answer to an action by the owner. (*r*)

1012. *Joint bailments to common carriers.*— Where a box delivered to a carrier to be carried, contained things belonging to each of the plaintiffs separately, but none in which they had a joint ownership, it was held that nevertheless there was a joint bailment in respect of which they might sue jointly. (*s*)

1013. *Parties to be made defendants—Carriage of goods and passengers over distinct lines of railway.* —We have already seen that, where goods are delivered to, and received by, a railway company to be carried to a particular destination, the railway company receiving the goods is the party to be sued for the loss of or damage to them, although the loss or damage has been sustained on the line of a second or third railway

---

(*p*) Freeman v. Birch, 1 N. & M. 420.

(*q*) Nicolls v. Bastard, 2 C. M. & R. 660.

(*r*) Coombs v. Bristol & Ex. Rali. Co., 3 H. & N. 1 ; 27 L. J., Ex. 269.

(*s*) Metcalfe v. Lond. & Br. Rail. Co., 4 C. B., N. S. 318 ; 27 L. J., C. P. 335.

company, to whom they have been delivered by the first railway company to be carried to their place of destination. The contract is made with the first railway company to whom they have been delivered, and to whom the hire for the entire journey has been paid ; (*t*) but both companies may, under certain circumstances, become joint contractors for the conveyance of the goods. (*u*) The same rule prevails with regard to the passenger and his luggage, so that, if one fare is paid and one ticket given for the entire journey, the contract is with the company issuing the ticket and receiving the money, and not with a second or third railway company over whose line the passenger is traveling in order to reach his destination. (*x*) And the company with which the contract is made will be liable for the negligence of such other railway company, the contract being that due care shall be used in carrying the passenger from one end of the journey to the other, so far as is within the compass of railway management. (*y*) But every railway company which allows its railway to remain open for public traffic is responsible to passengers who sustain injury from the line being unsafe and dangerous, although such persons are conveyed along it in the carriages of some other company. (*z*)

1014. *Damages in actions against carriers.*— Generally speaking, when articles of merchandise, such

---

(*t*) Brist. & Exeter Rail. Co. v. Collins, 7 H. L. C. 231. Coxon v. Gt. West. Rail. Co., 5 H. & N. 274 ; 29 L. J., Ex. 165.

(*u*) Hayes v. South Wales Rail. Co., 9 Ir. Com. Law Rep., C. P. 474.

(*x*) Mytton v. Mid. Rail. Co., 4 H. & N. 621 ; 28 L. J., Ex. 385. Great Western Ry. Co. v. Blake, 7 H. & N. 987 ; 31 L. J., Ex. 346. Buxton v. North-Eastern Ry. Co., L. R., 3 Q. B. 349 ; 37 L. J., Q. B. 258.

(*y*) Thomas v. Rhymney Ry. Co., L. R., 6 Q. B. 266 ; 40 L. J., Q. B. 89. But see Wright v. Midland Ry. Co., L. R., 8 Ex. 137 ; 42 L. J., Ex. 89.

(*z*) Birkett v. Whitehaven, &c., Rail. Co., 4 H. & N. 738 ; 28 L. J., Ex. 348.

as corn, hops, hemp, &c., are delivered to a carrier to be carried to a market town, and the carrier fails to deliver them in the ordinary course, and the goods come to a fallen market, the difference between the marketable value of the goods at the time they would have been sold if they had been carried according to contract, and their marketable value at the earliest period at which they could have been brought to market after their delivery to the consignee, will be the measure of damages recoverable. (*a*) If the goods have been lost altogether, the consignee is not restricted to the value of the goods at the place where they were delivered to the carrier to be carried ; but, if their marketable value was greater at the place of destination than at the place of consignment, the consignee is entitled to recover that difference, as being a loss likely to arise in the ordinary course of trade. (*b*) If there is no market at the place of delivery, the damages must be ascertained by taking into consideration, in addition to the cost price and expense of transit, the reasonable profit of the importer. (*c*) Where goods were delivered to a carrier by sea to be carried from Glasgow to Vancouver's Island, and on the arrival of the ship at the latter place they could not be found, it was held that the true measure of damages was the cost of replacing the lost articles in Vancouver's Island, with interest at 5 per cent. on the amount until judgment, by way of compensation for the delay. (*d*) [1]

In an action against a common carrier for loss sus-

(*a*) Rice v. Baxendale, 30 L. J., Ex. 371. O'Hanlan v. Gt. Western Rail. Co., 6 B. & S. 484 ; 34 L. J., Q. B. 154.

(*b*) O'Hanlan v. Gt. Western Rail.

Co., *supra.*

(*c*) British Columbia Saw Mill Co. v. Nettleship, L. R., 3 C. P. 499,

(*d*) Collard v. S. E. Ry. Co., 30 L. J., Ex. 393.

[1] Kyle v. Laurens R. R. Co., 10 Rich. 382.

tained by long delay in the delivery of articles of merchandise intrusted to him to be carried, whereby the consignee had lóst the season for selling them to advantage, and the marketable value of the articles was seriously diminished, it was held that the carrier was answerable for this loss, it being such as might naturally be expected to result from great delay in delivering articles of merchandise. (*e*)   But the plaintiff is not entitled to recover damages for loss of wages of workmen kept unemployed by reason of the non-arrival of the goods, or for loss of profit which might have been made if the goods had been delivered in due course, if the carrier had no notice of the purpose for which the goods were wanted ; (*f*) and if the carrier held the goods, at the time of the loss, in the character of a warehouseman, he can not, in general, be made responsible for more than the actual value of the goods. (*g*)[1]

(*e*) Wilson v. Lanc. & York. Rail. Co., 9 C. B., N. S. 632 ; 30 L. J., C. P. 233.

(*f*) Le Peinteur v. S. E. Rail. Co., 36 Law T. R. 170. Hadley v. Baxendale, 23 L. J., Ex. 179. Watson v.

Amberg., &c., Ry. Co., 15 Jur. 448; And see Horne v. Midland Ry. Co., L. R., 8 C. P. 131 ; 42 L. J., C. P. 59.

(*g*) Henderson v. N. E. R. Co., 9 W. R. 519.

[1] The rule of damages in cases of delay is stated *ante*, in note 1, p. 721. If the carrier's neglect is not the proximate cause, he is not liable, as where he is longer upon the route by reason of having a lame horse, and is so overtaken by a desolating flood. Morrison v. Davis, 20 Pa. St. 171. He is. not liable for a decline in the price of goods when the delay was inevitable ; Lepford v. Railroad Co., 7 Rich. 409 ; 13 Gray, 481 ; Galena, &c., R. R. Co. v. Roe, 18 Ill. 488 ; or he may be liable for interest on the value of the thing lost ; Kyle v. Laurens R. R. Co., 10 Rich. 382. Prospective profits will not be allowed to enter into the measure of damages. Redfield on Carriers, § 31. The value of the goods at the place of destination is the true rule of damages. Harris v. Panama R. R. Co., 3 Bosw. 7 ; Greeff v. Swetzer, 11 La. Ann. 324 ; Taylor v. Collier, 26 Ga. 122 ; Dean v. Vaccaro, 2 Head. 488 ; Davis v. New York, &c., R. R. Co., 1 Hilt. 543 ; Michigan, &c., R. R. Co. v. Carter, 13 Ind. 164 ; Spring v. Haskell, 4 Allen, 112.

If the plaintiff, being the consignor of horses, or other articles, makes a declaration of value which is below their real value, in order to get them carried at a lower rate of charge, he will be bound by his declaration of value, and can not recover more than he has himself declared. (*h*)

1015. *Contracts for the transmission of messages by electric telegraph—Limitation of liability.*—Acts of Parliament under which electric telegraph companies are incorporated, generally provide that the telegraph shall be open for the sending and receiving messages by all persons alike, without favor or preference subject to any reasonable regulations made by the company. It has been held to be a reasonable regulation for the company to stipulate that they will not be responsible for mistakes made in the transmission of messages, unless the messages are repeated, and an additional payment is made for such repetition of the message. (*i*) If a telegraph company negligently makes a mistake in the transmission of a message, it is liable to the sender only, and not to the receiver, although the latter may have acted on the message so erroneously transmitted, and may have sustained damage by so doing. (*k*) [1]

(*h*) McCance v. Lond. & North-West. Rail. Co., 34 L. J., Ex. 39.

(*i*) McAndrew v. Elect. Tel. Co., 17 C. B. 13.

(*k*) Playford v. The United Kingdom Electric Telegraph Company, Limited, L. R., 4 Q. B. 706 ; 38 L. J., Q. B. 249.

When goods are damaged, the owner can not refuse to receive them, and sue the carrier for total loss; Shaw v. South Carolina R. R. Co., 5 Rich. 162 ; but the carrier is only liable for the damage; Id. Michigan, &c., R. R. Co. v. Bivens, 13 Ind. 263.

[1] Telegraph companies are common carriers; but they will not be subjected to the same severe rule of responsibility of common carriers of merchandise, but held liable only for negligence, or willful misconduct. Leonard v. Albany, &c., Telegraph Co., 41 N. Y. 544 ; De Rutte v. New York, &c., Telegraph Co., 1 Daly, 547 ; New York & Washington Tele-

1016. *Proof of a jus tertii by the common carrier.*—A common carrier is not estopped from disputing the title of the person from whom he has received goods to be carried, or from disputing the title of the consignee, and showing that the real ownership of the goods is vested in some third party who has come forward and claimed the goods and received them from the carrier. (*l*)

(*l*) Sheridan v. New Quay Co., 4 C. B., N. S. 618 ; 28 L. J., C. P. 58. Cheesman v. Exall, 6 Exch. 344, over- ruling Laclough v. Towle, 3 Esp. 114.

graph Co. v. Dryburg, 35 Pa. St. 298; Parks v. Alta, &c. Telegraph Co., 13 Cal. 422; Western, &c., Telegraph Co. v. Carew, 15 Mich. 525; Breese v. United States Telegraph Co., 45 Barb. 274; Binney v. New York, &c., Telegraph Co., 18 Md. 341; Shearman & Redfield on Negligence, 556; Ellis, v. American Telegraph Co., 13 Allen, 226. "The degree of care which a telegraph company is bound to use may be called 'ordinary,' if we measure the meaning of that word solely by reference to the kind of care which a man of ordinary prudence would use in telegraphing for himself. But as compared with almost any other kind of business, the care required of a telegrapher would be called 'great care.'" Shearman & Redfield on Negligence, § 557. So it has been held culpable negligence in a telegraph company to keep an operator who does not know of the existence of an adjoining town; Western, &c., Telegraph Co. v. Buchanan, 35 Ind. 430; or the mistake of one letter in a word, which caused a loss of many hundred dollars; N. Y. & Washington Telegraph Co. v. Dryburg, 35 Pa. St. 298. It is said that, although the contract is between the telegraph company and the sender of the message, the receiver may sue upon it, since it is for his benefit; Shearman & Redfield on Negligence, § 560; citing as to the right of a third person to sue upon a contract made for his benefit. Lawrence v. Fox, 20 N. Y. 268; Burr v. Beers, 24 Id. 171; Steman v. Harmon, 42 Pa. St. 49.

END OF VOL. II.

Lightning Source UK Ltd.
Milton Keynes UK
UKHW040801070119
335137UK00010B/256/P